# Tom Swan's C++ Primer

# Tom Swan's C++ Primer

*by Tom Swan*

PUBLISHING

A Division of Prentice Hall Computer Publishing
11711 North College, Carmel, Indiana 46032 USA

# © 1992 by Tom Swan

International Standard Book Number: 0-672-30188-1

Library of Congress Catalog Card Number: 92-61310

95  94  93  92      4  3  2  1

Interpretation of the printing code: the rightmost double-digit number is the year of the book's printing; the rightmost single-digit number, the number of the book's printing. For example, a printing code of 92-1 shows that the first printing of the book occurred in 1992.

## Trademarks

*Composed in Carmel, Indiana by Prentice Hall Computer Publishing*

*Printed in the United States of America*

*To my lifelong friend Jere Eshelman, who had the good sense to install a hot tub where I often recovered from many long hours at the computer terminal.*

# Overview

**1** Discovering C++ ...................................................................... 1

**2** Making Statements and Building Structures ....................... 63

**3** Functions: Programming in Pieces ................................... 149

**4** Pointers About Pointers ..................................................... 211

**5** Class Objectives ................................................................. 295

**6** Building a Class Library—Part 1 ..................................... 387

**7** Building a Class Library—Part 2 ..................................... 437

**8** Files and Directories ......................................................... 521

**9** Advance Your C++ Knowledge ......................................... 587

**10** Cross-Compilation Tools ................................................. 661

Appendix A   Reserved Words .......................................... 703

Appendix B   Operator Precedence .................................. 705

Bibliography ...................................................................... 707

Index .................................................................................. 711

# Contents

Preface ................................................................. ixx
Introduction .......................................................... xxiii

**1    Discovering C++**                                                    **1**
A C++ Anatomy Lesson ...................................... 1
    Streams ........................................................ 5
    A Note about Semicolons ............................... 7
    Comments about Comments ............................ 8
    Identifiers .................................................... 12
    Case: A Sensitive Issue ................................ 12
    Keywords .................................................... 13
    Punctuators ................................................. 13
    Separators ................................................... 13
    Header Files ................................................ 14
Variables ........................................................... 15
    Initializing Variables with Definitions ........... 17
    Initializing Variables with Assignments ......... 19
    Scoop on Scope ........................................... 20
    Initializing Global and Local Variables ......... 23
Input and Output ............................................. 25
    Output Streams ........................................... 25
    Old-Style Output ......................................... 27
    Formatted Output ........................................ 28
    Input Streams ............................................. 34
    Formatted Input .......................................... 35
    A Simple Decimal-to-Hex-and-Octal Converter .......... 37
Constants .......................................................... 38
    Types of Constants ...................................... 39
    Literal Constants ........................................ 39
    Defined Constants ....................................... 44
    Declared Constants ...................................... 46
    Enumerated Constants .................................. 48
    Assigning Enumerated Element Values ........... 52

Operators ............................................................................. 53
    Operators and Precedence ................................................. 54
    Increment and Decrement Operators ................................. 54
    Expressions ...................................................................... 57
Questions and Exercises ........................................................ 59

**2    Making Statements and Building Structures          63**

Advanced Operators ............................................................. 64
    Good Relations ................................................................. 65
    Introducing *if/else*, the Decision Maker ......................... 67
    Making Sense out of Logical Operators ............................ 70
    Forget Me Not .................................................................. 73
    Bitwise Operators—Programming
        One Bit at a Time ......................................................... 73
    Shifty Operations ............................................................. 82
    Combined Assignments—Expressive Shorthand .......... 84
So It Flows ........................................................................... 85
    A Proper *exit* .................................................................. 86
    Reducing Complexity ....................................................... 88
    Filters and *while* Statements .......................................... 90
    Making Decisions with *if/else* ........................................ 93
    The Ol' *switch*eroo .......................................................... 97
    Using *switch* Statements ............................................... 100
    Upside Down *do/while* Statements ............................... 102
    C++'s Most Popular Statement—The *for* Loop .......... 105
    Multiple *for*-Loop Elements ......................................... 107
    Do-Forever Loops ........................................................... 108
    Taking a *break* .............................................................. 109
    The Plot *continues* ........................................................ 110
    Avoiding *goto* ............................................................... 112
Data Structures—Sand Castles in RAM ........................... 114
    Structures for Safe Keeping ............................................ 114
    Nested Structures ........................................................... 122
    Preserving the *union* .................................................... 123
    Vectoring in on Arrays ................................................... 126
    Making the Grade ........................................................... 130
    Initializing Arrays .......................................................... 132
    Arrays and the Multiple Dimension .............................. 133
    The True Character of Strings ........................................ 137

Character Array Initializations .................................. 138
Arrays and Pointers .................................................. 138
Fielding Bits ............................................................. 140
Sizing Up Your Variables ......................................... 144
Questions and Exercises .......................................... 147

## 3 Functions: Programming in Pieces — 149

Keeping It Simple ................................................... 150
Writing Your Own Functions ................................. 150
Designing from the Top Down ............................... 153
Functions and Their Variables ................................ 162
Local Variables ....................................................... 163
External Variables .................................................. 165
Register Variables ................................................... 168
Static Variables ...................................................... 170
Functions that Return Values ................................. 172
Parameter Passing .................................................. 178
One if by Value; Two if by Reference ..................... 179
Default Arguments ................................................ 188
Recursion: Programming with Mirrors ................... 194
Inline Functions ..................................................... 200
Turning Point ........................................................ 203
Questions and Exercises .......................................... 209

## 4 Pointers about Pointers — 211

Declaring Pointers .................................................. 212
Pointer Dereferencing ............................................ 213
Pointers and Type Checking ................................... 216
Null and Void Pointers .......................................... 216
Casting Roles for Pointers to Play .......................... 218
Near and Far Pointers ............................................ 222
Pointers to System Locations ................................. 224
Far Pointers and the Keyboard ............................... 226
Managing Your Memory ......................................... 232
Pointers to Structures ............................................. 236
Out of Memory ..................................................... 238
Why Use Dynamic Variables? ................................. 239
Creating Dynamic Lists .......................................... 241
Dynamic Arrays ..................................................... 251

Reserving Memory with *malloc* ...................................252
Pointers as Function Arguments ......................................259
Pointers to Functions .................................................264
Pointers and Arrays.....................................................270
    Pointer Arithmetic ................................................273
    Arrays of Pointers.................................................273
Functions that Return String Pointers .............................276
String Functions ........................................................278
    Common String Functions ....................................278
    Joining Strings ....................................................281
    Comparing Strings ...............................................281
    Searching Strings .................................................282
Command-Line Arguments ...........................................284
    Character Arguments ............................................287
    Numeric Arguments .............................................290
Questions and Exercises................................................292

**5   Class Objectives                                   295**

Go to the Head of the Class ..........................................297
    Creating Classes ..................................................300
    Inline Member Functions .....................................305
    Classes Are Data Types .........................................308
    Introducing Constructors......................................311
    Class Tactics .......................................................314
Compiling the Elevator Simulation .................................319
Using Header Files ......................................................322
The Person Class .........................................................325
    *person* Data Members ..........................................328
    The *person* Collection Class....................................328
    *person* and *persCollection* Member Functions ..............329
The Floor Class ..........................................................342
    Implementing the *floor* Class .................................344
The Elevator Class .......................................................353
    Implementing the *elevator* Class .............................355
Introducing Inheritance................................................365
    Using Inheritance ................................................366
The Building Class .......................................................374
    Replacement Member Functions .............................376
    Implementing the *building* Class .............................377

Completing the Elevator Simulation ................................381
Questions and Exercises.......................................386

**6  Building a Class Library—Part 1                              387**

Last Things First—WinTool .....................................388
  Compiling WINTOOL .........................................389
  The wintool.h Header ........................................390
  Pointers to Class Variables ..................................395
  Pointers to Derived Classes ..................................399
  Virtual Functions and Polymorphism ......................400
  Polymorphism in Action .....................................404
  Early and Late Binding ......................................408
  The WINTOOL.CPP Main Program ......................408
  Static Member Functions ....................................410
Mixing OOP and Non-OOP Code ...........................420
  The KEY Module ............................................420
  Defining KEY Values ........................................425
  Testing the KEY Module ....................................426
  Error Handling ..............................................428
  Testing the ERROR Module ...............................433
Questions and Exercises.......................................435

**7  Building a Class Library—Part 2                              437**

First Things Last—The Class Library ..........................438
  Class Hierarchies.............................................438
  At the Root of the Library ...................................439
  The item.h Header ...........................................440
  Protected Members ..........................................441
  Choosing Among *private*, *public*, and *protected*...........443
  Destructors ..................................................444
  Using the *item* Class.........................................445
  The ITEM.CPP Module......................................448
  *this* Is Where It's At ........................................449
A Class for Lists .................................................452
  The list.h Header .............................................453
  Using the *list* Class ..........................................455
  The LIST.CPP Module ......................................459
A Class for Strings ..............................................462
  The stritem.h Header.........................................463

Multiple Constructors ...................................................464
Using the *strItem* Class ..............................................466
The STRITEM.CPP Module ......................................467
Making Lists of Strings .................................................471
A Class for *Windows* .........................................................473
The window.h Header ....................................................473
Static Member Functions .............................................478
Static Member Members ..............................................479
Overloaded Constructors ..............................................480
Reference Functions ......................................................481
Designing Displays with Windows ............................482
The WINDOW.CPP Module .....................................487
A Class for Selections .........................................................499
The selector.h Header ...................................................500
Multiple Inheritance .....................................................501
Using the *selector* Class ...............................................502
The SELECTOR.CPP Module ....................................505
A Class for Commands .......................................................510
The command.h Header ...............................................511
Using the *command* Class ............................................513
Recap ....................................................................................518
Questions and Exercises .....................................................518

## 8   Files and Directories

File and DOS Functions .....................................................522
Text Files ..............................................................................522
Basic Text-File Techniques .............................................523
Creating Text Files..........................................................524
Formatted Output ..........................................................527
Errors from File Functions ............................................527
Reading Text Files ..........................................................529
Reading Text One Character at a Time .....................529
Reading Text One Line at a Time................................531
Sorting Text Files ............................................................534
Data Files ..............................................................................540
Basic Data-File Techniques ...........................................540
Reading and Writing Data Files ..................................541
Writing Binary Values to Disk .....................................541
Reading Binary Values from Disk ................................544

Creating Database Files ................................................ 547
Reading Database Files ................................................ 550
Working with Directories ................................................ 554
Determining Free Space on Disk .............................. 554
Changing the Current Directory ............................... 555
Displaying a Directory ................................................ 557
Decoding Directory Information .............................. 560
Modifying Directory Entries ..................................... 564
A Class for Directories .................................................... 567
The tscdir.h Header ................................................... 567
Using the Directory Classes ...................................... 569
The TSCDIR.CPP Module ....................................... 572
Directory Navigator ................................................... 577
READ: An OOP Text-File Reader ................................. 579
Compiling and Using READ ..................................... 579
The READ.CPP Program ......................................... 580
Questions and Exercises .................................................. 584

**9    Advancing Your C++ Knowledge                    587**
Good Friends and Neighbors ........................................... 588
Friend Classes ............................................................ 589
Mutual Friend Classes ............................................... 593
Friend Functions Part 1 ............................................ 594
Friend Functions Part 2 ............................................ 596
Function Overloading ...................................................... 599
Name Mangling Revisited ......................................... 599
The *overload* Keyword .............................................. 602
Overloading Conventional Functions ....................... 602
Overloading Class Member Functions ...................... 603
Operator Overloading ...................................................... 604
Overloading Operator Member Functions ................ 609
Overloading Unary Operators .................................... 611
Tips for Successful Operator Overloading ................. 613
Increment and Decrement Operators ........................ 614
Overloading Array Indexing ............................................ 615
User-Defined Type Conversions ............................... 619
Overloading the Assignment Operator ........................... 623
Copying Class Objects ............................................... 625
Memberwise Initialization ......................................... 626

Copying Pointer Members ........................................... 629

The Copy Constructor ................................................. 631

Memberwise Assignment .............................................. 632

Calling *operator*= from a Copy Constructor ............... 635

Copying Derived Class Objects .................................... 637

Overloading and Memory Management .......................... 637

Assignments to *this* .................................................. 638

Overloading *new* ..................................................... 638

Overloading *delete* .................................................. 640

Overloading Streams .................................................. 641

Overloading Output Streams ....................................... 642

Overloading Input Streams ......................................... 644

Miscellany .................................................................. 645

Other I/O Streams ..................................................... 646

Conditional Expressions ............................................. 647

Resolving Global Function Conflicts ........................... 648

Default Status of Inherited Classes ............................ 650

Pointers to Member Functions .................................... 651

Virtual Base Classes ................................................... 655

Now That You've Learned C++.................................... 657

Differences Between C and C++ ................................. 657

Using Other C++ Compilers ....................................... 658

Questions and Exercises ............................................. 659

**10    Cross-Compilation Tools                       661**

Building the Library .................................................... 662

The Compiler Identifier Symbol .................................. 664

The Automated MAKE Files ....................................... 665

MAKE File Options ..................................................... 665

Using the Cross-Compilation Library ........................... 669

The tscdefs Header .................................................... 669

The dosgfree Module .................................................. 676

The tscdisp Module .................................................... 677

The form Module ....................................................... 688

The msleep Module ..................................................... 690

The pbin Module........................................................ 692

The ZTCFLUSH Module ............................................. 694

Compiling Your Own Programs ........................................696
    Compiling with Borland C++ 3.0 and 3.1 .................697
    Compiling with Microsoft C/C++ 7.0 .......................698
    Compiling with Turbo C++ 3.0 ...............................698
    Compiling with Zortech C++ 3.0 ............................699
Converting to Other
    C++ Compilers ..........................................................699

**A    Reserved Keywords                                         703**

**B    Operator Precedence                                       705**

**Bibliography                                                   707**

**Index                                                          711**

# Preface

I decided to write this C++ Primer in answer to the many requests I have received for a Borland C++ version of my book *Learning C++*. Soon after I began working on the project, I had the bright idea (that turned out to be greatly diminished in brilliance, as I'll explain in a moment) to include a few other C++ compilers. Why should I stop with Borland C++? Why not include Turbo C++, Microsoft C/C++, and Zortech C++ as well?

The very concept of writing a multi-compiler book on C++ programming set my heart pounding. While I dreamed of my future book's best-seller status, however, I soon began to hear another sort of pounding—the sound one's fist makes when striking a desk. From the start, I encountered trouble.

I would convert one program to Borland C++ only to discover that, upon compiling with Microsoft C/C++, certain changes were required. No problem, I thought: just revise the code and recompile. After doing that, and after compiling successfully with Microsoft C/C++, I would then discover (to my exasperation) that the code no longer worked with Borland C++. So, I would make more revisions, requiring more testing with both of these compilers. Of course, then I would tackle the Zortech C++ version and, after revising the program, invariably the result would no longer work as it did with the Borland and Microsoft products. There is only one word to describe my feelings at these moments: *Argghhhhh!*

I nearly gave up, but by this time I was so annoyed at my lack of progress that I was determined to succeed. Why *shouldn't* I be able to cross-compile C++ programs with products that are advertised to support the AT&T C++ 2.1 standard? The answer was obvious: currently available C++ compilers aren't as cross-compatible as their manufacturers would have you believe.

So, I scrapped every program I had revised—the listings were a mess, anyway, and they were filled with ugly conditional compilation statements, making them difficult to read and unsuitable for publication. I started over, this time with a simple plan to guide my way. When I encountered a statement that worked in one compiler but not in another, I wrote a *new* statement for a hypothetical language element—a new function name, for example, or a macro symbol. I then implemented that element in a manner that was compatible with all of my target compilers, and that could easily be converted to support other compilers and future versions.

The result was a library of routines and header files containing various symbols that promote better harmony among C++ compilers from Borland, Microsoft, and Zortech. The complete cross compilation library, including all source code, is included on the diskette bound into this book's back cover. As you will see when you examine the book's listings, there are very few places in which conditional compilation statements are needed to cross-compile programs. This fact remains true even for programs that use special features such as direct-video output—features that typically extinguish all hope of compiling programs with multiple compilers.

From writing this book, I learned an important lesson: *Compatibility is in the eye of the manufacturer.* I also discovered that writing cross-compatible C++ programs is much more difficult than I had expected. If you need to write similarly cross-compatible code, you might find my library routines useful. You might also avoid breaking your fist on your desk as I nearly did.

*Tom Swan*
*CompuServe ID: 73627,3241*

**Note:** Some of this book's listings and text are similar to portions of my book *Mastering Borland C++*. The elevator simulation, class library, and windowing capabilities, however, are completely original (as revised from *Learning C++*). Also, this C++ Primer uses a pure C++ approach in programs that in *Mastering Borland C++* employ a mix of ANSI C and C++ techniques. If you have both books, you might gain insights into the C and C++ languages by comparing these similar programs.

# Acknowledgments

**M**ost books are the result of a team effort, and this book is no exception. Special thanks are due all members of the team that worked long and hard on *Tom Swan's C++ Primer*, especially Erik Dafforn, Gregory Croy, Richard Swadley, Neweleen Trebnik, Becky Freeman, Carla Hall-Batton, and others in the editing, art, production, and sales departments at Sams Publishing. I'm also indebted to my wife and assistant Anne Swan, who read the manuscript and made many useful suggestions. Many thanks to all of you for your valuable contributions.

# Introduction

**M**any computer language primers are written for one manufacturer's programming language and a specific computer or operating system. Many other programming books are written in a more general fashion—to support all ANSI C or C++ compilers, for example.

This book falls somewhere in between. The programs on the accompanying diskette are generally compatible with AT&T C++ Version 2.1, but they are specifically designed for use with five MS-DOS C++ compilers. You can compile every program in this book using any of the following products:

- Borland C++ 3.0

- Borland C++ 3.1

- Microsoft C/C++ 7.0

- Turbo C++ 3.0

- Zortech C++ 3.0

You might also be able to use other versions of AT&T C++ 2.1 compilers. Chapter 10, "Cross-Compilation Tools," discusses the various functions, conditional compilation symbols, and header files I developed for writing cross-compatible C++ code.

Read the following notes for system requirements and for instructions on installing the files from this book's accompanying diskette. Then, turn to the section later in this introduction for instructions about configuring the installed files for your C++ compiler.

# Requirements

**T**o use this book and the files on the accompanying diskette, you need to have the following minimum hardware and software:

- One or more of the compiler products: Borland C++ 3.0, Borland C++ 3.1, Microsoft C/C++ 7.0, Turbo C++ 3.0, or Zortech C++ 3.0.

- An IBM PC or 100% compatible system that is capable of running your chosen compiler. Borland C++ and Turbo C++ require an 80286 or higher-numbered processor, Microsoft C/C++ requires an 80386 or higher processor, and Zortech C++ requires an 8086 or higher processor.

- A hard disk drive with enough free space to hold the compiler and its related files, plus enough space for this book's listings. You need about 10 megabytes in addition to the disk space required by your compiler. (Installation requires about 2 megabytes, but you need an additional 8 megabytes to hold all of the programs after compiling. As you read each chapter, you can delete individual compiled .EXE program files and .OBJ code files to save space.)

- Enough RAM to satisfy your compiler's memory requirements. (My system has 16 megabytes of RAM, but 2 megabytes should be plenty for Borland C++, Turbo C++, and Microsoft C/C++. Zortech C++ needs only 640K of RAM.)

- MS-DOS 3.31 or higher. (I use and recommend MS-DOS 5.0.)

- You do not need Microsoft Windows, but if you run Windows, you can install and compile the book's listings in a DOS-prompt window. (I use Windows 3.1. You can also use Version 3.0.)

**Note:** See the README file on the accompanying diskette for additional information and late-breaking news. You can use any plain-text editor to read the file.

# Installing the Diskette

The files on the accompanying diskette are compressed to save space. Before using the files, you must decompress them using a supplied utility program. Follow these steps:

**Note:** You *must* install this book's files in a subdirectory. Do not attempt to install the files to a disk's root directory such as C:\ or D:\, which can hold only a limited number of files.

1. Create a directory on your hard drive. (I name my directory TSC for "Tom Swan's C++ Primer," but you can use another name if you want.) Copy all files from the diskette to the new directory. For example, if the diskette is in A: and your hard drive is C:, enter the following commands at a DOS prompt:

```
c:
cd \
md tsc
copy a:*.* c:\tsc
```

2. Change to your TSC directory. With the supplied LHARC.EXE program in the current directory, run the UNPACK.BAT batch file to dearchive all files. Enter the commands

```
c:
cd \tsc
unpack
```

3. The UNPACK.BAT file creates a series of subdirectories, and then extracts files from the .LZH archives and stores the files in these subdirectories.

4. After dearchiving, delete all .LZH files from the hard drive directory. For example, enter the command

```
del *.lzh
```

# Files and Directories

After installing the files, your disk contains a new main directory (C:\TSC) plus several subdirectories. Unless you have a good reason to reorganize the files, it's best to use the supplied directory structure. The automated MAKE files (which run the compiler and linker) expect to find certain files in specifically named locations. If you shuffle files around, you might have trouble compiling the programs.

The following table lists the subdirectories in C:\TSC and describes the files in each location. Use the table as a guide while you explore the files on disk.

> **Note:** Listings and related files for Chapter 10, "Cross-Compilation Tools," are stored in C:\TSC\LIB\SOURCE. There is no directory C:\TSC\C10.

**Directory organization**

| Directory | Files |
|-----------|-------|
| C:\TSC | Batch files, MAKE includes, and miscellaneous |
| C:\TSC\ANSWERS | Answers to exercises (complete programs only) |
| C:\TSC\C01 | Listings for Chapter 1 |
| C:\TSC\C02 | Listings for Chapter 2 |
| C:\TSC\C03 | Listings for Chapter 3 |
| C:\TSC\C04 | Listings for Chapter 4 |
| C:\TSC\C05 | Listings for Chapter 5 |
| C:\TSC\C06 | Listings for Chapter 6 |
| C:\TSC\C07 | Listings for Chapter 7 |
| C:\TSC\C08 | Listings for Chapter 8 |
| C:\TSC\C09 | Listings for Chapter 9 |
| C:\TSC\INCLUDE | Cross-compilation library header (.h) files |
| C:\TSC\LIB | Cross-compilation library (.LIB) files |
| C:\TSC\LIB\SOURCE | Cross-compilation library source code files |

# Compiling and Running Programs

The outer C:\TSC directory contains several files that simplify the steps required to compile the book's programs. The following table lists these files and their target compilers.

> **Hint:** To save a little disk space, you can delete files for compilers other than yours. You might, however, want to save these files in case you acquire a different compiler in the future.

## Files in C:\TSC

| File | Compiler | Purpose |
| --- | --- | --- |
| LHARC.EXE | none | Compresses or decompresses .LZH files |
| LHARC.MAN | none | Instructions for using LHARC.EXE |
| MAKEBTC.BAT | Borland C++ Turbo C++ | Compiles all programs for Borland C++ or Turbo C++ |
| MAKEBTC.INC | Borland C++ | Included by Borland C++ MAKE files |
| MAKEMSC.BAT | Microsoft C/C++ | Compiles all programs for Microsoft C/C++ |
| MAKEMSC.INC | Microsoft C/C++ | Included by Microsoft C/C++ MAKE files |
| MAKEZTC.BAT | Zortech C++ | Compiles all programs for Zortech C++ |
| MAKEZTC.INC | Zortech C++ | Included by Zortech C++ MAKE files |
| README | none | Notes and late-breaking news |
| ROOTBTC.INC | Borland C++ Turbo C++ | Specifies root directory for Borland C++ and Turbo C++ |
| ROOTMSC.INC | Microsoft C/C++ | Specifies root directory for Microsoft C/C++ |
| ROOTZTC.INC | Zortech C++ | Specifies root directory for Zortech C++ |
| SETBCC.BAT | Borland C++ | Sample setup batch file for Borland C++ |
| SETMSC.BAT | Microsoft C++ | Sample setup batch file for Microsoft C/C++ |

*continues*

**Files in C:\TSC continued**

| File | Compiler | Purpose |
|------|----------|---------|
| SETTCC.BAT | Turbo C++ | Sample setup batch file for Turbo C++ |
| SETZTC.BAT | Zortech C++ | Sample setup batch file for Zortech C++ |
| TURBOC.INC | Turbo C++ | Include file for Turbo C++ MAKE files. Must be renamed to MAKEBTC.INC. |
| UNPACK.BAT | none | Creates subdirectories and decompresses .LZH files. Not needed after installation. |

Before attempting to compile the programs, you need to make a few changes to one or more files. First, change to your installation directory. For example, enter the commands

```
c:
cd \tsc
```

Next, turn to one of the following sections for your compiler and version number. If your compiler is not listed, see Chapter 10, "Cross-Compilation Tools," for hints about modifying the cross-compilation library. You must configure the files for *each* compiler that you plan to use.

**Note:** For best results, do not attempt to configure your system for use with more than one vendor's compiler at a time. Use batch files to prepare environment variables and the system PATH according to your compiler's requirements. You can then run the batch files to switch between different compilers. C++ compilers use many files that have the same name but have very different contents. Make sure that your compiler can find the files it needs.

# Borland C++ 3.0

**L** oad the file ROOTBTC.INC into your text editor. The file has two symbols that specify the location of Borland C++ (CPPROOT) and the location of this book's files (TSCROOT). Modify the pathnames assigned to these symbols. For example, if you install Borland C++ and this book's files on drive C:, you might edit the commands to

```
CPPROOT = c:\borlandc
TSCROOT = c:\tsc
```

Before compiling programs, run the sample SETBCC.BAT batch file. Edit the commands in this file to set the system PATH. If you already configure your system for Borland C++—by using commands in AUTOEXEC.BAT, for example—you do not need to run SETBCC.BAT. Be sure to include your Borland C++ BIN (binaries) directory on the PATH. For example, SETBCC.BAT might include the line

```
path=c:\dos;c:\borlandc\bin
```

You should now be able to compile programs. For a test, change to the directory for Chapter 1, and run MAKE. For example, enter the commands

```
c:
cd \tsc\c01
make -fmakefile.btc
```

There is no space between the option -f and the filename. After compiling the programs, you can modify one of the listing files (ENUM.CPP, for example), save the new program, and reenter **make -fmakefile.btc** to recompile only the modified file. You can also modify more than one file in a directory. The automated MAKE utility is smart. It compares compiled- and source-file dates and times then recompiles only the files that are out of date.

The automated MAKE files create a new file named TURBOC.CFG, which contains options and directory settings. You can delete this file at any time, but don't delete the default TURBOC.CFG located in C:\BORLANDC\BIN.

To compile all programs in all chapters, run the MAKEBTC.BAT batch file program. Change to C:\TSC, and type **makebtc** for brief instructions. Type **makebtc all** to compile every program. (Don't try this unless you are prepared not to use your computer for a while—as long as 15 minutes to 1/2 hour, depending on your computer's speed.) Type **makebtc** *n* to compile programs in an individual chapter. Typing **makebtc 2**, for example, compiles the programs for Chapter 2.

The C:\TSC\LIB directory has similar batch files to compile the cross-compilation library. The library is supplied in compiled form. You need to recompile it only if you modify files in C:\TSC\LIB\SOURCE, or to update the TSCBCC.LIB file for a new compiler version. To recompile the library, change to C:\TSC\LIB and enter **buildbtc**.

> **Note:** You can use the Borland C++ integrated development environment (IDE) editor to examine and modify program source files. To compile directly in the IDE, you have to create a project file (.PRJ) for each program. To the project, add the program's name plus TSCBCC.LIB. You also have to add files for multiple-file programs as listed in this book. Add C:\TSC\INCLUDE and C:\TSC\LIB to the IDE's directory settings. You can then press Ctrl+F9 to compile and run. Press Alt+F5 to view a program's output. Creating projects for many small programs is so much trouble, however, it's probably best to use the automated MAKE files as described in this introduction. You can still use the IDE to edit program source files, but I suggest that you use the File|DOS shell command to return to a DOS prompt for compiling and running programs.

# Borland C++ 3.1

F ollow the instructions for Borland C++ 3.0. All programs are compatible with compiler versions 3.0 and 3.1. You might, however, make some optional adjustments to various symbols as described in the section "Using MAKE Files" later in this chapter.

# Microsoft C/C++ 7.0

L oad the file ROOTMSC.INC into your text editor. The file has two symbols that specify the location of Microsoft C/C++ (CPPROOT) and the location of this book's files (TSCROOT). Modify the pathnames assigned to these symbols. For example, if you install Microsoft C/C++ and this book's files on drive C:, you might edit the commands to

```
CPPROOT = c:\c700
TSCROOT = c:\tsc
```

Before compiling programs, run the sample SETMSC.BAT batch file. Edit the commands in this file to set environment variables and to prepare the system PATH. Add C:\TSC\LIB and C:\TSC\INCLUDE to your normal LIB and INCLUDE environment variables. For example, I use the commands

```
set lib=c:\c700\lib;c:\tsc\lib
set include=c:\c700\include;c:\msc\include
```

Also be sure to include your Microsoft C/C++ BIN (binaries) directory on the PATH. For example, SETMSC.BAT might include the line

```
path=c:\c700\bin;c:\dos
```

After running SETMSC.BAT, you should now be able to compile programs. For a test, change to the directory for Chapter 1, and run MAKE. For example, enter the commands

```
c:
cd \tsc\c01
nmake -f makefile.msc
```

Type a space between the option -f and the filename. After compiling the programs, you can modify one of the listing files (ENUM.CPP, for example), save the new program, and reenter **nmake -f makefile.msc** to recompile only the modified file. You can also modify more than one file in a directory. The automated MAKE utility is smart. It compares compiled- and source-file dates and times and then recompiles only the files that are out of date.

> **Note:** Microsoft names its automated MAKE utility NMAKE. Throughout this book, I refer to this program by its common name MAKE. When running the program, however, you must enter **nmake**.

To compile all programs in all chapters, run the MAKEMSC.BAT batch file program. Type **makemsc** for brief instructions. Type **makemsc all** to compile every program. (Don't try this unless you are prepared not to use your computer for a while—as long as 15 minutes to 1/2 hour, depending on your computer's speed.) Type **makemsc** *n* to compile programs in an individual chapter. Typing **makemsc 2**, for example, compiles the programs for Chapter 2.

The C:\TSC\LIB directory has similar batch files to compile the cross-compilation library. The library is supplied in compiled form. You need to recompile it only if you modify files in C:\TSC\LIB\SOURCE, or to update the TSCMSC.LIB file for a new compiler version. To recompile the library, change to C:\TSC\LIB and enter **buildmsc**.

> **Note:** You can also compile programs using the Programmer's WorkBench (PWB) supplied with Microsoft C/C++. To compile directly in PWB, use the **P**roject|**N**ew project command to create a project for each program. Enter the program name, choose **S**et, and select the C++ and DOS EXE options from the resulting screen. Add the program's .CPP filename plus TSCMSC.LIB (in C:\TSC\LIB) to the project. Choose **S**ave List and compile. Creating projects for many small programs is so much trouble, however, it's probably best to use the automated MAKE files as described in this introduction. You can still use PWB to edit program source files, but I suggest that you compile and run programs directly from DOS.

# Turbo C++ 3.0

L oad the file ROOTBTC.INC into your text editor. The file has two symbols that specify the location of Turbo C++ (CPPROOT) and the location of this book's files (TSCROOT). Modify the pathnames assigned to these symbols. For example, if you install Turbo C++ and this book's files on drive C:, you might edit the commands to

```
CPPROOT = c:\tc
TSCROOT = c:\tsc
```

Next, rename MAKEBTC.INC to BORLANDC.INC, thus preserving this file in case you later upgrade to Borland C++. Then, rename TURBOC.INC to MAKEBTC.INC. For example, from a DOS prompt, enter the commands

```
ren makebtc.inc borlandc.inc
ren turboc.inc makebtc.inc
```

**Note:** Reverse these steps to reset to the original filenames. For example, in the future, to reconfigure for Borland C++ programming, enter the following commands (but *don't* type these lines now):

```
ren makebtc.inc turboc.inc
ren borlandc.inc makebtc.inc
```

Before compiling programs, run the sample SETTCC.BAT batch file. Running the batch file automatically swaps the TURBOC.INC and MAKEBTC.INC files, as explained previously, in case you forget this step. Edit the commands in this file to set the system PATH. If you already configure your system for Turbo C++—by using commands in AUTOEXEC.BAT, for example—you do not need to run SETTCC.BAT. Be sure to include your Turbo C++ BIN (binaries) directory on the PATH. For example, SETTCC.BAT might include the line

```
path=c:\dos;c:\tc\bin
```

You should now be able to compile programs. For a test, change to the directory for Chapter 1, and run MAKE. For example, enter the commands

```
c:
cd \tsc\c01
make -fmakefile.btc
```

There is no space between the option -f and the filename. After compiling the programs, you can modify one of the listing files (ENUM.CPP, for example), save the new program, and reenter **make -fmakefile.btc** to compile only the modified file. You can also modify more than one file in a directory. The automated MAKE utility is smart. It compares compiled- and source-file dates and times, then recompiles only the files that are out of date.

The automated MAKE files create a new file named TURBOC.CFG, which contains options and directory settings. You can delete this file at any time, but don't delete the default TURBOC.CFG located in C:\TC\BIN.

To compile all programs in all chapters, run the MAKEBTC.BAT batch file program. Type **makebtc** for brief instructions. Type **makebtc all** to compile every program. (Don't try this unless you are prepared not to use your computer for a while—as long as 15 minutes to 1/2 hour, depending on your computer's speed.) Type **makebtc _n_** to compile programs in an individual chapter. For example, typing **makebtc 2** compiles the programs for Chapter 2.

The C:\TSC\LIB directory has similar batch files to compile the cross-compilation library. The library is supplied in compiled form. You need to recompile it only if you modify files in C:\TSC\LIB\SOURCE, or to update the TSCTCC.LIB file for a new compiler version. To recompile the library, change to C:\TSC\LIB and enter **buildtcc**.

> **Note:** You can also compile programs using the integrated development environment (IDE) editor supplied with Turbo C++. The steps are the same as for the Borland C++ IDE (see "Borland C++ 3.0" earlier in this introduction). It's probably best, however, to use the automated MAKE files as described in this introduction. You can still use the IDE to edit program source files, but I suggest that you compile and run programs directly from DOS.

# Zortech C++ 3.0

L oad the file ROOTZTC.INC into your text editor. The file has two symbols that specify the location of Zortech C++ (CPPROOT) and the location of this book's files (TSCROOT). Modify the pathnames assigned to these symbols. For example, if you install Zortech C++ and this book's files on drive C:, you might edit the commands to

```
CPPROOT = c:\zortech
TSCROOT = c:\tsc
```

Before compiling programs, run the sample SETZTC.BAT batch file. Edit the commands in this file to set environment variables and to prepare the system PATH. Add C:\TSC\LIB and C:\TSC\INCLUDE to your normal LIB and INCLUDE environment variables. For example, I use the commands

```
set lib=c:\zortech\lib;c:\tsc\lib
set include=c:\zortech\include;c:\tsc\include
```

Also be sure to include your Zortech C++ BIN (binaries) directory on the PATH. For example, SETZTC.BAT might have the command

```
path=c:\zortech\bin;c:\dos
```

After running SETZTC.BAT, you should now be able to compile programs. For a test, change to the directory for Chapter 1 and run MAKE. For example, enter the commands

```
c:
cd \tsc\c01
make -fmakefile.ztc
```

There is no space between the option `-f` and the filename. After compiling the programs, you can modify one of the listing files (ENUM.CPP, for example), save the new program, and reenter `make -fmakefile.ztc` to compile only the modified file. You can also modify more than one file in a directory. The automated MAKE utility is smart. It compares compiled- and source-file dates and times, then recompiles only the files that are out of date.

To compile all programs in all chapters, run the MAKEZTC.BAT batch file program. Type `makeztc` for brief instructions. Type `makeztc all` to compile every program. (Don't try this unless you are prepared not to use your computer for a while—as long as 15 minutes to 1/2 hour, depending on your computer's speed.) Type `makeztc n` to compile programs in an individual chapter. Typing `makeztc 2`, for example, compiles the programs for Chapter 2.

The C:\TSC\LIB directory has similar batch files to compile the cross-compilation library. The library is supplied in compiled form. You need to recompile it only if you modify files in C:\TSC\LIB\SOURCE, or to update the TSCZTC.LIB file for a new compiler version. To recompile the library, change to C:\TSC\LIB and enter `buildztc`.

**Note:** You can also compile programs using the Zortech WorkBench (ZWB). Of all the integrated editor-compiler development environments, ZWB is among the easiest to use. First, change to a directory (C:\TSC\C01, for example) and copy MAKEFILE.ZTC to MAKEFILE with no extension. From the DOS prompt, enter `zwb name.cpp` where *name* is a program name. When the file appears in the ZWB editor, make any changes to the text, and save the modified file to disk. Then press Shift+F7 (or use the Compile|Make command) to compile. Select File|Shell to return to DOS and run the compiled code file. Type `exit` to return to ZWB.

# Using MAKE Files

**B**ig programs are typically constructed from many separate modules, similar in size to this book's listing files. In fact, this book has much in common with a typical large software project composed of multiple parts and pieces. Studying how this book's files are organized might help you to plan the directory and file layouts for your next programming project.

If you are just beginning to learn C++, you might want to skip this section and go straight to Chapter 1. If, however, you want to learn more about how this book's automated MAKE files work, read on.

To keep a large program's pieces up to date, professional programmers often use a MAKE utility (called NMAKE in Microsoft C/C++). MAKE examines the dates and times of source- and object-code files, and automatically recompiles only the modified files plus any other files on which the modified files depend.

MAKE reads a text file (called the MAKE file) that contains compiler and linker commands. Actually, MAKE can issue *any* DOS command, and it can run most programs and utilities. Typical MAKE files have three kinds of commands: macros, dependency rules, and DOS command lines:

- *Macros* are optional but save typing and can increase a MAKE file's clarity. They look like this: $(CCLL). MAKE-file macros are similar to #defined symbols in a C++ program.

- *Dependency rules* state which files depend on others. If A.CPP uses another module, B.CPP (that is, A.CPP *depends on* B.CPP), MAKE automatically recompiles A.CPP, B.CPP, or both to keep the program's .EXE code file up to date.

- MAKE issues *DOS commands* when it detects a dependent file out of date relative to other files on which the file depends. Typically, MAKE issues command-line compiler and linker commands, but it can issue any DOS command.

This book uses a variety of complex MAKE files, which include (read from disk) other files. The following sections describe the contents of various MAKE files on this book's disk. To select compiler options, you can modify a MAKE file's symbols and then recompile the programs.

**Note:** In the following sections, *xxx* stands for BTC (Borland C++ and Turbo C++), TCC (Turbo C++), MSC (Microsoft C++), or ZTC (Zortech C++). Replace *xxx* with the appropriate 3-letter symbol to locate the file that applies to your compiler.

# MAKEFILE.xxx MAKE Files

Each directory that has one or more program source files also includes a MAKE file. Running the compiler's MAKE utility and supplying a MAKE-file name compiles the directory's source files to create object (.OBJ) and executable (.EXE) code files on disk.

This book's MAKE files begin by including two .INC files from the immediately preceding directory. For example, MAKEFILE.BTC for Borland C++ and Turbo C++ begins with the commands

```
!include "..\rootbtc.inc"
!include "..\makebtc.inc"
```

Other compiler MAKE files have similar commands, which differ somewhat in form. Including ROOTBTC.INC creates the root directory symbols CPPROOT and TSCROOT (described in the next section, "ROOTxxx.INC Include Files"). Including MAKEBTC.INC creates other symbols that specify various compiler options (see "MAKExxx.INC Include Files").

Each chapter has its own MAKEFILE.xxx files. Similar files are also provided for answers to exercises in C:\TSC\ANSWERS and for the cross-compilation library source files in C:\TSC\LIB\SOURCE.

When executed alone, MAKE and NMAKE automatically read a file named MAKEFILE. To take advantage of this fact, copy your compiler's MAKEFILE.xxx files to new files named MAKEFILE with no extension. For example, if you are using Borland C++ or Turbo C++, enter the commands

```
c:
cd \tsc\c01
copy makefile.btc makefile
```

You can do the same for Microsoft C/C++ and Zortech C++, but substitute MAKEFILE.MSC or MAKEFILE.ZTC for MAKEFILE.BTC in the COPY command.

Repeat these steps for each chapter directory, for C:\TSC\ANSWERS, and for C:\TSC\LIB\SOURCE. If you are using Borland C++, Turbo C++, or Zortech C++, rather than enter **make -fmakefile.xxx** to compile a chapter's programs, you now can simply type **make** to compile all out-of-date programs in the current directory. (Type **nmake** for Microsoft C/C++.)

This technique is especially handy when using a programmer's editor that lets you run DOS commands, or that has a "shell to DOS" option. Without leaving your editor, save any changes you have made to program source files and issue a **make** command. You then can run the resulting program; if any errors occur, you can return to your editor, fix the problems, and try again.

> **Note:** Do *not* rename or delete the MAKEFILE.xxx files. If you do, the automated batch files in C:\TSC and in C:\TSC\LIB that need these files will no longer work.

MAKE files contain many lines like these:

```
depends: turboc.cfg\
        welcome.exe comment.exe variable.exe\
        scope.exe dt.exe format.exe\
```

This command associates multiple .EXE executable code files with a symbol named depends (it could have a different name). These code files are called targets. The depends symbol is needed only to satisfy MAKE's syntactical requirements, permitting a single MAKE file to compile multiple .EXE programs in the same directory.

Each line ends with a backslash to continue the command on the next line. A blank line or a line ending without a backslash terminates the command. The file TURBOC.CFG is needed only by Borland C++ and Turbo C++. MAKE files for Microsoft C/C++ and Zortech C++ do not create this file.

MAKE next hunts for dependency rules that describe how to construct each of the target .EXE files. These rules have the general form

```
welcome.exe: welcome.cpp
  $(CCLL) $(CLFLAGS) welcome $(TSCLIB)
```

File WELCOME.EXE is one of the targets—a file that MAKE attempts to create. Following on the same line are a colon and the name of one or more files on which the target depends. In this case, WELCOME.EXE depends on WELCOME.CPP. If you change WELCOME.CPP, thus causing this file's date and time to be later than the date and time of WELCOME.EXE, MAKE issues the command on the next line, which must be indented.

> **Hint:** To add new programs to MAKE files, insert the program's .EXE filename among others associated with depends, then add a dependency rule. Use an existing rule as a guide.

The command (the second line in the preceding example) must be preceded by one or more blanks. It can be any DOS command, but typically runs a compiler or linker. Symbols like $(CCLL) are macros that expand to the text associated with the symbol in parentheses. CCLL in this case is the name of a compiler and linker control program (BCC for Borland C++, TCC for Turbo C++, CL for Microsoft C/C++, or ZTC for Zortech C++). The macro $(CLFLAGS) specifies compiler options. The macro $(TSCLIB) gives the name of this book's cross-compilation library.

Though complex, MAKE files greatly simplify the tedious chore of typing lengthy compiler commands and options at a DOS prompt. Professional programmers use MAKE files very similar to those described here, although in many cases, there is only one target .EXE or .OBJ file in each directory.

> **Note:** MAKE files for Borland C++ and Turbo C++ use echo commands to create a configuration file TURBOC.CFG in the current directory. This configuration file specifies pathnames and options, which might be too long to supply directly to the compiler. (Borland C++ and Turbo C++ do not use environment variables to specify pathnames, and long paths can easily exceed the command-line's length limit, usually 128 characters.) Microsoft C/C++ and Zortech C++ can use environment variables to specify directory paths, and these compilers do not require similar configuration files.

# ROOTxxx.INC Include Files

These files supply root directories for the compiler and for this book's programs. Pathnames may include a drive letter. For example, C:\TSC is a legal pathname. You may specify multiple directories as in C:\EXAMPLES\TSC, but a path may not be a root directory. A path such as C:\ is *not* permitted. (You cannot install this book's files in a disk's root directory.)

ROOTxxx.INC files exist only in this book's installation directory—C:\TSC, for example. The following table lists the symbols in ROOTxxx.INC files.

**ROOTxxx.INC symbols**

| Symbol | Description | Example |
| --- | --- | --- |
| CPPROOT | Compiler root directory | = c:\borlandc |
| TSCROOT | This book's root directory | = c:\tsc |

# MAKExxx.INC Include Files

MAKE files also include MAKExxx.INC files, located in the C:\TSC or other directory. Borland C++ MAKE files, for example, include MAKEBTC.INC, which creates symbols that specify the compiler name, various directory paths, options, and other items.

The following table lists the symbols in MAKExxx.INC files. MAKE files for specific compilers may not need every one of these symbols. Examples in the table are for Borland C++. See the MAKEMSC.INC and MAKEZTC.INC files for sample Microsoft C/C++ and Zortech C/C++ settings.

**MAKExxx.INC symbols**

| Symbol | Description | Example (Borland C++) |
| --- | --- | --- |
| CC | Compiler name | = bcc |
| CCLL | Compiler and linker name | = bcc |
| CDEBUG | Debugging option | = |
| CFLAGS | Compile-only flags | = -c -Od -g1 |

| Symbol | Description | Example (Borland C++) |
|--------|-------------|------------------------|
| CLFLAGS | Compile and link flags | = -Od -g1 |
| INC | Include (.h) pathname(s) | = $(TSCROOT)\include... |
| LIB | Library (.lib) pathname(s) | = $(TSCROOT\lib... |
| MODEL | Memory model | = s |
| TSCLIB | Cross-compilation library | = tscbcc.lib |
| WARN | Warning level | = -w |

The default settings are purposely restrictive. If you want full debugging information to be included so you can run your compiler's debugger to examine compiled programs, set CDEBUG to -v for Borland C++ and Turbo C++, to /Zi for Microsoft C/C++, or to -g for Zortech C++. This option greatly increases the sizes of .EXE and .OBJ files, however, and to save disk space, leave CDEBUG set to a blank command. *Do not delete this or any other symbol.* Instead, to disable a symbol, add a new command and convert the original into a comment preceded with # so you can later restore the default setting. For example, you might change the WARN command to

```
# WARN = -w
WARN =
```

Assign various options to CFLAGS, but do not delete option -c. This option is needed to compile separate modules to .OBJ code files, which are linked to other similar files for creating a finished .EXE code file.

The similar CLFLAGS symbol specifies compiler and linker options. It's typically the same as CFLAGS minus -c, but it could have a different set of options.

**Note:** CFLAGS and CLFLAGS are purposely set for maximum restrictions. For example, all warnings are enabled, no code optimizations are permitted, and in the case of Borland C++ and Turbo C++, just one warning aborts a compilation. These settings help keep beginning programmers on the straight and narrow path to C++ proficiency, but they might be too restrictive for pros. If you want to use another set of options, edit CFLAGS and CLFLAGS before compiling.

The INC and LIB symbols specify include- and library-pathnames. For Borland C++ and Turbo C++ users, these two symbols must be complete paths. For example, by default, MAKEBTC.INC sets these symbols to

```
INC = $(TSCROOT)\include;$(CPPROOT)\include
LIB = $(TSCROOT)\lib;$(CPPROOT)\lib
```

Microsoft C/C++ and Zortech C++ rely on environment variables named INCLUDE and LIB to specify similar paths. The INC and LIB symbols are not defined for these compilers.

The MODEL symbol specifies a memory model letter (s by default for the small memory model). You may compile programs using any of your compiler's memory models—just change the letter, for example, to m (medium memory model). (There's little or no benefit to be gained by changing memory models for this book's programs. You might, however, want to use a different model in your own programs, in which case you would need to recompile any of this book's modules that you use.)

> **Note:** If you change the memory model, you must rebuild the cross-compilation library, which is supplied only in small memory-model form. See "BUILDxxx.BAT Batch Files" later in this introduction.

The TSCLIB symbol specifies the name of this book's cross-compilation library. For example, MAKEMSC.INC sets TSCLIB like this:

```
TSCLIB = tscmsc.lib
```

The TSCMSC.LIB file, located in C:\TSC\LIB, contains the cross-compilation library in compiled form, ready for linking to Microsoft C/C++ programs. Each compiler has its own precompiled library. The TSCLIB symbol specifies only a filename, not a complete path.

The symbol WARN specifies a warning level. All warnings are enabled by default, but you can change the level if you want. (The option -w enables warnings in Borland C++, but -w- is needed for Zortech C++. Microsoft uses an altogether different option, /WX. Compare MAKExxx.INC files for other option differences.)

Finally, in MAKExxx.INC files there is a strange-looking command called an *implicit rule*. This rule looks like a dependency rule in a MAKE file. For example, here is the implicit rule from MAKEBTC.INC for Borland C++:

```
.cpp.obj :
  $(CC) $(CFLAGS) $.
```

This rule tells MAKE how to compile .OBJ files that depend on .CPP files. With this single implicit rule, MAKE attempts to compile MODULE.CPP into the target file MODULE.OBJ by using the rule's specified command (the second line in this example). Because MAKExxx.INC uses an implicit rule for constructing .OBJ files, individual MAKE files need only specify .OBJ targets. They don't have to issue explicit dependency-rule commands to compile separate modules.

Each MAKExxx.INC file has an implicit rule for creating .OBJ code files. The forms of these commands differ among the various compilers, but the results are the same.

## MAKExxx.BAT Batch Files

As mentioned earlier, your C:\TSC or other installation directory has batch files such as MAKEMSC.BAT for compiling all programs with a single command. If you don't use these batch files, you can delete them and enter individual **make** commands for each chapter.

## BUILDxxx.BAT Batch Files

Don't delete these batch files. Located in C:\TSC\LIB, the BUILDxxx.BAT files automate the complex chore of rebuilding this book's cross-compilation library.

Programmers use the word "make" to describe interim compilations—the process of keeping a complex program up to date by compiling only the minimum number of files. The word "build" typically describes the process of recompiling all modules, whether required or not. At many software companies, the latest "build" refers to the current release version of a program.

You can compile the cross-compilation library files as you do other programs listed in this book. Change to C:\TSC\LIB\SOURCE, and use the appropriate MAKEFILE.xxx file for your compiler. This does not, however, create the compiled .LIB file. To do that, you must run the BUILDxxx.BAT file in C:\TSC\LIB. For example, to rebuild the Microsoft C/C++ library, enter the commands

```
c:
cd \tsc\lib
buildmsc
```

Though different in form, each BUILDxxx.BAT batch file performs these three essential tasks:

1. Copies all .h header files from C:\TSC\LIB\SOURCE to C:\TSC\INCLUDE.

2. Runs the MAKE (or NMAKE) utility to compile the library source files.

3. Runs the compiler's library utility (TLIB for Borland C++ and Turbo C++, LIB for Microsoft C/C++, or ZORLIB for Zortech C++).

The last step creates the appropriate .LIB file for each compiler. (You can delete the .LIB files for compilers that you don't have. If you delete the wrong .LIB file, just rebuild the library.) Be sure to rebuild the library if you upgrade to a new compiler version.

> **Note:** When rebuilding the cross-compilation library, you might receive numerous warnings about files that are not in the library. You can safely ignore these warnings, but unfortunately, you can't turn them off.

# Summary

- This book teaches C++ programming. You can use Borland C++ 3.0, Borland C++ 3.1, Microsoft C/C++ 7.0, Turbo C++ 3.0, or Zortech C++ 3.0 to compile all of the book's programs.

- Install the accompanying diskette according to directions in this introduction. The files on the diskette are compressed. Before using the files, you must decompress them.

- After installation, configure this book's files for your compiler. Instructions are included in this introduction for each supported compiler and version. Be sure to include your compiler's BIN directory on the system PATH.

- To simplify compilation, this book uses automated MAKE files, similar to those that professional programmers use for compiling complex programs. This chapter explains how to use MAKE (named NMAKE in Microsoft C/C++).

- You might want to copy your compiler's MAKE files to new files named MAKEFILE with no extension. For example, if you are using Borland C/C++, copy MAKEFILE.BTC to MAKEFILE in most directories. You can then type **make** (**nmake** for Microsoft C/C++) at a DOS prompt to compile programs in the current directory.

- After installing the accompanying diskette, configuring your system, and trying the MAKE files, turn to the next chapter to begin learning how to program in C++.

# Discovering C++

T his chapter will help you discover what C++ is and how easy it is to use. If you
know Pascal or C, so much the better. You can skim this chapter as a guide to
how C++ differs from those popular, and in many ways similar, languages. I'll assume
only that you know a few basics, such as what bits and bytes are, how to give DOS
commands, and how to run programs.

I'll begin at the beginning (a good place to start) with an introduction to the parts
of a C++ program—items shared by all programs in this book. After that, I'll cover a
lot of ground quickly, exploring streams, constants, variables, input and output, and
operators. Nearly all C++ programs use one or more of these fundamentals, so take the
time to go through the examples and run the sample listings. The discoveries you make
now will be invaluable later.

## A C++ Anatomy Lesson

A ll C++ programs are related—in other words, their skeletons share some of the
same bones. A good way to learn how those bones are connected is to dissect a
small sample program like WELCOME.CPP (Listing 1.1). To compile the program—that is, to convert the program's text into executable code—change to this
chapter's directory on disk. For example, from a DOS prompt, enter the commands

```
c:
cd \tsc\c01
```

If you haven't done so already, copy your compiler's MAKE file to a new file named MAKEFILE (with no extension):

- For Borland C++ or Turbo C++, enter **copy makefile.btc makefile**

- For Microsoft C/C++, enter **copy makefile.msc makefile**

- For Zortech C++, enter **copy makefile.ztc makefile**

Next, if you are using Borland C++, Turbo C++, or Zortech C++, enter **make** to compile the chapter's programs. If you are using Microsoft C/C++, enter **nmake**. After compilation, run WELCOME by typing its name, or use your normal method for running DOS programs.

**Note:** From now on, compile and run sample listings this same way in each new chapter. If the MAKE utility doesn't seem to do much, check whether the programs are already compiled, a fact that MAKE determines. If you receive errors, consult this book's introduction for setup instructions. You must install the accompanying diskette, decompress the files, and configure your compiler (assign environment variables and set the system PATH, for example) before you can compile programs.

### Listing 1.1. WELCOME.CPP.

```
1: #include <tscdefs.h>
2: #include IOSTREAM_H
3:
4: int main()
5: {
6:    cout << "Welcome to C++ programming!\n";
7:    return 0;
8: }
```

I added the line numbers and colons at left for reference. If your editor displays the current line number, use the printed numbers to locate specific lines on-screen.

Skip lines 1–2 for now (I'll explain these later) and train your sights on lines 5–8, which form the substance of this small program. Taking out lines 6–7 leaves the shell:

```
int main()
{
}
```

This is called a function—one of C++'s most important features. In this case, there's only one function named main(). It returns an integer value, of type int. In other C++ programs, there might be dozens, or even hundreds or more functions of unique names written in this same form. But no matter how many functions a program has, it must have one and only one function called main(). When a C++ program runs, it always begins at main().

> **Note:** Don't confuse the term *function* with mathematical functions. Functions in C++ may perform mathematical chores, but they don't have to. In C++, functions are specifically-named groups of instructions that perform one or more actions. As you'll learn, a function's actions are completely up to you to define.

The empty parentheses after the function name tell the compiler that the function receives no information from the outside world. Later, you'll learn how to list parameters inside the parentheses, allowing functions to process incoming information. For example, you might pass to main() a command-line option or a filename that you want the program to use.

The left and right braces that follow the function name and its parentheses surround the function's body. Returning to Listing 1.1, you can see that main()'s body contains two lines of programming:

```
{
  cout << "Welcome to C++ programming!\n";
  return 0;
}
```

Because of the surrounding braces, the compiler knows that the enclosed programming lines—called statements—belong to function main(). Generally speaking, a statement is anything in a program that performs an action when the program runs.

The first statement in WELCOME.CPP writes a line of text to the standard output, usually the display (more on this later). The second statement returns the value 0 to the startup code that executed main(). (A program's startup code prepares internal values needed by various functions.) The statement could return a different value as an error code, which another program (or DOS) receives. By convention, zero means no error. All C++ main() functions should have a similar return statement, or you can also write them like this:

```
void main()
{
}
```

The word void means "nothing." Declared with a void return type, this main() function returns nothing and does not require a return statement. You can also leave out the return type altogether:

```
main()
{
  return 0;
}
```

C++ assumes that a typeless function returns an int value, so this form requires a return statement. I've used this popular style for main() functions throughout this book.

Everything else in a C++ program is either a declaration, a definition, an expression, or an instruction for the compiler to do something during compilation. Typically, declarations give the compiler some information, such as the format of a new data type. Definitions create space for storing values in memory, such as a variable of a previously declared data type. Expressions like 1 + m are evaluated to a single value. Other instructions may alter the way the compiler works, or they may compile different sections of the program's text based on various conditions.

Don't be concerned about memorizing all these terms. Authors and even experienced programmers frequently mix up the words *declaration* and *definition* anyway, and you can't rely on all texts to use the phrases consistently. At this early stage, it's more important for you to understand the purpose of C++ braces—to group one or more statements, expressions, declarations, or definitions as a unit that attaches to something immediately above. Together, the braces and the programming inside are called a block—a collection of items you want the compiler to treat as one.

# Streams

When you run the sample program, you see that it displays the message *Welcome to C++ programming!* There are different ways to accomplish similar output operations, but the most convenient method in C++ is to use an *output-stream statement.* Take a close look at Listing 1.1's sample output-stream statement:

```
cout << "Welcome to C++ programming!\n";
```

First comes the name of the output-stream object, cout, short for "character output." (By the way, I like to pronounce cout and similar words as "see out," not "kout." This makes cryptic phrases in programs sound better to my inner ear, but if you want to say "kout," I won't argue.) The object cout is the output's destination—a place where you can send information that you want the program to display or print in character form.

The double-character symbol << represents the stream's output symbol. It's one symbol even though it's composed of two characters. The symbol appears to point to cout, implying that the items to the right flow in that direction toward the destination object at the left, like water flowing down a stream to the sea. At the source of the program's stream is the string

```
"Welcome to C++ programming!\n"
```

The double quotes tell the compiler to take the enclosed text literally—that is, not to process the quoted characters as programming statements or other instructions. The \n symbol—another single symbol composed of two characters—is called the *newline character.* Inserting \n inside a string (it doesn't have to be at the end) causes the program to start a new line on the terminal or printer.

A good way to learn how output streams work is to try several on your own. Load WELCOME.CPP into your editor. Then add these lines inside main()'s body, between the opening and closing braces:

```
cout << "Welcome ";
cout << "to ";
cout << "C++ programming!\n";
```

**Hint:** After making these changes, save them to disk, go to a DOS prompt, and type **make**. For Microsoft C/C++, type **nmake**.

Notice that these three lines produce the same results as the original program. Because the first two lines do not end with \n, the program displays them on the same line. Try adding \n inside the closing quotes near the end of the first two lines. What happens now when you run the program?

Another way to produce similar results is to use a single output-stream statement with multiple parts. For example, you can write:

```
cout << "Welcome " << "to\n"
     << "C++ programming!\n";
```

Examine this and the preceding example carefully. Run them in sample programs and observe the results. In the first example, there are three statements, each ending with a semicolon—C++'s statement terminator. All statements in C++ programs must be terminated with semicolons. (That's "terminated" as in "ended," not "terminated" as in the movies.) In the second example, there are three strings, but there is only one statement, divided into two lines. C++ ignores line endings in the text, and it doesn't matter if you write statements on one line or several.

In general, you can write output-stream statements in this form:

```
cout << a << b << ... << c;
```

Items a, b, and c flow to the output-stream object cout. You can string together as many items this way as necessary, typing them on one line or separate lines:

```
cout << a
     << b
     << ...
     << c;
```

In each case, a semicolon terminates the statement, not each line. You can also split long strings over several lines to make typing easier. For example, insert this statement into Listing 1.1:

```
cout << "There was a young lady named Bright, \
Whose speed was far faster than light; \
She set out one day, \
In a relative way, \
And returned home the previous night.\n";
```

That's one output-stream statement, and it writes a single string. The backslashes at the end of each line tell the compiler to join the previous characters with those on the next line. The compiler ignores and throws away the backslash and any following spaces. When you run the program, you'll see that the limerick is displayed as one string (probably on two lines if your terminal automatically wraps around at the right border). To display the verses on separate lines, you need to insert \n symbols at their ends. Notice that there are only two quote marks—one at the beginning of the string and one at the end. There is no limit to the length of a string you can create with this trick.

> **Note:** The phrase "no limit" may rub some people the wrong way. Of course, there has to be a limit—you can't store a 100M-long string on a 20M hard disk. You also can't type more characters than there are hydrogen atoms in the universe. But there's no reason to be so technically finicky. Generally, "no limit" means the compiler imposes no specific limit on a construction.

We'll return to streams, strings, and characters later. Until then, try writing your own programs, using Listing 1.1 as a guide. (If you have trouble compiling your own programs, see "Compiling Your Own Programs" in Chapter 10, "Cross-Compilation Tools.") Display various strings. Insert one or more \n newline characters inside your test strings at different places to see the effect this symbol has.

# A Note about Semicolons

At first, one of the most difficult lessons to learn about C++ is where to use semicolons. Look one last time at Listing 1.1. As you can see, the statements at lines 6–7 end with a semicolon, but the other line endings are bare. All statements must end with semicolons. As I mentioned earlier, a semicolon terminates a statement, telling the C++ compiler that it has reached the statement's end. Because a semicolon, and not a new line, ends a statement, you can write single statements like this on multiple lines:

```
cout << "This is "
    << "one statement, "
    << "not three.\n";
```

There is only one semicolon at the end of the last line, so C++ reads that text as if you had written

```
cout << "This is one statement, not three.\n";
```

Don't try to memorize a lot of semicolon rules. At first, you'll probably insert semicolons where they don't belong and leave them out where they do. The trick to learning where semicolons go is to learn the elements of C++. Observe which of those elements require terminating characters. Eventually, semicolon placement will seem natural and obvious.

> **Note:** If you happen to use a semicolon in the wrong spot, the compiler displays an error message. Even experienced C++ programmers accidentally misuse semicolons, so don't be concerned if you receive many of these error messages at first.

## Comments about Comments

While writing this book, I made many notes on the side, reminding myself to expand a thought, research a fact, or insert a program listing in the text. Editors also insert notes to ask me to clarify a badly worded sentence. (With luck, and their skill, none will remain by the time you read this.)

Comments in programs are exactly like those notes. They are private messages for your eyes only, or perhaps for another programmer's eyes. To insert a comment into a program, surround it with the double-character symbols /* and */. Here are a few sample comments that might appear at the beginning of a program:

```
/* Title: MYPROGRAM by Mr. Software */
/* Revision 1.00B -- all bugs fixed (I hope) */
/* Original author skipped town */
```

Comments in this style may extend over one or more lines, and many programmers like to preface their files with a descriptive section like this:

```
/*  welcome.cpp by Tom Swan
 *  Date: 6/1/1998
 *  Revision: 1.0
 */
```

The vertical asterisks are merely an illusion—they have no practical significance. If you look carefully, you'll see that this text is a single comment starting with /* and reading left to right until reaching the */ symbol on the fourth line. The compiler completely ignores everything else in between, including the two extra asterisks that align with those in the two comment brackets.

You also can insert comments inside statements, although this often leads to confusing programs. Try adding this statement to Listing 1.1:

```
cout << "No comment " /*Oh, yeah?*/ << "here!\n";
```

Running this statement displays the string *No comment here!* The compiler ignores the comment /*Oh, yeah?*/ in the middle of the line.

Comments bracketed with /* and */ are called C-style comments. You can use them in C or C++ programs. In addition to this basic comment style, C++ also adds a second kind of comment, which is not available in C. A C++ comment must appear at the end of a line or on a line by itself. A C++ comment begins with a double slash. Here are the same comments used earlier but converted to C++ style:

```
// welcome.cpp by Tom Swan
// Date: 6/1/1998
// Revision: 1.0
```

When the compiler encounters a // symbol, it ignores all text from that point to the start of the next line (which might be another comment). This means that you can't use // inside statements, only at their ends. You also can't write multiline C++ comments. Typically, you'll use C++ comments to notate individual statements:

```
cout << "Your name? ";  // Prompt for user's name
```

The statement writes *Your name?* The comment after the end of the statement is a private note that describes the statement's purpose.

C++ and C comments can also be nested. Nesting is useful for temporarily removing a section of a program while hunting for bugs (because it's often helpful to delete programming to see what effect that has on a problem):

```
/*
cout << "Doesn't display";    // Output one string
cout << "Neither does this";  // Output another string
*/
```

Due to the C-style comment brackets on the first and last lines, the compiler ignores everything else in between—including the two C++ comments at the ends of the middle two lines.

To delete an entire line temporarily, just add // at the beginning. For example,

```
// cout << "Your age? "; // Prompt for user's age
```

Even though the line already ends in a C++ comment, the slashes at the front of the line cause C++ to ignore everything to the right—including that original comment at the end of the line.

Listing 1.2, COMMENT.CPP, demonstrates C and C++ comment styles, showing how to use // to create a distinctive "box" at the beginning of a listing and how to use C-style comments to insert multiline comments in programs.

### Listing 1.2. COMMENT.CPP.

```
 1: // comment.cpp -- Demonstrates C and C++ comment styles
 2:
 3: #include <tscdefs.h>
 4: #include IOSTREAM_H
 5:
 6: /////////////////////////////////////////////////
 7: // Author   : Tom Swan
 8: // Revision : 2.0  05/16/1992   Time: 07:15 am
 9: // Purpose  : Demonstrates C++ comment styles
10: /////////////////////////////////////////////////
11:
12: main()
13: {
14:   cout << "A Brief C++ Commentary\n";  // Display title
15:   cout << "\n";  // Display blank line under title
16:
17: /* This paragraph demonstrates that
18: C-style comments can occupy more
19: than one line. */
20:
21:   cout << "// This is not a comment.\n\n";
22:
23:   cout << "/* This also is not a comment.*/ \n\n";
24:
25:   cout /* This is a comment. */ << "This text is displayed.\n";
26:   return 0;
27: }
```

When you run COMMENT, you see that the compiler ignores any comment brackets inside strings. This happens because a string's double quotes tell the compiler to stop processing text as programming, but to take that text literally. This goes for comment brackets too. Inside a string's quotes, comment brackets are treated just like any other characters.

Characters like \n are called *escape characters*. The double symbol represents a newline code that, when written to the display, causes the cursor to drop down a line and move over to the far left. So, you might ask, how can you display the two characters \n? That's easy. Just repeat the backslash:

```
cout << "A \\n character begins a new line.\n";
```

C++ interprets the escape code \\ as a command to print a single backslash. The following n in this statement is therefore written as a character.

Most listings in this book begin with a C++ comment similar to the one at line 1 in the preceding example. This line identifies the program by filename and describes what it does. As you may have discovered on your own, the accompanying disk files end with a copyright notice and revision history that look something like this:

```
// Copyright (c) 1990,1992 by Tom Swan. All rights reserved
// Revision 1.00    Date: 07/14/1990    Time: 11:33 am
// Revision 2.00    Date: 05/16/1992    Time: 07:12 am
// 1. Converted for Borland C++ 3, Microsoft C/C++ 7, Zortech C++ 3
```

I inserted these lines at the end of most files so I could easily remove the lines from the printed listings, but still have the line numbers match the lines in your text editor. Most programmers put their copyright notices and other details at the beginning of their files. That way, the lines pop into view when the file is edited.

> **Note:** Always check the revision history number and date. I may update the files on disk from time to time to correct any errors discovered after the listings were printed in the book.

A second comment sample in Listing 1.3, NOTHING.CPP, uses a C comment and a C++ comment for no other reason than to explain that this program does nothing. The program is one of the smallest you can write in C++.

### Listing 1.3. NOTHING.CPP.

```
1: // nothing.cpp -- A mere shell of a program
2:
3: main()
4: {
```

*continues*

**Listing 1.3. continued**

```
5:   // This program does nothing!
6:   return 0;  // Needed to prevent compiler warning
7:   }
```

# Identifiers

Identifiers are unique symbols that you type into programs. The function name `main` minus its parentheses is an identifier—it identifies the function by name. Well-chosen identifiers are your primary tool for writing programs that make sense.

C++ recognizes many native identifiers such as `main`. Others are up to you to invent and use. Identifiers may contain only upper- or lowercase letters, digits, and underlines, and they may be any length. (Specific C++ compilers may impose an upper limit on identifier length—perhaps 127 characters—but you probably would never need an identifier of that length anyway.) In addition, identifiers must begin with an upper- or lowercase letter from A to Z, as in `fn1` or `Catch22`. The identifier `123abc` is not legal; `abc123` is.

You can also use underlines to separate words in long identifiers such as `head_count` and `bottom_of_the_barrel`. However, don't put underlines at the beginning of identifiers. C++ accepts identifiers such as `_value` and `__overandunder`, but you risk causing a conflict with system identifiers that often begin similarly.

# Case: A Sensitive Issue

C++ is case-sensitive, and all symbols count. This means that `keyPress`, `keypress`, and `key_press` are different identifiers, even though they seem similar to our eyes. For this reason, it pays to adopt a typing style and stick to it. If you mix styles in your programs—using uppercase at some times, and lowercase at others—you'll just make life with programming more difficult than necessary.

Most C++ programmers prefer to type identifiers in lowercase. Words such as `XYCOORD` and `PAYMENT` appear to shout from the screen, and a display full of uppercase text can obscure the program's logic. In lowercase, `xycoord` and `payment` don't crowd the screen and are easier on the eyes. Many people also prefer to write multi-word identifiers as arrayOfNames instead of array_of_names or arrayofnames. Any of these styles is okay as long as you use it consistently. (I use upper- and lowercase, and I rarely capitalize the initial letter. Alternatively, you could write ArrayOfNames.)

# Keywords

Keywords are identifiers that C++ reserves for its own use. Sample keywords include auto, float, signed, void, and while. These are symbols that you may not use for your own purposes—they have special meanings to the compiler, and those meanings can't be changed.

Appendix A lists all reserved C++ keywords, but don't try to memorize that list—just consult it when you suspect that you have accidentally used a reserved keyword for another purpose. You'll learn C++'s keywords as you read about each one. Before finishing this book, you'll meet them all.

# Punctuators

You already know that a semicolon terminates C++ statements. Technically, a semicolon is a *punctuator*. The left and right braces you learned about earlier are also punctuators.

A punctuator is a kind of abbreviated keyword. It's a symbol (which might be composed of one, two, or three characters) with special meaning to the compiler. The full set of C++ punctuators includes these symbols:

```
#  ()  []  {}  ,  :  ;  ...
```

As with other keywords and symbols, it's best to learn about punctuators as you meet them. Their uses are mostly intuitive, and you don't have to memorize this list now.

# Separators

Separators differ from punctuators in one important way—they're invisible! Because separators are nowhere to be seen, the term *white space* describes them. C++ separators include blanks, tabs, carriage returns, and line feeds embedded in text.

Usually, C++ ignores white space, as long as you don't use spaces inside identifiers, numbers, and other words and symbols that belong together. All white space is the same to C++, which explains why statements can be written on multiple lines. To C++, it's all the same if two statements are divided by a carriage return or a blank. In fact, in place of the common indented style demonstrated in Listing 1.1, you could write the `main()` function on a single line like this:

```
main() { cout << "Welcome to C++ programming!\n"; return 0; }
```

The compiler cares only that the parts and symbols in `main()` are properly separated and punctuated. C++ doesn't care if those separations are line endings or blanks. Obviously, though, this unusual style makes programs more difficult to read and to debug.

# Header Files

Most of the sample listings in this book begin with a couple of lines like these:

```
#include <tscdefs.h>
#include IOSTREAM_H
```

The `#include` directive is a command that tells the compiler to read the contents of another file, called an *include file*. The first line here, for example, tells the compiler to read tscdefs.h and to process that file's contents exactly as though the file's text appeared at this spot.

Header files typically contain declarations, definitions, and other instructions that many programs can share. (By convention, in this book, header filenames are printed in lowercase. Other filenames are in uppercase.) The file tscdefs.h declares this book's cross-compilation library symbols. Other header files declare many other items, such as functions and data types.

Because the tscdefs.h filename is inside angle brackets, the compiler looks for the file in one or more preset directories. (In the introduction, you configured your compiler to recognize this book's installation directories, one of which, probably C:\TSC\INCLUDE, contains tscdefs.h.) If that line had been written as

```
#include "tscdefs.h"
```

the compiler would look for the file in the current directory. Surrounding a header filename with quote marks is useful for including header files that are needed by programs in the current directory, but aren't generally needed by other programs that you write.

Throughout this book, you will encounter many instances of another kind of #include directive that looks like this:

```
#include IOSTREAM_H
```

Although this command might appear to read a file named IOSTREAM_H, that's not exactly what happens. IOSTREAM_H is not a filename because it is not quoted or written inside angle brackets. IOSTREAM_H is a *macro*—a symbol that the compiler replaces with other text. In Borland C++, Microsoft C/C++, and Turbo C++, for example, the line is translated into

```
#include <iostream.h>
```

After translating the macro symbol, the compiler reads the contents of the iostream.h header file. Among other items, iostream.h declares the symbols used by output stream statements such as the cout statements you examined earlier. If you don't include the proper header file, the compiler will have no information about what cout means, and the compilation will end with an error message.

I/O streams in Zortech C++ are declared in a different header file, iostream.hpp. For that compiler, the IOSTREAM_H symbol is translated accordingly to

```
#include <iostream.hpp>
```

Another compiler might translate IOSTREAM_H to yet another filename. Using the IOSTREAM_H symbol rather than a literal filename permits the same line in the program's source text to work correctly with multiple compilers.

> **Note:** The IOSTREAM_H symbol is one of several similar devices that I developed specifically so this book's examples can be compiled with multiple C++ compilers. For more information on this topic, see Chapter 10, "Cross-Compilation Tools."

# Variables

In C++, a variable is a named location in memory (see Figure 1.1). Variables can store all sorts of data—strings, numbers, and multipart structures. A variable typically has a name that describes its purpose, and in general, you're free to use any names you like for your program's variables. As the figure illustrates, the name points to the location where the value is stored, although you can ignore that fact and just use the name in a program as though it is the value.

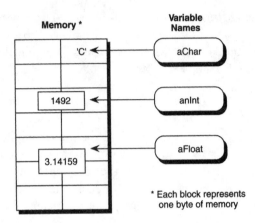

**Figure 1.1.** A variable is a named location in memory where a value is stored.

All variables have one common characteristic: an associated data type. This means that, in addition to choosing an appropriate name for a variable, you also have to tell the compiler what kind of information you want it to store. Table 1.1 lists C++'s common data types, showing examples of each, a type's size in bytes, and the range of values that variables of a type can hold.

**Table 1.1. Common C++ Data Types.**

| Data Type | Example | Size | Minimum | | Maximum |
|-----------|---------|------|---------|---|---------|
| char | 'c' | 1 | 0 | ... | 255 (or ASCII) |
| short | -7 | 2 | -32,768 | ... | 32,768 |
| int | 1024 | 2 | -32,768 | ... | 32,767 |
| long | 262144 | 4 | -2,147,483,648 | ... | 2,147,483,637 |
| float | 10.5 | 4 | 1.5E-45 | ... | 3.4E38 (approx) |
| double | 0.00045 | 8 | 5.0E-324 | ... | 1.7E308 (approx) |
| long double | 1e-8 | 10 | 3.4E-4932 | ... | 1.1E4932 (approx) |

> **Note:** All C++ compilers do not necessarily store variables of certain data types in the same number of bytes. The information in Table 1.1 applies to most MS-DOS C++ compilers, although exact value ranges may differ. Never write programs that rely on a data type to have a specific size or value range. A `char` variable, however, always occupies one byte.

To create a variable in a program, start with the data type and finish with an identifier and semicolon. For example, this line creates a `char` variable named `yesno`:

```
char yesno;
```

This statement is called a *definition* because it defines space for storing a variable in memory—in this case, a character in a single byte of space. You can insert this and other variable definitions just about anywhere—inside a function, outside a function, between other statements, in a block, and so on. As you'll learn, however, the location of definitions affects the way the compiler creates space for storing variables and can also affect the way a program runs. For now, I'll define all variables either above the function `main()` or just after `main()`'s opening brace, two of the most typical locations for variables.

## Initializing Variables with Definitions

There are two ways to initialize variables—that is, to give them starting values. The first way is probably the best in most cases, because it combines the definition of a variable with the assignment of its initial value:

```
char yesno = 'Y';
```

This creates a variable `yesno` of type `char` and assigns to that variable the character *Y*. By *assigns,* I mean "stores in memory at the location represented by the variable's name." This definition is similar to the preceding one, but ends with an equal sign and the value to store in the variable. Here are two more samples:

```
int counter = 1;
float weight = 155.5;
```

Variable `counter` is of type `int` and is assigned the initial value of 1. Variable `weight` is of type `float` and is assigned the initial value of 155.5. If you insert these definitions into a test program, you can display their values with statements such as these:

```
cout << "yesno = " << yesno << '\n';
cout << "counter = " << counter << '\n';
cout << "weight = " << weight << '\n';
```

When you compile these statements, the compiler replaces the variables yesno, counter, and weight with instructions that retrieve the associated values from memory. The compiler then converts the values to text form, which the output-stream statements display. Because each variable is bound to a specific data type, C++ knows that it should display yesno as a character, counter as an integer, and weight as a floating-point number.

Listing 1.4, VARIABLE.CPP, demonstrates how to initialize variables of all data types from Table 1.1. Each variable definition assigns a starting value in a form that's appropriate for each data type. Output-stream statements then display those values.

## Listing 1.4. VARIABLE.CPP.

```
 1: // variable.cpp -- Common variables
 2:
 3: #include <tscdefs.h>
 4: #include IOSTREAM_H
 5:
 6: main()
 7: {
 8:    char slash = '/';
 9:    short month = 3;
10:    int year = 1991;
11:    long population = 308700000L;
12:    float pi = 3.14159;
13:    double velocity = 186281.7;
14:    long double lightYear = 5.88e12;
15:
16:    cout << "Date = " << month << slash << year << '\n';
17:    cout << "Population of the U.S.A. = " << population << '\n';
18:    cout << "Pi = " << pi << '\n';
19:    cout << "Velocity of light = " << velocity
20:         << " mi./sec." << '\n';
21:    cout << "One light year = " << lightYear << " mi." << '\n';
22:    return 0;
23: }
```

VARIABLE displays each of the variables defined at lines 8–14. The output-stream statements at lines 16–21 display these values, using forms that are appropriate for the variables' data types. On-screen, you see

```
Date = 3/1991
Population of the U.S.A. = 308700000
Pi = 3.14159
Velocity of light = 186281.7 mi./sec.
One light year = 5.88e+012 mi.
```

# Initializing Variables with Assignments

Another way to initialize variables is to use separate assignment statements after defining the variables. For example, instead of line 8 in Listing 1.4, you can create the variable with the following definition:

```
char slash;
```

Then, later in the program, you can use an assignment statement to store a value in slash:

```
slash = '/';
```

The compiler interprets the equal sign as an instruction to assign the value on the right to the variable on the left. More exactly, the compiler generates code to store a value representing an ASCII slash character in a memory location reserved for the variable named slash (see Figure 1.2).

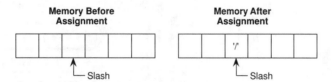

**Figure 1.2.** The assignment statement slash = '/'; stores an ASCII slash character at the location reserved for the slash variable.

You can also assign values to the other variables in Listing 1.4. For example, add this statement after line 14:

```
population = -500;
```

When you run the modified program, it displays the population of the U.S.A. as –500. Obviously, that value is incorrect, but it shows how an assignment can replace a variable's initial value. This is an important characteristic of variables. A program can change a variable's value as often as necessary, and every time the program assigns a value to a variable, the new value replaces the old.

No matter which of the two methods you decide to use for assigning values to variables, initializing variables in programs is important. If you forget to assign starting values to variables, the variables use whatever values exist in memory at the variables' reserved locations. Uninitialized variables are responsible for all sorts of programming bugs—from incorrect bank balances to faulty satellite orbits. To avoid such problems in your own code, be sure to give all variables starting values.

# Scoop on Scope

Statements can refer to variables, but only if the variables are within the same scope. The scope of a variable extends to the boundaries of its defining block.

Figure 1.3 shows a sample program (not included on disk) that contains nested blocks inside the main function. The sample program is artificial, but it demonstrates how scope limits the visibility of variables.

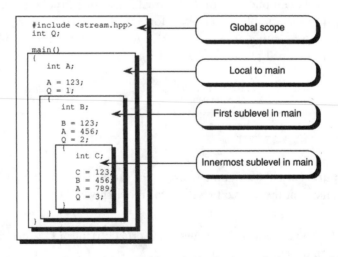

**Figure 1.3.** The scope of a variable extends only to the boundaries of the block that defines it.

The figure illustrates several important facts about scope. First, the global scope includes the entire program. This means that the integer Q is accessible to all statements, no matter where they are located. Q is a global variable—its scope extends to the four corners of the program's world.

Definitions inside main()'s braces, such as the integer A, are local to main(). Thus, only statements inside main()—that is, within the same scope as main()'s block delimited with braces—may use A. Any statements outside this block may not use A. (In this sample program, there are no such statements.) In fact, outside its defining block, A doesn't even exist in memory!

Farther inside main() is a nested block, labeled in the figure "First sublevel in main." Because the block is nested inside main()'s primary block, the nested block can use its own definition of B plus the integer A defined on the outer layer. The nested block also can use the global variable Q. Nested blocks can always "see" the definitions in their surrounding blocks. However, those outer layers can't "see" into the inner nest. This means that if you insert a statement immediately after A = 123, the program would no longer compile:

```
B = 456;
```

That won't work inside the block that's "Local to main" because B exists only within its defining block. main()'s primary block can't access B because B's scope is nested inside that outer level. Similarly, the statements inside the first sublevel in main() can't use the definitions inside the next and innermost level labeled "Innermost sublevel in main" in the figure. On this level, a fourth integer, C, is defined. As the figure illustrates, statements inside this innermost block can use all the variables defined in the program, but only this block can use C. Statements outside the innermost block can't see into this inner sanctum nested deeply in main().

A good way to think about nested blocks and scope is to imagine a house with rooms built inside one another. Windows in each room are made of one-way glass through which a room's occupant can look to the outside. Because the glass is one-way only, anyone outside can't see into inner rooms. The contents of a room are private except to the room's occupants (the block's statements) and to the occupants of other rooms nested inside this one.

For another example of how scope limits access to variables, compile and run Listing 1.5, SCOPE.CPP.

## Listing 1.5. SCOPE.CPP.

```
 1: // scope.cpp -- Demonstrate nested scopes
 2:
 3: #include <tscdefs.h>
 4: #include IOSTREAM_H
 5:
 6: int outer = 100;      // Global variable
 7:
 8: main()
 9: {
10:    int inner = 200;   // Local variable
11:
12:    cout << "outer = " << outer << '\n';
13:    cout << "inner = " << inner << '\n';
14:    {
15:      int noseeum = 300;
16:      cout << "noseeum = " << noseeum << '\n';
17:    }
18: //   cout << "noseeum = " << noseeum << '\n';
19:    return 0;
20: }
```

SCOPE defines three variables: outer, inner, and noseeum. The first definition at line 6 is global to the program. All statements in all scopes, no matter how deeply nested, can read and write this global variable. Line 10 is different—it is located inside main()'s block (between the braces at lines 9 and 20). This is an example of a local variable, a variable defined inside a block. The third variable definition at line 15 is also local, but it is nested inside a small block delimited by the braces at lines 14 and 17. Only statements inside this block's scope can read and write noseeum.

Prove this fact to yourself by removing the // comment symbol from the beginning of line 18, and activating the cout statement there. When you compile the modified program, the compiler reports an error even though this statement is identical to the one at line 16. The reason for the error is that noseeum is available only to statements within its scope. The statement at line 18 is outside that scope and therefore can't look in to "see" noseeum inside the inner level. (Undo your change to SCOPE before continuing.)

Note: In practice, there's no good reason to create nested blocks inside other blocks as SCOPE does for demonstration purposes. In future chapters, you'll learn practical uses for nested blocks to group statements inside control statements—but more on that later.

# Initializing Global and Local Variables

Even though they appear similarly in programs, global and local variables are stored differently in memory. The compiler allocates fixed space in a memory area called the data segment for all global variables. This memory stays put during the program's execution, and any variables in that memory keep their values while the program runs. If a statement assigns 100 to the global variable x, that variable equals 100 until another statement changes it, no matter what else the program does.

Local variables don't work that way. Instead of storing them in the program's data segment, the compiler creates temporary space for local variables. This space is part of another segment called the *stack*, which grows and shrinks as needed to accommodate information pushed onto it. That same information can then be popped from the stack, which shrinks when data is removed from its top. Using this device, C++ allocates space for variables when they are in scope. When a variable is not in scope, no stack space is assigned to the variable. Not only is that variable out of scope, it doesn't even exist in memory.

Another sample program demonstrates some of the important differences between global and local variables. Compile and run Listing 1.6, GLOBAL.CPP.

### Listing 1.6. GLOBAL.CPP.

```
1: // global.cpp -- Demonstrate global and local variables
2:
3: #include <tscdefs.h>
4: #include IOSTREAM_H
5:
6: int global = 100;
7: int globalDefault;
8:
9: // Disable warning: Possible use of variable before use
```

*continues*

## Listing 1.6. continued

```
10:
11: #ifdef __TSC_BTC__
12:   #pragma warn -def
13: #endif
14:
15: main()
16: {
17:   int local = 200;
18:   int localDefault;
19:
20:   cout << "global = " << global << '\n';
21:   cout << "local  = " << local  << '\n';
22:   cout << "globalDefault = " << globalDefault << '\n';
23:   cout << "localDefault  = " << localDefault  << '\n';
24:   return 0;
25: }
```

Lines 6 and 7 define two global variables. The first, global, is similar to other global definitions you've examined. Because it is a global variable, global is accessible by any statement and is stored in a fixed location in the program's data segment. Line 7 defines another global variable, globalDefault, but does not assign a starting value to the variable.

**Note:** The directives at lines 11–13 disable a warning given by Borland C++ and Turbo C++ when variables are used before being defined. The warning is expected because the purpose of this program is to demonstrate the effects of using variables in this usually improper way. Line 11's directive #ifdef __TSC_BTC__ tells the compiler to process subsequent lines only if the symbol __TSC_BTC__ is defined. Because this symbol is defined only if you are using Borland C++ or Turbo C++, line 12 is effective only for those compilers. Other compilers have similar symbols declared in tscdefs.h. The #endif directive at line 13 resets the compiler to normal running. Lines 11–13 are called a *conditional compilation directive.* These directives are messy, cumbersome, and best avoided. I have tried to reduce the number of conditional compilation directives in this book's programs, but unfortunately, a few are still needed.

By definition, all uninitialized variables like globalDefault at line 7 are assigned the starting value 0 when the program runs. You can rely on this fact—globalDefault is guaranteed to equal 0 unless another statement changes its value. Because line 6 specifies an initial value for global, however, that variable equals 100, not 0, when the program runs.

The two local variables at lines 17–18 use the same forms as the global definitions. Line 17 assigns a starting value to local, which the program displays. Line 18 does not assign a starting value. Even so, when the sample program runs, it still displays some value for localDefault.

That value illustrates one of the most important differences between global and local variables. Uninitialized globals are guaranteed to equal 0 when the program runs. Uninitialized locals come with no similar warranty. Because local variables are stored temporarily on the stack, they have whatever values were left in that space from a previous operation. Those values might be 0, but they also might be something else. In no case can you rely on local variables having any specific starting values.

# Input and Output

Loading information into memory and transferring that information from there to somewhere else are two jobs that probably occupy the lion's share in the jungle of statements that make up most programs. A program's input and output (I/O) statements are responsible for all comings and goings—displaying text on terminals, for example, and also printing reports, prompting for responses from users, and communicating with remote systems over telephone lines.

## Output Streams

Previous sample programs used output-stream statements to display strings and the values of variables. Listing 1.7, DT.CPP, shows a more practical example of these techniques, displaying the date and time.

**Listing 1.7. DT.CPP.**

```
 1: // dt.cpp -- Display the date and time
 2:
 3: #include <tscdefs.h>
 4: #include IOSTREAM_H
 5: #include <dos.h>
 6:
 7: main()
 8: {
 9:   DOS_DATE_T today;
10:   DOS_TIME_T theTime;
11:
12:   DOS_GETDATE(&today);
13:   cout << "The date is " << (int)today.month
14:        << "/" << (int)today.day << "/" << today.year << "\n";
15:   DOS_GETTIME(&theTime);
16:   cout << "The time is " << (int)theTime.hour << ":";
17:   if (theTime.minute < 10)
18:     cout << '0';
19:   cout << (int)theTime.minute << ":";
20:   if (theTime.second < 10)
21:     cout << '0';
22:   cout << (int)theTime.second << "\n";
23:   return 0;
24: }
```

There are a few items in DT.CPP you haven't learned about yet. For example, lines 9–10 define two structures named today and theTime. Lines 12 and 15 call library functions to read the date and time into these structures. Two other possibly unfamiliar statements at lines 17 and 20 use if statements to perform actions based on specified conditions. Also, line 5 includes the dos.h header file, which declares the date and time structures and functions that the program uses.

Don't be concerned with fully understanding the formats of DT.CPP's unfamiliar items. You will return to these items in future chapters. For now, concentrate on how the program uses output-stream statements to display text, characters, and the values that represent dates and times. These statements are similar to the samples you've seen in earlier listings, except for one difference. For example, at line 22 is the statement:

```
cout << (int)theTime.second << "\n";
```

The construction (int)theTime.second is called a *type cast*. Like a director casting a play, a type cast in C++ assigns new roles for variables to perform. In this case, the variable is second, a single-byte char contained in the structure theTime. The expression theTime.second tells the compiler to use the second *member* of theTime. Recall that char variables can store small values or ASCII characters. In this case, the program uses a char variable to store small integer values, not characters. However, because I didn't want to display seconds as ASCII characters, I had to tell the compiler to show the value as an integer. Prefacing the variable with (int) does this by casting char to type int.

## Old-Style Output

When reading C and C++ programs, you'll often run into statements such as these:

```
printf("Enter your name: ");
printf("Your balance is $%d\n", balance);
```

These are roughly equivalent to C++'s output-stream statements. The function printf() writes argument values in parentheses on the standard output, usually the display. The first statement displays a simple string. The second displays a string also, but uses a special notation (%d) to mark the locations of other values to be inserted in the output. In this case, the value to be inserted is a variable named balance, which printf() converts to characters and inserts at the marked location in the string for output. Running the program displays

```
Your balance is $75.68
```

> **Note:** To use printf() in C++ programs, insert the directive #include <stdio.h> at the beginning of your program. Because output streams can accomplish everything that printf() can, however, they're usually superior to printf().

# Formatted Output

Plain output streams don't always produce the needed effects. For example, writing an integer value named count displays the variable's value in decimal:

```
cout << "The count is " << count;
```

To display count and other values in hexadecimal or octal requires you to modify the output stream's default action for a data type. First, add this line to the beginning of your program, after #include <tscdefs.h>:

```
#include IOMANIP_H
```

Like IOSTREAM_H, the macro symbol IOMANIP_H is translated to an appropriate filename for your compiler. For Borland C++, Microsoft C/C++, and Zortech C++, the directive becomes

```
#include <iomanip.h>
```

Zortech C++ names this file iomanip.hpp, but the file's contents are similar in purpose. In the file are several *I/O manipulators* that you can insert in output stream statements. For example, use the oct, dec, and hex I/O manipulators to display octal, decimal, and hexadecimal values. These examples show how:

```
cout << "The octal count is " << oct << count;
cout << "The decimal count is " << dec << count;
cout << "The hexadecimal count is " << hex << count;
```

The I/O manipulators cause the count values to be formatted differently than without any manipulation.

Another manipulator, setw, aligns or justifies values within a certain number of character columns. To use setw, insert the number of columns in parentheses, and add the result to any output stream statement:

```
cout << "The count is " << setw(10) << dec << count;
```

This statement displays the value of count in decimal, adding spaces to the left to fill at least 10 character columns. If the number of columns is less than needed to display the value, it will be displayed correctly, but it won't be aligned as expected.

Listing 1.8, JUSTIFY.CPP, demonstrates how to use I/O manipulators. The program displays integers in octal, hexadecimal, and decimal, with and without using setw to justify the results. The program also displays a character and a string value.

**Listing 1.8. JUSTIFY.CPP.**

```
 1: // justify.cpp--Justifying characters and strings
 2:
 3: #include <tscdefs.h>
 4: #include IOSTREAM_H
 5: #include IOMANIP_H
 6:
 7: char *cutline = "\n------------------------------\n";
 8:
 9: main()
10: {
11:   int value = 249;
12:   char c = 'X';
13:   char *s = "I Brake for Butterflies";
14:
15:   cout << cutline << "Left justified:" << cutline;
16:   cout << value       << '\n';
17:   cout << hex << value << '\n';
18:   cout << oct << value << '\n';
19:   cout << c           << '\n';
20:   cout << s           << '\n';
21:
22:   cout << cutline << "Right justified:" << cutline;
23:   cout << setw(30) << dec << value << '\n';
24:   cout << setw(30) << hex << value << '\n';
25:   cout << setw(30) << oct << value << '\n';
26:   cout << setw(30) << c   << '\n';
27:   cout << setw(30) << s   << '\n';
28:   return 0;
29: }
```

Three variables at lines 11–13 create integer, character, and string values for the demonstration. Line 13 creates a pointer named s that points to the first character of the string delimited by double quotes. (Pointers are an advanced topic explained in Chapter 4, "Pointers About Pointers.") The output-stream statements at lines 15–20 show the default appearances of each variable, using hex and oct I/O manipulators to convert value to hexadecimal and octal. It's not necessary to use other manipulators such as dec, chr, and str because these are the default formats for integer, character, and string values.

Lines 22–27 show the same variables displayed within 30 columns. The only differences between these statements and the previous ones are the setw arguments and the use of dec at line 23 to reset output to decimal.

> **Note:** A bug in Borland C++ 3.0 and Turbo C++ 3.0 prevents setw from working correctly with single characters. For those compilers, line 26 does not display the character c justified in 30 columns. The problem was repaired in Borland C++ 3.1. Microsoft C/C++ and Zortech C++ justify characters correctly.

Even fancier formatting is possible in output streams with another function named form(). In this book's predecessor, *Learning C++*, form() was supplied with C++. More recent versions of C++ no longer have a form() function, much to the dismay of programmers who use it in their code.

This book adds the form() function back to C++, although my version is a tiny bit different from the original. To use my form() function, use these directives

```
#include <tscdefs.h>:
#include <form.h>
```

It would take pages of text to describe all that form() can do. (See Chapter 10, "Cross-Compilation Tools," for more information.) A sample program, Listing 1.9, FORMAT.CPP, goes a long way in demonstrating how form() can display values in a variety of formats.

## Listing 1.9. FORMAT.CPP.

```
 1: // format.cpp -- Demonstrate formatted output
 2:
 3: #include <tscdefs.h>
 4: #include IOSTREAM_H
 5: #include <form.h>
 6:
 7: main()
 8: {
 9:    int value = 0x79AF;
10:    unsigned long ulongValue = 123456789UL;
```

```
11:    long longValue = -123456789L;
12:    double pi = 3.14159;
13:    double balance = 572.63;
14:    char *name = "Judy";
15:    char buf[256];
16:
17:    cout << form(buf, "Plain decimal         = %d\n", value);
18:    cout << form(buf, "Signed decimal        = %+d\n", value);
19:    cout << form(buf, "Right justified        = %10d\n", value);
20:    cout << form(buf, "Plain hexadecimal      = %x\n", value);
21:    cout << form(buf, "Prefaced hexadecimal   = %#x\n", value);
22:    cout << form(buf, "Uppercase hexadecimal = %#X\n", value);
23: #ifdef __TSC_ZTC__
24:    cout << form(buf, "Binary                = %b\n", value);
25: #endif
26:    cout << form(buf, "Unsigned long decimal = %lu\n", ulongValue);
27:    cout << form(buf, "Signed long decimal   = %+ld\n", longValue);
28:    cout << form(buf, "Floating point        = %f\n", pi);
29:    cout << form(buf, "Scientific notation   = %e\n", pi);
30:    cout << form(buf, "Default notation      = %g\n", pi);
31:    cout << form(buf, "FP precision 10       = %.10f\n", pi);
32:    cout << form(buf, "%s's balance          = $%8.2f", name, balance);
33:    cout << '\n';
34:    return 0;
35: }
```

As in other sample programs in this chapter, FORMAT begins by defining several test variables at lines 9–14. The first three output statements (lines 17–19) display the int variable value, using output-stream statements and form(). These statements display the following lines:

```
Plain decimal   = 31151
Signed decimal  = +31151
Right justified = 31151
```

Take a good look at line 17. The percent sign inside the string tells the form() function to insert a value at this location in the resulting string. The percent sign (%) is called an *escape character* because it temporarily causes form() to "escape" from normal processing and treat the next characters specially. In this case, the d after the percent sign indicates that you want to display an integer value in decimal. That integer—in this case, value—must then follow the formatting string after a separating comma.

31

> **Note:** The form() function uses a character buffer, declared at line 15. This buffer, an example of an array (described in Chapter 2, "Making Statements and Building Structures") is where form() temporarily stores the function's resulting string. You must supply this buffer—a fact that was not true in form()'s original design. It is your responsibility to create a buffer that is large enough to hold the resulting string.

The second output stream statement (line 18) expands the formatting instruction to %+d. The plus sign tells form() to display a signed value, adding a + or - sign as needed. Without the plus sign in the formatting instruction, form() adds a minus sign to negative values, but does not add a plus sign to positive ones.

The third output stream statement (line 19) uses the formatting instruction %10d. This is similar to using the setw and dec I/O maniuplators to display value in decimal within 10 character columns. As you can see when you run the program, this statement shoves value toward the right.

Lines 20–22 display the same value variable but use formatting instructions %x, %#x, and %#X. The first of these lines displays values in unornamented hexadecimal. The second prefaces values with 0x, C++'s standard hexadecimal indicator. (0x9f, for example, represents the hexadecimal value 9f.) The output statement at line 22 is nearly the same as line 21, but displays the output in uppercase. On-screen, these three statements produce these lines:

```
Plain hexadecimal     = 79af
Prefaced hexadecimal  = 0x79af
Uppercase hexadecimal = 0X79AF
```

If you have Zortech C++, in addition to displaying decimal and hexadecimal formats, form() can display values in binary. The formatting instruction for this is %b. Using that instruction, line 24 displays this value:

```
Binary = 111100110101111
```

Borland C++, Microsoft C/C++, and Turbo C++ have no similar capability to display binary values, and this is one of the very few programs in this book that produce different output for different compilers. Because line 24 works only with Zortech C++, the conditional compilation directives at lines 23 and 25 select that line only if the __TSC_ZTC__ symbol is defined. That symbol won't be defined for any other compiler, and thus this line is skipped for the Borland and Microsoft compilers.

To display long-integer values—which typically are larger than int values, and can therefore represent larger quantities, though not under all operating systems (see Table 1.1)—use the formatting instructions %ld or %lu. The d stands for decimal; the u for unsigned decimal. Lines 26–27 write these lines on-screen:

```
Unsigned long decimal = 123456789
Signed long decimal   = -123456789
```

The form() function also handles a variety of display formats for floating-point values. As lines 28–31 show, you can display values in standard decimal notation (%f), in scientific notation (%e), or in decimal or scientific notations depending on the quantity of the value (%g).

To display floating-point values using a different precision from normal, follow the percent sign with a decimal point and the number of significant digits to use. For example, the instruction %.10f outputs floating-point values in decimal format, using 10 significant digits after the decimal place. Here are samples of the floating-point instructions displayed by the statements at lines 28–31:

```
Floating point       = 3.141590
Scientific notation  = 3.141590e+000
Default notation     = 3.14159
FP precision 10      = 3.1415900000
```

The statement at line 32 shows a typical use for the form() function in output-stream statements—displaying multiple values inserted into one string. Examine this statement carefully:

```
cout << form(buf, "%s's balance = $%8.2f", name, balance);
```

Inside the form() function's opening double quote, the instruction %s specifies the location for another string to be inserted. After a few other characters, a second instruction %8.2f tells form() to insert a floating-point value using a total of 8 character positions with 2 significant digits after the decimal place. Running this statement displays the line

```
Judy's balance = $  572.63
```

Notice that line 32 specifies four arguments inside form()'s parentheses: the temporary buffer (buf), the formatting string in quotes, and the two values name and balance. Those two values are needed to account for the two formatting instructions %s and %8.2f inside the formatting string. When using form(), you must specify exactly as many values after the formatting string as there are formatting instructions inside that string. There is no limit to the number of instructions and values you can insert in form() strings. (Or perhaps I should say there's no practical limit.)

> **Note:** The form() function uses the same notations as printf(), supplied with most C and C++ compilers. You can use only form(), but not printf(), in output-stream statements.

# Input Streams

Until now, sample programs in this chapter have done little more than send information to the outside world—that is, the display. It's time to consider the other side of the coin: how to get information from "out there" into a program. For the moment, I'll limit "out there" to the keyboard, but eventually, you'll learn ways to get information from other sources.

The simplest way to get responses entered at the keyboard is to use an *input-stream statement.* For example, these two statements prompt for and read an integer value into a variable defined as int countDown:

```
cout << "Start countdown from? ";
cin >> countdown;
```

The first line uses an output-stream statement to display a prompt. The second uses an input-stream statement to read a response into the countdown variable. In that statement, cin represents the source of the input—here the standard character input, meaning the keyboard (unless input has been redirected by a DOS command). The symbol >> represents the stream's action, indicating that the information flow is from left to right—that is, from the source (cin) to its destination (countdown).

As you can see, input and output streams are similar. They just use different stream objects (cin instead of cout), and they direct the information flow from left to right (>>) instead of from right to left (<<).

Although it's probably more common to read one variable at a time with an input-stream statement, you can read multiple values by stringing them together, similar to the way you can display multiple values in output streams. For example, to prompt for the values v1 and v2, you can write statements such as these:

```
cout << "Enter v1 v2: ";
cin >> v1 >> v2;
cout << form(buf, "v1=%d  v2=%d\n", v1, v2);
```

The first line prompts for the two values. The next line reads those values from cin into v1 and v2. After that, a second output-stream statement uses form() to display the entered values. Because the input-stream statement lists both values together, when the program runs, you must enter your responses by typing a blank character between them or by pressing Enter. If you prefer to enter values one at a time, use statements like these instead:

```
cout << "Enter v1: ";
cin >> v1;
cout << "Enter v2: ";
cin >> v2;
cout << form(buf, "v1=%d  v2=%d\n", v1, v2);
```

# Formatted Input

When you use input streams to read numeric values, it's important to consider what happens if your program's users enter characters other than digits and numeric punctuation characters. To see how this problem can cause headaches for your code, compile and run Listing 1.10, NUMIN.CPP.

### Listing 1.10. NUMIN.CPP.

```
 1: // numin.cpp -- Simple way to input numbers
 2:
 3: #include <tscdefs.h>
 4: #include IOSTREAM_H
 5:
 6: main()
 7: {
 8:   double fp;      // A floating point value
 9:   long k;         // A long int value
10:
11:   cout << "Enter a floating point value: ";
12:   cin >> fp;
13:   cout << "Value entered is: " << fp << '\n';
14:   cout << "Enter an integer value: ";
15:   cin >> k;
16:   cout << "Value entered is: " << k << '\n';
17:   return 0;
18: }
```

Run NUMIN, and type a floating-point value such as 3.14159. Press Enter, and type an integer value such as 100. Press Enter again, and the program runs smoothly, pausing for input and displaying the values you type.

Run NUMIN again, but this time enter a nonsense value such as XQ45. When you press Enter, instead of pausing for the next input, the program displays apparently random output values (or it might display 0) and ends.

This odd behavior occurs because input streams expect their information to be in the correct formats. Although input streams reject badly formatted input, they consider even simple typing mistakes to be serious errors. Worse, the slightest problem causes subsequent input statements to fail. Obviously, a finished program has to deal with these kinds of problems—it can't just display random values and halt as NUMIN does.

C++ streams can detect errors with methods explained in later chapters. Meanwhile, you can use another (and possibly the best overall) solution to error handling: Read input into character strings and then convert those strings to integers, floating-point values, and other binary forms. Because you can type anything into a string variable, you can use this technique to perform your own error checking, or you can simply ignore any errors. If you type ABC instead of 123, the program may use an incorrect value, but at least the code won't "crash and burn" just because you pressed the wrong keys. Listing 1.11, ATONUMS.CPP, demonstrates how to read input values into strings and convert those values to other data types.

## Listing 1.11. ATONUMS.CPP

```
 1: // atonums.cpp -- Demonstrate safe way to input numbers
 2:
 3: #include <tscdefs.h>
 4: #include IOSTREAM_H
 5: #include <stdlib.h>
 6:
 7: main()
 8: {
 9:   double fp;      // A floating point value
10:   long k;         // A long int value
11:   char s[80];     // 80-character string for input
12:
13:   cout << "Enter a floating point value: ";
14:   cin >> s;
```

```
15:    cout << "Original entry: " << s << '\n';
16:    fp = atof(s);
17:    cout << "After converting to double: " << fp << '\n';
18:    cout << "Enter an integer value: ";
19:    cin >> s;
20:    cout << "Original entry: " << s << '\n';
21:    k = atol(s);
22:    cout << "After converting to long: " << k << '\n';
23:    return 0;
24: }
```

ATONUMS runs like NUMIN, prompting and pausing for floating-point and integer values. This time, however, when you enter nonsense values like ABCDEFG, instead of causing problems, the program simply assigns the value 0 to variables. A more sophisticated program might go even further to detect typing mistakes and repeat the input statements, letting users correct their errors, but even this simplified sample behaves more reasonably than a program that outputs values at random and halts.

The new program has a few features you haven't seen before. Because some of these features are declared in the header file stdlib.h, the program includes that file at line 5. Also new are the assignment statements at lines 16 and 21. These statements call two functions declared in stdlib.h, atof() (ASCII to floating point) and atol() (ASCII to long). As their names suggest, these functions translate strings of ASCII characters to floating-point and long-integer values. Usually, you'll assign those values to variables as in this statement:

```
fp = atof(s);
```

This statement calls atof(), which processes the string argument s in parentheses, and then passes back the resulting value. In this case, the result is a floating-point value assigned to fp.

# A Simple Decimal-to-Hex-and-Octal Converter

Combining input and output streams with the formatting functions you learned about so far leads to a useful C++ program. For example, Listing 1.12, CONVERT.CPP, prompts for numbers and then displays your entries in decimal, hexadecimal, and octal. Use the program to convert values in decimal to these other number bases (or radixes).

**Listing 1.12. CONVERT.CPP.**

```
 1: // convert.cpp -- Convert integers to hex and octal
 2:
 3: #include <tscdefs.h>
 4: #include IOSTREAM_H
 5: #include <stdlib.h>
 6:
 7: main()
 8: {
 9:   long value;
10:   char s[80];     // 80-character string for input
11:
12:   cout << "Value? ";
13:   cin >> s;
14:   value = atol(s);
15:   cout << "Decimal="      << dec << value
16:        << "  Hexadecimal=" << hex << value
17:        << "  Octal="      << oct << value << '\n';
18:   return 0;
19: }
```

# Constants

Constants are values that don't change when a program runs. You'll see many examples of constants throughout this book's sample programs, and you should get into the habit of using constants correctly in your own code.

Because constants can't change, they provide programs with a reliable bedrock on which you can build other foundations. The unchanging constants give you confidence that your structures won't fall apart because of unexpected changes in critical values. For example, it is senseless to make the value of PI a variable.

Note: Constants like PI in C and C++ are typically written in all uppercase, although that's not required. Because constants typically are not used as frequently as other symbols in programs, uppercase letters make a constant's name stand out clearly in a long listing.

Good use of constants helps make a program's logic clear by associating recognizable names with values. Again, PI is a good example—the letters PI are probably recognized even by people who don't know PI's value by heart.

In other cases, constants are useful for representing values that change only rarely. In a program that stores test scores, for instance, you might create a constant named MAX_SCORES and associate that identifier with a value, perhaps 10. If the maximum number of scores later changes to 15, all you have to do is revise that constant and recompile. There's no need to hunt through the program to change every instance of 10 to 15.

## Types of Constants

In C++ programs, there are four kinds of constants:

- Literal constants

- Defined constants

- Declared constants

- Enumerated constants

Literal constants are the most common variety. They are values such as 123, 3.14159, or "Enter your name" that you type directly into the program's text. Defined constants are identifiers that you associate with literal constant values. Defined constants are the same as literal constants; they just have names. Declared constants are like variables: Their values are stored in memory, but the compiler refuses to let you change them. Enumerated constants let you associate an identifier such as Color with a sequence of other names like Red, Blue, and Green.

## Literal Constants

When encountering a literal constant like 100, the compiler determines the value's data type from its form. In a sense, C++ "knows" that 100 is an integer value. It also knows that 5.5 is a floating point value and that "Bees make honey" is a string. The form of a literal constant determines its data type, which can be any of the types listed earlier in Table 1.1 for variables. In fact, the *Example* column of that table lists examples of literal constants for each of C++'s fundamental data types.

Because the compiler determines a constant's type from its form, it is important to enter constant values in the correct formats. The sample constants in the next sections for each of C++'s fundamental data types will help you learn those forms.

## Character Constants

Like a double-edged sword, a char constant can cut two ways. Usually, chars represent symbols in the ASCII character set and are enclosed in single quotes. Examples of char constants are '$', 'U', 'z', and '?'. Because these symbols are represented internally as values from 0 to 255, chars can also be used for numbers in that same range. This makes char convenient for storing small values in exactly one byte of space.

That brings up a sore subject in programming—whether a data type holds signed or unsigned values. Signed values represent negative and positive quantities; unsigned values represent only positive numbers. The four integer types—char, short, int, and long—are signed by default. To make these types represent unsigned values, preface the type name with the keyword unsigned. A few samples clarify this idea:

```
char sc = 10;
unsigned char uc = 255;
short ss = -12345;
unsigned short us = 65535;
int si = -12345;
unsigned int ui = 65535;
long sl = -999999;
unsigned long ul = 999999;
```

In place of char sc, you could also write signed char sc. The same is true of the other integer types, which are signed by default. Although unsigned char constants can represent values from 0 to 255, signed char constants (the default for type char) can represent values from –128 to +127. A similar fact is true for unsigned int constants, which can range from 0 to 65535; signed int constants can range from –32768 to +32767. (These values are typical for MS-DOS C++ compilers, but might be different for compilers on other operating systems.)

If you have trouble visualizing the relationship between signed and unsigned value ranges, examine Figure 1.4, a familiar number line with 0 in the center. Imagine that the range of values for an integer data type, which is stored in a fixed number of bits, is a box of a fixed "length." Mentally position that box so that its left end is at zero, representing the range of unsigned values in that unsigned data type. Now shift the line halfway toward the left. After that, the left half of the line represents negative values, but the highest positive value has been lowered. Visualizing signed and unsigned values with a number line explains why signed data types can represent fewer positive values than their unsigned counterparts.

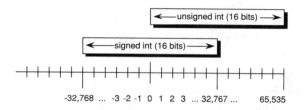

-32,768 ... -3 -2 -1 0 1 2 3 ... 32,767 ...    65,535

**Figure 1.4.** A familiar number line shows that signed and unsigned ranges are the same "lengths," but represent different ranges of value. Only signed data types can represent negative values.

As explained earlier, to enter chars that you can't type directly on the keyboard, you can use an escape code like '\n' to represent a newline character. Table 1.2 lists other escape codes that C++ recognizes. You can use these symbols as individual char constants (surrounded by single quotes) or in strings (surrounded by double quotes).

**Table 1.2. Character Escape Codes.**

| Escape Code | Meaning | ASCII value(s) Dec | Hex | Symbol(s) |
|---|---|---|---|---|
| '\a' | Bell | 7 | 07 | BEL |
| '\b' | Backspace | 8 | 08 | BS |
| '\f' | Form feed | 12 | 0C | FF |
| '\n' | New line | 13 10 | 0D 0A | CR LF |
| '\r' | Carriage return | 13 | 0D | CR |
| '\t' | Horizontal tab | 9 | 09 | HT |
| '\v' | Vertical tab | 11 | 0B | VT |
| '\\' | Backslash | 92 | 5C | \ |
| '\'' | Single quote | 39 | 27 | ' |
| '\"' | Double quote | 34 | 22 | " |
| '\?' | Question mark | 63 | 3F | ? |
| '\000' | ASCII octal | all | all | all |
| '\x00' | ASCII hexadecimal | all | all | all |

Because the backslash precedes these symbols, you must enter a backslash by typing that character twice like this: `'\\'`. Also, because quote characters have special meaning, you must type them as `char` constants by preceding them with a backslash. The prefaced question mark in the table is required only when using trigraphs (three-character symbols that begin with ?) to form certain symbols on some terminals. For example, the trigraph `??<` represents an opening brace, `{`. On PCs, you don't have to use trigraphs, and therefore, you can type question marks directly in strings.

At the bottom of Table 1.2 are two special escape sequences, `\000` and `\x00`. The zeros in these symbols represent digits, which can stand for any ASCII character value. For example, to insert the β symbol into a string, which some programmers use to represent "beta" test versions for their programs, you can write

```
"Version v7.54\xE1"
```

In place of `\xE1`, the compiler inserts the ASCII value `0xe1` hexadecimal. To represent values in octal, replace `x` with a digit from 0 to 7, such as `\341`. Either way, the result is this string:

```
"Version v7.54β"
```

## String Constants

Strings should be no strangers to you by now. In C++, strings can be any length, and they can contain any characters that you can type between two double quotes. Strings can also contain any of the escape codes listed in Table 1.2.

In memory, strings are represented by a series of ASCII character values plus 0, or null. The null character marks the end of the string and is inserted automatically by C++ at the end of string constants. To represent null values, C++ defines the symbol NULL as a constant in various header files (typically in stddef.h, stdio.h, stdlib.h, and string.h.) To use NULL in a program, include one or more of these files rather than define NULL with a line such as

```
#define NULL 0
```

Although that works, header files for other C++ compilers may define NULL differently based on various requirements, so it's best to let C++ define NULL for you.

> **Note:** In this book, the uppercase NULL is the symbol that (typically) represents zero. The word null refers to a null character (which has the ASCII value 0), or a null pointer (described in Chapter 4, "Pointers About Pointers.")

Because strings end with null, don't use double quotes to represent single characters. If you do, you can waste space. For example, "J" is a string that takes two characters—one to represent the *J* and another for the invisible null character at the end of the string. 'J' is a single character. It takes only one byte of space, and it does not require a terminating value.

## Whole Number Constants

When typing short, int, and long values, you normally can enter the number you need and not be concerned with its type. If you enter 1024 into a program, C++ treats that value as type int. If you type 999999, C++ probably assumes the value is long (because 65,535 is the maximum unsigned int value for typical MS-DOS C++ compilers).

There are a few less obvious details associated with whole number constants in programs. Remember these points:

- Never use commas or other punctuation in whole numbers. Enter 123456, not 123,456.

- To force a value to be long, end it with a capital L. For example, 1024 is type int, but 1024L is type long. Usually a trailing L is necessary only when mixing values of different types in expressions, and when you must force the result of that expression to be a certain type.

- To force a value to be unsigned, end it with a capital U. You can combine U and L to create unsigned long constants such as 3452UL.

## Floating Point Constants

Like whole numbers, floating-point constants represent values within a fixed number of bits (see Table 1.1). However, floating-point values are always signed, and they are best used for representing approximations rather than exact counts.

As I mentioned before, you can enter floating-point constants in the usual way—1.2 and –555.99, for example. Or you can use scientific notation, following a whole number with E and a positive or negative exponent. A positive exponent means to move the decimal place that many times to the right. A negative exponent means to move it to the left. The value `2.5E4` is equivalent to 25000; `4.257E-3` is the same as 0.004257.

# Defined Constants

Literal constants are common and useful, but they also lack clarity. For instance, what is 53? It could be somebody's age or the number of potatoes in a sack. Because literal constants like 53 might confuse readers of your programs (including you, months after you construct the code), it's a good idea to give names to values that help jog your memory about what the values represent.

One way to give a constant a name is to use a `#define` macro. Here are some samples:

```
#define PAYOFF 53
#define NEWLINE '\n'
```

These are not statements, and for that reason, they do not end with semicolons. They're control lines, or macros, and they do not take up any space in the compiled code. In the body of a program, the compiler replaces a `#defined` symbol with the associated text. For example, consider this statement:

```
cout << "Payoff was $" << PAYOFF << NEWLINE;
```

C++ replaces `PAYOFF` and `NEWLINE` with the text associated with those symbols, 53 and `'\n'`, in this case.

In complex settings, named constants can lend a great deal of clarity to programs. In fact, some programmers never use literal whole number constants other than 0 and 1 (and sometimes –1). They assign descriptive names to all other values such as `FACTOR`, `RATE`, and `TAX`.

> **Note:** Macros in C++ are far less common than they are in C. Macros are a kind of minilanguage built into C and C++ that uses #define to create complex commands. For reasons that will not be clear until much later in this book, other C++ features can do anything macros can do. I use only simple #defines in my own programs, and I suggest that you do the same.

Most of the time, you'll use #define as illustrated in Listing 1.13, DEFINE.CPP. The program associates several literal constants of various C++ data types, giving the values recognizable names. The main() function then uses those names in output-stream statements. DEFINE uses all uppercase for the constant identifiers—a typical style that makes the names stand out on the page.

### Listing 1.13. DEFINE.CPP.

```
 1: // define.cpp -- Demonstrate #defined constants
 2:
 3: #include <tscdefs.h>
 4: #include IOSTREAM_H
 5:
 6: #define CHARACTER        '@'
 7: #define STRING           "Tom Swan's C++ Primer"
 8: #define OCTAL            0233
 9: #define HEXADECIMAL      0x9b
10: #ifdef __TSC_ZTC__
11:    #define BINARY           0b10011011
12: #endif
13: #define DECIMAL          155
14: #define FLOATING_POINT   3.14159
15:
16: main()
17: {
18:    cout << CHARACTER       << '\n';
19:    cout << STRING          << '\n';
20:    cout << OCTAL           << '\n';
21:    cout << HEXADECIMAL     << '\n';
22: #ifdef __TSC_ZTC__
23:    cout << BINARY          << '\n';
```

*continues*

**45**

**Listing 1.13. continued**

```
24: #endif
25:   cout << DECIMAL          << '\n';
26:   cout << FLOATING_POINT << '\n';
27:   return 0;
28: }
```

Each of the seven constants at lines 6–14 is associated with the text to the right of the identifier in uppercase. Only Zortech C++ can directly display binary values in output stream statements, so line 11 is compiled only for that compiler. All values are aligned vertically to make them easier to read. A single space is all that's required to separate an identifier from its value. C++ ignores the extra spaces used here.

You can also add a comment after a #define control line. To do this, insert at least one space and a double slash after the constant's value:

```
#define FLOATING_POINT  3.14159    // Value for Pi
```

Or you can use C-style comments:

```
#define FLOATING_POINT  3.14159    /* Value for Pi */
```

# Declared Constants

A second way to create constants in programs is to preface a normal variable definition with the keyword const. The compiler rejects any statements that attempt to change values defined as const.

Listing 1.14 demonstrates how to create constants with const. Compare this program with DEFINE.CPP. Notice that the const definitions specify data types, end with semicolons, and are initialized like variables. The earlier #defined symbols do not specify data types, do not use the assignment operator (=), and do not end with semicolons.

**Listing 1.14. CONST.CPP.**

```
1: // const.cpp -- Demonstrate declared constants
2:
3: #include <tscdefs.h>
4: #include IOSTREAM_H
5:
```

```
 6: const char   CHARACTER      = '@';
 7: const char   STRING[]       = "Tom Swan's C++ Primer";
 8: const int    OCTAL          = 0233;
 9: const int    HEXADECIMAL    = 0x9b;
10: #ifdef __TSC_ZTC__
11:   const int   BINARY         = 0b10011011;
12: #endif
13: const int    DECIMAL        = 155;
14: const float FLOATING_POINT = 3.14159;
15:
16: main()
17: {
18:   cout << CHARACTER       << '\n';
19:   cout << STRING          << '\n';
20:   cout << OCTAL           << '\n';
21:   cout << HEXADECIMAL     << '\n';
22: #ifdef __TSC_ZTC__
23:   cout << BINARY          << '\n';
24: #endif
25:   cout << DECIMAL         << '\n';
26:   cout << FLOATING_POINT << '\n';
27:   return 0;
28: }
```

Except for the STRING constant at line 7, the constant identifiers are declared the same way in the DEFINE and CONST programs. (Here again, only Zortech C++ can display binary values directly, so line 11 is included only for that compiler.) In CONST.CPP at line 7, STRING ends with square brackets ([ ]). You'll understand the purpose of this better after you learn about arrays, which are symbolized by brackets. The brackets after STRING tell C++ to create an array of characters—in other words, a string of multiple char values. Without the brackets, the compiler would consider this line to define a single char, not an array of them. The brackets aren't needed in the DEFINE program because #defined constants simply associate text with symbols; the compiler doesn't care what that text is composed of until the symbol is used.

Another significant difference between #defined constants and those created with const is when the compiler evaluates a value. For instance, suppose you write

```
#define X 5
#define Y X + 10
```

As you might expect, X is associated with the value 5. Y is associated with the expression X + 10. Be careful with such definitions. They can introduce bugs! Only the *text* X + 10 is associated with Y, not the *result* of that expression. This may cause surprising consequences in statements like this:

```
cout << "X = " << X << " Y = " << Y;
```

When C++ compiles that statement, it inserts the *text* 5 and the *text* X + 10 in place of X and Y. The expression X + 10 is evaluated only later when the program is compiled. Because of this, if the program executes the following lines before the output-stream statement:

```
#undef  X
#define X 10
```

then X will have a different value when the statement is compiled; and, therefore, so will the expression X + 10. (The #undef control command undefines a symbol previously created with #define. Undefining a symbol throws that symbol away—necessary to avoid an error if you later redefine the same symbol with another #define.)

There are two other advantages to using const to create constants in programs instead of #define. One, the compiler can often generate more efficient code with const constants. Two, because the definitions specify data types, the compiler can immediately check whether the literal constants in the const definitions are in the correct forms. With #define, the compiler can't perform similar checks until a statement uses the constant identifier, making any errors in the constant more difficult for you to recognize if the program fails to compile.

A prime disadvantage of const symbols is that their values occupy data space at runtime. A #defined symbol exists only in the program text, and its value is typically inserted directly into compiled code. Many C++ programmers use #define instead of const because of this fact.

# Enumerated Constants

Some things just naturally go together: paper and pens, gears and motors, ice and snow. To categorize such lists, you might give them names like implements, gizmos, and badWeather. In programs, to represent these kinds of lists, you might begin by defining a few constants:

```
#define PAPER 0
#define PEN 1
```

You can then use PAPER and PEN to make programs more readable, making the compiler do the hard work of replacing the descriptive names with the associated values 0 and 1. The values have no special meanings; they serve only to give the identifiers substance so that they can be used in statements.

You'll see this idea applied often in programs, and there's nothing wrong with the technique. Instead of defining individual constants, however, you can use *enumerated constants* to create categorized lists that accomplish the same goal. The classic example of an enumerated constant is a list of colors, which you might declare as:

```
enum Colors {Red, Orange, Yellow, Green, Blue, Indigo, Violet};
```

This associates the constant elements listed between the braces—Red, Orange, ..., Violet—with the identifier Colors, the name assigned to this new data type. The keyword enum tells the compiler that these items should be enumerated—that is, associated with sequential numbers. When processing this directive, the compiler assigns a value starting with 0 to each enumerated element so that Red is equivalent to 0, Orange is 1, and so on. The compiler enumerates the identifiers so you don't have to.

After declaring a new enumerated data type, you can create variables of that type just as you do for other data types. For example, to define a variable of type Colors, you can write:

```
Colors favoriteColor = Indigo;
```

This creates a variable named favoriteColor of type Colors and assigns to that variable the initial value Indigo. Because favoriteColor is a variable, an assignment statement can also give it a new value like this:

```
favoriteColor = Orange;
```

By using const, you can define a constant, perhaps named lastingColor, that other statements can't change:

```
const Colors lastingColor = Red;
```

As these samples show, enumerated constants greatly enhance a program's readability. In a program, if you come across an uncommented statement acolor = 4, you have to track down the meaning of 4 in a reference to find out what color the program is using. The assignment acolor = Blue, however, is perfectly clear on its own.

Listing 1.15, ENUM.CPP, shows a few more examples of enumerated constants, and it illustrates some of the ways programs can use them.

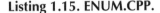

## Listing 1.15. ENUM.CPP.

```
 1: // enum.cpp -- Demonstrate enumerated types
 2:
 3: #include <tscdefs.h>
 4: #include IOSTREAM_H
 5:
 6: enum Language {Assembly, Basic, C, CPP, Fortran, Pascal} language;
 7: enum Scale {Do, Re, Mi, Fa, Sol, La, Ti};
 8: enum {False, True};
 9:
10: main()
11: {
12:    Scale tone = La;
13:    int timeFlies = True;
14:
15:    language = CPP;
16:    cout << "language = " << (int)language << '\n';
17:    cout << "tone = " << (int)tone << '\n';
18:    cout << "timeFlies = " << timeFlies << '\n';
19:    return 0;
20: }
```

Line 6 declares the enumerated type Language. Because Language is a type, it is capitalized by convention. At the end of this same line, the declaration also defines a variable named language, which (again, by convention) is not capitalized. As you can see, line 15 then assigns one of the listed Language elements to the variable.

Note: This typical capitalization style is used by many C and C++ programmers. Data types are capitalized, variables are not, and constants are written in all uppercase. Although enumerated symbols like Assembly and False in Listing 1.15 are constants, I prefer not to type them in all uppercase so I can tell them apart from #defined constants. These are not hard-and-fast regulations, and you are free to invent your own capitalization rules.

Line 7 declares only a new type, not a variable. The declaration associates the data type name Scale with music's sol-fa symbols, Do, Re, Me, Fa, Sol, La, and Ti. After the program creates the `Scale` data type, line 12 defines a variable `tone` of type `Scale` and also assigns to `tone` the initial value `La`.

Line 8 demonstrates how to create unnamed enumerated data types, which are occasionally useful. In this sample, the elements `False` and `True` add these Boolean values to C++. (Note: tscdefs.h also defines `TRUE` and `FALSE` `#defined` constants.) As with other enumerated types, using these names in statements that deal with the truth or falsity of various conditions makes programs more readable than if those same statements used the literal constant values 0 and 1.

Line 13 uses `True` to define and initialize the variable `timeFlies`. It's possible to assign `True` or `False` to `int` variables this way because those symbols were listed in an unnamed enumerated type at line 8. If the program had declared the type in the usual way with a name:

```
enum Boolean {False, True};
```

the definition at line 12 would no longer compile. C++ is strict about assigning values to variables—in all cases, the data types must agree. Even though the underlying elements `True` and `False` are associated with integer values 0 and 1, because they are now declared in the named `Boolean` type, C++ allows assigning the symbols only to variables of that same type.

But there's nothing wrong with using a data type name in an `enum` declaration like `Boolean`. To create a variable of that type, you can change line 13 to

```
enum Boolean timeFlies = True;
```

If you make this change, line 18 also needs to be changed. An output stream doesn't know what a `Boolean` data type is (without modification, it recognizes only standard C++ data types). To display the value of `timeFlies` requires a type cast:

```
cout << "timeFlies = " << (int)timeFlies << '\n';
```

When you run Listing 1.15, you'll have this same problem with displaying the other two enumerated data types. Even though it seems as though the output-stream statements in lines 16–18 should display the enumerated constant elements `CPP`, `La`, and `True`, the program instead displays these values:

```
language = 3
tone = 5
timeFlies = 1
```

Because output streams don't know what `Scale` and `Language` are, the output statements must cast values of these types to type `int`. Furthermore, identifiers associated with the enumerated data types exist solely in the program text. When the program runs, the elements are converted to the numbers that this sample code displays.

# Assigning Enumerated Element Values

Usually, it's best to let the compiler assign sequential values to enumerated data type elements. But when the need arises, you can change the values that the compiler associates with each element. For example, suppose that you are writing a program to play chess. You might begin by creating an enumerated data type that lists the piece names:

```
enum Piece {Pawn, Knight, Bishop, Rook, Queen, King};
```

By design, the compiler assigns the values 0 to Pawn, 1 to Knight, 2 to Bishop, and so on, up to 5 for the King. However, it would be more useful if the enumerated values reflected the relative importance of each piece—information that the program could use to calculate the computer's next move. To assign specific values to the enumerated elements, follow one or more elements with an equal sign and the value you want:

```
enum Piece {Pawn = 2, Knight = 6, Bishop = 7, Rook = 10,
  Queen = 18, King = 10000};
```

These values correspond with standard chess-piece values; a knight is worth three pawns, a rook is worth five pawns, and so on. I doubled these values because a bishop is typically worth 3.5 pawns (just a little more valuable than a knight). It's not possible to assign floating-point values like 3.5 to enumerated elements—only integer values are allowed. Doubling the standard rates keeps the ratios the same (2 x 3.5 = 7).

You don't have to assign values to every element as in this sample. After the last explicit assignment, the compiler starts the next element with the next value in sequence. For example, consider this declaration:

```
enum TrafficLight {Green, Yellow = 10, Red};
```

In this case, Green equals 0, Yellow equals 10, and Red equals 11. If any elements came after Red, they would have increasing values starting with 12. You can also assign more than one explicit value, giving those between increasing values in sequence:

```
enum Error {No_Error, Err_Memory, Err_Input, Err_Output,
  Err_Disk = 100, Err_Read, Err_Write, Err_Notfound,
  Err_Keyboard = 200, Err_Badkey, Err_Digit_Expected,
  Err_Printer = 300, Err_Nopaper, Err_Jammed};
```

In the error enumerated type, No_Error equals 0—the default starting value for all enumerated types. Because successive symbols increase by one automatically unless the type specifies another value, Err_Memory, Err_Input, and Err_Output equal 1, 2, and 3, respectively. Err_Disk begins a new sequence starting at 100. After that, symbols begin increasing by one again, so Err_Read equals 101, Err_Write is 102, and Err_Notfound is 103. Similarly, Err_Keyboard and Err_Printer begin new sequences at 200 and 300. The symbols following these two equal 201, 202, 301, 302, and so on.

As a result of this design, you can add new error names—for example, inserting Err_Eof (end of file) at the end of the second line without changing the underlying values of the other symbols. When you need to create enumerated data types of elements with values that match other constants (such as operating system error numbers, I/O-port values, and other fixed quantities), the capability to start new sequences inside an enum type declaration is extremely useful. Most of the time, however, you can let C++ choose the element values for you.

# Operators

C++ is loaded with operators—symbols that perform various operations on their arguments. The lowly plus sign (+) is an operator. In an expression, as you might expect, it adds two values:

```
a = b + c;
```

The symbols a, b, and c could be of any numeric data types, and the effect is fairly obvious: b is added to c, and the result is assigned to a.

The equal sign in that expression is itself an operator, and it has the unique capability of copying a value on the right to the memory location represented by the symbol on the left. Two terms represent this description: *rvalue* and *lvalue*. (These are not programming symbols, but you'll find them in other C and C++ references, so you should understand what they mean.) In general, an *rvalue* is something that can appear on the right side of an equal sign, and *lvalue* is something that can appear on the left. With minor exceptions, *rvalues* are temporary items, usually the results of expressions like b + c, and *lvalues* are the names of variables or other constructions that refer to places in memory where values can be stored.

Technical terms like *rvalue* and *lvalue* are not as important to memorize as compiler instruction manuals and some references would have you believe. The purpose of a = b + c is pretty darn obvious whether or not you can identify which part is the *rvalue* and which is the *lvalue*. Just be aware of these terms in case you encounter them elsewhere, such as in compiler error messages.

# Operators and Precedence

Of course, C++ has a few more operators in addition to the plus sign. Besides the usual + (plus), - (minus), / (divide), and * (multiply), there are operators that create functions, operators for arrays, operators that increment and decrement values, and complex operators that perform more than one job at a time. As you read this book, you'll see all these operators in action.

Appendix B lists C++'s operators and also shows their precedence levels. In normal use, operators of higher precedence perform their operations in expressions before operators of lower precedence. For example, the expression to the right of the equal sign in the statement

```
a = b + c * d;
```

multiplies c and d and then adds that product to b before assigning the total to a. The expression works this way because the times operator (*) has a higher precedence than +. To force a different evaluation order, use parentheses:

```
a = (b + c) * d;
```

There's no need to enclose the entire expression in parentheses, although you can write ((b + c) * d) if you want. The = operator in C++ has a lower precedence than *; therefore, the entire expression is evaluated before the result is assigned to a.

Regardless of precedence level, operations inside parentheses are always completed before operators outside get their chance to act. In this sample, the parentheses force the addition to occur before the multiplication, which may give different results depending on the initial values of b, c, and d.

# Increment and Decrement Operators

Two of C++'s most intriguing operators, which are also available in C, are ++ (increment) and -- (decrement). The ++ operator (pronounced "plus plus") adds one to its argument. The -- operator ("minus minus") subtracts one.

> **Note:** C++ ("C plus plus") takes its name from the ++ operator. It's one step beyond its predecessor language, C.

A few examples show how useful the increment and decrement operators can be:

```
i = i + 1;   // Add 1 to i
i++;         // Same as above
j = j - 1;   // Subtract 1 from j
j--          // Same as above
```

The first line adds 1 to an int variable i, assigning the result of that addition back to i and replacing i's original value. The effect, of course, is to increment i by 1—an operation neatly performed by the second line. The expression i++ has the identical result of i = i + 1, but requires you to type the variable name only once. Similarly, the third line subtracts 1 from another int variable j. The fourth line is shorter and is functionally identical to the line above.

A concept that strikes some people as strange at first is that expressions such as i++ have actions (increasing i by 1), and they also have values (the value of i before the increase). The concept might be clearer if you consider that (b + c) (an expression) also has a value—the value of the two elements added together.

Normally, if you do nothing else with an expression's value—usually storing it in memory—the value just floats away. But the expressions i++ and j-- are special; they perform an action on their arguments (incrementing i and decrementing j), and they also have values. However, because the operator follows its argument, the value of the expression i++ equals the original value before the increment takes effect. In other words, if i equals 100, i++ has the value 100 and increases i to 101—an action with significance in expressions like this:

```
j = i++;
```

Again, if i equals 100, this expression sets j to 100 before ++ increments i. The expression does not assign i + 1 to j as many people assume on first glance. In fact, the preceding expression is just a convenient way to write these statements:

```
j = i;
i = i + 1;
```

If you remember this expanded version, you'll never forget that the value of i++ equals i. This is always true when the ++ operator follows its argument. But, if the ++ or--operators appear in front of their arguments, they take effect before the expression's value is formed. Once again, assuming that i equals 100, this statement, like the previous ones, increments i:

```
j = ++i;
```

However, because ++ appears before i, the operator increments i before the result is assigned to j; therefore, after the assignment, if i was originally 100, both i and j now equal 101. Expressions like j = ++i are simply shorthand for these two statements:

```
i = i + 1;
j = i;
```

The only difference between i++ and ++i is the value of the expression. The effect on the target variable is the same—both forms increment i. Similarly, both i-- and --i subtract 1 from i, but the expression values of i++ and i-- equal i. The expression values of ++i and --i equal the original value of i plus or minus 1.

When you don't assign the result of ++ and -- to a variable, it doesn't matter whether the operator precedes or follows its argument. Assuming that the following identifiers are int variables, these statements increment each of those variables by one:

```
weight++;    // weight = weight + 1
balance++;   // balance = balance + 1
score++;     // score = score + 1
```

Placing the operators first gives the identical results:

```
++weight;    // weight = weight + 1
++balance;   // balance = balance + 1
++score;     // score = score + 1
```

Most programmers follow arguments with ++, but the choice is yours to make. However, you don't have this same option when using ++ and -- in complex expressions or in assignment statements. For example, this statement

```
n = (x++) * (y--);
```

does not give the same results as the following expression for all values of x and y:

```
n = (++x) * (--y);
```

In the first case, the ++ and -- operators follow their arguments; therefore, n is assigned the product of x * y. In the second case, the operators precede their arguments, thus giving those expressions the results after the increments take place. In this second example, n is assigned the product of (x + 1) * (y - 1). In both examples, the effects on the final values of x and y are identical.

Using ++ and -- takes practice and careful thought at first, but eventually, you'll find these special operators among the most useful in C++. A sample program will help make the concepts clear. Compile and run Listing 1.16, INCDEC.CPP. Enter test integer values to see the effects of applying ++ and -- on variables equal to the values you supply.

## Listing 1.16. INCDEC.CPP.

```
 1: // incdec.cpp -- Demonstrate increment (++) and decrement (--) operators
 2:
 3: #include <tscdefs.h>
 4: #include IOSTREAM_H
 5: #include <form.h>
 6:
 7: main()
 8: {
 9:   int b, v, k;
10:   char buf[80];
11:
12:   cout << "Enter an integer value: ";
13:   cin >> v;
14:   k = v;  // Save value of v for each output statement
15:   cout << "\n     Before  During  After\n";
16:   v = k; b = v++; cout << form(buf, "v++%8d%8d%8d\n", k, b, v);
17:   v = k; b = v--; cout << form(buf, "v--%8d%8d%8d\n", k, b, v);
18:   v = k; b = ++v; cout << form(buf, "++v%8d%8d%8d\n", k, b, v);
19:   v = k; b = --v; cout << form(buf, "--v%8d%8d%8d\n", k, b, v);
20:   return 0;
21: }
```

Run INCDEC and enter a value such as 100, which the program assigns to an int variable v. Four output-stream statements in lines 16–19 then display the value of v before, during, and after applying the operators ++ and -- in front of and after v. When examining the displayed values, remember that you are seeing the results of the expressions, not necessarily the final value of v after an operator is applied to it.

# Expressions

Computers are great at crunching numbers. Who hasn't used one to chew up a formula and spit out the results? Expressions are a computer language's number crunchers—a way for you to give instructions to a program about what it should do with various values.

In this chapter, you learned about input and output, variables and constants, and expressions and operators. Combining these elements—by no means the whole C++ story—lets you write useful programs that can quickly give answers to complex problems.

As an example, Listing 1.17, TAX.CPP, implements the answer to a simple problem in algebra. Given a dollar amount such as $155.76, and a tax rate of 0.06, what is the retail price of the item, and how much tax was charged? Before running the listing, you might want to try writing your own program to give the correct answer for any value and tax rate.

## Listing 1.17. TAX.CPP.

```
 1: // tax.cpp -- Calculate list price knowing tax rate and price paid
 2:
 3: #include <tscdefs.h>
 4: #include IOSTREAM_H
 5: #include <stdlib.h>
 6: #include <form.h>
 7:
 8: main()
 9: {
10:    double list, paid, rate, tax;
11:    char s[80];  // Input string and form() buffer
12:
13:    cout << "Price paid? ";
14:    cin >> s;
15:    paid = atof(s);
16:    cout << "Tax rate (ex: .06)? ";
17:    cin >> s;
18:    rate = atof(s);
19:    list = paid / (1 + rate);
20:    tax = paid - list;
21:    cout << form(s, "List price = $%8.2lf\n", list);
22:    cout << form(s, "Tax paid   = $%8.2lf\n", tax);
23:    return 0;
24: }
```

You should have little trouble understanding how TAX.CPP works. The program contains nothing you haven't seen before. After defining a few local variables at lines 10–11, input- and output-stream statements prompt for prices and tax rates. To prevent errors, responses are stored in a string (s) and converted to floating point values. Then, two assignment statements at lines 19–20 use expressions to calculate the list price and tax paid, displayed by two more output statements at lines 21–22.

This completes your introduction to C++. As TAX.CPP illustrates, you have learned enough of the language to write simple programs. Before continuing with the next chapter, try to complete some of the exercises that follow. You can finish them all by using only the fundamental elements of C++ introduced in this chapter. (If you get stuck, you'll find the answers to the exercises in the back of this book.)

As you use the features covered in this chapter to write your own C++ programs, you'll soon realize that something is missing. Programs often need to make decisions—to change course based on various conditions and to execute the same statements more than once. You'll notice also that simple variables can't store more complex items such as database records and arrays of multiple values. To accomplish these and other goals, you need to learn about C++'s advanced operators, and you'll need ways to alter the flow of a program, bending its normal straightforward course to follow new paths. As you'll learn in the next chapter, these features alone can add an amazing level of power to C++ programs.

# Questions and Exercises

1.1. Write a program that prompts for your first name, and then prints a message that includes the name you enter.

1.2. Explain the significance of the symbols //, /*, and */ in these lines:

```
/* Prompt for input */
cout << "Enter value: ";   // Prompt for a value
cin >> value;              // Get value from user
```

1.3. Write the smallest possible C++ program that compiles and runs.

1.4. Which of these identifiers are legal: myMoney, 2for1, _max, max_Value, $Balance, A_L_P_H_A_B_E_T_. How can you prove your answer?

1.5. Write a program that displays C++'s punctuators.

1.6. Explain what white space is and what it's used for.

1.7. Enter the following program into a file named OUT.CPP. The program demonstrates two ways to write text to the standard output (usually the display). Unfortunately, when you compile OUT, you receive an error from the compiler. Why? Fix the program so it runs.

```
main()
{
    cout << "\nSample C++ output stream statement";
    printf("\nSample C and C++ printf() statement");
    return 0;
}
```

1.8. What data type or types can store the values 145540, 145.543, and 10? What is the smallest type that can store those values?

1.9. With a single line of code, define a variable named `alpha` of type `char` and assign the character `'A'` to the variable.

1.10. What are the two main differences between a local and a global variable?

1.11. Write a statement to display the value 134 justified to the right of a 12-character column.

1.12. Write a program to display the following line where the values 64, 10, 11, 27, and 1300.76 are stored in integer variables named age, month, day, year, and a floating point variable balance:

```
Age = 64, Birth Date = 10/11/27, Balance = $1300.76
```

1.13. Write two programs that prompt for a floating point value named `rainFall` (the exact name doesn't matter). Use an input-stream statement in the first program to store your response directly in the variable. Use a string in the second program and convert that string to a floating point value. Why is the second method safer?

1.14. Write a program that displays the sentence `"It's raining "dogs and cats"` `in here!"` including the four double quotes and apostrophe.

1.15. Write a program that assigns the single quote character (`'`) to a character variable, and then displays that variable.

1.16. Write a program that declares two constants named `MIN` equal to 1 and `MAX` equal to 999. Display the constants in output-stream statements.

1.17. Create an enumerated data type named `Flowers` with the elements `Rose`, `Carnation`, `Orchid`, and `Gardenia`.

1.18. If count equals 98, what do the expressions count++, ++count, count--, and --count equal if executed in that order? What is the final value of count? Predict the results and then insert the statements into a program to prove your answers.

1.19. The circumference of a circle equals its diameter times PI. Write a program that prompts for the diameter of a circle and displays the circle's circumference.

# Making Statements and Building Structures

**C**omputer programs operate a lot like engines. They burn fuel (use data) and perform work (execute statements). Without fuel, the engine won't go, and, without an engine, the fuel may as well stay in the ground.

Most programs need both fuel and a working engine—that is, data and statements—to perform useful jobs. As you may expect, C++ has a variety of data types for storing information in memory. It also has a number of statement forms that, among other tasks, can make decisions, repeat actions, and select matching elements from a set of values.

Learning C++'s fundamental data structures and statement types isn't difficult. In fact, when you first meet them, these elementary programming tools may seem almost too simple to be of much practical use. This is natural, and it illustrates one of the reasons that many people never advance beyond a simple knowledge of programming with a general-purpose language like C++ (or C or Pascal). They memorize the basics—the way they might commit to memory a list of parts in a machine shop—but they fail to learn how to combine those parts to create programs that can shift computers into high gear.

For that reason, instead of documenting each data structure and statement form one by one as a compiler manual might do, in this chapter, I'll introduce C++ data and statement fundamentals in (mostly) practical settings. You'll learn not only *what* a structure is, but *how* you can apply it to solve problems. Later chapters will expand this "learn by doing" theme.

This chapter begins with C++'s advanced operators, which let you (among other things) write programs that can make decisions and manipulate bits in memory—two seemingly unrelated topics that, like religion and politics, have more in common than many people suppose. You'll also learn how to alter the flow of a program, making certain statements execute based on various conditions—a simple concept that gives most programs their true power.

> **Note:** Compile and run the listings in this chapter as you did the examples in Chapter 1, "Discovering C++." Try also to modify the statements to add personal touches—to display a title when the program starts, to modify a constant value, or to perform I/O with a custom twist. Making changes to existing programs and then seeing the effects of those changes is a great way to learn C++ and to gain more experience with programming in general. If you have trouble compiling programs, see the Introduction. Also see "Compiling Your Own Programs," in Chapter 10, "Cross-Compilation Tools."

# Advanced Operators

In the preceding chapter, you learned about some of C++'s operators—symbols that perform actions on their arguments. For example, the plus sign (+) is an operator with an obvious purpose—adding two values.

In this section, you'll meet some of C++'s less obvious operators, which can compare values, evaluate expressions, and manipulate bits in memory. You'll also learn how to use handy shorthand notations for writing expressions.

# Good Relations

C++'s *relational operators* compare values. Suppose you need to determine whether a count variable is less than 10. To do that, you can use the less-than relational operator (<) to compare count and a target value in an expression such as count < 10.

When a program executes a relational expression like that, it *evaluates* its arguments to produce a true or false result, which a program can then use to decide what to do next. Obviously, count is either less than 10 or it's not; there's no middle ground to consider. The expression count < 10 is therefore either true or false. The same is true of all relational expressions that use one or more of the operators listed in Table 2.1. In every case, expressions that use these operators evaluate to a single true or false result.

**Table 2.1. Relational operators.**

| Operator | Description | Example |
|----------|-------------|---------|
| < | Less than | (a < b) |
| <= | Less than or equal | (a <= b) |
| > | Greater than | (a > b) |
| >= | Greater than or equal | (a >= b) |
| == | Equal | (a == b) |
| != | Not equal | (a != b) |

**Note:** Internally, C++ reduces a relational expression to an integer value 0 for false or nonzero (usually 1) for true. Store this fact in the back of your mind. You'll need it later.

You can use any of the operators in Table 2.1 in expressions to compare two integer, character, or floating-point values. (Comparing strings requires more work—more on that in Chapter 4, "Pointers About Pointers".) Notice especially that the symbol for equality is *two* equal signs (==), not one. The expression (a == b) evaluates to true only if a and b represent the same value. The expression (a = b) *assigns* the value of b to a. Confusing these two nearly identical expressions is one of the most common mistakes that C++ (and C) programmers make. Worse, the compiler frequently allows you to interchange the relational expression and assignment statements, so it's up to you to use the correct forms.

The first sample program in this chapter, Listing 2.1, MILES.CPP, uses relational operators in a typical way—to have users choose options from a menu displayed on-screen. In this case, the problem is to convert miles and kilometers or to quit without making a calculation. Depending on which choice you make, the program performs different actions. When you run MILES, enter 1 and then a number of miles to convert to kilometers. Enter 2 and a number of kilometers for the equivalent in miles, or enter 3 to quit. Also try entering other values to see how the program deals with illegal menu choices.

## Listing 2.1. MILES.CPP.

```
1: // miles.cpp -- Miles to Kilometers converter
2:
3: #include <tscdefs.h>
4: #include IOSTREAM_H
5:
6: #define MILES_PER_KM 0.6214
7: #define KMS_PER_MILE 1.6093
8:
9: main()
10: {
11:   int choice;
12:   double km, miles;
13:
14:   cout << "\nMiles and Kilometers Converter\n";
15:   cout << "-----------------------------\n";
16:   cout << "1 : Miles to kilometers\n";
17:   cout << "2 : Kilometers to miles\n";
18:   cout << "3 : Quit\n\n";
19:   cout << "Enter 1, 2, or 3: ";
20:   cin >> choice;
21:
22:   if (choice == 1) {
23:     cout << "Miles? ";
24:     cin >> miles;
```

```
25:     km = miles * KMS_PER_MILE;
26:     cout << miles << " miles = " << km << " kilometers\n";
27:     }
28:     else if (choice == 2) {
29:     cout << "Kilometers? ";
30:     cin >> km;
31:     miles = km * MILES_PER_KM;
32:     cout << km << " kilometers = " << miles << " miles\n";
33:     }
34:     else if (choice != 3)
35:       cout << "Illegal choice!";
36:     return 0;
37:     }
```

# Introducing *if/else,* the Decision Maker

MILES.CPP uses a statement form that I'll dissect for you later in more detail. This statement, called if/else, is C++'s main decision maker. It's simple to use—just add a relational expression in parentheses after the keyword if and then type the statements you want the program to perform *if* that expression evaluates to true. For example, to display the value of a variable count only if that value is greater than 100, you could use the statement

```
if (count > 100)
  cout << "Count = " << count << '\n';
```

Only if count is greater than 100 does the output-stream statement execute. If count is less than or equal to 100, the program completely skips the statement. The expression (count > 100) *must* be enclosed in parentheses.

Small if statements like this one can be written on a single line. You can write the preceding statement as

```
if (count > 100) cout << "Count = " << count << '\n';
```

Either form is correct; C++ cares nothing about how a program looks, only that its parts and pieces are in place. Putting the output statement on its own indented line makes the program easier to read, and this is the style that most C++ programmers prefer to use.

To make an if statement "decide" whether to perform more than one statement, surround those statements with braces. This is called a *compound statement* or a *block*. In the preceding chapter, you learned that blocks can nest inside other blocks, creating levels or scopes in a program. A more practical use for blocks is to create compound statements that combine one or more statements into a *single* statement. For example, using a block, you can revise the previous sample to execute two statements if count is less than or equal to 10:

```
if (count <= 10) {
  cout << "Count is less than or equal to 10\n";
  cout << "Count = " << count << '\n';
}
```

This if statement is composed of two output stream statements, but syntactically, it's a single statement, and it can go wherever single statements are allowed in a program. This is a powerful tool. Anywhere you can write a single statement, you can *always* insert a compound statement delimited with braces. In this way, you can make programs execute multiple statements even though the language specifications may tell you that only a single statement is allowed at such and such a place.

The positions of the braces aren't critical. They could go anywhere as long as they mark or *delimit* the compound statement that should execute only if the relational expression is true. As in the sample before this one, the indentations are purely stylistic; they have no effect on the program's outcome. Every programmer, it seems, has a unique brace and indentation style, and you're free to pick a style that suits you. The style shown here is one of the most popular, and it isolates the fragment nicely in the program text, making it stand out clearly. However, some programmers insist on placing all braces on separate lines like these:

```
if (count <= 10)
{
  ...
}
```

> **Note:** Although most compound-statement blocks consist of at least two statements, surrounding a single statement with braces does no harm.

Getting back to Listing 2.1, MILES.CPP, examine lines 22–27 to see another sample compound if statement. In this case, if the menu selection variable choice equals 1 (note the double equal sign), the four statements surrounded by braces execute. If choice is not 1, the program skips these statements and continues at line 28.

At that line, you see an example of the if statement's alter ego, else. An else clause, which is always optional, executes a statement or block if the if's relational expression is false. In other words, if displays the value of count if it's greater than 100, but if not, you can display an error message by writing

```
if (count > 100)
  cout << "Count = " << count << '\n';
else
  cout << "ERROR: Count is not greater than 100\n";
```

Either or both of the target statements after if and else can be surrounded by braces to allow multiple statements in those locations:

```
if (count > 100) {
  // statements to execute if expression is true
} else {
  // statements to execute if expression is false
}
```

The else clause can also begin a new if statement, as in line 28 of MILES.CPP. This is handy for selecting one of a number of possibilities:

```
if (choice == 1) {
  // statements to execute for choice == 1
} else if (choice == 2) {
  // statements to execute for choice == 2
} else if (choice == 3) {
  // statements to execute for choice == 3
} else {
  // statements to execute for all other choice values
}
```

The final else clause in this construction executes if all other relational expressions in the preceding if statements evaluate to false. Lines 34–35 of MILES.CPP use this same idea a little differently:

```
else if (choice != 3)
  cout << "Illegal choice!";
```

If choice is 3, the program simply quits. If choice is not 3, it must be a value not listed in the menu, and the program displays an error message. Considerations like these—what to do when a value falls outside a specified range or when it doesn't match known possibilities—are important to ponder. Always do your best to write `if`/`else` and other statements that take all potential events into account.

# Making Sense out of Logical Operators

As you learned in the previous section, you can use relational operators to write expressions that perform actions based on the truth or falsehood of various conditions. Logical operators expand on this idea, giving you the means to evaluate multiple relational expressions to a single true or false result. For example, suppose that you want to display the value of count only if it's *between* 1 and 100. One way to do that is for a program statement to combine the results of two relational expressions using C++'s *logical AND* operator, `&&`:

```
if ((count >= 1) && (count <= 100))
  cout << "Count = " << count << '\n';
```

You could also write the statement in a form that resembles the one used by mathematicians to express a value within range of high and low limits, as in *1 <= count <= 100:*

```
if ((1 <= count) && (count <= 100))
  cout << "Count = " << count << '\n';
```

Either way, in both of these samples, the `if` statement's relational expression `((1 <= count) && (count <= 100))` is true only if count represents a value from 1 to 100. To reach that conclusion, C++ evaluates the two inner relational expressions, and then it combines the results using the rules for logical AND, which gives a true result only if one argument *and* another are both true.

> **Note:** Actually, C++ employs a concept known as *short-circuit expression evaluation.* This means that as soon as the result of a complex relational expression is known beyond a doubt, C++ stops evaluating other parts of that expression. For example, if count equals 0, the program "knows" that the full expression `((1 <= count) && (count <= 100))` is false as soon as it evaluates the first inner expression `(1 <= count)`, and there's no reason to evaluate the second half of the complete expression. This helps keep programs running fast by eliminating wasteful execution of purposeless code.

Another logical operator is the *logical OR*, represented in C++ by the symbol ¦¦. As with &&, you can use ¦¦ to create complex relational expressions, for example, to execute statements if one condition *or* another is true:

```
if ((count == 1) ¦¦ (count == 100))
  cout << "Count is 1 or 100\n";
```

The effect of this sample is to execute the output stream statement only if count equals 1 or 100. Any other values cause the full relational expression to be false, skipping the output statement. You can also create even more complex expressions by using parentheses judiciously to combine && and ¦¦:

```
if (((1 <= count) && (count <= 100)) ¦¦ (count == -1))
  cout << "Count is -1 or is between 1 and 100\n";
```

Here the output-stream statement executes only if count is a value between 1 and 100, or if it equals –1. Try to work through the logic until it's clear—even simple expressions like this one can be difficult to decipher. For that reason, it's often just as well to use multiple if statements to improve the program's clarity:

```
if ((1 <= count) && (count <= 100))
  // Statement if count is a value from 1 to 100
else if (count == -1)
  // Statement if count is -1
```

Listing 2.2 demonstrates how to use the && logical operator to calculate a vehicle's gas consumption and report whether the fuel use is poor, good, or excellent. Run the program, enter your starting and ending odometer reading, and then the number of gallons of fuel purchased. The program uses these figures to report the average miles per gallon traveled. (The units are arbitrary, and you can just as well enter kilometer readings and liters purchased, but in that case, you'll probably want to change the prompts and other messages.)

## Listing 2.2. GAS.CPP.

```
1: // gas.cpp -- Gas consumption calculator
2:
3: #include <tscdefs.h>
4: #include IOSTREAM_H
5: #include <stdlib.h>
6:
7: main()
8: {
```

*continues*

## Listing 2.2. continued

```
 9:    double start, end, gallons, miles, consumption;
10:
11:    cout << "Enter starting odometer reading: ";
12:    cin >> start;
13:    cout << "Enter ending odometer reading: ";
14:    cin >> end;
15:    if (start > end) {
16:      cout << "Odometer readings are reversed\n";
17:      exit(1);
18:    }
19:    cout << "Enter gallons purchased: ";
20:    cin >> gallons;
21:    miles = 1 + (end - start);
22:    consumption = miles / gallons;
23:    cout << "Consumption = " << consumption << " miles per gallon\n";
24:    cout << "Your vehicle's fuel use is ";
25:    if (consumption < 20.0)
26:      cout << "poor\n";
27:    else if ((consumption >= 20.0) && (consumption < 25.0))
28:      cout << "good\n";
29:    else
30:      cout << "excellent\n";
31:    return 0;
32: }
```

After prompting for starting and ending odometer readings, GAS.CPP uses an if statement and relational expression to detect whether start is greater than end (see lines 15–18). If so, the program displays an error message and halts by executing exit(1)—a standard function that you haven't seen before. Using exit() to halt a program causes it to pass back to DOS the value inside parentheses, in this case 1. A batch file can retrieve this value by examining the DOS variable errorlevel, and taking an appropriate action if that value is not 0. You'll see other examples of this technique in later programs.

Note: Before you can use exit(), you must include the header file stdlib.h as GAS.CPP does at line 5. The exit() function is declared in that file—it's not native to C++.

A second and more complex `if` statement at lines 25–30 displays a message that tells you if your vehicle's gas consumption is poor, good, or excellent. Line 25 uses a simple relational expression to detect `consumption` values less than 20. Line 27 uses a logical AND operator and two relational expressions to handle values above 20 and less than 25. A final `else` clause takes care of any values greater than or equal to 25. (You might adjust the literal constants in these statements if you are converting GAS.CPP to report on kilometers per liter or other units.)

The important lesson to learn from GAS.CPP is how relational expressions and logical operators change the way the program operates. GAS.CPP "decides" which of several statements to execute based on relational expressions, all of which evaluate to true or false results. Using relational expressions and `if`/`else` statements lets the program change course based on its input data—a simple but complete example of how data and action cooperate in programs to create meaningful results.

## Forget Me Not

In addition to the relational operators that take two arguments, C++ also has one unary relational operator called *not* and represented by an exclamation point (!). The *not* operator reverses the result of a relational expression, changing true to false, or false to true. To execute a statement if a condition is *not* true, you can write something like this:

```
if (!(count < 100))
  cout << "Count is >= 100" << '\n';
```

The expression (`!(count < 100)`) is actually two. First, the inner expression (`count < 100`) evaluates to true or false. Then the *not* operator is applied to that result, flipping its value. The final effect is to execute the output statement only if `count` is *not* less than 100. Of course, the expression (`count >= 100`) gives the same result and is simpler.

## Bitwise Operators—Programming One Bit at a Time

A little bit goes a long way in programming. In many computer languages, it's difficult to manipulate lone bits in memory, but not in C++. As in C, programmers can write high-level C++ statements that operate on low-level details—for example, to control hardware registers by setting and resetting specific bits at certain addresses in the computer's memory space where those registers are logically located. C++ is a high-level language, but it doesn't prevent you from writing code that operates at the system level.

Another reason for accessing bits in memory is to store information in the smallest possible space. For example, a certain bit in a database record could represent a fact's current status: 1 for yes and 0 for no, or 0 for male and 1 for female. A series of bits could also represent a set of values: If bit 1 is set, value A is considered to be in the set; if bit 2 is set, value B is in the set; and so on.

Many programmers prefer to use assembly language for low-level programming that manipulates memory and hardware on a bit-by-bit level. But it's probably easier to use C++'s *bitwise operators* listed in Table 2.2. With these operators, you can manipulate single bits in integer values, with results that are comparable in speed and efficiency to assembly language.

**Table 2.2. Bitwise operators.**

| Operator | Description |
|----------|-------------|
| & | Bitwise AND |
| ¦ | Bitwise inclusive OR |
| ^ | Bitwise exclusive OR |
| << | Shift bits left |
| >> | Shift bits right |
| ~ | Form one's complement |

In expressions, the first three bitwise operators in Table 2.2 combine two values according to the rules for logical AND (&), OR (¦), and exclusive OR (^). Three sample programs, TAND.CPP, TOR.CPP, and TXOR.CPP, demonstrate the effects of these operators and also make useful tools for previewing the effects of logical expression values you plan to use in other projects. (The *T* in these program names stands for *Test; XOR* is a common abbreviation for *exclusive OR*.) The three programs are nearly identical except for the operators they demonstrate. Run each one and enter two values separated by a blank, for example **1234 7**. If you press Enter by accident after the first value, just enter the second alone and press Enter again.

> **Note:** When using bitwise operators, be careful not to confuse the first two, &
> and ¦, with the logical operators && and ¦¦. As with the relational == and
> assignment = operators, C++ allows you to use the wrong operator in many
> cases without a whimper. It's up to you to use these operators correctly.
> Another significant difference is that C++ always evaluates all of any expres-
> sion that uses one or more bitwise operators. In the expression (A ¦ B) & C,
> for instance, A, B, and C are always evaluated. In the similar looking, but very
> different logical expression (A ¦¦ B) && C, the expression represented by C
> would not be evaluated if (A ¦¦ B) is false. In that case, the entire expression
> would then have to be false, and C++ stops evaluating logical expressions as
> soon as the outcome is certain.

Listing 2.3 shows the first of the three test programs, TAND.CPP.

## Listing 2.3. TAND.CPP.

```
 1: // tand.cpp -- Test program for bitwise AND
 2:
 3: #include <tscdefs.h>
 4: #include IOSTREAM_H
 5: #include <form.h>
 6:
 7: #if (defined __TSC_BTC__) ¦¦ (defined __TSC_MSC__)
 8: #include <pbin.h>  // Print binary function
 9: #endif
10:
11: main()
12: {
13:   unsigned int v1, v2, v3;
14:   char buf[80];
15:
16:   cout << "Enter values to AND: (ex: 1234 15) ";
17:   cin >> v1 >> v2;
18:   v3 = v1 & v2;
19: #ifdef __TSC_ZTC__
20:   cout << form(buf, "      %5u  %#06x  %016b\n", v1, v1, v1);
21:   cout << form(buf, "AND   %5u  %#06x  %016b\n", v2, v2, v2);
```

*continues*

## Listing 2.3. continued

```
22:    cout << "======================================\n";
23:    cout << form(buf, "        %5u   %#06x   %016b\n", v3, v3, v3);
24: #else   // Borland C++ and Microsoft C/C++
25:    cout << form(buf, "        %5u   %#06x   ", v1, v1); pbin(v1);
26:    cout << form(buf, "AND     %5u   %#06x   ", v2, v2); pbin(v2);
27:    cout << "======================================\n";
28:    cout << form(buf, "        %5u   %#06x   ", v3, v3); pbin(v3);
29: #endif
30:    return 0;
31: }
```

> **Note:** Of all the programs in this book, TAND.CPP and the similar ex-
> amples that follow are among the least compatible between the Borland,
> Microsoft, and Zortech C++ compilers. Only Zortech C++ can display binary
> values directly. The other compilers require the use of a function, pbin()
> (print binary value), explained in Chapter 10, "Cross-Compilation Tools."
> Several conditional compilation directives (see lines 7–9, 19, 24, and 29)
> select different sections of the program's text depending on which compiler
> you are using.

Line 18 in TAND.CPP uses the rules for *bitwise AND* (see Table 2.3) to combine two unsigned int values v1 and v2. This statement also assigns the result of that combination to a third variable, v3. Lines 20–28 display the three values, using form to show the unsigned, hexadecimal, and binary forms of each value and the result of the bitwise combination.

## Table 2.3. Rules for bitwise AND.

| A | & | B | == | C |
|---|---|---|----|---|
| 0 | & | 0 | == | 0 |
| 0 | & | 1 | == | 0 |
| 1 | & | 0 | == | 0 |
| 1 | & | 1 | == | 1 |

As Table 2.3 shows, the result of combining two values *A* and *B* with the *bitwise AND* operator is 1 only if the two original bits are also 1. In all other cases, the result is 0. Run TAND.CPP and enter various test values to illustrate these rules.

A typical use for the bitwise AND operator is to mask a portion of a value, allowing only part of that value to *pass through* to the result. For example, run TAND and enter **1021 15**. The 1021 represents the original value. The 15 is called a *mask*. Here's what you see on-screen:

```
      1021   0x03fd   0000001111111101
AND     15   0x000f   0000000000001111
======================================
        13   0x000d   0000000000001101
```

The mask allows bits in the original value to pass through to the result. Any place a 1 appears in the mask, the result contains the same bit as in the original value. Any place a 0 bit appears, a 0 appears in the result. The 0 in the mask *blocks* the bit in the original from passing through.

The next program, Listing 2.4, TOR.CPP, demonstrates the *bitwise inclusive OR* operator.

### Listing 2.4. TOR.CPP.

```
 1: // tor.cpp -- Test program for bitwise inclusive OR
 2:
 3: #include <tscdefs.h>
 4: #include IOSTREAM_H
 5: #include <form.h>
 6:
 7: #if (defined __TSC_BTC__) || (defined __TSC_MSC__)
 8: #include <pbin.h>  // Print binary function
 9: #endif
10:
11: main()
12: {
13:   unsigned int v1, v2, v3;
14:   char buf[80];
15:
16:   cout << "Enter values to OR inclusively: (ex: 1234 15) ";
17:   cin >> v1 >> v2;
18:   v3 = v1 | v2;
```

*continues*

## Listing 2.4. continued

```
19: #ifdef __TSC_ZTC__
20:    cout << form(buf, "     %5u  %#06x  %016b\n", v1, v1, v1);
21:    cout << form(buf, "OR   %5u  %#06x  %016b\n", v2, v2, v2);
22:    cout << "======================================\n";
23:    cout << form(buf, "     %5u  %#06x  %016b\n", v3, v3, v3);
24: #else  // Borland C++ and Microsoft C/C++
25:    cout << form(buf, "     %5u  %#06x  ", v1, v1); pbin(v1);
26:    cout << form(buf, "OR   %5u  %#06x  ", v2, v2); pbin(v2);
27:    cout << "======================================\n";
28:    cout << form(buf, "     %5u  %#06x  ", v3, v3); pbin(v3);
29: #endif
30:    return 0;
31: }
```

TOR.CPP combines the two unsigned int values v1 and v2 using the rules for bitwise inclusive OR (see Table 2.4) or just *bitwise OR*. In this case, the result of using the ¦ operator is 1 if either or both bits in the two arguments are 1. The result is 0 only if both bits are also 0.

## Table 2.4. Rules for bitwise OR.

| A | ¦ | B | == | C |
|---|---|---|----|---|
| 0 | ¦ | 0 | == | 0 |
| 0 | ¦ | 1 | == | 1 |
| 1 | ¦ | 0 | == | 1 |
| 1 | ¦ | 1 | == | 1 |

The bitwise OR operator is often used to insert bits into values. Suppose that a variable contains the value 152, or 10011000 in binary. To change the 6th and 8th bits to 1, use a mask value of 5. Try this by running TOR and enter **152 5**. On-screen, you'll see

```
       152  0x0098  0000000010011000
OR       5  0x0005  0000000000000101
       ======================================
       157  0x009d  0000000010011101
```

The result contains all of the bits from the original with the bits of the mask inserted where 0s appeared before. This technique is useful for setting bits in registers and other variables without disturbing other bits already there.

Listing 2.5, TXOR.CPP, illustrates how to use the bitwise exclusive OR operator.

## Listing 2.5. TXOR.CPP.

```
 1: // txor.cpp -- Test program for bitwise exclusive OR
 2:
 3: #include <tscdefs.h>
 4: #include IOSTREAM_H
 5: #include <form.h>
 6:
 7: #if (defined __TSC_BTC__) || (defined __TSC_MSC__)
 8: #include <pbin.h>  // Print binary function
 9: #endif
10:
11: main()
12: {
13:     unsigned int v1, v2, v3;
14:     char buf[80];
15:
16:     cout << "Enter values to OR exclusively: (ex: 1234 15) ";
17:     cin >> v1 >> v2;
18:     v3 = v1 ^ v2;
19: #ifdef __TSC_ZTC__
20:     cout << form(buf, "     %5u  %#06x  %016b\n", v1, v1, v1);
21:     cout << form(buf, "XOR  %5u  %#06x  %016b\n", v2, v2, v2);
22:     cout << "=====================================\n";
23:     cout << form(buf, "     %5u  %#06x  %016b\n", v3, v3, v3);
24: #else  // Borland C++ and Microsoft C/C++
25:     cout << form(buf, "     %5u  %#06x  ", v1, v1); pbin(v1);
26:     cout << form(buf, "XOR  %5u  %#06x  ", v2, v2); pbin(v2);
27:     cout << "=====================================\n";
28:     cout << form(buf, "     %5u  %#06x  ", v3, v3); pbin(v3);
29: #endif
30:     return 0;
31: }
```

TXOR demonstrates how the *bitwise exclusive OR* operator (^) works. Line 12 combines v1 and v2 according to the rules listed in Table 2.5, which shows that only if the two argument bits are *different* is the result 1. If the arguments are both 0 or both 1, the result is 0.

**Table 2.5. Rules for bitwise exclusive OR.**

| A | ^ | B | == | C |
|---|---|---|----|---|
| 0 | ^ | 0 | == | 0 |
| 0 | ^ | 1 | == | 1 |
| 1 | ^ | 0 | == | 1 |
| 1 | ^ | 1 | == | 0 |

Knowing how, when, and why to apply the &, |, and ^ operators takes practice. As I mentioned before, & is frequently used to mask bits in values, usually to force some bits to zero while allowing other bits to remain unchanged. For another example, run TAND and enter **45001 15**. This displays

```
        45001   0xafc9   1010111111001001
AND        15   0x000f   0000000000001111
====================================
            9   0x0009   0000000000001001
```

Notice how the value 15 decimal, or 1111 in binary, serves as a mask, allowing the four rightmost bits in 45001 to pass through to the result on the bottom. All other bits, whether they are 0 or 1 are forced to 0 by the zeros in the mask. This property is characteristic of a bitwise AND—bits equal to 1 in the mask allow bits in the other argument to pass through. Bits equal to 0 block bits, no matter what their values.

You can also use bitwise AND to reset individual bits to 0. For example, run TAND and enter **45001 65534**. All bits except the rightmost in 65534 equal 1, and combining that value with another therefore forces the rightmost bit in the original value (45001) to 0.

The | (bitwise OR) operator is typically used for the opposite purpose—to set bits to 1 without disturbing other bits in an integer. To see the difference between & and |, run TOR and enter the same values you entered for TAND, **45001 15**.

```
        45001   0xafc9   1010111111001001
OR         15   0x000f   0000000000001111
==========================================
        45007   0xafcf   1010111111001111
```

This time, instead of serving as a mask, the value 15 (1111 in binary) forces the lower 4 bits to ones. Bits on the top pass through the zeros in the mask. This property is useful for setting individual bits. For instance, run TOR again and enter **45000 1**. As you can see, this sets the rightmost bit to 1, leaving the other bits undisturbed.

The ^ (bitwise exclusive OR) operator's properties are almost enough to make one believe in magic. The rules for XOR state that a 1 bit appears in the result only if the original two bits are different. Because of this, the XOR operator can serve as a toggle to turn 1 bits to 0 and 0 bits to 1. To see how to use XOR for this purpose, run TXOR and enter the same values, **45001 15**, that you've been using for other bitwise operators. Compare the result with the TAND and TOR tests you ran earlier:

```
        45001   0xafc9   1010111111001001
XOR        15   0x000f   0000000000001111
==========================================
        44998   0xafc6   1010111111000110
```

Unlike the other two tests, the XOR operator toggled the four rightmost bits in the top value from 1 to 0 and from 0 to 1, effectively converting 1001 to 0110. Bits on top of 0 bits in the mask (the second value), are undisturbed. This becomes even more interesting when you run TXOR again and enter the result from the previous experiment along with the *same* mask, **44998 15**.

```
        44998   0xafc6   1010111111000110
XOR        15   0x000f   0000000000001111
==========================================
        45001   0xafc9   1010111111001001
```

The result is the original value from the previous test, a strange but true characteristic of XOR. Applying the same operator twice with the same mask restores the original value!

Graphics programs often make use of this property to allow shapes to move on-screen without disturbing images in the background. Displaying an image by XORing its bits with other bits that represent shapes already on display, and then using the identical mask to XOR those same bits again, displays an image on top of another, then wipes the background clean without disturbing the original picture.

Another use for XOR is encryption, where a mask is XORed with all bytes in a file, thus scrambling their contents. To restore the original file contents, that same operation is simply repeated. Although this simple scheme is easily broken, more sophisticated algorithms still make use of XOR's special capability to restore original values just by applying the same mask twice.

## Shifty Operations

So far, you've examined only three of C++'s six bitwise operators (see Table 2.2). The other three allow expressions to shift bits left and right and to complement all bits in integers, changing zeros to ones and ones to zeros.

If you've done any 80x86 assembly language programming, you'll recognize the left shift (<<) and right shift (>>) operators as corresponding with similar processor instructions shr and shl. In addition to their ability to move bits around in values—which imaginative programmers put to all sorts of uses—shifting bits left and right are useful operations for performing fast integer multiplications and divisions by powers of 2.

Use C++'s bitwise shift operators in expressions such as (v1 << 2) (shift the value in v1 left by two bits) and (v1 >> 1) (shift the value in v1 right by two bits). Remember that like other expressions, the operators do not change the argument values, but instead evaluate those arguments to produce a result, which you probably should assign to another variable or use as part of a complex expression.

> **Note:** You may have noticed an unfortunate resemblance between the shift operators and I/O streams. However, even though these statements use the same symbols, because they are used so differently, it's unlikely you'll confuse them in practice. C++ *never* confuses them and can easily determine whether >> and << are shift operators or I/O stream symbols from the context of the program.

On disk are two programs TSHL.CPP and TSHR.CPP, which demonstrate the left and right shift operators. Because these programs are nearly identical to TAND.CPP, TOR.CPP, and TXOR.CPP, they aren't listed here.

Run TSHL first, and enter the values **4 1**. Notice that the result is 8, or 4 * 2. Run TSHL again and enter **10 4**. This time the result is 160, or $10 * 2^4$. As this shows, shifting values left a bit at a time gives the same results as multiplying those same values by successive powers of 2. Because computers typically can shift bits faster than they can multiply—which is true even with a math coprocessor—when you need to multiply by powers of 2, it's usually wise to employ bit shifts rather than multiplications.

Similarly, shifting integers right effectively divides values by successive powers of 2. Compile and run TSHR and enter test values such as **160 4** and **32767 8**. Prove to yourself that shifting values right divides those values by powers of 2.

The final bitwise operator in C++ is represented by the symbol ~, but it works a little differently from the other bitwise operators. Instead of taking two arguments, ~ is a unary operator that is applied to a value at right (similar to the way the NOT operator (!) works). For example, the expression ~count complements the value of count, toggling all 1 bits to 0 and 0 bits to 1. Like other operators (except for ++ and --), this does not change count directly, and you'll need to use the result in an expression or assign it to another variable, as Listing 2.6, TCOMP.CPP, demonstrates. Run the program and enter values like **15** or **12345** to experiment with ~.

**Listing 2.6. TCOMP.CPP.**

```
 1: // tcomp.cpp -- Test program for bitwise complement
 2:
 3: #include <tscdefs.h>
 4: #include IOSTREAM_H
 5: #include <form.h>
 6:
 7: #if (defined __TSC_BTC__) || (defined __TSC_MSC__)
 8: #include <pbin.h>  // Print binary function
 9: #endif
10:
11: main()
12: {
13:   unsigned int v1, v2;
14:   char buf[80];
15:
16:   cout << "Enter value to complement: ";
17:   cin >> v1;
18:   v2 = ~v1;
```

*continues*

**Listing 2.6. continued**

```
19: #ifdef __TSC_ZTC__
20:   cout << form(buf, "       %5u   %#06x   %016b\n", v1, v1, v1);
21:   cout << "=====================================\n";
22:   cout << form(buf, "COMP   %5u   %#06x   %016b\n", v2, v2, v2);
23: #else    // Borland C++ and Microsoft C/C++
24:   cout << form(buf, "       %5u   %#06x   ", v1, v1); pbin(v1);
25:   cout << "=====================================\n";
26:   cout << form(buf, "COMP   %5u   %#06x   ", v2, v2); pbin(v2);
27: #endif
28:   return 0;
29: }
```

Combining the complement operator with other operators, often &, can sometimes be useful. For example, to set the second bit in a value count to 1, you can write

```
count = count & ~1;
```

This is the same as executing count = count & 65534. Although the purpose of an expression like count & ~1 is anything but crystal clear, you'll see it often in C++ and C programs. In your own code, be sure to document exactly what you are attempting to achieve with expressions like this, and use the test programs in this and previous sections to verify the results.

## Combined Assignments—Expressive Shorthand

Look again at that last sample statement in the previous section, count = count & ~1. It takes the value of count, applies the & operator to the one's complement of 1, and then assigns the result back to count. In this and similar cases where an operation is to be performed on a variable and then assigned right back, C++ allows a special operator shorthand known as a *combined assignment*.

To create a combined assignment operator, add an equal sign to any of the symbols +, -, *, /, %, <<, >>, &, ^, or |. For example, instead of count = count & ~1, you can write

```
count &= ~1;
```

C++ interprets the combined operator as an instruction to perform an operation on the initial value (count in this case) and then assign the result back to that same variable. Here are a few more samples with comments that show the equivalent longhand expressions:

```
count += 10;       // count = count + 10;
count *= 2;        // count = count * 2;
count *= count;    // count = count * count;
count %= 16;       // count = count % count;
```

Try to use these shorthand forms whenever possible. In many cases, the results will be no different, but sometimes, the compiler will be able to generate more efficient code for a combined assignment operator than for the equivalent longhand expressions. It's difficult to predict reliably when the shorthand forms will produce such benefits, so it's best to use them when you can. In any case, the results probably are never less efficient than the longhand, although some people find the short forms a bit harder to read. If you find them confusing, add a comment, as shown in the previous samples, to explain what's going on.

That wraps up C++'s operators. With what you have learned so far, you can write some very sophisticated expressions, manipulate bits in integer values, and use the results of expressions to make decisions. By now, however, you may also have noticed a deficiency in all of the sample listings you've compiled so far. In every case, the programs begin at the top and race like mad to the finish. Of course, most computer programs don't work that way. Instead, they loop around, jump from one section to another, and don't quit until you tell them to. The next section explains how to add these capabilities and others to your code.

# So It Flows

C++ programs start with the first statement inside main()'s block and continue to execute one statement after the other until reaching the block's closing parenthesis. At least that's true unless a statement does something to change the normal top-to-bottom flow of a program. I like to call statements in this category *program flow statements,* although that's not an official term. They're also known as *control structures.*

A program flow statement controls the order in which other statements execute. Those other statements can be of any kind—assignments, expressions, and other program flow statements. Program flow statements can halt programs dead in their tracks, make decisions, choose matching elements from sets, and repeat one or more statements. All of these actions are what give programs personality. Without program flow statements, programs simply start at the top and keep going until they run out of steam. With program flow statements, you can write programs that run until a planned event occurs or until *you* tell them to stop.

# A Proper *exit*

Left to their own devices, C++ programs stop after executing the final statement in main(). After that, DOS usually regains control so that you can give commands and run other programs.

Another way to halt a program is to execute an exit() statement, which you saw earlier in GAS.CPP. This passes an unsigned integer value back to DOS, which a batch file can retrieve by examining errorlevel. Before using exit(), a program must include the stdlib.h header file.

Listing 2.7, YESNO.CPP, puts this idea to practical use and also demonstrates how exit() affects the normal top-to-bottom flow of a program. YESNO solves a problem with DOS batch files—the lack of a batch file command to prompt a user for a yes or no answer and then change course based on the response. Compile YESNO.CPP now, but don't run the program just yet. I'll let you know when to do that.

**Listing 2.7. YESNO.CPP.**

```
 1: // yesno.cpp -- Return ERRORLEVEL=0 (No), 1 (Yes)
 2:
 3: #include <tscdefs.h>
 4: #include IOSTREAM_H
 5: #include <stdlib.h>
 6: #include <ctype.h>
 7:
 8: main()
 9: {
10:   char answer;
11:
12:   cout << "Type Y for yes, N for no: ";
13:   cin >> answer;
14:   answer = (char)toupper(answer);
15:   if (answer == 'Y')
16:     exit(1);
17:   else
18:     exit(0);
```

```
19:    cout << "This statement never executes!\n";
20:    return 0;
21: }
```

Line 14 in YESNO.CPP assigns the value of `toupper(answer)` to `answer`, a variable of type `char` that holds the response to the prompt at line 11. (Because `toupper()` returns type `int`, its value must be type cast to `(char)`, so that value can be assigned to the `char` answer.) In other words, if `answer` currently equals `'y'`, line 13 changes answer to `'Y'`. This makes the `if` statement in line 14 easier to write because it doesn't have to test whether a response is in upper- or lowercase.

The result is that either line 16 or 18 executes depending on the answer. Any answer other than yes—for example, pressing the X key—is considered a no response. Consequently, line 18 never executes—the `if`/`else` statement at lines 15–18 guarantees that the program's normal flow will be interrupted by one of the two marked `exit()`s. I added line 19 only to demonstrate the finality of `exit()`. You can remove this statement if you want.

Technically, `toupper()` is a *macro,* which C++ expands to the necessary commands to convert letters to uppercase. Other symbols passed to `toupper()`—digits and punctuation, for example—are unchanged. To use `toupper()`, a program must include the ctype.h header as YESNO.CPP does at line 6.

A similar macro, `tolower()`, also declared in ctype.h, converts characters to lowercase. Here are a few samples of `toupper` and `tolower` with the results listed in comments to the right:

```
toupper('a');    // == 'A'
toupper('#');    // == '#'
tolower('Q');    // == 'q'
toupper('3');    // == '3'
```

**Note:** Macros like `toupper()` in C++ and in C can be very complex, and some programmers use them extensively. Strictly speaking, however, macros are not part of the C++ language, and you don't need to master them in order to write C++ programs.

Listing 2.8, TESTYN.BAT, demonstrates how to use YESNO.CPP. With YESNO.EXE and TESTYN.BAT in the current directory, enter **testyn** to run the batch file from the DOS prompt. When you see the message, Type Y for yes, N for no:, type **Y** or **N** and press Enter. You'll then receive a message telling you whether you answered yes or no and proving that the batch file was able to determine that answer by examining errorlevel at line 7.

**Listing 2.8. TESTYN.BAT.**

```
 1: echo off
 2: rem
 3: rem * Test YESNO.CPP
 4: rem
 5: echo Continue program?
 6: yesno
 7: if errorlevel == 1 goto YES
 8: echo You answered no!
 9: goto end
10: :YES
11: echo You answered yes!
12: :END
```

**Note:** The errorlevel test at line 7 in Listing 2.8 is deceiving. Although written if errorlevel == 1, the effect is the same as the C++ statement if (errorlevel >= 1). In DOS batch files, == performs the same job as >= in C++.

# Reducing Complexity

There's another way to write YESNO.CPP that doesn't require an if statement and that reduces the size of the program text. As I said before, exit() ends a program and passes an unsigned integer value back to DOS. Instead of writing expressions like exit(0) and exit(1), which specify literal constants inside the parentheses, you can replace those values with any expression that evaluates to an unsigned integer.

For example, consider the expression

```
(toupper(answer) == 'Y')
```

This compares the result of `toupper(answer)` with `'Y'`, leaving in its wake the value 0 if the expression is false or 1 if it's true. Because the expression's value is passed to DOS via `exit()`, there's no reason to go to all the trouble in Listing 2.7 at lines 15–18 to test whether answer equals `'Y'` and execute either `exit(0)` or `exit(1)`. Instead, it's possible to eliminate that entire section by passing the expression result directly to `exit`:

```
exit((toupper(answer) == 'Y'));
```

Be sure that you understand how and why this works. If expressions like this throw you, take them apart, starting with the innermost items. First, `toupper()` operates on answer, converting that character to uppercase. Then, `==` compares the result with `'Y'`. The result of *that* expression is false (0) or true (1), and this is the value that the program passes to `exit()`.

Using the results of expressions this way—and taking advantage of the fact that C++ represents false as 0 and true as 1—is a common trick. You'll see it used time after time. However, because such expressions are difficult to understand without carefully examining the code, they can obscure the program's purpose. For that reason, adding a comment to explain what's happening is probably a good idea.

Listing 2.9, YESNO2.CPP shows how to pass a relational expression directly to `exit()` to shorten the original YESNO program. After compiling YESNO2.CPP, delete YESNO.EXE and rename YESNO2.EXE to YESNO.EXE. Then run the TESTYN.BAT batch file to verify that both versions of the program operate identically.

## Listing 2.9. YESNO2.CPP.

```
1: // yesno2.cpp -- Shortened version
2:
3: #include <tscdefs.h>
4: #include IOSTREAM_H
5: #include <stdlib.h>
6: #include <ctype.h>
7:
8: main()
9: {
```

*continues*

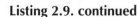

**Listing 2.9. continued**

```
10:    char answer;
11:
12:    cout << "Type Y for yes, N for no: ";
13:    cin >> answer;
14:    exit((toupper(answer) == 'Y'));
15:    return 0;
16: }
```

# Filters and *while* Statements

A *filter* is a useful kind of program that takes every character you can throw at it, performs some operation on that input, and writes the result to the standard output. By using filters along with DOS's redirection symbols < (*take input from*) and > (*send output to*), you can process text files stored on disk without having to do a lot of fancy programming: opening, reading, and writing files—subjects covered later.

You can also connect multiple filters using a pipe, represented by a vertical bar ¦. A pipe lets one filter pump its output to the input of another filter, which can direct the information flow to yet another filter and so on. Connecting filter programs this way constructs sophisticated DOS commands out of relatively simple building blocks. For example, using the DOS SORT and FIND filters, you can type a command such as the following to list a sorted directory of files and subdirectories created or updated on July 20, 1990:

```
dir ¦ find "7-20-90" ¦ sort
```

Using the redirection symbols, you can send the contents of a text file to a filter and then write the processed result to a new file. To sort a file named MYNAMES.TXT, you can type

```
sort < mynames.txt > sorted.txt
```

This directs the contents of MYNAMES.TXT to SORT and then writes the sorted text lines to a new file named SORTED.TXT.

Writing your own filters with C++ is easy and takes only a few lines of programming. Typically, a filter program uses a statement form called a `while` statement, also called a `while` *loop*. A `while` loop repeats another statement or block *while* a condition remains true. For example, if `count` is an `int` variable, the following `while` loop displays 1 through 10:

```
count = 1;
while (count <= 10)
  cout << count++ << '\n';
```

Try writing your own test program to execute this loop. Remember to define the variable int count; and insert the preceding lines inside main(). Notice how the output stream statement both displays the current value of count and increments that variable using the ++ operator. This ensures that the relational expression (count <= 10) eventually becomes true. If it didn't, the while loop would never end—that is, until you reboot or pull the computer's plug.

You can also execute a compound block of statements in a while loop by enclosing the block with braces in the usual way. In general, a multistatement while loop has the form

```
while (expression) {
  // statements to execute while expression is true
}
```

The (expression) can be any expression that evaluates to a true or false result. To use a while loop in a filter, the program needs some way to *get* input characters and *put* those characters to the standard output.

Listing 2.10, FILTER.CPP, shows how to accomplish that goal with a while loop that copies the standard input to the standard output. The program serves as a shell for more elaborate filters to come, but it can be used to copy text files. Of course, DOS already has COPY and XCOPY commands that work more rapidly and can copy other kinds of files as well. The purpose of FILTER.CPP is to demonstrate the mechanics of writing filter programs, not to replace those DOS commands.

**Note:** If you try to run a filter program like FILTER by simply typing its name—as you do to run other programs—DOS expects you to supply input manually for the program. This can seem to make the computer "hang." If you do this by accident, or after you're done typing input for a filter, press Ctrl+Z, DOS's end-of-file character, to return to the DOS prompt.

## Listing 2.10. FILTER.CPP.

```
 1: // filter.cpp -- Filter shell (copies input to output)
 2:
 3: #include <tscdefs.h>
 4: #include IOSTREAM_H
 5:
 6: main()
 7: {
 8:   char c;
 9:
10:   while (cin.get(c))
11:     cout.put(c);
12:   return 0;
13: }
```

Carefully examine lines 10–11 in FILTER.CPP. The while loop continually executes cin.put(c) while the expression (cin.get(c)) is true. You have seen cout and cin before in input and output stream statements. Here these objects are used differently. The expression cin.get(c) calls a function named get() that *belongs* to cin. The expression cout.put(c) calls a similar function, put(), that belongs to cout.

You'll return to the concept of functions belonging to objects later in this book when you examine classes. For now, think of cin as an object from which information comes. To read one character of that input, use the expression cin.get(c), where c is a variable of type char. To write a character, use the expression cout.put(c). The expression cin.get(c) returns a true value until the input (the keyboard, for example) returns EOF, or the "end of file" character. When that happens, cin.get(c) returns false, and the while loop ends.

Meanwhile, the loop continually gets characters and writes them to cout. Normally, cin is associated with the operating system's standard input (the keyboard by default), and cout is associated with the standard output (the display, usually). This simple program, then, merely copies the standard input to the standard output.

To run FILTER, enter the command **filter <filter.cpp**. This copies the contents of FILTER.CPP to the standard output. To copy FILTER.CPP to a temporary file named TEMP.TXT, type the command **filter <filter.cpp >temp.txt**. To print a file, type **filter <filter.cpp >prn**.

> **Note:** Be careful when specifying an output filename after the > redirection symbol or the append-to symbol >>. If you type the name of an existing file, the filter erases that file permanently without warning. This is true for all filter programs, not just those written in C++.

## Making Decisions with *if/else*

Earlier, you learned how to write decision-making statements with if/else. Combining that concept with a while loop filter makes it possible to write a program like Listing 2.11, LINENUM.CPP, which attaches line numbers to the lines in a text file.

### Listing 2.11. LINENUM.CPP.

```
 1: // linenum.cpp -- Counts number of lines in a text file
 2:
 3: #include <tscdefs.h>
 4: #include IOSTREAM_H
 5: #include IOMANIP_H
 6:
 7: #define NEWLINE '\n'
 8:
 9: main()
10: {
11:   char c;
12:   int linenum = 1;
13:
14:   cout << endl << setw(4) << dec << linenum << ": " << flush;
15:   while (cin.get(c)) {
16:     if (c == NEWLINE) {
17:       linenum++;
18:       cout << endl << setw(4) << dec << linenum << ": " << flush;
19:     } else
20:       cout << c << flush;
21:   }
22:   return 0;
23: }
```

After compiling LINENUM.CPP, type a command such as **linenum <linenum.cpp** to preface every line in LINENUM.CPP with a line number and colon, similar to the line numbers printed with the listings in this book. Or enter the command **linenum <linenum.cpp >temp.txt** to add line numbers to LINENUM.CPP and write the results to TEMP.TXT, which you can then examine with the DOS TYPE command, or with your text editor.

LINENUM works by first writing the initial line number with an output-stream statement at line 14. The `endl` symbol in this statement starts a new line, exactly the same as writing the escape code `'\n'`. (To use `endl`, include `IOMANIP_H` as done here at line 5.)

The `while` loop beginning at line 15 is identical to the one in FILTER. But, this time, instead of sending every input character to the standard output, an `if/else` statement at lines 16–20 examines the value of each character returned by `cin.get(c)`. If a character equals the symbol `NEWLINE`, defined at line 7, the `if` statement increments `linenum`, starts a new output line, and writes the *next* line number. If `c` is any character other than `NEWLINE`, the `else` clause writes that character to the standard output. The effect is to attach a line number in front of every new line.

Notice the uses of `flush` and `endl` in the output stream statements. These are called I/O manipulators. To use them, first include the `IOMANIP_H` header as demonstrated at line 5. The symbol, defined in tscdefs.h, is translated at compile time to an appropriate filename such as iomanip.h or iomanip.hpp.

The `endl` manipulator writes a newline character (or characters) to an output stream. The statement

```
cout << "This is a sentence." << endl;
```

is functionally equivalent to

```
cout << "This is a sentence." << '\n';
```

Insert the `flush` manipulator to ensure that output is written at the expected time:

```
cout << "Write this NOW!" << flush;
```

Without `flush`, the quoted sentence might be stored in a buffer and written only later after the buffer becomes full, or upon some other condition. To force output to be written now, use `flush`.

> **Note:** There are other ways to write LINENUM, which has two tiny flaws. As listed here, the program numbers the first nonexistent line in a zero-length file, and it appends an extra line number if the last line in the file ends with NEWLINE. These are minor annoyances, and the program is still useable, but after you know more about C++, you may want to refine LINENUM to take care of these problems.

Another example, Listing 2.12, WORDS.CPP, uses a similar while loop to count the number of words, characters, and lines in a text file. The program also demonstrates some new C++ techniques you haven't seen before.

### Listing 2.12. WORDS.CPP.

```
 1: // words.cpp -- Count words in standard input
 2:
 3: #include <tscdefs.h>
 4: #include IOSTREAM_H
 5: #include IOMANIP_H
 6: #include <ctype.h>
 7:
 8: #define NEWLINE '\n'
 9:
10: main()
11: {
12:    char c;
13:    int words, chars, lines, insideWord;
14:
15:    words = chars = lines = insideWord = 0;
16:    while (cin.get(c)) {
17:      chars++;
18:      if (c == NEWLINE) {
19:         lines++;
20:         chars++;
21:      }
22:      if (insideWord)
23:         insideWord = !isspace(c);
24:      else {
25:         insideWord = !isspace(c);
```

*continues*

## Listing 2.12. continued

```
26:      if (insideWord)
27:         words++;
28:      }
29:   }
30:   cout << chars << " total character(s)" << endl;
31:   cout << words << " word(s)" << endl;
32:   cout << lines << " line(s)" << endl;
33:   return 0;
34: }
```

To use WORDS, compile the program and give a DOS command such as **words <words.cpp**. In a moment, you'll see a report of the total number of characters, words, and lines in WORDS.CPP. Substitute the name of any plain ASCII text file for WORDS.CPP to see a report on that file's contents.

Of course, WORD.CPP can't read; therefore, it defines a "word" to be any series of characters separated by *white space*—that is, any tab, line feed, vertical tab, form feed, newline, or blank. Lines 23 and 25 detect these characters by using the isspace() macro declared in ctype.h. Other similar macros are isalpha(), isdigit(), islower(), and isupper().

Line 15 in WORDS.CPP demonstrates a shorthand technique for assigning the same value to a series of variables. In general, for int variables a, b, and c, instead of writing

```
a = 0;
b = 0;
c = 0;
```

you can accomplish the same tasks on one line:

```
a = b = c = 0;
```

This also works for other types of variables, as long as all are the same type, and all should be initialized to the same value.

WORDS.CPP employs another technique that you'll find useful in many situations. Variable insideWord of type int is known as a *flag*. Its sole purpose is to store a true (1) or false (0) value that the program can inspect to determine whether a certain condition exists at that time.

In this program, that condition is whether or not the while loop is currently reading the characters in a word (insideWord is true). If so, line 23 assigns the result of !isspace(c) to insideWord. This changes insideWord to false when the loop finds the *next* space character, which marks the end of the current word. (Remember, ! means *not*.) If insideWord is false, lines 25–27 set insideWord according to the current character. If the loop has reached the beginning of a word, the if statement at lines 26–27 increments the words counter.

> **Note:** There are many ways to write WORDS.CPP. For example, see Exercise 2.8, which eliminates the duplicated statements at lines 23 and 25.

# The Ol' *switch*eroo

When a program must select one of several actions, it can use a series of if/else statements. For example, suppose that you want the program to change gears depending on whether a char variable c equals 'A', 'B', or 'C'. To do that, you can write

```
if (c == 'A')
  // statement for 'A';
else if (c == 'B')
  // statement for 'B';
else if (c == 'C')
  // statement for 'C';
else
  // statement for all other characters;
```

Any or all of the single statements represented by comments here could also be compound blocks surrounded with braces. There's nothing wrong with this type of lengthy if/else construction, but another C++ statement called a switch lets you accomplish the same goals with a much clearer form that resembles a table. In this statement, the *cases* ('A', 'B', and 'C' in this example) mark the sections that should execute if the *selector* (c here) matches those values. Here's the switch statement version of the previous if/else:

```
switch (c) {
  case 'A':
    // statement(s) for 'A';
    break;
```

```
case 'B':
  // statement(s) for 'B';
  break;
case 'C':
  // statement(s) for 'C';
  break;
default:
  // statement(s) for all other characters;
}
```

The statement begins with the keyword switch and an expression in parentheses. This expression must reduce to an integer or character, and the case selectors must be character or integer constants or constant expressions (in other words, expressions with all constant arguments, no variables). The result of the switch expression—here, simply the value of c—is compared with every subsequent case selector constant, each of which must end with a colon. Only the statements below the first matching case are then executed. The case values must be unique, but they do not have to be in any particular order.

The multiple break statements mark the end of each case's statements. Without break, the program would simply start executing statements with the first matching case value and continuing to the end of the switch statement. If none of the case values matches the switch statement's expression, the statements following the optional default: case at the end are executed.

Unlike other C++ flow statements, multiple statements for cases inside a switch statement do not need to be surrounded by braces. In other words, it is not necessary to write

```
switch (c) {
  case 'A': {
    statement;
    statement;
    break;
  }
  case 'B': {
    statement;
    break;
  }
  default: {
    statement;
  }
}
```

The extra braces are unnecessary and confusing. Instead, write such code like this:

```
switch (c) {
  case 'A':
    statement;
    statement;
    break;
  case 'B':
    statement;
    break;
  default:
    statement;
}
```

Once again, pay close attention to the break keywords, which mark the end of each case section. This holdover from the C language, which has the identical switch statement, is one of C and C++'s weakest foundations. Misuse break and your code may crumble. For example, if you forget the break after the last statement at the end of a case, the statements in the *next* case will begin to execute! Suppose that by accident you write

```
switch (c) {
  case 'A':
    statement1;
    statement2;    // ???
  case 'B':
    statement3;
    break;
  default:
    statement4;
}
```

If c equals 'A', statement1 and statement2 execute as expected. But, because the case 'A' section fails to include a break after statement2, statement3 will also execute when c is 'A'. Usually, this is not intentional. However, there are rare times when this switch-statement quirk is advantageous. Selectively leaving out breaks allows one case section to *fall through* to the next, thus executing multiple cases for a single matching selector. Experience teaches that the risks of bugs far outweigh the benefits of such designs, and in most cases, you're probably wise to end every case section with a break.

To match more than one case for a given value, list them after each other this way:

```
switch (c) {
  case 'A':
  case 'B':
  case 'C':
    statement1;
    statement2;
    statement3;
    break;
  case 'D':
    statement4;
    break;
}
```

This code executes statements 1 through 3 if c equals 'A', 'B', or 'C'. Usually, it's much clearer to use multiple case selectors this way than to write the equivalent if statement:

```
if ((c == 'A') || (c == 'B') || (c == 'C')) {
  statement1;
  statement2;
  statement3;
} else if (c == 'D')
    statement4;
```

Both forms give identical results, and you can use whichever is appropriate.

Because the default: selector in a switch statement always comes last, it doesn't need to have a break, though it can. Also, the default: is optional—if you are absolutely sure that the switch statement's cases cover *every* possible expression value or if you don't need a default action for unmatched cases, you can safely leave out the default: section.

# Using *switch* Statements

A switch statement comes in handy any time a program needs to select among several possible actions based on the result of an expression or variable that evaluates to a character or integer value. A typical example where a switch statement works well is a program that displays a menu of choices. To select a choice, you type its first letter. Inside the program, a switch statement examines the characters you type and executes various statements for each selection.

To demonstrate how this works, Listing 2.13, MENU.CPP, displays a simple menu of four choices, A(dd, D(elete, S(ort, and Q(uit. The parentheses in these names remind you that typing the first letter of each choice selects that operation. Although this example doesn't actually add, delete, or sort any real information, you can use MENU as a shell for your own designs that need a simple program menu.

## Listing 2.13. MENU.CPP.

```
 1: // menu.cpp -- Using switch to create a simple program menu
 2:
 3: #include <tscdefs.h>
 4: #include IOSTREAM_H
 5: #include <stdlib.h>
 6: #include <ctype.h>
 7:
 8: #define INUSE 1
 9:
10: main()
11: {
12:   char choice;
13:
14:   while (INUSE) {
15:     cout << "\nMenu: A(dd D(elete S(ort Q(uit: ";
16:     cin >> choice;
17:     switch (toupper(choice)) {
18:       case 'A':
19:         cout << "You selected Add\n";
20:         break;
21:       case 'D':
22:         cout << "You selected Delete\n";
23:         break;
24:       case 'S':
25:         cout << "You selected Sort\n";
26:         break;
27:       case 'Q':
28:           exit(0);
29:           break;
30:       default:
31:         cout << "\nIllegal choice. Try again!\n";
32:     }
33:   }
```

*continues*

**Listing 2.13. MENU.CPP.**

```
34: #if (defined __TSC_MSC__) || (defined __TSC_ZTC__)
35:   return 0;  // MSC and ZTC requires this, though it's unreachable
36: #endif
37: }
```

> **Note:** Line 35 executes the usual return statement that ends main(). In this case, however, the statement is compiled only for Microsoft C/C++ and Zortech C++. Borland C++ and Turbo C++ correctly determine that this program can't possibly execute the return statement.

In line 8, a #define control line associates the value 1 with the identifier INUSE. Because 1 represents true, the while expression (INUSE) in line 13 always evaluates to true. In other words, this while loop runs "forever," meaning that another statement must provide a way to end the program. Here, the case for 'Q' executes exit(0), halting the program when you select the Q(uit command.

Carefully study the cases in the switch statement at lines 17–32. In another program, you could insert statements at these locations to handle each menu choice. Notice how break marks the end of each case. To prove that break is needed, type // in front of line 23 to convert it into a comment, and then compile and run the modified test. When you enter D to select the D(elete option, the program reports that you selected D(elete and S(ort, which is obviously wrong. The missing break causes the case for 'D' to *fall through* to the case for 'S'.

# Upside Down *do/while* Statements

A kind of upside-down while statement performs one or more actions *until* an expression is true. This statement form is called the do/while. To use it to count to 10, you could write

```
int count = 1;
do {
  cout << count << '\n';
  count++;
} while (count <= 10);
```

This is similar to the way a plain while loop works, except that the expression that controls whether the loop repeats or ends comes at the bottom of the construction, not at the top. Also, a do/while loop requires both keywords—do at the beginning and while at the end. Statements to execute come between do and while. Because of this special design—two keywords separated by statements to execute—most programmers type the braces even when there's only one statement inside. For example, the previous loop can be rewritten like this:

```
do {
  cout << count << '\n';
} while (++count <= 10);
```

Technically, you can remove the braces and just write

```
do
  cout << count << '\n';
while (++count <= 10);
```

However, you'll almost never see that form of do/while, and you probably should include the braces to make the loop stand out clearly on the page.

The key difference between a while and a do/while loop is that while loops may never execute if the controlling expression is false at the start. But a do/while loop *always* executes its statements at least once because the program doesn't evaluate the controlling expression until it runs through those statements one time. For example, if count equals 10, the following while loop effectively does nothing:

```
while (count < 10) {
  cout << "This never executes\n";
  count++;
}
```

Using a do/while loop causes the statements inside to execute at least once. Again, if count equals 10, consider what happens if you write

```
do {
  cout << "This executes one time\n";
  count++;
} while (count <= 10);
```

Even though count already equals 10 at the start of the loop, the two statements inside execute once because the program doesn't evaluate the terminating condition (count <= 10) until running through the loop the first time.

In practice, while loops tend to be more common than do/while, although both have uses. A good way to decide which to use is to ask the question, "Is there a condition when this loop should not execute, not even once?" If the answer is yes, a while loop is appropriate. If the answer is no—in other words, if the statements in the loop *must* execute at least once—use a do/while.

Listing 2.14, HEAD.CPP, shows do/while in action. The program is a filter that writes the first 10 lines of input to the standard output. This can be useful for examining the contents of text files when you don't want to list the entire file with the DOS TYPE command, a file lister, or your text editor.

### Listing 2.14. HEAD.CPP.

```
 1: // head.cpp -- Write first 10 lines of input to output
 2:
 3: #include <tscdefs.h>
 4: #include IOSTREAM_H
 5: #include IOMANIP_H
 6: #include <stdlib.h>
 7:
 8: #define MAXLINE 10
 9: #define NEWLINE '\n'
10:
11: main()
12: {
13:   char c;
14:   int linenum = 1;
15:
16:   while (cin.get(c) && (linenum <= MAXLINE)) {
17:     if (c == NEWLINE) {
18:       linenum++;
19:       cout << endl;  // Flush output and start new line
20:     } else
21:       cout << c;
22:   }
23:   return 0;
24: }
```

To use HEAD, enter a DOS command such as **head <head.cpp** or specify any other text file after the < redirection symbol. The program displays the first 10 lines from the file. If you want to change this number, change the value in line 8 to the maximum number of lines you want HEAD to display.

The program repeats the statements at lines 16–22 until linenum exceeds the constant MAXLINE. Two if statements inside this loop examine characters returned by cin.get(c), ending the program early at line 16 if this expression returns false before at least 10 lines are written. The second if statement watches for a NEWLINE character to come along; in which case line 18 increments linenum, and line 19 starts a new line. Line 20 sends other characters on their way to the standard output as in previous filters.

You might want to try your hand with while and do/while loops by rewriting HEAD.CPP using while. In this example, there's no compelling reason to use either statement type, and they both can do the job equally well.

# C++'s Most Popular Statement—The *for* Loop

When you know, or when a program can calculate in advance, the number of times a statement block should execute, a for statement is usually the best choice for writing a loop. All for statements have these elements:

- The keyword for

- A three-part expression in parentheses

- A statement or block to execute

A for loop combines these elements, using this general layout:

```
for (statement; expression1; expression2) {
  // statement(s) to execute
}
```

Inside the parentheses after the for keyword are three elements that control the loop's action. First comes a *statement,* which is executed a single time before the loop begins. Usually, this initializes a variable used by the next two elements. The first of these, *expression1,* is a relational expression that the for statement tests at the beginning of the loop. The second, *expression2,* is executed at the bottom of the loop after the statements to execute are done.

The preceding description will make much more sense when you compare it to an equivalent while loop that executes the identical steps:

```
statement;
while (expression1) {
  // statement(s) to execute
  expression2;
}
```

The `statement`, `expression1`, and `expression2` may be any statements and expressions that could appear in other places. For example, using `for` to display the digits 1 through 10, you could first define an `int` variable `count` and then write

```
for (count = 1; count <= 10; count++)
  cout << count << '\n';
```

This is *exactly* equivalent to the `while` loop:

```
count = 1;
while (count <= 10) {
  cout << count << '\n';
  count++;
}
```

Although the effects of the two loops are identical, the `for` loop is more concise and, after you learn how to put `for` loops together, you'll find them to be easier to read and understand than equivalent `while` statements. Also, a `for`'s "business" is neatly stowed inside parentheses at the top of the loop, but a `while`'s mechanisms are strewn throughout the loop. This makes `for` a little better at documenting what it does without requiring you to add comments to explain the statement's intentions.

A sample program shows a `for` loop in action. Listing 2.15, ASCII.CPP, displays a chart of the ASCII characters for the values 32 to 127.

## Listing 2.15. ASCII.CPP.

```
 1: // ascii.cpp -- Display ASCII chart
 2:
 3: #include <tscdefs.h>
 4: #include IOSTREAM_H
 5:
 6: main()
 7: {
 8:   char c;
 9:
10:   cout << '\n';
```

```
11:    for (c = 32; c < 127; c++) {
12:      if ((c % 32) == 0) cout << '\n';
13:      cout << c;
14:    }
15:    cout << '\n';
16:    return 0;
17: }
```

The for loop in ASCII.CPP (lines 11–14) initializes the unsigned char variable c to the value 32. (As you learned in Chapter 1, chars can hold ASCII characters or small integer values in the range –128 to 127. Unsigned chars can store values from 0 to 255.) After setting c to 32, the for loop tests whether the first expression is true. If so, it executes the statements inside the for's block, in this case, the two statements at lines 12 and 13. After that, the for loop executes its final expression, in this program, c++. This increments the for loop's *control variable*.

Usually, a control variable will be an int or char variable, but it doesn't have to be. Anything that you can test in a relational expression will do. Also, you can define the variable separately as in this fragment:

```
int i;
for (i = 1; i <= 10; i++)
  cout << i << '\n';
```

Or you can define and initialize the variable directly in the for statement:

```
for (int i = 1; i <= 10; i++)
  cout << i << '\n';
```

When a variable like i in these samples is needed only inside the loop, this is the best plan.

## Multiple *for*-Loop Elements

You can separate multiple for-loop elements with commas to perform more than one initialization and expression in the same loop. For instance, to count an int variable i from 0 to 9 and at the same time count another int j from 9 down to 0, you can write

```
int i, j;
for (i = 0, j = 9; i <= 9; i++, j--)
  cout << "\ni=" << i << "  j=" << j;
```

As with other less-complex `for` loops, this one is easier to understand when compared to the equivalent `while` statement:

```
int i, j;
i = 0;
j = 9;
while (i <= 9) {
  cout << "\ni=" << i << "  j=" << j;
  i++;
  j--;
}
```

In the `for`-loop version, each element separated by commas becomes a separate statement in the `while` construction. Despite the extra business in the `for` loop, however, there are still only three sections: the initialization and the two expressions. The sections are separated by semicolons; the multiple elements in each section are separated by commas. Technically, there's no limit to the number of elements you can string together with commas in a `for` loop, but it's rare to use more than a couple at a time. As the preceding examples show, even two additional elements make the statement difficult to read.

# Do-Forever Loops

Make sure that your `for` loops contain an expression such as `c++` that advances the condition expressed in the first expression towards a false result. In other words, if the first expression is (`c < 128`) as it is here, the second expression should do something to `c` to make that expression evaluate to false some time later. If you don't do this, the `for` loop may get "stuck." The simplest example of a stuck `for` loop is

```
for (;;) ;      // Loop "forever"
```

This loop initializes nothing, tests no condition, and advances no control variable. The two semicolons inside parentheses are required as place holders for the missing elements. The space before the final semicolon is optional, but avoids a warning from the compiler that it may be extraneous. This is an example of a *null statement*—empty except for its terminating semicolon. The space in front of the semicolon makes it clear that the invisible statement is intentional and is not a typing error.

Although this *do-nothing* or *do-forever* loop may seem silly, it can be useful. You might use it to halt a program, forcing people to switch off power or to reboot, or you can use it in an interrupt-driven environment, where an external signal from a device such as a modem or a timer causes another action to occur. In that case, the do-forever loop pauses the program until the awaited event wakes up another portion of the code.

# Taking a *break*

It's sometimes useful to interrupt a while, do/while, or for loop in progress. To do that, insert a break statement, as Listing 2.16, BREAKER.CPP, demonstrates.

### Listing 2.16. BREAKER.CPP.

```
 1: // breaker.cpp -- Demonstrate break statement
 2:
 3: #include <tscdefs.h>
 4: #include IOSTREAM_H
 5:
 6: main()
 7: {
 8:   int count;
 9:
10:   cout << "\n\nfor loop:\n";
11:   for (count = 1; count <= 10; count++) {
12:     if (count > 5) break;
13:     cout << count << '\n';
14:   }
15:   cout << "\n\nwhile loop:\n";
16:   count = 1;
17:   while (count <= 10) {
18:     if (count > 5) break;
19:     cout << count << '\n';
20:     count++;
21:   }
22:   cout << "\n\ndo/while loop:\n";
23:   count = 1;
24:   do {
25:     if (count > 5) break;
26:     cout << count << '\n';
27:     count++;
28:   } while (count <= 10);
29:   return 0;
30: }
```

BREAKER contains a for loop (lines 11–14), a while (17–21), and a do/while (lines 24–28), all of which count from 1 to 10 using an int variable, count. However, in each case, a break statement interrupts the loop before count reaches the loop's target value. Because of the statements at lines 12, 18, and 25, the three loops count only to 5 before stopping.

A break statement is useful for error handling inside complex for and other loops. It can also provide a means to exit a do-forever loop as the following fragment illustrates:

```
for (;;) {
  cout << "\nMenu: A(dd D(elete Q(uit: ";
  cin >> choice;
  choice = toupper(choice);
  if (choice == 'A')
    cout << "You selected Add\n";
  else if (choice == 'D')
    cout << "You selected Delete\n";
  else if (choice == 'Q')
    break;
}
```

This is similar to the while loop in Listing 2.13, MENU.CPP, but uses a do-forever for loop to execute menu choices. After displaying the menu and reading a character into a char variable choice, a series of if/else statements select various actions for 'A' and 'D'. If choice equals 'Q', the break statement ends the do-forever loop, continuing the program after the for block's closing brace.

## The Plot *continues*

While break immediately exits a loop, a similar statement continue forces a loop to start its next iteration from the top. Listing 2.17, CONTINUE.CPP, demonstrates the difference between the two statement forms.

### Listing 2.17. CONTINUE.CPP.

```
1: // continue.cpp -- Demonstrate continue
2:
3: #include <tscdefs.h>
4: #include IOSTREAM_H
```

```
 5:
 6: main()
 7: {
 8:   int count;
 9:
10:   cout << "\nStarting for loop with continue...\n";
11:   for (count = 1; count <= 10; count++) {
12:     if (count > 5) continue;
13:     cout << count << '\n';
14:   }
15:   cout << "After for loop, count = " << count;
16:   cout << "\n\nStarting for loop with break...\n";
17:   for (count = 1; count <= 10; count++) {
18:     if (count > 5) break;
19:     cout << count << '\n';
20:   }
21:   cout << "After for loop, count = " << count;
22:   return 0;
23: }
```

CONTINUE uses two for loops (lines 11–14 and 17–20) to count up to 10, similar to the way Listing 2.16 works. In this case, however, line 12 inside the first for loop executes a continue statement if count is greater than 5. Line 18 inside the second for executes break. Except for this difference, the loops are identical.

When you run the program, you'll see that both for loops count up to 5 and stop. After the first loop, however, the value of count is 11. After the second, it's 6. This is because the continue statement in the first loop causes the expression count++ to execute while the break in the second causes the loop to end immediately.

A continue statement in any for loop jumps immediately to the control expression in parentheses. In other words, given this loop,

```
for (statement; expression1; expression2) {
  if (expression3) continue;
  // statement(s) to execute
}
```

if expression3 is true, the continue statement immediately causes expression2 to be evaluated, and any following statements (those marked by the comment here) are skipped during this iteration. Similarly, a continue in a while or do/while statement causes the loop's relational expression to be evaluated immediately.

# Avoiding *goto*

I hesitate to tell you about this one—some people are convinced that goto statements hatch more bugs than a bayou. That may not be true, but in practice, I find that gotos, which let code jump from place to place, are rarely of much use. If I discover a need for a goto, it usually means my program needs redesigning. In fact, I've probably used more gotos in this paragraph than I ever have in my programs.

On the other hand, you shouldn't avoid a goto if one solves a problem for you. At the very least, you should be familiar with how goto works in case you come across one in somebody else's code. The goto statement is easy to use. First, insert a label—any unique identifier ending with a colon—before any statement. Then use a goto statement to continue the program at the marked location. For example, to use gotos to count from 1 to 10, you can write

```
int count = 1;
TOP:
cout << count << '\n';
count++;
if (count <= 10)
  goto TOP;
```

I completely agree with goto's detractors that such a "loop" is a disgrace: It doesn't even look like a loop. The equivalent for and while loops listed earlier are much easier to read and have obvious effects. The goto version requires hand work to trace through each line in order to figure out what the statements do. Still, it works, which is about all you can say in its favor.

The place where a goto is sometimes useful is inside a deeply nested series of if statements when some condition occurs and the program needs to fly the nest—that is, to start execution with the statement following the nested ifs.

```
for (;;) {
  for (...) {
    while (...) {
      if (done == TRUE)
        goto FASTEXIT;
    }
  }
}
FASTEXIT:
// statements to execute following the goto
```

Here, a goto exits the three nested if statements inside a do-forever for loop. This is similar to the way a break statement works, except that in this case, because the ifs are nested inside each other, replacing the goto with a break would exit only the innermost if.

Sometimes, a goto is also useful in a complex switch statement where a case needs to jump to another case. There's no other way to do this without goto, although there are probably other ways to design the code so that it doesn't require so much jumping around. In general, you can write

```
switch (c) {
  CASEA:
  case 'A':
    // statement(s) for 'A';
    goto CASEC;
  case 'B':
    // statement(s) for 'B';
    goto CASEA;
  CASEC:
  case 'C':
    // statement(s) for 'C';
    break;
}
```

If c equals 'A', the statements for the first case execute, followed by the statements for case 'C'. If c equals 'B', those statements execute, followed by those in case 'A', followed in turn by those in 'C'. If c equals 'C', only those statements execute.

Notice that the labels—CASEA: and CASEC:—are *not* case selectors, as are case 'A': and case 'B':. They are labels that mark locations inside a switch statement. However, the labels don't belong to that statement, and they could be named anything: BANANA:, AQ120x:, or L99:. The gotos simply cause the program to begin running from somewhere in the middle of the switch statement at the labeled locations.

> **Note:** Please don't get the idea that I'm recommending you write programs this way. You should be aware of this special use for gotos embedded inside switch statements, but you should hunt for alternatives until you turn blue before resorting to such nonsense in your own work.

# Data Structures—Sand Castles in RAM

**C**omputer memory chips are made with silicon, literally from plain ol' sand. Like sand particles, memory is just a pile of bits without form. To give form to memory, C++ has several features that impose structures on memory the way sand castles impose structure on sand. Data structures are still composed of memory bits, and sand castles are still composed of sand particles. Both are simply fresh ways to view the same raw material.

In this section, you'll meet C++ data structures, which let you collect variables, store information in arrays, and manipulate bits using techniques that are usually more convenient than the bitwise operators described at the beginning of this chapter. I'll also explain more about strings. Up to now, you've been using strings without paying close attention to some important details about their structure. It's time to dig deeper into what strings really are.

## Structures for Safe Keeping

When you have a set of variables, you can collect them in a structure with the `struct` keyword. This creates a new data type with the capability of reserving enough memory to hold many related variables in one place.

A typical example where `struct` is useful is a database program set up to store records that contain a variety of members. For example, suppose that you are the president of a weight reduction club and you need to store the names, weights, and phone numbers of the club's members. You might use a series of variables such as

```
char  name1[]  = "Marta";
float weight1   = 142.5;
char  phone1[] = "803-555-1212";
char  name2[]  = "Mel";
float weight2   = 165.0;
char  phone2[] = "209-555-1212";
char  name3[]  = "Bobbi";
float weight3   = 135.0;
char  phone3[] = "none";
```

Separately typing each name, weight, and phone number gets tedious fast and clutters the program with confusing variables. Worse, if you need to insert or delete a name, you'll have to write new statements that work with each variable. This is too messy to be practical.

A better method is to create a new data type that can store names, weights, and phone numbers together. You can then write statements that operate on that kind of structure and, therefore, on any club member's information. To do this, start by declaring the data type with `struct`:

```
struct Member {
  char name[31];
  float weight;
  char phone[13];
};
```

Rather than use literal numbers like 31 and 13, it's usually best to define contants like these:

```
#define NAMELEN 31
#define PHONELEN 13
```

and then use the constants in the structure's declaration:

```
struct Member {
  char name[NAMELEN];
  float weight;
  char phone[PHONELEN];
};
```

The end results are the same, but the constants make it easier to change the lengths of the name and phone members, and also make it possible for other statements in the program to use the correct lengths.

Either way, the `struct` declares a new data type named Member, with the capacity to store three members: name (a 30-character string), weight (of type `float`), and phone (a 12-character string). Don't forget the required semicolon at the end of the declaration after the closing brace. (This is easy to forget because statement blocks, which look similar to `struct` declarations, do not end with a semicolon.) Always remember also that a `struct` data type does not reserve any memory for storing information; it merely creates a blueprint that tells the compiler the nature of the structure. The members look like they define variables, but because the declarations appear inside a `struct`, they don't.

After creating a struct type, you can create variables of that type just as you do for other data types:

```
Member oneMember;
```

The preceding creates a variable named oneMember of type Member. It reserves space for all of the members declared inside the struct, in this case, a 30-character string, a floating point value, and another 12-character string. (The strings include one extra byte each for null terminators.) Here's another sample:

```
struct SampleStruct {
  float aFloat;
  int anInt;
  char aString[8];
  char aChar;
  long aLong;
};
```

This SampleStruct contains five members, all of different sizes. After declaring the struct, you can define variables of the new data type:

```
SampleStruct sampleVar;
```

This reserves space for variables of each of the five members declared in type SampleStruct and points sampleVar to the first of those members. In memory, the bytes for these members are packed tightly together (see Figure 2.1).

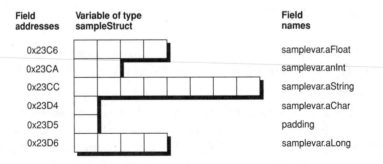

**Figure 2.1.** The bytes for each member in a struct variable are stored consecutively in memory.

> **Note:** In some cases, a `struct` variable's size might be greater than the sum of the sizes of the declared members. This is because C++ compilers can pad members containing an odd number of bytes so that every member begins at an even-numbered address. (See the single byte labeled `padding` in Figure 2.1.) The reason for this is to keep the program running fast on systems powered by 16-bit 80x86 processors, which can read data more quickly from even addresses than from odd ones. See the `sizeof` operator later in this chapter for a method of determining the exact sizes of `struct`s.

You can also declare a `struct` data type such as `Member` and create a variable `m1` of that type in one statement:

```
struct Member {
  ...
} m1;
```

Written this way, `m1` is a variable of type `Member`; you don't have to define the variable separately. If you don't want to create a named data type, however—for example, when you only need a single `struct` variable of a certain type—use a nameless `struct` like this:

```
struct {
  int a;
  float f;
} onemember;
```

Declared that way, `onemember` is a variable that contains all the members listed between braces, in this sample, an `int` and a `float`.

These forms are perfectly acceptable, but it's more common to declare a `struct` data type separately and then to define one or more variables of that type. Using the `Member` declaration again, to create a variable `m1` and assign values to each of the `struct`'s members, you can write

```
Member m1;         // Define variable m1 of type Member
strcpy(m1.name, "Tom");   // Assign string to name
m1.weight = 155;   // Assign value to weight
strcpy(m1.phone, "812-555-1212");   // Assign string to phone
```

Variable m1 is a structure of type `Member`. It has the three members declared in `Member`, each of which is accessible by following the variable name with a period and the member name. This is sometimes known as *dot notation.* The period, or "dot," relates the variable with the members that it contains. The expressions `m1.name`, `m1.weight`, and `m1.phone` are *fully qualified,* meaning that they contain enough information to let the compiler treat them as simple types. The expression `m1.weight` is an integer variable and is treated exactly the same as variable `count` defined as `int count`. You can't write `m1 = "Tom"` because `m1` is of type `Member`. It's not a string. The qualified expression `m1.name` is a string, and you can assign a character string to it by calling a library function such as `strcpy()`.

To copy characters to a `name` member in the structure, use the statement

```
strcpy(m1.name, "Tom");
```

You can't assign `"Tom"` directly to `m1.name`. That would be convenient, but assigning literal strings to variables simply isn't permitted by C++. The `strcpy()` function in this case copies the characters T, O, and M, plus a null terminating byte, to `m1.name`. (You'll learn more about functions later.)

As with other variables, you can define and initialize a `struct` with a single statement. To do this, insert member values in braces after the variable's definition:

```
member m1 = { "Anne", 110, "676-555-1212" };
```

Each member must be separated from the next by a comma. Be sure to allocate enough space to hold the characters plus a null terminating byte at the end of each string. (Note the semicolon at the end.) Also, you can't skip any members, but you can stop before assigning values to every one. For example, to assign only a `name` and `weight` to a `Member`, leaving the `phone` member uninitialized, you could write

```
Member m2 = { "Kathy", 112 };
```

After declaring a `struct` data type and defining one or more variables of that type, you can assign values to those variables, write their values to the display, use them in expressions, and so on. To demonstrate some of these possibilities, suppose that you need to track the models, speeds, capacities, and other facts about the computer systems in your company. You decide to store this information in a `struct` named `computer`. Listings 2.18, compdb.h, and 2.19, COMP1.CPP, show some of the required statements to write the database program.

## Listing 2.18. compdb.h.

```
 1: // compdb.h -- Computer data base header file
 2:
 3: enum Boolean {False, True};
 4:
 5: struct Computer {
 6:   char *model;             // Computer's model name
 7:   char *cpu;               // Type of CPU
 8:   char *display;           // Type of installed display
 9:   float speed;             // Speed in mHZ
10:   int numflop;             // Number of floppy drives
11:   int hdcapacity;          // Hard drive capacity in megabytes
12:   float memcapacity;       // Memory capacity in megabytes
13:   enum Boolean modem;      // Whether a modem is installed
14: };
```

## Listing 2.19. COMP1.CPP.

```
 1: // comp1.cpp -- Computer data base demonstration #1 using struct
 2:
 3: #include <tscdefs.h>
 4: #include IOSTREAM_H
 5: #include "compdb.h"
 6:
 7: main()
 8: {
 9:   Computer mysystem;
10:
11:   mysystem.model       = "ALR 386/2";
12:   mysystem.cpu         = "80386";
13:   mysystem.display     = "MDA";
14:   mysystem.speed       = 16.0;
15:   mysystem.numflop     = 1;
16:   mysystem.hdcapacity  = 40;
17:   mysystem.memcapacity = 2.0;
18:   mysystem.modem       = False;
19:
20:   cout << "\nMy old system:\n\n";
21:   cout << "Model ...... " << (mysystem.model)     << endl;
```

*continues*

**Listing 2.19. continued**

```
22:    cout << "CPU ........ " << (mysystem.cpu)       << endl;
23:    cout << "Display .... " << (mysystem.display)  << endl;
24:    cout << "Speed Mhz .. " << (mysystem.speed)     << endl;
25:    cout << "No. floppies " << (mysystem.numflop)  << endl;
26:    cout << "HD Capacity  " << (mysystem.hdcapacity)  << " mb" << endl;
27:    cout << "Memory ..... " << (mysystem.memcapacity) << " mb" << endl;
28:    cout << "Modem ...... ";
29:
30:    if (mysystem.modem)
31:      cout << "True\n";
32:    else
33:      cout << "False\n";
34:    return 0;
35: }
```

These two listings are the first of many sample programs stored in multiple files. Listing 2.18 is a header file that declares a few common items, including the struct that stores the facts about your company's computers. Other programs that need to create variables of type Computer can simply #include this file—they don't have to redeclare the data type. This saves typing and keeps the common declarations in a single location so that if it becomes necessary to modify the members in a computer, only one file needs editing.

> **Note:** compdb.h uses the construction char *model and similar declarations. These are examples of *pointers,* a topic covered in Chapter 4. For now, just think of this as another way to create string variables, for example, one named model. I'll explain more about this data type format later in this chapter.

Notice that the #include "compdb.h" statement at line 5 in COMP1.CPP surrounds the header filename with quotes rather than angle brackets. The quotes tell the compiler to look for the file in the current directory.

**Note:** Pay attention to the listing filenames. If they end in .h (or, sometimes, .hpp or .hxx), they are header files. Compile only the files that end in .CPP.

Line 9 in COMP1 defines a variable named mysystem of type Computer. It can do this because it included the declaration for the Computer struct back at line 5. Lines 11–18 assign values to each member in mysystem, using dot notation. Then lines 20–28 display these same values, again using dot notation to "get to" the separate members in the structure.

In every case, the only difference between the statements in COMP1 and those you've seen before is the presence of the structure name and its qualifying dot. Structures are simply collections of variables that behave like others defined as loners. The key difference in a struct is that you can safely assume that all of the variable's members are stored one after the other in memory. (Some C++ compilers might insert filler bytes between a struct's members, however.) With individual variables, even those defined next to each other in the source text, you can make no such assumption.

Listing 2.20, COMP2.CPP, is similar to COMP1.CPP but uses a single statement at lines 8–17 to define and initialize mysystem. This is a convenient method for initializing structures, and you should become familiar with the format. The rest of the listing is identical to COMP1.CPP. Because line 6 includes compdb.h, there's also no need to repeat the declaration for a Computer structure in this new program— a space-saving technique especially valuable in large programs containing dozens of struct declarations.

## Listing 2.20. COMP2.CPP.

```
1: // comp2.cpp -- Computer data base demonstration #2 using struct
2:
3: #include <tscdefs.h>
4: #include IOSTREAM_H
5: #include IOMANIP_H
6: #include "compdb.h"
7:
```

*continues*

**Listing 2.20. continued**

```
 8: main()
 9: {
10:   computer mysystem = {
11:     "Everex 386/25",        // model
12:     "80386",                // cpu
13:     "VGA",                  // display
14:     25.0,                   // speed
15:     2,                      // numflop
16:     660,                    // hdcapacity
17:     16.0,                   // memcapacity
18:     False                   // modem
19:   };
20:
21:   cout << "\nMy new system:\n\n";
22:   cout << "Model ...... " << (mysystem.model)      << endl;
23:   cout << "CPU ........ " << (mysystem.cpu)        << endl;
24:   cout << "Display .... " << (mysystem.display)    << endl;
25:   cout << "Speed Mhz .. " << (mysystem.speed)      << endl;
26:   cout << "No. floppies " << (mysystem.numflop)    << endl;
27:   cout << "HD Capacity  " << (mysystem.hdcapacity) << " mb" << endl;
28:   cout << "Memory ..... " << (mysystem.memcapacity) << " mb" << endl;
29:   cout << "Modem ...... ";
30:
31:   if (mysystem.modem)
32:     cout << "True\n";
33:   else
34:     cout << "False\n";
35:   return 0;
36: }
```

# Nested Structures

One struct can nest inside another to create a complex data type with a world of possibilities for storing all sorts of information. For instance, in a name and address database, you may want to include information about the personal computer that your correspondents own. Instead of redeclaring all the members you just designed in the previous listings, you can *nest* a Computer structure inside the new struct:

```
struct Person {
  char *name;
  char *address;
  int age;
  Computer comp;
};
```

Declared this way, a person is a struct with four members: the person's name, address, age, and comp. The first three members are identical in form to those you've seen before. The last is of type Computer, the struct declared in compdb.h. To create a variable oneperson and assign a name, address, and age, you can write

```
Person oneperson;
oneperson.name = "George";
oneperson.address = "543 West End Ave.";
oneperson.age = 32;
```

However, to assign values to the comp member requires a bit more effort. Because this member is a structure of type Computer nested inside another structure of type oneperson, use dot notation along with *both* data type names in order to qualify the expression to reach the Computer data type's members:

```
oneperson.comp.model   = "AT Clone";
oneperson.comp.cpu     = "80286";
oneperson.comp.display = "Hercules";
```

In a way, this resembles the way subdirectories on your computer's disk nest inside each other. For example, you've probably used directory pathnames such as C:\ZDEMO\EXAMPLES to refer to a location where a set of files are stored. In a similar way, a fully qualified struct expression uses dots rather than backslashes to refer to a location in memory where data is stored along with other related members. The expressions give the compiler the information it needs to pinpoint exactly where in memory the individual members in structures are stored.

# Preserving the *union*

Unions are nearly identical to structures, and in fact, if you're not careful, you can easily confuse the two with disastrous results. Although structures and unions have near twin-like forms, they are related more like cousins than identical twins.

As you learned in the previous section, structures collect various members into one convenient package. A `struct` lets you store related variables together, as you might need to do for keeping database records. Unions, declared with the `union` keyword, also store multiple members in one package. But instead of placing those members one after the other, in a union, all members overlay each other at the *same* location.

This may seem odd at first, but there are many times when a union comes in handy. The most common use is to design a data type that can be used as two or more different types. For example, you can create a union with a `float` member, but also treat that member as a `char` or a `long`. That doesn't mean C++ unions convert members from one type to another. They don't. The bytes in memory that store the information for each member are just interpreted as one data type for some statements and another for other statements. Consider a union declared as

```
union SampleUnion {
  float aFloat;
  long aLong;
}
```

In a variable of type `SampleUnion`, members `aFloat` and `aLong` are stored at the same address (see Figure 2.2). This means that if a program assigns a value to `aFloat`, it will also change `aLong`. It doesn't mean that there are two variables in the union. There's only one value represented two ways.

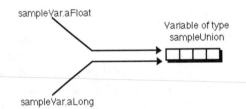

**Figure 2.2.** A union stores its data members at the same location.

An example will help make unions clear. Compile Listing 2.21, UNION.CPP, and run the program. Are you surprised at the result? Before reading on, try to figure out how the program works.

**Listing 2.21. UNION.CPP.**

```
1: // union.cpp -- Demonstrate unions
2:
3: #include <tscdefs.h>
4: #include IOSTREAM_H
5:
6: main()
7: {
8:   union charint {
9:     char c;
10:    int i;
11:  } ci;
12:
13:   int i;
14:
15:   for (i = 65; i < 91; i++) {
16:     ci.i = i;      // Assign i to ci.i
17:     cout << ci.c;  // Display c member in ci
18:   }
19:   return 0;
20: }
```

To understand how UNION displays the alphabet, look closely at lines 8–11. These lines declare a union named charint with two members, a char c and an int i. Except for the union keyword, this is the identical form used by struct declarations. In fact, any members that can go in a struct (which includes any of C++'s data types) can also go in a union. To keep the program simple, line 10 defines a variable ci of type charint. But you could also create union variables in the usual way:

charint anothervar;

Any of the methods discussed earlier for declaring struct types and variables also apply to unions. Lines 15–18 in UNION.CPP execute a for loop that cycles an int variable i from 65 to 90. On each pass through the loop, line 16 assigns the value of i to ci.i, using the same dot notation that struct expressions employ to "get to" the i member in ci. Line 17 then displays the *other* member in the union, the char variable c. Even though no statements assign any values to c, the program still displays the alphabet. Obviously, something is changing c.

That something is the assignment at line 16. Because all members in a union overlay each other, assigning a value to one member affects others in the variable. In this example, assigning the values 65 to 90—the ASCII codes for the letters A through Z—to i also assigns those same values to c, which the program displays.

# Vectoring in on Arrays

Like structures and unions, arrays also collect multiple pieces of information. Unlike those other data types, however, arrays always store one or more variables of the *same* type. A simple analogy is a stack of dishes, all of the same size and shape, but not necessarily the same color. Each dish (array element) sits next to its neighbors on the stack (the array). To retrieve a certain dish from the stack in order to inspect its color, you might count from the top down to the dish you want. You could then say that dish number 5 is red or dish number 12 is purple. In arrays, those numbers are called *indexes.*

All arrays have two main characteristics. First, they are declared to hold one or more variables of a certain data type. For example, an array might hold variables of type float. Another might hold variables of type int or a struct that you declared earlier in the program.

The second telling characteristic of arrays is their size. When defining arrays, you must choose in advance how many elements of the array's type you plan to store in the array. This is important because the compiler can only reserve enough memory for the array if you tell it how many items you will store there. Simply stated, the compiler multiplies the number of items by the size of each one and reserves that many bytes for the array.

> **Note:** Using pointers, it's possible to write programs that calculate array sizes at runtime and allocate space for an array. With this technique, you can design programs that create arrays of varying sizes on demand. I'll return to this subject in Chapter 4.

A demonstration of arrays shows how to create and use them. Listing 2.22 declares, fills, and displays an array (appropriately named array).

## Listing 2.22. ARRAY.CPP.

```
 1: // array.cpp -- Demonstrate arrays
 2:
 3: #include <tscdefs.h>
 4: #include IOSTREAM_H
 5: #include IOMANIP_H
 6:
 7: main()
 8: {
 9:   int array[100];    // Define array of 100 integers
10:   int index;         // Index for accessing array elements
11:
12: // Fill array with values from 0 to 99:
13:
14:   for (index = 0; index <= 99; index++)
15:     array[index] = index;
16:
17: // Display array contents forwards and back:
18:
19:   cout << "\nArray values from [0] to [99]:\n";
20:   for (index = 0; index <= 99; index++)
21:     cout << setw(8) << dec << array[index];
22:
23:   cout << "\nArray values from [99] down to [0]:\n";
24:   for (index = 99; index >= 0; index—)
25:     cout << setw(8) << dec << array[index];
26:   return 0;
27: }
```

Line 9 shows how to define arrays in C++. The definition is similar to others you've seen before, but adds square brackets around a literal constant after the variable name. The two brackets are C++'s array symbol:

```
int array[100];
```

That creates an array of 100 integers stored consecutively in memory. Each of the integers in the array is a distinct variable with its own space (see Figure 2.3).

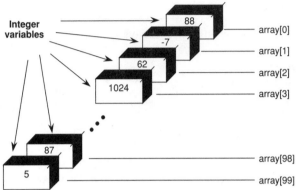

**Figure 2.3**. An array of 100 integers.

To get to one of the elements in the array—for example, to display its value—specify the element you want by its index number inside brackets after the array name. For example, to display the value of the integer at index location 3, write

```
cout << array[3];
```

Because the array is declared to contain int values, the effect of this statement is equivalent to passing any other int variable to cout. In this case, the statement displays the value of the fourth element.

Why does array[3] refer to the fourth element and not the third? The answer is that the first element in all C++ arrays have the index number 0, not 1. In other words, to display the first five int values in array, you could write

```
cout << array[0] << '\n';
cout << array[1] << '\n';
cout << array[2] << '\n';
cout << array[3] << '\n';
cout << array[4] << '\n';
```

Of course, doing this is much easier (and more efficient) with a for loop:

```
for (i = 0; i <= 4; i++);
  cout << array[i] << '\n';
```

The idea is the same in both cases. To display the first five array elements, use index values 0, 1, 2, 3, and 4. In the first sample, literal values (0, 1, ..., 4) were used for the index values. In the second, an int variable i specifies the index. Both methods are equally useful. You can also index arrays with expressions:

```
cout << array[i + k];
```

Any expression, variable, or constant that represents or evaluates to an integer value makes a legal array index.

Turning back to the ARRAY.CPP demonstration, take a look at lines 14–15. Here, a `for` loop cycles the `int` variable `index` through the values 0 to 99. Line 15 then assigns the value of the `index` to each array element. It can do this because the array is declared to hold `int` variables (see line 9). After that, lines 19–21 display the values in the array, again cycling `index` from 0 to 99 in a `for` loop. Lines 23–25 do the same, but display the values in reverse order.

> **Note:** Take care to assign values only to allocated array positions. If you declare an array as `int array[5]`, for example, the compiler accepts a statement such as `array[100] = 2` even though that stores a value in a position outside of the array's boundaries. This is a very common, easy to make, and usually disastrous error, as it might overwrite another value stored in memory.

A good use for arrays is to store multiple `struct` variables. For example, to create an array of 50 `Computer` records (using the declarations in compdb.h, Listing 2.18), you could write

```
Computer systems[50];
```

That defines an array named `systems` with enough space to hold 50 `Computer` `struct` variables—a more convenient structure than 50 individual `Computer` variables. To change the name of the sixth `Computer` record, you can write

```
systems[5].name = "PS/2";
```

As with the simple arrays of `int` variables, the array name (`systems`) is followed by square brackets and an index value (`[5]`). C++ recognizes that part of the expression as referring to one array element—in this case, one `Computer` record. Because that record is a `struct`, in order to get to its members, the statement qualifies the reference by using dot notation and the member name (`name`).

Combining data types this way—arrays of `struct` that contain other members, maybe even other arrays of some other type—is a powerful concept. In general, you are free to combine simple data types such as `int` and `float` with `structs`, `unions`, and `arrays` to build all sorts of sand castles in your programs.

# Making the Grade

Another sample program shows how arrays can be used to store information that a program can use later. Listing 2.23, GRADE.CPP, lets you enter up to 18 test scores into an array. It then uses that information to compute the average grade. (The 18-score limit simplifies the program's output. You can change this value in line 9 if you need to enter more than 18 grades.)

## Listing 2.23. GRADE.CPP.

```
 1: // grade.cpp -- Grade average calculator
 2:
 3: #include <tscdefs.h>
 4: #include IOSTREAM_H
 5: #include IOMANIP_H
 6: #include <stdlib.h>
 7: #include <form.h>
 8:
 9: #define MAXGRADES 18
10:
11: double grades[MAXGRADES];  // Array of grade values
12:
13: main()
14: {
15:    int i, numgrades;
16:    double total, average;
17:    char buf[80];
18:
19: // Prompt user for grades, and store values in array:
20:
21:    for (numgrades = 0; numgrades < MAXGRADES; numgrades++) {
22:      cout << "Enter grade #" << (numgrades + 1) << "(-1 to quit): ";
23:      cin >> grades[numgrades];
24:      if (grades[numgrades] < 0) break;
25:    }
26:    if (numgrades <= 0) exit(0);  // No grades entered
27:
28: // Display the values stored in the array:
29:
30:    cout << "\n\nGrades:\n\n";
```

```
31:   for (i = 0; i < numgrades; i++)
32:     cout << setw(2) << dec << (i + 1) << ':'
33:           << form(buf, "%8.2f", grades[i]) << '\n';
34:
35: // Total the scores:
36:
37:   total = 0.0;
38:   for (i = 0; i < numgrades; i++)
39:     total += grades[i];
40:
41: // Compute and display the average:
42:
43:   average = total / numgrades;
44:   cout << "\nTotal scores    = " << form(buf, "%8.2f", total);
45:   cout << "\nNumber of grades = " << setw(5) << dec << numgrades;
46:   cout << "\nAverage grade    = " << form(buf, "%8.2f", average);
47:   return 0;
48: }
```

Line 11 defines the grades array and specifies its elements to be of type double. Notice how the constant MAXGRADES is used in place of a literal value in the brackets. That same constant is then used in line 21 to limit the number of for loops that are performed. Because of this design, to change the array size, just modify the value in line 9 and recompile. Both the array size (line 11) and statement (line 21) are then automatically adjusted.

Line 23 is an input stream statement that stores a new value directly in an array element, grades[numgrades]. That expression is treated exactly as a variable of type double—the array's element type. The expression grades[numgrades] *is* a double variable. If d is a variable of type double, the statement cin >> d performs identically to cin >> grades[numgrades]. The first reads a value into a lone double variable; the second reads a value into a double stored in an array.

Other statements in GRADE display the values entered in the array, calculate the average score, and display the results. Run the program several times and examine the statements as you enter values. Be sure that you understand how the values in grades are used.

> **Note:** If you have trouble with line 39, remember from earlier how combined operators work. Here, the statement adds the current total and a grade value and is equivalent to the more wordy assignment `total = total + grades[i]`.

# Initializing Arrays

When you define an array of any type, like other variables, its values may or may not be initialized. If an array is global, all the bytes that belong to the array's elements are set to 0. You can prove this by compiling and running a test program containing these lines:

```
int array[10];
main()
{
  int i;
  for (i = 0; i <= 9; i++)
    cout << "\narray[" << i << "] == " << array[i];
}
```

The `for` loop displays 0 for all 10 array values. Try a second test, but this time move the `int array[10];` definition to between the opening brace and the `for` statement. Now when you run the program, it displays values seemingly chosen at random.

This happens because arrays behave like all variables in C++. Global variables are initialized to 0 by default, but variables that are local to a function (`main` in this case) are not initialized to any specific values. You must perform all initializations with statements.

One way to initialize an array is to assign values to all array elements. To do this, you can use a `for` loop such as

```
for (i = 0; i <= 9; i++)
  array[i] = 0;
```

This sets every array value to 0. Of course, if your program is going to assign other values to array positions anyway, it doesn't have to pre-assign other values to the arrays. Still, it's a good idea to initialize arrays (and other variables) to prevent bugs caused by using variables that have unpredictable values.

Another way to initialize arrays is to list constant values in braces after the array definition. C++ reads each listed value and assigns it to successive array positions. For example, to initialize a 10-integer array to the values 10 down to 1 and then display those values in reverse-declaration order, you can write

```
int countdown[10] = {10, 9, 8, 7, 6, 5, 4, 3, 2, 1};
for (i = 9; i >= 1; i--)
  cout <<"\ncountdown[" << i << "] == " << countdown[i];
```

# Arrays and the Multiple Dimension

Arrays such as int array[100] and Computer systems[50] are *flat*—they have only one dimension. These and similar arrays are like boxes that you can stack in no other way but straight up. Sometimes, however, arrays need to be two dimensional, like a honeycomb in a beehive or like mail boxes in a post office.

On your desk is another example of an array that needs more than one dimension—your computer's display. The rows and columns on-screen are easily represented by a two-dimensional data structure containing 25 rows and 80 columns. In C++, you could define this as an array using the definition

```
char display[25][80];
```

Defined with two sets of brackets and sizes, display is technically an *array of arrays* capable of storing 25 80-character arrays of type char. However, it's often easier to visualize such an array as having rows and columns, like a computer screen. Here's another sample:

```
int multi[6][8];
```

The array multi is an array of 6, 8-integer arrays, but most people simply view this as a structure having six rows and eight columns with integer values stored at the intersections (see Figure 2.4).

Because multidimensional arrays are stored as arrays of arrays, there are two ways to refer to the array's elements. The expression multi[4] or multi[2] refers to one 8-integer array or row. To read or write an individual integer stored in that row, add a second index expression. For example, to display the value of the integer stored in the fourth row at the sixth column, you can write

```
cout << multi[3][5];
```

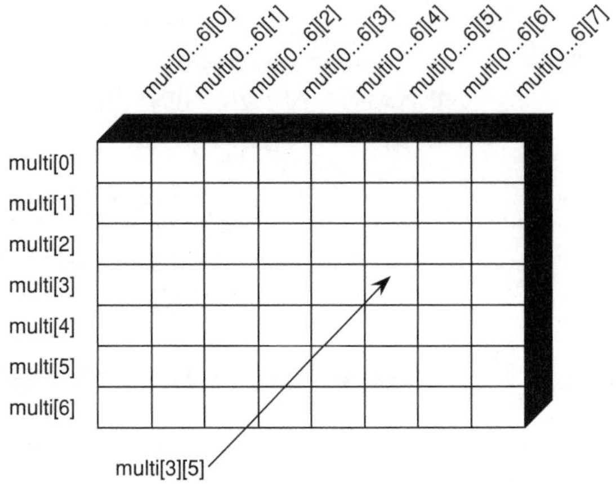

**Figure 2.4**. A two-dimensional array is an array of arrays, but you can also view it as a single structure that has rows and columns.

As I mentioned before, all arrays are indexed from 0 in C++, a rule that includes those with multiple dimensions. For that reason, the fourth row is indexed by [3]; the sixth column by [5]. To display all integers in multi, you could use a nested for loop:

```
for (int row = 0; row <= 6; row++) {
  for (int col = 0; col <= 7; col++)
    cout << dec(multi[row][col], 8);
  cout << '\n';
}
```

> **Note:** Some languages allow combined array indexes using a single set of brackets, as in the expression array[row, col]. In C++, this must be converted to array[row][col]. However, the results are the same.

Multidimensional arrays are tailor-made for storing a series of facts covering various categories. A made-up example demonstrates the idea nicely. (With a little work, the program I'm going to discuss could make a useful utility.) Suppose that you are the manager in an office of busy people, and you want to find out what times everyone has free for group meetings. One way to do this is to stick your head out your office door and ask everyone when they want to get together. If that doesn't work, you might consider writing a computer program to search an array of meeting times, looking for slots that everyone has free.

Listing 2.24 shows how to solve this problem with a multidimensional array. Run the program and enter an employee number from 0 to 3. Then enter the hours from 8 to 17 (5 pm) for which this person has scheduled an appointment. Enter –1 when you're done typing the hours. Then type another employee number and enter scheduled hours for that person. Repeat these steps for up to 4 employees and then enter a final –1 to end. The program displays a chart of the current schedule and lists possible meeting times when all employees are free.

## Listing 2.24. MEETING.CPP.

```
 1: // meeting.cpp -- Multidimension array demonstration
 2:
 3: #include <tscdefs.h>
 4: #include IOSTREAM_H
 5: #include IOMANIP_H
 6:
 7: #define NUMEMPLOYEES 4
 8: #define NUMHOURS 10
 9: #define STARTHOUR 8
10:
11: #define JOE 0
12: #define SAM 1
13: #define PAULA 2
14: #define MARY 3
15:
16: int schedule[NUMHOURS][NUMEMPLOYEES];
17:
18: main()
19: {
20:   int empnum, hour;
21:
22: // Enter employee appointments:
23:
24:   for (;;) {
25:     cout << "Employee number? (-1 to quit): ";
26:     cin >> empnum;
27:     if (empnum < 0) break;
28:     if (empnum >= NUMEMPLOYEES) {
29:       cout << "Employee number is out of range\n";
30:       continue;
31:     }
```

*continues*

## Listing 2.24  continued

```
32:     for (;;) {
33:       cout << "Hour of appointment? (8-17, -1 to quit): ";
34:       cin >> hour;
35:       if (hour < 0) break;
36:       if ((STARTHOUR <= hour) && (hour < STARTHOUR + NUMHOURS))
37:         schedule[hour - STARTHOUR][empnum] = 1;
38:       else
39:         cout << "Hour is out of range\n";
40:     }
41:   }
42:
43: // Display schedule:
44:
45:   cout << "\nSchedule:\n";
46:   cout << "           Joe      Sam      Paula    Mary\n";
47:   for (hour = 0; hour < NUMHOURS; hour++) {
48:     cout << setw(2) << dec << (hour + STARTHOUR) << ":00";
49:     for (empnum = JOE; empnum < NUMEMPLOYEES; empnum++) {
50:       cout << '\t';
51:       if (schedule[hour][empnum] != 0)
52:         cout << 'X';
53:     }
54:     cout << '\n';
55:   }
56:
57: // Calculate hours when all employees can meet:
58:
59:   cout << "\nPossible meeting times:\n";
60:   for (hour = 0; hour < NUMHOURS; hour++) {
61:     int k = 0;
62:     for (empnum = 0; empnum < NUMEMPLOYEES; empnum++) {
63:       k += schedule[hour][empnum];
64:     }
65:     if (k == 0)
66:       cout << setw(2) << dec << (hour + STARTHOUR) << ":00\n";
67:   }
68:   return 0;
69: }
```

After preparing several constants, MEETING declares a two-dimensional array schedule at line 16. As programmed here, the schedule array has room for 10 hourly appointments for four employees. Imagine this structure as having rows for hours and columns for the employees.

Two do–forever for loops at lines 24 and 32 control the entry portion of the program. Two break statements and one continue provide an exit path from the otherwise endless loops. The statement at line 37 stores 1 in an appointment slot for the employee and hour that you enter. The program considers 1 to mean this hour is filled. Any slots containing 0 are free.

Lines 45–55 use the information stored in the schedule array to display the appointments for all employees. Study line 51 carefully. It checks the values at schedule[hour][empnum]. If this value is not 0, the program displays an X for this hour and employee. If the value is 0, the program skips this position, leaving it blank on-screen.

After displaying the full schedule, lines 60–67 search for rows (hours) that contain all 0s, indicating a free period for every employee. To do this, the values in each array position are summed in a variable k. If the sum is 0, this hour is free, and line 66 displays the hour as a candidate for a group meeting.

When examining MEETING.CPP, pay close attention to the way constants such as STARTHOUR and NUMHOURS are used to calculate array indexes. Because all arrays in C++ use indexes that start at 0, having arrays of hours indexed by values from 8 to 17 requires careful programming. (Of course, you could just declare an array of 24 hours and waste the unused slots, but I wanted to show examples of typical index calculations because you'll probably have to deal with similar problems sooner or later.)

> **Note:** To be truly useful, MEETING.CPP should be able to read a file that lists employee schedules. After reading about C++ file handling techniques in Chapter 8, you might want to modify this program to make it easier to use.

# The True Character of Strings

Now that you have a clear picture of arrays, you're ready to consider the true nature of strings. What is a string? If you answered "an array of characters," you're right on the button. As you've seen in other sample listings, to declare an 80-character string, you simply write

```
char string[80];
```

That, of course, is just an array definition that creates a variable named string with room for 80 char elements. In C++, a string is an array of characters; there is no "string" data type as there is in other programming languages, such as Pascal and BASIC.

Despite the lack of an explicit string data type, however, C++ does give special status to arrays of char. As you know, you can create and initialize a string this way:

```
char firstPresident[] = "George Washington";
```

This is still an array of char, but instead of requiring you to fill in a literal size in the brackets, C++ simply counts the number of characters between the double quotes and uses that number to reserve space for the array, here named firstPresident. The characters from the string "George Washington" are then stored in that space.

## Character Array Initializations

Like other arrays, you can initialize arrays of char by listing individual elements in braces after the array's definition. Usually, however, it's easiest just to assign a string as in the previous samples. If you prefer, however, you can initialize a character array like this:

```
char kbtype[7] = {'Q', 'W', 'E', 'R', 'T', 'Y', 0};
```

The 0 after the list of characters supplies the string with its required null terminator. The result is identical to

```
char kbtype[7] = "QWERTY";
```

except that C++ automatically supplies the terminating null (0) byte at the end of the string.

## Arrays and Pointers

You've also seen another kind of string declaration in previous programs. For instance, char *model in COMPDB.H declares a variable named model that *points* to a string. The asterisk tells C++ that model is a pointer to one or more char variables stored at a location in memory. Despite the lack of brackets in the defnition, C++ allows `model` to be used as an array. For instance, you can assign a literal string to `model` with

```
system.model = "XT Clone";
```

This is similar to the earlier assignments to arrays that use brackets. C++ does not copy any characters, however, to carry out string pointer assignments. Instead, the program simply assigns the string's address to the `model` pointer.

The similarity between pointers like `char *model` and arrays such as `char model[18]` is more than just superficial. Arrays in C++ are implemented as pointers. Suppose that you define an array like this:

```
int array[10];
```

When the compiler processes this definition, it allocates space for 10 integers and assigns the address of the first integer to the variable `array`. It may appear as though `array` stores the integers inside itself, but in the program's compiled code, `array` is implemented as a pointer to the array's first element. As you learned earlier, to display the third item for an array defined like this, you can write

```
cout << array[2];
```

Now consider the same declaration using a pointer:

```
int *arrayPtr;
```

Because arrays in C++ are implemented as pointers, even though `array` is defined differently, you can still write a statement like this to display the second element:

```
cout << arrayPtr[1];
```

Watch out, however. The bracketed definition `int array[10]` reserves space in memory for an array of 10 integers. The equivalent definition `int *array` reserves space *only for a pointer named* array. It does *not* reserve any space for integers. When an array is defined as a pointer, you'll have to take additional steps to reserve memory in which to store the array's elements. It's too early to list those steps here; I'll get back to them in Chapter 4, "Pointers About Pointers."

> **Note:** That's enough about pointers for the moment. Don't be concerned if the details seem a bit fuzzy; most people have trouble understanding the relationship between arrays and pointers on a first reading. For now, you need to know only that variables defined as `char x[10]` and `char *x` are
>
> *continues*

*continued*

functionally equivalent, meaning you can use x in many of the same ways in program statements. Both definitions create pointers to memory where characters are stored, but only the one with brackets reserves memory for those characters.

## Fielding Bits

It often happens that members in a structure will never exceed a certain small value. For example, in a database of facts on parents, a member that represents the number of children is unlikely to be higher than 15 and will usually be 2 or 3. A member that represents a person's sex will need only a single bit if 0 is taken to mean male and 1 female. Such a structure might look like this:

```
struct person {
  unsigned age;        // 0 ... 99
  unsigned sex;        // 0=male, 1=female
  unsigned children;   // 0 ... 15
};
```

That takes six bytes, assuming two bytes per int member. Unfortunately, there's lots of wasted space in this structure. For example, sex requires only a single bit to hold its value, and the other 15 bits in that int are never used. If the structure could *pack* the information into a smaller space that takes only as many bits as needed to represent each member, it could squeeze out most of those wasted bits.

The way to do this is to use a *bit field,* which resembles a structure—it uses the same struct keyword—but specifies the number of bits that each field occupies within the size of an int (16 bits on PCs). Here's how the previous structure looks when converted to a bit-field:

```
struct person {
  unsigned age : 7;         // 0 ... 127
  unsigned sex : 1;         // 0=male, 1=female
  unsigned children : 4;    // 0 ... 15
  unsigned : 4;             // Not used
};
```

Following each field name with a colon and unsigned literal value packs that field into the specified number of bits in the structure, which can total up to 16 bits for all such fields. In this sample, 7 bits are allotted for the age field. Because an unsigned integer can range from 0 to 127 when represented in binary by 7 bits, the age of a person in this record is similarly limited. The other two fields, sex and children, are also packed into 1- and 4-bit spaces, limiting the ranges of values these fields can hold.

> **Note:** The official minimum size limit of a bit field is the same as an int. There's no set rule, however, about whether a bit field structure may be larger than the size of an int, and each C++ compiler is free to construct bit fields differently. Using them can make your programs difficult to transfer to other C++ compilers and operating systems.

The last field in the person bit field is unnamed. This is a place holder and is used to keep the total number of bits at 16. A place holder is optional but is usually included to account for every bit in a structure. You may also use more than one place holder to force fields to begin at certain bits. For example, here's a fictitious sample with three place holders marked Not used:

```
struct hardware {
  unsigned reset : 1;      // 0 ... 1
  unsigned level : 4;      // 0 ... 15
  unsigned : 1;            // Not used
  unsigned selector : 2;   // 0 ... 3
  unsigned : 3;            // Not used
  unsigned active : 1;     // 0 ... 1
  unsigned : 4;            // Not used
};
```

Structures with multiple place holders are often necessary to match the fixed bits stored in a register. For example, an input port might define certain bits to mean various things: Whether a byte is available, what the status of the port is, whether it's ready to send another byte, and so forth. You could use a bit field structure to read that information into a program, but you might have to use place holders to force some fields to match the positions of specific values.

Use bit fields as you do members in other structures. For example, to display the age and number of children in a Person bit field, you could write

```
Person p;
...
cout << "\nAge      = " << p.age;
cout << "\nChildren = " << p.children;
```

Unlike many other computer languages, in C++, you don't have to extract the bits from the structure, and you don't have to use logical operators to isolate field values from their neighbors. Instead, just use the fields as though they were integers. C++ takes care of the messy details of extracting and inserting the packed bit fields in the structure without disturbing other bits there. Of course, you must be careful not to assign values greater than a field can represent. Except for this detail, you can use bit fields as though they were separate unsigned integer variables.

> **Note:** Bit fields must be declared in `struct` structures. Bit fields are not allowed in unions.

Listing 2.25, EQUIP.CPP, shows how to use bit fields to extract information packed inside computer hardware. The program uses a bit field structure to interpret the information returned by a function named `_bios_equiplist`, which is declared in the header file bios.h. Run the program to detect how many disk drives, serial ports, and printers are installed, whether a game adaptor is available, and the startup video mode of your PC.

## Listing 2.25. EQUIP.CPP.

```
 1: // equip.cpp -- Display list of computer's equipment
 2:
 3: #include <tscdefs.h>
 4: #include IOSTREAM_H
 5: #include <bios.h>
 6:
 7: struct Equipment {
 8:   unsigned hasdiskette : 1;
 9:   unsigned : 1;                // Not used
10:   unsigned planar : 2;
11:   unsigned videomode : 2;
12:   unsigned numfloppy : 2;
13:   unsigned : 1;                // Not used
14:   unsigned numserial : 3;
```

```
15:    unsigned gameadaptor : 1;
16:    unsigned : 1;                // Not used
17:    unsigned numprinters : 2;
18: };
19:
20: union TwoTypes {
21:    Equipment eq;       // The bit field structure
22:    int k;              // Same bytes as an integer
23: };
24:
25: main()
26: {
27:    TwoTypes t;
28:
29:    t.k = _bios_equiplist();   // Get list as integer
30:    cout << "\nNumber of printers          " << t.eq.numprinters;
31:    cout << "\nGame adaptor installed (1)   " << t.eq.gameadaptor;
32:    cout << "\nNumber of serial ports       " << t.eq.numserial;
33:    cout << "\nNumber of diskette drives    ";
34:    if (t.eq.hasdiskette)
35:      cout << (t.eq.numfloppy + 1);
36:    else
37:      cout << 0;
38:    cout << "\nInitial video mode (2)       " << t.eq.videomode;
39:    cout << "\nPlanar RAM size (3)          " << t.eq.planar;
40:    cout << "\n\n(1): 0=FALSE, 1=TRUE";
41:    cout << "\n(2): 1=40x25 color, 2=80x25 color, 3=monochrome";
42:    cout << "\n(3): 3=64K on XTs\n";
43:    return 0;
44: }
```

EQUIP.CPP declares a bit field named Equipment at lines 7–18. Inside this structure are a number of fields and place holders (marked with the comment Not used). These fields are positioned to match the values stored in your system's toggle switches (or perhaps in a small amount of battery-powered RAM). Using a bit-field structure to extract these values makes it easy to display them, as shown at lines 30–39.

The program also shows good use of a union. Lines 20–23 declare TwoTypes as a union with two overlayed fields, eq of type Equipment and k of type int. Because Equipment is a 16-bit bit field, and because an int also occupies 16 bits, the two fields in this union exactly overlay each other.

The program then defines a variable of type TwoTypes (line 27) and assigns the result of the _bios_equiplist function to t.k—in other words, to the int k field in the t union. The compiler would reject a direct assignment to the eq field because, even though the int and Equipment fields are the same size, they are different data types.

After assigning the function value to t.k, the statements at lines 30–39 use the other field (t.eq) in the union to extract the bit-field values from this same value. As this shows, the union makes it easy for the program to manipulate the values as an integer (t.k) and as a bit field structure (t.eq).

> **Note:** Bit fields typically restrict programs to running on specific hardware. Running EQUIP on anything but a true-blue PC, AT, PS/2, or clone may cause the program to fail. Also, because the code relies on the declarations in bios.h, it might not compile with another C++ compiler. That's not to discourage you from using bit fields, only to point out that doing so usually makes a program totally dependent on a specific computer system. Because the int data type may be a different size on other systems, if you want your code to be portable, it's probably best to use plain structs rather than bit fields. However, if you write your program carefully and *never* assume that a bit field is in a specific location, it *may* be possible for your bit fields to work correctly on more than one type of system.

## Sizing Up Your Variables

Now that we are talking about system-dependent items, this is a good place to introduce one last C++ operator, sizeof. Use sizeof to determine the number of 8-bit bytes occupied by a variable or a data type. For example, to display how many bytes float occupies, you can write

```
cout << "Size of float = " << sizeof(float);
```

C++ replaces the expression sizeof(float) with the number of bytes that a float variable takes in memory. You can use sizeof to determine also the size of an array, union, bit field, or other structure. Just put the name of the variable or data type in parentheses after sizeof and use the expression where you might use an unsigned int.

Listing 2.26, SIZEOF.CPP, demonstrates how to use sizeof. Run the program to determine the sizes of all basic C++ data types. The program makes a useful test that you can compile and run with other compilers or even on other computer systems. Do this to compare one compiler's assumed sizes for fundamental data types.

### Listing 2.26. SIZEOF.CPP.

```
 1: // sizeof.cpp -- Determining the sizes of variables
 2:
 3: #include <tscdefs.h>
 4: #include IOSTREAM_H
 5:
 6: // Disable warning: "xxx is defined but never used..."
 7:
 8: #if (defined __TSC_BTC__)
 9:   #pragma warn -use
10: #elif (defined __TSC_MSC__)
11:   #pragma warning( disable : 4101 )
12: #endif
13:
14: main()
15: {
16:   char c;
17:   short s;
18:   int i;
19:   long l;
20:   float f;
21:   double d;
22:   long double ld;
23:
24:   cout << "Size of char ...... = " << sizeof(c)  << " byte(s)\n";
25:   cout << "Size of short ..... = " << sizeof(s)  << " byte(s)\n";
26:   cout << "Size of int ....... = " << sizeof(i)  << " byte(s)\n";
27:   cout << "Size of long ...... = " << sizeof(l)  << " byte(s)\n";
28:   cout << "Size of float ..... = " << sizeof(f)  << " byte(s)\n";
29:   cout << "Size of double .... = " << sizeof(d)  << " byte(s)\n";
30:   cout << "Size of long double = " << sizeof(ld) << " byte(s)\n";
31:   return 0;
32: }
```

> **Note:** Lines 8–12 disable a warning for Borland C++, Turbo C++, and Microsoft C/C++. These compilers issue the warning to inform you that one or more variables in the program are declared but never used. Because this example merely displays the sizes of its variables, the warning is safely ignored. Notice how conditional compilation statements select two different #pragma options (commands to the compiler) depending on the compiler you are using. Zortech C++ does not warn you about unused variables.

Careful programmers use sizeof to write system-independent programs. Instead of assuming an int variable takes two bytes, a statement can use the expression sizeof(int). Compiling this expression on a different system gives the program a way of determining how many bytes an int occupies on the new machine.

You can also use sizeof to determine the sizes of structures and arrays. Specify either a data type identifier or the name of a variable in parentheses after sizeof. For example, using the declaration of a Computer struct in compdb.h (Listing 2.18), include that file and use a statement like this to display the struct's size in bytes:

```
#include "compdb.h"
cout << "Size of a Computer struct = " << sizeof(Computer);
```

Or replace Computer with the name of any array to determine its size:

```
int array[100];
cout << "Size of array = " << sizeof(array);
```

Using sizeof this way is preferable to assuming that an array or structure takes a certain number of bytes. Also, because C++ compilers can insert padding bytes to keep fields in structs aligned to even addresses, sizeof is the *only* reliable way to determine a struct's true size. Just summing the sizes of a struct's members might not give an accurate result.

You've now seen most of C++'s operators and data structures in action. With these elements, and with the help of program-flow statements like for and while, you can write sophisticated programs that repeat actions and make decisions. Unfortunately, as your programs grow larger, you'll begin to notice that main() tends to expand like a hot-air balloon with its valve stuck open. Unless you do something to relieve the pressure, sooner or later, the balloon will burst.

And, unless you do something to prevent overstuffing main() with statement after statement, your programs may also burst as they become more difficult to create and maintain. Good programmers avoid writing long main() functions. Instead, they divide their programs into small, manageable chunks. Like main(), those chunks are called functions. The next chapter explains what functions are and how you can use them to write complex C++ programs while you never work on more than small, easy-to-understand pieces of the code at a time.

# Questions and Exercises

2.1. In relational expressions, what values does C++ use internally to represent true and false?

2.2. Explain the difference between == and =.

2.3. Write a program using a loop that prompts for a value between 1 and 100. If someone types a value outside of that range, the program should display an error message and redisplay the prompt.

2.4. Write the equivalent while statement for the following for loop (assume counter is type int):

```
for (counter = 0; counter > -8; counter--) {
  cout << "\nValue of counter = " << counter;
  cout << "\n---";
}
```

2.5. Using bitwise operators, write a program that limits the range of an int variable to 0 through 31.

2.6. Write a program that encrypts a string after you enter a password, then recovers that same string. Use the bitwise XOR operator in your answer.

2.7. Write a program that passes an integer value to DOS for a batch file to receive through the errorlevel variable.

2.8. Write a version of WORDS.CPP (Listing 2.12) that eliminates the duplicate statements at lines 20 and 22.

2.9. Write a filter program that converts input strings to uppercase.

2.10. Write a program that determines whether an integer value is odd or even.

2.11. Write for, while, and do/while loops that display the alphabet. Insert your loops into a switch statement that lets people select which loop variety to run.

2.12. Why do programmers frown on using goto statements?

2.13. Create a a structure that can store the date and time.

2.14. Define an array of 50 date and time structures from Exercise 2.13.

2.15. Write a program to display a string's characters separated by blanks. If you type ABCDEFG, the program should display A B C D E F G.

2.16. Pack your data and time structure into one or more bit fields. How many bytes does the bit field save? Use sizeof to prove your answer.

# Functions: Programming in Pieces

A *function* is a kind of miniprogram inside a program. Functions collect various statements under a single name that a program can then use one or more times to execute those statements. Functions save space by reducing repetition, and they make programming easier by giving you a way to divide a large project into small, easy-to-handle modules.

If you've programmed in BASIC or assembly language, you'll recognize functions as being similar to subroutines. If you know Pascal, you'll notice that functions are equivalent to Pascal procedures *and* functions. If you have a background in C, you should still read this chapter. Functions look much the same in C and C++, but looks can be deceiving, and there are many differences between C and C++ functions that you'll want to learn.

# Keeping It Simple

**B**eginners often think that learning about functions is where C++ programming starts to "get hard." Not so. *The main reason for using functions is to keep programs simple.* Functions modularize a program by dividing it into manageable pieces. With functions, you can write major programs while working on only a few relatively small, simple chunks of code at a time.

You've already seen one function in every program listed so far—main(). As you know, when a C++ program runs, it begins by executing the first statement inside main(). You've also used *library functions*—those that are provided with C++ and declared in header files. When you called _bios_equiplist() in EQUIP.CPP (Listing 2.25), you saved the effort that you would have had to spend writing that function's instructions yourself.

As those sample programs show, library functions can serve as specialized tools for constructing new programs. Instead of reinventing a tool, if the right one exists in the C++ library, you can just use it as is. In this way, functions extend the C++ language by providing custom commands that you can pull in and use as needed to solve problems.

## Writing Your Own Functions

The key to writing good functions is to choose good tasks for functions to perform. A "good" task is one with a narrow, clear purpose. For example, a clearDisplay() function might clear the display. A factorial() function might compute the factorial of a number. But it's probably not a good idea to write a function named clearDisplayAndComputeTheFactorial(). That's way too much for one function to bite off and chew.

It's also important to choose good function names such as clearDisplay(), factorial(), promptForInput(), and showErrorMessage(). Even without seeing those functions in use, you already have some idea what they do. Good function names can make C++ statements read more like stories than computer programs. You can use any unique identifiers for function names, but your programs will be easier to read and maintain if you create names that describe what functions accomplish. If you name your functions fn64(), axp9b(), or other equally cryptic names, you'll need to add comments to the code to explain what's going on. With good function names, program statements are self-documenting, and comments are often unnecessary.

Listing 3.1 demonstrates how to create functions in C++ programs.

## Listing 3.1. FNCOUNT.CPP.

```
 1:  // fncount.cpp -- Function demonstration
 2:
 3:  #include <tscdefs.h>
 4:  #include IOSTREAM_H
 5:  #include IOMANIP_H
 6:
 7:  void countup(int value);
 8:  void countdown(int value);
 9:
10:  main()
11:  {
12:    countup(20);
13:    countdown(10);
14:    return 0;
15:  }
16:
17:  void countup(int value)
18:  {
19:    int i;
20:
21:    cout << "\n\nCounting up\n";
22:    for (i = 1; i <= value; i++)
23:      cout << setw(8) << dec << i;
24:  }
25:
26:  void countdown(int value)
27:  {
28:    int i;
29:
30:    cout << "\n\nCounting down\n";
31:    for (i = value; i >= 1; i--)
32:      cout << setw(8) << dec << i;
33:  }
```

When writing your own functions, type them into the program text just as you do function main(). Most programmers insert functions after main() as done here in lines 14–30, but that's not a requirement, and functions can precede main() if you prefer. In general, for all of a program's functions *except* main(), you need to carry out these three steps:

- Declare a prototype that describes the function

- Use the function in at least one statement

- Write the function's body

FNCOUNT implements these goals. First, it declares two *function prototypes* at lines 7–8. A function prototype describes the name of the function (countup() and countdown()), determines what kind of value the function returns (void in this case, meaning *no return value*), and lists any parameters in parentheses that the function needs (such as int value). Each prototype declaration ends with a semicolon.

Function prototypes tell the compiler the name and nature of the functions in the program. You must declare a prototype for every function in your program *before* the program uses that function. For that reason, function prototypes are usually placed above main(). This also lists the prototypes in a convenient spot where you can examine and modify them.

Lines 12–13 *call* the two functions countup() and countdown(). "Calling a function" simply means that you type the function's name in a statement or expression. When C++ compiles the program, it replaces the function names with code that executes the statements collected inside the functions. Usually, C++ performs this task by inserting a machine language subroutine call instruction, transferring control to the address where the function is stored.

In addition to declaring a function's prototype and to calling the function from another statement, you also have to write the statements that perform the function's actions. The function's implementation describes what the function does. When you implement the function's body, usually by typing it after the end of main(), begin with the function's prototype minus the semicolon at its end. This first line in the function's implementation is called the *function declaration*. Inside a subsequent pair of opening and closing braces, declare the variables and write the statements that belong to the function. For example, here's the implementation of function countup() from FNCOUNT:

```
void countup(int value)
{
  int i;
```

```
  cout << "\n\nCounting up\n";
  for (i = 1; i <= value; i++)
    cout << setw(8) << dec << i;
}
```

You'll recognize this format as nearly identical to the one used by main(). A function may define variables such as int i for its own use, and it may include statements, control structures, and any other items that you've come across in other sample listings inside the main() function.

You must be sure to implement every function prototype (see 26–33 in FNCOUNT.CPP for another example). To put that into a rule: *For every function prototype, there must be a corresponding implementation of that function.* The prototype and function declaration—for example, lines 8 and 26—also must agree exactly. In this way, the compiler helps you write reliable programs by insisting that the function prototypes match their implementations. Of course, it wouldn't make any sense to design and use a function prototype as returning a float value but then to implement that function to return type int. In a large program with hundreds of functions, however, it's all too easy to make that kind of mistake. C++'s strict rules about prototyping functions guard against using functions improperly—a common mistake that C programmers know all too well. (ANSI C does not require function prototypes.)

**Note:** When designing functions, try to keep them short. A good rule of thumb is to limit your function lengths to one printout page, about 55 or 60 lines. Even that's fairly long, and you should try to keep most functions below about half that size. At first, you may have trouble meeting this goal, but it's a good one to strive for. Experience teaches that simple functions are easier to write and maintain, especially months or years after you write them. Do yourself a favor now, and keep your functions as small as you can.

# Designing from the Top Down

You may have heard the phrase "top-down programming." This isn't some obscure scientific term. It's a description of an approach to the craft of programming. When practicing top-down programming, the general idea is to begin with a broad concept—the goal you are trying to achieve. You then chisel that concept into smaller and smaller chunks, carving out the details of a complex project until you reach rock bottom. At that point, you have an assortment of easy-to-implement definitions suitable for converting to C++ functions. By implementing these small, purposeful functions, you can write major applications while never working on more than a few simple lines of code at a time.

For example, suppose that you are writing a program to play checkers. That's the main goal—to play the game of checkers, and starting the ball in motion might be all that function `main()` does:

```
main()
{
  playCheckers();
  return 0;
}
```

Then, in function `playCheckers()`, you'd call other functions to initialize a new game board, make moves, check if a player has won or lost, and so on. A diagram of all the modules and submodules that make up the finished program resembles an organizational "tree"—like those managers use to chart a company's departments. (See Figure 3.1.)

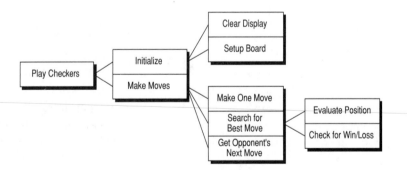

**Figure 3.1.** Top-down programming divides a complex job into modules. Diagramming those modules shows their relationship to the program—here a fictitious (and incomplete) game of checkers.

Unfortunately, like most theories, top-down programming in practice is a bit more difficult than these descriptions make it sound. There are several reasons for this. Projects may be poorly defined at the start, project managers may misunderstand key goals, and while implementing the details, programmers may discover a need to refashion code that was already finished and tested. Still, top-down programming has an important role to play, and you should learn how to apply the concept when designing your own code. I'll get back to this idea in Chapter 5 when I introduce C++ object-oriented features. As you'll learn then, object-oriented programming patches many of the flaws in top-down programming.

To understand more about functions and to explore how you can use them in top-down fashion, in this section, you'll complete a small program that checks for mismatched braces and parentheses in C++ source-code files. It's a common error to leave out a closing brace in a statement block or to forget to match every opening and closing parenthesis in a complex expression. If you receive errors during compilation that you don't understand, you can use the program to eliminate a mismatched brace or parenthesis as the cause.

The first step is to sketch what the program should do. It will have to read characters from a text file, keep track of encountered braces and parentheses, and display the results. For a professional appearance, the program should also display a brief welcoming message. Instead of writing the instructions right off the bat in C++, I'll use *pseudocode* to describe the program's design. Pseudocode is a free-form approximation of statements that look like those in a real program but can't be compiled. Designing programs with pseudocode is like penciling in the figures for a painting you'll finish with oils when you get back to the studio. Here's the "main loop" in pseudocode:

```
welcome user to program
open the input file
while (nextcharacter != EOF) {
  count braces and parens
}
display results
close the file
```

This is a complete program, although it isn't yet in a form that C++ can compile. The pseudocode describes the program, but doesn't include every tiny detail. This completes the forest. Next, it's time to plant a few trees.

At this stage, after settling on the outer design, I like to rewrite the pseudocode in a form that's as close as possible to the final program. I do this by replacing the pseudocode descriptions with function names. The functions don't yet exist, and the program will not yet compile, but this lets me see whether my design is on track before going further:

```
main()
{
  char c;

  welcome();
  openfile();
  while ((c = fgetc(fp)) != EOF)
     countchars(c);
  showresults();
  fclose(fp);
}
```

I replaced "welcome user to program" with welcome(), a call to a function of that name. Similarly, I converted "open the input file" to openfile(), another function call.

As you become more experienced with the top-down method, you'll discover that you can invent your function names directly. Instead of writing "welcome user to program" in the pseudocode design, you'll just write welcome(). That's fine, but don't make the mistake of adding too many details too early. Concentrate on one level at a time. When you're satisfied with that level, then go below decks to polish the trim.

There are two items in this example you haven't seen before. The while loop calls fgetc() for a character from a file, represented here as fp. This is a file-handling function declared in stdio.h, which the program must include. That and other header files contain function prototypes for the C++ library. You might want to use your editor to examine stdio.h and study the prototypes. You can also print copies of the various header files supplied with your compiler. These printouts give you a handy reference to the requirements of the standard function library.

> **Note:** Chapter 8 covers file handling in more detail. In this chapter, I'll introduce only the file concepts required to understand how the sample programs work.

Another file-handling function from stdio.h, fclose(), closes the file opened by openfile(). DOS limits the total number of files available to programs; therefore, your program's functions should always close files when they're done using them. This recovers the space used by DOS and releases a file *handle* for the program to use for other purposes. Handles are just identifying numbers that DOS assigns to open files. (When a program ends, it automatically closes any open files.)

So far so good. The program's outer layer is coming together. It calls several functions, even though those functions don't exist yet. The next step is to create the function prototypes, which describe each function more completely:

```
void welcome(void);
void openfile(void);
void countchars(char c);
void showresults(void);
```

You can optionally omit the void keyword, declaring parameterless functions as:

```
void welcome();
void openfile();
void countchars(char c);
void showresults();
```

Either form is acceptable in C++. In ANSI C, however, you must insert void. I find the former style clearer, but if you prefer to leave out void, you may do so without harm.

The program's main() function calls these four functions, none of which returns any values. For that reason, the prototypes all begin with the keyword void. (Think of the word *void* as meaning *nothing*, not as *invalid*. A void function is not at all like a *void* check.) Next come the function names—welcome(), openfile(), countchars(), and showresults. After each of those names are any parameters that the function requires. Three functions have none, represented by another void in parentheses. However, countchars() needs a character to count, so the prototype tells the compiler about that character by listing (char c) after the function's name.

Notice how the parameter declaration (char c) resembles a variable definition. In fact, that's what a parameter is—a variable that the function receives from its caller. However, parameters are special in the sense that they don't exist until the caller passes a value, called an *argument,* to the function. The declaration (char c) simply tells the compiler what to expect. It doesn't create a character named c until the program runs. For this reason, you don't even need to name the variable, and you could write the prototype this way:

```
void countchars(char);
```

This gives the compiler everything it needs to know about the function: its return value (void meaning none), its name (countchars) and the data type of any parameters (char). Even though this style of nameless parameters is permitted in C++, I prefer to include parameter names in my prototypes. A function that requires more than one parameter helps document the code. For example, the prototype

```
void proto(int, int, int);
```

is permissible. But I prefer to write something like this:

```
void proto(int count, int min, int max);
```

Implementing the countchars() function demonstrates the final stage in the top-down design method. Here's how I wrote that function:

```
void countchars(char c)
{
  if (c == '(') openparen++;
  else if (c == ')') closeparen++;
  else if (c == '{') openbrace++;
  else if (c == '}') closebrace++;
}
```

Because this is the real McCoy, the function declaration now requires a full accounting of its parameters—data types *and* names. It's not enough to write (char) for the single parameter used by countchars(). In the function implementation, all parameters must have names. Statements inside the function (but nowhere else) can then use the parameter names to "get to" the values passed as arguments to the function.

The body of the function consists of a four-part if/else statement that inspects the value of the character passed to the function. Inside the function, the statements refer to the char parameter by its name c. You could use any name you want here, even the same names used elsewhere. Function parameters are available only to the function's statements—in other words, within the same *scope*, or bounds. Outside of the function's scope, the parameters don't exist.

Examine how this sample function compares the parameter c with literal braces and parentheses. Matches increment one of four variables, openparen, closeparen, openbrace, and closebrace. Next, it's time to define those variables:

```
int openparen, closeparen, openbrace, closebrace;
```

By making the four variables global (defined outside of main), they are automatically initialized to 0. For that reason, there's no need to include statements to assign starting values to them.

The program is shaping up. All that remains is to complete the other three functions. As you can see from this small demonstration, top-down programming lets you focus on one small section of the program at a time. Instead of worrying about how to open files, read characters, and perform other necessary jobs, you concentrated on completing the outer design and then spent time on one function, countchars(). You completed that function *out of context,* leaving the rest of the program for another time.

The final result is Listing 3.2, BP.CPP. You should be able to understand most of the program, except, that is, for the file handling details. (I'll explain those items in a moment.) Try to pick out the function prototypes, and study the implementations for each function.

## Listing 3.2. BP.CPP.

```
 1:   // bp.cpp -- Count braces and parentheses in C++ programs
 2:
 3:   #include <tscdefs.h>
 4:   #include IOSTREAM_H
 5:   #include IOMANIP_H
 6:   #include <stdio.h>
 7:   #include <stdlib.h>
 8:
 9:   void welcome(void);
10:   void openfile(void);
11:   void countchars(char c);
12:   void showresults(void);
13:
14:   int openparen, closeparen, openbrace, closebrace;
15:   char filename[128];
16:   FILE *fp;
17:
18:   main()
19:   {
20:     char c;
21:
22:     welcome();
23:     openfile();
24:     while ((c = fgetc(fp)) != EOF)
25:       countchars(c);
26:     showresults();
27:     fclose(fp);
28:     return 0;
29:   }
```

*continues*

## Listing 3.2. continued

```
30:
31:  void welcome(void)
32:  {
33:    cout << "\n\nBraces and Parentheses Counter";
34:    cout << "\nby Tom Swan.\n" << flush;
35:  }
36:
37:  void openfile(void)
38:  {
39:    cout << "\nFilename? " << flush;
40:    gets(filename);
41:    fp = fopen(filename, "r");    // Open file for reading
42:    if (!fp) {
43:      cout <<"\nError opening file\n" << flush;
44:      exit(1);
45:    }
46:  }
47:
48:  void countchars(char c)
49:  {
50:    if (c == '(') openparen++;
51:    else if (c == ')') closeparen++;
52:    else if (c == '{') openbrace++;
53:    else if (c == '}') closebrace++;
54:  }
55:
56:  void showresults(void)
57:  {
58:    if (openparen < closeparen)
59:      cout << "\nMissing " << (closeparen - openparen)
60:           << " ( character(s)";
61:    else if (openparen > closeparen)
62:      cout << "\nMissing " << (openparen - closeparen)
63:           << " ) character(s)";
64:    else
65:      cout << "\nParentheses match";
66:
67:    if (openbrace < closebrace)
68:      cout << "\nMissing " << (closebrace - openbrace)
69:           << " { character(s)";
```

```
70:    else if (openbrace > closebrace)
71:      cout << "\nMissing " << (openbrace - closebrace)
72:           << " } character(s)";
73:    else
74:      cout << "\nBraces match";
75:    cout << "\n\n" << flush;
76:  }
```

Function openfile (lines 37–46) uses a few C++ features you haven't seen before. After displaying a message that prompts you to enter a filename (and flushing the output because the string doesn't end with a newline character), line 40 calls gets(), a function declared in stdio.h. You can use this function to let people type characters into string variables, such as the filename string defined at line 15. There are other ways to read strings into programs, but gets() works well enough. (It doesn't prevent you from typing too many characters, so it's best to define strings of at least 128 characters, the maximum that the standard PC keyboard input buffer can hold.) After getting the file's name, the program executes

```
fp = fopen(filename, "r");
```

Variable fp is declared at line 16 as type FILE *, which stdio.h declares. The asterisk creates a *pointer* to a FILE, a concept you'll meet again in Chapter 4. A FILE variable is a struct that contains the fields C++ needs to keep track of open files. Normally, you don't need to use these fields directly, although you can study them in stdio.h if you want. Instead, most programs only need to create a FILE * variable such as fp and assign to it the result from a function like fopen().

That function's job is to instruct DOS to find a file by name on disk, to prepare various internal variables to let other statements read the file's contents, and to return the address of a FILE structure, which this program saves in fp. The "r" in the function call specifies "read only access," meaning that subsequent statements are allowed to read the file's contents, but not write new data. (In Chapter 8, I'll show you other ways to open files.)

After opening the file, an if statement at line 42 tests fp to see whether it contains a valid address. If fopen() failed for some reason—usually because it couldn't find a file of the specified name—it returns null, which as you know, is represented by the value 0 or the macro NULL. If fopen() succeeds, it returns a nonzero value that the program can then use to refer to the opened file. Because 0 represents false in C++, and nonzero values represent true, the if statement can test fp as though it were an int variable:

```
if (!fp) {
  cout <<"\nError opening file\n" << flush;
  exit(1);
}
```

The expression (!fp) means "if fp is false," and is exactly equivalent to (fp == 0) or (fp == NULL). The shorthand expression if (!fp)... is a typical C and C++ trick that you'll see time and again. Some people prefer the longer forms, but both styles are acceptable and there's no reason not to use the shorthand.

**Hint:** To make the shorthand expressions easier to remember, I like to pronounce if (!fp)... mentally as "if fp *is not* valid." Pronounce if (fp)... as "if fp *is* valid." Memorize these tips and you'll never misuse these common shorthand expressions.

To see the effect of these statements, run BP and enter a filename that you know doesn't exist. The program displays an error message and exits. Always deal with similar possibilities in your own programs. Many C++ functions are designed to return the results of their operations, and it's your responsibility to check those results to see whether the functions encountered any errors. Forgetting or ignoring errors returned by functions is sure to lead to bugs.

# Functions and Their Variables

Just about the only task you can't perform inside a function is to declare another function. Aside from that, you can insert statements and variables of all types inside functions.

Defining variables in a function limits those variables for the function's private use. A variable inside a function can be "seen" only by statements that are also in that same block. Statements in other functions can *never* peer over another function's shoulders in order to read or write variables defined there. A function's boundaries are like impenetrable stone walls.

This is not a limitation but a main advantage of the way functions work. Because the scope of a function's *local variables* is limited to the statements inside that function, you can be certain of a few helpful facts:

- Inside a function, unless you explicitly change a variable's value, that variable can't be changed by any statements outside of the function.

- The names of local variables do not have to be unique. Two, three, or more functions can all define variables named count. Each such variable is distinct, and each belongs only to its declaring function.

- Local variables in functions do not exist in memory until the function runs. This conserves memory by letting multiple functions share the same memory for their local variables (but not at the same time). This is an important concept—more on it in the next section.

## Local Variables

In addition to having a restricted scope, local variables are special for another reason. They exist in memory only when the function is active—that is, only while the function's statements are executing. When the function is not running, its local variables do not occupy even one bit of memory. They simply do not exist at all.

This apparent magic is accomplished by storing variables on the computer's stack, an area of memory that grows and shrinks as needed by the program. When a function begins running, it expands the stack by enough space to hold local variables declared in the function. When the function ends, the stack shrinks by the same amount. Then the next time that same function runs, the process repeats, again expanding the stack to hold variables and shrinking it when the function is done.

Between the time a function runs and the next time it is called to action, other functions may also run. If they also declare local variables, their values might be stored in the *same* locations on the stack used by other local variables declared in now inactive functions. In this way, functions share the same memory for their local variables, and it's possible for the total number of bytes of all local variables in a program to exceed the amount of available RAM without running out of memory!

As a consequence of this design, however, you can't store values in local variables and then expect those variables to have the same values the next time the function runs. In the meantime, another function may have stored its own variables in the same locations on the stack, overwriting those values. While the function runs, its variables are protected, but when the function is inactive, its variables do not exist, and their values are thrown away.

A short program demonstrates these ideas. Listing 3.3, LOCAL.CPP, declares three functions at lines 6–8. One function, pause(), displays a message and waits for you to press the Spacebar. The other two functions define and display local string variables.

## Listing 3.3. LOCAL.CPP.

```
1:  // local.cpp -- Local variables demonstration
2:
3:  #include <tscdefs.h>
4:  #include IOSTREAM_H
5:  #include IOMANIP_H
6:  #include <conio.h>
7:
8:  void pause(void);
9:  void function1(void);
10: void function2(void);
11:
12: main()
13: {
14:   function1();
15:   return 0;
16: }
17:
18: void pause(void)
19: {
20:   cout << "Press <Spacebar> to continue..." << flush;
21:   while (getche() != ' ') ;
22: }
23:
24: void function1(void)
25: {
26:   char s[15] = "Philadelphia\n";
27:
28:   cout << "\nBegin function #1.   s = " << s;
29:   pause();
30:   function2();   // Call function2 from function1
```

```
31:    cout << "\nBack in function #1. s = " << s;
32:  }
33:
34:  void function2(void)
35:  {
36:    char s[15] = "San Francisco\n";
37:
38:    cout << "\nBegin function #2.   s = " << s;
39:    pause();
40:  }
```

The first thing to notice about LOCAL is that both of the two local variables at lines 26 and 36 have the same name (s). Because local variables are visible only inside the function that declares them, there is no conflict. Each variable is distinct even though it has the same name as the other.

The second important observation to make is at line 30, where function1() calls function2() (lines 34–40). During this time, while function2() runs, function1() is in suspended animation. function1() is still active, but it has transferred control *temporarily* to function2(). Because function1() remains active during this time, its local variables retain their values. Line 31 proves this by displaying the value of s after function2() returns control to its caller. This also shows that the two local variables are distinct even though they share the same name. Running LOCAL displays

```
Begin function #1.   s = Philadelphia
Press <Spacebar> to continue...
Begin function #2.   s = San Francisco
Press <Spacebar> to continue...
Back in function #1. s = Philadelphia
```

As you can see, after calling function2(), the local s string in function1() retains its value ("Philadelphia"). Though they share the same name, the two local variables do not occupy the same space.

# External Variables

Most of the time, you declare a local variable in a function by just inserting its data type and name inside the function's block. Local variables use the same forms as global variables declared outside of main() or as variables local to main(). There are no differences in form between local and global variables—only differences between where and how those values are stored in memory.

But sometimes the standard ways don't cut the mustard, and you need other means to declare variables. For example, suppose that a function needs to use a value that *another* function initializes. Because local variables exist only temporarily while their declaring function is running, a plain local variable won't solve this problem.

Listings 3.4, EXTERN1.CPP, and 3.5, EXTERN2.CPP, demonstrate one way to write functions that can share variables. To simulate a situation that occurs in many larger programs, the demonstration program is stored in two files. Compiling combines the files to create a single program, EXTERN1.EXE. Run this program to execute the test.

## Listing 3.4. EXTERN1.CPP

```
 1:  // extern1.cpp -- Extern variable demonstration part 1
 2:
 3:  #include <tscdefs.h>
 4:  #include IOSTREAM_H
 5:
 6:  void getfloat(void);
 7:
 8:  float f;
 9:
10:  main()
11:  {
12:    getfloat();
13:    cout << "Value of float = " << f;
14:    return 0;
15:  }
```

## Listing 3.5. EXTERN2.CPP

```
 1:  // extern2.cpp -- Extern variable demonstration part 2
 2:
 3:  #include <tscdefs.h>
 4:  #include IOSTREAM_H
 5:
 6:  void getfloat(void)
 7:  {
 8:    extern float f;
```

```
 9:
10:     cout << "Enter floating point value: ";
11:     cin >> f;
12:   }
```

The problem to solve is this: How can a function in a separate source-code file use a variable defined in another file? One solution is to declare the local variable with the extern keyword, as I did here at line 8 in EXTERN2.CPP. By prefacing the declaration with extern, you are telling the compiler that this variable's space is defined elsewhere. You are saying "Don't create space on the stack for float f. Another part of the program will take care of allocating some memory for this variable."

That happens in EXTERN1.CPP at line 8, which declares the variable with the same name (f) and data type (float) as in the other file. The extern keyword in the getfloat() function tells the compiler to assume that f is defined elsewhere. Later, when the separate files are linked, the declarations are combined so that they all refer to the same location in memory.

Variable f in getfloat() is a local variable in the sense that its scope is limited *in this source-code file* to that function. No other function can "see" f unless it also declares it to be extern. This is a safety measure that prevents any old function from changing the value of f.

There's no limit on the number of times you can declare the same variable extern, but you can define space for it only once. This makes extern suitable for header files that are included in multiple modules. You can declare a program's variables extern in the header file and include that file in all modules that need to use the variables. In the main module, you then define each global variable.

> **Note:** Try not to use extern too frequently. There are superior ways to pass information between functions. In general, use extern only to refer to global variables that are defined elsewhere. Because this creates permanent space for the variables, most local variables should *not* be extern.

# Register Variables

A *register variable* looks the same as any other local variable, but instead of being stored on the stack, it's placed directly in a processor register such as si or bx. Because there are a limited number of registers, and because those registers are limited in size, the number of register variables that a program can create at once is severely restricted.

To declare a register variable, preface it with the register keyword. For example, to create an integer variable k and place it in a register, use this local-variable declaration:

```
register int k;
```

A register variable must be local to a function; it can never be global to the entire program. You also can't make register variables external to a function by using the extern keyword. Only pure local variables can be placed in registers.

Using the register keyword does not guarantee that a value will be stored in a register. That will happen only if a register is available. If there aren't enough processor registers to go around, C++ ignores the register keyword and creates the variable locally as normal. Declaring register variables is only a suggestion to the compiler that it should try to place this value in a register if it can.

Why do that? Because operations on values in registers are usually faster than those same operations when performed on values stored in memory. Used in critical code, register variables can boost performance by reducing the number of times the program has to access the computer's slower and less accessible memory circuits. Register variables can help optimize a program's performance by giving the CPU direct access to a program's key values.

> **Note:** Borland C++, Microsoft C/C++, Turbo C++, and Zortech C++ use register variables by default for the first one or more local variables declared in a function. Other C++ (and many C) compilers do the same; therefore, a local variable might be placed in a register even if you *don't* use the register keyword. By *not* using the register keyword, you let the compiler decide which values to place in registers, and the code may actually run faster than if you choose register variables yourself. Using register variables correctly is a tricky business. The only reliable way to decide whether one is appropriate is to test the code extensively. Also, never write programs that rely on values stored in specific registers.

Listing 3.6 demonstrates register variables and shows how to use register's opposite, volatile, when you *don't* want C++ to store a value in a processor register. The program counts from 1 to 100 twice, first using a register variable k (line 16) and then using a volatile (nonregister) variable at line 25.

## Listing 3.6. REG.CPP.

```
 1:  // reg.cpp -- Register variable demonstration
 2:
 3:  #include <tscdefs.h>
 4:  #include IOSTREAM_H
 5:  #include IOMANIP_H
 6:
 7:  void useregister(void);
 8:  void usevolatile(void);
 9:
10:  main()
11:  {
12:    useregister();
13:    usevolatile();
14:    return 0;
15:  }
16:
17:  void useregister(void)
18:  {
19:    register int k;
20:
21:    cout << "\nCounting with a register variable\n";
22:    for (k = 1; k <= 100; k++)
23:      cout << setw(8) << dec << k;
24:  }
25:
26:  void usevolatile(void)
27:  {
28:    volatile int k;
29:
30:    cout << "\nCounting with a volatile variable\n";
31:    for (k = 1; k <= 100; k++)
32:      cout << setw(8) << dec << k;
33:  }
```

When you run REG.CPP, you'll probably notice no difference in speed between the two functions `useregister()` and `usevolatile()`. This goes to show that register variables are beneficial only in critical places. Most of the time, it won't make much difference if a value is stored in memory or in a register.

Be aware also that register variables can have other consequences. In Chapter 4, for instance, you'll learn how to find a variable's address in memory. Because a register variable isn't stored in memory, it doesn't have an address and it won't be possible for statements to refer to the variable by its location.

Use `volatile` for values that must be stored in memory, either because you need to find the addresses of those values or because other statements may change a local variable in ways that C++ will not know about. For example, if an external event such as a subroutine activated by an interrupt stores values in memory, those values must not be stored in registers.

Use `register` variables for a `for`-loop's control variable or in the conditional expression for a `while` statement that must run at top speed. But don't expect too much from `register`—it's no cure-all for a poor design, and using it does not guarantee a boost in performance.

> **Note:** The `register` keyword is available in all modern C++ (and C) compilers. Obviously, however, different computer systems have different registers, and a program that relies on values being placed in a processor register may not run correctly if ported to another system. Remember that using `register` does not guarantee that a value will be stored in a register.

# Static Variables

Earlier, I stressed that local variables are temporary—they exist only while their declaring function is active, and they do not retain their values between calls to that function.

Rules are made to be broken, and you can break this one by declaring a local variable `static`. A `static` variable is local to its function, but like a global variable, it is stored in a fixed memory location. For this reason, a `static` variable retains its values between calls to a function. Unlike normal local variables, a `static` variable is initialized only one time (provided that initialization is included in the variable's definition).

An example helps to show the difference between a static and a plain local variable. Run Listing 3.7, STATIC.CPP, to execute two for loops that call two functions, next1() and next2(). As you can see, although the loops and functions are nearly identical, their output is different.

## Listing 3.7. STATIC.CPP.

```
 1:  // static.cpp -- Demonstrate static variables
 2:
 3:  #include <tscdefs.h>
 4:  #include IOSTREAM_H
 5:
 6:  int next1(void);
 7:  int next2(void);
 8:
 9:  main()
10:  {
11:    int i;
12:
13:    cout << "\nCalling next1():\n";
14:    for (i = 1; i <= 10; i++)
15:      cout << " " << next1();
16:    cout << "\nCalling next2():\n";
17:    for (i = 1; i <= 10; i++)
18:      cout << " " << next2();
19:    return 0;
20:  }
21:
22:  int next1(void)
23:  {
24:    static int value = 1;      // Static variable
25:    return value++;
26:  }
27:
28:  int next2(void)
29:  {
30:    int value = 1;             // Normal local variable
31:    return value++;
32:  }
```

The first for loop (lines 14–15) calls next1(), which declares an int variable value as static (line 24). It also initializes this variable to 1, an action that occurs only the first time the function runs. The function returns value++ at line 24, passing the value of value back to the calling statement and then incrementing value. Because the static variable retains its value between calls to next1(), the for loop displays 1 2 3 4 5 6 7 8 9 10.

The second for loop (lines 17–18) calls next2() (lines 28–32), which also declares an int variable value, but leaves out the static keyword. Because of this, value in next2() exists only temporarily and does not retain its value between function calls. The result of value++ at line 31 is thrown out when the function ends. When the for loop calls next2() again, the function recreates space for value and again initializes that space to 1. This second loop displays 1 1 1 1 1 1 1 1 1 1, proving that the pure local value does not retain its value between function calls.

> **Note:** A static variable is stored in a fixed location in memory. For this reason, you should use static sparingly. Unlike plain local variables, which exist temporarily and can share the same memory on the stack, all static variables in a program take up permanent storage which is not available for any other purpose while the program runs.

# Functions that Return Values

The previous sample program (Listing 3.7, STATIC.CPP), used a return statement to pass a value back to the caller of a function. Until now, most functions in this book were declared as void, meaning they return no value:

```
void centerText(int x, int y);
```

Declaring function centerText() as void tells the compiler that this function does not pass any value back to its callers. To use a function declared with a void return value, simply type its name in a statement, supplying values for any arguments in parentheses:

```
centerText(10, 15);
```

Other kinds of functions perform calculations and return the results for use by other statements. For example, let's say you need a function that sums three integers. You could declare the function's prototype like this:

```
int threesum(int a, int b, int c);
```

The `int` data type replaces the `void` you've seen in other prototypes. Typing `int` in front of the function name tells the compiler that `threesum()` *returns* an `int` value. Because the function returns a value, its name can appear inside an expression such as

```
int sum = threesum(10, 18, 25);
```

The effect of this is to call `threesum()` with the three arguments 10, 18, and 25. After the function finishes, it passes the result (10 + 18 + 25) back to the caller. That value is then assigned to `sum`, an `int` variable.

In order for all of this to work, `threesum()` has to perform its job correctly. It has to add the three arguments and return the result, using a `return` statement this way:

```
int threesum(int a, int b, int c)
{
  return (a + b + c);
}
```

The parentheses around the `return` statement's expression are optional. You could also write that statement as

```
return a + b + c;
```

When the function runs, it adds a + b + c and uses `return` to pass that sum back to the caller. Many statements can call `threesum()` with any three values to add, and the function will faithfully sum those values and pass back the result.

Functions that return values are useful to solve all sorts of problems. Many times, functions that return values perform mathematical operations, but there are exceptions. A function might return a pointer to a variable (see chapter 4), or it might return an error code. For example, it's typical to declare a function like this:

```
int openFiles(void);   // Returns true if successful
```

This function executes `return (1)` if it's successful. If the function encounters an error, it executes `return (0)`, passing back C++'s value for false. Without filling in every detail, the function's body might be coded along these lines:

```
int openFiles(void)
{
```

```
unsigned errorCode;   // > 0 = error
...   // Statements that "open files"
return (errorCode == 0);
}
```

The function declares a local variable errorCode, in which other statements (not shown) store a value representing any errors that occur, for example, if a file isn't found on disk. The final statement in openFiles evaluates the expression (errorCode == 0), which is true only if no errors were detected earlier. The result of this expression is passed back to the function's caller by return. Another statement can then call openFiles in an if statement:

```
if (!openFiles()) {
  cout << "\nERROR opening files!\n" << flush;
  exit(1);
}
```

Reading the expression if (!openFiles()) as "if *not* openFiles" or as "if openFiles does *not* succeed" makes the sense of this fragment perfectly clear. By using return to pass a true (1) or false (0) value back to its caller, the function tells the if statement whether the function's actions were successful. The if statement detects any errors, and halts the program if the function fails, giving the program the capability of detecting and dealing with problems.

Commonly, functions return mathematical values. Using a function to perform a calculation and return the result saves space by storing the formula's statements in one place. Other statements that need to use the same formula can then call the function. By building a library of math functions, you can concentrate on writing new code instead of reinventing your formulas every time you begin a new project. If you make a mistake in a function's calculations, you need only fix the problem in one place.

C++ already has many mathematical functions, such as pow() (power) and sin() (sine). These are common enough to warrant a place in the C++ library. Other functions you can create yourself. For example, programs often need to find the *factorial* of a number, which equals the product of all integer values in sequence from 1 to that number. The factorial of 3 is 6 (1 * 2 * 3). The factorial of 8 is 40,320 (8 * 7 * ... * 1), and so on.

Listing 3.8 shows how to write a factorial function and puts that function to good use. For small input values, the program calculates what's known as a *combinatorial coefficient*—a mouthful of a phrase that describes a method of calculating the number of ways to arrange a certain number of items. For example, if you are the manager of an ice cream parlor and you want to know the number of triple-dipper ice cream cones you can make from 28 flavors, you can use the formula for a combinatorial coefficient to calculate the answer.

**Note:** I got the idea for this section from *Innumeracy,* by John Allen Paulos, a superb book on "mathematical illiteracy and its consequences." If you like numbers, don't miss this intriguing book.

## Listing 3.8. COCO.CPP.

```
 1:  // coco.cpp -- Combinatorial coefficients
 2:
 3:  #include <tscdefs.h>
 4:  #include IOMANIP_H
 5:
 6:  long factorial(int number);
 7:
 8:  main()
 9:  {
10:    int i, selections, elements;
11:
12:    cout << "Number of selections? ";
13:    cin >> selections;
14:    cout << "Out of how many elements? ";
15:    cin >> elements;
16:    double answer = elements;
17:    for (i = 1; i < selections; i++)
18:      answer *= --elements;
19:    cout << "Nonunique combinations = " << answer << '\n';
20:    answer /= factorial(selections);
21:    cout << "Unique combinations   = " << answer << '\n';
22:    return 0;
23:  }
24:
```

*continues*

**Listing 3.8. continued**

```
25:  long factorial(int number)
26:  {
27:    long value = 1;
28:
29:    while( number > 1 )
30:      value *= number--;
31:    return value;
32:  }
```

Run COCO and enter two values: the number of selections (3 for the triple-dipper example) and the number of elements from which to make those selections (in this case, the 28 flavors). The program then displays the number of nonunique combinations, or 19,656. This represents the total number of ice cream cones you can make if you consider chocolate-peach-banana to be a *different* flavor than peach-chocolate-banana. This value equals 28 * 27 * 26—the total number of ways to arrange 28 items in groups of three.

However, if you advertise your parlor as having 19,656 flavors, your customers might question whether you have crossed the line that divides truth in advertising from fraud. You probably should promise to supply only the total number of *unique* flavor combinations that can be made from 28 flavors. This value equals the total number of nonunique combinations divided by the factorial of the number of selections (3), or in this case, 3,276 (19,656 / 6). This makes sense if you consider that, for any three flavors, there are exactly 6 ways to arrange the scoops. In other words, if you give each flavor a number from 1 to 3, the list of possible combinations of those three flavors is 1-2-3, 1-3-2, 2-1-3, 2-3-1, 3-1-2, and 3-2-1. That's six ways to make three. Because this holds for all sets of flavors, dividing the total number of nonunique combinations by 6 equals the number of *unique* sets of three flavors that are possible to make from all *nonunique* combinations.

Getting back to C++, this formula is easy to implement by first calculating the number of nonunique combinations (lines 17–18) and dividing that answer by the factorial of the number of selections (line 20). The `factorial()` function at lines 25–32 is a good example of a mathematical function that returns a value to its caller:

```
long factorial(int number)
{
  long value = 1;
```

```
  while (number > 1)
    value *= number--;
  return value;
}
```

Examine the function closely and be sure you understand how it operates. The function receives a value (number) from its caller. It declares one local variable (value) initialized to 1. A while loop cycles while number > 1 and during each of those cycles, it multiplies value * number, assigning the result of that expression back to value and reducing number on each pass. You should recognize the shorthand used in this statement, but in case you're struggling with this, here is the equivalent of value *= number — written "the hard way:"

```
value = value * number;
number = number - 1;
```

The final statement in factorial() executes return value, which passes the result of value back to the function's caller. Because value is a local variable inside factorial(), it doesn't exist outside the function, and you may wonder how it's possible for a function to pass such a value back. The answer is that a function makes a *copy* of the value that it passes back via return. It's not the actual *variable* value that gets passed, but only a copy of that value. As a result, a statement can use factorial() in an expression:

```
answer /= factorial(selections);
```

When C++ executes that line, it calls factorial with the current value of selections. The function takes that value, calculates its factorial, and returns the result. C++ then finishes the statement by dividing answer by the value returned by the function. The statement then assigns the final result of the calculation to answer.

As you can see here, functions are great for hiding messy implementation details. Instead of having to write yet another while loop, store the result of that calculation in a temporary variable, and then use that value to compute the answer, the statement simply calls factorial() as though the function was a native C++ command. Using the function lets you forget about how that function is implemented. The details are hidden, and you don't have to think about them. You can assume that factorial() gives the correct answer and use the function directly in statements.

When coding complex expressions, using functions this way can reduce a program's complexity and also help ensure that the code works correctly. Of course, if your functions are buggy, any expressions that use them might give wrong results.

Most of the time, however, if you take the time to test your functions thoroughly, you'll find that using numerous functions is a good way to write programs that run correctly the first time through.

> **Note:** Function-return values might be stored temporarily on the stack, in some other memory, or in one or more CPU registers. C++ doesn't guarantee anything about the locations of return values. However, a compiler manual will usually explain how it implements values returned by functions. Normally, you can ignore these details. After all, one of the reasons for using a high-level language like C++ is to let the compiler do the dirty work like deciding where to store temporary function-return values.

# Parameter Passing

In previous sections, you examined functions that received *arguments* from callers. For example, the factorial() function uses a single argument, a number that the function is to process:

```
long factorial(int number);
```

Inside the function prototype's parentheses is a variable declaration int number. This declaration has the same form as a local variable, except that it doesn't end with a semicolon. As I mentioned earlier, in the prototype, it's not necessary to give the variable a name and you could also write the line this way:

```
long factorial(int);
```

But I prefer to include the name; it helps me remember the purpose of the values I plan to pass to the function. For example, suppose that you need to write a graphics routine to draw a circle. (This is just a hypothetical example—don't bother to compile it.) You might declare the function prototype like this:

```
void circle(int x, int y, int diameter);
```

The three values x, y, and diameter obviously establish the location and size of the circle. Without the names, the prototype is still technically correct, but it's anything but clear:

```
void circle(int, int, int);
```

I'll use named parameters in (almost) all functions from now on. To use the fictitious `circle` function, you must pass as many arguments as declared in `circle`'s prototype. For example, to draw a circle, you might use the statement

```
circle(5, 10, 100);
```

When the function runs, it *receives* the three arguments. At this time, variable x equals 5, y is 10, and `diameter` is 100. The parameters receive their *actual values* from the arguments passed to the function. Keep these key points in mind:

- A function prototype declares the *parameters* that it expects to receive from a caller.

- To call the function, a statement passes *arguments* to the function's parameters, one argument of the correct data type for each declared parameter.

- Inside the function, statements use the named parameters the same way as they use other local variables in the function. When the program runs, the parameters receive copies of the actual values passed to them by callers.

This last point is one of the most important concepts to learn about function parameters. Normally, a function receives a *copy* of any arguments passed to the function's parameters. Returning to the `factorial()` function again, consider what happens in the statement

```
answer /= factorial(selections);
```

This statement passes a copy of the value `selections` to `factorial()` for processing. When the function runs, it retrieves this value from its parameter number. In effect, C++ performs an assignment `number = selections` and then calls `factorial()`. Inside the function, because number now holds a copy of `selections`' value, `factorial()` can change number (it doesn't) without affecting the original `selections`.

# One if by Value; Two if by Reference

Normally, parameters in C++ functions receive copies of values passed as arguments to those functions. As explained in the previous section, if a program calls `factorial` with an expression such as `q = factorial(n)`, and assuming that q is a `long` and n is an `int` variable, you can be 100% certain that `factorial()` does not change the value of n. The function receives a *copy* of n, and it can't reach back and change the original variable's value.

Because function parameters receive copies of argument values, those arguments are said to be "passed by value." The actual variables aren't passed to the function. Only copies of those values are passed. (See Figure 3.2.)

But there are times when you need exactly the opposite capability. For example, suppose you need a function that prompts a user to enter a number. You begin by writing

```
void prompt(int n)
{
  cout << "Enter a value: " << flush;
  cin >> n;   // ???
}
```

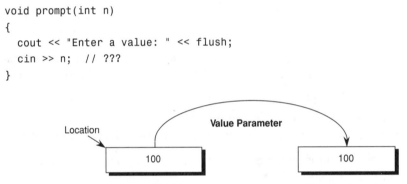

**Figure 3.2.** A value parameter receives a copy of an argument value passed to a function.

Next, you write a statement to call the function, passing it the value of a local variable, perhaps named newvalue:

```
main()
{
  int newvalue;

  prompt(newvalue);   // ???
  cout << "newvalue = " << newvalue << flush;
}
```

The trouble is, prompt receives a copy of newvalue in its parameter n. And, even though the function executes cin >> n to let you enter a value for n, that value is thrown away when the function ends. Remember, like local variables, parameters exist only as long as the function is active. Assigning new values to parameters doesn't change the value of a variable passed to a function as an argument.

**Time out:** By now, you should be able to collect fragments from this text into a file, shape them into the correct forms, and compile them to experiment with the concepts discussed here. If you're not already doing this, start now. Learn to be your own teacher. If you find this hard, start by loading a copy of a program from the diskette that comes with this book. Cut the meat from that program and replace it with the fragments printed here. Remember to add prototypes for all functions before calling them in main or elsewhere. If you get stuck, consult Chapter 10 under the heading "Compiling Your Own Programs."

There are a couple of ways to solve this sticky problem: How can a function pass values back to arguments passed to a function parameter? One solution is to redesign a function like prompt() to return a value, using a prototype such as

```
int prompt(void);
```

And then, back in main(), you could write

```
newvalue = prompt();
```

There's nothing wrong with this approach, except that now, the function has to declare a local variable, read a value into that variable, and use a return statement to pass it back to the caller:

```
int prompt(void)
{
  int temp;   // temporary variable

  cout << "Enter a value: " << flush;
  cin >> temp;
  return (temp);
}
```

That will work, but it seems to require more work than necessary. I also liked that original statement:

```
prompt(newvalue);
```

To my eye, the purpose of this is clear—to prompt somebody to enter a new value. In general, programs that are understandable are easier to fix and maintain, but, the problem remains: How can prompt change newvalue directly? The answer is to pass the parameter by *reference*.

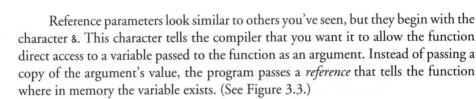

Reference parameters look similar to others you've seen, but they begin with the character &. This character tells the compiler that you want it to allow the function direct access to a variable passed to the function as an argument. Instead of passing a copy of the argument's value, the program passes a *reference* that tells the function where in memory the variable exists. (See Figure 3.3.)

The reference that a function receives is the variable's address. Passing an argument by reference is just another way of saying "passing the address of the argument." With a reference parameter, the new function prototype is

```
void prompt(int &n);
```

And the function's implementation is now

```
void prompt(int &n)
{
  cout << "Enter a value: " << flush;
  cin >> n;
}
```

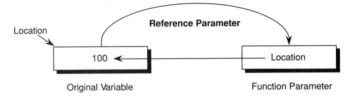

**Figure 3.3.** A reference parameter receives a reference to a variable passed as an argument to a function.

That's much simpler than the previous version, which declared and passed a local variable back in a return statement. The new function simply declares n to be a reference parameter. Because of that, when cin >> n executes, the value you type is assigned directly to the argument passed to prompt. In other words, when main() executes

```
prompt(newvalue);
```

the input stream statement operates as though it were written

```
cin >> newvalue;
```

Another sample program, Listing 3.9, REF.CPP, shows the difference between value and reference parameters. The program prompts twice for you to enter a "new value." Enter 100 each time. Only the second time does the program correctly report the value you enter. As you'll see, a reference parameter makes the difference between code that runs correctly and code that's broken (but not beyond repair).

## Listing 3.9. REF.CPP.

```
 1:  // ref.cpp -- Value and reference parameters
 2:
 3:  #include <tscdefs.h>
 4:  #include IOSTREAM_H
 5:
 6:  void prompt1(int n);
 7:  void prompt2(int &n);
 8:
 9:  main()
10:  {
11:    int newvalue = 0;
12:
13:    prompt1(newvalue);
14:    cout << "After prompt1, newvalue = " << newvalue;
15:    prompt2(newvalue);
16:    cout << "After prompt2, newvalue = " << newvalue;
17:    return 0;
18:  }
19:
20:  void prompt1(int n)
21:  {
22:    cout << "\n\nEnter new value: ";
23:    cin >> n;
24:  }
25:
26:  void prompt2(int &n)
27:  {
28:    cout << "\n\nEnter new value: ";
29:    cin >> n;
30:  }
```

REF has two functions, prompt1() and prompt2(), implemented at lines 20–30 and prototyped at lines 6–7. The functions are identical except for their names and the presence of an & character in front of their single int parameters. In prompt1(), parameter int n is a *value parameter*. When a statement calls the function, it passes a copy of an argument value to the function parameter. In prompt2(), parameter int &n is a *reference parameter*. When a statement calls this function, it passes a reference to the original argument.

Running the program shows what a difference a single character (&) can make. Line 13 calls prompt1(newvalue), passing the value of newvalue to prompt1. When line 23 reads a new value into n, the program simply throws that value away without changing the original newvalue. But, when line 15 makes a similar call to prompt2(newvalue), line 29 also reads a new value into n. Because that's a reference parameter, this action now stores the value you enter directly back to newvalue.

When you use value and reference parameters, keep these important facts in mind:

- Value parameters (declared without &) receive copies of argument values passed to them.

- Assignments to value parameters in a function *never* change the original argument's values passed to the parameters.

- Reference parameters (declared with &) receive the address of argument values passed to them.

- In a function, assignments to reference parameters change the original arguments' values.

Usually, you can use value and reference parameters in exactly the same ways. But there is a difference. When passing arguments to parameters, you'll sometimes use the names of variables. At other times, you'll pass literal values. For example, suppose you have a function that positions the cursor at an X and Y coordinate on a display. The prototype might look like this:

```
void gotoxy(int x, int y);
```

Because x and y are declared as value parameters, it's possible to pass a mix of variables and literal values to them:

```
int x, y;

x = 5;
y = 10;
gotoxy(x, y);
gotoxy(0, 24);
gotoxy(0, y);
gotoxy(x, 1);
```

The same is not possible with reference parameters, which require an argument to be a variable—in other words, to be stored in a location that has an address. Obviously, this must be so for reference parameters to receive the addresses of arguments passed to them. For that reason, you can pass to reference parameters only arguments that have addresses:

```
void gotoxy(int &x, int &y);
```

Declared that way, only the first of the previous calls to gotoxy would be accepted by the compiler. The calls that specify literal values, such as 0, 24, and 1, are rejected because those values aren't stored in memory. Literal constants do not have addresses; therefore, programs can't pass them to a function's reference parameters.

This leads to a good rule of thumb for deciding whether to use value or reference parameters. If a function needs only the value of arguments to perform a job, value parameters are appropriate. If a function needs to pass values back to a caller, and if doing that with a return statement isn't convenient—for example, to pass back two or more values—reference parameters are probably the best choice.

> **Note:** All function parameters in C are passed by value. C has no equivalent to the reference parameters in C++.

Let's look at a practical use for value and reference parameters. Listing 3.10, BOX.CPP, prompts you to enter four display coordinate values (two pairs of two values). It then draws a box on-screen using the values you enter as the positions of the box's upper left and bottom right corners. You can use similar functions in your own programs to create good-looking displays where text is divided on-screen into neatly outlined boxes.

## Listing 3.10. BOX.CPP.

```cpp
1:   // box.cpp -- Display text boxes
2:
3:   #include <tscdefs.h>
4:   #include IOSTREAM_H
5:   #include DISP_H
6:
7:   void getcoords(int &toprow, int &topcol, int &botrow, int &botcol);
8:   void drawbox(int toprow, int topcol, int botrow, int botcol);
9:
10:  main()
11:  {
12:    int toprow, topcol, botrow, botcol;
13:
14:    disp_open();
15:    getcoords(toprow, topcol, botrow, botcol);
16:    disp_move(0, 0);
17:    disp_eeop();
18:    drawbox(toprow, topcol, botrow, botcol);
19:    disp_move(24, 0);
20:    disp_close();
21:    return 0;
22:  }
23:
24:  void getcoords(int &toprow, int &topcol, int &botrow, int &botcol)
25:  {
26:    cout << "\nEnter top row and column (ex: 3 7): ";
27:    cin >> toprow >> topcol;
28:    cout << "Enter bottom row and column (ex: 20 64): ";
29:    cin >> botrow >> botcol;
30:  }
31:
32:  void drawbox(int toprow, int topcol, int botrow, int botcol)
33:  {
34:    disp_box(0, DISP_NORMAL, toprow, topcol, botrow, botcol);
35:  }
```

In addition to showing off value and reference parameters, BOX demonstrates another way to display text on-screen. The method, which I'll use in other listings, employs Zortech C++'s display package. To make the package's commands available, you must include the disp.h header file as BOX does at line 5.

**Note:** Chapter 10, "Cross-Compilation Tools," describes how I implemented the Zortech C++ display package for Borland C++, Turbo C++, and Microsoft C/C++. To use the display package in a way that permits programs to compile with all of these compilers, #include DISP_H as shown at line 5. You also must include tscdefs.h, as shown at line 3. If you are using Zortech C++, then you can #include disp.h directly.

After that, you're ready to use display commands to write text to the screen. Unlike other methods you've examined for this purpose, the display package lets you display all 256 characters available on PCs, including the normal ASCII set plus various Greek letters, line-drawing shapes, and other symbols that are useful for creating good-looking screens. (Another program in this chapter, ASC.CPP, Listing 3.15, uses the display package to show the full set of extended ASCII symbols available on most PCs.)

To use the display package, you first have to initialize it. This detects the type of display on your computer, and prepares other internal variables to let your programs run under a variety of conditions. You don't need to select among various display types. Just call disp_open() before using most other display commands. For example, to initialize the display package, clear the display, move the cursor to midscreen, display a message, and quit with the cursor on the bottom line, you can write

```
#include <tscdefs.h>
#include DISP_H
main()
{
  disp_open();                      // Initialize display package
  disp_move(0, 0);                  // Send cursor to row 0, col 0
  disp_eeop();                      // Erase to end of page
  disp_move(12, 32);                // Send cursor to row 12, col 32
  disp_printf("Display package");   // Display some text
  disp_move(24, 0);                 // Send cursor to last row
  disp_close();                     // Close display package
}
```

This is a complete program. You can type it into your editor, save it, compile, and run. (Be sure to link non-Zortech C++ programs to TSCxxx.LIB, however, as explained in the Introduction.) The comments explain what each line does. I'll explain other display-package functions as needed for future listings.

In BOX.CPP, examine the function prototypes at lines 7–8. Notice that the functions getcoords() and drawbox() declare the same four parameters. However, in getcoords(), the parameters are passed by reference (declared with &). In drawbox(), the parameters are passed by value (no &). The reason for this should be obvious: The purpose of getcoords() is to *return* (get) new values for each of its four parameters; the purpose of drawbox() is only to use those values, not to change them.

Lines 24–30 show how getcoords() directly enters new values into the argument variables passed to the function from line 15. Because getcoords()' parameters are passed by reference, the input statements directly change the original argument variables passed to the function.

Lines 32–35 use copies of those values to draw a box on-screen. Function drawbox() doesn't need to pass any values back to its caller, so value parameters are appropriate here. To display a box on-screen, line 34 calls disp_box(), another function in the display package. The first argument to disp_box() selects the box's type; try values from 0 to 4 to see the different styles available. The second argument to disp_box() selects the kind of display mode. Replace DISP_NORMAL with DISP_REVERSEVIDEO to change the box's display attribute (or color on a color monitor). The last four arguments represent the box's coordinates.

Because drawbox() declares value parameters, you can also pass literal values to the function. For example, load BOX.CPP into your editor and insert this line just after the drawbox() statement at line 18:

```
drawbox(0, 0, 24, 79);
```

If drawbox() declared its parameters to be passed by reference, the compiler would not accept that statement. However, because the parameters are passed by value, literal values are okay. The effect is to draw another box around the display's borders and around (or on top of) the box you defined by entering coordinate values to the prompts.

# Default Arguments

In everyday terms, a default argument might be one that you have regularly with your boss or a "friend" at work, but in C++, a *default argument* is a parameter that a caller to a function doesn't have to supply. Default arguments might also be named optional parameters. If you pass a value to one, it uses that value. If you don't pass a value to an optional parameter, it uses a default value as the argument.

This is a very useful device, especially when designing functions that perform one way in the absence of certain input, but do something else on demand. For example, here's a function named dashes that displays a certain number of dash characters at any screen location:

```
void dashes(int row, int col, int num, int c = '-');
```

The function's prototype specifies four int values. The first two, row and col, let you choose where the first dash is to appear. Next, num holds the number of dashes to display at this location. And the final parameter is the character to use. In addition to the usual data type (int) and variable name (c), the parameter declaration includes an assignment and a default literal value (= '-'). C++ interprets this construction to mean "if the caller supplies an argument for this parameter, use that argument's value; otherwise, use the default value specified in the declaration."

You can now call dashes in one of two ways. First, to display 40 dashes at row 4, you can write

```
dashes(4, 0, 40);
```

Even though the function prototype specifies four parameters, because the last parameter includes a default argument value, you don't have to supply that value when calling the function. In this case, C++ compiles the program as though you had written

```
dashes(4, 0, 40, '-');
```

However, if you want to change the character used by the function, you can write

```
dashes(4, 0, 40, '+');
```

The explicit argument overrides the default specified in the prototype. Now, the function will display plus signs instead of dashes.

When implementing a function prototype that declares default arguments, don't repeat the assignments. Just write the function as you normally would if none of the parameters had default argument values. For example, here's one way to implement the dashes function:

```
void dashes(int row, int col, int num, int c)
{
  disp_move(row, col);
  while (—num >= 0)
    disp_putc(c);
}
```

The default assignment to c appears only in the prototype, not in the implementation's function declaration. A few other rules to memorize when using default arguments are:

- Default arguments must be passed by value. A default argument's name can't be passed by reference (prefaced with an & character).

- Default argument values (the n in the declaration int x = n) may be literal values or const definitions. They may *not* be variables. In other words, if n were declared int n, int x = n would be rejected as a default parameter. If n is declared as const int n = 1, the declaration will be accepted.

- All default arguments must come last in the function prototype. After the first default argument, all subsequent arguments must also include default values.

This last point is important and also has implications that affect how programs can call functions with default arguments. A small example helps to explain the rule:

```
void f(int width, float v = 3.14159, char q = '$');
```

Although it's just for demonstration, function f shows a typical case that uses default parameters. The first parameter, width, could not be declared anywhere else. Placing it between v and q, or at the end of the parameter list, is not allowed. Both of f's default parameters come last in the parameter list, as they must.

When calling f, a program must specify a width. You always have to supply argument values for a function's normal parameters. But, a program has the option of including v and q. These are legal calls:

```
f(10);
f(10, 5.5);
f(10, 5.5, '@');
```

The first call specifies no overriding values for the default arguments. The second specifies a value for v, overriding the default assignment of 3.14159. The third overrides both defaults, also specifying a character '@' for q in place of its default '$'. However, the following sort of call is not allowed:

```
f(10, , '#');   // ???
```

The compiler rejects this statement because it attempts to skip one of the default parameters. In all cases, C++ requires you to supply overriding values for all default arguments starting with any one of those declared by the function. You can't skip others in between. If a function prototype is declared like this:

```
void g(int a = 1, int b = 2, int c = 3, int d = 4);
```

then you have the option to use any of these function calls:

```
g();
g(9);
g(9, 8);
g(9, 8, 7);
g(9, 8, 7, 6);
```

However, there is no way to supply override values, say, to parameters a and d while skipping b and c. Unfortunately, this does not compile:

```
g(9, , , 6);    // ???
```

**Note:** I surely wish that C++ default parameters allowed skipping arguments by accepting place-holding commas as in that dysfunctional sample. If they worked this way, default function arguments would be much more useful.

Another good use for default parameters is to add new parameters to existing function declarations without having to modify programming that calls those functions. For example, suppose that you are writing a simulation of an audio circuit, and you write this function and declaration:

```
#define MAXVOLUME 100
void setVolume(int level);
```

You call this function from a dozen or more statements strewn throughout various modules. The function sets the simulation's volume level, limiting it to the MAXVOLUME constant. Later, you discover that you need to add a *variable* maximum; therefore, the constant is no longer useful. One solution is to make MAXVOLUME a global variable, but that's not usually wise because it makes the variable too accessible to other statements, and might cause a bug to creep into the code. Another is to add a parameter to setVolume():

```
void setVolume(int level, int maxLevel);
```

Now, you also have to hunt through the source text and change every use of setVolume() to include an argument for the new parameter. A better plan is to give maxLevel a default value:

```
void setVolume(int level, int maxLevel = MAXVOLUME);
```

After making this alteration, you can write new statements like setVolume(n, 50) to change a volume and limit it to 50. Previous statements such as setVolume(quiet) work as they did before, giving maxLevel the default value specified by the constant MAXVOLUME.

> **Note:** There are other ways to deal with modifications to programs that help keep existing code intact—a good idea for preventing bugs. (You know: "if it isn't broken, don't fix it.") I'll explain more about the subject in Chapters 5 and 9, which cover object-oriented programming techniques and a feature in C++ called *overloading*.

As a final example of default arguments, Listing 3.11, CENTER.CPP, demonstrates a useful function that centers text on the display. You can copy this function into your own programs to display titles, prompts, for help screens, and so forth.

### Listing 3.11. CENTER.CPP

```
 1:  // center.cpp -- Center text on-screen
 2:
 3:  #include <tscdefs.h>
 4:  #include IOSTREAM_H
 5:  #include DISP_H
 6:  #include <string.h>
 7:
 8:  #define MAX_LEN 64
 9:
10:  void center(int row, int col, char *s, int width = 0, int fill = '-');
11:
12:  char s[MAX_LEN];      // String to center
13:
14:  main()
15:  {
16:    int length;    // Length of string
17:
18:  // Prompt for a string to center
19:    cout << "Enter a string: ";
```

```
20:    cin.get(s, MAX_LEN, '\n');
21:    length = strlen(s);      // Get length of string
22:
23:  // Prepare display
24:    disp_open();
25:    disp_move(0, 0);
26:    disp_eeop();
27:
28:  // Display string using all defaults
29:    center(10, 40, s);
30:
31:  // Display string with only fill default
32:    center(12, 40, s, length + 8);
33:
34:  // Display string with no defaults
35:    center(14, 40, s, length + 16, '*');
36:
37:    disp_move(24, 0);
38:    disp_close();
39:    return 0;
40:  }
41:
42:  void center(int row, int col, char *s, int width, int fill)
43:  {
44:    int wd2;     // Width divided by 2
45:    int c;       // for-loop control variable
46:
47:    if (width > 0) {
48:      wd2 = width / 2;
49:      for (c = col - wd2; c <= col + wd2; c++)
50:        disp_pokew(row, c, (DISP_NORMAL * 256) + fill);
51:    }
52:    disp_move(row, col - (strlen(s) / 2));
53:    disp_printf(s);
54:  }
```

Function center in CENTER.CPP (lines 42–54) makes good use of default parameters. As the prototype at line 10 shows, the width and fill arguments are optional. Unless you supply override values for these items, the width will default to 0 and the fill character will be a dash '-'. To use the function to center text on-screen, execute a statement such as

```
center(10, 40, " C++ Primer ");
```

**193**

That will display the string in quotes at row 10. The center of the string will be at column 40. To surround the quote with dashes, use a statement like this:

```
center(10, 40, " C++ Primer ", 24);
```

Supplying the width argument 24 displays dashes around the string. The two extra blanks inside quotes make a nicer title line:

```
----- C++ Primer ------
```

By overriding both of the default argument values, you can control the width of the string and the character used at each end. For example, to display asterisks rather than dashes, you can write

```
center(10, 40, " C++ Primer ", 24, '*');
```

Study how the center() function works (lines 42–54 in CENTER.CPP). The function first checks whether width is greater than 0; it will be only if a statement overrides that default value. If width is greater than 0, a for loop calls disp_pokew() to insert a character into the display. (I'll explain more about this function later.) Lines 52–53 then display the string passed to the function on top of any characters drawn with the previous for loop.

You won't use default arguments all the time, but as these samples show, the arguments are useful for designing functions that operate in different ways depending on the values you pass to them. If a parameter isn't always needed, consider making it optional by giving it a default value in the function's prototype. This can go a long way toward making functions easier to use.

# Recursion: Programming with Mirrors

Computers owe their existence, in part, to the need for putting things in order. Today, modern computers of all kinds spend a good bit of their time sorting data. Most database programs include instructions to sort records alphabetically on a text field or numerically on a field such as a ZIP code or a customer balance.

C++ has a sorting function that I'll explain how to use in Chapter 9. It's instructive, however, to write your own sorting function, and it's useful to have one in your personal library for the times when you don't want to use the standard code in the library.

One of the most famous sorting *algorithms* is called *Quicksort*, and it was invented by C. A. R. Hoare. (For those who are getting started with programming, an *algorithm* is a method for solving a problem and is often described in step-by-step terms that are suitable for converting to computer language statements.) Basically, the Quicksort algorithm divides a set of data over and over, matches items in pairs, and swaps items repeatedly until all items are in order.

There are many ways to implement a Quicksort algorithm in a computer program, but one of the simplest uses a concept known as *recursion*. Recursion is what happens when a function calls itself during the course of its own actions. At first, the idea of a function calling itself may strike you as strange, but there's nothing magical about it, and it's a useful technique to know.

**Note:** For a complete description of the Quicksort and other sorting algorithms, see Donald E. Knuth's *The Art of Computer Programming,* Vol. 3, *Sorting and Searching,* Addison Wesley.

A simple program demonstrates how to use recursion to count from 1 to 10—nothing exciting, but a good way to learn what recursion is. Compile and run Listing 3.12, RECOUNT.CPP. See whether you can figure out how it works before reading the descriptions that follow the listing.

### Listing 3.12. RECOUNT.CPP.

```
1:  // recount.cpp -- Count from 1 to 10 using recursion
2:
3:  #include <tscdefs.h>
4:  #include IOSTREAM_H
5:  #include IOMANIP_H
6:
7:  void recount(int top);
8:
```

*continues*

**Listing 3.12. continued**

```
 9:  main()
10:  {
11:    recount(10);
12:    return 0;
13:  }
14:
15:  void recount(int top)
16:  {
17:    if (top > 1)
18:      recount(top - 1);
19:    cout << setw(4) << dec << top << flush;
20:  }
```

Look closely at function recount() at lines 15–20. Line 17 tests the value of parameter top. If that value is greater than 1, the statement calls recount()—the same function that is now executing. For this call, the program passes to the function the result of the expression top - 1.

When a function calls itself this way, it starts over from the top. The same physical code in memory runs again, but because local variables and parameters are created on the stack when a function runs, a completely new set of those variables and parameters is reserved for each recursive call.

When the recursively called function ends, it picks up where it left off at the place where the function called itself. This action resembles what you see when you look into a mirror when there's another mirror behind you. The endless series of reflections are caused by mirror A reflecting mirror B, which reflects mirror A's reflection, which reflects B's, and so on.

Unlike light's capacity to shine, a computer's stack can grow only so large, and too many recursive calls can quickly lead to a stack overflow by reserving too many fresh sets of variables and parameters for each recursion. When using recursion, you must be certain to provide a well-lighted exit, in this case, the if statement at line 17.

Think this through. Suppose you call the function with recount(3). When recount() calls itself, it passes the value of top - 1. When the function begins again, the freshly allocated top argument now equals 2. Because 2 is larger than 1, the if statement again calls recount(). Again it passes top - 1 as the argument. On this third restart of recount(), top equals 1. This time, however, the if statement fails, causing the program to *fall through* to the output stream statement at line 19. That statement displays the value of top, which now equals 1. Then the function ends, causing the previous call to the function to pick up where it left off, executing the output statement and displaying the value of top as it was on that level, or 2. This repeats again and again until reaching the bottom level of function calls, displaying the initial value for top, or 3. The result is to display 1 2 3.

When you run RECOUNT, you'll see that it displays the numbers 1 through 10. To count up to higher values, change the starting value in line 11. (If you use a value that's too high, the computer might run out of stack space, which in extreme cases, could force you to reboot, although that probably won't happen.)

Now that you have an idea of how recursion works, let's see it in action in a more useful setting. Listing 3.13, SORTER.CPP, demonstrates one way to sort an array of values. You can use similar methods in programs to sort other kinds of data.

## Listing 3.13. SORTER.CPP.

```
 1:  // sorter.cpp -- Array sorter
 2:
 3:  #include <tscdefs.h>
 4:  #include IOSTREAM_H
 5:  #include IOMANIP_H
 6:  #include <stdlib.h>
 7:  #include <time.h>
 8:
 9:  #define ARRAYSIZE 100
10:
11:  void fillArray(void);
12:  void displayArray(char *s);
13:  void quicksort(int left, int right);
14:  void sortArray(int n);
15:
16:  int array[ARRAYSIZE];       // Array of integers
17:
18:  main()
19:  {
20:    fillArray();
21:    displayArray("Before");
22:    sortArray(ARRAYSIZE);
23:    displayArray("After");
24:    return 0;
25:  }
```

*continues*

## Listing 3.13. continued

```
26:
27:  // Fill global array with values taken at random
28:  void fillArray(void)
29:  {
30:    int i;
31:
32:    srand((unsigned)time(NULL));        // Randomize generator
33:    for (i = 0; i < ARRAYSIZE; i++)     // Fill array
34:      array[i] = rand();
35:  }
36:
37:  // Display contents of array before and after sorting
38:  void displayArray(char *s)
39:  {
40:    int i;
41:
42:    cout << '\n' << s << " sorting:\n";
43:    for (i = 0; i < ARRAYSIZE; i++)
44:      cout << setw(8) << dec << array[i] << flush;
45:  }
46:
47:  // Quicksort algorithm by C. A. R. Hoare
48:  void quicksort(int left, int right)
49:  {
50:    int i = left;
51:    int j = right;
52:    int test = array[(left + right) / 2];
53:    int swap;
54:
55:    do {
56:      while (array[i] < test) i++;
57:      while (test < array[j]) j--;
58:      if (i <= j) {
59:        swap = array[i];
60:        array[i] = array[j];
61:        array[j] = swap;
62:        i++;
63:        j--;
64:      }
```

```
65:    } while (i <= j);
66:    if (left < j) quicksort(left, j);
67:    if (i < right) quicksort(i, right);
68:  }
69:
70:  // Sort n elements in global array
71:  void sortArray(int n)
72:  {
73:    if (n > 1) quicksort(0, n - 1);
74:  }
```

The key feature to observe about SORTER is the way lines 66 and 67 call the quicksort() function recursively. These two statements are *inside* quicksort(); therefore, calling quicksort() from these locations causes the function to start over from the top with a brand new set of local variables and parameters. The if statements in the recursive calls provide the well-lighted exits that prevent the function from calling itself "forever," that is, until running out of stack space.

SORTER defines a global array at line 16, which it fills with values selected at random in function fillArray() (lines 28–35). In that function, line 32 calls srand() to "seed" a random-number generator. This scrambles the generator's starting value so that rand() produces a different sequence each time the program runs. If the program didn't perform this step, the values from rand() at line 34 would be the same for each new run. To use the srand() and rand() functions, include the stdlib.h and time.h headers as shown at lines 6–7.

**Note:** It may strike you as odd that random sequences may be repeated each time you run a program. Doesn't that mean they aren't random? The answer is no. A random sequence is "random" if values in that sequence can't be predicted from previous values. Numeric sequences are "random" simply because they follow no ordained pattern.

Line 34 assigns a value selected at random to the global array variable, one value for each space in the array. Function rand() returns an integer value. Calling it returns the next number from the current random sequence.

After filling the array and displaying its initial values (see function `displayArray()` at lines 38–45), the program calls `quicksort()` to rearrange the values in the array. By comparing values and exchanging those that are out of order—and by dividing the array into sections to avoid examining the same pairs of values too many times, which would slow the action considerably—the function puts the array of values into numeric order. Finally, the program displays the same array, showing its contents after sorting.

# Inline Functions

C alling functions takes time—not much time, but enough to make a difference in performance when a program calls a function many thousands of times. To call a function, the compiled program has to save the address of the current location on the stack. It also has to "push" onto the stack any argument values needed by the function. Finally, the code executes a `call` assembly language instruction to start the function's ball rolling.

You don't need to know all those underlying details about function calls to write most C++ programs. Just be aware that, when all those details are taken together, they waste time. In critical applications, you may be able to eliminate some of the overhead associated with function calls by declaring them `inline`.

An `inline` function may contain any statements and perform any actions that normal functions can. Unlike a normal function, however, the `inline` variety does not have a prototype, and it's usually declared before `main()`. That's not a requirement; `inline` functions need to be declared only before they are used, not necessarily before `main()`. But they are usually stored in header files, and because those files are usually included into a program before `main()`, this is the most common place to insert `inline` functions.

To create an `inline` function, insert the `inline` keyword in front of a normal function declaration and body. For example, here is an `inline` function that adds 10 to a parameter n:

```
inline int add10(int n) { return (n + 10); }
```

Let's take that one element at a time. First, comes the `inline` keyword. Next, comes the function declaration (`int add10(int n)`), which is no different than other declarations you've seen. The function returns an `int` value, and it specifies one parameter, `int n`.

The major difference is the body of the function, which appears immediately after the declaration. The statement inside braces returns the result of the expression (n + 10). In a larger inline function, there could be more than one statement, with each statement terminated by a semicolon. Notice the semicolon at the end of the single statement in this sample. Some people are confused by this because there is no semicolon after the brace. If you examine the same code written in the usual one-line-per-element style, you'll see that it's no different from the single-line version:

```
inline int add10(int n)
{
  return (n + 10);
}
```

I wrote the inline() sample on one line because that's the style most C++ programmers prefer. But there's no technical reason for writing the code that way, and you can type inline functions on multiple lines if you want.

When the compiler encounters a statement that uses an inline function, as in this sample,

```
int x;
x = add10(5);
```

instead of calling add10() as it would for a normal function, the compiler inserts the function's body *directly into the program.* In other words, the compiler *expands* the second line of this example as though it had been written

```
x = 5 + 10;
```

This is a silly example, of course, but you can see that processing the expression 5 + 10 in line with the rest of the program takes less time than calling a function with all its associated overhead.

Most of the time, you'll use inline functions inside a for or other loop that executes many times and that must run as fast as possible. For another example, compile and run Listing 3.14, CONE.CPP.

## Listing 3.14. CONE.CPP.

```
1:  // cone.cpp -- Use an inline function to find the volume of a cone
2:
3:  #include <tscdefs.h>
4:  #include IOSTREAM_H
```

*continues*

## Listing 3.14. continued

```
 5:
 6:   #define Pi 3.14159265
 7:
 8:   inline float cone(float radius, float height)
 9:     { return ((Pi * (radius * radius) * height) / 3.0); }
10:
11:   main()
12:   {
13:     float radius, height, volume;
14:
15:     cout << "Enter cone's radius at base: ";
16:     cin >> radius;
17:     cout << "Enter cone's height: ";
18:     cin >> height;
19:     volume = cone(radius, height);
20:     cout << "Cone's volume = " << volume;
21:     return 0;
22:   }
```

Lines 8–9 declare an `inline` function that calculates the volume of a cone. After prompting you for the cone's radius and height (lines 15–18), the statement at line 19 assigns the result of the `cone()` function to a variable `volume`, which the program displays in an output statement at line 20.

Instead of calling `cone()`, however, at line 19, C++ expands the inline function by replacing the expression to the right of the equal sign with the instructions declared in the function back at line 9. As in the previous examples, this use of `inline` functions isn't required here; a few milliseconds (or however much time it takes) difference between calling a function and expanding its statements in line will hardly matter, and `cone()` may as well be a regular function.

Don't hesitate, however, to use `inline` functions if you need to give a loop the sharpest possible edge in performance. When doing so, be aware of these restrictions and suggestions:

- The compiler might ignore the `inline` keyword. Usually, it will do this if you try to create an `inline` function that is too large. The exact limit is difficult to predict, but if your `inline` functions exceed a few statements, C++ might convert them to regular functions.

- Numerous `inline` functions can greatly expand the final size of a compiled program. If you call a large `inline` function 100 times, the compiler faithfully expands that function in 100 places!

- If you are familiar with C, you have probably used macros to create instructions that are roughly similar to C++ `inline` functions. In most cases, `inline` functions are easier to write than macros, and the type checking of parameters—which, for example, ensures that you don't use a floating-point value where only an integer is allowed—gives the program an added measure of safety.

- Remember that the benefits from `inline` functions are likely to be small except in the most critical of applications. Don't make the mistake of converting all functions to the `inline` kind. This is *not* a good way to optimize most programs for better performance.

# Turning Point

Y ou'll be pleased (and maybe a tad surprised) to learn that you've now passed the halfway mark in your quest for learning C++. In fact, you're further than halfway. You've already met most all there is to know about C++ fundamentals, and you've seen most of the tools in action that you'll use to write your own C++ programs.

Don't be *too* surprised, though. C++ is a terse language with only the minimum number of native features required to write programs. That doesn't mean that C++ is simple-minded. C++'s relatively simple set of fundamental commands can be combined in unlimited ways, and you haven't learned about two of C++'s more advanced features: pointers and classes, which I'll cover in the next two chapters.

Before doing that, however, this is a good place for you to review what you know about C++ so far. Be sure that all of the material in previous chapters is clear. Run and study the sample listings again, and be sure you understand how they work. Write a few test programs, complete the exercises at the ends of this and the previous two chapters if you haven't done that already. The better you learn the fundamentals in these three chapters, the easier you'll be able to pick up the more advanced material to come.

Listing 3.15, ASC.CPP, is a useful program for marking this turning point in your goal to learn C++. It's the longest program listed so far, and it's a useful utility to boot. Instead of chapter 2's simple ASCII chart displayed by ASCII.CPP

(Listing 2.15), the all new ASC shows all 256 characters available on PC screens. After compiling and running the program, use the cursor keys to highlight any character and see its ASCII value in decimal and hex in the upper right corner. Press Esc to quit.

## Listing 3.15. ASC.CPP.

```
 1:  // asc.cpp -- Interactive ASCII chart
 2:
 3:  #include <tscdefs.h>
 4:  #include DISP_H
 5:  #include <stdio.h>
 6:
 7:  #define ESC 27
 8:  #define TOPROW  3
 9:  #define TOPCOL  7
10:  #define BOTROW 21
11:  #define BOTCOL 73
12:
13:  void showChart(void);
14:  void showASCII(unsigned c, int attrib);
15:  void movecursor(unsigned c);
16:  void showvalues(unsigned c);
17:  int rowasc(unsigned c);
18:  int colasc(unsigned c);
19:
20:  int oldc;  // Previously displayed character
21:
22:  main()
23:  {
24:    unsigned c = 1;  // Currently highlighted character
25:    unsigned key;    // Command from keyboard
26:
27:    disp_open();                      // Initialize display package
28:    showChart();                      // Display ASCII chart
29:    movecursor(c);                    // Initialize cursor position
30:    while ((key = getch()) != ESC) {  // Get user command
31:      switch (key) {
32:        case 'H': c -= 32; break;     // Move up
33:        case 'P': c += 32; break;     // Move down
34:        case 'K': c--; break;         // Move left
35:        case 'M': c++; break;         // Move right
36:      }
```

```
37:      c %= 256;          // Make sure c is in range 0 ... 255
38:      movecursor(c);     // Highlight and report on character c
39:    }
40:    disp_move(24, 0);   // Move cursor to last line before ending
41:    disp_close();       // Close the display package
42:    return 0;
43: }
44:
45: void showChart(void)
46: {
47:    unsigned c = 0;   // for-loop control variable
48:
49: // Clear display
50:
51:    disp_move(0, 0);
52:    disp_eeop();
53:
54: // Display box and ASCII characters inside
55:
56:    disp_box(3, DISP_NORMAL, TOPROW, TOPCOL, BOTROW, BOTCOL);
57:    for (c = 0; c <= 255; c++)
58:      showASCII(c, DISP_NORMAL);
59:
60: // Display other text on-screen
61:
62:    disp_move(TOPROW - 1, TOPCOL);
63:    disp_printf("Cursor keys move; Esc quits");
64:    disp_move(BOTROW + 1, TOPCOL);
65:    disp_printf("Tom Swan's C++ Primer");
66:    disp_move(BOTROW + 1, BOTCOL - 22);
67:    disp_printf("Interactive ASCII Chart");
68: }
69:
70: // Display one ASCII character using a display attribute
71: void showASCII(unsigned c, int attrib)
72: {
73:    disp_pokew(rowasc(c), colasc(c), (attrib * 256) + c);
74: }
75:
76: // Return row number for character cListing 3.15.
```

*continues*

## Listing 3.15. continued

```
 77:   int rowasc(unsigned c)
 78:   {
 79:     return(2 + TOPROW + ((c / 32) * 2));
 80:   }
 81:
 82:   // Return column number for character c
 83:   int colasc(unsigned c)
 84:   {
 85:     return(2 + TOPCOL + ((c % 32) * 2));
 86:   }
 87:
 88:   // Unhighlight old character and highlight a new one
 89:   void movecursor(unsigned c)
 90:   {
 91:     showASCII(oldc, DISP_NORMAL);
 92:     showASCII(c, DISP_REVERSEVIDEO);
 93:     oldc = c;
 94:     showvalues(c);
 95:   }
 96:
 97:   // Display character and its ASCII value in decimal and hex
 98:   // Microsoft C/C++ doesn't reposition cursor after disp_printf()
 99:   //   so I move the cursor manually before calling disp_eeol()
100:
101:   void showvalues(unsigned c)
102:   {
103:     disp_move(TOPROW - 1, TOPCOL + 35);
104:   #if (defined __TSC_MSC__)
105:     int k = disp_printf("Character =     ASCII = %d  %#x", c, c);
106:     disp_move(TOPROW - 1, TOPCOL + 35 + k);
107:   #else
108:     disp_printf("Character =     ASCII = %d  %#x", c, c);
109:   #endif
110:     disp_eeol();
111:     disp_pokew(TOPROW - 1, TOPCOL + 47, (DISP_NORMAL * 256) + c);
112:   }
```

After you read ASC's text, you'll discover that this program is different from earlier examples that simply print a few numbers or display some text and quit. ASC carefully formats the screen. It clears the display of old text. It centers its lines, and it draws a stylish box around the "main action." These items aren't just fluff. Many programs succeed or fail based on how well their interface lets people interact with the program's operation. Later chapters show other ways to design good looking screens with a "class library" of objects for displaying text in pop-up windows—but more on that later.

ASC also takes advantage of C++'s rich function library, including the display-package functions introduced earlier. Statements in ASC are collected into well-named functions, which are short and to the point. This makes the text clear, and you should be able to understand the program by reading the statements a couple of times. Also read the comments as a guide through ASC's operation. If you find any of the statements in ASC unintelligible, you need to go back over this and the previous two chapters. There isn't anything in the program that you haven't met before.

But there are a few areas that might give you a little trouble. One is at line 37, which assigns to c the result of c *modulo* 256. This is just the remainder left after dividing c by 256. Because that remainder has to be a value from 0 to 255, the effect is to limit c's value to that same range. This is a useful trick to remember, and the most frequent reason for using the C++ modulo operator %.

A second element of ASC that needs explanation occurs twice. (Earlier, I promised to explain this.) In function showASCII at line 73, you find the statement

```
disp_pokew(rowasc(c), colasc(c), (attrib * 256) + c);
```

The first two arguments call the two functions rowasc() and colasc(), which together return the row and column coordinate where character c is displayed. The calls to these functions occur *before* the program calls disp_pokew(). It passes the values from those functions to the value parameters declared by disp_pokew(). This is a common use for functions and avoids code like this:

```
int row, col;

row = rowasc(c);
col = colasc(c);
disp_pokew(row, col, ...);
```

Instead of calling the functions and saving their results in variables such as row and col, you can just call the functions and pass their values as arguments directly. However, you can do this only for value parameters. You can't pass a function result (which you should consider to be constant) to a reference parameter. Reference parameters, you'll recall, must refer to an address of a variable somewhere in memory. Function return values don't have defined addresses.

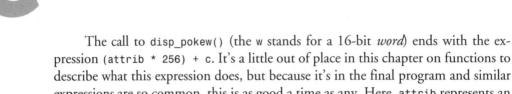
The call to disp_pokew() (the w stands for a 16-bit *word*) ends with the expression (attrib * 256) + c. It's a little out of place in this chapter on functions to describe what this expression does, but because it's in the final program and similar expressions are so common, this is as good a time as any. Here, attrib represents an attribute to use for displaying a character. Various attribute values control the color of characters, or on monochrome screens, whether a character is displayed in bold, is underlined, blinks, and so forth.

Multiplying attrib by 256 has the opposite effect as the modulo expression described earlier. Because the value 256 is a power of 2, multiplying any value by 256 effectively shifts that value into the upper 8 bits of a 16-bit integer. In other words, if attrib equals 7, multiplying that value by 256 equals 1792. In binary, the shifting action is easier to see:

```
    7      0000 0000 0000 0111
x 256      0000 0001 0000 0000
          ─────────────────────
 1792      0000 0111 0000 0000
```

As this shows, the multiplication by 256 shifts the bits that represent 7 in binary to the left eight places, in a sense opening up a hole of eight 0s at the end of the value. Adding the value of a character in the ASCII range 0 to 255 to this intermediate result drops that value into the hole. For example, if c is 65 (the ASCII value for the character 'A'), adding c to 7 x 256 equals 1857, or in binary,

```
0000 0111 0100 0001
```

The addition affects only the lower 8 bits. It doesn't change the upper 8 bits in any way. Using this trick, the expression (attrib * 256) + c *combines* the value of attrib and the value of c into a single 16-bit word, provided, of course, that the two uncombined parts are no larger than can be represented in 8 bits. This packed format—two 8-bit quantities squeezed into a 16-bit word—is inserted directly in the PC's video display buffer by calling disp_pokew() to display a character in its selected colors (or other attributes).

That may be a long-winded explanation of a relatively simple process, but the method for combining two 8-bit bytes into a 16-bit word is a good one to know and comes in handy all the time. In general, given two 8-bit values A and B in the range 0 to 255, you can combine those values into one 16-bit word C by using the expression

```
C = (A * 256) + B;
```

To extract the original two values from C, use these expressions:

```
B = C % 256;
A = (C - B) / 256;
```

Even better, use logical operators (shifts, ANDs, and ORs) rather than mathematical ones to perform these same tasks. Because the logical operators relate directly to similar assembly language instructions, the equivalent expressions probably run more efficiently. You also may find the results of using logical operators easier to visualize, if you have a good understanding of the binary number system (see Chapter 2's sample programs TAND, TOR, TSHR, TSRL, and others).

To combine the two values A and B into C, using a logical shift left (<<) and a logical OR (¦), use the expression

```
C = (A << 8) ¦ B;
```

That shifts A left 8 bits and "ORs in" the value of B. To extract the original two values from C, use these expressions:

```
A = (C >> 8);
B = (C & 0x0ff);
```

# Questions and Exercises

3.1. Describe some of the reasons for using functions.

3.2. What's the difference between a function prototype and a function implementation? Where are the prototype and implementation usually stored in relation to function main()?

3.3. How do you call a function?

3.4. What keyword represents "no return type?"

3.5. What is the one item that a function can't declare?

3.6. Write a function that uses one or more register variables, and an identical function that uses common variables. Compare the disk sizes of the two functions inserted into a sample program. Are the sizes the same? If not, why not?

3.7. Write a function that knows how many times it was called. You may *not* use any global variables in the program.

3.8. Listing 3.8, COCO.CPP, calculates a combinatorial coefficient. Extract the necessary statements from this program, and create a function named coco() that returns the correct answer for this formula. What parameters does the function need? What data type should it return?

3.9. Write one or more functions that prompt for and return two int values within a specified range. The function(s) should require one value to be less than or greater than the other.

3.10. Design a single function area() that can calculate the area of a square *and* a cube. (Hint: use default parameters.)

3.11. Write a recursive version of the factorial function from Listing 3.8, COCO.CPP.

3.12. Convert your factorial function from Exercise 3.12 into an inline function. What effect will this have on the size of a program?

3.13. How many times can you declare a variable to be extern? Where is a good place to store extern declarations, and what are they good for?

3.14. Write a function that accepts two char parameters and returns those values packed into an unsigned 16-bit integer.

3.15. Write a function similar to the one in Exercise 3.15 that can extract the two 8-bit char values packed into an unsigned integer passed to the function as an argument.

# Pointers about Pointers

"**T**he point I'm trying to make is... I'd like to point out that... Didn't I tell you it's not nice to point?! Could you point me to the nearest exit? Only point a weapon at something you are sure you want to hit. Why don't you just get to the point?"

Our world is filled with pointers. The ideas of an arrow pointing out a one-way street and a finger pointing to a destination are natural and intuitive. Why then, do many programmers think of pointers in programming as though they were poison spears with the programmers' names written on them?

I don't know the answer, but there's no reason for you to have any reservations about using pointers. Forget what you may have heard about pointers causing bugs in code. That's rubbish. Pointers don't cause bugs. People do. You can learn how to use pointers successfully. Many programmers have done so, and you can be one of them.

This chapter describes C++ pointer fundamentals. Along the way, I'll "point out" tips and tricks that will help you to use pointers effectively in your programs. You can write programs without pointers, but as you'll learn, pointers offer practically unlimited control over memory storage in ways that put other techniques to shame.

# Declaring Pointers

**T**o create a pointer, add a space and an asterisk after any data type identifier. For example, int p creates a plain integer, but int *p creates a pointer *to* an integer. (Some programmers place the asterisk after the data type, writing int* p rather than int *p. It's all the same to the compiler, but I prefer to use the form int *p.) Regardless of how you create pointers, remember these key facts:

- A pointer is a *variable* just like any other.

- A pointer variable contains an *address* that points to another location in memory.

- Stored at that location is the *data* that the pointer addresses.

A pointer points to a value in memory. If you declare a variable like this:

```
int *ptr;
```

you are telling the compiler that the variable ptr is a pointer to an integer stored somewhere else in RAM. (See Figure 4.1.)

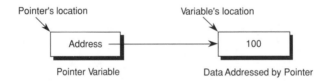

**Figure 4.1.** A pointer is a variable that contains an address.

Like all variables, ptr requires initializing before use. If you fail to initialize a pointer, its address might equal a leftover value from another operation. When you initialize a pointer, you give it an address that you know points to a valid location in memory. Uninitialized pointers are like arrows spilled from a quiver—a bunch of dangerous pick-up sticks that can point every which way.

There are several ways to initialize pointers—most of which are covered in this chapter—but the results are identical. Initializing a pointer gives that pointer the address of its target data. After initialization, you can then use the pointer to reference the addressed data.

There is a significant difference, however, between normal variables and those addressed by pointers. Programs can manipulate pointers in ways that can't be applied to normal variables. By altering, reassigning, and tweaking the address held by a pointer, it's possible to create many interesting data structures such as lists, trees, and stacks that use pointers as links to items in memory. In this way, pointers operate as chains connecting variables that may be stored anywhere and making it possible to design structures that grow and shrink to accommodate whatever you want to store in them. Pointers also let you peek into memory to extract and even change values that belong to DOS, to the ROM BIOS, or to the CRT's display buffer. With pointers, all bytes in memory are at your disposal.

# Pointer Dereferencing

After defining a pointer variable, the next step is to initialize the pointer and to use it to address some target data in memory. Using a pointer to "get to" its target is called *dereferencing the pointer*. When you dereference a pointer, you tell the compiler to use the data addressed by the pointer rather than the address value that the pointer contains. In all expressions involving a pointer, you must specify whether you intend an operation to use a pointer's address or to use the data stored at that location.

Listing 4.1, ALIAS.CPP, demonstrates the concepts of creating, initializing, and dereferencing a pointer variable. These are the most important details to learn about pointers, and you should run the sample program several times until the statements and their effects are perfectly clear.

**Listing 4.1. ALIAS.CPP.**

```
1:  // alias.cpp -- Demonstrate alias pointers
2:
3:  #include <tscdefs.h>
4:  #include IOSTREAM_H
5:
6:  char c;              // A character variable
7:
```

*continues*

**Listing 4.1. continued**

```
 8:  main()
 9:  {
10:    char *pc;       // A pointer to a character variable
11:
12:    pc = &c;
13:    for (c = 'A'; c <= 'Z'; c++)
14:      cout << *pc;
15:    return 0;
16:  }
```

Are you surprised at ALIAS's output? Running the program displays the alphabet—nothing to shake the earth, but consider *how* the program accomplishes this simple task. The only output statement is at line 13. That statement does not refer to the character variable c, to which the for loop at line 12 assigns the characters 'A' through 'Z'. If the output statement doesn't use the character variable directly, how can it display the letters that c contains?

To understand the answer to this riddle, first examine line 10, which creates a pointer variable named pc. The pointer is *bound to* a variable of type char by the definition char *pc. If the declaration was char pc;, pc would be a simple character variable. Written as char *pc; with the asterisk, pc is a *pointer* to a character variable stored somewhere in memory. However, at this early stage in the program, pc doesn't yet address any valid location. Like all variables, the pointer requires initializing before use.

Line 12 accomplishes that job by assigning to pc the address of variable c. The expression &c means "the address of c." In general, you can use the & character in a similar way to obtain the address of any variable. The expression &value is the address where value is stored; &myStruct is the address where a structure named myStruct is located, and so forth.

Because pc is a pointer, C++ allows programs to assign addresses to it. By executing the statement pc = &c, the program assigns the address of the variable c to pc. After this, pc points to c. Both pc and c then refer to the *same* location in memory. (See Figure 4.2.)

Consider this. If the variable c, which is stored somewhere in memory, and pc, which points to that same location, refer to the same data, changing one must affect the other. This is how ALIAS works. The for loop at lines 13–14 cycles c through the letters 'A' through 'Z'. Because pc addresses the same location where c is stored, using the pointer in the output statement at line 14 displays the value of c. Technically speaking, pc is called an *alias* because it serves as another name for c.

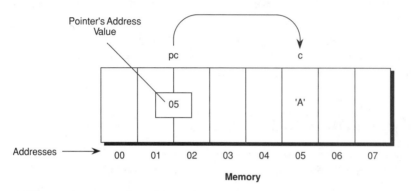

**Figure 4.2.** pc and c address the same memory location.

**Note:** All pointers are not aliases, only those that point to the location where another program variable is stored.

Look closely at the output statement cout << *pc at line 14 in ALIAS.CPP. Notice the asterisk in front of the pointer's name. This symbol tells C++ to dereference the pointer—in other words, to use the data that the pointer addresses. In this case, the data is a character, and therefore, the statement displays that character's value. C++ knows that pc addresses a character because the program declared it to be bound to a char data type back at line 9.

Load ALIAS.CPP into your editor and change the output statement to cout <<c;. Running the modified program produces the same results as the original. This proves that both c and pc refer to the same location in memory. To use a plain variable like c, you need to type only its name. To use the data addressed by a pointer,

you must dereference that pointer by prefacing its name with an asterisk as in *pc. The expression pc refers to the pointer itself as a variable. The expression *pc refers to the data that the pointer addresses. In fact, to C++, the expression *pc *is* a char variable no different from c.

When you dereference other pointers, think of them as variables of their bound data types. For a pointer declared as float *fp, the expression *fp in a statement is treated identically to a common float variable. For a pointer declared as myStructType *mstp, the expression *mstp is identical to a plain variable of type myStructType. The expressions fp and mstp are pointers; in other words, they are address values. The expressions *fp and *mstp refer to variables of the data types bound to the pointers when the program declared them.

## Pointers and Type Checking

Because pointers are bound to specific data types, C++ can verify that you don't accidentally assign the address of one sort of data to the wrong kind of pointer. If you declare a pointer to float, you can't assign to it the address of a character or an integer. For example, this will never work:

```
float *fp;
char c;
fp = &c;    // ???
```

Because c is a char variable and fp is bound to a variable of the float data type, C++ does not allow assigning c's address to fp. All similar assignments are checked for data-type consistency—one of the ways that C++ helps you to write programs that run correctly.

When you receive a "type mismatch" (or similar) compiler error for a statement that assigns an address to a pointer variable, check that the pointer's bound data type is the same as the addressed item's. There is a way to get past this rule, as the next section explains, but in general, C++ demands that pointer variables actually address variables of the same data types bound to the pointers in their declarations.

## Null and Void Pointers

You now know how to declare a pointer (add a space and asterisk to a data type), initialize it (assign an address to the pointer), and dereference it to use the addressed data (preface the pointer's name with an asterisk). Two other important and related concepts are null and void pointers.

A null pointer points nowhere in particular. It's like an arrow without a tip or a sign that's fallen onto the ground. A null pointer is C++'s way of saying that, at least for the moment, "this pointer does *not* address any valid data in memory."

The purpose of a null pointer is to give programs a way of knowing when a pointer addresses valid information. To give null a useable value in programs, C++ defines NULL as a macro equivalent to 0. Typically, NULL is defined in the header files stddef.h, stdio.h, stdlib.h, and string.h. You must #include one or more of these headers before you can use the NULL macro. Or, you can define NULL at the top of your program (or in a custom header file) with the line

```
#define NULL 0
```

> **Note:** Usually, it's best to include a system header file than to define NULL yourself. Other C++ compilers might alter NULL's definition to accommodate different memory models, operating systems, or other conditions.

Like all global variables, global pointers are initialized to 0. Because null and 0 are equivalent, if you declare a pointer fp this way:

```
float *fp;     // fp == null
main()
{
  ...
}
```

you can be 100 percent certain that fp equals null when the program begins. If, however, you declare fp or any other pointer as a local variable in a function, like all local variables, the pointer has no particular value when the function runs:

```
void f(void)
{
  float *fp;  // fp == ???
  ...
}
```

Declared as a local variable, a pointer is uninitialized; its contents are unpredictable, and therefore, the pointer might point anywhere. Before using such a pointer, it's vital that you give it a valid address. Usually, the compiler warns you if you use a variable or pointer before initializing it. Ignoring this warning for common variables may cause trouble, but if you ignore such warnings for pointers, the program may store information at a random location in memory—a sure road to disaster. Using an uninitialized pointer may overwrite other data, DOS, or even the program itself, and it's a nasty bug to find and fix. Luckily, you can avoid this problem easily by *always* initializing your pointer variables.

Throughout this book, listings have used the void keyword to stand for "nothing in particular." Like a void function that does not return any value, a void pointer points to no specific type of data. Create a void pointer like this:

```
void *noWhereLand;
```

The void pointer noWhereLand may address any location in memory, but the pointer is not bound to a specific data type. Similar void pointers may address a float variable, a char, or an arbitrary location, perhaps one belonging to DOS or to the ROM BIOS. Think of void pointers as generic vehicles for addressing data without having to specify the type of that data in advance.

> **Note:** Don't confuse null and void pointers. A null pointer does not address any valid data. A void pointer addresses data of an unspecified type. A void pointer may equal null if it doesn't currently address any valid data. Null is a value; void is a data type without form.

## Casting Roles for Pointers to Play

A typical use for void pointers is to address buffers—large blocks of RAM used to store data, often coming in from a file or on its way out to another file or device such as the printer. One way (not necessarily the best) to create buffers is to first define some memory and then create one or more pointers to address that location in RAM:

```
char buffer[1024];    // A 1,024-byte buffer
void *bp;             // A pointer to nothing in particular
...
bp = &buffer;         // Address buffer with bp
```

This fragment defines buffer as an array of 1,204 char elements. Pointer bp is then declared to address void, meaning that C++ allows the program to assign to bp the address of a variable of any data type. The last line assigns buffer's address (&buffer) to bp. At this point, bp addresses buffer, but there's a problem here that needs fixing. Because bp is a pointer to void, a statement can't dereference the pointer to get to the data it addresses. This won't work:

```
cout << *bp;     // ???
```

As you have learned, the expression *bp should dereference bp, but because that pointer addresses nothing in particular, C++ is unable to know what to do with this statement. Does *bp address a char, a float, a struct, or an int? There's no way for C++ to know the answer, and for that reason, the compiler rejects the statement.

To get out of this dilemma, you must tell C++ what data type a void pointer addresses. This requires a *pointer type cast* expression, which temporarily binds the pointer to a data type that C++ knows about. A pointer type cast is your way of telling the compiler to "treat this pointer as though it addresses a variable of type X." You can use a type cast to change the bound type of any pointer temporarily, but you *must* use a type cast before you can refer to data addressed by a void pointer.

Listing 4.2, VOID.CPP, demonstrates pointer type casts and also contains a useful function that you can extract for your own programs. When you run the program, you'll see that it displays the values and addresses of variables and pointers. To perform those actions, the program makes good use of void pointers.

## Listing 4.2. VOID.CPP.

```
 1:  // void.cpp -- Type-cast demonstration
 2:
 3:  #include <tscdefs.h>
 4:  #include IOSTREAM_H
 5:  #include IOMANIP_H
 6:  #include <dos.h>
 7:
 8:  void disp_pointer(void *p);
 9:
10:  main()
11:  {
12:    char buffer[1024];
13:    void *bp;
```

*continues*

## Listing 4.2. continued

```
14:
15:    bp = buffer;          // Assign buffer address to bp
16:    *(char *)bp = 'A';    // Store character via pointer
17:    buffer[1] = 'B';      // Store character directly
18:    buffer[2] = 0;        // Insert null after "AB"
19:    cout << "address of buffer = ";
20:    disp_pointer(buffer);
21:    cout << "data in buffer = ";
22:    cout << (char *)bp;
23:    return 0;
24: }
25:
26: void disp_pointer(void *p)
27: {
28:    cout << hex << FP_SEG(p) << ":" << hex << FP_OFF(p) << endl;
29: }
```

Line 8 shows how to declare a function that receives an untyped pointer as a parameter, in this case, void *p. This expression states that disp_pointer's single parameter p is a pointer to data of no particular type. You can use this technique to pass pointers of any type to a function. Eventually, however, you must state what type of data the void pointer addresses. For example, line 19 executes

```
disp_pointer(&value);
```

As you learned earlier, prefacing any variable with & creates an expression that C++ evaluates as the address of that variable. An address is a pointer, so it's perfectly okay for the statement to pass the address of value to disp_pointer's void *p parameter. Likewise, the statement at line 20

```
disp_pointer(buffer);
```

passes buffer's to disp_pointer. Though buffer is declared as an array of char values (see line 12), C++ treats buffer as a pointer to the first char value in the array, and it's okay to pass buffer as a pointer to a pointer parameter such as void *p in disp_pointer(). (Later in this chapter, I'll explain more about the relationship between pointers and functions.)

Inside the disp_pointer() function at lines 26–29, a seemingly complex statement actually performs a simple job—displaying the value of a pointer passed to the function:W

```
cout << hex << FP_SEG(p) << ":" << hex << FP_OFF(p) << endl;
```

If you find such statements difficult to understand, you are not alone. Take the pieces one at a time, and you'll see that the line is not as complicated as it appears. First the statement displays FP_SEG(p) in hexadecimal, next a colon, then FP_OFF(p). The endl symbol finishes the statement with a new display line.

The statement takes advantage of the fact that the value of a pointer—in other words, the address that the pointer holds—is composed of two parts, a segment and an offset. Ignoring the complexities of expanded and extended memory found in most PCs today, all addresses in memory can be expressed with these two values. The address space is *segmented*—divided into 16-byte chunks called paragraphs. To find a value in RAM, the processor starts at a chunk address represented by a segment register, usually DS or ES. It combines that address with the value of another register representing the offset from that segment boundary. Together, the two values pinpoint a variable's location in memory.

Two functions (they could be coded as macros, but they're still used as functions) FP_SEG() and FP_OFF() return an unsigned int value representing any pointer's segment and offset values. Although it appears lengthy, the output statement at line 28 simply passes the void pointer p to these two functions and displays the resulting word values with the help of hex. (It's common to express addresses in hexadecimal, but you could show them in decimal, too.)

The key point to learn about VOID.CPP is the way function disp_pointer() accepts a void pointer parameter, which could represent the address of a variable of *any* data type. For example, insert these definitions and statements between lines 13 and 14:

```
float f = 3.14159;
float *fp = &f;
cout << "*fp = " << *fp << endl;
cout << "address held by fp = ";
disp_pointer(fp);
```

The first line defines a float variable named f and initializes its value to 3.14159. The second line defines a pointer to float named fp and assigns the address of f to that pointer. The fp pointer now addresses the same location where the value of f is stored. After these lines, an output stream statement displays the value of f using the dereferenced pointer expression *fp, proving that fp does address the same location where f is stored in memory. The last two lines then display the address of fp. As this shows, disp_pointer()'s void pointer parameter accepts fp even though it addresses a specific data type (`float`). You can always assign the value of *any* pointer to a `void` pointer variable or function parameter.

> **Note:** Obviously, programs that rely on a PC's segmented memory are highly dependent on the hardware. Other computer systems may or may not use a segmented address architecture, and programs written to recognize a PC's addressing peculiarities won't run on those systems without modification. If your programs need to run on different computers, it's wise to avoid coding them to expect pointer address values to have a specific format.

# Near and Far Pointers

Whether a pointer is *near* or *far* is another highly system-dependent aspect of C++ pointers. These terms do not refer to the relative locations of pointers. Despite their names, they don't always have much to do with how far away an addressed variable is in memory.

Instead, the words near and far refer to the internal format used to represent the addresses stored in pointers. A *near pointer* takes 2 bytes (one 16-bit word). A *far pointer* takes 4 bytes (two 16-bit words). Listing 4.3, NEARFAR.CPP, demonstrates this difference.

**Listing 4.3. NEARFAR.CPP.**

```
 1:  // nearfar.cpp -- Demonstrates near and far pointers
 2:
 3:  #include <tscdefs.h>
 4:  #include IOSTREAM_H
 5:
 6:  // Disable warning: "xxx declared but never used"
 7:
 8:  #if (defined __TSC_BTC__)
 9:  #pragma warn -use
10:  #endif
11:
```

```
12:  main()
13:  {
14:    float *fp1;          // A "near" pointer
15:    float far *fp2;      // A "far" pointer
16:
17:    cout << "\nSize of fp1 = " << sizeof(fp1) << " bytes";
18:    cout << "\nSize of fp2 = " << sizeof(fp2) << " bytes";
19:    return 0;
20:  }
```

NEARFAR defines two pointers to float, fp1 and fp2. The two pointers are identical except for their names and the presence of the keyword far in the second definition at line 15. Using the expression far * tells the compiler that you want to represent this pointer with a full 4 bytes rather than the usual 2. When you run the program, it displays

```
Size of fp1 = 2 bytes
Size of fp2 = 4 bytes
```

The difference between the two pointers is that fp1 can hold addresses restricted to the range 0 to 65,535. On PCs, this value represents an offset from a fixed location (the segment value), which the program and operating system select at runtime. The far pointer represents an address using a full four bytes—two for the segment value and two for the offset. Because of this, a far pointer can point to any location in a PC's memory, not just addresses offset from a fixed segment boundary. (Again, I am purposely ignoring the complexities of expanded and extended RAM plus the 32-bit addressing capabilities of newer 80x86 processors.)

Before going any farther out on this highly system-dependent limb, you need to understand that far pointers are not part of the "pure" C++ definition. They were added to the C++ compilers supported by this book in order to allow programs to deal with a PC's segmented memory architecture. It's possible to write useful C++ programs without using a single far keyword, and for most purposes, that's probably a good idea. Also, when using different memory models, plain pointers might be far in nature even though you didn't declare them that way.

However, there are times when only a far pointer will do. For example, when you need to address external variables that belong to the operating system, there's no reason not to use system-dependent far pointers. You know the program will run only on PCs anyway, and the code may as well include system-dependent features. Let's examine a couple of cases that put these ideas into practice.

# Pointers to System Locations

Listing 4.4, CRTSTAT.CPP, demonstrates a useful trick for programs that will run on PCs, and it shows how to use far pointers to access system information.

### Listing 4.4. CRTSTAT.CPP.

```
 1:  // crtstat.cpp -- Get CRT's mode and number of columns
 2:
 3:  #include <tscdefs.h>
 4:  #include IOSTREAM_H
 5:  #include IOMANIP_H
 6:  #include <dos.h>
 7:
 8:  main()
 9:  {
10:  #if (defined __TSC_BTC__) || (defined __TSC_ZTC__)
11:     char far *mode = (char far *)MK_FP(0x0040, 0x0049);
12:     int far *cols = (int far *)MK_FP(0x0040, 0x004a);
13:  #elif (defined __TSC_MSC__)
14:     __segment dos_seg = (__segment)0x0040;
15:     char __based(dos_seg) *mode;
16:     int  __based(dos_seg) *cols;
17:     mode = (char __based(dos_seg) *)0x0049;
18:     cols = (int  __based(dos_seg) *)0x004a;
19:  #endif
20:     int imode = *mode;
21:     cout << "CRT startup mode = " << dec << imode << endl;
22:     cout << "CRT columns      = " << dec << *cols << endl;
23:     return 0;
24:  }
```

**Note:** Borland C++, Turbo C++, and Zortech C++ use identical means for assigning explicit addresses to pointers. Microsoft C/C++ requires a different method. The following text discusses both techniques.

Except for Microsoft C/C++, lines 11 and 12 in CRTSTAT define and initialize two far pointers, mode and cols. The first pointer addresses a char variable (in other words, a single 8-bit byte value). The second pointer addresses an int. Each of these pointers is initialized using a macro MK_FP (make far pointer), defined in the dos.h header file. (Even though it's a macro, you use MK_FP as a function. Examine the dos.h header file if you want to know how MK_FP is constructed.)

The result of MK_FP is a far pointer containing a 16-bit segment value and a 16-bit offset. Both mode and cols use the same segment value—0x0040, the base address in hexadecimal where DOS and the PC's ROM BIOS routines store various system variables. The offsets (0x0049 and 0x004a) in the two initialization assignments represent the offset addresses from the fixed base. These addresses locate values specifying the system's startup video mode and the number of columns available for text displays.

After these setup chores, mode and cols address the appropriate system values inside the segment at 0x0040. You can use similar techniques to assign other known addresses to pointer variables in order to read and even change system-dependent variables. Obviously, changing system variables requires a thorough knowledge of how PC's operate. Even a simple modification could have disastrous results, so be careful when using these methods.

Microsoft C/C++ uses an entirely different method for assigning addresses to pointers. As line 14 shows, the first job is to define a __segment variable, dos_seg here. To this variable, assign the type-cast segment address that you want to use—0x0040 in this case.

Next, define a __based pointer, such as *mode at line 15. A __based pointer is *based* on a segment value, here supplied as dos_seg in parentheses. The resulting mode pointer at line 15 is identical to the pointer at line 11—it just takes more effort to define. The int pointer cols at line 16 is defined similarly, using the same segment base.

Finally, assign the explicit address values as demonstrated here in lines 17–18. You must enter complex type-cast expressions (the ones in parentheses), or the compiler will reject the assignments.

The rest of the code is the same for all compilers. Two output stream statements at lines 21–22 display the system variables by dereferencing the pointers. Because *mode addresses a char value, however, line 20 first assigns that value to int imode, thus setting imode to the addressed character's ASCII value. If line 21 used *mode directly, it would write a character. (You could also type-cast *mode by writing (int)*mode rather than assigning *mode to a temporary int variable.)

The expression *cols evaluates to the int value stored at the location addressed by cols, representing the number of columns available on the terminal. No type cast or temporary variable is needed to display *cols.

> **Note:** To reduce the system dependency of your programs, isolate statements that refer to specific memory locations. A good way to do that is to insert system-dependent statements in functions. When porting your code to another computer, you can replace the functions and reduce the amount of work required to modify the code for a different environment.

## Far Pointers and the Keyboard

Another example shows how to use far pointers to sense whether someone is pressing the Alt, Crtl, Shift Left, or Shift Right keys. The program also detects the current state (on or off) of the Insert, Caps Lock, Num Lock, and Scroll Lock keys. This can be a useful technique in programs that need to check for keypresses that combine a letter key and one or more of these other keys.

Compile and run Listing 4.5, KEYSTAT.CPP. Then press any of the keys just mentioned. (These key names are also displayed on-screen for reference.) Notice that some of the keys turn on (1) and off (0) as soon as you press and release them and that the program distinguishes between the left and right shift keys. Other keys such as Caps Lock and Num Lock toggle on and off. To quit the program, simultaneously press and hold the three keys Crtl, Alt, and Shift-Left.

### Listing 4.5. KEYSTAT.CPP.

```
1:  // keystat.cpp -- Keyboard status and bit field demonstration
2:
3:  // Note: Press Ctrl+Alt+Left-shift to quit
4:
5:  #include <tscdefs.h>
6:  #include IOSTREAM_H
7:  #include DISP_H
8:  #include <dos.h>
9:  #include <string.h>
```

```
10:
11:   #include <stdlib.h>
12:
13:   struct keyboard {
14:     unsigned shiftRight  : 1;      // Keyboard flags
15:     unsigned shiftLeft   : 1;
16:     unsigned ctrl        : 1;
17:     unsigned alt         : 1;
18:     unsigned scrollLock  : 1;
19:     unsigned numLock     : 1;
20:     unsigned capsLock    : 1;
21:     unsigned insert      : 1;
22:     unsigned             : 8;      // Not used
23:   };
24:
25:   int cmpkeys(void far* p1, void far* p2);
26:
27:   main()
28:   {
29:     // Pointer to key state
30:   #if (defined __TSC_BTC__) ¦¦ (defined __TSC_ZTC__)
31:     keyboard far *keys = (keyboard far *)MK_FP(0x0040, 0x0017);
32:   #elif (defined __TSC_MSC__)
33:     __segment dos_seg = (__segment)0x0040;
34:     keyboard __based(dos_seg) *keys;
35:     keys = (keyboard __based(dos_seg) *)0x0017;
36:   #endif
37:
38:     keyboard oldkeys;      // Holds copy of last known key state
39:     int done = 0;          // True (1) when user quits program
40:
41:     disp_open();           // Initialize display package
42:     disp_move(0, 0);       // Move cursor to upper left corner
43:     disp_eeop();           // Clear to end of page (clears screen)
44:
45:     while (!done) {
46:       disp_move(0, 0);
47:
48:   // Display states of various keys
49:
50:       disp_printf("Keyboard State\r\n");
```

*continues*

227

**Listing 4.5. continued**

```
51:     disp_printf("\r\nState bits (press and release):");
52:     disp_printf("\r\n <Insert> ....... %d", keys->insert);
53:     disp_printf("\r\n <Caps lock> .... %d", keys->capsLock);
54:     disp_printf("\r\n <Num lock> ..... %d", keys->numLock);
55:     disp_printf("\r\n <Scroll lock> .. %d", keys->scrollLock);
56:     disp_printf("\r\n\nShift bits. (press, hold, and release):");
57:     disp_printf("\r\n <Alt> ......... %d", keys->alt);
58:     disp_printf("\r\n <Ctrl> ........ %d", keys->ctrl);
59:     disp_printf("\r\n <Shift left> ... %d", keys->shiftLeft);
60:     disp_printf("\r\n <Shift right> .. %d", keys->shiftRight);
61:     disp_printf("\r\n\nPress above keys to change state");
62:     disp_printf("\r\nPress <Ctrl>-<Alt>-<shiftLeft> to quit");
63:
64:     disp_move(24, 0);
65:     done = (keys->alt && keys->ctrl && keys->shiftLeft);
66:     oldkeys = *keys;  // Save key state in oldkeys
67:     // Pause until state changes
68:     while (cmpkeys((void far *)&oldkeys, keys)) ;
69:   }
70:   disp_move(24, 0);    // Move cursor to bottom line
71:   disp_close();        // Close the display package
72:   return 0;
73: }
74:
75: // Return true (1) if bytes at p1 and p2 are the same
76: int cmpkeys(void far* p1, void far* p2)
77: {
78:   return *(char far *)p1 == *(char far *)p2;
79: }
```

In addition to showing a good use for far pointers, KEYSTAT also demonstrates how to address struct variables with pointers. Lines 13–23 declare a bit-field structure named keyboard. Each member of this structure matches the bits that are stored in memory by the ROM BIOS when you press certain keys. Inspecting this value, called the *keyboard flag byte,* and extracting its various bits gives programs the capability to detect whether specially named keys are toggled or being pressed.

Line 25 declares a prototype for the function cmpkeys(), which returns true (1) if the bytes addressed by the void far pointers p1 and p2 are equal. If those bytes differ, the function returns false (0). Comparing before and after values of the keyboard flag byte gives the program a way to detect a change in a key's status.

To address the keyboard flag byte, at line 31 the program uses MK_FP to create a far pointer named keys. Lines 33–35 create a similar pointer using a __based segment as explained previously. For all compilers, the address assigned to keys is 0x0040:0x0017, the location of the keyboard flag byte. (A good PC reference lists the addresses of this and other system variables.) Notice that keys is a far pointer to a keyboard structure. (In Microsoft C/C++, __based pointers are far by definition.) Declaring the structure and then defining a pointer bound to that same type makes it easy to extract formatted information stored in memory.

Most of KEYSTAT's action occurs inside a long while loop (lines 45–69). Lines 50–62 display text using the display package's disp_printf() routine, which operates like the printf() and form() functions. Here, the %d escape codes (in most of the formatting strings) are replaced with the value of a bit field in the keyboard structure.

> **Note:** In Borland C++ and Turbo C++, when calling disp_printf(), use the two escape codes \r\n to perform a carriage return where in printf(), you would simply use \n. The \r escape code is interpreted as a carriage return; \n is interpreted as a line feed. Together, the two symbols start a new display line. In Microsoft C/C++ and Zortech C++, \r is not needed as \n translates to a carriage return *and* a line feed. Using \r for these compilers as in KEYSTAT.CPP, however, does no harm.

By the way, like other library functions, display functions such as disp_printf() are not part of the C++ language. You might not find this function on another system—like that Cray supercomputer you've been meaning to drive home one of these days.

Let's closely examine one of the disp_printf() statements in KEYSTAT.CPP. The statement contains a symbol you haven't seen before. Line 45 is as good as any:

```
disp_printf("\r\n <Shift left> ... %d", keys->shiftLeft);
```

In the formatting string, I typed a %d escape code to be replaced by the value of the shiftLeft bit field in the keyboard structure addressed by the keys pointer.

Because keys is a pointer, to locate a field in the structure requires using the -> symbol. This picks out an individual field in the structure that keys addresses.

Recall from Chapter 2, "Making Statements and Building Structures," that a period is the usual way of qualifying a structure's name and one of its members. If keysvar is a variable of type keyboard, you could access the shiftLeft member and others like this:

```
keyboard keysvar;
cout << keysvar.shiftLeft;
```

Because keys is a pointer and not a keyboard variable, however, you must use another symbol to get to the members in the addressed structure. The reason for this is obvious if you consider that the illegal expression keys.shiftLeft would mean "the shiftLeft member in the pointer keys." That's senseless—there aren't any structure members in a pointer. Pointers hold addresses, not structures. Instead, you must use keys->shiftleft, which stands for "the shiftLeft member in the keyboard structure addressed by the keys pointer."

> **Hint:** The -> symbol resembles an arrow, which is a good way to remember that you can use it only with a pointer that points like an arrow to a variable in memory. Also, when you use -> to refer to an addressed structure member, you do not also have to dereference the pointer name with an asterisk.

You can see other uses of -> at line 65 in KEYSTAT which sets a variable done to true or false. This determines whether the while loop continues or ends. The assignment to done uses two logical ANDs (&&) to combine the bits that represent the Alt, Crtl, and Shift Left keys. Only when all three of these bit fields equal 1 is the result of this expression 1, which sets done to true and causes the while loop to end.

While running KEYSTAT, you probably noticed that the program somehow manages to detect each change in the keyboard flag byte. To make this happen, line 66 assigns the flag's value to a variable named oldkeys. Because oldkeys is a keyboard structure, the assignment dereferences keys to obtain the flag's current value:

```
oldkeys = *keys;
```

Remember that when C++ dereferences a pointer prefaced with an asterisk, it considers that expression to be a variable of the pointer's declared data type. In the case of keys, that data type is a keyboard structure. Thus, *keys *is* a keyboard variable and so is oldkeys. C++ allows assignments between variables of the same data types (except for arrays, which I'll get to momentarily), and the assignment simply transfers the value addressed by keys to the memory reserved for the oldkeys variable.

Also take a look at the way line 57 calls cmpkeys with two void pointers to pause until the keyboard flag byte changes state:

```
while (cmpkeys(&oldkeys, keys)) ;
```

Because oldkeys is a variable, it's necessary to use the & operator to find that variable's address. However, keys is a pointer; it already *is* an address, and for that reason, the program can pass it directly to cmpkeys. The space before the semicolon is not accidental, but technically, it is optional. The space lets the compiler know that this while loop is supposed to wait until an external condition changes the conditional expression inside parentheses. Some C++ compilers display a warning message if you forget to add the space. They do this because such constructions are rarely needed, and you may have accidentally inserted a semicolon incorrectly at the end of a while or other loop's starting line.

> **Note:** If you remove the blank before the semicolon at the end of line 68—simulating a common typographical error that mistakenly terminates a while statement at its opening line—among the five compilers supported by this book, only Zortech C++ displays a warning. Borland C++, Turbo C++, and Microsoft C/C++ do not recognize this construction as a possible error.

Line 78 inside cmpkeys shows how to cast the function's two void pointers to new types. At the same time, it dereferences the recast pointers to access the addressed data. This single statement in the function may appear unreadable at first:

```
return *(char far *)p1 == *(char far *)p2;
```

Constructions like *(char far *)p1 throw most people for a loop on a first meeting. Taking this line apart shows that it's really not that complex. You know that p1 is a void far pointer. Like all void pointers, it doesn't address any data type in particular, so the statement must use a type cast expression to tell C++ what kind of data p1 addresses. In this case, the data type is a single byte, represented in C++ by char.

To have C++ treat p1 as char far *, the statement uses the type cast expression (char far *). This much of the statement

(char far *)p1

tells C++ to consider p1 the same as if the program had declared it to be char far *.

So far so good, but there's more to cover in this statement. The asterisk in front of the expression *(char far *)p1 dereferences the pointer, just as the asterisks in simpler constructions like *pint and *pfloat dereference those typed pointers. This dereferencing tells the compiler to use the data addressed by p1 as temporarily recast to a far pointer to char.

Returning to line 68 in KEYSTAT, you'll see a similar expression that recasts and dereferences the void pointer p2. It then returns the result of the comparison of the two bytes addressed by p1 and p2. Study this construction well—you'll see (and use) it time and again.

# Managing Your Memory

As you've seen many times so far, programs can create variables that are global or local. Global variables are stored at fixed locations in the program's data segment, and all functions can use those variables. Local variables are stored on the stack and exist only while their declaring functions are active. It's also possible to create variations of global variables that are static, meaning they are stored in a fixed location but are available only to the module (that is, the text file) or function that declares them.

All of those kinds of variables share one common characteristic: They are defined when you compile the program. When you compile definitions like int x or float *fp, the compiler reserves (defines) space for storing values of the declared data types.

But there's another way to create variables that delays their definition until the program runs. Such variables are *dynamic*—they are stored in a block of memory known as the *heap*, but their locations aren't known until runtime. Dynamic variables are also called *pointer-addressable variables* because they are always addressed by a pointer. As Figure 4.3 shows, a pointer defined as int *p can address a variable allocated space on the heap. Using that pointer, a program can store values at locations determined at runtime.

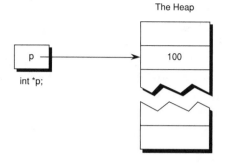

The Heap

p

int *p;

100

**Figure 4.3.** Pointer variables can address dynamic variables.

There are several ways to reserve space on the heap for dynamic variables. The first is the easiest; use the C++ new operator. For example, suppose that you want to create a string, but you don't know how much space to reserve for the string variable until the program runs. You can begin by defining a string pointer:

```
char *string;  // A string pointer
```

Variable string is a pointer to type char. At that location (which doesn't yet exist) will be a string of zero or more characters, ending in a null (ASCII 0) byte. Suppose there also is an int or unsigned variable named size that specifies how big the string should be. To reserve that much space at runtime and to assign to string the address of the reserved memory, the program executes

```
string = new char[size + 1];
```

The new operator returns the address of newly reserved memory. After new is the data type of the item you plan to store in that memory. C++ uses this data type to determine how much space to allocate. In this case, the type is an array of char equal to the value of size plus 1. The expression adds 1 to size to reserve space for the string's null byte at the end. (The program also assumes that size is not negative.)

After reserving memory with new and assigning its address to string, the program can use that pointer to "get to" the assigned memory space. For example, to read characters from the keyboard into the string (size should be at least 128 in this case), you can execute

```
gets(string);
```

You can display the current value of string—that is, the ASCII characters addressed by the string pointer—in an output stream statement:

```
cout << string;
```

Later, when you are done using the memory allocated to string, you can dispose of it. This makes that memory available for future variables created with new. To dispose of memory addressed by a pointer, use the delete operator followed by the name of the pointer that addresses the memory to be reclaimed:

```
delete s;
```

Because you reserved space with new, you can use delete to dispose exactly that same space. C++ saves the size of a reserved memory block with that block—which, by the way, also implies that the actual amount of reserved memory will be a few bytes more than you request. Also, there may be additional overhead that C++ stores along with allocated memory to keep track of it.

When deleting arrays, you can use a special form of delete with square brackets attached. For you can delete a string s with the statement:

```
delete[] s;
```

Technically, this form of delete is required only if the deleted array has objects of a class type—a subject for later. Zortech C++ does not recognize this form.

> **Note:** Only delete memory that you allocate with new. Never pass any other pointers to delete; the results of disposing memory not allocated by new could be catastrophic.

In general, you can use new to reserve space for any data type or an array of elements of any type. Here are a few more samples that show how to use new in programs. First, create a few pointers of various types:

```
int *ip;      // ip is a pointer to int
float *fp;    // fp is a pointer to float
long *lp;     // lp is a pointer to long
```

Remember that, when you define pointers, like all variables they are not initialized (unless they are global variables, in which case they are initialized to null). To reserve some memory and assign that memory's address to each pointer, use statements like these along with the new operator:

```
ip = new int;      // Reserve space for an int
fp = new float;    // Reserve space for a float
lp = new long;     // Reserve space for a long
```

After these statements run, ip, fp, and lp address reserved space on the heap. That space is guaranteed to be at least large enough to hold values of the declared data types (int, float, and long). The values stored in the heap are not yet initialized, but equal the values previously stored in the newly reserved locations.

You should also test each pointer to see whether new failed. If new can't allocate the requested space, it returns null. Usually, instead of putting all your faith in the computer, you should follow each use of new with a statement like this:

```
ip = new int;               // Reserve memory
if (!ip)                    // If pointer ip is not valid
  error("Out of memory");   //  then call error()
```

After defining pointers and reserving heap space with new, you can use the newly created dynamic variables stored on the heap by dereferencing the pointers in the usual way. Examine these statements, which assign values to each of the three variables defined and initialized earlier:

```
*ip = -1234;       // Assign value to int addressed by ip
*fp = 3.14159;     // Assign value to float addressed by fp
*lp = 99999L;      // Assign value to long addressed by lp
```

Prefacing each pointer with an asterisk tells the compiler to refer to the addressed location, in other words, the space reserved on the heap for values of the declared types. The assignments store values at those heap locations. Similarly, to use the data stored on the heap, you must dereference the pointers as in these statements:

```
cout << *ip << '\n';  // Display value at ip
cout << *fp << '\n';  // Display value at fp
cout << *lp << '\n';  // Display value at lp
```

These uses of pointers to memory reserved on the heap by new are no different from the uses you saw in earlier examples. Regardless of where a pointer points, you dereference that pointer in exactly the same way. Dynamic variables are so called because they are created at runtime on the heap by new and disposed by delete or delete[]. However, they are used just like other variables created by other means.

# Pointers to Structures

Creating simple variables dynamically as in the previous samples may strike you as being silly. If so, you're right—it is. Pointers to integers or floating-point values take up about the same amount of space as the data the pointers address. For that reason, simple variables are best created as you've seen in other listings—as global or local variables directly in the program's text.

Pointers come into their own when they address larger or more complex variables, for example, a struct, an I/O buffer, or an array of values. To create pointers to structures, first declare the struct data type and then allocate space for one or more structures by using new as you did in Listing 4.5, KEYSTAT.CPP. Finally, assign the address of the dynamic structure variable to a pointer and use that pointer to refer to the variable in memory. As an example of this technique, Listing 4.6, DSTRUCT.CPP, declares a structure named xyrec, creates space for a variable of that type, and then uses a pointer to store and display data held in the reserved memory.

**Listing 4.6. DSTRUCT.CPP**

```
 1:  // dstruct.cpp -- Dynamic structure demonstration
 2:
 3:  #include <tscdefs.h>
 4:  #include IOSTREAM_H
 5:  #include <stdlib.h>
 6:
 7:  struct xyrec {
 8:    int x;
 9:    int y;
10:  };
11:
12:  main()
13:  {
14:    xyrec *xyp;   // xyp is a pointer to an xyrec structure
15:
16:    xyp = new xyrec;   // Reserve space for an xyrec variable
17:    if (!xyp) {        // Make sure that new worked
18:      cout << "\nOut of memory!";
19:      exit(1);
20:    }
```

```
21:    xyp->x = 10;   // Assign 10 to x member in structure at xyp
22:    xyp->y = 11;   // Assign 11 to y member in structure at xyp
23:    cout << "x = " << xyp->x << "; y = " << xyp->y;
24:    return 0;
25: }
```

**Note:** Technically, you should always delete any allocated memory. Simple examples such as this one and others in this book simply end—any allocated memory is thrown away when the program returns to DOS.

Lines 7–10 declare a structure of two int members, x and y. This structure might be useful in a program that plots points on a graphics display. Instead of storing the locations of various points separately in variables like x1 and y1, with the xyrec struct, a program can define a variable as xyrec xy and then use statements like xy.x = 5 and xy.y = 100 to store coordinate values in the x and y structure members.

To do the same with a pointer requires using the -> operator introduced earlier. First, line 14 defines a pointer named xyp which is bound to the struct data type, xyrec. Remember that this and similar definitions create space only for the pointer. No space is yet reserved for storing information in memory.

That happens at line 16, which uses new to reserve enough space (and possibly a few bytes of overhead) to hold one xyrec variable. The statement assigns the address of the allocated memory to the pointer variable xyp. After this, xyp addresses a dynamic variable of type xyrec ready to use. Before doing that, however, lines 17–20 perform the ever-important task of checking that new worked. (In this small example, it's likely there will be enough space for one teensy structure, but it's still a good idea to check.)

Now that space is reserved for an xyrec and the address of that space is assigned to xyp, the program can use the newly created variable. Lines 21–23 demonstrate this by first assigning the values 10 and 11 to the structure's x and y members and then displaying those same values in an output stream statement. Figure 4.4 illustrates how the heap and the program's variables are organized in memory.

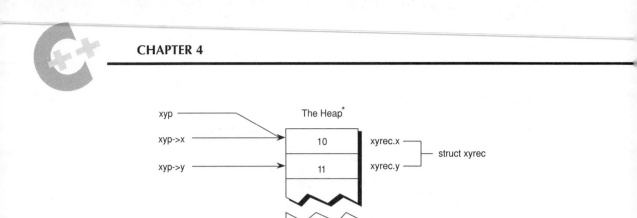

**Figure 4.4.** After creating a dynamic `struct` variable on the heap, a pointer `xyp` can be used with the `->` operator to address the structure's members.

Notice that in each of the assignments at lines 21–22, and in the output statment at line 23, the program uses the `->` operator along with the pointer's name to refer to a member in the dynamic `struct` variable. The pointer `xyp` addresses the full structure stored on the heap. The expressions `xyp->x` and `xyp->y` address individual members in that structure. As I mentioned before, you do not need to dereference the pointer in these cases with an asterisk—C++ knows from `->` that you mean to use the addressed information.

## Out of Memory

For small to medium programs, there's usually plenty of memory available on PCs. The pool of available RAM is more of a lake than an ocean, however, and large programs can easily run out of room. If you allocate too many dynamic variables or load resident programs into memory, `new` may not be able to satisfy your request to reserve heap space.

Although I hinted at this subject before, it's worth repeating. Every time you call `new`, test whether the space you requested was actually reserved. If not, `new` returns null and does not reserve *any* space. Even if the amount you request is only one byte too large for the amount of space available, `new` refuses to allocate any memory unless it can reserve it all. For this reason, after every use of `new`, you should check the results, amending the earlier statement to

```
string = new char[size + 1];
if (!string) {
  cout << "\nOut of memory!";
  exit(1);
}
```

> **Note:** Because null and C++'s value meaning false both equal zero, some people use expressions like if (string == NULL) rather than if (!string). (Pronouce this as "if string is not valid.") I used to prefer the long form, but I have changed my thinking and now use the shorter and more popular style.

# Why Use Dynamic Variables?

There are many advantages (and some drawbacks) that dynamic variables bring to C++. Among their strong points are the capabilities for dynamic variables to

- Determine a variable's size at runtime. This is useful for creating arrays and buffers that grow and shrink to accommodate whatever you need to store in them.

- Form lists that link multiple dynamic variables using pointers to form a chain of data in memory. Such chains have many uses, for example, storing information related to a variable number of disk files or storing lists of strings in a text editor.

- Use all memory available to a program without knowing or having to calculate in advance how much memory is free until the program runs.

The main disadvantage of dynamic variables occurs after creating and disposing many of them during a program run. When C++ creates a dynamic variable, it reserves a block of memory from an area called the heap. After a program is done using a dynamic variable, it can dispose of it to reclaim the previously reserved space. This returns that space to the heap's available pool of memory for use by other dynamic variables.

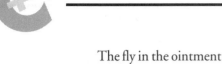

The fly in the ointment is that a disposed variable might be surrounded by other dynamic variables that are still in use. This creates a "hole" in memory equal to the size of the disposed item. Unless the next variable the program creates dynamically is no bigger than that hole, this area of memory can remain unusable.

One or two such holes won't make much difference, as long as there's plenty of other free memory available. But when a program creates and disposes hundreds of variables, a condition known as *fragmentation* can occur. Figure 4.5 shows what can happen after a program has disposed numerous variables, leaving tiny holes in memory between other dynamic items. Those items are strewn through memory, chopping it up into pieces that are too small to be used for new variables. The result is plenty of free memory in total, but all of it fragmented uselessly into small chunks.

The Heap

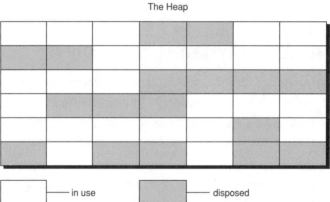

**Figure 4.5.** After disposing numerous variables, available memory (shaded boxes) may be fragmented or divided into unconnected regions.

A badly fragmented heap can make life with pointers extremely unattractive. Unfortunately, C++ doesn't have the capability to collect disposed fragments into one large space that the program could use for new variables. Such a feature is known as a *garbage collector* because it collects all the disposed garbage bytes discarded in the heap. (Maybe we should call it a dump?) C++ has a lot of features, but it lacks a garbage collector.

One answer to this problem is to reserve only large structures, preferably of the same sizes or of sizes that are multiples of some fixed value. For example, you could add dummy members to pad structs to 32, 64, 128, and 256 bytes, all of which are powers of 2 and multiples of 16. Because C++ will combine adjacent disposed areas, this may help to reduce the number of small unusable fragments.

Another answer is to allocate a large space for arrays of structs. Then write your own functions to use these spaces as needed. Instead of disposing individual structs, you would keep track of which structs in the array are in use. This method may be wasteful because it reserves a large amount of memory at once, but it lets the program rely on space being available as needed.

One other possible answer is to tap into the heap manager and change the way new and delete work. This is a highly advanced subject that I'll touch on later in Chapter 9, "Advancing Your C++ Knowledge." Writing your own memory management routines is an ambitious project, and most programmers will not have to follow that route, but it's good to know that C++ offers the capability to let you provide a custom heap manager if that becomes necessary.

# Creating Dynamic Lists

The old law that the data should structure the program is as true today as it was when Brian W. Kernighan and P. J. Plauger coined the phrase in their 1974 book, *The Elements of Programming Style*. Always keep this advice in mind. The more planning you do on the layout of the data, the easier it will be to write the code. This concept will be even more important when you start to use C++'s object-oriented features introduced in the next chapter.

Many programs need to store multiples of some data type, often a struct. When the exact number of those items is impossible to predict until the program runs, and if an array is inappropriate, you should consider storing the items as a list. This takes a bit more work than creating an array (see Chapter 2, "Making Statements and Building Structures"), but the results are often worth the effort. Lists can grow and shrink as needed to store zero, one, or more items in memory. They also tend to use available heap space efficiently by letting the list structure weave in and out of other items (even other lists) stored in the heap at the same time.

For example, a series of filenames in the current directory is a good use for a list. You might also store a list of strings to sort into alphabetic order. We'll see these and other uses for lists in this and in future chapters.

Stacks are a good place to begin learning about lists. If you've done any assembly language programming, you undoubtedly know about the system stack that stores return addresses for subroutine calls plus other items such as register values saved on the stack for restoring later. There's a system stack for all programs, including those written in C++. But it's also possible to create your own stacks as dynamic data structures. You can then *push* (insert) and *pop* (retrieve) variables of any kinds from your program's custom stacks.

All stacks share some of the same properties: they grow to accommodate new items pushed onto the stack, and they shrink as items are popped from the stack for the program's use. Like cards in a deck (not a *stacked* deck, that is), a stack's top item is the only one available; to get to the items below, you must remove those above. This means that, as you push items onto the stack (place new cards onto the deck), you can pop those items off (deal out the cards) in last-in, first-out order. There's an acronym for this, LIFO. A stack is a LIFO data structure. There are also FILO (first-in, last-out) and FIFO (first-in, first-out) variations on this basic scheme, but I'll stick to the more common LIFO variety here.

Figure 4.6 shows the evolution of a stack as values (represented by the numbered boxes) are pushed onto the top of the stack. A pointer (sp) always addresses the top item. To retrieve items, they must be popped from the top of the stack in the reverse order they were pushed there before.

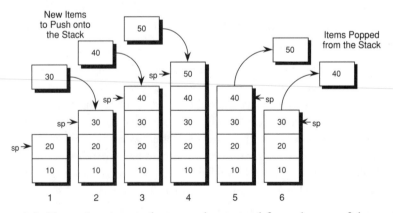

**Figure 4.6.** To retrieve items, they must be popped from the top of the stack in the reverse order they were pushed.

Listing 4.7, STACK.CPP, creates two stacks. The program also demonstrates how to manage a linked list of items created dynamically at runtime with the new operator. When you run STACK, press A to add new items to the *Item list.* Press D to delete items from that list and push them onto a second stack named the *Avail list.* If you delete more items than available on the Item list, the program creates new items automatically. For demonstration purposes, only integer values are stored on the stacks. The program can handle other kinds of data, however, with only minor changes.

## Listing 4.7. STACK.CPP.

```
 1:  // stack.cpp -- Implement a linked list stack
 2:
 3:  #include <tscdefs.h>
 4:  #include IOSTREAM_H
 5:  #include DISP_H
 6:  #include <conio.h>
 7:  #include <stdlib.h>
 8:  #include <ctype.h>
 9:
10:  struct item {
11:    int data;        // Could be any data
12:    item *next;      // Points to next item in list
13:  };
14:
15:  typedef item *Itemptr;   // Create Itemptr data type
16:
17:  // Function prototypes
18:  void push(Itemptr newitem, Itemptr &list);
19:  void pop(Itemptr &newitem, Itemptr &list);
20:  void showlist(Itemptr p, int &y);
21:  void display(void);
22:  void additem(void);
23:  void delitem(void);
24:  void clearscreen(void);
25:
26:  Itemptr avail;        // The "avail" stack
27:  Itemptr itemlist;     // The "item" stack
```

*continues*

**243**

## Listing 4.7. continued

```
28:
29:  main()
30:  {
31:    int done = FALSE;     // When TRUE, program ends
32:    int c;                // User command character
33:
34:    disp_open();
35:    while (!done) {
36:      display();
37:      disp_move(24, 0);
38:      disp_printf("A-dd, D-elete, Q-uit");
39:      c = getch();
40:      switch (toupper(c)) {
41:        case 'A': additem(); break;
42:        case 'D': delitem(); break;
43:        case 'Q': done = TRUE;
44:      }
45:    }
46:    return 0;
47:  }
48:
49:  // Push newitem onto list. Modifies list pointer.
50:  void push(Itemptr newitem, Itemptr &list)
51:  {
52:    newitem->next = list;  // Item's next now points to list
53:    list = newitem;        // List now points to new item
54:  }
55:
56:  // Pop newitem from list, or create a new item if list is empty
57:  void pop(Itemptr &newitem, Itemptr &list)
58:  {
59:    if (list == NULL) {    // If list is empty...
60:      newitem = new item;  //  Create new item
61:      newitem->data = -1;  //  Initialize data to -1
62:    } else {               // Else...
63:      newitem = list;      //  Pass back item at top of list
64:      list = list->next;   //  Adjust list to next item
65:    }
66:  }
67:
68:  // Display contents of list addressed by p
```

```
69:  void showlist(Itemptr p, int &y)
70:  {
71:    while (p) {
72:      disp_move(++y, 0);
73:      disp_eeol();
74:      disp_printf("%d", p->data);
75:      p = p->next;    // Address next item in the list
76:    }
77:  }
78:
79:  // Display the avail and item stacks
80:  void display(void)
81:  {
82:    int y = 1;
83:
84:    clearscreen();
85:    disp_move(y, 0);
86:    disp_printf("Avail list:");
87:    showlist(avail, y);
88:    y += 2;
89:    disp_move(y, 0);
90:    disp_printf("Item list:");
91:    showlist(itemlist, y);
92:  }
93:
94:  // Add item with random data to item stack
95:  void additem(void)
96:  {
97:    Itemptr newitem;
98:
99:    pop(newitem, avail);        // Get or create new item
100:    if (newitem->data < 0)      // If this is a new item
101:      newitem->data = rand();   // Assign random data to it
102:    push(newitem, itemlist);    // Put new item onto item stack
103:  }
104:
105:  // Delete item from item stack. Save same item on avail stack
106:  void delitem(void)
107:  {
108:    Itemptr newitem;
109:
```

*continues*

## Listing 4.7. continued

```
110:    pop(newitem, itemlist);     // Get new item from item stack
111:    push(newitem, avail);       // Save item on avail stack
112:  }
113:
114:  // Clear the display
115:  void clearscreen(void)
116:  {
117:    disp_move(0, 0);
118:    disp_eeop();
119:  }
```

To understand how STACK operates, start with the data structures. (This is also a good plan of attack for investigating other programs you've never seen before.) The key data structure in STACK is item, a struct declared at lines 10–13:

```
struct item {
  int data;
  item *next;
};
```

The int data member in item could store any kind of data, or perhaps, one or more pointers to other items created dynamically at runtime. To modify the program for other uses, you'll want to replace this member or add new ones. Member item *next looks like the pointers you've declared before, but uses a technique that's new. Notice that the member's type (item *) refers to the *same* structure in which the member is declared. In other words, next is a pointer to an item variable, which contains another member named next, which points to another item variable, and so on. Each item is linked to the next by the next pointer. Together, the linked items form a list. (See Figure 4.7.)

Usually, C++ prevents you from referring to undeclared items, but in this special case—creating a pointer to a structure inside that same structure—the compiler breaks its own rule. It does this to allow creating *recursive data structures,* those that refer to other variables of the same types. Like recursive functions that can call themselves, recursive data structures can point to other items that are exactly like themselves.

To refer to items stored on a linked list of item structures, line 15 uses typedef (type define) to create a new data type named Itemptr:

```
typedef item *Itemptr;  // Create Itemptr data type
```

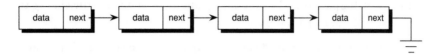

**Figure 4.7.** Store pointers in structure members to link multiple variables of the struct type together, forming a list.

The declaration tells the compiler that Itemptr and item * mean the same thing. Either can be used to create a pointer to an item structure. Using typedef to create a pointer data type this way is merely a convenience—it allows statements and other declarations to use the identifier Itemptr rather than item *. This can reduce the number of confusing asterisks in the program text.

After taking care of these details and declaring several function prototypes, the program is ready to create two lists. This is done at lines 26 and 27, which define two Itemptr variables named avail and itemlist. Because these are global variables, they are automatically initialized to null at runtime.

These two pointers are usually known as *list heads,* or *root pointers.* They point to the first item on a list, which points to the next item, which points to the next, and so on until reaching the end of the list. As Figure 4.7 shows at far right, a list's end is often drawn using an electrical grounding symbol. A program can know when it has reached the end of a list by examining the next member in an item. If that member equals null, it's the last in the list; otherwise, it points to another item.

Two functions, push() and pop(), use these careful definitions to create stacks of item structures in memory. The push() function at lines 50–54 is the simpler of the two, so let's take it apart first:

```
void push(Itemptr newitem, Itemptr &list)
{
  newitem->next = list;
  list = newitem;
}
```

Pay close attention to the two parameters, newitem and list. The first is an Itemptr—a pointer to an item. The second is the same, but is passed by reference (&) rather than by value. As you learned in Chapter 3, "Functions: Programming in Pieces," this means that any changes made to list inside the function will affect the pointer variable passed to the function by another statement. Any change to newitem, however, will not be passed back.

The first statement inside push() assigns the value of list (in other words, the address that this pointer holds) to the next member in the structure addressed by newitem. The item addressed by newitem now points to the same item that list addresses; newitem is linked (pushed) onto the list.

The second line inside push then assigns the value of newitem to list. Because list is passed to the function by reference, this assignment directly changes the argument passed to push. Suppose that someitem addresses an item in memory. To push that item onto the avail stack, the program could execute

```
push(someitem, avail);  // Push someitem onto avail stack
```

When this statement calls push(), the function first sets someitem->next to where avail points (or to null if avail equals null). Then it changes avail to point to someitem. Verify these actions on paper, a blackboard, or by hand-tracing Figure 4.8. The process of linking items onto lists is much easier to visualize by working through a few examples on your own than it is to read a description of how the linking works.

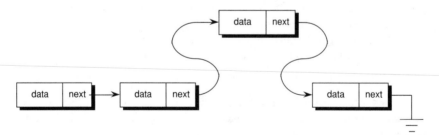

**Figure 4.8.** Pushing items onto a list links those items to others previously joined by similar operations.

The second key function in STACK is pop() (lines 57–66), which reverses push()'s accomplishments. The function's declaration is similar to push()'s, but this time, both parameters `newitem` and `list` are passed by reference. This means that if the function changes either of these two pointers, it directly affects the arguments passed to the function by a calling statement:

```
void pop(Itemptr &newitem, Itemptr &list)
{
  if (list == NULL) {
    newitem = new item;
    newitem->data = -1;
  } else {
    newitem = list;
    list = list->next;
  }
}
```

It's a grievous error to pop more data than is available on a stack—sort of like digging into your pockets too deeply and poking a hole in the fabric. For this reason, `pop()` first checks whether `list` is null. If so, the stack is empty, and `list` addresses no valid `item` structure in memory.

In that event, the function uses `new` to create a new `item`, assigning the address of this structure to the `newitem` argument passed to the function. At the same time, `pop()` initializes the `data` member in the item to –1. I did this just so you could see on-screen the items created by this section when you try to delete more items than are available. (To see the effect, run the program and press D a few times.) You can remove this statement when using the programming in your own code.

> **Note:** To keep its logic simpler, STACK doesn't perform any error checking. In your own code, however, you should always test the result passed back from `new`.

If `list` is not null, the function assumes the pointer addresses at least one `item` variable. To return that `item` to the caller—the reason that a statement is called `pop()` in the first place—the function assigns the address of `list` to `newitem`. Now `newitem` addresses the current top of the stack. So that the next call to `pop()` returns the next item from the list, the last statement in `pop()` assigns the value of the next member to

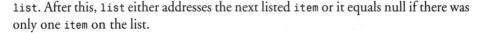

list. After this, list either addresses the next listed item or it equals null if there was only one item on the list.

That covers the basics of how STACK pushes and pops items to and from a list. Next, turn to function additem() at lines 95–103. First, this function calls pop(), which may seem strange; if pop() removes an item from the stack, why call it when we want to add a new one? The reason for this is because, as I explained a moment ago, pop() executes new to create a new item when the stack is empty, or in this case, when avail equals null. Either way, the effect is to return the address of an item structure addressed by newitem. In additem(), an if statement examines this address to see whether it equals –1. If so, the program assigns a value at random to the item's data member and calls push() to store it on the itemlist. In short, additem() calls pop() to get an item variable from the avail stack or to create a new item, possibly assigns new data to it, and then calls push() to save the item on the other stack.

> **Note:** The data member is set to –1 here only for demonstration purposes. You can remove data and the associated tests for its value if you want to incorporate STACK into your own programs.

The opposite function, delitem() at lines 106–112, is even simpler than additem(). First, the function calls pop() to delete the topmost item from itemlist. Then push() transfers this item to the avail stack. The effect is to transfer one item from the stack addressed by itemlist to the stack addressed by avail. (If itemlist is null when calling pop(), a new item with its data member initialized to –1 is created and transferred to avail.)

One other function in STACK contains a few techniques that you haven't seen before. Function showlist() (lines 69–77) is responsible for displaying the lists of values that you see on-screen when you run the program. It does this with a while loop that cycles until an Itemptr pointer p passed as an argument to the function equals null:

```
while (p) {            // i.e. while (p != NULL)
  disp_move(++y, 0);
  disp_eeol();
  disp_printf("%d", p->data);
  p = p->next;   // Address next item in the list
}
```

The intention is for p to address the first item in a linked list. Before displaying the value of the data addressed by p with the disp_printf() function, the loop executes disp_eeol() to clear the line of any leftover characters.

The final statement in the while loop assigns the value of the next member in the item addressed by p to p. Think about what this does. If next contains the address of the next item in the list, the assignment of p->next to p causes p to point to that item. On the next pass through the loop, p will then point to the next item and so on until next equals null—the value that marks the last item in the list. This also ends the while loop.

As a result of these actions, the while loop causes p to point to each item in a list, no matter where those items are stored. They might be stored one after the other physically, but, more likely, they will be scattered in various locations. Because of this, following the next pointers is the *only* way to locate a list's items. The pointers form a kind of chain, with each link attaching two items. The while loop pulls in the string of items like a winch winding up a chain until reaching the last link.

# Dynamic Arrays

One good use for new is to create dynamic arrays. Instead of having to declare an array's size in the program's text, with new, you can allocate space on the heap for an array at runtime. This lets the program itself decide how big to make an array.

The usual method for creating arrays is to add brackets and a value after the array's name. For example, this creates an array of 100 floating-point numbers:

```
float af[100];
```

When you don't know how many items to allow for, create a pointer to the data type you need to store in the array. Then, use new to reserve space at runtime for as many items as you need:

```
int n = 100;
float *afp = new float[n];
if (!afp)
  error("Out of memory");
```

The value of n might come from a calculation, or it might be entered by an operator. In the second statement, operator new allocates space for 100 floating-point variables. The statement assigns the address of that space to the afp pointer. You can then use that pointer as an array of float:

```
cout << "Fifth element = " << afp[4];
```

Later, I'll return to the subject of using pointers as arrays. First, let's examine other ways to allocate memory on the heap.

# Reserving Memory with *malloc*

The new and delete operators belong to the C++ language, not to C, which has other ways for reserving memory for dynamic variables. These same methods are also available in C++, and it's a good idea to understand how they work.

The most common technique is to call a library function named malloc() for "memory allocation." Before you can call malloc(), include the stdlib.h header file. Alternatively, when you don't need all the other declarations in stdlib.h, in Borland C++ and Turbo C++ you can instead include alloc.h or malloc.h. In Microsoft C/C++, you can include malloc.h.

You can then call malloc() to reserve a number of bytes and to assign the address of the first of those bytes to a pointer:

```
char *sp;          // sp is a pointer to char
sp = malloc(129);  // Reserve 129 bytes
if (!sp)           // Call error function
  error();         //  if malloc() fails
```

After the first line defines pointer sp, the second line calls malloc() with the value 129 in parentheses. This reserves a space of 129 bytes and assigns the address of the first byte of that space to sp. However, if malloc() returns null, there wasn't enough room in memory to satisfy the request for new storage, and the program needs to take evasive action. In this fragment, the if statement calls function error() (not shown).

A similar function, calloc(), also reserves memory, but requires a different set of arguments. Pass the number of items to reserve and the size of a single item to calloc() and assign the resulting address to a pointer:

```
int *bp;
bp = calloc(1024, sizeof(int));
```

The first line defines a pointer bp to type int. The call to calloc() attempts to reserve 1024 int-sized chunks of memory and then assigns the address of the first byte of the first chunk to bp. Unlike malloc(), which sets aside the requested memory but doesn't initialize that memory, calloc sets all reserved bytes to 0. As usual, if the function can't reserve as much space as you request, it returns null, and you should follow each call to calloc() with a test for this condition. In this sample, because an int takes 2 bytes, the statement reserves 2,048 bytes of memory. On another system, an int may take more or less room, which would change the outcome. Even so, the statement ensures that, no matter what int's size, unless calloc() returns null, bp will address an area of reserved memory that can hold 1,204 integer values.

Used this way, sizeof() can help you to write system-independent programs. Generally, calling malloc() or calloc() to reserve space for a certain number of variables is better than statements such as malloc(2048) which assumes an int's size will always be 2 bytes—a dangerous assumption to make.

> **Note:** The function name calloc() may stand for *clear and allocate*. No doubt some reader will know, but despite searching a dozen references, I could not find the origin of this word. It might also mean *core allocation*, a reference to early "core" memory made from magnets.

Although it's probably best to use new and delete, malloc() comes in handy for allocating buffers—large spaces into which you can stuff bytes for various purposes. Listings 4.8 and 4.9, popup.h and POPUP.CPP, show a good example of this. (Be sure to have both files in the current directory when compiling.) The program uses malloc() to create buffers for storing text behind a series of "windows." When you run the program, you'll see these windows—in color, if you have a color display—pop up on top of each other at random locations. After the tenth window appears, press the Spacebar ten times to remove each window, exposing the ones below. Actually, though, there aren't any windows "below" the ones on top. It's just an illusion brought to you by malloc() and a few pointers.

## Listing 4.8. popup.h (1 of 2).

```
1:  // popup.h -- Header file for popup.cpp
2:
3:  #define MAXWINDOW 10        // Maximum number of windows
4:  #define MAXCOLOR 7          // Maximum background color (min = 0)
5:  #define MAXROW 22           // Maximum row number (min = 0)
6:  #define MAXCOL 79           // Maximum column number (min = 0)
7:  #define WHITE 15            // Color number for whiter than white
8:  #define MONOCHROME 7        // Monochrome display mode number
```

*continues*

253

## Listing 4.8. continued

```
 9:
10:   struct winrec {               // Window record
11:     unsigned short * bufptr;    // Saved text. Null if window is closed
12:     unsigned trow;              // Top row number
13:     unsigned lcol;              // Left column number
14:     unsigned brow;              // Bottom row number
15:     unsigned rcol;              // Right column number
16:     int attribute;              // Background & foreground color
17:   };
18:
19:   typedef winrec *Winrecptr;   // Define winrecptr data type
20:
21:   // Function prototypes
22:
23:   void error(char *errmsg);
24:   void pause(void);
25:   int randrange(int low, int high);
26:   void openWindow(Winrecptr wrp, int backcolor, unsigned trow,
27:     unsigned lcol, unsigned brow, unsigned rcol);
28:   void displayText(Winrecptr wrp, char *message);
29:   void closeTopWindow(Winrecptr wrp);
```

## Listing 4.9. POPUP.CPP (2 of 2).

```
 1:   // popup.cpp -- Display overlapping "pop-up" windows
 2:
 3:   #include <tscdefs.h>
 4:   #include IOSTREAM_H
 5:   #include DISP_H
 6:   #include <conio.h>
 7:   #include <stdlib.h>
 8:   #include <time.h>
 9:   #include <form.h>
10:   #include "popup.h"
11:
12:   #if (defined __TSC_BTC__) ¦¦ (defined __TSC_MSC__)
13:   #include <msleep.h>
14:   #endif
15:
```

```
16: main()
17: {
18:   int wnum;
19:   unsigned trow, lcol, brow, rcol;  // Window coordinates
20:   winrec buffer[MAXWINDOW];          // Array of winrecs
21:   char cbuf[80];                     // Buffer for form()
22:
23:   srand((unsigned)time(NULL));       // Randomize
24:   disp_open();                       // Initialize display package
25:
26: // Display MAXWINDOW windows at random locations and colors
27:
28:   for (wnum = 0; wnum < MAXWINDOW; wnum++) {
29:     trow = randrange(0, MAXROW / 2);        // Set top row
30:     lcol = randrange(0, MAXCOL / 2);        // Set left column
31:     brow = randrange(trow + 4, MAXROW);     // Set bottom row
32:     rcol = randrange(lcol + 12, MAXCOL);    // Set right column
33:     openWindow(
34:       &buffer[wnum],             // Pass winrec pointer
35:       randrange(1, MAXCOLOR),    // Background color
36:       trow, lcol, brow, rcol);   // Location
37:     displayText(&buffer[wnum], form(cbuf, "Window #%d", wnum + 1));
38:   }
39:
40: // Close windows one by one
41:
42:   disp_move(24, 0);
43:   disp_printf("Press <Space> to erase top window...");
44:   for (wnum = MAXWINDOW - 1; wnum >= 0; wnum--)
45:     closeTopWindow(&buffer[wnum]);
46:   disp_move(24, 0);     // Move cursor to last row
47:   disp_close();         // Close display package
48:   return 0;
49: }
50:
51: // Display error message and quit
52: void error(char *errmsg) {
53:   disp_move(24, 0);              // Move cursor to last row
54:   disp_close();                  // Close the display package
55:   cout << "ERROR: " << errmsg;   // Display error message
56:   exit(1);                       // Return to DOS
57: }
```

*continues*

## Listing 4.9. continued

```
58:
59:  // Pause for a keypress (no message displayed)
60:  void pause(void)
61:  {
62:    getch();      // Wait for any keypress
63:  }
64:
65:  // Return random number from low ... high
66:  int randrange(int low, int high)
67:  {
68:    return low + (rand() % ((high - low) + 1));
69:  }
70:
71:  // Open a new window at these coordinates and fill with color.
72:  // Background color is ignored on monochrome displays.
73:  void openWindow(Winrecptr wrp, int backcolor, unsigned trow,
74:    unsigned lcol, unsigned brow, unsigned rcol)
75:  {
76:    int bcolor, tcolor;   // Border color, text color
77:    unsigned bufsize;     // Saved-text buffer size
78:
79:  // Determine color to use for background and foreground
80:
81:    if (disp_getmode() == MONOCHROME) {
82:      bcolor = DISP_REVERSEVIDEO;          // Monochrome display
83:      tcolor = bcolor;
84:    } else {
85:      bcolor = (backcolor << 4) + WHITE;   // Color display
86:      tcolor = bcolor - WHITE;
87:    }
88:
89:  // Calculate number of bytes needed to save text behind window
90:
91:    bufsize =
92:      ((brow - trow + 1) * (rcol - lcol + 1)) * sizeof(unsigned);
93:
94:    wrp->bufptr = (unsigned short *)malloc(bufsize);  // Reserve buffer
95:    if (!wrp->bufptr)            // If that fails, return
96:      return;                    //   leaving bufptr == NULL
```

```
97:
98:    // Save text behind window in buffer just created
99:
100:     disp_peekbox(wrp->bufptr, trow, lcol, brow, rcol);
101:     wrp->trow = trow;    // Save coordinates and color, too
102:     wrp->lcol = lcol;
103:     wrp->brow = brow;
104:     wrp->rcol = rcol;
105:     wrp->attribute = tcolor;    // Text color
106:
107:    // Pause and then display the window
108:
109:     msleep(250);    // Pause for 1/4 second
110:     disp_fillbox(((bcolor * 256) + ' '), trow, lcol, brow, rcol);
111:     disp_box(0, bcolor, trow, lcol, brow, rcol);
112: }
113:
114:    // Display some text inside this window (assumes that window is
115:    // frontmost on display)
116:    void displayText(Winrecptr wrp, char *message)
117:    {
118:      if (wrp->bufptr == NULL) return;  // Exit if window not open
119:      disp_move(wrp->trow + 2, wrp->lcol + 2);
120:      disp_setattr(wrp->attribute);
121:      disp_printf(message);
122:      disp_setattr(DISP_NORMAL);
123:    }
124:
125:    // Close window using winrec struct addressed by wrp. Assumes that
126:    // this window is frontmost on display.
127:
128:    void closeTopWindow(Winrecptr wrp)
129:    {
130:      if (wrp->bufptr == NULL) return;  // Exit if window not open
131:      pause();
132:      disp_pokebox(
133:        wrp->bufptr, wrp->trow, wrp->lcol, wrp->brow, wrp->rcol);
134:      free(wrp->bufptr);    // Dispose buffer
135:      wrp->bufptr = NULL;  // Prevent further use of buffer
136:    }
```

> **Note:** Lines 12–14 in POPUP.CPP include msleep.h for Borland C++, Turbo C++, and Microsoft C/C++. These lines provide the `msleep()` function, similar to that function in Zortech C++. Calling `msleep()` pauses for a certain number of milliseconds, slowing the program so you can see what it does. See also Chapter 10, "Cross-Compilation Tools."

Despite the program's size, POPUP.CPP (Listing 4.9) contains very little that you haven't seen before. To understand how the program works, it's probably best to start with the header file in Listing 4.8. Most important is the `winrec` structure at lines 10–17 and the `Winrecptr` (pointer to a `winrec` structure) type at line 19. The structure collects various details about a window's location and color, and also has a member `bufptr` declared as `void *`. This untyped pointer will address a block of memory that saves a copy of the text "behind" a window. Redisplaying that text on top of where the window appears is how POPUP causes pop-up windows to pop *off*. Also, if this pointer is null, POPUP considers the window closed.

The main program in Listing 4.9 stores an array of `winrec` records in `buffer` (line 20). A `for` loop (lines 28–38) creates several variables to open a window at a random location on-screen and then calls `openWindow()`. To `openWindow()`, the program passes the address of one of the `winrec` variables in the `buffer` array (see line 34) along with other items that tell the function where to place the window and what color to use for its background. After this, the program displays the window's number (line 37). Lines 44–45 call `closeTopWindow()` to close each window one by one when you press the Spacebar.

Line 94 inside function `openWindow()` calls `malloc()` to reserve space for the buffer that will store the text behind a new window, which is not yet visible. Notice how the next line tests whether the result is null. If so, the function immediately returns (line 96). This prevents an accidental (and disastrous) use of a null pointer. Because null equals 0, writing data to the location addressed by a null pointer (if you can get away with doing that) would overwrite the system's interrupt vectors—pointers to various system routines—stored in low memory. To say the least, this is a serious mistake!

If all proceeds normally, line 100 calls `disp_peekbox()` to save the text now on display where the window will appear in the buffer space reserved a moment earlier. The rest of the function saves other details about the window in the `winrec` variable passed to `openWindow()` and then displays the window with calls to `disp_fillbox()`

and disp_box() (lines 110–111). Line 109 calls msleep() to delay each window's appearance by about 1/4 second so that you can see the windows one by one as they are drawn. You can remove this line to open windows at full speed.

The other new area in POPUP is in function closeTopWindow() (lines 128–136). There, disp_pokebox() "closes" a window by redisplaying the text saved earlier by disp_peekbox(). After this, free deletes the memory where that text is stored. Even though this program doesn't reuse that space, deleting the memory would be necessary in a more active setting that opens and closes many windows. Also notice how line 135 sets the bufptr pointer to null, a safety measure that helps prevent using a disposed pointer.

**Hint:** Never use the memory addressed by a pointer passed to free or delete. That memory has been returned to the general pool from where new, malloc(), and calloc() obtain fresh memory space. To help prevent accidents, it's a good idea to set disposed pointers to null. That way, before using a pointer, a simple check like if (!p) tells whether a pointer has been disposed or addresses a valid memory space.

# Pointers as Function Arguments

Pointer function parameters are more common in C than in C++. The reason for this fact is simple (and no doubt aggravatingly clear to C experts in the audience). C lacks C++'s reference parameters (those declared with &). To pass an argument to a function for direct use, a statement must pass the *address* of that argument to a pointer parameter. In C, it's your responsibility to crank out the mechanics that make reference parameters work automatically in C++.

Still, it's a good idea to know how to pass arguments by address to function pointer parameters. Sometimes it is more convenient to design functions that way, and many library functions are designed to take pointer parameters. Learning the technique will also make it easier for you to read published C listings, which frequently declare function pointer parameters.

Because you already know how to use C++ reference parameters, compare that method with C's pointer parameters. Suppose that you create a structure to keep track of high and low temperatures:

```
struct temperature {
  float high;
  float low;
};
```

You plan to use `temperature` in a program that keeps track of high and low readings from a thermometer somehow attached to the computer. A key function in that program reads the current temperature and modifies the appropriate member, `high` or `low`, in a `temperature` structure passed by reference to the function. In C++, this is easy to write:

```
void recordtemp(temperature &t)
{
  float current;

  getcurrenttemp(current);
  if (current > t.high)
    t.high = current;
  else if (current < t.low)
    t.low = current;
}
```

The `temperature` parameter `&t` is passed by reference. This means that a statement can call `recordtemp()` with a `temperature` variable passed as an argument, and the function will deposit the correct values (if necessary) directly in that variable:

```
temperature thetemp;
recordtemp(thetemp);
```

Because `recordtemp`'s parameter is passed by reference, the function directly operates on the `thetemp` variable. If the parameter were not declared with `&`, the function would operate on a *copy* of that argument's value. Except for the `&` character, however, the function statements are identical regardless of whether a parameter is passed by value or by reference. Even though the parameter `&t` is a pointer that addresses the actual variable passed as an argument (`thetemp` in this case), this detail is conveniently hidden by the compiler, making the function easier to write and maintain.

The same is not true in C, which does not have reference parameters. In C, *all* parameters are passed by value. For that reason, to refer back to an actual argument requires passing that argument's address to a parameter pointer. Here's the same recordtemp() function written in C (the code also works in C++):

```c
void recordtemp(temperature *t)
{
  float current;

  getcurrenttemp(current);
  if (current > t->high)
    t->high = current;
  else if (current < t->low)
    t->low = current;
}
```

Now the statements in the function must be aware that t is a pointer and not a variable. Instead of using expressions like t.high and t.low to refer to members in the structure, statements must use the symbol ->. Also, although not shown here, it's necessary to dereference the pointer t using *t in expressions that need to refer to the addressed information. To call the function, you must use the form recordtemp(&t), passing the address of t to the pointer parameter.

**Note:** Don't confuse the & (address of) operator in statements with C++'s unique & (reference parameter) symbol. Although both use the same character, their contexts are different. Both C and C++ can use & as an operator in expressions that evaluate to the addresses of identifiers, for example, &var. However, only C++ can use & in a function declaration to create reference parameters that are passed by address to a function. In C, a declaration like int f(int &var) is not allowed.

Although less common than in C, pointer arguments are still useful in C++ programming, especially when a function needs to operate on arguments of more than one data type. Listing 4.10, SWAP.CPP, shows an example.

## Listing 4.10. SWAP.CPP.

```
 1:  // swap.cpp -- Use pointers to swap any two same-size variables
 2:
 3:  #include <tscdefs.h>
 4:  #include IOSTREAM_H
 5:  #include <stdlib.h>
 6:  #include <string.h>
 7:
 8:  struct rec {          // Sample structure to swap
 9:    char *title;
10:    char *author;
11:    int pages;
12:  };
13:
14:  // Function prototypes
15:  void swapbytes(void *p1, void *p2, unsigned size);
16:  void showrecs(char *s);
17:
18:  rec r1, r2;          // Two rec global variables
19:
20:  main()
21:  {
22:  // Assign test values to the global variables
23:    r1.title = "The C++ Programming Language 2nd Ed";
24:    r1.author= "Bjarne Stroustrup";
25:    r1.pages = 669;
26:    r2.title = "C++ Primer";
27:    r2.author= "Tom Swan";
28:    r2.pages  = 1133;
29:
30:  // Display variables before and after swapping
31:    showrecs("Before");
32:    swapbytes(&r1, &r2, sizeof(r1));
33:    showrecs("After");
34:    return 0;
35:  }
36:
37:  // Swap size bytes addressed by p1 and p2
38:  void swapbytes(void *p1, void *p2, unsigned size)
39:  {
40:    unsigned char t;     // Temporary place to hold each byte
```

```
41:    char *c1 = (char *)p1;
42:    char *c2 = (char *)p2;
43:
44:    while (size--> 0) {
45:      t = *c1;
46:      *c1++ = *c2;
47:      *c2++ = t;
48:    }
49: }
50:
51: // Display values of r1 and r2
52: void showrecs(char *s)
53: {
54:    cout << "\n\n" << s << "\n=============";
55:    cout << "\nr1.title  = "  << (r1.title);
56:    cout << "\nr1.author = "  << (r1.author);
57:    cout << "\nr1.pages  = "  << (r1.pages);
58:    cout << "\n\nr2.title  = " << (r2.title);
59:    cout << "\nr2.author = "  << (r2.author);
60:    cout << "\nr2.pages  = "  << (r2.pages) << '\n';
61: }
```

Although just a demonstration, the SWAP program contains a function that you'll want to keep around for your own programs. The function, swapbytes(), can swap the values of two variables, no matter what their data types and sizes. Line 15 declares the function's prototype:

```
void swapbytes(void *p1, void *p2, unsigned size);
```

The first two parameters p1 and p2 are pointers to void. Whenever you need general purpose pointers that can address variables of any types, declare them like this. The third parameter equals the size in bytes of the variables to be swapped. The function assumes that the pointers address two variables of at least this size. Usually, the two variables should be of the same types, although they don't have to be.

Because void pointers can hold the addresses of any variables, using swapbytes() is easy. Just insert the address-of operator & in front of each argument to swap, as at line 35:

```
swapbytes(&r1, &r2, sizeof(r1));
```

This swaps r1 and r2, two global variables defined at line 18 of type rec, a structure declared earlier at lines 8–12. Notice how the sizeof operator at line 32 calculates how many bytes to swap. Using sizeof this way instead of specifying a literal value avoids swapping the wrong number of bytes.

SWAP displays the before and after values of r1 and r2, proving that swapbytes() is doing its job. The function assigns pointers p1 and p2 to two temporary char pointers, c1 and c2, at lines 41–42. It then executes a while loop that performs the swap.

While size is greater than 0 (and decrementing size at the same time with the— operator), the loop executes three statements. The first statement assigns the byte addressed by c1 to a temporary char variable t. The second statement assigns the byte at c2 to the address where c1 points. The third statement assigns t to where c2 points. The last two statements also apply the increment operator ++ to each pointer. This advances the pointers to address the next bytes in line to be swapped on the next pass through the loop.

You could rewrite the while loop to include the type-cast expressions directly, and do away with the assignments at lines 41–42.

```
while (size--> 0) {
  t = *(char *)p1;
  *((char *)p1)++ = *(char *)p2;
  *((char *)p2)++ = t;
}
```

Unfortunately, however, this alternative loop does not compile with Microsoft C/C++, which reports the error, "++ needs lvalue." Apparently, Microsoft C/C++ does not permit type-cast pointers to be incremented with ++ or decremented with —. Borland C++, Turbo C++, and Zortech C++ compile this loop with no errors.

In the program, I wrote the function the "hard way," to make it easier to understand, and so it would work with all C++ compilers. Most C++ programmers would prefer the preceding style, even though it's more cryptic and doesn't work with Microsoft C/C++.

# Pointers to Functions

So far in this chapter, you've spent a lot of time examining pointers to data. As you've seen, a program can declare pointers to any type of variable, structure, or array. Also, functions can declare pointer parameters to allow statements to pass the addresses of arguments to those functions.

It's also possible to create pointers to functions. Instead of addressing data, function pointers point to executable code. Dereferencing a pointer to data lets statements read and write values stored in memory. Dereferencing a pointer to a function causes that function to run.

The trick to learning how to create pointers to functions is to investigate why the obvious approach doesn't work. As you know, to create a pointer to a variable, you preface the variable's name with an asterisk. For example, this creates a pointer named myptr to a variable of type float:

```
float *myptr;
```

Without the asterisk, myptr would be a plain float variable. With the asterisk, it's a pointer *to* a float variable. However, this same rule doesn't work exactly the same for function pointers. Suppose that you want to create a pointer to a function that returns a float value. You might try to do this by declaring the function's prototype prefaced with an asterisk, the way you create other pointers:

```
float *myfnptr(void);   // ???
```

That appears to create a function pointer named myfnptr that addresses a function with no parameters that returns float. The declaration is faulty, however, because the asterisk binds with float, not with myfnptr. Despite appearances, what the previous command line creates is a function that returns a pointer to a float value! It is as though you wrote

```
(float *)myfnptr(void);
```

This might be useful in other circumstances, but it's not what was intended. To create a pointer to a *function* that returns a float value, surround the asterisk and function name with parentheses:

```
float (*myfnptr)(void);
```

The parentheses tell the compiler that the asterisk binds to the function name, not its data type. This is the correct way to create function pointers. Some programmers also add a space between the asterisk and function name to make their intentions perfectly clear:

```
float (* myfnptr)(void);
```

Either method is correct, but adding the space can make function pointer declarations easier to spot in a lengthy text file. If the function requires parameters, add them as usual inside parentheses in the function's parameter list:

```
float (* myfnptr)(int x, int y);
```

That sets up a pointer to a function that returns a `float` value and requires two integer arguments. To call such a function from a statement, first initialize the pointer to address a real function written in the usual way. Like all pointers, before using one that addresses a function, you must initialize the pointer to address executable code. Suppose that the function you want to call via a pointer is named `thefunction()`. You can assign its address to `myfnptr` like this:

```
myfnptr = &thefunction;
```

You don't, however, need to use the `&` operator. The name of a function is synonomous with the function's address, and you can simply write

```
myfnptr = thefunction;
```

Don't add parentheses as you do when you call the function! This is *not* correct:

```
myfnptr = thefunction();  // ???
```

You don't want to *call* the function; you just want to assign its address to `myfnptr`.

Assigning a function address to a pointer is similar to assigning addresses of variables to data pointers, but using function pointers requires some careful programming. After assigning `thefunction()`'s address to `myfnptr`, call the function like this:

```
float answer;
answer = (* myfnptr)(5, 10);
```

If the function requires no arguments, leave the final parentheses blank:

```
answer = (* myfnptr)();
```

These statements call the function addressed by `myfnptr`. Of course, you could always call the function directly without using a pointer:

```
answer = thefunction();
```

When using the pointer, however, you must add the parentheses and asterisk to the function pointer's name. As in the declaration, the extra space between the asterisk and function name is optional, and you could write

```
answer = (*myfnptr)();
```

Now that you've seen the basic forms, look at a program that puts a function pointer to good use. Listing 4.11, PLOT.CPP, plots a graph of a mathematical function. As you'll see when you examine the statements, using a pointer to that function makes it easy to replace it with another mathematical function to plot.

### Listing 4.11. PLOT.CPP.

```
1:  // plot.cpp -- Plot a function
2:
3:  #include <tscdefs.h>
4:  #include IOSTREAM_H
5:  #include DISP_H
6:  #include <conio.h>
7:  #include <math.h>
8:  #include <time.h>
9:
10: #if (defined __TSC_BTC__) ¦¦ (defined __TSC_MSC__)
11: #include <msleep.h>
12: #endif
13:
14: #define XSCALE 20        // X display adjustment
15: #define YSCALE 10        // Y display adjustment
16: #define XMIN 0           // Display coordinate ranges
17: #define XMAX 78
18: #define YMIN 0
19: #define YMAX 24
20:
21: // Define pointer to float function with an int parameter
22: typedef float (* pfptr)(int x);
23:
24: // Function prototypes
25: void pause(void);
26: void yplot(int x, float f);
27: float afunction(int x);
28:
29: main()
30: {
31:    int x;
32:    pfptr pf = afunction;
33:
```

*continues*

## Listing 4.11. continued

```
34:     disp_open();          // Initialize display package
35:     disp_move(0, 0);      // Move cursor to upper left corner
36:     disp_eeop();          // Clear screen
37:     for (x = XMIN; x <= XMAX; x++)    // Cycle for range of x
38:       yplot(x, (* pf)(x * XSCALE));   // Plot function result
39:     pause();                          // Wait for keypress to end
40:     return 0;
41:   }
42:
43:   // Wait for a keypress, then continue
44:   void pause(void)
45:   {
46:     getch();
47:   }
48:
49:   // Plot value of f on y axis at x
50:   void yplot(int x, float f)
51:   {
52:     disp_move(YSCALE + (f * YSCALE), x);
53:     msleep(50);           // Optional. Remove to plot at full speed
54:     disp_putc('*');       // Display asterisk on graph
55:   }
56:
57:   // The function to plot
58:   float afunction(int x)
59:   {
60:     return sin((x * M_PI) / 180.0);
61:   }
```

This small example doesn't show the full value of using a function pointer. In a larger program where this program might be only one of many related modules, it would be tedious to change the function name or to have to recompile the entire module just to plug in a new plot function. Function pointers make that easy.

A pointer to a function can simplify the job of replacing one function with another. So that other places in the program can create function pointer variables of the same type, a typedef declaration at line 22 declares the design for a pointer to the plot function:

```
typedef float (* pfptr)(int x);
```

Except for `typedef`, this construction is similar to the function pointer described before. Instead of creating a pointer *variable,* this line creates a new *data type* named `pfptr` (plot-function pointer). Other places in the program can then use that new data-type identifier to create function-pointer variables. For example, line 32 creates a pointer named `pf` of type `pfptr` and initializes it at the same time to address a function named `afunction()`:

```
pfptr pf = afunction;
```

At this point, `pf` addresses `afunction()`, which is written elsewhere. (In a larger program, the function would probably reside in a separate module, and a statement would pass `pf` to the plot module.) Look carefully at `afunction()`'s prototype at line 27 and at its implementation at lines 58–61. The function's declaration matches that of the function pointer's:

```
float afunction(int x);
```

After assigning the address of this function to `pf`, PLOT calls the function at line 38 inside a `for` loop. The call to the function is used as an argument to another function, `yplot`:

```
yplot(x, (* pf)(x * XSCALE));
```

This statement calls `yplot()` to plot one value on-screen. The first parameter is simply the `x` coordinate value—the column where this value should be plotted. The second argument uses the form `(* pf)()` to call the function addressed by `pf`. To this function, the expression passes the argument `(x * XSCALE)`, representing the y coordinate value for the plot. Dereferencing `pf` with the expression `(* pf)()` causes the program to call the function addressed by `pf`, or in this case, `afunction()`. This calculates a formula (here, the sine of a value representing an angle). The function returns a `float` value, which is then passed to `yplot()` for plotting.

As you can see from this section, function pointers can be tricky to use and to set up. (Use the samples here as guides the next time you need to create a function pointer.) A good place for function pointers is in precompiled library routines to which you can pass function pointers to force a routine to call a new function in your own program. (Chapter 8, "Files and Directories," lists a program, SORTTXT.CPP, that demonstrates how to call functions via pointers this way with the `qsort()` library function.)

Now, back to a subject I promised to complete earlier—one that confuses even expert C programmers from time to time—pointers and arrays. As you are about to learn, in C and C++, these are just birds of the same feather.

# Pointers and Arrays

**M**ost people who are learning C++ or C are surprised to discover that arrays and pointers are one and the same. All array names are actually pointers, and all pointers actually address arrays.

Sound strange? If so, consider the nature of an array. As you learned in Chapter 2, "Making Statements and Building Structures," an array stores one or more variables of the same data type in memory. Those variables are stacked up like jets over O'Hare. The array name locates the start of the array. In that sense, the array identifier in a C++ program (and in C) acts like a *pointer* to the first element in the array.

A simple example proves this important concept. Run Listing 4.12, ARRAYPTR.CPP. As you can see, the program assigns integer values to an array and then uses indexing (the normal technique) to display that value. It also uses the array name as a pointer to do the same, proving that the array name *is* a pointer.

**Listing 4.12. ARRAYPTR.CPP.**

```
 1:  // arrayptr.cpp -- Show relationship between arrays and pointers
 2:
 3:  #include <tscdefs.h>
 4:  #include IOSTREAM_H
 5:
 6:  #define MAX 10       // Size of array
 7:
 8:  void showFirst(void);
 9:
10:  int array[MAX];       // Global array of MAX integers
11:
12:  main()
13:  {
14:    array[0] = 123;    // Assign value using indexing
15:    showFirst();       // Display value both ways
16:    *array = 321;      // Assign value using pointer
17:    showFirst();       // Display value both ways
18:    return 0;
19:  }
20:
```

```
21:  void showFirst(void)
22:  {
23:    cout << "array[0] = " << array[0] << '\n';  // Via index
24:    cout << "*array   = " << *array   << '\n';  // Via pointer
25:  }
```

Line 10 declares a global array of int values. Line 14 assigns the value 123 to the first element in the array using the index expression [0]. After this, showFirst() displays that value. At line 23, an output stream statement uses the expression array[0]—the normal way of selecting an array element with an index value.

The next line (24) displays the same value, but instead of the brackets and an index value, the statement treats array as though the program had declared it as a pointer. In fact, that's exactly what array is—a pointer to its arrayed elements. The expression *array in line 24 dereferences the pointer to "get to" the addressed data and is exactly equivalent to the expression array[0].

This idea may be easier to visualize if you think about what the compiler must do in order to process an indexed array expression such as array[4]. To "find" the fifth element in the array (remember, the first element is at index 0, so the fifth is at index 4, not 5), the compiler has to

- Locate the start of the array. Let's call it start.

- Calculate the distance from start to the indexed element. In this case, the array contains 2-byte integers, so the fifth element is 4 * 2, or 8 bytes beyond the first. Call this value the offset.

- Add offset to start, creating a pointer to the fifth element.

It is this pointer that the program actually uses when the program executes an expression such as i = array[4]. To make that assignment work, the compiler creates instructions to form a pointer (call it p) to the fifth element in array. It then executes i = *p to complete the assignment. You don't see any of this happening, of course, but it's useful to know what's going on underfoot.

Although it's usually best to let C++ handle the details of array addressing, it's sometimes useful to take that job away from the compiler and use pointers to address array elements directly. For example, run Listing 4.13, PTRARRAY.CPP.

## Listing 4.13. PTRARRAY.CPP.

```cpp
 1:   // ptrarray.cpp -- More about arrays and pointers
 2:
 3:   #include <tscdefs.h>
 4:   #include IOSTREAM_H
 5:
 6:   #define MAX 10        // Size of array
 7:
 8:   void showFirst(void);
 9:
10:   int array[MAX];       // Global array of MAX integers
11:
12:   main()
13:   {
14:     int *p = array;    // p is an int pointer to array
15:     int i;             // i is a plain int variable
16:
17:   // Fill array with values from 0 to MAX - 1
18:     for (i = 0; i < MAX; i++)
19:       array[i] = i;
20:
21:   // Use pointer p to display the array's values
22:     for (i = 0; i < MAX; i++)
23:       cout << *p++ << '\n';
24:
25:   // Use pointer p to display one array value
26:     p = &array[5];
27:     cout << "\narray[5] = " << array[5];
28:     cout << "\n*p ..... = " << *p;
29:     return 0;
30:   }
```

This program is similar to the previous one, but it shows how to use pointers to access any element in an array, not only the first. Line 14 defines a pointer variable p as a pointer to type int, the same type as the array's elements (see line 10). Line 14 also assigns the address of array to p. Using the address-of operator here as in &array would not be correct and will not compile. Remember, array *is* a pointer; therefore, you can assign it directly to another pointer that's bound to the same type (int in this case).

Lines 18–19 use normal indexing to fill array with a few values from 0 to MAX -1. After that, a second for loop at lines 22–23 displays the contents of the array. This time, however, the program uses the pointer p rather than array indexing to refer to each value in array.

Carefully study the expression *p++ in the statement at line 23. There are two actions occurring here. The first dereferences *p, returning the value of the int variable that p addresses. After this, the increment operator ++ advances p to the next int in array. As a result, the loop displays all array elements exactly as though you had written array[i] rather than *p++.

## Pointer Arithmetic

You might wonder how it's possible for an expression like *p++ to advance p to the address of the next item in memory. In this case, those items are integers, which for the compilers supported by this book, take two bytes each. For this reason, so that p++ advances p to the next integer value—not to the next byte—C++ has to add 2, not 1, to p.

That's exactly what happens. The compiler uses p's data type to calculate how many bytes to advance p in an expression such as *p++. Likewise, *p-- subtracts 2 from the address held in p. When adding and subtracting pointers and values, C++ considers the values to represent *units* of the data types that the pointers address. If a pointer ap addresses a 10-byte structure, ap++ advances the address in ap by 10 bytes. You never have to calculate these details, but you should be aware that C++ multiplies values added and subtracted to and from pointers by the size of the addressed data.

You can also use pointer arithmetic expressions such as p += 10 to advance p 10 units from its present position. And you can compare pointers, using expressions like (p1 < p2). But these are turbulent waters. Although the compiler accepts such statements, they may not work correctly with far pointers.

## Arrays of Pointers

A useful construction is an array of pointers. Each element in such an array points to the "real" data located elsewhere. This is a good way to keep track of many items of different sizes—a series of strings loaded from a text file, for example. If those strings were stored in fixed string variables, perhaps declared as char c[128], each 80-character string would waste 48 bytes. Multiplied by a few hundred lines, that much waste can add up quickly.

> **Note:** Because PC compilers use segment and offset values to represent far pointers, it's possible for two different combinations of those values to address the identical location in memory. Pointer comparison expressions do not take this fact into account, and for that reason, they may fail. Every C++ compiler, it seems, has its own rules and regulations for comparing segmented pointer values, but if you intend to write portable code, it's probably best to avoid these techniques and not write programs to rely on pointer comparisons.

Listing 4.14, READSTR.CPP, shows how to avoid such waste. The idea is to create an array of pointers, allocate just enough storage to hold each string, and save a pointer to that string in the array. Despite the fact that the array itself takes some memory, this plan tends to save space because most strings will not be of the same lengths.

### Listing 4.14. READSTR.CPP.

```
1:  // readstr.cpp -- Read strings into dynamic variables
2:
3:  #include <tscdefs.h>
4:  #include IOSTREAM_H
5:  #include IOMANIP_H
6:  #include <stdio.h>
7:  #include <string.h>
8:
9:  #define MAX 3      // Maximum number of strings
10:
11: char *readstring(void);
12:
13: main()
14: {
15:   int i;              // i is an index into the following
16:   char *array[MAX];   // an array of MAX char pointers
17:
18:   cout << "Enter " << MAX << " strings:" << endl;
19:   for (i = 0; i < MAX; i++)
20:     array[i] = readstring();   // Save pointer to each string
```

```
21:    cout << "\n\nYour strings are:" << endl;
22:    for (i = 0; i < MAX; i++)
23:      cout << array[i] << '\n';  // Display strings via pointers
24:    for (i = 0; i < MAX; i++)
25:      delete array[i];          // Delete allocated string memory
26:    return 0;
27:  }
28:
29:  // Read string
30:  char *readstring(void)
31:  {
32:    char buffer[128]; // buffer for reading each string
33:
34:    gets(buffer);              // Read string from user or stdin
35:    return strdup(buffer);  // Allocate and return string copy
36:  }
```

Although READSTR is just a demonstration, the principles are the same no matter how many strings you need to hold in memory. Line 16 defines an array of pointers to type char. Each element in the array is a pointer. By storing the strings in memory, and saving the address of each string's first character in the array, the program demonstrates a convenient way to find its strings, no matter where they are stored.

Function readstring() (lines 30–36) prompts you to enter one string (or you can enter a DOS command such as **readstr <file.txt** to pass strings from a file to the program). Line 34 calls gets() to read a string into a local buffer. After this, line 35 calls strdup() to allocate exactly enough memory on the heap to hold the string's characters and copy the enter characters to that space. The address of the allocated memory is returned as the function result.

This means that line 20 receives from readstring() the address of a newly allocated string in memory. By saving these addresses in the array of char pointers, the program can easily display or perform other operations on the strings, as lines 22–23 demonstrate. Notice that there is no need to dereference the pointers in the array at line 23. C++ understands that strings (arrays of char) are represented by char pointers. Remember, arrays and pointers are equivalent, and for that reason, pointers to char do not require special treatment to let C++ know that it should treat the pointer as the address of a string.

> **Note:** This brings up an interesting point. If C++ treats a pointer to char as addressing a string—that is, an *array* of characters—how do you declare a pointer to a *single* character? The answer is, you don't. A single character takes one byte of memory. Declaring a pointer, which takes two or more bytes, to address a single char would be silly. However, if you need only one character addressed by a pointer declared as char *p, the expression p[0] does the trick. Because p, a pointer, is equivalent to an array, indexing p with [0] returns a single char element at the address specified by p.

# Functions that Return String Pointers

C hapter 1, "Discovering C++," lists a program DT.CPP that displays the date and time. By calling string functions in the C++ library, it's possible to write that same program with fewer statements.

String functions return a pointer to type char. Because C++ considers such pointers to address strings, you can pass any string function's result directly to a parameter declared as char * or as const char * (including const tells the compiler not to permit assignments to the addressed data). Listing 4.15, THEDATE.CPP, for example, calls the string function asctime() to convert the date and time into an ASCII string. This function's prototype is in the header file time.h, which the program includes at line 5.

### Listing 4.15. THEDATE.CPP.

```
1:   // thedate.cpp -- Improved date and time display
2:
3:   #include <tscdefs.h>
4:   #include IOSTREAM_H
5:   #include <time.h>
6:
7:   main()
8:   {
9:     time_t t;
```

```
10:
11:    time(&t);
12:    cout << asctime(localtime(&t));
13:    return 0;
14:  }
```

THEDATE defines a variable t of type time_t—also declared in time.h. Line 11 passes the address of t to time(), which expects to receive a pointer to a variable of this type. In time.h, you'll find that time() is declared as time(time_t *);. Its single parameter is a pointer to type time_t.

The time() function copies the date and time in binary format to the structure addressed by the pointer you pass to the function. Then line 12 passes t's address to function localtime(), which converts the raw date and time information into a structure that asctime() requires. That function converts this information to a string displayed here in an output-stream statement. The result is a line like this:

```
Tue Jun 30 10:23:36 1992
```

Cascading functions inside functions as at line 12 is a common practice. When dealing with string functions, however, be aware that when a function returns type char *, that pointer (unless equal to null) addresses space that's best treated as temporary. String functions do not return strings. They return *pointers to strings*. The characters that belong to that string are stored somewhere in memory, of course, but the next time you call the same function, it will probably use that same memory for the next string.

For this reason, you'll almost certainly introduce bugs into your programs if you write code like this:

```
char *sp;  // sp is a pointer to a string
sp = asctime(localtime(&t));  // ???
cout << sp;
```

This dangerous practice saves the result of asctime() in a string pointer, sp. It then displays the string by passing the pointer to cout. Although this will probably work, the program may fail later if it again executes asctime() or another string function, which may change the string that sp addresses.

To guard against this possibility, if you need to save the results of a string function, first create new storage to hold a string of the same length as the string at the address returned by asctime() or another string function. Then use the strdup()

function declared in string.h. This function calls `malloc()` to allocate memory to hold a string passed to the function as a `char` pointer. It then copies the characters addressed by that pointer into the newly allocated memory. Finally, it returns the address of that memory, which you can save in a pointer so that you can find the copy of the string later. Here's one way to accomplish all of this:

```
char *sp;  // sp is a pointer to a string
sp = strdup(asctime(localtime(&t)));
cout << sp;
```

This inserts the call to `asctime()` inside a call to `strdup()`. Now, the program can be certain that sp addresses a string that won't change unexpectedly. After the program is finished using the copied string, delete its memory by calling `free()`:

```
free(sp);
```

# String Functions

Supplied with C++ are a rich set of functions that operate on strings. Most of these functions return pointers to strings, and most take one or more string pointers as parameters. You've already seen one of these functions, `strdup()`, in action. With what you have learned about arrays and pointers—and especially about pointers to arrays of characters—you're ready to begin using `strdup()` and other C++ string functions in your own programs.

I'll cover a few of the more common string functions here. For descriptions of others, look up function names in your C++ compiler's reference.

> **Note:** To use the string functions described in this section, insert the directive `#include <string.h>` at the beginning of your program.

## Common String Functions

Copying one string to another doesn't work as you might expect it to, especially if you have some experience with BASIC or Pascal. If s1 and s2 are both `char *` pointers, this assignment does *not* make a copy of the string addressed by s2:

```
s1 = s2;
```

That copies the *pointer* s2 to s1, not the characters addressed by s2; therefore, after the assignment, s1 and s2 address the *same* string in memory. Sometimes this can be useful, and there's nothing technically wrong with the statement. Just be sure that it accomplishes what you expect.

Dereferencing the pointers is also no help:

```
*s1 = *s2;
```

That copies only *one* character addressed by s2 to the memory addressed by s1 (to which you should be careful to allocate at least one byte beforehand).

**Note:** When two or more pointers address the same memory space allocated on the heap, you *must* be careful never to delete or free more than one of those pointers. Deleting the same allocated memory space more than once will corrupt the heap and cause your program to fail. There are no exceptions to this rule!

To copy the characters addressed by one string pointer to space addressed by another, call strcpy(). For example, this copies the string addressed by a character pointer source to the memory addressed by a similarly declared character pointer destination:

```
char *source;
char *destination;
...
strcpy(destination, source);
```

Two observations are important here. One, the "direction" is right to left (from source to destination), which is easy to mix up. Second, the memory addressed by destination must be large enough to hold the characters in the string addressed by source. If there's not enough room to hold the string, the statement may overwrite other variables or code in memory, causing a serious problem.

To make sure that destination addresses enough space, use statements like these:

```
destination = new char[strlen(source) + 1];
if (!destination)
  error("Out of memory");
strcpy(destination, source);
```

Using `strlen()` to find the length of the source string, and allocating that much space plus one byte, ensures that `destination` addresses enough space to hold the string copy plus a null terminator byte.

You'll find `strlen()` useful in many other situations. The function returns an integer value equal to the number of characters in a string, but *not* including the string's null terminator. Even a zero-length string has a terminating byte, and therefore, occupies at least one byte of memory.

To make it easier to copy strings of different sizes, you can also use `strncpy()`. This is similar to `strcpy()`, but takes a third argument specifying how many characters to copy from the source to the destination:

```
strncpy(destination, source, 10);
```

That copies 10 characters addressed by `source` to the memory addressed by `destination`. If the source string is longer than the space allocated to `destination`, the function does *not* terminate the new string with a null. For that reason, it's usually a good idea to fill the `destination` string with nulls before calling `strncpy()`. Assuming that n represents the number of bytes, one way to do this is to follow `strncpy()` with

```
int n = 11;
destination = new char[11];
strncpy(destination, source, 10);
destination[n - 1] = 0;
```

The statements allocate 11 bytes to `destination` (enough room for 10 characters plus a null terminator). Then `strncpy()` copies up to 10 characters from `source` to `destination`. To make sure that the copied string is terminated correctly, the final statement assigns an ASCII null (0) to the last byte allocated to `destination`.

Another way to copy strings is to use `strdup()`. Like `strcpy()` and `strncpy()`, `strdup` copies a string. Unlike those other functions, however, `strdup()` also allocates space on the heap to hold the new copy. The function returns `char *`, and you will usually assign it to a character pointer like this:

```
destination = strdup(source);
```

This is one of my favorite string functions. Assuming that `source` addresses a character string, the statement allocates just enough space to hold those characters. It assigns the address of the space to `destination` and copies the characters addressed by `source` (including the null terminator) to the newly allocated space. If enough free memory is not available to hold the string copy, `strdup()` returns null. Always follow each use of `strdup()` with a check of the results:

```
destination = strdup(source);
if (!destination)
  error("Out of memory");
```

# Joining Strings

When you need to join two or more strings, call strcat() or strncat(). (The *cat* stands for *concatenate,* meaning "to join.") Suppose that you have these three string pointers:

```
char *lastName = " Lincoln";
char *firstName = "Abraham";
char *name;
```

You can join Abe's first and last names by first allocating some space to name and then calling strcat():

```
name = new char[strlen(lastName) + strlen(firstName) + 1];
strcpy(name, firstName);
strcat(name, lastName);
cout << name;
```

The call to strcat() attaches a copy of the string addressed by lastName onto the end of the string addressed by name. The function returns a pointer to the result, letting you use it directly. For example, the last two lines could be written

```
cout << strcat(name, lastName);
```

This still attaches lastName's string to name's, but also returns the address of the final result so it can be written to cout. A similar function, strncat(), adds a third parameter that specifies the number of characters to copy:

```
strncat(name, lastName, 5);
```

The statement copies up to 5 characters or strlen(lastName), whichever value is smaller, from lastName to the end of name.

# Comparing Strings

Comparing two strings is another operation that may not work as you expect it to. As with copying strings, if a program has two string pointers s1 and s2, this expression does *not* compare the strings addressed by the pointers:

```
if (s1 == s2)
  cout << "The strings are equal!\n";   // ???
```

The expression (s1 == s2) compares the two *pointers,* not the characters they address. Dereferencing the pointers doesn't help:

```
if (*s1 == *s2)
  cout << "The strings are equal!\n";    // ???
```

Looks good, but it compares only the first character addressed by each pointer, not the full strings at those locations. To do that, call the strcmp() function:

```
if (strcmp(s1, s2) == 0)
  cout << "The strings are equal!\n";
```

This is the correct way to compare two strings. The strcmp() function returns an int value less than 0 if the string at s1 is alphabetically less than the string at s2. It returns 0 if the two strings are equal. It returns a positive value if the string at s1 is alphabetically greater than the string at s2. To test whether s1 is greater than s2, you can write

```
if (strcmp(s1, s2) > 0)
  cout << "The first string is greater!\n";
```

A similar function, strcmpi(), takes upper- and lowercase into consideration when comparing the strings. Replace strcmp() with strcmpi() when you *don't* want case to matter. In other words, strcmp("A", "a") is less than 0; strcmpi("A", "a") equals 0.

## Searching Strings

Programs that break down strings into their components, an action called *parsing,* can use several string functions for searching one string for occurrences of characters and other strings.

One such function is strchr(), which locates the first character in a string that matches a given argument. For example, to find a period in a string addressed by a pointer named filename, you can write

```
char *filename = "TEST.DAT";
cout << strchr(filename, '.');
```

If the character in the second argument to strchr isn't found in the string addressed by the char * in the first argument, strchr returns null. If it can find the specified character, it returns a pointer to it of type char *.

It's important to realize that `strchr` returns a character pointer, which can be treated as another string that starts somewhere in the middle of the original. However, `strchr` does *not* copy the string, so you must be aware that you now have two pointers addressing the same characters. To copy the tail of a string after searching it for a specific character, use statements like these:

```
char *filename = "TEST.DAT";
char extension[4] = "none";
char *p;

if ((p = strchr(filename, '.')) != NULL)
  strcpy(extension, p);
cout << extension;
```

Try running this sample and then change `"TEST.DAT"` to `"TEST"`. The function call `strchr(filename, '.')` returns a character pointer to the first period in the string addressed by `filename`, or it returns null, a condition the `if` statement carefully checks before using the data addressed by p.

To find the last occurrence of a character, use `strrchr()`. For example, `strrchr(filename, 'X')` returns a pointer to the last X in the string addressed by `filename`. If there are no Xs in the string, `strrchr()` returns null.

You can also search for the occurrences of one string inside another. To do this, call `strstr()`:

```
char *source = "ABCDEFGHIJKLMNOPQRSTUVWXYZ";
char *pattern = "MNOP";
char *p;

if ((p = strstr(source, pattern)) != NULL)
  cout << p;
```

This searches for the string addressed by `pattern` inside the string addressed by source, setting p to the address of the first matching character or to null if no match was found. The output stream statement displays the string starting with the matching character.

To ignore differences between upper- and lowercase arguments passed to `strstr()`, call `strlwr()` for both strings before the search:

```
char *source = "ABCDEFGHIJKLMNOPQRSTUVWXYZ";
char *pattern = "mnop";
char *p;

strlwr(source);
strlwr(pattern);
if ((p = strstr(source, pattern)) != NULL)
  cout << p;
```

This converts all characters in both `source` and `pattern` strings to lowercase before calling `strstr()`. (If you don't want to alter the original strings, use `strcpy()` or `strdup()` to make copies of them and pass those copies to `strlwr()`). You can also call `strupr()` to convert strings to uppercase rather than lowercase if you prefer.

Because `strlwr()` and `strupr()` return pointers to their string arguments, you can use them directly in a statement:

```
if ((strstr(strlwr(source), strlwr(pattern))) != NULL)
  cout << "\nFound " << pattern << " in " << source;
```

# Command-Line Arguments

Y ou've undoubtedly used programs that accept command-line arguments. When you enter a command like **ztc thedate** to compile THEDATE.CPP, the argument `thedate` is passed to ZTC.COM for processing.

Other programs often let you select various options, for example, by entering -s or /m to change the way a program operates. Passing instructions to programs this way is convenient, and it eliminates the need for a program to prompt users for required and optional details.

Writing programs that can pick up arguments passed on the command line is not difficult. The first step is to change the way you declare function `main()`. In place of the usual empty parentheses, add two parameters this way:

```
main(int argc, char *argv[])
{
  ...
}
```

The first parameter, argc (argument count), is a plain integer. It represents the number of arguments passed to main(). An "argument" is defined as any unbroken sequence of characters.

The second parameter is an array of char pointers. The empty brackets indicate that the array's size is not fixed but is determined at runtime. C++ guarantees that argv (argument vectors, or pointers) will hold as many char pointers as specified by argc. Together, the two variables make it easy to pick up arguments passed to a program on the command line.

> **Note:** Remember always that char *argv[] declares an array of char pointers, *not* an array of strings. Each element in argv is a pointer that addresses a string stored somewhere in memory. Forgetting this fact is a common source of bugs. Figure 4.9 illustrates the relationship between argv and its collection of argument strings.

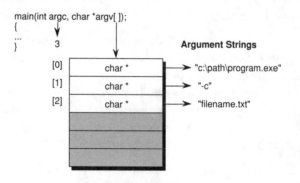

**Figure 4.9.** How argument strings are organized in memory after calling a fictitious program with the command line **c:\path\program -c filename.txt**.

A simple program demonstrates how to access arguments passed to a C++ program. Listing 4.16, CMDLINE.CPP, also makes a useful test for investigating the forms of arguments that another program will receive. When designing new code to pick up command-line arguments, run CMDLINE and type test arguments, for example **cmdline arg1 myname.txt -s -p/x**. The program simply displays all of the arguments you pass to it. It doesn't take any action on them, so feel free to experiment.

## Listing 4.16. CMDLINE.CPP.

```
 1:  // cmdline.cpp -- Demonstrate command-line arguments
 2:
 3:  #include <tscdefs.h>
 4:  #include IOSTREAM_H
 5:
 6:  main(int argc, char *argv[])
 7:  {
 8:    while (--argc > 0)
 9:      cout << *++argv << '\n';
10:    return 0;
11:  }
```

Though it's only a shorty, CMDLINE shows the three essential elements that most command-line processing programs need. First, line 6 declares main() as described earlier, adding the argc and argv parameters. When the program runs, it passes to main() the number of command-line arguments in argc. It also passes an array of char pointers in argv. These pointers address each argument string.

The while loop at line 8 decrements argc before testing whether it's greater than 0. This means that if argc equals 1 at the start of the program—indicating that there is one argument to process—the statement at line 9 will never execute. The reason for this is that argv always addresses at least one argument: the pathname of the currently running program. If you need this pathname string, you can retrieve it by using the expression argv[0] or just *argv. Either of these expressions selects a single char pointer from the start of the argv array.

Line 8 in CMDLINE demonstrates a typical trick with command-line arguments. The expression displays one string addressed by argv:

```
cout << *++argv << '\n';
```

Think this through. Because argv is an array, you can treat it as a pointer. Applying the ++ operator to argv advances that pointer to the next element in the array—in other words, to the next string pointer. Applying the dereference symbol * to the result retrieves one char pointer from the array, which C++ treats as the address of a string.

Another way to access the string pointers in the argv array is to index that variable as an array. For example, argv[2] locates the third command-line string pointer. Either method—indexing or using argv as a pointer—is acceptable, and you should be familiar with both of these common techniques. To demonstrate this, replace lines 8 and 9 in CMDLINE.CPP with this `for` loop:

```
for (int i = 0; i < argc; i++)
  cout << argv[i] << '\n';
```

This shows that you can index `argv` as an array of `char` pointers or use it as a pointer to an array of type `char *` elements as in the original program. When you run the modified CMDLINE, enter **cmdline aaa bbb ccc**. You'll see those three arguments along with the program's pathname.

> **Note:** Versions of MS-DOS and PC DOS earlier than 3.0 are not capable of passing the current program's pathname to programs. When running under those DOS versions, `argv[0]` addresses a zero-length string, and the previous changes will not work as expected. If your own programs require pathnames to their own files, run that program only on DOS versions 3.0 or later or include programming that lets people enter a pathname manually when `strlen(argv[0])` equals 0.

# Character Arguments

A common use for command-line arguments is to pass *switches* to a program to select one or more options. For example, a sorting program might accept commands like `sort -d myfile` to sort the contents of MYFILE in descending (-d) order.

By tradition, option letters are preceded by dashes (-d) or slashes (/d). This distinguishes the letters from filenames, which normally don't begin with those same characters. (However, DOS permits filenames to begin with a dash, but not a slash, which can play havoc with this scheme.)

There are many ways to retrieve command-line options, and most programmers develop their favorite methods. Listing 4.17, OPTIONS.CPP, demonstrates one way to accomplish this. Run the program and type commands such as **options -a, options -b -c,** or **options /a -c** to test the results of applying the fictitious option letters a, b, and c. The program detects these options and displays them for confirmation. You might want to convert the program into a function that you can add to any program needing options from the command line.

## Listing 4.17. OPTIONS.CPP.

```
 1:  // options.cpp -- Command-line options demonstration
 2:
 3:  #include <tscdefs.h>
 4:  #include IOSTREAM_H
 5:  #include <stdlib.h>
 6:  #include <ctype.h>
 7:
 8:  enum {False, True};
 9:
10:  int aoption = False;
11:  int boption = False;
12:  int coption = False;
13:
14:  main(int argc, char *argv[])
15:  {
16:    char ch;
17:
18:    while (--argc > 0) {
19:      ch = (*++argv)[0];  // ch = first char of next argument
20:      if ((ch == '-') || (ch == '/')) {
21:        ch = toupper((*argv)[1]);  // ch = second char of argument
22:        switch (ch) {
23:          case 'A':
24:            aoption = True;
25:            break;
26:          case 'B':
27:            boption = True;
28:            break;
29:          case 'C':
30:            coption = True;
31:            break;
32:          default:
33:            cout << "Unknown option letter " << ch << '\n';
34:            exit(1);
35:        }
36:      }
37:      else {
38:        cout << "Unknown option switch " << ch << '\n';
39:        exit(2);
40:      }
```

```
41:    }
42:    cout << "Results (0=False, 1=True):\n";
43:    cout << "aoption = " << aoption << '\n';
44:    cout << "boption = " << boption << '\n';
45:    cout << "coption = " << coption << '\n';
46:    return 0;
47: }
```

Lines 10–12 declare three options, `aoption`, `boption`, and `coption`. These global variables are declared as type `int` and are intended to be `True` (1) or `False` (0). Even though C++ initializes global variables to 0, I assigned default `False` values here for clarity. You don't have to do this in your own programs.

Line 18 begins a `while` loop similar to the one in CMDLINE.CPP. The loop cycles while — `argc` is greater than 0—once for each command-line argument passed to the program but skipping the program's pathname.

Line 19 sets local variable `ch` to the first character of the next argument. Examine this line carefully. You can use this technique to extract characters from command-line strings:

```
ch = (*++argv)[0];
```

The expression in parentheses should look familiar; it's identical to the similar one in CMDLINE.CPP. As there, `*++argv` advances and dereferences the `argv` pointer to the next `char` pointer in the array. C++ evaluates this much of the expression as a `char` pointer—a pointer to a string. Because a string is an array of `char` variables, applying the index `[0]` to the `char` pointer retrieves the first character from that string.

In general, to extract a single character from a string, use brackets and an index value such as `s[5]` or `mystring[23]` as you do for any other array. The parentheses in the expression `(*++argv)[0]` are required because `argv` is *not* a pointer to a string. The expression `argv[0]` is a char pointer. The expression `(*argv)[0]` is a char variable in the string addressed by `argv[0]`. (Remember, expressions like `argv[0]` and `*argv` are equivalent because of the relationship between arrays and pointers.)

Lines 19–20 in OPTIONS test whether `ch` is a dash or a slash, indicating that the next character should be an option letter. Line 20 picks up that character with the assignment expression

```
ch = toupper((*argv)[1]);
```

Spend a moment examining the expression (*argv)[1]. First, (*argv) dereferences the argv pointer to *another* pointer, which addresses a string. Second, the index expression [1] selects the second character of that string. This should be the option letter, which a call to the toupper() function converts to uppercase. (The "function" toupper() might be implemented as a macro, but even so, it's used as a function.)

> **Note:** Shouldn't line 21 test the length of the argument before indexing the string's second character? What if the string is only one character long? Think about this. If the first character in the string is a dash or a slash, and if that's the only character in the string, the next "character" will be the string's null terminator, which the program will ignore. In many cases, however, it is a good idea to make sure that strings (and other arrays) have valid information in them before applying index expressions to reference that data.

A large switch statement at lines 22–35 completes the job of detecting command-line options by setting the three global variables to True for their letters. OPTIONS then displays the results at lines 42–45.

# Numeric Arguments

In addition to passing strings as command-line arguments, it's frequently useful to pass numeric values to programs. For example, Listing 4.18, COLUMN.CPP, accepts commands such as column 1 12. This specifies the starting column number (1) and width of the column (12) that you want to extract from the standard input. One way to use COLUMN is to enter the command dir ¦ column 1 12, which lists a disk directory, passes each full line of that directory listing to COLUMN, and extracts 12 columns of text starting with column 1. The result is a list of filenames minus the other information, such as the date and time, normally listed with directory entries. (The result also contains a few lines of extraneous information that you can ignore.)

**Listing 4.18. COLUMN.CPP.**

```
1:  // column.cpp -- Extract a column from input lines
2:
```

```
 3:   #include <tscdefs.h>
 4:   #include IOSTREAM_H
 5:   #include IOMANIP_H
 6:   #include <stdlib.h>
 7:
 8:   #define NEWLINE '\n'
 9:
10:   main(int argc, char *argv[])
11:   {
12:     char c;                // I/O character
13:     int cstart, cend;      // Start and end column numbers
14:     int cpos = 0;          // Column position on current line
15:
16:   // Display instructions if 1 or 0 arguments entered
17:     if (argc < 3) {
18:       cerr << "COLUMN  v1.00  (c) 1991 by Tom Swan\n";
19:       cerr << "To use: Enter column number and width\n";
20:       cerr << "Example: dir ¦ column 1 12\n";
21:       exit(1);
22:     }
23:
24:   // Calculate starting and ending columns
25:     cstart = atoi(argv[1]);
26:     cend = cstart + atoi(argv[2]) - 1;
27:     if (cstart < 1)
28:       cstart = 1;
29:     if (cend < cstart)
30:       cend = cstart;
31:
32:   // Copy selected column from input lines to output
33:     while (cin.get(c)) {
34:       cpos++;
35:       if (c == NEWLINE) {
36:         cout << endl;
37:         cpos = 0;
38:       } else if ((cstart <= cpos) && (cpos <= cend))
39:         cout << c;
40:     }
41:     return 0;
42:   }
```

Because COLUMN requires two arguments, lines 17–22 test whether argc is less than 3. If so, the program displays a reminder about how to use it—a good idea in most programs that need specific numbers of arguments. Remember that argc is always at least 1 because the first argument string is the program's pathname. To test whether there are at least n arguments available, argc should be greater or equal to n+1.

After checking that there are at least two arguments available, COLUMN extracts each string and converts it into an integer value. It does this at lines 25–26 with the assignment statements:

```
cstart = atoi(argv[1]);
cend = cstart + atoi(argv[2]) - 1;
```

The expressions argv[1] and argv[2] retrieve the second and third command-line arguments. (The program's pathname is at argv[0], the first argument.) This is another illustration of the way that argv can be treated as an array of character pointers. Indexing argv as an array is probably the easiest method when you simply need to access arguments in full, as in this program.

Each of the two argument strings is then passed to atoi() (ASCII to integer). This converts the arguments to integer values that are used to calculate cstart and cend, representing the starting and ending columns to cut from the input. The while loop at lines 33–40 uses these values to write text from these columns; text in other columns is ignored.

**Note:** Lines 27–30 check the values of cstart and cend, altering them so that cstart is never less than 1 and that cend is greater or equal to cstart. This shows another way to deal with data entry errors. Instead of stopping the program with an error message, if someone enters the wrong values—for example, typing **column -5 -12**—the program simply adjusts the arguments to a reasonable range.

# Questions and Exercises

4.1. Show the definitions for creating a pointer named pfloat to a variable of type float, a pointer named string to type char, and a pointer prec to a struct named customer.

4.2. What does a pointer variable contain?

4.3. Given a pointer named `fp` to type `float`, write an output-stream statement that displays the value addressed by `fp`.

4.4. What does the phrase "dereferencing a pointer" mean?

4.5. Suppose a program defines a variable named `bigValue` of type `double`. Using a pointer, define an alias named `aliasPtr` for `bigValue`. Write a statement that uses `aliasPtr` to display `bigValue`'s value.

4.6. What is the main difference between null and `void`?

4.7. Suppose a program defines a `void` pointer `p` that addresses an `int` value in memory. Write an output-stream statement that uses `p` to display that value.

4.8. A program defines a pointer `counter` to a variable of type `double`. Write two statements that show the size of the pointer and the size of the data addressed by the pointer.

4.9. In most models of PCs, address 0x0040:0x006C contains a 4-byte integer that stores the current number of clock ticks since startup. (One clock tick equals about 0.055 seconds.) Write a program to display this value.

4.10. Write a program to allocate space for a string on the heap, and then prompt for and store in that space characters entered at the keyboard. Display the results to prove that they are inserted into your string.

4.11. Write a program that creates an array of 100 floating point values on the heap. Include statements that fill the array with values and then display those values in a table.

4.12. Given the following `struct`, write a program to create space for a `record` variable on the heap, assign the address of that space to a pointer `rp` (record pointer), and use the pointer to assign test values to each of the `struct`'s members:

```
struct record {
  int count;
  double balance;
  char *title;
};
```

4.13. Using the same struct from Exercise 4.12, write a program to allocate fresh space on the heap for an 80-character string. Assign the address of this space to the `title` member in a `record` variable that's also stored on the heap.

4.14. After assigning heap space to a variable of type `record` in Exercise 4.12, and assiging heap space to the `title` member in the `struct`, what statement or statements are required to delete these spaces from the heap?

4.15. What value does `new` return if that function can't fulfill a request to reserve heap space?

4.16. What is "fragmentation?"

4.17. Create a `struct` that keeps a string's length in a member along with a pointer to the string's characters. Write a function that assigns a string and length to a variable of your new data type. What advantage does your function offer over using common string functions and the `strlen()` function?

4.18. Show three equivalent statements using `new`, `malloc()`, and `calloc()` that reserve space for an array of 100 integer values on the heap. Show the statements required to delete the reserved space in each case.

4.19. Write a function that removes extra blanks from the end of a string. The function does not have to alter the physical size of the string. (Hint: Remember that a byte equal to 0 marks the end of a string of characters.)

4.20. Declare a pointer `fp` to a function that returns type `double` and takes two parameters, one of type `int` and one of type `float`. Write a statement that calls the function. (If you want to complete the program, you can implement the function to multiply an `int` and `float` arguments and return the result.)

4.21. Write a program named MULT that accepts two floating-point arguments from the DOS command line and displays the product of those values.

# Class Objectives

S o far, you've learned most of C++'s fundamentals, you've studied many sample programs, and you may even have written a few of your own. If so, how did you begin? Like most programmers, you probably started with an idea, maybe scratched a few notes, and then started typing. Perhaps you copied one of the sample programs in the previous four chapters as a template for your new design. At the very least, you probably referred to some of the programming in this book for guidance.

Building on other programmers' code (or on your own past efforts) is a natural way to work. But suppose that you need to tackle a heftier project. How would you proceed? One way would be to apply the top-down design principles outlined in Chapter 3, "Functions: Programming in Pieces." With this concept, or *paradigm,* you begin with the larger goals—for example, to play chess, to compute a spreadsheet, or to sort a database file—and work toward finishing the details—to move pieces, to evaluate expressions, and to compare records. Eventually, you will write low-level code to carry out small, well-defined functions that perform easily understood tasks. In this way, the job of writing even the most complex software reduces to the relatively simple steps of creating small functions that even novice programmers should be able to handle. With luck, you'll be able to refashion existing functions from your personal library to fit the new code.

**CHAPTER 5**

Unfortunately, as experienced programmers will tell you, this solid theory frequently develops serious flaws in practice. A strict top-down approach fails to recognize that software specifications often change after projects are well under way. During coding, programmers typically discover fundamental errors in the design, requiring retooling from the top and recoding of functions that were already tested. This wastes time and effort, and it increases the likelihood that new bugs will be introduced into code that was already done and tested.

To "solve" these problems, software companies and programmers have traditionally started new projects by writing detailed specifications about what a program is supposed to accomplish. Today's software houses and consultants typically require customers to approve detailed specifications before any work begins. Worse, customers are often discouraged from changing their minds later, even when a change might be justified. ("Sorry, but you signed off on that spec weeks ago. We can't change the size of the database fields now. It's too late!")

Such rigidity is the death of software. As its name suggests, *software* needs to be malleable so that it can mold to fit changing needs. It's unreasonable to expect people to choose perfect goals from the outset of a complex project. Software should be able to grow, not strictly from the top down, but from the inside out to meet new demands without requiring a complete rewrite just to incorporate minor changes. Programmers should be able to reuse their well-tested functions and build on the foundations laid down by others.

Few people would disagree with that statement, but why then, is such an obvious concept so poorly realized in so much existing code? Just think of the mountain of wasteful programming that probably exists on your computer's disk drive. It's a good bet that most programs in your collection have dozens of similar display functions, input routines, and expression parsers programmers rewrote from scratch only because the subroutines they composed for their previous programs didn't exactly fit the score for the new ones. Wouldn't it be great if there was an alternative—a way to build flexibility into software while making the code more reusable for future projects?

There is. Like top-down design, *object-oriented programming,* or OOP, is a paradigm that can help you to create programs that are easy to modify and that contain functions and other declarations that are simple to reuse. Among C++'s strong points are its many features that let programmers use object-oriented programming techniques. Unlike "pure" OOP languages, which require you to use OOP for everything a program does, C++ is a *hybrid* language that mixes OOP and non-OOP methods. With C++, you can use OOP where it does the most good, but you don't have to abandon what you've learned about conventional programming as described in the previous four chapters. You can mix and match as you please.

While introducing C++'s OOP capabilities in this chapter, I'll also explain some of the reasons that OOP is gaining in popularity among programmers. Understanding how and why others are turning to OOP is a good way to learn the fundamentals of this new wave in software design. By studying certain problems with conventional programming, and seeing how OOP solves those problems, you'll be able to put OOP into practice in your own work without having to wade through a lot of theory that, unfortunately, seems to flood many current OOP texts.

We'll begin with a general problem that OOP is particularly good at solving— making computers simulate actions in the real world, for example, the movement of shoppers passing through a mall or the flow of traffic in a busy city. As you'll see, OOP simplifies the job of writing programmed simulations by letting you focus on the properties of the system instead of making you fuss with time-consuming details about how a program ties its many pieces together. Instead of working towards the far-off goal of a finished program, to write the simulation in C++, you'll spend most of your efforts designing objects that model the system's elements—its buttons, switches, vehicles, people, or whatever items contribute to the events you are trying to simulate. In C++, these objects are called *classes.*

# Go to the Head of the Class

**A** *class* is to OOP what a `struct` is to conventional C++ (and C). Classes combine, or *encapsulate,* functions and the data on which those functions operate. This is the heart of OOP—the binding of action and data into new data types that "know" what they are supposed to do. As Figure 5.1 illustrates, in conventional programming, data is passed to functions, which may pass modified (or new) data back. In OOP, a class encapsulates data and functions, making their relationship part of the program's structure.

A simple example shows the value of C++ classes. Suppose that you've been assigned the job of writing a program to simulate the ups and downs of a bank of elevators in an office building. Your goal is to make it easy to test various schemes and to see how many people can be moved through the system in a given amount of time. Just for fun—and to prove to your boss that you are indeed working hard on the problem—you decide to include a visual display of the elevators in action.

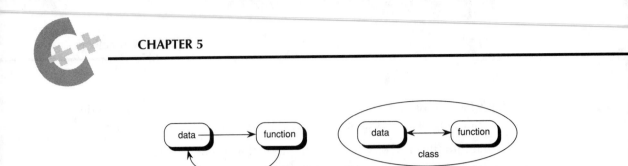

Figure 5.1. In conventional programming, data is passed to and from functions. In object-oriented programming, classes encapsulate data and functions.

At this stage in the program's development, only a few rough goals exist. You know that the code will simulate the movements of people and elevators. You know that it will have to update the display to show the simulation in progress. There are numerous other details to consider, but for now, that much will serve as a starting place. At least it's possible to sketch out the main program's design. Listing 5.1, SIMULATE.CPP, shows my first crack at the problem.

## Listing 5.1. SIMULATE.CPP.

```
 1:  // simulate.cpp -- Sample C++ simulation
 2:
 3:  #include <tscdefs.h>
 4:  #include IOSTREAM_H
 5:  #include "action.h"
 6:
 7:  action theAction;
 8:
 9:  main()
10:  {
11:    theAction.display();
12:    while (theAction.continues()) {
13:      theAction.perform();
14:      theAction.display();
15:    }
16:    theAction.results();
17:    return 0;
18:  }
```

As the simulation develops, I'll list the files in the order I created them originally. This will give you a better sense about how to think in OOP's terms—a hurdle most people have some difficulty with at first. Following the top-down philosophy, I started by writing the program's outer module and `main()` function. Lines 3–5 include the usual tscdefs.h and IOSTREAM_H header files plus another called action.h, which doesn't exist yet. I'm assuming action.h will contain various declarations needed for the simulation.

One of those declarations will be a new data type named `action` (see line 7). An `action` will be a C++ class. It will contain everything there is to know about this simulation. The `action` class will store data associated with the events being simulated, and it will perform various calculations and operations on that data. The `action` class will be a black box, a magic module, a completely self-contained unit that, folks, will require absolutely no maintenance. In no cases will statements outside of the class be permitted access to `action`'s data; the class itself will handle every detail needed to step through the simulation.

Four of those steps are `perform()`, `display()`, `results()`, and `continues()`. Lines 11–16 call these functions in a `while` loop to run the simulation, update the display, and so forth. I probably wouldn't have to explain all this. A glance at SIMULATE's source code should give you a rough idea of what the program is doing. But don't be concerned about how the program accomplishes these tasks. Just accept for now that the `action` class can hold (encapsulate) the fuel (data) and the engine (functions) that will power the simulation.

As you examine SIMULATE.CPP, you may notice that its statements differ in one significant way from those in conventional C++ programs. Instead of calling `perform` and other functions directly, the program uses statements such as `theAction.perform()` and `theAction.continues()`. Similar to the way expressions access data members in structures, these statements use dot notation to call functions associated with `theAction`, which the program defines at line 7 as an object of the `action` class. In fact, except for a few exceptions I'll get to later, referring to an object of a class data type is the *only* way a program can call a class's functions.

> **Note:** If you have any experience with other OOP languages, you're probably familiar with the concept of *message passing*. In a "pure" OOP language, the statement theAction.perform() is said to pass a message named perform() to an object named theAction. The object receives the message and acts on it. With C++ and other hybrid OOP programming languages, the distinction between passing messages and calling functions is unimportant—they are only different models of the same machinery.

## Creating Classes

That an object like theAction can contain functions is one of the backbones of OOP. Because theAction specifies the functions that operate on itself, it's completely self contained. The *only* way to call theAction's functions is to refer to them through that object.

Unless you're familiar with another OOP language, you may not appreciate the value of encapsulating data and objects this way. If so, a short program will show some of the benefits of the OOP way. Listing 5.2, BUTTON.CPP, creates a class named button that a program can "push."

**Listing 5.2. BUTTON.CPP.**

```
1:  // button.cpp -- Creating a class
2:
3:  #include <tscdefs.h>
4:  #include IOSTREAM_H
5:
6:  class button {
7:  private:
8:    int isUp;
9:  public:
10:    void push(int upDown);
11:    int state(void);
12:  };
13:
14:  main()
15:  {
```

```
16:     button myButton;
17:
18:     myButton.push(1);
19:     cout << "\nButton state = " << myButton.state();
20:     myButton.push(0);
21:     cout << "\nButton state = " << myButton.state();
22:     return 0;
23:   }
24:
25:   void button::push(int upDown)
26:   {
27:     isUp = upDown;
28:   }
29:
30:   int button::state(void)
31:   {
32:     return isUp;
33:   }
```

When you run BUTTON, it displays the state of an object named myButton of type button (see line 16). In this demonstration, a button is considered to be "pushed" if its state equals 1. It is not "pushed" if its state is 0.

The button class at lines 6–12 describes everything needed to simulate a button. Notice how the declaration resembles a struct. First comes the class keyword, followed by the class name (button). A pair of parentheses delimit the items inside the class, which are divided into two sections marked private: and public:

```
class button {
private:
  int isUp;
public:
  void push(int upDown);
  int state(void);
};
```

Items, or *members,* in a class's private section are strictly to be used by the class's functions. Except from inside those functions, no statement may refer to a class's private members. Only items declared in the class's public section are visible from outside of the class. Any statement anywhere in a program may refer to a class's public members. Statements outside the class may *never* refer to the class's private declarations. (See Figure 5.2.)

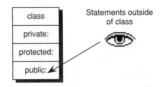

**Figure 5.2.** Statements outside of a class can "see" only the class's public members. Private members are strictly for the class's own use. Protected members are described later in this book.

If you don't specify either the `private:` or `public:` keywords, all members of a class default to private status. Usually, data members are placed in a class's private section, and member functions are stored publicly; therefore, most classes will have a `public:` section or there would be no way for a program to access any of the class's members. But that's only a guideline, not a rule. Members and functions may be declared either privately or publicly. There's also a third section header called `protected:`, which I'll describe in Chapter 7, "Building a Class Library—Part 2."

In the sample `button` class, there is one private data member, an `int` member named `isUp`. There are also two public member functions, `push()` and `state()`. These functions carry out whatever the class is supposed to do—in this case, push a button and return a button's current state. The member functions are just prototypes, similar in form to the prototype functions you've seen in earlier listings. The prototypes describe the functional details of these class members.

As with all prototype functions, you must implement class member functions somewhere in the program. BUTTON does this at lines 25–33. For example, the completed `push()` function is

```
void button::push(int upDown)
{
  isUp = upDown;
}
```

This resembles a typical function definition but includes the name of the class plus a double-colon symbol (`::`) in front of the function name. Adding `button::` to the function name this way uniquely identifies the function to the compiler as a member of the class and not just an ordinary function named `push()`. Because of this notation, other classes may declare functions named `push()`, and the program may include a common C++ `push()` function that is not a member of a class. Because the implementations of those functions all begin with unique declarations, such as `button::push()`, `anotherclass::push()`, or simply `push()`, there's no possibility of a conflict between these identically named functions.

> **Note:** Consider how important it is to be able to invent new classes and never have to worry about using names that conflict with others in a large program. This is a real boon to software development, especially in projects maintained by several people. You are free to use any names you want for class member functions. It is simply *not possible* to create a conflict with another function of the same name that may exist elsewhere.

Except for the class name and double-colon symbol, the `push()` member function looks the same as a common function. In fact, it is the same! The implementations of class member functions and classic C++ functions are identical except for their declaration lines. Anything a common function can do, a member function can do as well.

There are a few differences in the way a class member function can access other class members, however. For example, in `push()`, there's a single statement that assigns the value of parameter `upDown` to the private data member `isUp`. Because `push()` belongs to the same class as `isUp`, it can refer to that data member directly. Statements outside of the class can't do that.

The second member function in `button` returns the current value of `isUp`. Again, the function implementation is similar to a common C++ function, but it includes the class name and a double-colon symbol in the declaration line:

```
int button::state(void)
{
  return isUp;
}
```

Classes typically need functions to return the values of private data members. Because `isUp` is private to the class, only member functions in the class can "see" this variable. Statements outside of the class must call functions like `state()` to obtain a private data member's value. This rule, which may seem arbitrarily restrictive to you now, lets you change the way a class stores its data without having to modify any code outside of the class. In a large program, this can greatly simplify modifications by limiting the amount of required work to a small section of the code.

Next, have a look at BUTTON's `main()` function. After defining an object `myButton` of type `button`, the program executes these four statements:

```
myButton.push(1);
cout << "\nButton state = " << myButton.state();
myButton.push(0);
cout << "\nButton state = " << myButton.state();
```

First, `myButton.push(1)` calls the `push()` member function, which sets the private `isUp` member to 1. The second line then displays the current state of the button by calling `myButton.state()`. The next two lines are similar, but pass 0 to the `push()` function, resetting the button's state.

Programming this same example in a conventional way reveals some of the benefits of the OOP method, which small examples like BUTTON tend to obscure. OOP shines in large projects, and it's difficult to demonstrate OOP's value in small samples that could easily be written using non-OOP techniques. Instead of creating a `button` class, a programmer might solve this problem without OOP by

- Creating a button data type

- Writing functions that accept button parameters

After creating a structure or another data type, perhaps named `buttonType`, you might then write a function named `push(buttonType &b)` to operate on a variable of the new type. This will work, of course, but can also lead to bugs if you accidentally pass the wrong data type to the function (a situation that modern C and C++ compilers are better at catching than in the past) or if you pass an uninitialized pointer to the function, causing it to "push" heaven knows what value in memory.

The OOP approach neatly avoids these and other problems associated with passing data to functions. With OOP, data and function are one, which more closely mirrors the way the world works. To push a real button, you don't unscrew it, pass it to a button-pushing machine, and then plug it back into its socket. You just press it, and the button, which can be pushed, responds to the pressure of your finger.

This is what OOP does—it lets you create data types that have associated properties: buttons that can be pushed, wheels that can turn, and elevators that can travel up and down. Because of this encapsulation of data and code, programs are easier to maintain, and bugs are easier to find. If something goes wrong with a button object, you need to examine only the data and functions associated with a single class. You don't have to hunt around looking for errant statements that affect your data. *No* statements outside a class can access that class's private data.

# Inline Member Functions

After examining one or two OOP programs, you may object to calling functions for simple jobs like assigning values to integer variables. For example, to push a button, you have to write

```
myButton.push(1);
```

Obviously, a simple assignment such as `int aButton = 1` would be more efficient. Calling functions requires the program to push any arguments and a return address onto the stack, transfer control to the function's compiled code, and then clean up the stack when the function returns. Multiplied by thousands of functions in an even medium-size program, this amount of overhead can quickly add up to gross inefficiencies.

The solution is to use *inline member functions* where speed matters. Although inline member functions resemble the normal variety in their declarations and use, the compiled result is often as good as what you can achieve by "unrolling" your functions manually. In other words, although you write a statement like `myButton.push(1)`, the compiler generates inline code that directly assigns the value 1 to the data member in a button. With inline functions, there's no function call and therefore no overhead.

Performing this neat trick is simple—just include the function's inline statements in the class declaration. Listing 5.3, BUTTON2.CPP, shows how. It's the same program as BUTTON.CPP but defines all of a `button`'s member functions in line.

## Listing 5.3. BUTTON2.CPP.

```
 1:  // button2.cpp -- Inline member functions
 2:
 3:  #include <tscdefs.h>
 4:  #include IOSTREAM_H
 5:
 6:  class button {
 7:  private:
 8:     int isUp;
 9:  public:
10:     void push(int upDown) { isUp = upDown; }
11:     int state(void) { return isUp; }
12:  };
13:
14:  main()
```

*continues*

Listing 5.3. continued

```
15:  {
16:    button myButton;
17:
18:    myButton.push(1);
19:    cout << "\nButton state = " << myButton.state();
20:    myButton.push(0);
21:    cout << "\nButton state = " << myButton.state();
22:    return 0;
23:  }
```

The main function is identical in BUTTON and BUTTON2, proving an important point about inline member functions: Only their definitions are special. When used, inline functions appear and operate identically to normal member functions.

Lines 10 and 11 show how to define inline functions. Unlike the earlier example, this time there are no function implementations in the listing—the inline functions are complete. Until you get used to the format, however, inline functions may appear a little odd:

```
void push(int upDown) { isUp = upDown; }
```

Two rules to remember: There is no semicolon after the function declaration nor is there one after the closing brace. If you view this the way most functions are usually written, you'll see that the single-line style is no different from a usual multiline function implementation:

```
void push(int upDown)
{
  isUp = upDown;
}
```

Compare that character for character with the inline definition. The functions differ only in style; their contents are identical. In fact, you could write inline functions this way, though the one-line style is more common.

Don't forget to end the statement inside braces with a semicolon, as you must end all statements in C++. Again, this is identical to normal function forms—but the single-line style typically used for inline member functions may make the semicolon's position seem out of place.

There's no need to limit member functions to one statement. You can include multiple statements inside the braces. For example, a better push() function might force upDown to be 1 or 0:

```
void push(int upDown)
  { if (upDown == 0) isUp = 0; else isUp = 1; }
```

Notice where the semicolons go—at the end of the two statements, not after the end of the definition's closing brace. The common one-line style makes this hard to see, and you can write the statements on separate lines if you want:

```
void push(int upDown)
{
  if (upDown == 0)
    isUp = 0;
  else
    isUp = 1;
}
```

When C++ compiles a program that uses inline member functions, it inserts code to perform that function's actions for a specified class object. In place of myButton.push(1) the compiler inserts the statements defined inside the inline definition's braces. This eliminates all the usual overhead associated with function calls while letting you keep the program's text looking sharp.

But don't define every member function in line. There are several reasons why that would be a mistake. In general, inline member functions

- Increase the compiled code size. Inline functions can cause your program to take more room in memory.

- Are easily modified by programmers who have access to your class declarations but not to the implementations of your other function prototypes and classes.

- Are limited by the compiler to a small size. Although this limit is not exactly defined, if the compiler decides an inline function is too large, it will convert the code to a normal member function implementation.

- Cause the compiler to run out of memory sooner because it has to store all inline statements for inserting into the program.

- Might not be supported by all C++ compilers or may be supported in different ways. Never write code that relies on member functions being defined inline.

The second of these points is easily dealt with. Instead of coding inline member functions inside the class declaration, you can change the function implementations in BUTTON.CPP (Listing 5.2) to these:

```
inline void button::push(int upDown)
{
  isUp = upDown;
}

inline int button::state(void)
{
  return isUp;
}
```

Adding the keyword `inline` in front of the function declarations has the same effect as defining the inline member functions directly in the class. But there is one drawback to this approach: In addition to the `inline` keyword, you must insert the function implementations before they are used in a module. In BUTTON.CPP, this means you would also have to move the functions to above `main()`, or the compiler will treat them as common functions, and it will not insert the inline statements directly into the compiled code.

For debugging, C++ compilers from Borland, Microsoft and Zortech autmatically convert inline functions to normally called functions. You should be able to trace inline statements as you do those that are not inline.

## Classes Are Data Types

Now that you've seen a few examples of C++ classes, let's get back to the elevator simulation. Listing 5.1, SIMULATE.CPP, used a class named `action`, which called the class's member functions associated with the object `theAction`.

This is a key concept. A class is a data type, and like other data types, it can be used to define objects. This is no different from the way other data types are used. For example, an `int` is a data type, but you can't use `ints` directly to store values. Instead, you first have to define `int` *variables*. Then, you can store values in those variables like this:

```
int myValue;    // Define variable myValue of type int
myValue = 123;  // Store value 123 in myValue
```

Classes behave in exactly the same way; they are data types just like others built into the language. To use a class's members, you first have to create an object of the class. Then you can call its functions:

```
action theAction;  // Define object theAction of type action
action.display();  // Call display member function in theAction
```

Before using any members of a class, you must create an object of that class. Then you can call the class's public functions and use other public declarations belonging to that object.

> **Note:** Although it seems as though class objects *contain* their member functions, the actual code for those functions is *not* stored inside the class object. If you define six objects of class `action`, there is only one copy of `display()` and other class member functions in memory. However, distinct space for data members in a class is set aside for each class object. This mirrors the way other data types work. For example, you can create multiple `int` variables, but there's only one "plus" routine somewhere that can add two integers. In this sense, the plus operator behaves as though it were a member function named + in a class named `int`. You certainly wouldn't expect the compiler to create a new "plus" subroutine for each integer variable in a program!

Classes give you the means to create new data types that add to those supplied with C++ such as `int` and `float`. But unlike C++'s built-in types, the nature of a new class is completely up to you.

As BUTTON and BUTTON2 demonstrated, creating a new class is similar to creating a `struct` that you can then use to define variables. Listing 5.4, action.h, shows the declaration for the `action` class that Listing 5.1 uses and that other modules in this chapter will use in the final elevator simulation.

### Listing 5.4. action.h.

```
1:  // action.h -- Action header file
2:
3:  #ifndef __ACTION_H
```

*continues*

**Listing 5.4. continued**

```
 4:   #define __ACTION_H      1     // Prevent multiple #includes
 5:
 6:   class action {
 7:   private:
 8:     int timeAtStart;          // Seconds for simulation
 9:     int timeRemaining;        // Seconds remaining to end
10:   public:
11:     action();                 // The "constructor"
12:     int continues(void);
13:     void setTime(int secs);
14:     int getTime(void);
15:     void reduceTime(int secs);
16:     void perform(void);
17:     void display(void);
18:     void results(void);
19:   };
20:
21:   #endif   // __ACTION_H
```

The action.h header file shows a typical class declaration in C++. It also demonstrates how to organize a large program into headers and modules. In my programs, I prefer to use many small files, each with a distinct purpose. Rarely do my source code files contain more than a few hundred lines.

Because many other .h and .CPP files may include action.h in order to use the action class, it's possible that action.h will be included more than once during compilation. This is never allowed and produces an error when the class action identifier is redeclared. To avoid this tricky situation, which is very common in large programs, action.h begins with two *conditional directives:*

```
#ifndef __ACTION_H
#define __ACTION_H    1
```

The #ifndef directive evaluates the following argument (here __ACTION_H) as true (1) if that identifier was *not* previously defined in a #define directive. A similar directive #ifdef (not shown) evaluates as true if an identifier *was* previously defined. Each of these directives must be followed at some point by #endif (see line 21). The #define directive is the same as the one you have used to create constants in other programs. But in this case, it's used for a different purpose—to define a symbol named __ACTION_H.

Both `#ifndef` and `#ifdef` cause the compiler to compile whatever follows on subsequent lines only if the directives are true. As a result, these commands

```
#ifndef __ACTION_H
#define __ACTION_H     1
...
#endif
```

tell the compiler to skip everything between `#ifndef` and `#endif` if `__ACTION_H` was previously defined. If that symbol was not yet defined, the `#ifndef` directive will be true, and the compiler will compile every line between `#ifndef` and `#endif`. The first time this occurs, a `#define` directive immediately defines the `__ACTION_H` symbol; therefore, the *next* time this same file is read, that symbol will be defined and the compiler will skip every significant line in the file! This means that, if action.h is included a dozen times, the `action` class declaration is compiled only the first time, neatly avoiding the redeclaration conflict that would otherwise occur.

Other files can also test whether `__ACTION_H` is already defined and if so, avoid including that file:

```
#ifndef __ACTION_H
#include "action.h"
#endif
```

For better clarity, the listings in this chapter do not use this trick, but in a monstrous program, it may shave a few seconds from long compilations.

> **Note:** The notation used for symbols like `__ACTION_H` is just a convention. You can name any identifier for this purpose as long as it's unique. But the two underscores plus the filename with its usual period replaced by a third underscore pretty much ensures that the same symbol will not be defined elsewhere.

# Introducing Constructors

As in the `button` class, `action` declares a private section, this time containing two `long` integer members, `timeAtStart` and `timeRemaining`. Because these members are private to the class, only the class member functions may use them. There are eight such functions in `action`, none of which is defined in line (see lines 11–18). The first of these needs some explaining:

```
action();
```

As you can see from this function prototype, it has the same name as the `action` class. All such functions are called *constructors* and have the sole purpose of initializing objects of the class type. Unlike other function prototypes, constructors do not specify a `void` return type. In fact, they may *never* return a value. Constructors may specify a `void` parameter list (`action(void);`), although the form `action()` without `void` is more widely used and serves the same purpose. (It's possible for constructors to accept arguments, but in this example, `action()` requires none.) These small differences in form make it easy to pick out the constructors in a class declaration.

> **Note:** A constructor's counterpart is called a *destructor,* which is covered in Chapter 7, "Building a Class Library—Part 2."

Most programmers insert constructor prototypes immediately after the `public:` header in a class declaration. This is not a requirement, and the constructor may go anywhere in that section.

A class constructor runs automatically when you define storage for a class object. This means that, when SIMULATE (Listing 5.1) defines `theAction` with the line

```
action theAction;
```

the program automatically calls the class constructor function `action()` to initialize `theAction`. This is completely optional. If you don't include a constructor in a class, no code runs automatically when an object of the class comes into existence. But because it's so handy to be able to rely on this automatic initialization feature, most classes should have constructors.

> **Note:** The implementation for a constructor function is no different from any other member function. The only difference between a constructor and another member function is that the constructor runs automatically when storage is defined for a class object.

I'll explain more about constructors later. For the moment, just remember that a constructor

- Has the same name as the class

- May not return a value

- May declare a parameter list

- Runs automatically when space for a class object is defined

**Note:** Because theAction is a global object, the program defines its space before main() starts to run. This means that the constructor in the action class runs before main()'s first statement. At that time, the constructor initializes theAction object, preparing that object for use. If theAction was defined local to another function, the constructor would run when that function was called. If theAction is created on the heap, the constructor would run when that space was reserved. In all cases, constructors run automatically when space for the class object is defined.

You should have no trouble understanding the prototypes for the other member functions in the action class (see lines 12–18). Function continues() returns true as long as the class "wants" the simulation to continue. That will be so as long as timeRemaining is greater than zero. Functions setTime() and getTime() set and return the simulation time, and reduceTime() reduces the amount of time remaining. Function perform() activates the simulation, and display() shows what's happening. The last function, results(), displays a final report after the simulation is finished.

Take a moment to study action.h in Listing 5.4, and before continuing, be sure that you understand what each line does. You don't need to know how the action class performs its duties—just be comfortable with the format of the class's declaration. This is another benefit that OOP brings to programming. To learn how to use a new class, you need only study its declaration (assuming, that is, there's some documentation to go along with the source code as there is in this book). Rarely will you have to pick through the implementation of a class to understand how to use it. A well-designed class fully describes what it can do. Though you can't tell much about a book from its cover, the same isn't true of a C++ class. You *can* tell most of what you need to know about a class simply by reading its declaration.

Also examine how SIMULATE.CPP in Listing 5.1 calls the class functions through object theAction to run the simulation. The next step is to fill in those class member functions so that you can compile and run the SIMULATE test program and begin writing the elevator modules.

## Class Tactics

Even without looking at more than a few simple programs and class declarations, you've already met most of the class tactics that you'll employ in other C++ programs. So far, the elevator simulation has a main module SIMULATE.CPP that uses a class named action declared in action.h. Before SIMULATE is ready to be compiled and run, however, the program needs a few essential ingredients—the implementations for the functions that carry out the action class's duties. Creating a new class like action is like drawing the plans for a cabinet. After getting the design just as you want it, you've got to do some sawing and hammering before you can place books on the shelves.

Listing 5.5, ACTION.CPP, bangs out the function definitions for the action class members declared in action.h. You can now compile the full program (if you haven't already done so). As explained in the Introduction and in the beginning to Chapter 1, "Discovering C++," the easiest way to compile programs in this book is to run the automated MAKE utility supplied with your compiler. MAKE compiles the SIMULATE.CPP and ACTION.CPP modules, then links the resulting object-code files, SIMULATE.OBJ and ACTION.OBJ, to create the final SIMULATE.EXE program.

When you run the program, press the Spacebar to activate each pass through the simulation. At this early stage, the simulation merely counts the number of times through the main loop. The program displays this value plus the time at start and the time remaining. This doesn't look much like an elevator simulation, does it? But don't be concerned: You need to excavate more of OOP and C++'s grounds before you'll be ready to add elevator shafts to the program.

### Listing 5.5. ACTION.CPP.

```
1:   // action.cpp -- Action class module
2:
3:   #include <tscdefs.h>
4:   #include IOSTREAM_H
5:   #include IOMANIP_H
```

```
 6:   #include <conio.h>
 7:   #include "action.h"
 8:
 9:   // The action's "constructor." Runs when space for an action
10:   // object is defined.
11:
12:   action::action()
13:   {
14:     timeAtStart = 3600;              // Seconds to run simulation
15:     timeRemaining = timeAtStart;    // Time remaining to end
16:   }
17:
18:   // Return TRUE if time remaining is greater than 0. The program's main
19:   // loop continues the action until this function returns FALSE.
20:
21:   int action::continues(void)
22:   {
23:     return timeRemaining > 0;
24:   }
25:
26:   // Set time counters to this many seconds.
27:
28:   void action::setTime(int secs)
29:   {
30:     timeAtStart = secs;
31:     timeRemaining = timeAtStart;
32:   }
33:
34:   // Return time remaining for simulation.
35:
36:   int action::getTime(void)
37:   {
38:     return timeRemaining;
39:   }
40:
41:   // Reduce time remaining for simulation. Minimum resolution, or
42:   // "granularity," is one second. Can't reduce time to < 0.
43:
44:   void action::reduceTime(int secs)
45:   {
46:     if (secs > timeRemaining)
```

*continues*

## Listing 5.5. continued

```
47:      timeRemaining = 0;
48:    else
49:      timeRemaining -= secs;
50:  }
51:
52: // Perform the action. In this case, the function is just a shell.
53: // Later, we'll add programming to simulate a real action.
54:
55: void action::perform(void)
56: {
57:   cout << "\n\nAction! (Press <Space> to continue..." << flush;
58:   while (getch() != ' ') ;   // Pause for <Space> keypress
59:   reduceTime(900);           // Decrease time remaining 900 secs
60: }
61:
62: // Display the current action status. Calling display() is the only way
63: // a statement outside of the action object can access the timeRemaining
64: // value.
65:
66: void action::display(void)
67: {
68:   cout << "\n\nTime remaining: " << timeRemaining << " sec." << flush;
69: }
70:
71: // Display final results. As in action::display(), calling results() is
72: // the only way a statement outside of the action object can access the
73: // private data members in the action class.
74:
75: void action::results(void)
76: {
77:   cout << "\n\nSimulation results";
78:   cout << "\n==================";
79:   cout << "\nTime at start .. : " << timeAtStart << " sec." << flush;
80:   cout << "\nTime at end .... : " << timeRemaining << " sec.\n" << flush;
81: }
```

ACTION.CPP contains full function definitions for each of the member functions declared in action.h. One reason for storing these items separately is to let many other files such as SIMULATE.CPP include the action.h header file. That way, the main program (or another module) can use the elements in ACTION without forcing you to compile the entire program over and over for each change you make. Instead, you can compile each .CPP module individually. (MAKE does this automatically). In a program with dozens or more such modules, this can save a lot of time that would otherwise be wasted by needlessly recompiling source code that didn't change.

The division of classes into header and module files also lets software companies distribute compiled class libraries along with the associated headers. For example, if I were to distribute ACTION as a developer's tool, I could compile ACTION.CPP to create ACTION.OBJ. Then I could sell that *object-code* file plus action.h. You could include the header file in your own programs and link your code to my object code. But you would not be able to modify or learn my trade secrets. You may accuse a company that takes this approach of being overly protective of their sources, but later, you'll learn that OOP lets you build on commercial class libraries even if they don't come with full source code—often impossible to do with common subroutine libraries.

**Note:** All source code is included with this book for *all* functions, modules, headers, classes, and other listings. I just wanted to make that clear.

The first function in ACTION is the action() constructor (lines 12–16). As I explained earlier, the constructor runs automatically when an object of type action is constructed. Examine the contructor closely:

```
action::action()
{
  timeAtStart = 3600;            // Seconds to run simulation
  timeRemaining = timeAtStart;  // Time remaining to end
}
```

On a first meeting, the form of a constructor's implementation may seem confusing. You are not seeing double at the first line, action::action(). Remember, all member function implementations are uniquely identified by the class name plus a double-colon symbol (action::) in front of the member function name and parameter list (action()). (In this case, the parameter list is empty.) Although the double whammy looks redundant, `action::action()` simply tells the compiler that the `action()` constructor belongs to the `action` class. This format allows you to declare other non-OOP functions named `action()` without causing a conflict.

The two statements inside the `action()` constructor assign 3600 to the `timeAtStart` and `timeRemaining` private members in the class. This means that all objects of type `action` will be initialized for a simulation lasting 3600 seconds, or 1 hour, without the program having to "lift a finger." (The "seconds" are not necessarily in real time, however.)

But what if somebody later wants to change the simulation startup time to another value? Shouldn't you spend time now allowing for this possibility? That's always a difficult question, but in general with OOP, the answer can be "no" without causing problems down the road. As you'll see, it's not difficult to alter the fundamental nature of a class to accommodate situations like changing the startup time. OOP allows you to forge ahead and get the program working rather than waste time dealing with countless details about initializations, interfaces, and other items that may very well change tomorrow anyway.

This doesn't mean you don't have to do *some* planning, but it does mean that you won't be locked into a corner next week just because of the decisions you make today. In this example, you may as well let the `action` class initialize itself to 3600 seconds. You can always change this minor detail later without affecting any other parts of the program.

> **Note:** This is another benefit of encapsulating code and data. Because the two time members are private to the `action` class, you can be certain that no other statements outside the class depend on those values or change them directly. All references to the class's private data are in the class itself. If you need to modify the class, you can do so without causing a conflict with another module.

The other function implementations in ACTION.CPP have obvious purposes and use simple statements. Read the comments in the program to understand what each function does. Notice how the function declarations include the `action::` symbol that uniquely identifies each function as a member of the `action` class. Except for those declaration lines, the function forms and statements are no different from others you've seen. They use common C++ features, write to output streams, get characters from the keyboard, and so on. As this demonstrates, anything you can do in normal C++ functions you can do in class member functions. It's the declaration of classes as new data types and the use of objects of those types that separate C++ OOP from conventional C and C++ programming. You are free to use any and all OOP and non-OOP techniques *inside* class functions to specify the actions those functions are to perform.

# Compiling the Elevator Simulation

T he listings in the rest of this chapter complete the elevator simulation. Many of the elements in the coming listings will find their way into your own work, and examining a program of a non-trivial size will demonstrate many of the benefits of using C++ OOP techniques. As I mentioned earlier, I'll list the files in the order that I created them, though, of course, I didn't just sit down and write each file from start to finish. Like most programs, ELEVSIM grew in stages, and I made many changes to the files along the way.

Before I explain the first of the simulation's modules, it will be helpful for you to compile the program and run it. To do this, assuming you have followed the instructions in the Introduction for configuring your compiler, change to the directory that holds Chapter 5's listings (usually C:\TSC\C05). Copy the appropriate MAKE file for your compiler to a new file named MAKEFILE, with no extension. (You might already have performed this step.) For example, if you are using Microsoft C/C++, enter the commands

```
c:
cd \tsc\c05
copy makefile.msc makefile
```

Replace msc with btc for Borland C++ or Turbo C++. Replace msc with ztc for Zortech C++. After creating MAKEFILE, with your compiler's BIN directory in the current path (and after setting any required environment variables), enter **make** (**nmake** for Microsoft C/C++).

Examine MAKEFILE for the various commands required to compile the entire simulation. Each module is compiled separately, and the resulting .OBJ code files are linked to produce the final ELEVSIM.EXE program.

Using MAKE is practically essential for maintaining a large multifile program like this one. You can change an individual file (several such changes are suggested in this chapter), then simply rerun MAKE to compile only the modified modules.

Table 5.1 lists the files that make up the simulation. Notice that the ACTION files, which you already examined, are included in the portfolio.

**Table 5.1. Elevator simulation files.**

| *Filename* | *Description* |
| --- | --- |
| ACTION.CPP | Action class module |
| ACTION.H | Header file for ACTION.CPP |
| BUILDING.CPP | Building class module |
| BUILDING.H | Header file for BUILDING.CPP |
| ELEVATOR.CPP | Elevator class module |
| ELEVATOR.H | Header file for ELEVATOR.CPP |
| ELEVSIM.CPP | Main elevator simulation program |
| ELEVSIM.H | General simulation header file |
| FLOOR.CPP | Floor class module |
| FLOOR.H | Header file for FLOOR.CPP |
| PERSON.CPP | Person class module |
| PERSON.H | Header file for PERSON.CPP |

After compiling, run ELEVSIM to start the simulation. Your display will appear as illustrated in Figure 5.3. Along the left of the screen are the floor numbers 0 through 9, followed by indicators that tell whether the up (U) or down (D) buttons are pressed on these floors. The numbers to the right of those characters represent the number of people waiting for elevators.

The elevators are represented by small reverse-video boxes dangling from elevator cables—shown on-screen by vertical columns of colons. Each elevator shows its direction: Up, Dn, or none (--). At the top of the elevator's cable is the current floor number—what people normally see while waiting for a lift in front of closed elevator doors.

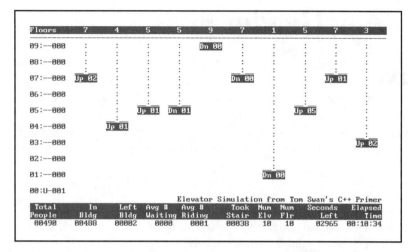

**Figure 5.3.** The elevator simulation's display.

Along the bottom of the display are several statistics that the program constantly updates as it runs. The first value shows the total number of people who have passed through the system. The next value represents the number of people now in the building. Until people begin to leave (the third statistic), this will be the same as the total number of people passing through the simulation. The fourth and fifth values show the running average number of people currently waiting for and riding in elevators. One of the goals of the simulation is to keep the number of riders high compared to the number waiting.

Sometimes, people will get tired of waiting for elevators and will decide to take the stairs (the fifth value at the bottom of the display). As a rule, these people also will live longer due to the increased activity of their heart muscles (just kidding).

The other statistics show the number of elevators, the number of floors, the number of seconds remaining in this simulation run, and the total elapsed time in hours, minutes, and seconds. You can easily change the number of elevators, the number of floors, and the decision logic to change the character of the simulation. As I explain the files, I'll suggest many such changes you might want to make.

# Using Header Files

**M**ost large programs need one main header file to describe various global facts. Also, it may be necessary to declare a few global variables for other modules to share. In general, it's not a good idea to use too many global variables. Local variables and dynamic structures on the heap tend to use memory more efficiently. Because any statement can modify a global variable's value, they also make debugging difficult. If something goes wrong with a global value, there's no telling where to begin searching for the fault.

But that doesn't mean you should *never* use globals. For example, the statistics displayed at the bottom of the elevator simulation may as well be global. The modules in the program need to update these values, and passing them around as function parameters is probably more trouble than it's worth.

Other global items in the simulation include several #defines, which set various parameters—for example, how long it takes for an elevator to travel between floors, how long an elevator waits at a floor before closing its doors, how many people can fit into an elevator at one time, and so on. Listing 5.6. elevsim.h, stores all these items and more in one handy package.

## Listing 5.6. elevsim.h.

```
 1: // elevsim.h -- General header file for elevator simulation
 2:
 3: #ifndef __ELEVSIM_H
 4: #define __ELEVSIM_H    1     // Prevent multiple #includes
 5:
 6: // Various constants. Don't change these.
 7:
 8: #define UP 1            // Value for direction == up
 9: #define DOWN -1         // Value for direction == down
10: #define NODIRECTION 0   // Value for direction == none
11: #define ESCKEY 27       // ASCII value for Esc key
12:
13: // Other constants. Okay to change with care. MAXPERSONS is limited by
14: // available memory--you may not be able to increase this value much
15: // beyond 1000 or so. Also, be sure to keep MAXELEVS and MAXFLOORS
```

```
16:    // within the ranges stated in the comments below. Values outside of
17:    // these ranges may work, but too many floors or elevators will turn the
18:    // simulation's display to mush.
19:
20:    #define MAXELEVS 10       // Number of elevators (1 to 10 only)
21:    #define MAXFLOORS 10      // Number of floors (2 to 10 only)
22:    #define MAXPERSONS 500    // Maximum people in building
23:    #define ELEVWAIT 15       // Min. seconds to wait at floors
24:    #define CAPACITY 24       // Maximum people in an elevator
25:    #define TRAVELTIME 5      // Seconds to travel between floors
26:
27:    // Formulas using rand() function to make various decisions.  Feel free
28:    // adjust these values to alter the simulation. WANTS_TO_ENTER controls
29:    // how frequently people enter the building. ENTER_DEST selects the
30:    // destination floor which must be within 1 to MAXFLOORS - 1. MAX_WAIT
31:    // determines how many seconds a person will wait for an elevator before
32:    // getting fed up and taking the stairs. BUSINESS controls how many
33:    // seconds people spend at their destination floors before going
34:    // elsewhere or leaving the building. LEAVING controls whether a person
35:    // will leave or go to another floor--it's currently set to force people
36:    // to decide to leave about 2/3 the time.
37:
38:    #define WANTS_TO_ENTER   rand() < 200
39:    #define ENTER_DEST       1 + (rand() % (MAXFLOORS - 1))
40:    #define MAX_WAIT         180 + (rand() % 180)
41:    #define BUSINESS         400 + (rand() % 6200)
42:    #define LEAVING          rand() < 22000
43:
44:    // Global variable declarations. These variables are defined in
45:    // elevsim.cpp and are the only global variables in the program except
46:    // for the building object (see elevsim.cpp). The program uses these
47:    // values to display the simulation statistics on the bottom line. All
48:    // other program variables are class objects or are local to class
49:    // functions.
50:
51:    extern unsigned totalPeople;     // Number of people handled
52:    extern unsigned inBuilding;      // People in building now
53:    extern unsigned leftBuilding;    // People who left building
```

*continues*

**Listing 5.6. continued**

```
54:   extern unsigned avgWait;       // Average no. people waiting
55:   extern unsigned avgRide;       // Average no. people in elevators
56:   extern unsigned tookStair;     // Number people who walked
57:   extern unsigned totalTime;     // Seconds simulation has run
58:
59:   #endif   //  __ELEVSIM_H
```

Several files include elevsim.h during compilation to access its declarations. Lines 8–11 list a few miscellaneous items that you should not change. Lines 20–25 define several parameters that can affect the simulation; these you can change, but only within the limits described in the comments. For example, try setting MAXELEVS to 2, or lower MAXFLOORS to 4 or 5 and set the number of elevators to 1. Having these values in one file is important because it lets you quickly modify the program without having to hunt through other source files. Just make your changes, save the modified header file to disk, and use MAKE to recompile.

The definitions at lines 38–42 in elevsim.h control the program's decision logic. All these definitions use the rand() function to obtain a value selected from a randomized sequence. Two of these expressions (WANTS_TO_ENTER and LEAVING) evaluate to true or false values that can be used in an if statement such as

```
if (WANTS_TO_ENTER) {
  // programming to have a person enter the building
}
```

The compiler replaces WANTS_TO_ENTER with the expression rand() < 200 listed in the #define at line 38. You could always type such expressions directly into if statements, of course, but using identifiers like WANTS_TO_ENTER makes the code more readable while keeping that and other logic expressions together in the header file where they are easily modified.

The other three symbols (ENTER_DEST, MAX_WAIT, and BUSINESS) choose the floor numbers to which people travel, select the maximum time that people will wait for elevators before deciding to take the stairs, and designate the amount of time that people will spend on floors attending to business before deciding to take an elevator to another floor or to leave the building. Feel free to alter any of these to modify the simulation's characteristics.

Finally in elevsim.h are several global variables, declared at lines 51–57 with the extern keyword. This allows other modules to refer to these variables, but it does not define storage space for them. A good place to do that is in the program's main module, in this case ELEVSIM.CPP, listed near the end of this chapter. As I mentioned earlier, these variables hold the values displayed along the bottom of the screen. With one exception, which you'll see later, these are the *only* global variables in the program.

> **Note:** If elevsim.h declared global variables directly, the compiler and linker would still be able to sort out the mess and create only one copy of each variable in memory. However, using extern in header files clearly indicates that the variables are defined elsewhere—a good source-code management practice.

# The Person Class

In many simulations, the goal is to let people pose "what if" questions, run the model, and observe the results. For example, you might want to answer the question, "If we have only 3 elevators, what happens when the volume of people increases to 350 at lunchtime?"

Another good reason to run simulated computer models is to investigate potentially harmful situations without injuring the test subjects. Flight simulators fall into this category.

> **Note:** I recently had the opportunity to sit in the cockpit of one of USAir's 747 flight simulators. The simulator is so realistic that a mistake during flight could actually injure the crew, and the software that drives the simulation has "crash prevention logic" built in to prevent real mishaps. Fortunately for my passengers, I did not have the time (or skill) to take off and test the software's reliability.

The elevator simulation in this chapter is of the "what if" variety. In a nutshell, the goal is to determine how many people a certain number of elevators can handle in a given amount of time. By varying the parameters to set up the test bed, the simulation quickly shows the effects of changes in the algorithms used to move elevators.

Before designing the elevators, however, we need some people to enter a building, travel to a destination, and then leave the system. For the purposes of writing this program, "people" are objects with properties—the property to exist on a certain floor or to be inside an elevator. The program creates the people it needs from a C++ class named person. Listing 5.7, person.h, declares this and one other class, persCollection (person collection).

## Listing 5.7. person.h.

```
1:  // person.h -- Header file for person.cpp
2:
3:  #ifndef __PERSON_H
4:  #define __PERSON_H      1      // Prevent multiple #includes
5:
6:  #include "elevsim.h"
7:
8:  class person {
9:  private:
10:    int floorNowOn;       // Floor (-1 if outside)
11:    int destination;      // Destination floor number
12:    int maxWaitTime;      // Aggravation level
13:    int waitingForElev;   // True (1) if waiting
14:    int takingStairs;     // True (1) if walking
15:    int elevNowIn;        // Elevator number (-1 if none)
16:  public:
17:    person();
18:    void action(void);
19:    int upwaiting(int floorNumber);
20:    int dnwaiting(int floorNumber);
21:    int loadIfWaiting(int elevNumber,
22:      int floorNumber, int &pdest);
23:    int loadIfGoing(int elevNumber,
24:      int floorNumber, int direction, int &pdest);
25:    int discharge(int elevNumber, int floorNumber);
26:  };
27:
```

```
28:  class persCollection {
29:  private:
30:    person pa[MAXPERSONS];  // Array of person objects
31:  public:
32:    void action(void);
33:    void numWaiting(int floorNumber, int &nup, int &ndn);
34:    int loadAny(int elevNumber,
35:      int floorNumber, int &pdest);
36:    int loadOne(int elevNumber,
37:      int floorNumber, int direction, int &pdest);
38:    int discharge(int elevNumber, int floorNumber);
39:  };
40:
41:  #endif   // __PERSON_H
```

Reading through person.h, you may wonder how I knew what to include in the person class. At this stage, I hadn't designed the other modules, and later on, I would make changes to person. The person.h listing, however, is almost identical to the one I wrote originally. I don't mean to pat myself on the back. I just want to point out a subtle benefit of OOP. When creating new classes, you'll be forced to consider your program's goals carefully. If you *don't* know what a class should contain, it's a sure sign that you need to think more about what you are trying to accomplish. In this program, I knew where I was headed, and therefore, I had a good idea what a person class needed to do. My planning paid off by making this class relatively easy to write.

Hint: When designing new classes, be careful not to fall into the common trap of throwing every old thing that comes to mind into the class declaration. If you don't have a good reason for adding a member to a class, leave it out; you can always add it later. When class declarations grow to page after page of members and functions, it may be a sign that you need to rethink your program's goals. Short and sweet is far preferable to big and juicy when it comes to C++ classes.

## *person* Data Members

Lines 10–15 declare six private data members, all of type int. These values record certain facts about a person object—what floor that person is on, the person's destination, and other information. The comments in the listing describe each variable. Most have obvious purposes. (The aggravation level represents the amount of time a person will wait for an elevator before taking the stairs.)

Remember, when a class object is created, C++ allocates new space for all of a class's members. This means that each person in the simulation will have its own set of the six members in the class's private section. The elevsim.h header file defines MAXPERSONS to be 500, so when this version of the program runs, there will be 500 sets of the six members in a person class, one set per person. (At 2 bytes per integer, the program's citizens occupy 6,000 bytes of space.)

Remember also that only the class's functions may access these private members. No other statement anywhere in the program has any access to a person's inner secrets. If it becomes necessary to change how person works—packing waitingForElev and takingStairs into a bit-field structure to conserve space, for example—the only affected functions are those that belong to this class. No statements outside this module have access to these variables, and changing them requires no modification to other parts of the program.

## The *person* Collection Class

The person.h header file also declares a second class, persCollection (see lines 28–39). The purpose of this class is to give the simulation a simple way to work with a large number of person objects. Instead of defining an array, a list, or another kind of data structure to hold the people that will pass through the simulation, the simulation simply creates one object of type persCollection.

In general, when a program needs a large number of objects, it's a good idea to provide a new class with functions to manipulate the population of the collected class objects, whatever they are. Because classes hide their inner details in the private section, collecting other objects into a class limits the program's access to those details. This can be important if you later need to modify the way the program stores its object collections. For example, in person.h, all people in the simulation are stored in an array pa of person objects (see line 30). Because *only* the persCollection functions at lines 32–38 may access that array, these are the *only* functions that will need modifying if you later decide to change the array into a list or, perhaps, to store "people" on disk and read them in as needed.

Another benefit of using a class to store collections of objects concerns efficiency. Instead of wasting time now trying to choose the best storage methods, you can use whatever works and go on to the next task. Later, after the program is up and running, you can return to each class and modify the data structures to improve performance.

Imagine how difficult this would be if the program itself defined an array of person objects for the simulation. To change that array to a list would require hunting through the program for every use of the array. The persCollection class neatly eliminates that tedious job. It *hides* the details of its implementation—not from you, but from other modules. This tends to keep modules autonomous, which in turn, makes them easier to maintain.

## *person* and *persCollection* Member Functions

Like most classes, person contains a number of public functions that perform the actions of the class. A person object is initialized by the person() constructor (declared in person.h at line 17), which along with other person member functions, are the only parts of the program permitted to access the class's private data members. This encapsulation of code and data is invaluable during debugging. If people start acting strangely, you can limit your diagnosis to the person class.

The class's member functions at lines 17–25 specify the actions that an object of type person may perform. Because the implementations of those functions (and those for the persCollection class) are lengthy, I'll list the PERSON.CPP module (Listing 5.8) in a slightly different way from other smaller programs in this book. The lines are numbered as usual, but the descriptions for various functions are scattered throughout the listing. Of course, despite being broken up here, PERSON.CPP is stored in one file on disk.

**Listing 5.8. PERSON.CPP.**

```
1:   // person.cpp -- Person class module
2:
3:   #include <tscdefs.h>
4:   #include <stdlib.h>
5:   #include "person.h"
6:
7:   // The person class constructor. Runs when a person object is
```

*continues*

**Listing 5.8. continued**

```
 8:  // constructed. Assigns defauts values to person data members.
 9:
10:  person::person()
11:  {
12:    floorNowOn = -1;      // Not in the building
13:    waitingForElev = 0;   // Not waiting for an elevator
14:    destination = -1;     // No destination assigned
15:    maxWaitTime = 0;      // Not waiting until next action
16:    takingStairs = 0;     // Not walking the stairs
17:    elevNowIn = -1;       // Not in any elevator
18:  }
19:
```

As is typical for C++ classes, the person() constructor (lines 10–17) initializes an object of this class type. In this case, the initialization steps are simple—they merely assign default values for each of the six member members in a person object. Because constructors run automatically when an object of the class is constructed, you can be certain that *all* people start their simulated lives with equal potential.

Try to design your own classes along these same lines. Instead of inserting initialization details into other member functions that you'll have to remember to call, place those statements into the class constructor. You can then forget about them and let C++ initialize your class objects automatically.

The next fragment from PERSON.CPP fills in the action() member function, which controls what a person does during each tick of the simulation's clock. To get a feel for the programming, scan the comments of this section before reading on. As I mentioned earlier, this and other listing fragments belong to the same PERSON.CPP file, but are divided here among the descriptions to reduce the number of pages you have to flip while reading the code.

**Listing 5.8. PERSON.CPP. (continued)**

```
20:  // Perform an action for this person. Called once for every tick of the
21:  // simulation's clock.
22:
23:  void person::action(void)
24:  {
25:
```

```
26:   // Decide whether a person outside should enter building.
27:
28:     if (floorNowOn < 0) {            // If not in bldg
29:       if (WANTS_TO_ENTER) {          // Decide to enter
30:         destination = ENTER_DEST;    // Select destination
31:         floorNowOn = 0;              // Enter on ground floor
32:         maxWaitTime = MAX_WAIT;      // Set aggravation level
33:         waitingForElev = 1;          // Person is waiting
34:         takingStairs = 0;            // Not taking stairs
35:         elevNowIn = -1;              // Not inside an elevator
36:         totalPeople++;               // Count people handled
37:         inBuilding++;                // Count people in bldg
38:       }
39:
40:   // If person is inside and waiting for an elevator, depending on the
41:   // person's aggravation level, decide whether to take the stairs and
42:   // walk to the destination floor.
43:
44:     } else {                         // If in bldg
45:       if (waitingForElev) {          // If inside and waiting
46:         if ((maxWaitTime--) <= 0) {  // Mark time waiting
47:           waitingForElev = 0;        // Tired of waiting
48:           takingStairs = 1;          // Take stairs instead
49:           maxWaitTime =              // 30 secs per floor
50:             30 * abs(destination - floorNowOn);
51:           tookStair++;               // Count people who walk
52:         }
53:       }
54:
55:   // If person is inside and is walking up or down the stairs, check if
56:   // that person has arrived. If so, set the amount of time the person
57:   // will spend on this floor.
58:
59:       else if (takingStairs) {
60:         if ((maxWaitTime--) <= 0) {  // Mark time walking
61:           floorNowOn = destination;  // Reached destination
62:           takingStairs = 0;          // Not walking on stairs
63:           maxWaitTime = BUSINESS;    // Time on this floor
64:         }
65:       }
```

*continues*

## Listing 5.8. continued

```
66:
67:   // If a person is not inside an elevator, that person must be on a floor
68:   // taking care of business. Check whether the person is done and select
69:   // another destination. Most people will decide to leave the building,
70:   // but some will travel to another floor.
71:
72:      else if (elevNowIn < 0) {        // If not inside an elevator
73:        if ((maxWaitTime--) <= 0) {    // Mark time on floor
74:          if (LEAVING)                 // Most people will want
75:            destination = 0;           //   to leave on floor 0
76:          else                         // Some will travel to
77:            destination = ENTER_DEST;  //   another floor
78:          if (destination == floorNowOn)  // Don't let people
79:            destination = 0;           //   travel to same floor
80:          maxWaitTime = MAX_WAIT;      // Set aggravation level
81:          waitingForElev = 1;          // Person is waiting
82:        }
83:      }
84:
85:   // Check for any person who is in the building, has arrived at the
86:   // ground floor, and is ready to leave the building.
87:
88:      if ((floorNowOn == 0) && (destination == 0)) {
89:        floorNowOn = -1;               // Send person outside
90:        leftBuilding++;                // Count people leaving
91:        inBuilding--;                  //   and no longer in bldg
92:      }
93:    }
94:  }
95:
```

The action() member function serves as a person's heartbeat. Several if statements examine the current state of a person object to determine whether that person is out of the building (floorNowOn < 0), riding in an elevator, or taking the stairs.

The simulation calls the `action()` function for each clock tick (a non-real time second) for each `person` in the system. To have people behave differently, the program uses a timing value `maxWaitTime`. When that value counts down to 0, depending on what a person is now doing, the object *changes states* and begins doing something else. In other words, when a `person`'s time on a floor is up, that `person`'s object will decide on its next destination, which is usually the ground floor. (All people enter and leave the building on the ground floor. There's no fire escape.)

Because it changes states this way, the programming in the `action()` function is often called a *state machine*. Unlike many functions that perform the same statements each time a program calls them, a state machine function may execute widely different operations every time it runs. A state machine like `action()` is a good way to model objects that assume different modes or states.

Although `action()` seems long, because of its state-machine nature, it's composed of relatively short parts. For example, lines 59–65 describe what happens if people are taking the stairs. First, the program subtracts one from `maxWaitTime` (line 60). If this causes the timing value to be less or equal to 0, the three statements at lines 61–63 are executed. These statements alter the values of the `floorNowOn`, `takingStairs`, and `maxWaitTime` data members in the object. The effect is to change a person's state from walking up or down the stairs to performing business on the destination floor. The *next* time the `action()` function runs for this same person, lines 72–83 will perform the steps required to have people take care of business on floors.

Also notice how `action()` uses the logical definitions from elevsim.h to make decisions. For example, line 74 uses `LEAVING` to decide whether a person should leave the building. By the way, those people who do leave are free to reenter the building later in a new incarnation.

The rest of the `person` member functions are short and simple. For instance, in the next fragment, two functions, `upwaiting()` and `dnwaiting()` return true or false to let the program know whether a `person` is waiting for an elevator.

## Listing 5.8. PERSON.CPP. (continued)

```
96:  // Return true if this person is now waiting for an up elevator
97:  // at the specified floor number.
98:
99:  int person::upwaiting(int floorNumber)
100: {
```

*continues*

## Listing 5.8. continued

```
101:    return ((waitingForElev         ) &&
102:            (floorNowOn == floorNumber) &&
103:            (destination > floorNowOn ));
104:  }
105:
106:  // Return true if this person is now waiting for a down elevator
107:  // at the specified floor number.
108:
109:  int person::dnwaiting(int floorNumber)
110:  {
111:    return ((waitingForElev         ) &&
112:            (floorNowOn == floorNumber) &&
113:            (destination < floorNowOn ));
114:  }
115:
```

Each of these two functions (lines 99–104 and 109–114) contains a single return statement. The expressions in each of those statements are similar, differing only in the test for whether a person's destination variable is less or greater than floorNowOn, which specifies a person's present location. The floorNumber parameter indicates on which floor the simulation is checking for people waiting for elevators.

As you learn more about OOP and C++, and as you write your own programs, you'll discover opportunities to create many such small functions with distinct purposes. This is always a good sign, because it means you have identified some of the atomic properties of a class. Lots of small functions are desirable—if you're concerned about efficiency, however, you can always convert them to inline code later.

Most functions, of course, will have more than only one statement. For example, loadIfWaiting() is a bit more complex than the previous two functions:

## Listing 5.8. PERSON.CPP. (continued)

```
116:  // Have person enter elevator if waiting for an elevator on this floor
117:  // regardless of direction. (Elevator is empty and the person will
118:  // determine its direction.) Return the person's destination in pdest to
119:  // simulate that person pressing one of the elevator's floor buttons.
```

```
120:
121:   int person::loadIfWaiting(int elevNumber,
122:     int floorNumber, int &pdest)
123:   {
124:     if (waitingForElev && (floorNowOn == floorNumber)) {
125:       waitingForElev = 0;        // Not waiting any longer
126:       elevNowIn = elevNumber;    // Save elevator number
127:       pdest = destination;       // Pass person's destination back
128:       return TRUE;               // Person got on board
129:     }
130:     return FALSE;                // Person did not get on board
131:   }
132:
```

Function `loadIfWaiting()` is one of the additions I made to `person` after creating the `elevator` class, which I haven't explained yet. Because the function's purpose has not been discussed and is out of context, it may be difficult to understand. When empty and directionless, an elevator calls `loadIfWaiting()` to allow one person to enter and choose the direction. This mirrors a real person getting into an idle elevator and pressing a floor button. In such cases, the first person to enter the elevator decides whether the lift travels up or down. To simulate the action of pressing a floor button, function `loadIfWaiting()` returns the `person`'s destination in the reference parameter `&pdest`.

**Note:** By the way, this is a typical situation. You write one class and discover the need for various functions in other classes. That's fine, and it helps to keep classes stripped of unnecessary functions. Don't insert every member function under the sun that *might* be needed. Stick to the necessities.

Another similar function, `loadIfGoing()`, lets others enter an elevator that is traveling in a known direction. If the elevator is going up, it will call `loadIfGoing()` to load as many people as possible going in that same direction. No doubt you've seen a group of people charge an elevator that's about to leave. Here's the function that simulates this typical mob scene:

## Listing 5.8. PERSON.CPP. (continued)

```
133:   // Load person if waiting for an elevator going in the specified
134:   // direction. Return the person's destination in pdest to simulate that
135:   // person pressing one of the elevator's floor buttons. Similar to
136:   // loadIfWaiting(), but loads only people going up or down.
137:
138:   int person::loadIfGoing(int elevNumber,
139:     int floorNumber, int direction, int &pdest)
140:   {
141:     int pdir;        // Person's direction, up or down
142:
143:     if (destination > floorNumber)
144:       pdir = UP;
145:     else
146:       pdir = DOWN;
147:     if (waitingForElev && (floorNowOn == floorNumber) &&
148:       (direction == pdir)) {
149:       waitingForElev = 0;
150:       elevNowIn = elevNumber;
151:       pdest = destination;
152:       return TRUE;
153:     }
154:     return FALSE;
155:   }
156:
```

Only a little more complicated than loadIfWaiting(), loadIfGoing() places a person inside an elevator if that person is waiting for a lift in the specified direction. Most of the programming in the function simply adjusts various data members in the object to represent a person's new state. This causes the action() function to select a different section when the simulation calls on it to advance people through the building.

Of course, after having people enter an elevator, they also need to be able to leave. This is handled by function discharge(), which completes the person class:

## Listing 5.8. PERSON.CPP. (continued)

```
157:   // If this person is in the specified elevator and is headed for the
158:   // designated floor number, make that person get off the elevator.
159:   // Return true if the person gets off; otherwise, return false. Set the
160:   // person's wait time to the number of seconds this person will remain
161:   // on the floor unless that floor is 0 in which case the person will
162:   // exit the building immediately.
163:
164:   int person::discharge(int elevNumber, int floorNumber)
165:   {
166:     if ((elevNowIn == elevNumber) && (destination == floorNumber)) {
167:       elevNowIn = -1;                 // Get out of elevator
168:       floorNowOn = destination;       // Set floor person is on
169:       if (floorNowOn != 0)
170:         maxWaitTime = BUSINESS;       // Set time to spend on floor
171:       return TRUE;                    // Person got off elevator
172:     } else
173:       return FALSE;                   // Person did not exit
174:   }
175:
```

As with most of the other member functions, this one simply adjusts data members in the class object to represent the new state of a person. In this case, when a person object leaves an elevator, it sets its maxWaitTime to a random number of seconds (specified by the BUSINESS symbol from elevsim.h). This causes that person to spend a certain amount of time on this floor. However, most people will leave the building on reaching floor 0. For the purposes of this simulation, the program assumes that a person is out of the building as soon as the person leaves the elevator. (You might imagine the building's doors are next to the elevator shaft.)

That's all there is to a person class. If you scan back through the previous 174 listing lines, you may be surprised to discover only simple statements that assign a few values and make a few decisions. One of the myths of object-oriented programming is that it tends to be more complex than conventional techniques. Not so. The design of a class may involve much planning, but its implementation is typically easier than in conventional programming. There's a good reason for this. By concentrating on what an object *does* instead of fretting about how that object is *used,* you limit your sights to the task at hand. If you can describe what an object is supposed to do, you can program it. And you can do that out of context from the rest of the program.

For another good example of how OOP helps to reduce a program's complexity, let's examine the persCollection class, which is stored along with person in the same PERSON.CPP module. Some programmers prefer to store only one class per module, but when the classes are intimately related as are these two, they're probably best stored together. Here's the first member function:

### Listing 5.8. PERSON.CPP. (continued)

```
176:  // Call action() function for every person. Runs once for every tick of
177:  // the simulation's clock.
178:
179:  void persCollection::action(void)
180:  {
181:    for (int i = 0; i < MAXPERSONS; i++)
182:      pa[i].action();
183:  }
184:
```

There is no constructor in the persCollection object. Always remember that constructors are optional: If you include one in a class, it is called when an object of the class is constructed. If you don't include a constructor, data members in a class object are not initialized and you might need to call a member function to perform various startup duties for newly constructed objects.

> **Note:** C++ automatically provides classes with a default constructor to satisfy various requirements—initializing an array of objects, for example, without requiring you to perform that task in a program statement. These default constructors, however, do not initialize any data members that you insert in a class. You can also define your own default constructor, which C++ can call automatically. For a class anyClass, the default constructor is declared as anyClass(); (no return value and no parameters).

You may wonder, if a persCollection object stores an array of person class objects, how do *those* individual person objects become initialized? And when does this occur?

The answer is the same as for all class objects: The default constructor is called when the objects of the class are defined. In this case, when the program defines space for an object of type persCollection, that space consists of an array of person objects (line 30 in person.h):

```
person pa[MAXPERSONS];
```

Array pa is a collection of person objects. MAXPERSONS specifies the number of those objects in the array. When C++ allocates space for the array, it calls the default person() constructor for *each* object in the array. Every object, then, is initialized by the person() constructor at lines 10–18 in PERSON.CPP. This happens automatically; you don't need to insert function calls into your program to the default constructor for an array of objects.

The automatic initialization of objects in programs has enormous benefits. It simplifies the program and helps reduce bugs caused by using uninitialized values— one of the most common errors programmers make. It also means you can use class objects without thumbing around in your code to make sure that the objects have been properly initialized.

Notice that there are two action() functions in the PERSON module, one belonging to the person class and the other to persCollection. The action() function in persCollection (see lines 179–183 in PERSON.CPP) calls the action function for every person object in the pa array. To put all the people through their paces, the program needs only call the collection's action() function.

In the person class, in file PERSON.CPP, the action() function is declared at line 23 as

```
void person::action(void)
```

In persCollection, in the same file, the action() function is declared similarly at line 179, but using a different class name:

```
void persCollection::action(void)
```

As these functions show, you can use the same names for class members without any conflict.

One of the jobs that persCollection needs to perform is to call member functions for every person object stored in the pa array. For instance, the numWaiting() function counts the number of people waiting for an elevator on a specified floor:

## Listing 5.8. PERSON.CPP. (continued)

```
185:   // Count number of persons waiting on a floor. Returns nup (number of
186:   // persons going up) and ndn (number of persons going down) on the
187:   // specified floor.
188:
189:   void persCollection::numWaiting(int floorNumber,
190:     int &nup, int &ndn)
191:   {
192:     nup = ndn = 0;
193:     for (int i = 0; i < MAXPERSONS; i++) {
194:       nup += pa[i].upwaiting(floorNumber);
195:       ndn += pa[i].dnwaiting(floorNumber);
196:     }
197:   }
198:
```

Here again, the persCollection class simplifies the main program by providing a high-level operation that accesses the individual person objects stored in the pa array. The function returns two int reference parameters, nup and ndn, representing the number of people waiting to travel up or down.

To determine these numbers, a for loop at lines 193–196 calls two functions for every person object, upwaiting() and dnwaiting(). As you recall from earlier, these functions return true (1) if a person is waiting for an elevator or false (0) if not. The program simply adds these function results to nup and ndn. This quickly counts the number of people traveling in both directions.

Be sure to understand the form of the expression pa[i].upwaiting(floorNumber). First, the array is indexed with pa[i], selecting an individual person object. The dot-notation expression calls the class member function upwaiting() for that person. The floorNumber parameter is passed to that function, using the same notation for passing arguments to common C++ functions.

A persCollection object can call person member functions this way because those functions are declared in the person's public section (see person.h, lines 16–25). Members of a class's public section are visible to statements outside of the class (including statements inside other classes, as in persCollection here.) But members of a class's private section are strictly hidden from view. Only member functions of that *same* class can access those items.

This same rule applies equally to all classes, even those in the same module. For example, although persCollection is declared in the same file as person, it has no access to person's private data. For that reason, statements like this one won't compile:

```
pa[i].destination = 5;  // ???
```

It's not possible for persCollection to refer directly to the destination member in a person object. That member is strictly for the use of the member functions in person.

> **Note:** Like most rules, it's possible to break the one in C++ that limits access to a class's private data members. However, because this chapter introduces OOP concepts, I'll take the "pure" approach here and postpone discussing the exceptions until later. As the program in this chapter demonstrates, it's possible (and desirable) to write complete programs that obey the fundamental rules about data hiding in class objects. Yes, you can break the rules. But you'll get more from C++ and OOP if you learn to play by those rules before you break them.

The three remaining functions in persCollection load people into elevators (loadAny() and loadOne()) and discharge an elevator's passengers traveling to a specified floor (discharge()). These functions operate much like the others, and you should be able to understand them by reading the comments in the listing:

### Listing 5.8. PERSON.CPP. (continued)

```
199:  // Load any person waiting for an elevator at this floor number.  Return
200:  // the person's destination in pdest so the elevator can begin traveling
201:  // in the necessary direction. Return true if a person is loaded, else
202:  // return false. If false, pdest is undefined.
203:
204:  int persCollection::loadAny(int elevNumber,
205:    int floorNumber, int &pdest)
```

*continues*

## Listing 5.8. continued

```
206:    {
207:      for (int i = 0; i < MAXPERSONS; i++)
208:        if (pa[i].loadIfWaiting(elevNumber, floorNumber, pdest))
209:          return TRUE;       // Person got on board
210:      return FALSE;          // No person got into an elevator
211:    }
212:
213:    // Load one person waiting for an elevator at this floor number, and
214:    // headed in the specified direction. Return true if a person is loaded,
215:    // else return false. Similar to loadAny, but loads only persons
216:    // traveling in a specified direction.
217:
218:    int persCollection::loadOne(int elevNumber,
219:      int floorNumber, int direction, int &pdest)
220:    {
221:      for (int i = 0; i < MAXPERSONS; i++)
222:        if (pa[i].loadIfGoing(elevNumber,
223:          floorNumber, direction, pdest))
224:          return TRUE;     // Person got on board
225:      return FALSE;        // No person got into an elevator
226:    }
227:
228:    // Discharge all persons in this elevator who are traveling to the
229:    // specified floor. Return number of people who got off elevator.
230:
231:    int persCollection::discharge(int elevNumber, int floorNumber)
232:    {
233:      int n = 0;     // Number of people who get off elevator
234:
235:      for (int i = 0; i < MAXPERSONS; i++)
236:        n += pa[i].discharge(elevNumber, floorNumber);
237:      return n;
238:    }
```

# The Floor Class

The simulation is moving along. Finished so far are some of the mechanical details needed to compile the program and to specify global definitions and variables. You've also examined two full classes: person and persCollection.

It's time to begin constructing the building. For this simulation, a "building" is simply a collection of floor objects. It's not important what's on those floors—only that people have somewhere to travel. Also, the program needs programming to model the up and down elevator buttons that simulated people press to call for an elevator. All these details go into the next two classes, floor and floorCollection in Listing 5.9, floor.h.

## Listing 5.9. floor.h.

```
1:  // floor.h -- Header file for floor.cpp
2:
3:  #ifndef __FLOOR_H
4:  #define __FLOOR_H        1      // Prevent multiple #includes
5:
6:  #include "person.h"
7:
8:  class floor {
9:  private:
10:    int floorNumber;   // Lobby is floor 0
11:    int up, down;      // 1 = up or down buttons pressed
12:    int np;            // Number of people waiting for elev
13:  public:
14:    floor();
15:    void setFloorNumber(int n) { floorNumber = n; }
16:    int downButton(void) { return down; }
17:    int upButton(void) { return up; }
18:    void resetUpButton(void) { up = 0; }
19:    void resetDownButton(void) { down = 0; }
20:    int getNumWaiting(void) { return np; }
21:    void setUpButton(void);
22:    void setDownButton(void);
23:    void showFloor(persCollection &thePersons);
24:  };
25:
26:  class floorCollection {
27:  private:
28:    floor fa[MAXFLOORS];     // Array of floor objects
29:  public:
30:    floorCollection();
31:    void showFloors(persCollection &thePersons);
32:    void resetButton(int direction, int floorNumber);
```

*continues*

343

**Listing 5.9. continued**

```
33:    int signalUp(int floorNumber);
34:    int signalDown(int floorNumber);
35:    int signalSameDir(int direction, int floorNumber);
36:    int avgWaiting(void);
37:  };
38:
39:  #endif    // __FLOOR_H
```

The floor class (lines 8–24) has the same general organization as a person. It declares a few variables in its private section and a few member functions in the public area. A floor has a number (floorNumber), two buttons (up and down), and keeps track of the number of people waiting for an elevator on this floor (np).

Also like the person.h header, floor.h declares a second class, floorCollection. This class holds all the floors in a building and performs several important functions that elevators need. As with persCollection, an array fa at line 28 declares a data structure for holding a collection of floor objects. Notice how the MAXFLOORS constant from ELEVSIM specifies the number of floors in the collection.

# Implementing the *floor* Class

One area where floor.h differs from person.h is its reliance on inline member functions (see lines 15–20). The inline functions greatly reduce the size of Listing 5.10, FLOOR.CPP, while adhering to good OOP practices of using class members to access data inside a floor object. Because the functions are written inline, there's no overhead to worry about as there would be with common functions that simply read or change a variable. Functions that are not inline are implemented in the usual way in the FLOOR.CPP module. Because this module is large, it is listed here in sections. Here's the first part:

**Listing 5.10. FLOOR.CPP.**

```
1:  // floor.cpp -- Floor class module
2:
3:  #include <tscdefs.h>
4:  #include DISP_H
5:  #include "floor.h"
```

```
 6:
 7:   // The floor class constructor. This function initializes an object
 8:   // (variable) of the floor class. Note: The collection of floors is
 9:   // expected to assign a floor number to each floor in a building.  Until
10:   // that happens, the floorNumber member is uninitialized.
11:
12:   floor::floor()
13:   {
14:      up = down = np = 0;     // Reset up and down buttons
15:   }
16:
```

First comes the floor constructor, which initializes an object of type floor. In this case, the constructor simply sets the up and down buttons and the np member to 0, using the classic C++ trick of stringing multiple assignments together. The statement up = down = np = 0; is equivalent to

```
up = 0;
down = 0;
np = 0;
```

Looking back at the declaration for the floor class, you'll notice that the constructor fails to initialize the floorNumber member. The reason for this omission points out a flaw in C++ that makes it difficult to initialize collections of objects requiring function arguments. In other words, to give each floor a different number, the constructor would have to be declared with a floor-number parameter, perhaps like this:

```
floor(int fn);
```

That's perfectly legal, and it's often useful for constructors to accept arguments this way. But the addition of the integer fn parameter poses a problem for C++ when another class such as floorCollection declares an array of floor variables. Earlier, you learned that the person class's default constructor is called automatically for every object in the pa array. The same event occurs for the fa array of floors, but it would *not* occur if the constructor declared one or more parameters (because the constructor would then not have "default constructor" status.)

In general, for an array of class variables like pa and fa, the constructor in the class is called automatically only if the constructor declares no arguments. Given this class,

```
class firstClass {
private:
```

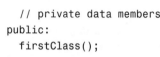
```
  // private data members
public:
  firstClass();
}
```

if you then define an array of five `firstClass` objects,

```
firstClass fca[5];
```

C++ calls the `firstClass()` default constructor for each of the objects stored in the `fca` array. But if the class is declared like this,

```
class firstClass {
private:
  // private data members
public:
  firstClass(int aValue);
}
```

C++ can't call the constructor automatically because it now declares a parameter, `int aValue`. In fact, C++ can't even compile the definition:

```
firstClass fca[5];
```

This simply doesn't give the compiler the information it needs to know how to initialize the objects. To do that, you might complete the definition this way:

```
firstClass fca[5] = { 5, 200, 19, 64, -12 };
```

Defined with initializing values inside braces, the array passes each value in turn (5, 200, ..., –12) to the class constructor, initializing the array's variables with those arguments. Unfortunately, this cements the definition in place, and the code now requires two changes to modify the number of variables stored in `fca`—the number in brackets, plus the initializing values. This complicates maintenance because this and similar definitions are likely to be buried inside one or more source modules.

Probably, a better solution is to declare another member function to complete the initialization of class variables. This is the approach I took in FLOOR, where the inline `setFloorNumber()` function assigns a value to the private `floorNumber` data member (see line 15 in floor.h, Listing 5.9). This allows the `floorCollection` object to initialize its array of `floor` objects automatically, but it also means I now have to remember to call `setFloorNumber()` for each object to complete its initialization.

> **Note:** Another way to deal with the construction of class objects in arrays is to declare more than one constructor. In that case, C++ calls the constructor that has no parameters (i.e. the default constructor) unless you specify one or more values in the array definition to pass to the constructors that have parameters. (I'll return to the advanced topic of multiple constructors in Chapter 7, "Building a Class Library—Part 2.")

After implementing the `floor` constructor, FLOOR.CPP fills in a medium-size function, `showFloor()` that handles the display details for each floor object:

### Listing 5.10. FLOOR.CPP. (continued)

```
17:  // Display a representation of this floor, showing its number and the
18:  // state of its up and down buttons.
19:
20:  void floor::showFloor(persCollection &thePersons)
21:  {
22:    int col = 0;
23:    int row = 20 - (floorNumber * 2);
24:    char uc = '-';
25:    char dc = '-';
26:    int nup, ndn;      // Number of persons going up and down
27:
28:  // Get number of persons waiting on floor going up or down.
29:
30:    thePersons.numWaiting(floorNumber, nup, ndn);
31:    np = nup + ndn;
32:    if (nup > 0) setUpButton();       // Sense up button push
33:    if (ndn > 0) setDownButton();     // Sense down button push
34:    if (up) uc = 'U';                 // Init up and down symbols
35:    if (down) dc = 'D';               //  for the display
36:
37:  // Display information for this floor.
38:
39:    disp_move(row, col);
40:    disp_printf("%02d:%c%c%03d", floorNumber, uc, dc, np );
41:  }
42:
```

The showFloor() member function differs in one significant way from others you've examined. Look closely at the function's declaration:

```
void floor::showFloor(persCollection &thePersons)
```

The function declares a single reference parameter &thePersons of type persCollection, the class from the person.h header file described earlier. The floor objects need to call functions in the collection of people entering the simulation, and it's through this parameter that the collection of floors gains access to those person objects. For example, line 30 in the preceding fragment calls the numWaiting() member function to retrieve the number of people in thePersons that are currently waiting for an elevator at this floor.

It's perfectly acceptable to pass objects as function parameters this way. Just as you can pass int and float arguments to common C++ functions, you can pass arguments of class data types. However, when a class is large, it's probably best to pass it by address, as done here with the & reference symbol, or as a pointer.

> **Note:** Because most classes protect their data members in private sections, passing objects by reference or as pointers to functions doesn't open the same dangerous doors that can lead to bugs in conventional programming. Even though the class variable is passed by address to a function, that function can *still* only access the private data by calling member functions. This increases the program's efficiency by passing small pointers rather than large objects on the stack while preventing functions from accidentally modifying data that should remain untouched.

Because the program calls showFloor() for every tick of the simulation's clock, I decided to include calls to setUpButton() and setDownButton() at lines 32–33, which set the floor's up or down buttons if there are any people waiting for an elevator at this floor. (In retrospect, it probably wasn't the best plan to perform these actions in the display function. If you modify the program, perhaps to display the elevators on a graphics screen instead of using only text, you'll have to remember to include these two calls.)

As with the person class, other functions in floor are simple and contain only simple statements. Again, in your own code, don't be concerned if you find that you are writing dozens of small functions like these. Small, tightly written functions lead to programs that are easy to maintain, and you can always convert them to inline definitions if you're concerned about speed. Here are the remaining two member functions in the floor class:

**Listing 5.10. FLOOR.CPP. (continued)**

```
43:  // Turn on the floor's up button, signaling that someone is waiting for
44:  // an elevator to travel to a higher floor. The up button on the top
45:  // floor is permanently off.
46:
47:  void floor::setUpButton(void)
48:  {
49:    if (floorNumber < MAXFLOORS - 1)
50:      up = 1;
51:  }
52:
53:  // Turn on the floor's down button, signaling that someone is waiting
54:  // for an elevator to travel to a lower floor. The down button on the
55:  // ground floor is permanently off.
56:
57:  void floor::setDownButton(void)
58:  {
59:    if (floorNumber > 0)
60:      down = 1;
61:  }
62:
```

A floor's setUpButton and setDownButton functions do what you probably expect—set the floor's up and down buttons that call for elevators to pick up waiting passengers. The functions also test whether this floor is on the ground or at the top of the building and prevent people from pressing the down button in the lobby or the up button in the penthouse.

That completes the floor class. As with the person class, a floor is a fairly simple object. Of course, one floor does not make a building, just as one person does not make a crowd. Like the people in the simulation, another class, floorCollection, stores a collection of floors as an array of floor objects. Like most classes, the collection includes a constructor to initialize all of the floors in the simulated building. The listing continues:

**Listing 5.10. FLOOR.CPP. (continued)**

```
63:  // The constructor for a floorCollection object. This function
64:  // initializes all floor objects in a collection—in other words, all of
65:  // the floors in the building.
66:
67:  floorCollection::floorCollection()
68:  {
69:    for (int i = 0; i < MAXFLOORS; i++)
70:      fa[i].setFloorNumber(i);    // Assign floor numbers
71:  }
72:
```

You might recall that the persCollection class had no constructor. As I've said before, constructors are optional; include one only if you want C++ to initialize objects of a class automatically when those objects are defined.

The reason floorCollection needs a constructor is to take care of the uninitialized floorNumber member in the floor objects. The constructor initializes that member by calling setFloorNumber() for each floor object in the fa array.

To make updating the display quick and easy, the floorCollection class also includes a function that calls showFloor() for every floor in the collection:

**Listing 5.10. FLOOR.CPP. (continued)**

```
73:  // Call showFloor() function for every floor. This function updates the
74:  // display for all floors in the building.
75:
76:  void floorCollection::showFloors(persCollection &thePersons)
77:  {
78:    for (int i = 0; i < MAXFLOORS; i++)
79:      fa[i].showFloor(thePersons);
80:  }
81:
```

Notice how the call to showFloor() at line 79 passes thePersons to that member function. Somewhere, the program declares an object of type persCollection and passes that object to showFloors() in the floorCollection class. The collection passes that same persCollection object to showFloor(), which takes care of the display details for that floor. All of this gives floor objects access to the person objects in the building while neatly hiding the mechanics about how persons are stored in memory. Instead of passing variables of rigid data structures from function to function, the program passes objects, which are easily modified if necessary to change how data is represented. These function calls, declarations, and parameters will need no modifications to accommodate changes in the storage details of a persCollection class.

Aim for this same degree of information hiding in your own programs. Use classes to hide the details of their implementations from functions that use objects of the class types. Classes that operate independently of other classes are easier to modify, a fact that you will appreciate in the future when it comes time to update your programs.

The last several functions in the floorCollection class contain no new features. Read the comments in the listing to understand what these functions do:

### Listing 5.10. FLOOR.C PP. (continued)

```
 82:   // Reset the up or down button for this floor
 83:
 84:   void floorCollection::resetButton(int direction, int floorNumber)
 85:   {
 86:     if (direction == UP)
 87:       fa[floorNumber].resetUpButton();
 88:     else if (direction == DOWN)
 89:       fa[floorNumber].resetDownButton();
 90:   }
 91:
 92:   // Return true if there are any floors above the specified floor
 93:   // signaling for an elevator in any direction.
 94:
 95:   int floorCollection::signalUp(int floorNumber)
 96:   {
 97:     for (int i = MAXFLOORS - 1; i > floorNumber; i--)
 98:       if (fa[i].upButton() || fa[i].downButton())
 99:         return TRUE;
100:     return FALSE;
101:   }
```

*continues*

## Listing 5.10. continued

```
102:
103:   // Return true if there are any floors below the specified floor
104:   // signaling for an elevator in any direction.
105:
106:   int floorCollection::signalDown(int floorNumber)
107:   {
108:     for (int i = 0; i < floorNumber; i++)
109:       if (fa[i].upButton() || fa[i].downButton())
110:         return TRUE;
111:     return FALSE;
112:   }
113:
114:   // Return true if a button in the specified direction (up or down) is
115:   // pressed on this floor. Elevators use this function to help decide
116:   // whether to stop at a floor. Returns false if no buttons are pressed
117:   // or if direction is not set.
118:
119:   int floorCollection::signalSameDir(int direction, int floorNumber)
120:   {
121:     if (direction == UP)
122:       return fa[floorNumber].upButton();
123:     else if (direction == DOWN)
124:       return fa[floorNumber].downButton();
125:     else
126:       return FALSE;
127:   }
128:
129:   // Return average number of people now waiting on all floors for an
130:   // elevator in any direction.
131:
132:   int floorCollection::avgWaiting(void)
133:   {
134:     int total = 0;
135:
136:     for (int i = 0; i < MAXFLOORS; i++)
137:       total += fa[i].getNumWaiting();
138:     return (total / MAXFLOORS);
139:   }
```

# The Elevator Class

**N** ow that we have floors and people, we're ready to tackle the final object in the simulation—the elevators. As with the other classes, the declaration for the elevator class is stored in a header file, elevator.h, Listing 5.11.

## Listing 5.11. elevator.h.

```
 1: // elevator.h -- Header file for elevator.cpp
 2:
 3: #ifndef __ELEVATOR_H
 4: #define __ELEVATOR_H    1     // Prevent multiple #includes
 5:
 6: #include "elevsim.h"
 7: #include "floor.h"
 8: #include "person.h"
 9:
10: class elevator {
11: private:
12:    int elevNumber;        // Elevator's number
13:    int timeToAction;      // Time in secs until next action
14:    int floorNumber;       // Current floor number
15:    int stopped;           // 1 == stopped at floor
16:    int direction;         // 1 == up, -1 == down, 0 == none
17:    int buttons[MAXFLOORS]; // Flr buttons (0 == off, 1 == on)
18:    int passengers;        // Number of passengers on board
19:    int buttonUp(void);
20:    int buttonDown(void);
21: public:
22:    elevator();
23:    int getPassengers(void) { return passengers; }
24:    void setelevNumber(int n);
25:    void showElevator(void);
26:    void setDirection(floorCollection &theFloors);
27:    int elevStopping(floorCollection &theFloors);
28:    void action(floorCollection &theFloors,
29:       persCollection &thePersons);
30: };
31:
32: class elevCollection {
```

*continues*

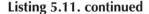

## Listing 5.11. continued

```
33:  private:
34:    elevator ea[MAXELEVS];   // Array of elevator objects
35:  public:
36:    elevCollection();
37:    void showElevators(void);
38:    void action(floorCollection &theFloors,
39:      persCollection &thePersons);
40:    int avgRiding(void);
41:  };
42:
43:  #endif   // __ELEVATOR_H
```

The `elevator` class declares several private data members at lines 12–18. Most have obvious purposes (see the comments to the right of each line). Line 17 declares an array named `buttons` that simulates the bank of floor buttons in real elevators. People push these buttons to tell the elevator to travel to a certain floor, and the elevator uses the values in this array to decide whether to travel up, down, or to stay where it is.

Lines 19 and 20 in the `elevator`'s private section declare two private member functions, `buttonUp()` and `buttonDown()`. As you'll see in the next listing, these functions let the elevator sense whether any buttons are pressed above or below the current floor. (I know little more about elevators than anyone else who's ridden in them, but I imagine there are circuits inside that perform similar jobs. These two functions at least simulate what I imagine goes on behind those locked panels inside real elevators.)

Usually, a class stores data members privately and makes all of its functions public. But as `elevator` illustrates, you can also make member functions private to a class. When you do, those member functions can be called *only* by other functions in this same class. No other statements outside of the `elevator` class can call `buttonUp()` or `buttonDown()`.

In this simulation, it doesn't matter whether `buttonUp()` and `buttonDown()` are private or public. However, this arrangement does mimic the way real elevators work; floors and people do not examine an elevator's internal circuits to determine which direction the lift is traveling. Only an elevator can do that—in real life and in the simulated environment here.

Like the person.h and floor.h header files, elevator.h also declares a collection class. Here, elevCollection declares an array ea of elevator objects (line 34), using the MAXELEVS constant from elevsim.h for the array size. The collection gives the program a simple means to access all of the elevators in the building, and it simplifies the job of revising the program if you later need to change the way elevator objects are stored in memory. In that case, all you need to do is rewrite the elevCollection class. No other parts of the program will require changes.

# Implementing the *elevator* Class

As you might expect, the implementations of the elevator and elevCollection member functions are the most complex in the simulation. Even so, there are almost no new elements in Listing 5.12, ELEVATOR.CPP, and you should be able to understand most of the code by reading the comments. I'll explain only the trickier parts in the listing.

**Listing 5.12. ELEVATOR.CPP.**

```
 1:  // elevator.cpp -- Elevator class module
 2:
 3:  #include <tscdefs.h>
 4:  #include DISP_H
 5:  #include "elevator.h"
 6:  #include <stdio.h>
 7:
 8:  // The elevator class constructor. This function runs for each elevator
 9:  // variable as it is constructed. It initializes the elevator's
10:  // location, number of people on board, etc.
11:
12:  elevator::elevator()
13:  {
14:     elevNumber = -1;          // Elevator number not assigned
15:     timeToAction = ELEVWAIT;  // Time elevator waits at floor
16:     floorNumber = 0;          // Current floor number
17:     stopped = 1;              // Elevator is stopped at floor
18:     direction = NODIRECTION;  // Elevator direction not set
19:     passengers = 0;           // No passengers on board
20:
```

*continues*

## Listing 5.12. continued

```
21:  // Reset all floor buttons inside elevator.
22:
23:    for (int i = 0; i < MAXFLOORS; i++)
24:      buttons[i] = 0;
25:  }
26:
```

The constructor initializes an elevator variable's data members. It also sets the buttons inside to 0 (off). As I've said before, this is typical: Most constructors do little more than initialize a few members and quit. Keep in mind too that these actions occur when the program allocates storage space for an elevator object. Programs don't call constructors directly.

A few other functions in the ELEVATOR module also perform simple jobs. While reading this code, imagine how elevators work, and try to picture in your mind how the program simulates a real elevator's actions. (The comments in the listing explain each function's purpose.)

## Listing 5.12. ELEVATOR.CPP. (continued)

```
27:  // Assign number to this elevator. The first elevator must be number 0,
28:  // the next 1, and so on. These numbers are not displayed.
29:
30:  void elevator::setelevNumber(int n)
31:  {
32:    elevNumber = n;
33:  }
34:
35:  // Return true if there are any buttons inside the elevator pressed for
36:  // floors above the current floor. Elevators use this function to
37:  // determine whether there are passengers traveling to higher floors.
38:
39:  int elevator::buttonUp(void)
40:  {
41:    for (int i = floorNumber + 1; i < MAXFLOORS; i++)
42:      if (buttons[i]) return TRUE;
43:    return FALSE;
44:  }
45:
```

```
46:   // Return true if there are any buttons inside the elevator pressed for
47:   // floors below the current floor. Elevators use this function to
48:   // determine whether there are passengers traveling to lower floors.
49:
50:   int elevator::buttonDown(void)
51:   {
52:     for (int i = 0; i < floorNumber; i++)
53:       if (buttons[i]) return TRUE;
54:     return FALSE;
55:   }
56:
57:   // Display this elevator, showing its direction, the number of people
58:   // travelling up and down, and the elevator cable.
59:
60:   void elevator::showElevator(void)
61:   {
62:     int row = 20 - (floorNumber * 2);     // Display row
63:     int col = 10 + (elevNumber * 7);      // Display column
64:     char buffer[3];                       // Number of passengers
65:
66:     if (floorNumber < MAXFLOORS - 2) {
67:       disp_move(row - 3, col);
68:       disp_puts("  :  ");                 // Display elevator cable
69:     }
70:     if (floorNumber < MAXFLOORS - 1) {
71:       disp_move(row - 2, col);
72:       disp_puts("  :  ");                 // Display more cable
73:       disp_move(row - 1, col);
74:       disp_puts("__:__");                 // Display elevator roof
75:     }
76:     disp_startstand();                    // Start reversed video
77:     disp_move(0, col + 2);
78:     disp_printf("%d", floorNumber);       // Floor # at top of screen
79:     disp_move(row, col);
80:     if (direction == UP)                  // Display direction
81:       disp_puts("Up ");
82:     else if (direction == DOWN)
83:       disp_puts("Dn ");
84:     else
85:       disp_puts("-- ");
86:     sprintf(buffer, "%02d", passengers);
```

*continues*

357

**Listing 5.12. continued**

```
87:      disp_puts(buffer);
88:      disp_endstand();                    // End reversed video
89:      if (floorNumber > 0) {
90:        disp_move(row + 2, col);          // Erase old elevator so
91:        disp_puts("      ");              //  it appears to move
92:        disp_move(row + 1, col);
93:        disp_puts("      ");
94:      }
95:    }
96:
```

> **Note:** To port the program to another system, or to convert the display from text to a more realistic-looking bit-mapped graphics system, you'll need to modify showElevator() to depict a single elevator, showing the direction, the number of passengers inside, and so on. OOP makes such modifications easier than conventional code because it encapsulates in the elevator class the data and code that represents a real elevator.

The next three functions, setDirection(), elevStopping(), and action(), control the movements of elevators during the simulation. Together, they implement an algorithm (see Figure 5.4) that specifies how elevators respond to various situations, what to do if buttons are pressed on other floors to signal for an elevator, whether to stop at a floor, and other tasks. I wrote the algorithm as an outline from which I coded the class functions; this is not C++, of course.

> **Note:** The elevator algorithm represents my casual observations about how elevators work, and it may not be complete. Although I've ridden in plenty of elevators, I've never built a real one. And after all, the purpose of this program is to demonstrate C++ classes in action, not to get you started with your own elevator company.

```
if elevator is stopped
  discharge any passengers
  if direction is not set
    load one passenger and set direction
  load another passenger travelling in current direction
  if ready to start moving
    if direction is not set
      decide on next direction (1)
    if direction is not set and not on ground floor
      set direction to down
    if direction is not set
      continue waiting on this floor
    else
      start moving
else if elevator is not stopped
  if elevator has reached the next floor
    change floor number
    decide on next direction (1)
    decide whether to stop at this floor (2)
    if stopping
      stop the elevator
    else
      continue moving

(1) decide on next direction
  if passengers are travelling to a higher floor
    set direction to up
  else if passengers are travelling to a lower floor
    set direction to down
  else if any floors above are signalling in any direction
    set direction to up
  else if any floors below are signalling in any direction
    set direction to down
  else
    set direction to none

(2) decide whether to stop at this floor
  stop if there are any passengers getting off here
  else stop if there are any passengers waiting for elevator in
      same direction
  else stop if this is the first floor
  else stop if this is the ground floor
  else stop if direction is none
  else don't stop
```

**Figure 5.4.** This algorithm, expressed in outline form, controls the movements of elevators in the simulation.

## Listing 5.12. ELEVATOR.CPP. (continued)

```
 97:   // Decide on the direction the elevator should travel next.
 98:
 99:   void elevator::setDirection(floorCollection &theFloors)
100:   {
101:     if (buttonUp()) direction = UP;
102:     else if (buttonDown()) direction = DOWN;
103:     else if (theFloors.signalUp(floorNumber)) direction = UP;
104:     else if (theFloors.signalDown(floorNumber)) direction = DOWN;
105:     else direction = NODIRECTION;
106:   }
107:
108:   // Decide whether elevator should stop at the current floor.
109:
110:   int elevator::elevStopping(floorCollection &theFloors)
111:   {
112:     if (buttons[floorNumber])
113:       return TRUE;                // Passengers getting off
114:     else if (theFloors.signalSameDir(direction, floorNumber))
115:       return TRUE;                // Persons waiting for elevator
116:     else if (floorNumber == 0)
117:       return TRUE;                // Stop at ground floor
118:     else if (floorNumber == MAXFLOORS - 1)
119:       return TRUE;                // Stop at highest floor
120:     else if (direction == NODIRECTION)
121:       return TRUE;                // No signals above or below
122:     else
123:       return FALSE;               // Keep moving
124:   }
125:
126:   // Perform all required actions for this elevator. This function runs
127:   // once for every tick of the simulation's clock.
128:
129:   void elevator::action(floorCollection &theFloors,
130:     persCollection &thePersons)
131:   {
132:     int pdest;                 // A person's destination
133:
134:     // Take care of actions for an elevator stopped at a floor. The "else"
135:     // clause to this statement handles actions for elevators currently
```

```
136:   // moving between floors. If elevator is stopped, the first job is to
137:   // discharge any passengers travelling to this floor.
138:
139:    if (stopped) {
140:      passengers -= thePersons.discharge(elevNumber, floorNumber);
141:
142:   // If the direction is not set (nobody on board), load one person and
143:   // set the direction to that person's destination. In other words, if
144:   // the elevator doesn't know where it's going, the first person to get
145:   // on board decides the elevator's direction.
146:
147:      if ((direction == NODIRECTION) && (passengers < CAPACITY)) {
148:        if (thePersons.loadAny(elevNumber, floorNumber, pdest)) {
149:          passengers++;                    // Count passenger
150:          timeToAction++;                  // Takes time to get in
151:          buttons[pdest] = 1;              // Press destination button
152:          if (pdest > floorNumber)         // First person on board
153:            direction = UP;                //  sets elevator's direction
154:          else
155:            direction = DOWN;
156:        }
157:      }
158:
159:   // If the direction is set (there's at least one person on board,)pick
160:   // up additional passengers waiting to go in that same direction. Stop
161:   // doing this when elevator becomes full. It takes some time to load
162:   // one person, so add 1 second to elapsed time.
163:
164:      if ((direction != NODIRECTION) && (passengers < CAPACITY)) {
165:        if (thePersons.loadOne(elevNumber,
166:        floorNumber, direction, pdest))    // Then if another person
167:        {                                  //  climbs on board...
168:          passengers++;                    // Count the newcomer
169:          timeToAction++;                  // Takes time to get in
170:          buttons[pdest] = 1;              // Press dest. button
171:          if (passengers >= CAPACITY)      // Leave immediately if
172:            timeToAction = 0;              //  elevator is full
173:        }
174:      }
```

*continues*

361

## Listing 5.12. continued

```
175:
176:    // If ready to start moving (elapsed time is 0 or less), perform final
177:    // actions before leaving for the next floor. For instance, If the
178:    // direction is still not set, then there are no passengers on board. In
179:    // that case, look for signals from other floors. If there are no
180:    // signals, head down unless on ground floor. If a new direction is
181:    // selected, reset the floor's up or down button and start moving.
182:
183:        if (timeToAction-- <= 0) {
184:          if (direction == NODIRECTION)
185:            setDirection(theFloors);
186:          if ((direction == NODIRECTION) && (floorNumber > 0))
187:            direction = DOWN;
188:          if (direction == NODIRECTION)
189:            timeToAction = ELEVWAIT;      // Stay at floor 0
190:          else {                          // Ready to start moving
191:            theFloors.                    // Reset floor up or
192:              resetButton(direction,      //   down button
193:              floorNumber);
194:            stopped = 0;                  // Tell elevator to move
195:            timeToAction = TRAVELTIME;    // Set time to next floor
196:          }
197:        }
198:      }
199:      else if (timeToAction-- <= 0) {     // If moved to next floor
200:        if (direction == UP)              // Change floor number
201:          floorNumber++;                  //   to go up,
202:        else
203:          floorNumber--;                  //   or down.
204:        setDirection(theFloors);          // Decide direction
205:        if (elevStopping(theFloors)) {    // If elevator should stop
206:          theFloors.                      // Reset floor up or
207:            resetButton(direction,        //   down button.
208:            floorNumber);
209:          stopped = 1;                    // Stop the elevator
210:          timeToAction = ELEVWAIT;        // Set wait time
211:          buttons[floorNumber] = 0;       // Reset button in elevator
212:        } else
```

```
213:        timeToAction = TRAVELTIME;     // Else keep moving
214:    }
215: }
216:
```

Most of the programming in these three functions, setDirection(), elevStopping(), and action() is simple and well explained in the comments. Notice how the function declarations at lines 99, 110, and 129 declare parameters of class types floorCollection and persCollection. The program passes objects of those types to the elevator::action() function, which gives elevators access to the collections of floors and people in the simulation.

Passing class objects to functions in other objects is a very useful technique. When designing a new class, instead of referring to global objects of another class type, consider declaring a parameter of that class in the function. This will make your program more adaptable to new situations because, instead of forcing the code to use one or more fixed global objects, statements can pass many different objects to your functions.

That finishes the actions of a single elevator. As I did with the person and floor classes, I also created a class that collects multiple elevator objects, elevCollection. As you'll soon see, this makes it easier for a program to work with a bank of elevators in the simulated building. And it simplifies the later job of modifying the inner storage details of that collection by encapsulating the details inside the class. Here are the function implementations:

### Listing 5.12. ELEVATOR.CPP. (continued)

```
217: // Elevator collection constructor. Runs when a variable of type
218: // elevCollection is constructed.
219:
220: elevCollection::elevCollection()
221: {
222:   for (int i = 0; i < MAXELEVS; i++)
223:     ea[i].setelevNumber(i);           // Assign elevator numbers
224: }
225:
226: // Display all elevators in the building. Calls showElevator function
227: // for every elevator object.
```

*continues*

## Listing 5.12. continued

```
228:
229:   void elevCollection::showElevators(void)
230:   {
231:     for (int i = 0; i < MAXELEVS; i++)
232:       ea[i].showElevator();
233:   }
234:
235:   // Call action() function for every elevator. This function runs for
236:   // every tick of the simulation's clock.
237:
238:   void elevCollection::action(floorCollection &theFloors,
239:     persCollection &thePersons)
240:   {
241:     for (int i = 0; i < MAXELEVS; i++)
242:       ea[i].action(theFloors, thePersons);
243:   }
244:
245:   // Return average number of passengers riding in all elevators.
246:
247:   int elevCollection::avgRiding(void)
248:   {
249:     int total = 0;
250:
251:     for (int i = 0; i < MAXELEVS; i++)
252:       total += ea[i].getPassengers();
253:     return (total / MAXELEVS);
254:   }
```

Again, most of the code is conventional C++. The constructor (lines 220–224) calls setelevNumber() for each object in the elevator array (ea) to assign unique numbers to each elevator in the collection. The showElevators() function (lines 229–233) calls showElevator() for every elevator, thus displaying the bank of elevators on-screen. The other functions perform similarly, calling functions for each of the elevator objects collected in elevCollection.

In your own programs, when you need more than one object of a class type, consider creating a new class to contain those objects. Have the main program call functions in the new class to access every object in a collection. In general, this is easier to manage than forcing a program to create its own collections—especially when the program needs to perform jobs on groups of objects.

The alternative leads to messy code. For example, I could have designed the ELEVATOR module as only a single `elevator` class. But then, the main program would need to define storage for the multiple elevators needed in the simulation. This means that if I would change the way elevators work, I might also have to modify the way the program stores multiple `elevator` objects in memory.

By instead creating the collection class `elevCollection`, I contain those details inside the module where they are easily modified. No statements other than those in `elevCollection` functions refer to the ea array; therefore, if I want to store elevators on the heap or create separate variables for them, I can do so by modifying the class without even reading any of the other parts of the program.

> **Note:** When creating collection classes similar to `elevCollection`, I find that it's helpful to use names for functions like `elevCollection::showElevators()` (plural) that call similar functions like `elevator::showElevator()` (singular). I also use plural names for objects of the collection type—`theElevators` of type `elevCollection`, and `theFloors` of type `floorCollection`. For individual objects of a class, I'd probably use singular names—`anElevator` of type `elevator`, for example, or `onePerson` of type `person`.

# Introducing Inheritance

**B**efore continuing with the final listings in the elevator simulation, it's time to consider one of OOP's major contributions to programming—*inheritance*. With this device, a new class can inherit all the properties of another class. In this way, classes can reuse existing programming.

Inheritance lets you mix and match data types in ways that are difficult if not downright impossible with conventional programming techniques. When writing new code, you can select classes with features that are close to those you need, inherit those classes into new classes, and then add new elements that describe how the new classes differ from their ancestors.

In a program that displays pop-up windows, for example, you might select a window class from another program, or perhaps, from a class library that you purchased from a software toolkit vendor. If the existing class doesn't have all the features you need—perhaps it displays only single-line titles, and you need a double-line one—you can simply create a new class that is derived from the existing one. Then you can add the missing details to display double-line titles without having to rewrite any other of the original class's properties.

> **Note:** The next two chapters explain how to create and use a window class similar to the hypothetical one mentioned here.

After using OOP in a few projects, you'll begin to appreciate just how valuable inheritance can be. Instead of revising subroutines to accommodate new specifications, you can inherit classes and add or replace programming to remold the class to a new design. With classes, you'll rarely if ever need to modify existing code to make it perform new tricks. With common subroutines, new demands often lead programmers to create many copies of similar routines, which are difficult to maintain and even harder to debug.

## Using Inheritance

When a new class inherits the properties of another class, the new class is called a *derived class*. The original class is called the *base class*. A derived class inherits the properties of a base class—all of the data members and functions in the base. Derived classes do not inherit constructors, however. They also do not inherit destructors (a topic for Chapter 7, "Building a Class Library—Part 2.") A derived class can also be a base class—in other words, one class can inherit the properties of another class, which may inherit the properties of a third class, and so on.

> **Note:** Some OOP texts use the terms *ancestor* and *descendant* to describe the relationship between base and derived classes. I'll use the more common C++ terms, *derived class* and *base class*.

To create a derived class, insert a colon and the base class name after the new class name. For example, suppose that you are writing a program to keep track of animal statistics. You might begin with a class named animal, declared at lines 8–14 in Listing 5.13, ANIMAL.CPP.

## Listing 5.13. ANIMAL.CPP.

```
 1: // animal.cpp -- Inheritance example
 2:
 3: #include <tscdefs.h>
 4: #include IOSTREAM_H
 5: #include <string.h>
 6: #include <stdlib.h>
 7:
 8: class animal {
 9: private:
10:   char name[30];    // The animal's name
11: public:
12:   animal(const char *s);
13:   const char *getName(void) { return name; }
14: };
15:
```

The animal class's private section declares a 30-character string to hold an animal's name. A public constructor (animal(const char *s)) initializes objects of the animal class. A single member function, getName(), returns an animal's name.

So far, this class is similar to others you've seen, but it is too general for direct use. Before the program declares any objects, it needs to create a few more specific classes. Here's one:

## Listing 5.13. ANIMAL.CPP. (continued)

```
16:  class mammal: public animal {
17:  private:
18:    int offspring;      // Number of offspring
19:  public:
20:    mammal(const char *s, int nc);
21:    int numOffspring(void) { return offspring; }
22:  };
23:
```

A mammal is a kind of animal, so the program declares mammal as a derived class that inherits properties from the animal base class. At line 16, the colon and words public animal after class mammal, tell C++ to import into mammal the data members and member functions from animal.

Declaring the base class to be public in a derived class tells C++ that the inherited properties should retain their original status. In other words, if the base class is public, public members from that class remain public in the derived class. Likewise, private members from the base class remain private. You could replace public with private, which makes all inherited members private, regardless of their original status:

```
class mammal: private animal {
```

However, if you specify a base class as private this way, a subsequent class that derives from mammal cannot use any of animal's members because those members are now private to mammal.

> **Note:** Chapter 7, "Building a Class Library—Part 2," describes a third category, protected, that you can use similar to private and public in class declarations.

The difference between public and private inherited classes might be easier to understand with a simple example. Suppose that you declare one class named A and then create a derived class B that inherits the properties of A:

```
class A {
  ...
}

class B: private A {
  ...
}
```

Class B derives from A. Everything in A is also in B (except for any constructors and destructors, which are never inherited). Because A is declared to be private to B, however, if you declare a third class C that derives from B,

```
class C: public B {
  ...
}
```

then C cannot use any of A's members, even if those members were originally declared in A's public section. Only B has access to the public members in A. C can use only the public items declared in B.

Carrying this one step further, if a fourth class D derives from C, because B is public to C, D can use everything declared publicly in B and C. But D can't reach back to the items in A.

> **Note:** If you don't specify either public, private, or protected for an inherited base class, the status defaults to private. This feature is a holdover from early C++ versions and should be avoided. Always preface a base class name with public, private, or protected in a derived class declaration.

Getting back to the animal farm, because mammal inherits the properties of its base class, a mammal has a 30-character name data member, it has an animal constructor, and it has a getName() function. To these inherited members, a mammal adds an int member (offspring), a new constructor (mammal()), and a member function (numOffspring()).

In this simple example, a mammal class records the average number of offspring at birth for this type of animal. That statistic differentiates the new class from the base. Instead of forcing you to create a new data type for a mammal, with C++ you design a new class by specifying only the items that differ from the members of an inherited ancestor class such as animal.

The program also needs to keep records on birds. A bird is an animal, of course, but it is not a mammal. So again, the demonstration creates a new class `bird` that inherits the properties of the `animal` class:

### Listing 5.13. ANIMAL.CPP. (continued)

```
24:  class bird: public animal {
25:  private:
26:    int eggs;          // Average number of eggs
27:    int nesting;       // True if builds nest
28:  public:
29:    bird(const char *s, int ne, int nests);
30:    int getEggs(void) { return eggs; }
31:    const char *buildsNest()
32:      { if (nesting) return "True"; else return "False"; }
33:  };
34:
```

As with `mammal`, at line 24, the derived `bird` class declares its base class with a colon and the base class name (`animal`). Because `animal` is declared to be `public` to `bird`, any further derived classes can also access the members in `animal`. For instance, suppose you declare the class

```
class extinct: public bird {
  ...
}
```

The derived `extinct` class inherits the properties of `bird`. Because `bird` also inherits from `animal` and because it did that by using the `public` keyword, the `extinct` class can use all of the public members of the `animal` class. This means an object of class `extinct` has a `name` member and a `getName()` function for retrieving that string.

In C++, it's typical for a class to be constructed on the foundations of many base classes. With inheritance, you can write code that builds on your previous work and on the work of others. Best of all, there's rarely any need to revise older code to meet the new specifications. The new programming simply inherits the old, updating the original design as needed to accommodate new situations as they arise. Of course, it might be necessary from time to time to cut out the deadwood from old classes, but in general, to handle new program requirements, classes and inheritance tend to preserve existing programming rather than force you to rewrite code that's already finished and debugged.

Classes that inherit properties from other classes can use the public members of the base class, just as though those members were declared in the derived class. The main section of ANIMAL plus two support functions show examples of this technique:

## Listing 5.13. ANIMAL.CPP. (continued)

```
35:   void showMammal(mammal &m);
36:   void showBird(bird &b);
37:
38:   main()
39:   {
40:     mammal homoSapiens("Homo Sapiens", 1);
41:     mammal gopher("Gopher", 9);
42:     mammal armadillo("Armadillo", 4);
43:     mammal houseMouse("House Mouse", 12);
44:
45:     bird woodDuck("Wood Duck", 15, FALSE);
46:     bird sandhillCrane("Sandhill Crane", 2, TRUE);
47:     bird loon("Loon", 3, TRUE);
48:
49:     cout << "\n\nMammals:";
50:     showMammal(homoSapiens);
51:     showMammal(gopher);
52:     showMammal(armadillo);
53:     showMammal(houseMouse);
54:
55:     cout << "\n\nBirds:";
56:     showBird(woodDuck);
57:     showBird(sandhillCrane);
58:     showBird(loon);
59:
60:     return 0;
61:   }
62:
63:   // Display functions
64:
65:   void showMammal(mammal &m)
66:   {
67:     cout << "\nName ............... " << (m.getName());
68:     cout << "\n Avg offspring ..... " << (m.numOffspring());
69:   }
```

*continues*

## Listing 5.13. ANIMAL.CPP. continued

```
70:
71:  void showBird(bird &b)
72:  {
73:    cout << "\nName .............. " << (b.getName());
74:    cout << "\n Avg no. eggs ...... " << (b.getEggs());
75:    cout << "\n Builds a nest ..... " << (b.buildsNest());
76:  }
77:
```

Lines 40–47 show how to define objects of a class type and pass arguments to the class constructors. The first of these declarations creates an object named homoSapiens of type mammal. It passes the two arguments "Homo Sapiens" and 1 to the mammal() constructor, which saves the string and value in the class object's data members. Earlier, you learned how to construct class objects with parameterless constructors (or with no constructors):

```
elevator anElevator;
```

To use a constructor that declares one or more parameters, just include the initializing values in parentheses after the object's name:

```
mammal gopher("Gopher", 9);
```

This *looks* like a function call, but it's not. It's an object definition. The effect, however, is to call the mammal's class constructor for the gopher object, passing a string and number to that constructor's parameters.

The other definitions are similar, but in the case of the bird objects at lines 45–47, an additional TRUE or FALSE parameter is passed to the constructor.

After defining the objects, the program calls two functions, showMammal() and showBird() (lines 65–76). Look carefully at lines 67 and 73. These each call the getName() member function in the mammal and bird reference arguments, m and b. Looking back at the declarations of these classes, you can see there is no getName() function. But there is a getName() function in the animal class that each of these new classes inherits. Objects of mammal and bird classes can call getName() because they inherited that function from animal.

Finally, the ANIMAL program implements the class constructors. Because two of the classes (mammal and bird) inherit the properties from class animal, their constructors require special treatment:

## Listing 5.13. ANIMAL.CPP. (continued)

```
78:  // Class constructors
79:
80:  animal::animal(const char *s)
81:  {
82:    strncpy(name, s, 29);
83:  }
84:
85:  mammal::mammal(const char *s, int nc) : animal(s)
86:  {
87:    offspring = nc;
88:  }
89:
90:  bird::bird(const char *s, int ne, int nests) : animal(s)
91:  {
92:    eggs = ne;
93:    nesting = nests;
94:  }
```

The animal constructor (lines 80–83) is the simplest case—it operates as a function that initializes an object of the class. In this case, the constructor calls strncpy() to copy up to 29 characters of a passed argument string s to the name member in the animal object. The constructor for the animal class is similar to those you've seen before.

The mammal and bird constructors are different. Like the animal constructor, these two initialize objects of their class by assigning values to data members. But they also include a new element at the end of their declarations: a colon and a parameter name in parentheses (see lines 85 and 90).

This special notation tells C++ to pass one or more arguments to the constructor of the base class. In other words, when the program constructs an object of the mammal class:

```
mammal dolphin("Dolphin", 1);
```

C++ calls the mammal constructor to initialize the dolphin object. It passes a string and a value to the parameters declared by the mammal constructor. When that constructor is called, (see line 85), it passes the first of these parameters (s) to the base constructor for animal, which saves this string in animal's name data member.

Chaining constructors this way is a fundamental tool in C++ programming. Each base constructor initializes the members (and possibly, performs other duties) for its class. Derived class constructors have to provide only the additional details needed to initialize objects of the derived class, and to specify which arguments or values should be passed to the base constructor.

We'll return to constructors and inheritance again—there are some other details about this subject that I'm purposely postponing. Before continuing with this chapter, be sure that you run the ANIMAL demonstration and that you understand how the derived classes `mammal` and `bird` inherit members from the `animal` base class.

> **Note:** Default constructors—those that have no parameters—do not have to be specified in a derived class's constructor. In such cases, the base constructors are still called automatically when variables of a derived class are defined.

# The Building Class

This chapter began with a simple demonstration of a simulation in its barest form (SIMULATE.CPP in Listing 5.1). That program used the declarations in action.h (Listing 5.4) implemented in ACTION.CPP (Listing 5.5). The purpose of SIMULATE was to provide a starting place. It served only as a shell to demonstrate a few fundamentals.

Was that earlier effort wasted? Not at all. Try running SIMULATE again. As you can see, this program's simple output of the time remaining when you press Spacebar bears no relation to an elevator. How can the new program make use of this earlier work?

The answer is *inheritance.* By inheriting the properties of the `action` class declared in action.h, the simulation can use the programming that's already completed and tested. Returning to our almost completed elevator simulation, Listing 5.14, building.h, puts this idea to the test.

## Listing 5.14. building.h.

```
 1:  // building.h -- Header file for building.cpp
 2:
 3:  #ifndef __BUILDING_H
 4:  #define __BUILDING_H    1      // Prevent multiple #includes
 5:
 6:  #include "action.h"
 7:  #include "person.h"
 8:  #include "floor.h"
 9:  #include "elevator.h"
10:
11:  class building: public action {
12:  private:
13:    persCollection thePersons;    // People in the system
14:    floorCollection theFloors;    // Floors in the building
15:    elevCollection theElevators;  // Elevators in the building
16:  public:
17:    int continues(void);
18:    void perform(void);
19:    void display(void);
20:  };
21:
22:  #endif   // __BUILDING_H
```

What is a building? For the purpose of writing the elevator simulation, a building is a collection of person, floor, and elevator objects. The building class encapsulates this notion in one neat package.

Line 11 declares the building derived class to inherit the properties of action—the simulation-engine class declared in action.h and used in the SIMULATE program. This means that a building variable has access to all the public members in action. (See Listing 5.4 or examine the action.h file to refresh your memory about these members.)

In addition to its inheritance from action, the derived building class adds three private data members of its own. These are thePersons, theFloors, and theElevators—declarations of the collection classes that group person, floor, and elevator objects. The new class is truly a high-level object. It inherits properties of another class (action), and it declares data members that are themselves objects—the collections of people, floors, and elevators that make up the program's simulated building.

# Replacement Member Functions

When you compare the derived building class in building.h with the base action class in action.h, you'll see that the three member functions in building have the identical names, return types, and parameter lists (void in these cases) as in the base. As a result, the derived member functions *replace* the same functions inherited from the base.

A building needs to make this modification because the original continues(), perform(), and display() member functions in action don't perform the jobs needed for the elevator simulation. But the other base functions such as setTime() and getTime() will do just fine, and the derived class can use these functions directly. It doesn't have to replace *every* member, only those that need additional capabilities for the new class.

This demonstrates a typical situation. A derived class inherits the properties of a base class. Some of the base class's member functions perform perfectly well. Others won't do at all and need rewriting. In that event, just redeclare the original member functions in the derived class as building does here. The program can then call the replacement functions without losing access to the inherited functions from the base.

Replacing member functions in a derived class is a primary tool for modifying how a class behaves. When replacing inherited functions, you must declare the functions identically in the derived class as in the base. For example, suppose a class named base has three functions:

```
class base {
public:
  void f1(void);
  int f2(void);
  float f3(void);
};
```

Then another class, derived, inherits the properties of base. At the same time, it replaces function f3():

```
class derived: public base {
public:
  float f3(void);
};
```

If the program now defines an object q of class derived and executes q.f3(), the f3() replacement function in derived will run, not the function inherited from the base. The statements q.f1() and q.f2() call the inherited functions in the base class. For this to work, however, the replacement function must have the identical return type, name, and parameter list.

> **Note:** When a derived class replaces a base class's member function, the original function doesn't disappear. It's still available, as the implementation of the building class shows in the next section.

# Implementing the *building* Class

Listing 5.15, BUILDING.CPP, implements the member functions declared in the building class. In this class, there is no constructor, and the listing begins with the first member function.

## Listing 5.15. BUILDING.CPP.

```
 1:  // building.cpp -- Building class module
 2:
 3:  #include <tscdefs.h>
 4:  #include DISP_H
 5:  #include <conio.h>
 6:  #include "building.h"
 7:
 8:  // Return true if building simulation should continue. Adds test for Esc
 9:  // keypress to action::continues().
10:
11:  int building::continues(void)
12:  {
13:    if (kbhit())                    // If there is a keypress,
14:      if (getch() == ESCKEY)        // And if it's the Esc key,
15:        setTime(0);                 //   set time remaining to 0
16:    return action::continues();     // Return ancestor fn result
17:  }
18:
```

The replacement function, continues(), in the building class takes over from the function of that same name in the base class, action, from which building derives. I needed to replace the original function because I wanted the program to recognize an Esc key press as a signal to end the simulation. In the original continues() function (see ACTION.CPP, Listing 5.5), the simulation ends only when time runs out. Because ELEVSIM might be programmed to run for hours, it needs an alternate exit. At the same time however, I did not want to do away with the original function because the simulation must still end when there's no time left.

Inheritance makes it easy to solve these kinds of problems. Lines 11–17 add the new check for any keypress (line 13), and if one is sensed through the kbhit() function, line 14 checks whether the key is Esc. If so, line 15 calls the setTime() function inherited from action to set the remaining time to 0. This forces the simulation to run out of time and end.

Examine line 16 carefully. The expression action::continues() calls the base class's continues() function, even though the derived building class replaces that member. The base class function is still available from inside the derived class. To call the original code, the program specifies the base class name and a double colon (action::). This tells C++ to call the member function in the base class instead of making a recursive call to the replacement function, which it would do without the action:: preface.

In the next fragment, a replacement function completely replaces the original code:

## Listing 5.15. BUILDING.CPP. (continued)

```
19:  // Perform the building's actions, that is, moving people in elevators
20:  // between floors. Each call to this function represents the passage of
21:  // one second (not necessarily in real time).
22:
23:  void building::perform(void)
24:  {
25:    thePersons.action();
26:    theElevators.action(theFloors, thePersons);
27:    reduceTime(1);      // One second passes
28:    totalTime++;        // Count seconds for time display
29:    disp_move(24, 64);  // Display time remaining
30:    disp_printf("%05d", getTime());
31:  }
32:
```

In the `action` base class, the `perform()` member function displayed a message, waited for you to press the Spacebar, and reduced the time remaining by 900 seconds. None of these dummy actions is appropriate for the elevator simulation; therefore, the replacement `perform()` member function in `building` does not call the original code.

Instead, the new `perform()` activates the elevator simulation by calling the `action()` functions in `thePersons` and `theElevators`—two of `building`'s three private data members. Line 27 calls the inherited `reduceTime()` function to reduce the time remaining by 1 second. It also increments a global variable (`totalTime`) and displays the time left.

These are very different operations than those performed by the original `perform()` function in the `action` base class. One of the myths of OOP is that derived classes closely resemble their base ancestors. That's not always true. Derived classes may *radically* alter what a base class does, using only the members that perform as needed. In this example, the new `building` completely replaces the `perform()` function, but it keeps the `getTime()` and other functions from the old simulation demo that don't need modifying. The result is an entirely new use for an old class—and an efficient use of existing programming.

> **Note:** Another key point here is the way the `building` class reuses `action`'s programming without requiring you to change one speck of the original code. You may have to write new code to replace an original member function, as in the new `perform()` function. But you do not have to hack apart the rest of the ACTION module to get it to work as needed in this new situation. As a result, you can still compile the original SIMULATE program even though the new simulation radically modifies the demonstration's `action` class. This concept—the preservation of base class declarations—has important consequences for documenting the evolution of a program. And it aids debugging by allowing old test modules to compile and run despite radical changes made to later versions.

Finally in the BUILDING module is the replacement `display()` function. As for `perform()`, the `display()` function's requirements of the elevator simulation are much different from the simple SIMULATE demonstration, and the new function completely replaces the old:

## Listing 5.15. BUILDING.CPP. (continued)

```
33:   // Update the display, showing current status of floors and elevators,
34:   // plus the people waiting on floors or traveling in elevators. Also
35:   // show current simulation statistics and the elapsed time on the bottom
36:   // row.
37:
38:   void building::display(void)
39:   {
40:     long t;
41:     unsigned hours = 0;
42:     unsigned minutes = 0;
43:     unsigned seconds = 0;
44:
45:     theFloors.showFloors(thePersons);
46:     theElevators.showElevators();
47:     avgWait = theFloors.avgWaiting();
48:     avgRide = theElevators.avgRiding();
49:     disp_move(24, 1);
50:     disp_printf(
51:       "%05u    %05u    %05u    %04u    %04u    %05u%5d%5d",
52:       totalPeople, inBuilding, leftBuilding, avgWait,
53:       avgRide, tookStair, MAXELEVS, MAXFLOORS);
54:     disp_move(24, 71);
55:     t = totalTime;
56:     if (t >= 3600) {
57:       hours = (unsigned)(t / 3600L);
58:       t -= (hours * 3600);
59:     }
60:     if (t >= 60) {
61:       minutes = (unsigned)(t / 60);
62:       t -= (minutes * 60);
63:     }
64:     seconds = (unsigned)t;
65:     disp_printf("%02d:%02d:%02d", hours, minutes, seconds);
66:   }
```

The new display() function calls the appropriate member functions in theFloors() and theElevators() (lines 45–46). This updates most of the display by calling on these objects to represent themselves on-screen.

The rest of the function calculates and displays various statistics on the bottom line. Except for the few calls to class member functions, the code is straightforward C++. Notice how lines 47 and 48 call on the class objects, theFloors and theElevators for the average number of people waiting for and riding in elevators.

# Completing the Elevator Simulation

A t last, light at the end of the tunnel! (Or maybe it's an elevator shaft.) Listing 5.16, ELEVSIM.CPP finishes the elevator simulation.

## Listing 5.16. ELEVSIM.CPP.

```
 1:   // elevsim.cpp -- Elevator simulation in C++
 2:
 3:   #include <tscdefs.h>
 4:   #include IOSTREAM_H
 5:   #include DISP_H
 6:   #include <stdlib.h>
 7:   #include <time.h>
 8:   #include "building.h"
 9:
10:   // Function prototype used only by main()
11:
12:   void initDisplay(void);
13:
14:   // Global variables. These are the only global variables used by the
15:   // simulation. Except for the main building object (theAction), the
16:   // variables hold the statistics displayed on the bottom line.
17:
18:   unsigned totalPeople;      // Number of people handled
19:   unsigned inBuilding;       // People in building now
20:   unsigned leftBuilding;     // People who left building
21:   unsigned avgWait;          // Average no. people waiting
22:   unsigned avgRide;          // Average no. people in elevators
23:   unsigned tookStair;        // Number people who walked
24:   unsigned totalTime;        // Seconds simulation has run
```

## Listing 5.16. ELEVSIM.CPP.

```
25:
26:   building theAction;            // Building simulation object
27:
```

In addition to the usual system header files at lines 3–7, the main ELEVSIM program includes building.h (line 8). With few exceptions, most of the code that drives the simulation is neatly hidden away in that file's building class declaration. Line 12 declares one of the exceptions: a lone function, initDisplay(), which ELEVSIM uses to initialize the display package. (See Chapter 10, "Cross-Compilation Tools," for more information about the display package functions.)

Lines 18–24 define storage for the global variables declared extern in elevsim.h. When many modules need to share the same globals, it's important that only one place in the program defines storage space for those variables. A good way to accomplish this is to declare the variables extern in a header file that other modules can include. Then define the global variables as done here in the main program. (You can also place the definitions into another file that the main module can include.)

Line 26 adds one additional global object to the previous group, theAction of type building. In this case, theAction is truly where the action is. This single object collects all the people, elevators, and floors for the simulation. It also provides access to the dozens of member functions covered earlier. In a way, theAction *is* the program; all that remains is to set the object into motion:

## Listing 5.16. ELEVSIM.CPP. (continued)

```
28:   // Note: Enable one of the optional msleep() statements below to slow
29:   // the simulation on a fast system.
30:
31:   main()
32:   {
33:     srand((unsigned)time(NULL));   // Randomize random-number generator
34:     initDisplay();                 // Initialize the display
35:     theAction.display();           // Display the elevators and labels
36:
37:   // This while-loop handles the entire simulation. It cycles while the
```

```
38:    // building object (named theAction) returns true through its
39:    // "continues()" function.
40:
41:      while (theAction.continues()) {
42:    //       msleep(1000);      // 1 real second == 1 simulated second
43:    //       msleep(250);       // 1/4 real second = 1 simulated second
44:    //       msleep(125);       // 1/8 real second = 1 simulated second
45:        theAction.perform(); // Perform all simulation actions
46:        theAction.display(); // Update the display
47:      }
48:
49:    // Perform an orderly exit.
50:
51:      disp_move(24, 0);     // Position cursor on last line
52:      disp_showcursor();    // Make cursor visible
53:      disp_close();         // Close display package
54:      return 0;
55:  }
56:
```

Most programs that are larger than a page or two benefit from a small main() function. If you find that you are inserting low-level details into main(), you may need to redesign the project. By the time you write the main() function, most of the work should be done. This is certainly true in ELEVSIM, where main() occupies only a few lines.

First, main() scrambles the random number generator (remove line 33 to repeat the *same* simulation for each new run). It then calls initDisplay() to prepare the screen and makes a single call to theAction's display() function to fill in the elevators and floors just before the simulation starts to roll. That happens in a while loop at lines 41–47, where the program calls perform() and display() while continues() reports that the simulation should go on. These three building-class member functions control the entire simulation.

Because this simulation does not run in real time, lines 42–44 suggest three ways to slow the action on fast systems. Enable one of these lines by removing the comment slashes at the beginning. The msleep() function pauses for a specified number of milliseconds. With none of these lines enabled, the simulation pace depends on your computer's speed.

Compare this while loop with the loop in SIMULATE.CPP (Listing 5.1, lines 12–15). The two loops are nearly in the same form, but the results—as you can see by running ELEVSIM—are not even close.

The rest of the program prepares the display, showing various static items that don't change during the simulation. There aren't any new elements in this function, and you should be able to understand how it works by reading the comments:

### Listing 5.16. ELEVSIM.CPP. (continued)

```
57:  // Initialize the display, showing various labels that remain unchanged
58:  // throughout the simulation. Also initialize the display
59:  // package for fast screen writes.
60:
61:  void initDisplay(void)
62:  {
63:    int i;
64:
65:    disp_open();                    // Initialize display package
66:    disp_move(0, 0);                // Move to "home" position
67:    disp_eeop();                    // Clear the display
68:    disp_hidecursor();              // Make cursor invisible
69:    disp_move(21, 33);              // Display title line
70:    disp_puts(
71:      "Elevator Simulation from Tom Swan's C++ Primer");
72:    disp_startstand();              // Begin reversed-video display
73:    disp_move(0, 0);
74:    disp_puts("Floors      ");
75:    for (i = 0; i < 10; i++)        // Show reversed video floor
76:      disp_puts("  0     ");        //   numbers at top of screen
77:    disp_move(22, 0);
78:    disp_puts(" Total        In     Left  Avg #   Avg #      ");
79:    disp_puts("Took  Num  Num   Seconds   Elapsed");
80:    disp_move(23, 0);
81:    disp_puts("People      Bldg     Bldg  Waiting Riding     ");
82:    disp_puts("Stair  Elv  Flr    Left      Time");
83:    disp_endstand();                // End reversed-video display
84:    disp_move(1, 0);
85:    for (i = 0; i < 10; i++)        // Display horzontal divider line
86:      disp_puts("--------");
```

```
87:
88:  // Display elevator cables. These are redrawn by the elevator
89:  // class as needed while elevators move.
90:
91:    for (int row = 2; row < 18; row++) {
92:      for (int col = 0; col < MAXELEVS; col++) {
93:        disp_move(row, 12 + (col * 7));
94:        disp_putc(':');
95:      }
96:    }
97:  }
```

That completes ELEVSIM and this chapter's introduction to C++ OOP features. There's more to the OOP story than I've shown you here, but you should now have a good grasp of the fundamentals and be comfortable with the concepts of

- Declaring classes

- Private and public data members

- Private and public member functions

- Constructors

- Inline member functions

- Inheritance

The remaining chapters in this book cover additional OOP features in C++, and now it's time to change course a little. You examined ELEVSIM in the order (more or less) that I wrote the code, wading through low-level objects until finally reaching the high level main() function at the end. In the next two chapters, you'll take the opposite approach, starting at the top of an existing class library, learning how to use it, and then taking it apart to see what makes it tick. This more closely resembles the way you'll dig into a commercial class library supplied by a toolkit vendor. As you'll discover next, one of the secrets to learning C++ is knowing how to read classes and to incorporate them into your own code.

# Questions and Exercises

5.1. What does the word "encapsulate" refer to in reference to C++ classes?

5.2. What kinds of functions may use private members declared in a class?

5.3. What do constructors do?

5.4. Design and test a class named rectangle that outlines a rectangular area on a computer screen.

5.5. Using the rectangle class from Exercise 5.4, create a derived class square that outlines a square region on a computer screen.

5.6. Convert to inline functions one or more member functions from the rectangle class in Exercise 5.3. If you already used inline member functions, convert them to the normal variety.

5.7. Using the button class from Listing 5.3 (BUTTON2.CPP), design a container class that can store several buttons.

5.8. Reprogram the elevator simulation to simulate two elevators in a 5-story building.

5.9. Reduce the frequency of new people entering the elevator simulation.

5.10. Double the amount of time it takes for an elevator to travel from one floor to the next in the elevator simulation.

# Building a Class Library—
# Part 1

L earning a new language like C++ is not the end of the road. It's merely a starting place for future explorations. Sooner or later, one journey most programmers take is to purchase a library of subroutines. For example, to write a graphics program, you could spend time developing your own graphics tools, or you could pick up a library of graphics functions to link to your code. As I've said before (and, no doubt, I'll say again) building on other programmers' work saves time and helps prevent bugs.

In time, many programmers also set out on a longer trip: They build their own programming libraries. If you can't find a library that suits your needs, at least plan to store your modules in reusable form. This is especially important when several programmers need to share modules from a common code pool. Surprisingly, however, programmers often rewrite the same modules over and over because it's *too hard* to reuse programming from other projects.

C++ class libraries—collections of class declarations and modules—are ideal for reducing that kind of wasteful effort. Unlike standard subroutine libraries, class libraries encourage you to use inheritance to build new software from tested classes, even if you don't have access to the original source files.

In this chapter and the next, I'll describe the workings of an extensive class library that you can use to create programs with pop-up windows and menus. The library contains a number of classes for creating lists, strings, selection lists, text windows, and program-command menus. All the library's source text is listed here and is stored on disk in C:\TSC\LIB\SOURCE. The library is also supplied in compiled library (.LIB) files located in C:\TSC\LIB. As usual, example programs are stored in chapter directories. This chapter's example program listings, for instance, are stored in C:\TSC\C06.

Learning how to use a new class library takes time and patience, and one of the purposes behind this chapter and the next is to suggest ways for cutting through the fog in a new library of programming tools. For that reason, instead of starting at the bottom of the class hierarchies as you did in the previous chapter, this time you'll start at the top, running a sample program that uses most of the class library's features. This will show you what the tools can do, rather than overwhelming you with endless details about how the code works, a common problem in the documentation of many commercial libraries.

After learning in this chapter what the class library can do, in the next chapter you'll delve into the programming behind the library's many classes. As I explain the various classes and programs in the library, I'll also point out many new C++ features you haven't met before.

# Last Things First—WinTool

T he program listed in this section, WINTOOL, will help you to design pop-up windows for your own programs. It will also show you more about how to use classes and OOP techniques in C++. With WINTOOL, you can design text-based windows using different attribute values for a window's border, background, and text. After selecting a window's attributes, you can plug WINTOOL's reported values into your own code to create windows with your chosen attributes. Figure 6.1 shows WINTOOL's main display.

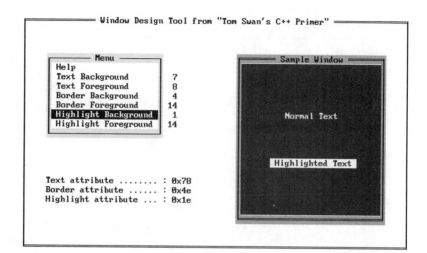

**Figure 6.1**. WINTOOL's main display. The program, a window-design utility, uses the class library described in this chapter and in Chapter 7, "Building a Class Library—Part 2."

## Compiling WINTOOL

WINTOOL uses many different modules, some of which are stored in C:\TSC\LIB\SOURCE. Table 6.1 lists all of the program's files. Compile WINTOOL as you have been compiling programs in other chapters. For example, if you are using Microsoft C/C++, from directory C:\TSC\C06, copy MAKEFILE.MSC to MAKEFILE and enter **nmake** at a DOS prompt. See the Introduction and Chapter 10, "Cross-Compilation Tools," if you experience any trouble during compilation. After compiling, run WINTOOL. Use the cursor keys to select one of the commands in the small box at upper left, and press Enter to change that item's value. The effect of each setting is shown instantly in the sample window at right. Press Esc to quit.

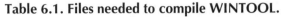

**Table 6.1. Files needed to compile WINTOOL.**

| Filename | Description |
| --- | --- |
| COMMAND.H | Class command module (no corresponding .CPP file) |
| ERROR.CPP | Error-handling routines module |
| ERROR.H | Header file for ERROR.CPP |
| ITEM.CPP | Class item module |
| ITEM.H | Header file for ITEM.CPP |
| KEY.CPP | Keyboard-handling routines module |
| KEY.H | Header file for KEY.CPP |
| LIST.CPP | Class list module |
| LIST.H | Header file for LIST.CPP |
| SELECTOR.CPP | Class selector module |
| SELECTOR.H | Header file for SELECTOR.CPP |
| STRITEM.CPP | Class stritem (string item) module |
| STRITEM.H | Header file for STRITEM.CPP |
| WINDOW.CPP | Class Window module |
| WINDOW.H | Header file for WINDOW.CPP |
| WINTOOL.CPP | The WINTOOL main program |
| WINTOOL.H | Header file for WINTOOL.CPP |

# The wintool.h Header

Like most programs, WINTOOL stores several constants and other declarations in a header file, Listing 6.1, wintool.h. In addition to its miscellaneous items, the file also declares two objects that demonstrate how to use the classes in this chapter to create menu-driven programs. As in Chapter 5, "Class Objectives," I'll explain this and other long listings in sections. On disk, of course, each listing is stored in a single file.

### Listing 6.1. wintool.h.

```
 1:  // wintool.h -- Header for wintool.cpp
 2:
 3:  #include <key.h>
 4:  #include <command.h>
 5:  #include <window.h>
 6:  #include <selector.h>
 7:
 8:  // Pop-up menu position, size, and other attributes
 9:
10:  #define MENU_ROW        4
11:  #define MENU_COL        5
12:  #define MENU_WIDTH      24
13:  #define MENU_HEIGHT     9
14:  #define MENU_TA         0x07
15:  #define MENU_BA         0x1f
16:  #define MENU_HA         0x70
17:  #define MENU_TYPE       1            // Single-line border
18:  #define MENU_TITLE      " Menu "
19:  #define MENU_POPUP      0            // Not pop-up, stationary
20:
```

Wintool.h begins with a few #include directives to bring in declarations from the class library. Header key.h prototypes keyboard-handling routines; command.h declares the command class, which menu-driven programs use to execute commands; window.h declares the Window class, which, as you might suppose, creates pop-up windows; and selector.h declares another class, selector, out of which you can create pop-up lists of items that users can select by moving a highlight bar up and down.

The #defines at lines 10–19 assign values to several constants used in WINTOOL's pop-up menu. These values describe the position, size, attributes, type, title, and style for the window on the left side of WINTOOL's main screen. (Run the program to see this if you haven't done so already.)

Most programs you'll create will need similar constant values. The first four constants in wintool.h specify the starting row and column of a window's top-left corner plus the window's width and height in characters. The three hexadecimal values represent the text (MENU_TA), border (MENU_BA), and highlight (MENU_HA) attributes used to display this window. WINTOOL's main job is to let you view the results of similar values, which you can use to create your own windows in other programs.

The final three MENU constants select the type of window, define its title, and specify whether the menu should be the pop-up kind or stationary. The MENU_TYPE value can be one of the values listed in Table 6.2, which can be used to create menus and other kinds of windows. These values are the same as those used by the display package's disp_box() function, described in Chapter 10, "Cross-Compilation Tools." MENU_POPUP can be 1 to have a menu disappear when you select a command, or set to 0 as done here to have the menu window remain visible until the program ends.

**Table 6.2. Menu and window border type values.**

| Value | Border Type |
| --- | --- |
| 0 | Double-line border |
| 1 | Single-line border |
| 2 | Solid border |
| 3 | Double-line horizontal, single-line vertical border |
| 4 | Single-line horizontal, double-line vertical border |

**Listing 6.1. wintool.h. (continued)**

```
21:  // Sample window position, size, and other attributes
22:
23:  #define SAMP_ROW       4
24:  #define SAMP_COL       44
25:  #define SAMP_WIDTH     31
26:  #define SAMP_HEIGHT    18
27:  #define SAMP_TYPE      3
28:  #define SAMP_TITLE     " Sample Window "
29:
30:  // Unique values identifying menu commands that call the same
31:  // command-object virtual function. That function uses these values
32:  // to determine which command called it.
33:
34:  #define CMD_TBG   0
35:  #define CMD_TFG   1
36:  #define CMD_BBG   2
37:  #define CMD_BFG   3
```

```
38:   #define CMD_HBG    4
39:   #define CMD_HFG    5
40:
```

The wintool.h header file continues at line 23 with a few more #defines. First are six constants that specify the position, size, type, and title for the sample window displayed on the right side of WINTOOL's main screen.

The six constants at lines 34–39, all of which begin with CMD_, list unique values that distinguish between some of the program's menu selections. When designing menu-driven programs using the classes in this chapter, you'll create new classes for each command. Many times, there will be one class per command in a menu. But at other times, several commands will be related and you'll want them to execute the same function, but to have a slightly different effect. In such cases, constants like the CMD_ values listed here let a single member function in a command determine which menu item called it.

## Listing 6.1. wintool.h. (continued)

```
41:   // Command classes for WinTool
42:
43:   class helpCommand: public command {
44:   public:
45:     helpCommand(): command(" Help") { }
46:     virtual void performCommand(void);
47:   };
48:
49:   class attrCommand: public command {
50:   public:
51:     attrCommand(const char *s, int cn): command(s, cn) { }
52:     virtual void performCommand(void);
53:   };
54:
55:   // Function prototypes for main program
56:
57:   void createMainWindow(void);
58:   void createSampWindow(void);
59:   void performCommands(void);
60:   void showColors(void);
61:   void showSample(void);
```

The wintool.h header file also declares two new classes, helpCommand and attrCommand. Each of these classes is derived from the command class, described later. In WINTOOL, the helpCommand object displays the program's help screen. The attrCommand object takes care of all other WINTOOL commands. In your own programs, you'd declare one or more similar classes for each command.

The two classes are similar. Each has a public constructor that initializes an object of its class. The two constructors illustrate the two basic ways you can create your own command objects. In helpCommand, the constructor is defined as

```
helpCommand(): command(" Help") { }
```

There are no parameters listed for helpCommand, and the constructor contains no statements of its own. The constructor performs only one task: It passes a literal string " Help" to its ancestor's constructor in the command class. This means that any objects of type helpCommand construct themselves with the command's name as it should appear in the program's menu. (The leading blank in " Help" moves the H one space to the right of the left border in the menu's window.)

The attrCommand constructor is similar to helpCommand's, but it lists two parameters, both of which are passed to the inherited constructor

```
attrCommand(const char *s, int cn): command(s, cn) { }
```

Because of this design, an object of type attrCommand must specify a string for the command's name (s) plus a unique value to identify the command (cn). Statements can use this information to create multiple instances of attrCommand objects, giving each of those objects unique names and integer values. As in the helpCommand class, the attrCommand constructor contains no statements of its own.

Lines 46 and 52 declare identically named performCommand() member functions. Each function is prefaced by the keyword virtual, making it possible for pointers to various command variables to select different performCommand() functions based on the type of addressed object. (The next two sections explain how virtual functions work.)

For each command object, performCommand() is the function that executes when the program's user selects the command from a menu. To create a menu-driven program, all you need to do is create a few classes like helpCommand and attrCommand, and to provide virtual performCommand() member functions for each. You then define objects of these classes, insert those objects into the program's menu, and the code itself determines which performCommand() function to execute based on a selected command.

Finally in wintools.h at lines 57–61 are five prototypes for functions that WINTOOL calls to execute various actions. These functions are not class members. In the next section, I'll explain what these functions do, although you can probably figure out their actions from the function names.

> **Note:** Keep in mind that C++ doesn't force you to use classes and object-oriented programming techniques in every corner of your code. You are free to mix OOP and conventional code, as I have done with the five plain function prototypes here.

# Pointers to Class Variables

In Chapter 5, "Class Objectives," you learned how to declare new classes and how to define objects of those class types. Class objects are sometimes called *instances* to distinguish them from objects of common C++ data types like int and double. I'll use the terms *object* and *class object* interchangeably.

> **Note:** In this book's ancestor, *Learning C++,* I shunned the term *class object.* Times have changed and the phrase apparently has won the popularity contest of how to address an instance of a class. I would not want to impede progress, so "class object" it is!

In many programs, you'll define class objects as local or global variables. For example, to create an object of a class named item, you could write

```
item myItem;
```

The object myItem is an instance of the item class. If item has a constructor with no parameters, the definition calls that constructor. If a constructor has one or more parameters, you can define an item object like this:

```
item myItem(x);
```

Here, x represents an argument passed to item's constructor for initializing the new object. It's also possible to pass more than one argument to a constructor:

```
item myItem(x, y, z);
```

This resembles a common function call, and in fact, that's exactly what it is— a call to the constructor in item. You never call a constructor as you call common functions. You always call constructors in tandem with the definition of a class object.

After defining objects as in the preceding three examples of MyItem, use dot notation to access the object's public members. For example, if the item class declares a member function named showItem(), you can call that function with the statement

```
myItem.showItem();
```

You can also create objects on the heap and assign the address of that allocated memory to a pointer. In Chapter 4, "Making Statements and Building Structures," you learned how to create pointers to common variables. To create and use a pointer to type float, you can write statements such as these:

```
float *fp;
fp = new float;
*fp = 3.14159;
cout << *fp;
delete fp;
```

The first line creates a new pointer named fp bound to the type float. The next line allocates space on the heap for a float variable. The third line assigns a value to the variable's space in memory. The fourth line displays the assigned value, and the last line deletes the allocated space, returning it to the memory pool used by future allocations. The third and fourth lines dereference fp to refer to the data addressed by fp.

You can use similar definitions and statements to allocate and use heap space for a class object. Suppose you declare this class

```
class aClass {
private:
  int value;
public:
  aClass() { value = 0; }
  int getValue(void ) { return value; }
  void putValue(int n) { value = n; }
};
```

Class aClass contains a single data member named value. The constructor aClass() sets value to 0. Member function getValue() returns value. Member function putValue() assigns a new value to value. (Without more substance, aClass isn't useful, but in the next sections, it will serve to demonstrate how to address class objects with pointers.)

To create an object of aClass, you could define a local or global variable as explained earlier, or you can call new to allocate space on the heap for the object:

```
aClass *acp;
acp = new aClass;
if (acp == NULL)
  error();
```

The first line defines a pointer named acp to an object of type aClass. The definition is identical in form to the float *fp definition that creates a pointer to a common data type; only the names are changed. The space for the object doesn't yet exist. That happens when the second line calls new to allocate memory for the object and assign the address of that space to acp. This statement is also identical in form to the preceding one that allocated memory for a float variable stored on the heap. As always, after calling new, you should check whether the pointer is null. If so, then new was unable to fulfill the allocation request. (I'll skip this step in future samples to save space, but *don't* skip this test in your code!)

If you're thinking that creating pointers to class objects is no different from creating pointers to other data types, you're right! Classes *are* data types, and you can use them in nearly all the same ways you can use other data types built into C++.

You can also define a pointer to a class object and call new to allocate space with a single stroke:

```
aClass *acp = new aClass;
```

Get used to this notation—you'll see it and put it to work often in C++ programs. It has the same effect as the first two lines in the previous fragment. The definition creates a pointer named acp to an object of type aClass, and it calls new to allocate space on the heap for that object, assigning the object's address to acp.

When you call new either in a definition or separately to allocate space on the heap for a class object, if that class declares a constructor, C++ calls the constructor automatically to initialize the object. For the hypothetical aClass, this means that the object's value field will be set to 0 without the program having to specify this action. C++ calls the class constructor for *every* new class object that the program defines.

After allocating space for a new class object, you can use the object's pointer to call public member functions declared for this class (or inherited from a base class). For example, to change value to 1234, you could write

```
acp->putValue(1234);
```

This notation is identical to that used to access struct fields addressed by a pointer. The -> symbol serves a similar purpose as the dot in dot notation—it selects a member of a structure or object. The effect of this example statement is to call the putValue() function for the object addressed by acp, and to assign the value 1234 to that object's private value data member.

It's also possible to pass arguments to constructors to initialize objects on the heap. Suppose you change the declaration of aClass to this:

```
class aClass {
private:
  int value;
public:
  aClass(int n) { value = n; }
  int getValue(void ) { return value; }
  void putValue(int n) { value = n; }
};
```

The only difference between this declaration and the previous one is the aClass constructor. In this new version, the constructor declares an int parameter n and assigns it to value. To create a pointer to an object of this class and allocate heap space for that object, you can write

```
aClass *acp = new aClass(4321);
```

This defines a pointer named acp to an object of type aClass. The statement calls new to allocate space on the heap for an aClass object, and it passes the literal value 4321 to the class constructor, which assigns that value to the object's copy of the private value data member. You must supply arguments for each parameter that a constructor declares, just as you must supply arguments for parameters in other functions.

Using the notation you learned about in Chapter 3, "Functions: Programming in Pieces," you can declare a default parameter in a constructor. For example, to make n optional, you could change the constructor in aClass to this:

```
aClass(int n = 0) { value = n; }
```

When you define an object of type aClass, you now have the option of supplying an argument for n's value. All the following statements are correct:

```
aClass v1;
aClass v2(10);
aClass *p1 = new aClass;
aClass *p2 = new aClass(20);
```

The first line defines an object of type aClass. Because no argument is passed to the constructor, the default value 0 is assigned to n. The second line specifies a new value for n, overriding the default. The third line defines a pointer p1 to an aClass object, allocated heap space by new. As in the first line, the default of 0 is passed to the constructor because no argument is supplied. The fourth line also calls new to allocate heap space and assign an address to p2. This line overrides the default value, passing 20 to the constructor.

It's also possible to declare more than one constructor in a class to allow a different object initializations. I'll explain more about this technique in Chapter 7, "Building a Class Library—Part 2," when I introduce the strItem (string item) class.

# Pointers to Derived Classes

Storing class objects on the heap helps programs use memory efficiently. But there's another benefit that goes with using object pointers. A pointer may address an object of a base class, or it may address any object of a class that is derived from that base.

The value of this concept may not be apparent now, but it's one of C++'s most important capabilities. Suppose you have one class named A and another class B derived from A. You can declare a pointer p to an object of type A:

```
A *p;
```

Pointer p may then address an object of type A. But here's the twist: p may also address an object of the derived class B even though you declared p to address objects of class A.

You can't perform the same sort of trick with pointers to C++ built-in types. Types like int and double are not classes and therefore, they can't serve as base classes for derived types. If they could, you'd be able to declare a higher-order floating-point data type, and all your pointers to type float could address the new type without your having to modify a single line of existing code.

With classes, you can do exactly that: create a class and define a pointer to objects of that class, and then create other derived classes from that base class. All your pointers to objects of the base class can then address the new derivations. That rule even holds true for pointers in code that's already compiled! How and why this concept is important will become evident as you examine the programming in this and the next chapter. To provide some additional background on the subject, the following few sections demonstrate one of the main benefits of using pointers of one class to address objects of classes derived from that class: *polymorphism.*

## Virtual Functions and Polymorphism

When a pointer addresses an object of a class, the actual type of that object might not be known until the program runs. For example, if you declare a pointer to a class of type A, at runtime the program may assign to that pointer the address of a derived object B.

Such assignments pose a problem, illustrated by a simple example. Here's class A's declaration:

```
class A {
private:
  int x;
public:
  void f(void);
};
```

Class A declares a private data member x and a single member function f(). The function stores a value in x:

```
void A::f(void)
{
  x = 1234;
}
```

The exact value doesn't matter, and the assignment merely represents the effect that any member function might have on the data in an object of a class type. Class B inherits A's properties. Here's B's declaration:

```
class B: public A {
private:
  int y;
public:
  void f(void);
};
```

Class B inherits all of A's properties; therefore, a variable of type B will have an x data member and a y data member declared in class B's private section. B also replaces f() with its own function f(), which acts on the private data stored in B:

```
void B::f(void)
{
  A::f();
  y = 4321;
}
```

B's implementation of function f() calls class A's function of the same name. To tell the compiler which of the identically named functions to call, the statement uses the notation A::f(). (You saw this technique in Chapter 5, "Class Objectives," when derived classes in ELEVSIM replaced functions in their base classes. There's nothing new here so far.) In addition to calling the base class f() function, the replacement function f() also assigns data to B's private y member. Again, that assignment represents the effect that any member function in a derived class might have on data members of the derived class.

All these declarations and function implementations work, and there's nothing wrong with them. Replacing member functions in derived classes is a useful technique, as ELEVSIM demonstrated in the previous chapter. But when a pointer addresses an object of the base class (A), a subtle problem arises. Suppose you define that pointer like this:

```
A *ap1 = new A;
```

Pointer ap1 addresses an object of class A. You can then write statements to use A's public members. There's only one such member in this example, the function f(). To call that function, you can use the statement

```
ap1->f();
```

As you probably expect, that calls function f() in class A for the object addressed by ap1. But here's the problem: Suppose you create another pointer and allocate space for an object of the derived class B

```
A *ap2 = new B;
```

C++ allows ap2, declared as a pointer to an object of the base class A, to address an object of the derived class B. Thinking all is well, you then execute this statement

```
ap2->f();
```

and you are surprised to discover that function f() in the base class A is called. Since ap2 addresses an object of type B, you want that statement to call the replacement function in B, not the original in A. But the code calls A's f() function, not B's. How can such a statement call B's function to initialize the data member declared in B (in this case, the integer y)?

The obvious solution is to declare the pointer to address an object of class B

```
B *ap2 = new B;
ap2->f();
```

Now the compiler knows that ap2 addresses an object of type B, and the second line calls function f() in B. However, while solving the problem, you've introduced another: You now have to declare *in advance* that ap2 addresses objects of class B. That might not be possible. Suppose, for example, that a single pointer addresses a list of class objects, many of which are of *different* derived classes. That's a typical case for object-oriented programs. Before the program runs, there's no way to tell what type of objects the pointer will address. How, then, can the program use a single pointer to call many different functions in those objects' derived classes?

The solution is to declare the functions *virtual.* A virtual member function in a class is identical to other member functions, but its prototype begins with the keyword virtual. Here are the two classes, A and B, with virtual f() functions:

```
class A {
private:
  int x;
public:
  virtual void f(void);
};

class B : public A {
private:
  int y;
public:
  virtual void f(void);
};
```

The only differences from the previous declarations are the two virtual keywords. Notice that the keyword comes *before* any return type, here void. The function implementations from before are exactly the same, and do not need corresponding virtual keywords. *Any* member function, but not a constructor, can be virtual.

With virtual functions in the two related classes, an amazing transformation takes place in the program. Consider what happens when you define a pointer to an object of class A. You call function f() to act on that object, and then delete the heap space addressed by p:

```
A *p = new A;
p->f();
delete p;
```

The statement p->f() calls function f() in class A. In another section of the program, you reuse that *same* pointer p, but this time you assign to the pointer the address of newly allocated space for an object of class B:

```
p = new B;
p->f();
delete p;
```

Here's where the magic comes in: The statement p->f() now calls the function declared in class B because that's the data type of the object addressed by p. Compare that statement with the preceding one that calls f() in class A. The two statements are identical, proving that *the object itself determines which virtual function is called!* This sleight of hand is called polymorphism.

In zoology, the word polymorphism describes the growth of different forms such as sponges that share the same properties. There's a wide variety of sponges in the seas, all of different sizes, shapes, and colors. Despite their differences, however, they are all still sponges, and they all serve the same purposes in life (such as life must be for a sponge). In programming, polymorphism refers to the capability of multiple class objects to change form at runtime while sharing the same function names—like function f() in the preceding samples.

A good example of polymorphism at work is a drawing program where shapes—circles, rectangles, and lines—are represented by classes. Each class derives from a base class, perhaps named shape. A pointer to shape might address an object of many derived types, for example, a circle, a rectangle, or another type of graphics object. At runtime, a virtual function named draw() in each class carries out the necessary instructions to draw the particular shape on-screen. The sample listing in the next section shows the basic design of this kind of program.

# Polymorphism in Action

Before continuing with WINTOOL, a simple example of polymorphism in action will help you to understand the value of virtual functions and polymorphism. Compile and run Listing 6.2, POLY.CPP.

### Listing 6.2. POLY.CPP.

```
 1:  // poly.cpp -- Demonstrate polymorphism
 2:
 3:  #include <tscdefs.h>
 4:  #include IOSTREAM_H
 5:
 6:  // Declare an abstract shape class
 7:
 8:  class shape {
 9:  public:
10:    virtual void draw(void) = 0;
11:  };
12:
13:  // Declare three derived classes that inherit the properties of
14:  // the shape class.
15:
16:  class circle: public shape {
17:  public:
18:    virtual void draw(void);
19:  };
20:
21:  class square: public shape {
22:  public:
23:    virtual void draw(void);
24:  };
25:
26:  class line: public shape {
27:  public:
28:    virtual void draw(void);
29:  };
30:
```

Lines 8–11 declare a class named shape. The class contains a single virtual member function, draw(). The notation = 0 at the end of the prototype tells C++ that draw() is a *pure virtual function,* and thus shape is an *abstract class.* The pure virtual function is only a prototype for a function in a derived class that you will supply later. A pure virtual function has no implementation, and you can't call it. Likewise, an abstract class is merely a schematic—you can't define an object of an abstract class like shape.

Abstract classes are useful for creating base classes from which other classes will derive common properties. Abstract classes also prevent programmers from defining objects of an incomplete class that's intended only as a sketch of the common parts that other derived classes will share.

Three such derived classes appear at lines 16–29. The circle, square, and line classes derive common properties from shape. Each of these classes declares a replacement function named draw(). Because the inherited draw() was declared to be virtual, the derivations *must* also use the virtual keyword at lines 18, 23, and 28.

The three replacement functions do not end with the = 0 notation as they do in the abstract base class. The program will create objects of the circle, square, and line classes, and, therefore, these classes must not be abstract. The reason for deriving these three new classes from shape is to give all the classes a common base. In a more complete program, the shape class might declare other common elements such as coordinate values, a color, and a size for the shape. The derived classes could then use these items (perhaps by calling public member functions) for a variety of purposes.

**Note:** The sample POLY program doesn't actually draw any shapes on-screen. But the principles the program illustrates are the same as they would be in a full-fledged graphics system.

## Listing 6.2. POLY.CPP. (continued)

```
31:  // The main program
32:
33:  main()
34:  {
35:    shape *p[3];          // Three shape pointers
```

*continues*

**Listing 6.2. continued**

```
36:
37:    p[0] = new circle;      // Allocate space for a circle
38:    p[1] = new square;      // Allocate space for a square
39:    p[2] = new line;        // Allocate space for a line
40:
41: // Call the virtual draw method in the object addressed by the
42: // pointers in the p[] array. Which virtual function actually
43: // executes is determined at runtime by the object itself.
44:
45:    for (int i = 0; i <=2; i++)
46:      p[i]->draw();
47:    return 0;
48: }
49:
```

POLY's main() function defines an array of three pointers to the abstract shape class. Lines 37–39 then call new to allocate space for objects of the three classes that are derived from shape. As I mentioned earlier, a pointer to a class may address objects of that class or of any derivation. In this example, however, the pointers would not be permitted to address an object of type shape because that class was designated to be abstract. You can *never* create objects of an abstract class, so the pointers in the p array can address *only* objects of classes that are derived from shape and that provide completed draw() member functions.

Lines 45–46 demonstrate how the relationships of derived classes to a common base can simplify programs. Here, a for loop cycles int i from 0 to 2, indexing the array of shape pointers, and calling the draw() member function for each object. (The "draw" functions in this small example simply display a message that confirms which function is called.)

Consider an important question: Which draw() function does the program call at line 46? The answer is: The program calls the draw() member function that belongs to the addressed object. Even though line 46 doesn't specify which draw() function to call, the program calls the correct function in the circle, square, and line class objects. *The objects themselves determine at runtime which draw() function should be called.*

You can demonstrate this effect by rearranging the order of the assignments to the pointer array at lines 37–39. You might also increase the size of the array, and use new to allocate space for several more circle or other shape derivations. No matter what kinds of objects you address with the array's pointers, you never need to modify the statement at line 46. That statement always calls the correct draw() function in whatever object p[i] happens to address.

Even more exciting: If the for loop at lines 45–46 were buried deeply inside a compiled module and even if you didn't have the source code to that module, the loop could still call new draw() member functions in classes that you derive from shape at a later time. You might create a new derived class sphere with its own virtual draw() function and insert a pointer to a sphere object into the p array. The for loop would call your new draw() function to draw a shape that didn't even exist when the programmer wrote the original statement at line 46!

Imagine the power this concept provides. In a graphics program, you can create new shapes, plug them into memory, and a precompiled program will be able to draw your designs. In a database, you can insert new data types, and the searching and sorting modules compiled earlier will be able to handle data of your new class types. In these and other cases, the original programmers would not have to know anything about your plans in order for them to write code that can use your custom objects.

POLY ends with the implementations of the three replacement virtual functions. These functions, which don't actually draw any shapes, are no different from common nonvirtual member functions.

## Listing 6.2. POLY.CPP. (continued)

```
50:  // The implementations of the three classes that derive from the base
51:  // class shape. Although declared to be virtual, the functions are no
52:  // different in form than nonvirtual member functions.
53:
54:  void circle::draw(void)
55:  {
56:    cout << "\nInside circle::draw()";
57:  }
58:
59:  void square::draw(void)
60:  {
61:    cout << "\nInside square::draw()";
62:  }
63:
```

*continues*

**Listing 6.2. continued**

```
64:  void line::draw(void)
65:  {
66:    cout << "\nInside line::draw()";
67:  }
```

# Early and Late Binding

C++ calls virtual functions differently than it does nonvirtual member functions. Normally, when a program calls a function, the compiler generates an instruction that transfers control to a fixed address in memory where the compiled code for the function is stored. Putting this in technical terms, C++ binds common function calls to static function addresses at compile time, a process known as *early binding*.

C++ does not call virtual member functions in that same way. When a statement or expression calls a virtual function, instead of generating code to call a static address, C++ creates instructions that look up the actual address of the function at runtime. That lookup action uses the object of the class to find the correct address of a virtual function, a process called *late binding*.

Late binding is the internal method by which C++ selects among virtual functions of the same names in related classes. To use late binding, all you have to do is declare a member function with the `virtual` keyword.

**Note:** Virtual functions require a program to perform an additional memory reference to look up a function's address. For this reason, there's a slight time penalty for using virtual functions that you don't have to pay when using nonvirtual functions. In most cases, this penalty is small compared to the benefits that late binding provides.

# The WINTOOL.CPP Main Program

You'll now be able to appreciate how WINTOOL uses polymorphism to call program commands. The main program, Listing 6.3, WINTOOL.CPP, begins with several declarations, a few global variables, and a simple `main()` function.

## Listing 6.3. WINTOOL.CPP.

```
 1: // wintool.cpp -- Select window attributes
 2:
 3: #include <tscdefs.h>
 4: #include IOSTREAM_H
 5: #include <form.h>
 6: #include "wintool.h"
 7:
 8: // Global variables
 9: int attributes[6] = {1, 15, 7, 0, 7, 0};
10: unsigned wta = 0x1f;
11: unsigned wba = 0x70;
12: unsigned wha = 0x70;
13: Window *mainWindow;
14: Window *sampleWindow;
15:
16: main()
17: {
18:   Window::startup();
19:   createMainWindow();
20:   createSampWindow();
21:   performCommands();
22:   delete sampleWindow;
23:   delete mainWindow;
24:   Window::shutDown();
25:   return 0;
26: }
27:
```

WINTOOL includes usual tscdefs.h and IOSTREAM_H header files, and also includes form.h so output stream statements can call the form() function (see Chapter 10, "Cross-Compliation Tools"). Line 6 includes wintool.h (see Listing 6.1), which loads other headers, making most of this book's class library available to WINTOOL.

Line 9 prepares an array of byte values, one per menu selection. These are the attributes you adjust while using the program to select window colors. Lines 10–12 create variables that WINTOOL uses to display the sample window in these colors. Change the default values listed here to alter the sample's initial colors.

Lines 13–14 declare two pointers to objects of type Window, a class that you can use to create pop-up text windows. In your own programs, each window needs a Window * pointer, and you can't define Window objects as global or local variables. In other words, objects of the Window and most other classes in this book's class library *must* be stored dynamically on the heap.

> **Note:** The preceding rule may seem highly restrictive, but it's common in OOP, where objects are commonly created dynamically at runtime. Many of the classes in the library contain code that deletes class objects stored on the heap, and those deletions will fail for local and global objects of the Window and other classes.

## Static Member Functions

In addition to calling a few internal functions and deleting the two Window objects at lines 22–23, the program's main() function initializes the Window class with the statements at lines 18 and 24. Any program that includes the window.h header (as WINTOOL.CPP does by including wintool.h) *must* call the startup() and shutDown() functions as done here:

```
Window::startup();
...
Window::shutDown();
```

Until now, all calls to member functions were associated with an object of their class. But these two statements are different. They do not call a function to act on a class object. They call functions that apply to the class as a whole.

For most classes, you normally define an object of the class and then use dot notation to call a member function. For example, assume that button is the class type; to call a push() function in button, you first need to define an object such as b1 of type button, and then execute a statement such as b1.push().

The Window class's startup() and shutDown() functions are different. They are *static member functions.* To call them, precede their names with double colons and the class name.

Static member functions such as startup() and shutDown() are useful for hiding system-dependent items inside a class. In this version of the Window class, startup() and shutDown() initialize and deactivate the display package described in Chapter 10, "Cross-Compilation Tools." Hiding system-dependent jobs like these in a class simplifies the job of porting programs to new environments. Because the dependent statements are buried inside the class, programs that use the class should not require changes to compile with different C++ compilers for which the same class is implemented.

## Listing 6.3. WINTOOL.CPP. (continued)

```
28:  // Create and display main program window
29:  void createMainWindow()
30:  {
31:    winStruct ws = {
32:      0, 0, 80, 25,    // row, column, width, height
33:      0x07,            // text attribute
34:      0x0f,            // border attribute
35:      0x70,            // highlight attribute
36:      3                // border type
37:    };
38:    mainWindow = new Window(
39:      ws, " Window Design Tool from \"Tom Swan's C++ Primer\" ");
40:    mainWindow->showWindow();
41:  }
42:
```

After main(), WINTOOL continues at function createMainWindow(). The function demonstrates how simple it is to create a pop-up window using the Window class. First, a struct of type winStruct (declared in window.h, and listed later) defines a few values that describe the window's position, size, attributes, and border type. These values have the same purposes as I described earlier for various constants in wintool.h (Listing 6.1). In your own programs, each window must have a similar structure.

Next, the program calls new to allocate heap space for an object of the Window class. Line 38 assigns the address of that space to a Window pointer named mainWindow. The arguments in this statement pass to the Window class constructor the winStruct variable ws and the window's title.

Use similar definitions and statements in your own code to create windows. For example, it takes only one line to create a pointer named myWP (my window pointer), allocate space for the Window class object, and assign the address of that object to myWP:

```
Window *myWP = new Window(ws, " My Window ");
```

This assumes that you also prepared a winStruct variable ws. After creating the Window object, you can use the pointer to call various Window member functions. For object, to display the window, use this statement:

```
myWP->showWindow();
```

Remember to use the pointer notation -> to access member functions in the class. Because you *must* allocate space for Window objects on the heap, you *must* use pointers along with the operator -> to call Window class member functions.

I'll explain other Window functions as you see them in WINTOOL. The Window class includes many functions that can display text, scroll lines, change attributes, and perform other actions inside pop-up windows.

## Listing 6.3. WINTOOL.CPP. (continued)

```
43:  // Create and display sample window
44:  void createSampWindow()
45:  {
46:    winStruct ws = {
47:      SAMP_ROW, SAMP_COL, SAMP_WIDTH, SAMP_HEIGHT,
48:      wta, wba, wha, SAMP_TYPE
49:    };
50:    sampleWindow = new Window(ws, SAMP_TITLE);
51:    sampleWindow->showWindow();
52:  }
53:
```

The next function, createSampWindow(), is similar to createMainWindow(). Instead of specifying literal values for window parameters, however, the code uses SAMP constants and the three global variables wta, wba, and wha to prepare the winStruct structure. The variables control the colors that change in the sample window when you select WINTOOL's attribute commands.

Using constants keeps the source text clean, and collects the constants in wintool.h, where they are easy to modify. Line 51 calls showWindow() to display the window addressed by the sampleWindow pointer.

## Listing 6.3. WINTOOL.CPP. (continued)

```
54:  // Create command menu and execute command objects
55:  void performCommands(void)
56:  {
57:    command *cp;           // Pointer to selected command
58:    winStruct ws = {
59:      MENU_ROW, MENU_COL, MENU_WIDTH, MENU_HEIGHT,
60:      MENU_TA, MENU_BA, MENU_HA, MENU_TYPE
61:    };
62:    selector *menu = new selector(ws, MENU_TITLE, MENU_POPUP);
```

The performCommands() function is more complex than the previous two, so I'll describe it in two stages. First, line 61 defines a pointer cp to an object of the command class—another in the class library that I'll explain in Chapter 7, "Building a Class Library—Part 2." This pointer gives the program a way to execute member functions for the command objects declared in wintool.h.

Lines 58–61 define a winStruct variable similar to that used for the main and sample windows. *Every* window needs to have a corresponding structure that describes the window's attributes. Line 62 is new:

```
selector *menu = new selector(ws, MENU_TITLE, MENU_POPUP);
```

This creates a selector object, another class in the library. A selector is a window in which you can select lines of text—in this case, the commands in WINTOOL's menu. Because selector is derived from Window, its constructor requires a winStruct object (ws) and a title (MENU_TITLE). It also needs a third argument, MENU_POPUP. This constant tells the selector object whether to keep the window visible after someone selects a line (0), or to hide the window at that time (1). If you don't specify this last argument, the default value is 1.

## Listing 6.3. WINTOOL.CPP. (continued)

```
63:    menu->insertItem(new helpCommand());
64:    menu->insertItem(new attrCommand(" Text Background",    CMD_TBG));
65:    menu->insertItem(new attrCommand(" Text Foreground",    CMD_TFG));
66:    menu->insertItem(new attrCommand(" Border Background",  CMD_BBG));
67:    menu->insertItem(new attrCommand(" Border Foreground",  CMD_BFG));
68:    menu->insertItem(new attrCommand(" Highlight Background", CMD_HBG));
```

*continues*

## Listing 6.3. continued

```
69:     menu->insertItem(new attrCommand(" Highlight Foreground",  CMD_HFG));
70:     showColors();
71:     while ((cp = (command *)(menu->getSelection())) != NULL) {
72:       cp->performCommand();
73:       showColors();
74:     }
75:     delete menu;
76:   }
```

Function performCommands() continues at lines 63–75 with several statements that demonstrate how to create a pop-up menu of commands. The menu pointer, to which the function just allocated space for an object of the selector class, is used to call that class's insertItem() member function. Each such call adds one command object to the menu. For example, line 63 creates and inserts the helpCommand object declared in wintool.h. Note how new is used here:

```
menu->insertItem(new helpCommand());
```

First, menu is dereferenced to access the insertItem() member function. That function requires a pointer to an object to insert in the selector addressed by menu. Instead of saving the result of new in a pointer, that result is simply passed directly to insertItem. What happens to the pointer? It's saved in memory on a list of commands. I'll explain later how that happens—for now, just become familiar with the use of new to pass an object pointer to a member function.

**Note:** You may have the urge here to hunt for insertItem()'s declaration. If so, you'll find it in list.h, not selector.h, in directory C:\TSC\LIB\SOURCE. The class selector is derived from the list class, which declares insertItem(). The list class in turn is derived from the item class. You'll examine the declarations of all these classes in time, and jumping ahead through the class hierarchy now may be more confusing than helpful. It's probably best to stick to the game plan—learn the high-level uses first before diving too deeply below the surface. But feel free to peek ahead if you want.

Line 64 shows a different way to insert commands into menus. Here, new allocates space for an object of type attrCommand. Because that class's constructor declares two parameters (see Listing 6.1, line 51), the statement must supply two arguments

```
menu->insertItem(new attrCommand(" Text Background", CMD_TBG));
```

The statement calls the insertItem() member function for the selector object addressed by menu. Using new allocates memory for an object of the attrCommand class. The statement also initializes the object with a string and the constant value CMD_TBG.

Use this kind of statement to insert commands for which the *same* member function will be called when users select the command from a menu. The CMD_TBG constant assigns a unique value to the program's Text Background command to distinguish this command from other attrCommand objects. Lines 65–69 insert similar commands with different titles and constant values.

The function continues at line 70 by calling showColors(), which displays the attribute values you see on-screen to the right of WINTOOL's menu. A while loop shows the correct way to get and execute commands from a pop-up menu:

```
while ((cp = (command *)(menu->getSelection())) != NULL) {
  cp->performCommand();
  ...
}
```

The control expression looks more complex than it is. As with all lengthy expressions, to understand this one, it's best to take it apart from the inside out. In order of execution, the elements are as follows:

- menu->getSelection() returns a pointer to a selected command object in the menu. The function returns null if you press Esc.

- (command *) casts the result of menu->getSelection() to a command pointer, so it can be assigned to cp. The menu pointer addresses a generic selection list, which in another program might select among other kinds of strings—for example, filenames from a disk directory. WINTOOL knows that the selections are menu commands, but the compiler doesn't. That's why recasting is needed.

- != NULL causes the while loop to continue as long as cp is not equal to null. When cp is null (indicating that you pressed Esc), the loop ends.

The effect of all this is to assign the address of a single command object to cp. The statement cp->performCommand() then executes that object's virtual member function—another example of polymorphism. The type of object cp addresses depends on which commands you select from the menu. The statement at line 77 executes *any* program command, similar to the way earlier examples called different virtual functions via pointers.

## Listing 6.3. WINTOOL.CPP. (continued)

```
77:  // Display current color attributes and sample window
78:  void showColors(void)
79:  {
80:    char buf[80];
81:
82:    for (int i = 0; i < 6; i++) {
83:      mainWindow->gotorc(MENU_ROW + i + 1, MENU_COL + MENU_WIDTH);
84:      mainWindow->puts(form(buf, "%2d", attributes[i]));
85:    }
86:    mainWindow->gotorc(16, 4);
87:    mainWindow->puts(form(buf, "Text attribute ........ : %#2x  ", wta));
88:    mainWindow->gotorc(17, 4);
89:    mainWindow->puts(form(buf, "Border attribute ...... : %#2x  ", wba));
90:    mainWindow->gotorc(18, 4);
91:    mainWindow->puts(form(buf, "Highlight attribute ... : %#2x  ", wha));
92:    showSample();
93:  }
94:
```

The next WINTOOL function, showColors(), demonstrates how to display text inside a window. Earlier, the program allocated space on the heap for a Window object, and assigned the address of that space to the mainWindow pointer. The showColors() function calls two Window class member functions for that object: gotorc() (go to row and column) and puts() (put string).

Rows and columns are relative to the window's borders. If wp is a pointer to an object of type Window, then the statement wp->gotorc(0, 0) sends the cursor to the upper left corner inside the window's boundaries. The "cursor" is only a logical position, not a visible symbol, where you want to display text.

Similarly, function puts() displays a string at the current cursor location. The string's characters are colored with the window's default attributes. ("Colors" on monochrome systems appear as bold, dim, underlined, and blinking text.) I'll show you how to select different attributes in a moment. If wp is a Window pointer, then wp->puts("C++ Primer") displays the quoted characters inside the window at the cursor's location. After that operation, the cursor is moved to the end of the string.

> **Note:** To format integer, floating-point, and other variables for display, include the form.h header and use the form() function as you do in output-stream statements. For example, to display an int value, you could use the statement wp->puts(form(buf, "value=%d", value));. The buf argument is a char array large enough to hold a temporary copy of the resulting string. See Chapter 10, "Cross-Compilation Tools," for more information about form().

### Listing 6.3. WINTOOL.CPP. (continued)

```
 95:  // Display sample window using selected attributes
 96:  void showSample(void)
 97:  {
 98:    winStruct ws = {
 99:      SAMP_ROW, SAMP_COL, SAMP_WIDTH, SAMP_HEIGHT,
100:      wta, wba, wha, SAMP_TYPE
101:    };
102:    sampleWindow->setInfo(ws);
103:    sampleWindow->gotorc(0, 0);
104:    sampleWindow->eeow();
105:    sampleWindow->gotorc(5, 9);
106:    sampleWindow->normalVideo();
107:    sampleWindow->puts("Normal Text");
108:    sampleWindow->gotorc(10, 6);
109:    sampleWindow->reverseVideo();
110:    sampleWindow->puts(" Highlighted Text ");
111:  }
112:
```

The showSample() function is similar to showColors(). This function displays the sample window using the colors you select from WINTOOL's menu. Because these colors will change, the function begins by calling the window's setInfo() member function and passing a winStruct variable containing the global attribute values. Use this technique to change an existing window's attributes. The function also calls eeow() (erase to end of window), normalVideo() (unhighlighted text), and reverseVideo() (highlighted text) to construct the sample window. All these functions—setInfo(), eeow(), and reverseVideo()—are members of the Window class. You can call them for any Window object.

### Listing 6.3. WINTOOL.CPP. (continued)

```
113:   // Implementation of the help command
114:   void helpCommand::performCommand(void)
115:   {
116:     winStruct ws = {
117:       2, 2, 76, 21,   // row, column, width, height
118:       0x1f,           // text attribute
119:       0x70,           // border attribute
120:       0x70,           // highlight attribute
121:       0               // border type
122:     };
123:     Window *helpWindow = new Window(ws, " WinTool Help ");
124:     helpWindow->showWindow();
125:     helpWindow->gotorc(8, 4);
126:     helpWindow->puts("No help available");
127:     helpWindow->gotorc(10, 4);
128:     helpWindow->puts("(Press <Esc> from main menu to quit program)");
129:     while (!keyWaiting()) ;
130:     getKey();
131:     delete helpWindow;
132:   }
133:
```

WINTOOL's helpCommand and attrCommand classes declare virtual performCommand() functions. These are the functions that run when you select a command from the program's menu. Lines 114–132 show the implementation for helpCommand's function, which runs when you select the Help command. (The function is unfinished. Exercise 6.8 asks you to complete this section.)

Most of the programming in the function should be familiar to you by now, except for the two statements at lines 129–130. There, a while loop calls keyWaiting() from the keyboard module explained later in the chapter. The empty statement at the end of the line causes the loop to pause the program until you press a key. Then, line 130 calls another of that module's functions, getKey(), to remove the keypress from the input buffer.

> **Note:** Be sure to use delete for any class objects you create with new, as done here at line 131. If you don't delete objects from the heap, they will remain in memory after the functions that created them end. This may cause the program to run out of room for new objects. For a graphic example of the errors that can occur by forgetting to delete objects when you're done using them, temporarily remove line 131, recompile, and run WINTOOL. Open the help window repeatedly. As you'll see, the window refuses to go away, and in time, the program halts when it runs out of memory.

### Listing 6.3. WINTOOL.CPP. (continued)

```
134:   // Implementation of the attributes command. Increments attribute
135:   // value for selected item, identified by cmdNum. Updates global
136:   // window attribute values.
137:
138:   void attrCommand::performCommand(void)
139:   {
140:     attributes[cmdNum] = ++attributes[cmdNum] % 16;
141:     wta = attributes[0] * 16 + attributes[1];
142:     wba = attributes[2] * 16 + attributes[3];
143:     wha = attributes[4] * 16 + attributes[5];
144:   }
```

The second performCommand() implementation in WINTOOL belongs to the attrCommand class. Recall from earlier in this chapter that several variations of this object were created and inserted in the program's menu. Statements in performCommand() use cmdNum to determine which variation was selected. The cmdNum variable is a member of the command, and is available to all descendants of that class (explained in Chapter 7, "Building a Class Library—Part 2").

In attrCommand's performCommand() function, cmdNum is used as an index to the attributes array of byte values that specify the sample window's colors. (In another setting, cmdNum might select one of several subfunctions to execute.) Line 140 increments the corresponding attributes entry for each attribute command you select. The next three statements assign the final attribute values to the global wta, wba, and wha variables. These values are used in a winStruct structure to change the appearance of the sample window (see line 108 in function showSample()).

That completes WINTOOL. You've now seen a full example of what the class library can do. You've learned about static functions, virtual functions, and polymorphism. And you've learned how to use some of the member functions in the Window class. Chapter 7, "Building a Class Library—Part 2," details that class and others in the library. Before turning to those subjects, however, you need to take a short side trip back to non-OOP land.

# Mixing OOP and Non-OOP Code

**B**eginners to OOP techniques tend to forget that C++ is a hybrid language. Everything in a C++ program does *not* have to be stored in a class. You can and should mix OOP and non-OOP techniques in the same programs.

The rest of this chapter lists two modules used by some of the member functions in the book's class library. The modules provide keyboard and error-handling support for programs that use the library. I could have invented classes for these items, but there seemed to be several good reasons not to do so. For one, there's only one keyboard on most computers, and programs would therefore need only a single object of a keyboard class. For another, operations such as getting keypresses and displaying error messages are global in nature. Hiding those operations inside class objects seemed pointless.

## The KEY Module

The first support module is stored in two files, key.h and KEY.CPP. The key.h header file (Listing 6.4) lists the prototypes for the three functions in KEY.CPP. The KEY.CPP file (Listing 6.5) implements the three function prototypes declared in key.h.

## Listing 6.4. key.h.

```
 1:  // key.h -- Header for key.cpp
 2:
 3:  #ifndef __KEY_H    //
 4:  #define __KEY_H          1      // Prevent multiple #includes
 5:
 6:  // Various key definitions. The values work only with the getkey
 7:  // function in the key module; they do not work with the getch and
 8:  // other standard key-input library functions.
 9:
10:  int getKey(void);
11:  int keyWaiting(void);
12:  void ungetKey(int k);
13:
14:  #endif   // __KEY_H
```

## Listing 6.5. KEY.CPP.

```
 1:  // key.cpp -- Keyboard routines
 2:
 3:  #include <conio.h>
 4:  #include "key.h"
 5:
 6:  int savedChar;  // Char saved by ungetKey()
 7:
 8:  // Wait for and return the next keypress. Displays nothing.
 9:  // Returns extended PC ASCII values from 0 to 255 for alphanumeric and
10:  // control keys. Returns negative values for function keys such as <F1>,
11:  // <End>, and <Home>. Constants for these keys are defined in key.doc.
12:  // Other similar constants (e.g. for <Alt>-key combinations) can be
13:  // created by taking the second character returned by getch() for that
14:  // key and subtracting 256 from the character's ASCII value.
15:
16:  int getKey(void)
17:  {
18:    int c;
```

*continues*

## Listing 6.5. continued

```
19:
20:    if (savedChar != 0) {    // If there's a saved char
21:      c = savedChar;         // Assign it to c
22:      savedChar = 0;         // Reset savedChar to none
23:    } else {
24:      c = getch();           // Else get next keypress
25:      if (c == 0)            // Check for function-key lead in
26:        c = getch() - 256;   // Return function key value < 0
27:    }
28:    return c;  // Return next keypress to caller
29:  }
30:
31: // Return true if a key was pressed and a character is waiting to be
32: // read, or if the program called ungetKey and a saved character is
33: // waiting to be reread.
34:
35: int keyWaiting(void)
36: {
37:    return (kbhit() || (savedChar != 0));
38: }
39:
40: // Undo the most recent call to getKey. Saves keypress value k in a
41: // global variable. That key will then be returned by the next call to
42: // getKey. Only one key value can be undone. If you call this routine
43: // without calling getKey, it erases the previously undone key.
44:
45: void ungetKey(int k)
46: {
47:    savedChar = k;
48: }
```

C++ has in its library several functions for getting keypresses. I find the standard approaches lacking in two main areas: function keys and the capability to *unget* a character previously received from the keyboard. (The C++ standard `ungetc()` function doesn't work for function keys.)

KEY solves these problems by representing keys as `int` values, not as ASCII characters. Because of this design, the number of keys a program can recognize is practically unlimited. Using int values to represent keys also makes it easy to work with function keys such as F1 and F8, as well as other named keys like Home and Page Down (labeled PgDn on some keyboards).

The KEY.CPP module begins at line 3 (Listing 6.5) by including the conio.h header, which declares the low-level input routines that KEY calls. The module also includes its own header, key.h.

Line 6 defines a variable, savedChar, used to store a key value passed to the ungetKey() function. This variable is declared outside any function; therefore, any function in the module can use it. However, since the variable is not declared extern, and is not mentioned in the key.h header file, other modules have no access to savedChar. This technique for hiding data in modules isn't as effective as hiding data in a class's private section. But it's a useful device when several functions in a module need to share a few small variables. Variables like savedChar take up permanent storage in the program's data segment, however.

Function getKey() at lines 16–29 reads the next keypress from the keyboard. Or, if ungetKey() saved a character in savedChar, getKey() returns that variable's value. An if statement at line 20 checks whether savedChar is 0. If not, the function returns savedChar and resets the variable to 0.

The else clause at lines 23–27 reads keypresses directly from the keyboard. The first statement in this section (line 24) shows the standard way to get a single keypress:

```
c = getch();
```

Notice that c is type int, not char. For alphanumeric and punctuation keys, getch() returns the equivalent ASCII value. But for function keys and other named keys, getch() returns 0. In that event, the *next* call to getch() returns a value that represents the actual key value.

This two-stage process for reading function keys and named keys overly complicates programs. For that reason, I like to convert function keys and named keys to negative values, as done here at line 26. With this technique, a program can use statements like the following to read any keypress:

```
int c;

if ((c = getKey()) < 0)
  doFunctionKey(c);
else
  doNormalKey(c);
```

The `if` statement calls `getKey()` and assigns the function result to an `int` variable c. If that value is less than 0, the program calls `doFunctionKey()` (not shown) to process a function key. If the value returned by `getKey()` is greater than 0 (it can't equal 0), then `doNormalKey()` (also not shown) handles the keypress.

Table 6.3 lists the values that `getKey()` returns for function keys and other named keys on PC keyboards. You may want to define constants of these same values to make your programs more readable. For example, you could insert the directive `#define KEY_F1 -197` into a header file, and then use statements such as

```
if (getKey() == KEY_F1)
  doSomething();
```

**Table 6.3. Function- and named-key values returned by** `getKey()`.

| *Key* | *Value* | *Key* | *Value* |
|-------|---------|-------|---------|
| F1 | –197 | Home | –185 |
| F2 | –196 | Cursor Up | –184 |
| F3 | –195 | Page Up | –183 |
| F4 | –194 | Cursor Left | –181 |
| F5 | –193 | Cursor Right | –179 |
| F6 | –192 | End | –177 |
| F7 | –191 | Cursor Down | –176 |
| F8 | –190 | Page Down | –175 |
| F9 | –189 | Insert | –174 |
| F10 | –188 | Delete | –173 |
| F11 | –123* | | |
| F12 | –122* | | |

*\* Not available on all keyboards*

Function `keyWaiting()` at lines 35–38 returns false (0) if no key is waiting to be read; otherwise, the function returns true (1). Use the function to detect keypresses with `if` statements such as the following:

```
if (keyWaiting()) {
  c = getKey();
  doSomething(c);
}
```

If a keypress is waiting to be read, the statement calls getKey() to read the key value and passes that value in an int variable c to doSomething() (not shown). This fragment also demonstrates how to read keypresses without pausing the program. If no key is waiting, the program continues after the if statement. If the program called getKey() without checking keyWaiting() and no key was waiting to be read, the program would pause until you pressed a key.

The keyWaiting() function calls the standard kbhit() function to detect keypresses waiting in the system's type-ahead buffer, a small amount of memory set aside by the PC ROM BIOS for storing key values as you type them. The keyWaiting() function combines the result of kbhit() with the result of the expression (savedChar != 0), using the logical OR operator ¦¦. For this reason, calling ungetKey() also causes keyWaiting to return true.

That function's implementation is at lines 45–48. Call ungetKey() to push a key value back to the keyboard (actually, into the module's hidden savedChar variable). Use this function to *unget* keys, but only one at a time. For example, to have a program "press" the Esc key, use the statement

```
ungetKey(27);
```

The next call to getKey() will return ASCII 27, the value for the Esc key. You can unget only one keypress this way. Each call to ungetKey() overwrites a previously saved character.

# Defining KEY Values

Listing 6.6, KEY.DOC, defines several constants equal to the values from Table 6.3. (This file is also stored on disk.) Include or copy the file into your programs that use the KEY module. The constants represent function- and named-key values returned by getKey().

**Listing 6.6. KEY.DOC.**

```
 1:  // Copy any of these definitions to modules that need to call KEY.CPP
 2:  // routines for function and special keys. These definitions could be
 3:  // included in key.h, but I removed them to conserve memory for the
 4:  // compiler.
 5:
 6:  #define KEY_F1     -197     // Function keys
 7:  #define KEY_F2     -196
 8:  #define KEY_F3     -195
 9:  #define KEY_F4     -194
10:  #define KEY_F5     -193
11:  #define KEY_F6     -192
12:  #define KEY_F7     -191
13:  #define KEY_F8     -190
14:  #define KEY_F9     -189
15:  #define KEY_F10    -188
16:  #define KEY_F11    -123     // Not recognized on all systems
17:  #define KEY_F12    -122     // "      "      "      "      "
18:
19:  #define KEY_HOME   -185     // Special-purpose keys
20:  #define KEY_UP     -184
21:  #define KEY_PGUP   -183
22:  #define KEY_LEFT   -181
23:  #define KEY_RIGHT  -179
24:  #define KEY_END    -177
25:  #define KEY_DOWN   -176
26:  #define KEY_PGDN   -175
27:  #define KEY_INS    -174
28:  #define KEY_DEL    -173
```

# Testing the KEY Module

Listing 6.7 demonstrates how to use the KEY module and serves as a useful utility for testing the values of various keys.

## Listing 6.7. TKEY.CPP.

```
 1:   // tkey.cpp -- Test KEY module
 2:
 3:   #include <tscdefs.h>
 4:   #include IOSTREAM_H
 5:   #include IOMANIP_H
 6:   #include "key.h"
 7:
 8:   #define KEY_ESC    27     // ASCII value for <Esc> key
 9:   #define KEY_SPACE 32      // ASCII value for <Spacebar>
10:
11:   main()
12:   {
13:     int c = 0;
14:
15:     cout << "Type any keys; <Esc> quits" << endl;
16:     while ((c = getKey()) != KEY_ESC) {
17:       cout << "\nc = " << c << flush;
18:       if (c >= KEY_SPACE)
19:         cout << " ASCII-(" << char(c) << ')' << flush;
20:       else if (c < 0)
21:         cout << " (Function or other named key)" << flush;
22:       else
23:         cout << " (<Ctrl> key)" << flush;
24:     }
25:     return 0;
26:   }
```

TKEY is one of several test programs (T stands for Test) included with the modules and classes in this chapter and the next. These test programs demonstrate how to use the book's class library. They also make useful tests to run if you modify the listings.

Run TKEY and press some key combinations not listed in KEY.DOC. For example, press Ctrl+Cursor-Left and Crtl+F4 to find the values that getKey() returns for these combined keys. You might want to add to KEY.DOC the constants for heavily used combinations.

# Error Handling

Every programmer, it seems, has a unique plan for handling errors in programs. What are the best ways to deal with disk errors, input errors, and other misdirections a program might take?

Maybe there's no *right* answer. But here are some general guidelines I've found useful:

- Don't halt programs or display error messages at the place where errors are detected. Call a function to perform this duty. Someday you might want to modify the methods used in your code to detect and handle errors. You'll make that task easier by calling a common error routine.

- Identify each error with a unique constant value. Once an error has been assigned a value, *never* reuse that value. (A truly horrible bug to trace is one that displays the *wrong* error message for a faulty condition.)

- Give your functions the capability to halt a program if an error occurs, or to postpone error handling until later. During development, you can just let programs halt when errors happen. In the finished product, you can replace the error handling with statements that display friendly messages rather than stopping the program.

The goal of a program's error-handling logic is to deal gracefully with goofups and foul balls. You should *always* consider the consequences of null pointers, bad input, and other error conditions. Never let a program follow a random course for problems that are easily trapped at the source.

The ERROR module in this section demonstrates one way to deal with errors in programs. The book's class library uses the functions in the module for error handling. You can also use ERROR in your own projects, even in those that don't incorporate the class library.

As usual, ERROR is divided into header and implementation files. Listing 6.8, error.h, is the header.

## Listing 6.8. error.h.

```
1:  // error.h -- Header file for error.cpp
2:
3:  #ifndef __ERROR_H
4:  #define __ERROR_H    1      // Prevent multiple #includes
```

```
 5:
 6: #define NOERROR      0      // Value for no error
 7: #define ERRMEM       1      // Out of memory
 8: #define ERRWININIT   2      // Window class not initialized
 9:
10: #ifndef NULL
11: #define NULL 0
12: #endif
13:
14: void error(int errnum, const char *s = NULL);
15: int geterror(int reset = 1);
16:
17: #endif   // __ERROR_H
```

Lines 6–9 define a few error codes used by the class library. You can add additional codes to this list. The value 0 represents "no error." Lines 10–12 define NULL as 0 if that macro is not already defined. (Use conditional directives like #ifndef and #endif as shown here to avoid redefining symbols defined in other header files that a program might include in addition to this header.)

Lines 14–15 declare two function prototypes. The first, error(), includes an integer errnum parameter. When calling error() to signal that something's amiss, pass in errnum an error code as an argument. The second parameter is optional. You can pass a string to this parameter to describe an error for which you haven't assigned a unique error code. For errors of this kind, errnum must be a value that error() doesn't know about (–1 is a good choice).

The second prototype, geterror(), retries the most recent error code. Use this function when you don't want error() to halt the program.

In the following sections, I'll explain both functions in more detail. ERROR.CPP, Listing 6.10, implements the error() and geterror() functions. The file isn't large, but it contains a few tricky features. For that reason, I'll list and describe the programming in small bites.

### Listing 6.9. ERROR.CPP.

```
1: // error.cpp -- Error-handling module
2:
3: #include <tscdefs.h>
```

*continues*

**Listing 6.9. continued**

```
 4:  #include IOSTREAM_H
 5:  #include IOMANIP_H
 6:  #include <stdlib.h>
 7:  #include "error.h"
 8:
 9:  int errornumber;   // Most recent error number passed to error()
10:  int errorignore;   // 0 = halt on error; 1 = don't halt on error
11:
```

The first few lines in ERROR.CPP include the usual header files, plus stdlib.h and error.h. At lines 9–10, the module defines two private variables, errornumber and errorignore. The first variable, errornumber, stores the error code of the most recent error passed to the error() function. The second variable, errorignore, is a flag that tells the module whether to halt on detecting errors, or to continue. Both variables are stored permanently in the program's data segment. Like the savedChar variable in KEY.CPP (see Listing 6.6, line 6), the variables are not accessible to programs that use ERROR.

Or, I should say, the variables are not *normally* available. A program can gain access to private variables defined in modules such as KEY.CPP and ERROR.CPP by declaring those variables to be extern. To use the private variables in ERROR, insert this line in your main program:

```
extern int errornumber;
extern int errorignore;
```

This tells the compiler (and linker) that the two values are defined in another module. As you can see, private variables like these two are not that private after all. Any program can easily gain access to the values by declaring them to be extern. For that reason, when you need to hide data from other modules, it's usually best to insert that data into a class and *not* to define variables as done here. Still, the technique is useful, and you should understand it. A test program, TERROR, following this section demonstrates how to use the extern declarations.

## Listing 6.9. ERROR.CPP. (continued)

```
12:  // Call error with error number argument. If errorignore == FALSE (the
13:  // default), program halts with error message. If errorignore == TRUE,
14:  // then program continues and the next statement should call geterror()
15:  // to determine whether the previous operation succeeded or failed.
16:
17:  void error(int errnum, const char *s)
18:  {
19:    errornumber = errnum;      // Save error number in global
20:    if (errorignore) return;   // Exit if not halting on errors
21:    if (s == NULL)             // If no string passed to function
22:      switch(errnum) {         // Assign literal string to s
23:        case ERRMEM:
24:          s = "Out of memory";
25:          break;
26:        case ERRWININIT:
27:          s = "Window class not initialized";
28:          break;
29:        default:
30:          s = "Unknown cause";
31:      }
32:    cout << "\n\nERROR: " << dec << errnum << ": " << s << endl;
33:    exit(errnum);                      // Halt program
34:  }
35:
```

When an error occurs in a program, call the error() function listed at lines 17–34. Most of the time, you'll pass only an error code as an argument to error(). For example, using the constants listed in error.h, the following statement signals an out-of-memory error:

```
error(ERRMEM);
```

At line 19, error() assigns the error-code argument to the global errornumber variable. The function then checks whether errorignore is true. If so, line 20 exits error immediately. If errorignore is false, the function continues with another if statement at line 21 that inspects the optional char * parameter s. If s equals NULL, error executes a switch statement that sets s to the address of a literal error message string based on one of the constants from error.h. If s is not NULL, the function skips this step.

The effect of these statements is to allow two ways to call `error()`. Most of the time, you'll execute statements such as

```
error(ERRWININIT);
```

If `errorignore` is false, the call to `error()` displays the message string "Window class not initialized" and halts the program by calling `exit` at line 33.

You can also call `error()` with an explicit string as the second argument. In this case, the error code doesn't matter; to prevent conflicts with other error constants, however, negative values are probably best:

```
#ifdef DEBUGGING
error(-154, "Internal bug. Please report at once.");
#endif
```

Surrounding such calls with `#ifdef` and `#endif` directives makes it easy to eliminate temporary error-handling statements in the final code. Include the line `#define DEBUGGING 1` to enable the statement; remove the `#define` to disable the temporary `error()` statement.

At line 32, the function displays an error-message string, and then calls `exit()` to halt the program. Line 33 also passes the current error code back to DOS. A batch file could examine `errorlevel` to retrieve this value.

Using the `errorignore` flag in `error()` gives programs the choice of halting or continuing after encountering errors. If you choose to continue (demonstrated by TERROR.CPP later), use the next function to examine the current error code.

## Listing 6.9. ERROR.CPP (continued)

```
36:    // Call geterror after setting errorignore to TRUE to determine whether
37:    // previous operation succeeded (geterror == 0) or failed (geterror ==
38:    // 1). If the optional reset parameter == 0, then the global
39:    // errornumber is NOT reset. If you do not supply this argument value
40:    // (or if it's not 0), then the global errornumber is reset to 0.  This
41:    // means that in normal use, only the first call to geterror returns
42:    // useful information.
43:
```

```
44:  int geterror(int reset)
45:  {
46:    int t = errornumber;
47:
48:    if (reset)
49:      errornumber = 0;
50:    return t;
51:  }
```

The geterror() function returns the value of errornumber. The statement geterror(0); calls the function but does *not* reset the global errornumber to 0. Call the function with no argument (or 1) to reset errornumber to 0. This action—a function modifying a global variable—is called a *side effect*. If a program isn't aware of the effect on the global value, and it calls geterror() two or more times for the same error, it will expect the function to return the same value each time. But that's not what happens, because the first call resets errornumber to 0, causing the second call to return 0, the value that represents no error.

Together, error() and geterror() provide all the error-handling logic that most programs will need. To halt the program with an error, pass an error code to error(). To continue the program, set errorignore to true (1), and use geterror() to detect whether other statements have called error() to signal an error condition.

The test listing in the next section demonstrates how to use the ERROR module.

## Testing the ERROR Module

The name of ERROR's test program, TERROR (Test Error), was purely accidental, but I couldn't have picked a better name. Dealing with errors in programs is a terror that most programmers would rather avoid. Listing 6.10, TERROR.CPP, shows how the ERROR module can make error-busting a little less terrifying.

**Note:** Running TERROR displays an error message. The program is *supposed* to do that. This is not a bug!

## Listing 6.10. TERROR.CPP.

```
1:   // terror.cpp -- Test ERROR Module
2:
3:   #include <tscdefs.h>
4:   #include IOSTREAM_H
5:   #include "error.h"
6:
7:   extern int errorignore;     // Gain access to errorignore flag
8:
9:   void test(int n);
10:
11:  main()
12:  {
13:    errorignore = 1;          // Do not halt on errors
14:    test(1);                  // Test with reset in geterror
15:    test(0);                  // Test without reset in geterror
16:    errorignore = 0;          // Halt on errors
17:    error(-154, "Internal problem. Please report at once!");
18:    cout << "\n\nIf you are reading these lines, there is an";
19:    cout << "\nerror in the ERROR module!";
20:    return 0;
21:  }
22:
23:  void test(int n)
24:  {
25:    int err;
26:
27:    if (n == 0)
28:      cout << "\n\nTesting geterror without reset";
29:    else
30:      cout << "\n\nTesting geterror with reset";
31:    error(ERRMEM);            // Out-of-memory error
32:    if ((err = geterror(n)) != NOERROR)
33:      cout << "\nError detected. Code = " << err;
34:    else
35:      cout << "\nError in ERROR: geterror failed to return code";
36:    cout << "\nSecond call to geterror = " << geterror();
37:  }
```

Line 7 declares errorignore external, gaining access to that normally private variable. Line 13 sets errorignore to 1, causing the error() function not to halt the program.

The next two lines call the test function, defined at lines 23–37. The test calls error(), passing the constant ERRMEM to simulate an out-of-memory error. Line 32 then calls geterror() to retrieve the error code saved by error(). In a real program, error() would probably be called inside another function, and a statement elsewhere would call geterror() for the result of that operation.

If parameter n is 0, then geterror() does not reset the internal errornumber on each call. If the parameter is 1, then geterror() resets errornumber to 0. Normally, you should not pass any parameters to geterror(). Doing so will reset the internal error code to 0, and the next call to geterror() will return 0 if there have been no intervening calls to error().

That finishes your tour of the non-OOP code in the book's class library. In the next chapter you'll examine the class hierarchies and the programming for the class member functions. You'll also investigate a few new C++ tricks.

# Questions and Exercises

6.1. Name the main reason class libraries are easier to use than conventional subroutine libraries.

6.2. Suppose canoe is the name of a class that contains a public member function declared as void row(void);. List the steps required to: a) define a pointer to an object of canoe; b) allocate space for a canoe object on the heap; c) assign the address of that object to your pointer; and d) call function row() for the new object.

6.3. List the declaration needed to make function row() in Exercise 6.2 virtual. Why might you want to do that?

6.4. What is polymorphism?

6.5. What do the terms *early binding* and *late binding* mean?

6.6. Describe a disadvantage of using virtual instead of nonvirtual member functions.

6.7. Write a short program that creates a window in the center of the screen, opens the window, and displays a message inside. (Hint: Use WINTOOL.CPP, Listing 6.3, as a guide. You'll need to include the window.h header file in your program, and you might also want to include key.h so you can insert a statement that waits for a keypress before ending the program. Because you haven't learned how to use the full LC++ class library, finishing this exercise might be difficult. But take a stab at it before looking up the answer.)

6.8. Finish the `performCommand()` function for WINTOOL's `helpCommand` class (see Listing 6.3, lines 114–132). Use `puts()` and `gotorc()` member functions from the `Window` class to display strings and move the cursor. Your text should describe how to use WINTOOL.

6.9. Discuss the possible advantages and disadvantages of converting to classes the conventional functions used by the KEY and ERROR modules listed at the end of the chapter.

6.10. Design and test a function that waits for someone to press a specific key—Esc or Spacebar, for example. Use the KEY module in your answer.

6.11. What values does `getkey()` return for keys F7, Ctrl+Q, and Alt+F9?

6.12. What steps do you need to take to prevent the `error()` function in the ERROR module from halting a program?

6.13. Write a program that uses the ERROR module and displays the error message "Red alert!". You do *not* need to modify files error.h or ERROR.CPP to solve this problem.

6.14. What's a "side effect?"

6.15. Design a class named `saveCommand` derived from the `command` class. You don't have to implement any member functions in `saveCommand`, just list the class declaration.

# Building a Class Library—
# Part 2

S ome say that learning object-oriented programming requires a mental shift, a fundamental change in the way programmers conceptualize how to solve problems with computers. Programmers who are comfortable with passing data to and from functions may not appreciate the value of encapsulating data and code inside classes. What good are classes if you can't figure out how to use them?

Learning the rules of C++ and OOP is the easy part. Learning how to apply those rules to solve problems is more difficult. In a few hours, anyone can memorize how to write class declarations, how to derive new classes from others, and how to declare and use member functions. But it can take a lifetime to learn how to weave useful programs from these simple threads.

From past mistakes, I've learned that a *wrong* way to pick up a new programming language is to study the language's parts individually and then start coding a major project. I would just as soon learn to fly by strapping on wings, biting on a propeller, and jumping off a cliff with a copy of some flight jockey's *How to Fly* manual open to Chapter 1.

A more sensible plan is to take a few lessons with someone who's been *up there* before. Ground your programs in the sound base of a class library, such as this book's class library described in this and the preceding chapters. Choose classes that are close to those you need. Then, use inheritance to customize the classes to provide the services required to get your program off the ground. Resist the natural urge to write every scrap of code yourself, at least until you've logged a few hours in the copilot's seat.

# First Things Last—The Class Library

**I**n Chapter 6, "Building a Class Library—Part 1," you examined a program, WINTOOL, that demonstrates some of the book's class library capabilities. Now that you have an idea of what the classes can do, you'll be able to understand how and why the low-level code operates as it does, and you'll be able to visualize new ways to apply that code in your own projects.

In this chapter, you'll examine each class in the library, starting at the base of the class hierarchy with a simple class named item from which all other classes are derived. Along with each new class, you'll also compile and run a demonstration program that illustrates how to use the class's public members. And, of course, you'll look at the source code that implements the class member functions. Study this code and read the comments carefully—the listings contain many tips and tricks that you can extract for your own work.

> **Note:** On disk, the class library files are located in the directory C:\TSC\LIB\SOURCE. Test programs for this chapter are located in the directory C:\TSC\C07.

# Class Hierarchies

Figure 7.1 shows the hierarchy of classes in the class library. Base classes to the left are connected to their derivations at right. For example, the diagram shows that command derives from the base class stritem, which in turn derives from the base class item. The `selector` class is marked with an asterisk to indicate that it derives from more than one base class (`list` and `Window`), and, therefore, appears more than once in the chart—a condition known as *multiple inheritance.*

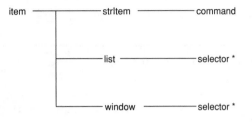

* inherits from multiple base classes

**Figure 7.1.** Standard hierarchy diagram showing derived classes that inherit properties from various base classes.

Other commercial class libraries will have similar diagrams. (If you find one that doesn't, get a different library!) Because many classes in a library will inherit members from other classes, just finding all that's in a derived class can be extremely difficult. Diagrams like the one in Figure 7.1 can help by showing class relationships, and you may want to construct similar charts for your own projects.

# At the Root of the Library

All classes in the book's class library derive from the base class `item` (see Figure 7.1). An `item` doesn't do much on its own. It simply gives other derived classes a common ancestor, and it also contains the basic mechanisms required to create lists of class instances in memory.

As you learn more about C++ and OOP, you'll discover that lists are as common in OOP as nuts in a squirrel's nest. Lists are convenient for creating *container classes* that can store a variety of items. Among other uses, a list might hold a menu of commands, filenames in a directory, or the lines from a text file. More on this subject later.

# The item.h Header

Listing 7.1, item.h, shows the header for the item class. Most of the text in this short file should be familiar to you, but there are two new elements you haven't seen before.

### Listing 7.1. item.h.

```
 1:  // item.h -- Header file for item.cpp
 2:
 3:  #ifndef __ITEM_H
 4:  #define __ITEM_H     1      // Prevent multiple #includes
 5:
 6:  class item {
 7:  protected:
 8:    item *left;          // Address item at "left"
 9:    item *right;         // Address item at "right"
10:  public:
11:    item();
12:    virtual ~item();
13:    item *link(item *ip);
14:    item *unlink(void);
15:    item *getleft(void) { return left; }
16:    item *getright(void) { return right; }
17:  };
18:
19:  #endif   // __ITEM_H
```

Before reading about item's new features, make sure that you understand the purpose of lines 8–9 and 13–14. The two item pointers left and right address instances of type item. As with structs, C++ allows pointer members inside a class to address objects of that same class. In this way, it's possible to declare pointers such as left and right that link objects of a class type (or any derivations) in chains, forming lists of the objects in memory.

The public member functions link() and unlink() carry out the instructions needed to make and break the linkage between items. To link two items, pass an item pointer to another item's link member. For example, if aItem and bItem are both pointers to item instances, you can link those instances with the statement

```
aItem->link(bItem);
```

That links the instance addressed by aItem to bItem's instance, which might be linked to another item in a list. The link function returns ip, allowing you to use it inside a nested function call such as

```
aItem->link(bItem->link(chain));
```

That links the instance at aItem to the one at bItem. The result is then linked to a third item, chain.

Call unlink to detach an item from a list. You can do this regardless of whether you previously called link(). To unlink the instance that bItem addresses, use the statement

```
bItem->unlink();
```

# Protected Members

The first new element in item.h is the protected keyword at line 7. Like public and private, protected (ended with a colon) begins a new section in the class, giving special status to all members listed below.

Members in a protected section are both private and public. They are private to statements outside the class. But they are public to statements inside a *derived* class. Members in a protected class section are visible to the class that declares them and to any classes derived from the class.

A simple example will help you to understand how protected members differ from those in private and public areas. Suppose you design a class named aClass with three data members

```
class aClass {
private:
  int A;
protected:
  int B;
public:
  int C;
  void f();
}
```

Integer A is visible only to member functions also in aClass. Statements in function f() (the implementation is not shown here) may access A directly. Function f() may also use integers B and C. All the members in the class are useable by statements

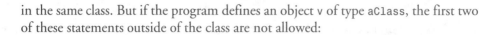
in the same class. But if the program defines an object v of type aClass, the first two of these statements outside of the class are not allowed:

```
v.A = 10;    // ???
v.B = 20;    // ???
v.C = 30;    // okay
```

A is private to the class; therefore, the statement can't access the A member directly. Likewise, B is protected—it too is invisible to statements outside the class. However, C is public, so any statement can refer to this member. (Public data items are considered to be bad form. I used one here only to demonstrate how protected members differ from private and public ones. Avoid public data members in your own code.)

Suppose you next declare a derived class that inherits the properties of aClass. Let's call this new class bClass:

```
class bClass: public aClass {
public:
  void g();
}
```

Because bClass inherits aClass's members, it can use the members declared in aClass's public and protected sections. But it can't use any of the base class's private members. For example, inside bClass's implementation of function g, the first of the following statements is not allowed:

```
A = 10;    // ???
B = 20;    // okay
C = 30;    // okay
```

Member A is private to the base class. A copy of this member exists in a object of the derived class type, but that member is visible by name *only* to member functions inside aClass. However, since B is in a protected section, the derived class can refer to B directly. The assignment to the public C is always allowed. Any statement, anywhere, anytime can use a class's public members.

Remember these rules: Private members can be used only by other members of the same class. Protected members can be used by members in that class and in any derived class. Public members can be used by any statement inside or outside the class. (See Figure. 7.2.)

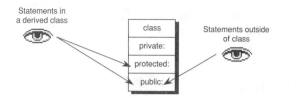

**Figure 7.2.** Private members are strictly for use by their class.

> **Note:** Chapter 9, "Advance Your C++ Knowledge," describes *friends,* a method for allowing unrelated classes access to private and protected declarations. Friends can be useful, but are best avoided because they bend the rules of OOP almost to breaking. The classes in this book's class library do not use friends.

# Choosing Among *private, public,* and *protected*

It takes careful planning, a healthy measure of intuition, a bit of luck, and much experience to decide whether members should be private, protected, or public. Three guidelines will help you to make the right decision:

- If there's any chance you'll want to change the data type of a class member, or if you want to isolate a member to make it difficult for statements outside the class to change the member's value, then make that member *private.*

- If a derived class will benefit greatly from direct access to a data member declared in a base class, make that member *protected.*

- Make *only* member functions *public,* never data members. Use inline member functions to provide fast access to private data members. Don't make data members public just to give programs quick access to values.

If you sidestep these guidelines, your programs might compile and run, but you might not be able to modify the class declarations without also having to alter statements that use the classes. In time you'll appreciate being able to enhance your existing programs by using inheritance and virtual functions without having to rewrite statements that already work perfectly well. You can always break the rules, but if you do, you should ask yourself why you are using OOP techniques to program your project. Maybe you shouldn't!

# Destructors

The second new element in item.h is called a *destructor* (see Listing 7.1, line 12). A destructor is the antithesis of a constructor, which, as you know, initializes new objects of a class. Like a constructor, a destructor has the same name as its class. To distinguish the destructor, it begins with the *difference symbol* ~ from mathematics. In the item class, the ~item destructor at line 12 is declared to be virtual, though other classes may declare nonvirtual destructors. The reason for making ~item virtual is to allow pointers to base class objects to call destructors in derived classes, similar to the way other virtual member functions allow pointers to base class objects to call replacement functions in derived classes.

What does a destructor do? In a nutshell, it cleans up any leftovers in a class object when that object goes out of scope. As you know, constructors initialize class objects. Destructors do the opposite—they *deinitialize* objects when a program is done using them.

Programs *almost never* call destructors directly. Instead, C++ generates instructions that call a class's destructor automatically when

- A local or global class object goes out of scope, or

- The program deletes a class object stored on the heap.

Other classes in this chapter declare destructors, and as you examine those classes, you'll learn more about how destructors work and why they are needed. Until then, here are a few important points about destructors to keep in mind:

- There can be only one destructor in a class.

- Destructors are often declared virtual, although they don't have to be.

- Destructors do not have parameters.

- Destructors do not have return data types (not even void).

- Destructors are optional. If a class doesn't need to clean up after itself, it doesn't need a destructor.

- Destructors are called automatically to deinitialize a class object. Programs almost never call destructors directly.

# Using the *item* Class

Listing 7.2, TITEM.CPP (test item), demonstrates how to use the item class. Because item does nothing on its own, the program derives a new class from item, derivedItem, to give the program something to do. While confirming that the ITEM module works correctly, the program also demonstrates a few key points about using constructors and destructors.

## Listing 7.2. TITEM.CPP.

```
1:  // titem.cpp -- Test item class
2:
3:  #include <tscdefs.h>
4:  #include IOSTREAM_H
5:  #include <item.h>
6:
7:  class derivedItem: public item {
8:  public:
9:    derivedItem();
10:   virtual ~derivedItem();
11: };
12:
13: main()
14: {
15:   item *ip1;
16:   item *ip2;
17:
18:   cout << "\nCreating new item on the heap";
19:   ip1 = new item;
20:   cout << "\nCreating new derivedItem on the heap";
21:   ip2 = new derivedItem;
22:   cout << "\nLinking the two items together";
23:   ip1->link(ip2);
24:   cout << "\nUnlinking derived item";
25:   ip2->unlink();
26:   cout << "\nDeleting the new item";
27:   delete ip1;
28:   cout << "\nDeleting the derived item";
29:   delete ip2;
30:   return 0;
31: }
```

*continues*

## Listing 7.2. continued

```
32:
33:  derivedItem::derivedItem()
34:  {
35:    cout << "\n Inside derivedItem's constructor";
36:  }
37:
38:  derivedItem::~derivedItem()
39:  {
40:    cout << "\n Inside derivedItem's destructor";
41:  }
```

Lines 7–11 declare a derived class named derivedItem. The class inherits all the properties of item, but not item's constructor and destructor. (Constructors and destructors are not inherited by derived classes.) To its inheritance, derivedItem adds its own constructor (line 9) and a new virtual destructor (line 10).

The main() function defines two pointers, ip1 and ip2, to objects of type item (see lines 15–16). Then, several output-stream statements display notes about what the program is about to do at each step in the test. First, line 19 allocates space for an item object, assigning the address of that space to ip1. Line 21 performs a similar job, but this time allocates space for a derivedItem object. The constructors for item and derivedItem automatically run at this time.

The statements at lines 19 and 21 illustrate that pointers to objects of a base class can address objects of a derived class. The reverse is not true. If you insert the following lines at line 17 in TITEM, you'll receive an error from the compiler:

```
derivedItem *ip3;  // Define pointer to derivedItem
ip3 = new item;    // ???
```

Pointers to a derived class may never address objects of a base class. However, pointers to base classes may address objects of derived classes. Figure 7.3 will help you to understand the purpose of this rule. A derived class inherits properties from a base class. In addition to those properties, a derived class usually adds new members that do not exist in the base. For that reason, a base class pointer can safely address an object of the derived type, which, after all, has an inherited copy of the data members that exist in the base class. But the base class does *not* have any of the new items added to the derived class; therefore, a pointer to the derived class can't address an object of the base class type. If a pointer to a derived class instance addressed a base class object, a statement might attempt to access a nonexistent data member, causing a serious bug. C++ prevents this kind of error by not permitting pointers to derived classes to address objects of a base class.

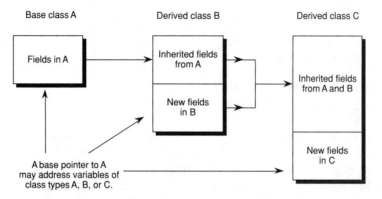

**Figure 7.3.** A pointer to a base class object may address objects of derived classes but pointers to derived classes may never address objects of a base type.

Lines 23 and 25 in TITEM call the link() and unlink() member functions declared in the item class. Even though ip2 addresses an object of derivedItem, line 25 can call the unlink() member function because derivedItem inherits item's members. The *same* unlink() function applies to objects of type item and to objects of type derivedItem.

Lines 27 and 29 delete the objects created by new earlier. Similar to the way constructors run when the new objects are constructed, destructors in a class run when the class objects are deleted. Line 40 in the derivedItem destructor displays a message that tells you when an object of this type goes out of scope.

There's more happening internally than is evident from running TITEM. When a derivedItem object is constructed at line 21, the class's constructor at lines 33–36 runs automatically. In addition, C++ calls the item class's constructor to initialize the members that derivedItem inherits from item. In other words, line 33 acts as though it had been written

```
derivedItem::derivedItem(): item()
```

C++ can call the item() constructor because it is a default constructor—one that declares no parameters. When constructors declare parameters, use a form similar to this to call constructors in ancestor classes.

These effects mean that, when TITEM executes the statement ip2 = new derivedItem at line 20, C++ generates code that

- calls the base class item's constructor

- then calls derivedItem's constructor.

Similarly, when the program deletes ip2, because derivedItem derives from item, C++ generates code that

- calls derivedItem's destructor

- then calls the base class item's destructor.

In general, constructors in base classes run *before* the constructors in derived classes. Destructors in base classes run *after* destructors in derived classes. These rules may be easier to remember if you think of class objects as buildings that are constructed from the base up (base class constructors run first), but are torn down starting at the top (base destructors run last).

# The ITEM.CPP Module

Finally in this section is the item class's implementation. At this stage, you know just about everything there is to know about item. You've examined its header file and compiled a test program. Armed with that knowledge, you should have little trouble understanding the low-level code in ITEM.CPP's text file (Listing 7.3). But there is one new element: a keyword with the unusual name this.

## Listing 7.3. ITEM.CPP.

```
 1:   // item.cpp -- Item class
 2:
 3:   #include <stddef.h>
 4:   #include "item.h"
 5:
 6:   // Disable Microsoft warning about unreferenced member functions
 7:   // that have been removed. The functions are inline and are used
 8:   // by other modules.
 9:
10:   #if (defined __TSC_MSC__)
11:   #pragma warning( disable : 4505 )
12:   #endif
```

```
13:
14:   // An item object's constructor. Automatically called when space is
15:   // allocated for a new item object.
16:
17:   item::item()
18:   {
19:     left = right = this;   // Point item to itself.
20:   }
21:
22:   // Item's destructor. Ensures that all items are unlinked from any
23:   // others before the item's memory is returned to the heap.
24:
25:   item::~item()
26:   {
27:     if (left != this)   // If item is linked to another,
28:       unlink();         //   unlink it.
29:   }
30:
```

# *this* Is Where It's At

The item constructor appears at lines 17–20. As in most constructors, the function initializes the data members in an instance of the class. Here, line 11 carries out that duty by assigning the same value to the left and right pointer members, which can address other item objects (and derivations) in lists.

The value assigned to left and right is a C++ keyword, this. The this keyword is a pointer that's available to all member functions in a class. The this pointer addresses the instance of the class that called the function. The this pointer is also available in constructors and destructors.

**Note:** The this pointer is passed as a hidden parameter to every nonstatic member function in a class. The pointer has the same type as a declared pointer to the class. In other words, in item's member functions, this has the type item *; therefore, C++ allows the assignment at line 19 to the left and right members, both of which are of that same type.

Assigning this to left and right causes the item object to point to its own instance in memory (see Figure 7.4). In this book's class library, an object that addresses itself is by definition not a member of any list, a fact other statements can use to determine whether an object needs to be detached from other objects.

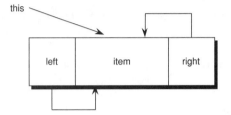

**Figure 7.4.** Assigning the this pointer to the left and right members in an item instance causes the item to address itself in memory.

One such moment comes in item's destructor at lines 25–29. Again, this is used to obtain the address of the instance that called the destructor. If the item's left pointer does not equal this, then that item must be attached to another, and line 28 calls the unlink() member function to detach the object. (The statement could just as well examine the right member for this purpose.) It's important to perform this step in the destructor, because the object is being destroyed (a statement, for example, might have deleted the object from memory). Just *before* that happens, the destructor has the opportunity to clean up any business inside the object—in this example, detaching the item from another. Deleting an item without detaching it from another could cause other items to address an instance that has been deleted. The destructor neatly prevents that error. All the program has to do is delete the class object.

In your own classes, you should use destructors to perform similar cleanup chores. Ideally, it should be possible simply to delete a class object (or end a function that defines a local class object) without having to perform additional duties. The best classes construct themselves when they are defined, and destroy themselves completely when they are deleted or go out of scope.

## Listing 7.3. ITEM.CPP. (continued)

```
31:   // Attach one item to another. Assuming A and B are pointers to items,
32:   // to attach a new item A to an existing item B, pass B to A's link
33:   // function. B may be attached to another item, or it may be solitary.
```

```
34:  // The item at A will then be linked to the "left" of B. If A is
35:  // already attached to another item, it will be unlinked from that item
36:  // before being attached to B.
37:
38:  item *item::link(item *ip)
39:  {
40:    if (ip ==  NULL)        // Ignore request to link to
41:      return NULL;          // a NULL item.
42:    if (left != this)       // If item is linked to another
43:      unlink();             // unlink it.
44:    right = ip;             // Adjust item's right and left
45:    left = ip->left;        // pointers to link to the item
46:    ip->left->right = this; // addressed by ip.
47:    ip->left = this;
48:    return ip;              // Return address of linked item.
49:  }
50:
51:  // Unattach this item from another. After calling unlink for any item,
52:  // you can be sure that the item is not an element of any list.  It's
53:  // okay to call unlink whether or not the item is currently joined to
54:  // another in a list. Return address of unlinked item, allowing
55:  // unlink() to be passed to another item* function parameter.
56:
57:  item *item::unlink(void)
58:  {
59:    left->right = right;     // Unlink the item by adjusting
60:    right->left = left;      //  the attached item's pointers.
61:    left = right = this;     // Point this item to itself.
62:    return left;             // Return item's address.
63:  }
```

Lines 38–63 implement the two public member functions in the item class. All classes derived from item inherit these functions, which can link and unlink multiple objects. (The next section explains how to use the functions to form lists.)

The link() function at lines 38–49 requires a single argument, a pointer ip to another item object. An if statement examines this argument, ending the function immediately if the pointer is null. This prevents a serious problem that would occur if a statement tried to link a null item to a list.

A second if statement at lines 42–43 compares the left pointer to this, which addresses the instance of the item that called the link() function. If these two pointers are not equal, then this item is attached to another, and line 43 calls unlink() to detach the item before linking. Because of this step, programs can call link() to move an item from one list to another. You don't have to detach an item in order to reattach it somewhere else.

Note that line 43 calls the unlink() member function directly. The statement does not preface unlink() in the usual way with the name of an object or a pointer to an object of the class. As you know, outside the class, you normally allocate space for an item object, and then use a statement such as p->unlink() to call the member function for the item instance addressed by p. Line 43 does not require a similar object, because *another statement already provided an object for link() to use.* Where is that object? It's at the location addressed by this. In other words, line 43 executes as though it were written

```
this->unlink();
```

Inside a member function, you can always call other member functions directly—except, that is, for private member functions inherited from a base class. When you call a member function as at line 43, C++ assumes that you mean to call it for the object addressed by this.

The rest of link() at lines 44–48 adjusts the left and right members in item to attach it to the item addressed by this. Finally, the function returns the address of the attached item, ip.

Member function unlink (lines 57–63) undoes what link() puts together. Again, the this pointer is used to obtain the address of the instance that called unlink(). After adjusting the left and right members to detach the item from another (if it's attached to one), line 53 assigns this to left and right. This reconfigures the item to its initial state, and ensures that any lists the item was attached to are kept sound. Finally, line 54 returns the address of the instance that called unlink().

# A Class for Lists

The list class in the book's class library is derived from item (see Figure 7.1). This means every list is also an item, and thus every list object inherits a copy of the data members, and it has access to nonprivate member functions, declared in item.

Like item, the list class doesn't do much on its own. The list class is a general-purpose container—it can hold whatever kinds of objects you want a list to store (up to the limits of available memory). All objects stored in a list must derive from the item class. However, the same list may store many different types of item derivations. Since list itself derives from item, a list can even be a list of lists.

## The list.h Header

The list class is declared in list.h, Listing 7.4. Notice that the file includes the declarations in item.h (see line 7). As a result, programs that include the list.h header automatically receive a copy of item.h.

### Listing 7.4. list.h.

```
 1:  // list.h -- Header for list.cpp
 2:
 3:  #ifndef __LIST_H
 4:  #define __LIST_H      1      // Prevent multiple #includes
 5:
 6:  #include <stdlib.h>
 7:  #include <item.h>
 8:
 9:  class list: public item {
10:  private:
11:    item *anchor;         // Anchors list head
12:    item *cip;            // "Current item pointer"
13:
14:  public:
15:
16:  // Constructor and destructor
17:
18:    list();
19:    virtual ~list();
20:
21:  // Inline member functions
22:
23:    int listEmpty(void)
24:      { return (anchor == NULL); }
```

*continues*

## Listing 7.4. continued

```
25:    int atHeadOfList(void)
26:       { return ((anchor != NULL) && (cip == anchor)); }
27:    int atEndOfList(void)
28:       { return ((anchor != NULL) && (cip == anchor->getleft())); }
29:    item *currentItem(void)
30:       { return cip; }
31:    item *firstItem(void)
32:       { return (cip = anchor); }
33:    void resetList(void)
34:       { cip = anchor; }
35:    void setCurrentItem(item *ip)
36:       { cip = ip; }
37:
38: // Other member functions
39:
40:    item *insertItem(item *ip);
41:    item *removeItem(item *ip);
42:    item *prevItem(void);
43:    item *nextItem(void);
44:
45: // Virtual member function
46:
47:    virtual void disposeList(void);
48: };
49:
50: #endif    // __LIST_H
```

Because list is derived from item, all list objects have left and right pointer members along with the new members, anchor and cip, declared in list at lines 11–12. Unlike the left and right members, however, anchor and cip are private to the class. No other classes or statements outside of list may use these two members directly. Because of this design, it's possible to modify the way list stores items in memory without affecting programs that use the class.

The anchor pointer addresses the first item in the list. Lists are circular in this implementation, and therefore, the anchor marks a list's beginning and end. The cip pointer addresses the current item object. This pointer floats from object to object, and is often used to scan all the item class objects in a list. (Because cip is private to the class, however, programs can't use the pointer directly.)

Lines 18–19 declare the `list` class constructor and destructor. Because the destructor is virtual, a pointer declared as type `list *` could address an instance of a derived class and still be deleted properly. Calling `delete` for such a pointer would call the proper virtual destructors in derived class objects.

The purpose of the functions at lines 23–36 should be obvious from their names. The function `listEmpty()`, for example, returns true if the list has no `item` objects. Each of these member functions is declared inline, which helps keep programs running fast. Low-level classes like `list` are good candidates for inline member functions. Chances are, many derivations will use these functions, and it makes good sense to use inline code to avoid the overhead required to call normal functions.

Four other nonvirtual member functions are prototyped at lines 40–43. The first of these, `insertItem()`, inserts new objects into a list. The second, `removeItem()`, performs the reverse job—it deletes an object currently in the list. Functions `prevItem()` and `nextItem()` help you write loops that scan all the objects in a list. You'll see examples of how to do this later.

The final member function is `disposeList()`, at line 47. This function is declared virtual so that statements compiled in this module can be redirected to a derived class's `disposeList()` function in the future. In this way, a derived class can declare its own `disposeList()` to clean up additional items added to the derivation. Any *existing* code that calls `disposeList()` will then be redirected at runtime to call the new `disposeList()` member function.

## Using the *list* Class

TLIST.CPP, Listing 7.5, demonstrates how to use the `list` class.

### Listing 7.5. TLIST.CPP.

```
1:  // tlist.cpp -- Test list class
2:
3:  #include <tscdefs.h>
4:  #include IOSTREAM_H
5:  #include <list.h>
6:
```

*continues*

## Listing 7.5. continued

```
7:    Class myItem : public item {
8:    private:
9:      int value;
10:   public:
11:     myItem(int n) { value = n; }
12:     void putValue(int n) { value = n; }
13:     int getValue(void) { return value; }
14:   };
15:
16:   void showList(void);
17:
18:   list *lp = new list;
19:
20:   main()
21:   {
22:     int i;
23:     myItem *mip;
24:
25:     cout << "\nAfter allocating new list";
26:     showList();
27:
28:     cout << "\n\nInsert 10 items into the list";
29:     for (i = 1; i <= 10; i++)
30:       lp->insertItem(new myItem(i));
31:     showList();
32:
33:     cout << "\n\nAdd 100 to listed item values";
34:     lp->resetList();
35:     do {
36:       mip = (myItem *)lp->currentItem();
37:       mip->putValue(mip->getValue() + 100);
38:       lp->nextItem();
39:     } while (!lp->atHeadOfList());
40:     showList();
41:
42:     cout << "\n\nDelete first 3 items from list";
43:     lp->resetList();
44:     for (i = 1; i <= 3; i++)
45:       lp->removeItem(lp->currentItem());
46:     showList();
47:
```

```
48:      cout << "\n\nDispose of all listed items";
49:      lp->disposeList();
50:      showList();
51:      return 0;
52:  }
53:
54:  void showList(void)
55:  {
56:      cout << "\nITEMS IN LIST: ";
57:      if (lp->listEmpty()) {
58:        cout << "List is empty";
59:        return;
60:      }
61:      lp->resetList();
62:      do {
63:        cout << ((myItem *)(lp->currentItem()))->getValue();
64:        cout << "   ";
65:        lp->nextItem();
66:      } while (!lp->atHeadOfList());
67:  }
```

To give a list object something to store, lines 7–14 in the test program declare a new class, myItem, derived from item. This new class inherits the data members and member functions from item, and fulfills the requirement that all objects stored on a list be derived from item. (Such objects do not have to be *immediately* derived from item. Another class could be derived from myItem and stored in a list. As long as a class has item as a base class, no matter how distantly related, that class's objects can be stored in a list object.) The derived myItem contains a single int member value (line 9) and also has a constructor (line 11) and two methods (lines 12–13) for accessing value.

Line 18 illustrates the correct way to define list instances, using new to allocate space for a list on the heap. In this case, the lp pointer (list pointer) is declared globally, but it could also be local to a function. It's important to realize that defining space for a list object does *not* reserve any space for listed objects. The statement at line 18 applies only to the lp pointer and the list object that the pointer addresses. This object is usually called the *list head,* or the *root.*

As in the TITEM test program, the bulk of TLIST consists of a series of test statements (lines 25–40) that demonstrate some of list's capabilities. Each section calls a local function, showList(), to display the values of the myItem instances currently stored on the list.

Line 30 shows how to insert new items into a list object, calling member function insertItem(). Calling new allocates space for a myItem object, to which the program passes i, thus giving new data to each newly constructed object.

After the program is finished inserting a few items, lines 33–40 scan the list and add 100 to each myItem value. Lines 34–39 illustrate how to perform this scan. In general, for a list addressed by lp, these steps access every listed instance:

```
lp->resetList();
do {
  doSomething(lp->currentItem());
  lp->nextItem();
} while (!lp->atHeadOfList());
```

The first line resets the list so that the next item examined is the first in the list. A do/while loop then cycles while the expression (!lp->atHeadOfList()) remains true. Function atHeadOfList() will be true when the previous statement, lp->nextItem(), advances the list back to its starting place. That will cause the negated expression to become false, thus ending the loop.

Inside the loop, the statement doSomething(lp->currentItem()) calls a hypothetical function named doSomething() (not shown) and passes the address of the current item object as an argument. Always use the expression lp->currentItem() to obtain the address of objects in a list.

Unfortunately, because currentItem returns type item *, a type cast is usually necessary to tell the compiler what kind of item derivative the function result addresses. For example, line 36 executes the statement

```
mip = (myItem *)lp->currentItem();
```

This assigns the result of currentItem() to mip, a pointer declared as type myItem *. Without the type cast (myItem *), the compiler would reject the assignment, because item * and myItem * are different types. You'll find many other situations that require similar type casts.

Instead of assigning a recast pointer to a temporary object like mip, you can also perform and use the cast expression directly. This leads to complex expressions such as the one at line 63, repeated here:

```
((myItem *)(lp->currentItem()))->getValue();
```

Compare this with the previous sample. The expression calls currentItem() for the list object addressed by lp. It casts the result (declared as an item *) to type myItem *. Then, it uses the pointer to call the getValue() member function in the myItem class. The parentheses are necessary to force the compiler to evaluate the expression parts in the correct order.

Writing such long expressions is tedious work. Although the names will change, however, the forms in other type-cast expressions will be nearly identical. I find that it helps to #define a macro for part or all of the expression. The macro name greatly simplifies multiple uses of the same expression. For example, you might define this macro:

```
#define DP ((derived *)(bp->baseFunction()))
```

Then, you can use DP in place of the confusing type cast:

```
DP->derivedFunction();
```

Using uppercase for the macro name reminds you that DP is not an object.

## The LIST.CPP Module

The implementation for the list class is surprisingly short. LIST.CPP, Listing 7.6, weighs in at just under 100 lines.

### Listing 7.6. LIST.CPP.

```
 1:   // list.cpp -- List class
 2:
 3:   #include <stddef.h>
 4:   #include "list.h"
 5:
 6:   // Disable Microsoft warning about unreferenced member functions
 7:   // that have been removed. The functions are inline and are used
 8:   // by other modules.
 9:
10:   #if (defined __TSC_MSC__)
11:   #pragma warning( disable : 4505 )
12:   #endif
13:
14:   // List constructor. Initializes an empty list when the list object
15:   // comes into being (i.e. is allocated storage). Note: because a
16:   // list is a descendant of an item, the item class constructor also
17:   // runs before the list constructor.
```

*continues*

**CHAPTER 7**

## Listing 7.6. continued

```
18:
19:  list::list()
20:  {
21:    anchor = cip = NULL;     // No listed or current items
22:  }
23:
24:  // List destructor. Like a snake eating itself by the tail, the
25:  // destructor disposes of all items (if any) on the list, and then
26:  // disposes of itself.
27:
28:  list::~list()
29:  {
30:    if (anchor != NULL)
31:      disposeList();
32:  }
33:
```

The list class constructor sets the anchor and cip members to null, indicating that the list is empty (see lines 19–22). Because list is derived from item, it's important to realize that the item constructor has already finished by the time the statements at line 21 execute. This fact is easy to miss when reading the source code of a derived constructor.

The destructor at lines 28–32 is called when a program uses delete to dispose of a list object. Line 30 first checks whether there are any objects on the list. If so, the destructor calls disposeList(), another list member function. The function deletes all listed objects, emptying the list before it too is disposed. Because of this automatic cleanup, you can delete a list object without having to check whether the list holds any data.

The rest of list's member functions use conventional C++ techniques, and you should have no trouble understanding the statements. Comments in the listing explain the functions and point out several highlights.

## Listing 7.6. LIST.CPP. (continued)

```
34:  // Insert a new item addressed by ip into a list object. The new item
35:  // is linked in front of (to the left of) the current item. To link an
```

```
36:   // item after another, find that item and call nextItem before calling
37:   // insertItem. Does nothing if argument is NULL. If list is empty, then
38:   // a new list is created with the single item at ip. Returns address of
39:   // inserted item or NULL.
40:
41:   item *list::insertItem(item *ip)
42:   {
43:     if (ip == NULL)                  // Ignore request to insert
44:       return NULL;                   //   a NULL item.
45:     if (anchor == NULL)              // If list is empty...
46:       return anchor = cip = ip;      //   start a new list
47:     return ip->link(cip);            // Else, link item into list
48:   }
49:
50:   // Remove the item addressed by ip from the list object. Also adjust
51:   // the anchor and cip pointers to make sure they do not address the
52:   // unlinked item. If the addressed item is the only one in the list,
53:   // then this function empties the list. Does NOT dispose the unlinked
54:   // item or call its destructor. After calling removeItem, the item
55:   // addressed by ip points to itself, and it can be used to begin a new
56:   // list, or it can be used as a free-floating object. Returns NULL or
57:   // the address of the removed item.
58:
59:   item *list::removeItem(item *ip)
60:   {
61:     if (ip == NULL)                  // Ignore request to remove
62:       return NULL;                   //   a NULL item.
63:     if (ip->getright() == ip)        // If list has only one item...
64:       anchor = cip = NULL;           //   then empty the list
65:     else {
66:       if (ip == anchor)              // Else adjust anchor and
67:         anchor = anchor->getright(); //   cip pointers to ensure
68:       if (cip == ip)                 //   they do not address the
69:         cip = cip->getright();       //   unlinked item.
70:     }
71:     return ip->unlink();             // Unlink item from list
72:   }
73:
74:   // Return a pointer to the previous item, the one to the "left" of the
75:   // current item. Also sets the current item pointer to that item.
76:   // Returns NULL if list is empty.
```

*continues*

**Listing 7.6. continued**

```
77:
78:  item *list::prevItem(void)
79:  {
80:    if (cip != NULL)          // If list is not empty
81:       cip = cip->getleft();  //  set cip to item at left.
82:    return cip;               // Return current item pointer.
83:  }
84:
85:  // Return a pointer to the next item, the one to the "right" of the
86:  // current item. Also sets the current item pointer to that item.
87:  // Returns NULL if list is empty.
88:
89:  item *list::nextItem(void)
90:  {
91:    if (cip != NULL)          // If list is not empty
92:       cip = cip->getright(); //  set cip to item at right.
93:    return cip;               // Return current item pointer.
94:  }
95:
96:  // Remove and delete all items (if any) in the list object. If items
97:  // have destructors, they are called for each item. Items are not
98:  // necessarily disposed in the order they were inserted.
99:
100: void list::disposeList(void)
101: {
102:   while (!listEmpty())
103:      delete removeItem(currentItem());
104: }
```

# A Class for Strings

S uppose that you need to store a bunch of strings in memory—it's probably one of the most common problems programmers contend with. Maybe you are writing a text editor and you need a convenient way to manage lines of text. Or maybe you need a simple way to display a set of instructions in a window. How would you attack these problems?

You could design arrays of type char. Or perhaps an array of char pointers would be suitable. Either of those solutions will work, but they come with a built-in danger: You might discover later that you picked the wrong data structure. If so, you'll have to waste time redesigning the code from scratch.

This is exactly the kind of calamity that OOP techniques help prevent. When you need a new kind of data structure, begin by examining the classes you have at your disposal. Ask whether there is a class that has at least some of the capabilities you need. Derive a new class from that class, inheriting the original class's properties. Then, customize the new class to perform whatever tricks you need.

To use this concept to solve the problem of storing strings in memory, review the classes you know about, item and list. A list can store any derivative of item; therefore, the logical place to begin is to create a string class that inherits the properties of item. Then it will be a simple matter to create lists of strings.

## The stritem.h Header

The strItem class declared in stritem.h, Listing 7.7, adds a little meat to item's bones. Because strItem is derived from item, a strItem object has a copy of all the data members in item, and can call all of item's public and protected member functions.

**Listing 7.7. stritem.h.**

```
 1:  // stritem.h -- Header for stritem.cpp
 2:
 3:  #ifndef __STRITEM_H
 4:  #define __STRITEM_H  1     // Prevent multiple #includes
 5:
 6:  #include <item.h>
 7:
 8:  class strItem: public item {
 9:  private:
10:    char *sp;
11:
12:  public:
13:
14:  // Constructors and destructor
15:
```

*continues*

## Listing 7.7. continued

```
16:     strItem(const char *s);
17:     strItem(const char *s, int maxLen);
18:     virtual ~strItem();
19:
20: // Member functions
21:
22:     virtual char *getString(void) { return sp; }
23:     void putString(const char *s);
24:     void putString(const char *s, int maxLen);
25: };
26:
27: #endif    // __STRITEM_H
```

Line 10 adds a new private member, sp, a char pointer. This pointer will address the characters that belong in instance of the strItem class. Because sp is private to the class, only member functions in strItem can use sp. The private sp pointer also ensures that if you revise strItem to store strings in a different manner, you won't have to change a single line of code in programs that use strItem's public members. Since only strItem's member functions can use sp, if you change that pointer to something else, at the most you obviously need to modify only strItem's functions. Encapsulation of data and code inside classes can greatly limit the time it takes to modify programs when data specifications change.

# Multiple Constructors

A new feature in strItem is the use of two constructors at lines 16–17. C++ lets you *overload* constructors of the same names as long as the declarations differ in at least one parameter. (You can also overload other kinds of functions, a subject covered in Chapter 9, "Advance Your C++ Knowledge.")

The first constructor, on line 16, requires a constant string argument. The second constructor, on line 17, requires a string and a maximum length. Because there are two constructors, you can create a new string by using the following statement:

```
strItem *sp = new strItem("A string of any length");
```

That defines a strItem pointer named sp, and uses new to allocate heap space for a strItem object. The literal string in quotes is passed to the first strItem constructor, which copies the string and assigns its address to the private sp pointer. To limit the size of the string, add a maximum-length value

```
strItem *sp = new strItem("A string of limited length", 10);
```

That creates a new strItem object limited to 10 characters. Because the statement uses two arguments, C++ calls strItem's second constructor—the one that declares parameters that match the arguments used in the statement. If the string argument is longer than the stated maximum (as it is here), the string is truncated before being copied and assigned by address to sp.

C++ differentiates between the two constructors by the differences in their parameters. Not every class will need multiple constructors, but overloading is vital for creating classes that need to be initialized in different ways.

Line 18 declares strItem's virtual destructor. The function runs when strItem objects are deleted, giving the objects the opportunity to clean up after themselves.

The other member functions at lines 22–24 give you three ways to read and write characters in strItem objects. Call getString() to obtain the address of a strItem's string. Notice that getString is implemented inline and is declared to be virtual. C++ allows you to write inline virtual functions, but the functions most likely will be converted to callable functions as though they were not declared inline. This restriction makes more sense if you remember that, in order to call a virtual function, C++ looks up that function's address at runtime. Inline functions do not have addresses, so for any virtual function that is declared inline, C++ converts that function to the more common callable variety. The syntax at line 22, however, is convenient as it permits short virtual functions to be written directly in a class declaration.

Call putString() to change the characters in strItem objects. As with the class's double constructors, function putString() is overloaded. To change the string of strItem objects addressed by sp, you can write

```
sp->putString("New string of any length");
```

To change the string but limit its length to a maximum number of characters, you can write

```
sp->putString("New string of limited length", 10);
```

C++ figures out which of the identically named functions to call based on the different arguments passed to the functions. Of course, I could have created two functions with different names, perhaps putString1() and putString2(). Overloading makes it unnecessary to invent different names for similar operations.

> **Note:** Declaring default parameters is another useful tool for creating constructors and functions that allow statements to pass different numbers of arguments. For example, I could have declared a single constructor as strItem(const char *s, int maxLen = 0), and a single putString() member function as void putString(const char *s, int maxLen = 0). Then, in the implementations for these functions, if maxLen were 0, the program would assume that a statement called the function with no specific length value, meaning that the entire string should be used.

## Using the *strItem* Class

A simple test program, TSTRITEM.CPP in Listing 7.8, demonstrates how to use the strItem class.

### Listing 7.8. TSTRITEM.CPP.

```
 1:   // tstritem.cpp -- Test strItem class
 2:
 3:   #include <tscdefs.h>
 4:   #include IOSTREAM_H
 5:   #include <stritem.h>
 6:
 7:   main()
 8:   {
 9:     strItem *a = new strItem("This is item A");
10:     strItem *b = new strItem("Another item B");
11:     strItem *c = new strItem("One more item C");
12:
13:     cout << (a->getString()) << '\n';
14:     cout << (b->getString()) << '\n';
15:     cout << (c->getString()) << '\n';
```

```
16:
17:     c->putString(a->getString());
18:     cout << "After assigning A to C, C == " << c->getString() << '\n';
19:     return 0;
20:  }
```

Lines 9–11 define three strItem pointers, a, b, and c. Each of these lines uses new to create one strItem object in memory and store the string argument in parentheses. Lines 13–15 then display the strings by calling the getString() member functions for each object. Line 17 shows how to copy one string to another, passing the result of a string item's getString() function to putString(). That statement creates a distinct copy of the original string.

You normally won't use the strItem class as demonstrated in TSTRITEM, although the class is useful for storing strings in memory. After describing the implementation for the class in the next section, I'll return to the problem of storing lists of strings in memory. The value of strItem will then be more apparent.

## The STRITEM.CPP Module

The strItem class is implemented in STRITEM.CPP, Listing 7.9. The module includes error.h and uses the error-handling functions described in Chapter 6, "Building a Class Library—Part 1," Listing 6.9, ERROR.CPP. To have objects deal with error conditions directly, leave errorignore in that module set to false. To deal with errors yourself, set errorignore to true and use geterror() to retrieve a possible error code after calls to strItem member functions.

### Listing 7.9. STRITEM.CPP.

```
1:  // stritem.cpp -- String item class
2:
3:  #include <string.h>
4:  #include "error.h"
5:  #include "stritem.h"
6:
7:  // Disable Microsoft warning about unreferenced member functions
8:  // that have been removed. The functions are inline and are used
9:  // by other modules.
```

*continues*

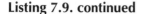

## Listing 7.9. continued

```
10:
11:  #if (defined __TSC_MSC__)
12:  #pragma warning( disable : 4505 )
13:  #endif
14:
15:  // Constructor. Create copy of string addressed by s as a new strItem
16:  // object. Argument may be NULL.
17:
18:  strItem::strItem(const char *s)
19:  {
20:    sp = NULL;      // Initialize private data member
21:    putString(s);   // Save argument string in object
22:  }
23:
24:  // Alternate constructor. Creates copy of string containing up to the
25:  // number of characters specified in maxLen. Argument may be NULL.  If
26:  // maxLen is 0 or less, allocate no space to string.
27:
28:  strItem::strItem(const char *s, int maxLen)
29:  {
30:    sp = NULL;                // Initialize private data member
31:    putString(s, maxLen);     // Save limited-length string
32:  }
33:
34:  // Destructor. Deletes space occupied by string and addressed by sp,
35:  // which may be NULL. Runs when a strItem object is deleted. Because
36:  // object is about to be deleted anyway, sp is not set to NULL.
37:
38:  strItem::~strItem()
39:  {
40:    delete[] sp;  // i.e. delete if sp != NULL
41:  }
42:
```

The two constructors at lines 18–22 and 28–32 set sp to NULL and then call one of the overloaded putString() member functions. In any constructor, you may call other member functions in the same class. Be aware, however, that the object might not be fully constructed until after the constructor finishes; therefore, you should not call any member functions that rely on members not yet initialized by the constructor.

If a constructor calls virtual functions declared in the same class, you should also carefully consider which functions are actually called. Inside a constructor, C++ does not look up virtual function addresses for the object being constructed. Instead, C++ generates direct calls to any virtual functions that are declared in the same class as the constructor.

> **Note:** In a constructor of a base class, calls to virtual member functions are fixed at compile time to the base class's declared virtual functions, even if a derived class replaces those functions and the object in construction is of the derived class. However, in the same class's destructor, calls to virtual functions operate normally, and are redirected to any replacement functions belonging to the object being destroyed. The general rule is, "In a constructor, virtual functions behave as common member functions." Only after a constructor is finished do virtual functions among derived class object begin to behave virtually.

The strItem destructor at lines 38–41 illustrates one of the most common uses for a destructor. The statement uses delete[] to dispose any memory allocated to sp. This works even if sp is null. It's okay to delete a null pointer. Deleting strItem pointers will call the destructor, which will clean up the object.

The STRITEM module continues in the next listing with the overloaded putString() functions.

### Listing 7.9. STRITEM.CPP. (continued)

```
43:  // Insert string into string object, replacing any string now
44:  // addressed.
45:
46:  void strItem::putString(const char *s)
47:  {
48:    delete[] sp;            // Dispose old string (if any)
49:    sp = NULL;              // Prevent accidental use of old pointer
50:    if (s == NULL) return;  // Exit if argument is NULL
51:    sp = strdup(s);         // Copy s to new string at sp
52:    if (sp == NULL)         // Test for strdup error
```

*continues*

## Listing 7.9. continued

```
53:      error(ERRMEM);           // Signal error copying string
54:  }
55:
56:  // Overloaded putString function. Same as putString above, but limits
57:  // the new string to maxLen characters.
58:
59:  void strItem::putString(const char *s, int maxLen)
60:  {
61:    int len;     // Length of string.
62:
63:    delete[] sp;               // Dispose old string (if any)
64:    sp = NULL;                 // Prevent accidental use of old pointer
65:    if (s == NULL) return;     // Exit if argument is NULL
66:    if (maxLen <= 0) return;   // If maxLen <= 0, exit with sp==NULL
67:    len = strlen(s);           // Set len to argument string length
68:    if (len > maxLen)          // If string is longer than maxLen
69:      len = maxLen;            //   limit len to maxLen
70:    sp = new char[len + 1];    // Create space for string + NULL
71:    if (sp == NULL)            // Test whether new() found enough memory
72:      error(ERRMEM);           // If not, signal out of memory error
73:    else {
74:      strncpy(sp, s, len);     // Else, copy len chars to sp
75:      sp[len] = NULL;          // Make sure string ends with NULL
76:    }
77:  }
```

Both putString() member functions delete any current string addressed by sp before assigning a new string. The functions also detect a null s argument. You can use this fact to recover memory allocated to strItem objects. Use the statement

sp->putString(NULL);

to delete characters in a string but not delete the strItem object. Zero-length, null strings are commonplace, and it's important for functions like putString() to deal with them in a sensible way.

The two functions also make good use of the ERROR module from Chapter 6, "Building a Class Library—Part 1." Lines 51 and 74 call conventional string functions to copy strings passed to strItem objects. If these operations fail, the functions call error(), passing the constant ERRMEM to indicate an out-of-memory condition. Unless you set errorignore to true, as explained in Chapter 6, these statements will halt the program if it runs out of memory.

# Making Lists of Strings

The strItem class neatly solves the problem of how to store a bunch of strings in memory. So far in this chapter, you've examined three classes: item, list, and strItem. A list may store any number of item objects or derivatives. Since strItem is derived from item, a list object can store strItem objects handily.

Test program TSTRLIST.CPP, Listing 7.10, demonstrates how to create string lists using the classes in this book's class library. Future programs will use similar techniques.

### Listing 7.10. TSTRLIST.CPP.

```
 1:  // tstrlist.cpp -- Test strItem class
 2:
 3:  #include <tscdefs.h>
 4:  #include IOSTREAM_H
 5:  #include <stritem.h>
 6:  #include <list.h>
 7:
 8:  #define CURRENT_STRING ((strItem *)(root->currentItem()))
 9:
10:  main()
11:  {
12:    list *root = new list;
13:
14:    root->insertItem(new strItem("First item in list"));
15:    root->insertItem(new strItem("Second item in list"));
16:    root->insertItem(new strItem("Third and last item in list"));
17:    if (root->firstItem() != NULL)
18:    do {
19:      cout << CURRENT_STRING->getString() << '\n';
20:      root->nextItem();
21:    } while (!root->atHeadOfList());
22:    delete root;
23:    return 0;
24:  }
```

The test program shows all the steps required to create lists of strings. Lines 5–6 include the stritem.h and list.h headers. Line 8 creates a macro CURRENT_STRING that executes the statement root->currentItem(), returning a pointer to the current item in a list addressed by a pointer root. The result of that expression is recast as (strItem *) so the macro can be used to call member functions for strItem class objects.

In function main(), line 12 creates a list pointer named root. It's not necessary to specify the kinds of data this list will store. A list object can store any other objects of classes derived from item. Lines 14–16 put this theory to the test, using new to allocate space for three strItem objects. The literal strings in quotes are passed to the strItem constructor to initialize each object. The result of new (a pointer to newly constructed strItem objects) is passed directly to the list's insertItem() member function.

Line 17 shows an alternate way to determine whether a list is empty; that is, if firstItem returns null. If the list at root is not empty, the program uses a do/while loop at lines 18–21 to display the listed strings. Line 19 calls the getString() member function in strItem, using the CURRENT_STRING macro to obtain and recast the pointer to the current item in the list. The macro saves typing and keeps the program text clean.

Consider the series of events that takes place when TSTRLIST uses delete at line 22. Remember that class objects are destroyed from the top down. First, the list destructor (lines 28–32 in LIST.CPP, Listing 7.6) calls disposeList(), (lines 100–104 in LIST.CPP), which deletes each item on the list. Those items' destructors are called automatically to delete each object. Finally, the item destructor finishes the cleanup job. The list class, as you might recall, is descended from item, so item gets the final crack at cleaning up descendant objects that are being deleted or that are about to go out of scope.

Think this through. When you compiled item and list, neither of those two classes knew about strItem's existence. However, the list destructor calls strItem's destructor to clean up each listed string instance. How can that be? How can code that was already compiled call a new function in a module you compiled *after* the one that's doing the calling?

Virtual functions are the answer. Look back to strItem's declaration (stritem.h, Listing 7.7). The destructor at line 18 is declared as virtual ~strItem();. Because the destructor is virtual, when a program uses delete to dispose of an item object, or of any object of a class descended from item, the program looks up the address of virtual destructor in the object being deleted. In this case, that object is of the class strItem;

therefore, the `list` destructor calls that object's destructor. Thanks to virtual functions, the code you compiled earlier in LIST can clean up a list of string instances by calling the new function you added later to STRITEM.CPP.

# A Class for *Windows*

W INTOOL in Chapter 6 showed off the capabilities of the `Window` class in this section. A window is like a small terminal in which you can display text, scroll lines up and down, select text attributes, and perform other operations. You can create as many `Window` objects as you like, limited only by available memory. Each new object can be displayed on top of others, creating overlapping windows. Removing a window on top exposes any others below—an illusion that makes the display appear to hold more information than is possible to show in the 80 rows and 25 columns of a typical PC screen.

The `Window` class is the most complex in this book's class library. The class demonstrates several key data-hiding features in C++ that you'll want to use in your own projects, especially in those that need to isolate system-dependent information inside a class. As in the previous sections, I'll explain the declarations in the header file, list a sample program, and then explain `Window`'s inner workings.

> **Note:** I was forced to capitalize the `Window` class name to avoid a conflict with the `window()` function in Borland C++ and Turbo C++. The only other alternative was to rename the class to something else, and capitalizing the class name seemed the least onerous solution, even though other class names like `item` and `list` are not capitalized. In *Learning C++*, `Window` is not capitalized.

## The window.h Header

The window.h header file, Listing 7.11, includes stdlib.h, stritem.h, and item.h. A `Window` class descends from `item` (as do all of the class library classes). After including window.h in your own programs, you do not have to include these other header files (although doing so does no harm).

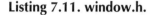

## Listing 7.11. window.h.

```
 1:  // window.h -- Header for window.cpp
 2:
 3:  #ifndef __WINDOW_H
 4:  #define __WINDOW_H       1      // Prevent multiple #includes
 5:
 6:  #include <tscdefs.h>
 7:  #include DISP_H
 8:  #include <stdlib.h>
 9:  #include <stritem.h>
10:  #include <item.h>
11:
12:  // Window information structure
13:
14:  struct winStruct {
15:      int row;            // Absolute row of top left corner
16:      int col;            // Absolute column of top left corner
17:      int width;          // Width of border
18:      int height;         // Height of border
19:      unsigned wtattr;    // Window normal text attribute
20:      unsigned wbattr;    // Window border attribute
21:      unsigned whattr;    // Window highlight text attribute
22:      int wtype;          // Border type (0 ... 4)
23:  };
24:
```

Lines 14–23 declare the winStruct structure. The members in winStruct describe the upper left row and column of a window's border, its width and height, its display attributes, and the border type. You've seen several examples of winStruct in Chapter 6. Every Window object needs a corresponding winStruct.

There are two main reasons I decided to collect Window details in the winStruct structure. The first reason is clarity. When functions need more than a few arguments, it's generally easier to store the value in a struct and pass that entire structure as an argument than it is to pass the values one by one. Try to avoid designing functions like this fictitious one that requires row, col, width, height, and other arguments:

```
void confusingFunction(int row, int col, int width, int height,
    unsigned wtattr, unsigned wbattr, unsigned whattr, int type);
```

Reading and using hundreds of similar functions in a large class library is enough to give anybody a whopping headache. A much clearer approach is to store the details in a struct, and then design functions like this with a parameter or two:

```
void clearFunction(winStruct &ws);
```

But there's another good reason to pass multiple arguments in a struct this way (usually by reference). You can save a lot of memory during compilation. The compiler has to store all the declarations you make, and numerous function parameters can quickly eat up a lot of space. Passing structures instead of individual arguments to functions conserves memory by helping the compiler store program symbols more efficiently.

The program might also run faster. To call confusingFunction(), the compiled program has to push each of the declared arguments onto the stack and then call the function. To call clearFunction(), it has to push only the address of a winStruct object. On the other hand, you'll probably need to assign individual values to the structure's members, so for a single function call, the time savings might be nil. Even so, passing structures is usually at least as fast if not faster than passing multiple objects around.

The next element of window.h is the Window class itself. Take the time to go through each line carefully—there are several items you haven't met before.

### Listing 7.11. window.h. (continued)

```
25: // Window class
26:
27: class Window: public item {
28: private:
29:
30: // Static data member (shared by all objects of class)
31:
32:    static int dispInitialized;  // True == display initialized
33:
34: // Private data members
35:
36:    int wbr;               // Window bottom row
37:    int wrc;               // Window right column
38:    int cr, cc;            // Logical cursor row, cursor column
39:    unsigned wca;          // Window current attribute
```

*continues*

**Listing 7.11. continued**

```
40:    strItem *wtitle;       // Pointer to window title strItem
41:    unsigned short *save;   // If NULL, text behind not saved
42:
43:  // Protected data members
44:
45:  protected:
46:    int isOpen;            // True if window is visible
47:    winStruct ws;          // Location, size, attributes
48:
49:  // Private member functions
50:
51:  private:
52:    unsigned short *saveBuf(void);
53:    void commonInits(void);
54:    void showOutline(void);
55:
56:  public:
57:
58:  // Static member functions
59:
60:    static void startup(void);
61:    static void shutDown(void);
62:
63:  // Constructors and destructors
64:
65:    Window();
66:    Window(winStruct &ws, const char *title);
67:    ~Window();
68:
69:  // Inline member functions
70:
71:    winStruct &getInfo()
72:      { return ws; }
73:    void reverseVideo(void)
74:      { wca = ws.whattr; }
75:    void normalVideo(void)
76:      { wca = ws.wtattr; }
77:
78:  // Other member functions
79:
```

```
80:     void showWindow();
81:     void hideWindow();
82:     void setTitle(const char *s);
83:     void setInfo(winStruct &ws);
84:     void gotorc(int row, int col);
85:     void puts(char *s);
86:     void scrollUp(int nrows);
87:     void scrollDown(int nrows);
88:     void eeol(void);
89:     void eeow(void);
90:   };
91:
92:   #endif    // __WINDOW_H
```

Like most class declarations, Window has private and public sections. Actually, it has *two* private areas—one beginning at line 28, and another at line 51. I organized the class this way merely for convenience (and to demonstrate that multiple private and other sections are possible). In any class, you can repeat the private, public, and protected keywords as often as you like. This can help you to organize the declarations in a complex class by keeping related members together in the text.

> **Note**: In a complex class like Window, I like to group private member functions in separate private areas (see lines 51–54). When creating a new class, I often need to create small functions I don't want host programs to use. For example, commonInits() carries out various common initializations that the class constructors need. I want host programs to use those constructors, but not to call commonInits() directly. Isolating this and other functions in a private section is a useful technique for preventing bugs caused by inappropriate function calls.

In addition to its private and public sections, Window also declares a protected area (lines 45–47). As you recall, members in a private section are strictly for use by member functions in the class. Members in a public section are available to statements in that class as well as to statements outside. Classes that derive from Window may directly use protected and public members in the base class. Because of this rule, a derivative of Window may use the isOpen and ws members directly (lines 46–47), but statements outside the class and its derivatives cannot do the same.

# Static Member Functions

In Chapter 6, you learned that to start up and shut down the Window class, a program must call two functions, preferably in main:

```
main()
{
  Window::startup();
  ...
  Window::shutDown();
  exit(0);
}
```

The startup() and shutDown() functions are declared at lines 60–61 in window.h. Each prototype is prefaced by the keyword static, which has special meaning when applied to member functions. Unlike common member functions, such as showWindow at line 80, a *static member function* is never available through an object of its class. In other words, if you create a window with

```
Window *myWin = new Window;
```

you can then execute statements such as myWin->showWindow() and myWin->eeow(). But you can't execute myWin->startup() and myWin->shutDown(). Those functions are static, and therefore do not receive a this pointer. Static functions are usually called by direct reference to the class name, as in the statements Window::startup() and Window::shutDown().

The primary use for static member functions is to initialize a global aspect of the class that should apply equally to all objects of that class. For example, in Window, it's necessary to initialize the Zortech display package before using any of that package's routines. Other compilers might not need similar initializations, but even so, this requirement provides a useful tool to add future startup chores without requiring programs to be revised. This job must be done only once; therefore, it would be a mistake to perform the initialization inside a class constructor because the constructor runs for *each* new object of the class. Storing the global initialization steps in a static member function makes it possible for a program to initialize the class for all future class objects.

Another benefit of static member functions is the isolation of low-level details inside the class. Without the startup() and shutDown() functions, it would be necessary for host programs to call the Zortech or other compiler's initialization functions before using Window. You could create other global functions for this purpose, but then the Window class would lose its autonomy, and it would have to *know* somehow that the display package was initialized.

Avoid making your classes dependent on global objects, global functions, or peculiar compiler requirements. When a class (not just an object of the class type) needs to be initialized in some fashion, consider storing the initialization code in a static member function. This approach will increase the portability of your programs, and will help prevent bugs by isolating low-level details inside the class.

**Note:** Common functions may also be declared static. Usually, this is done to prevent programs from gaining access to static functions stored separately in modules.

# Static Member Members

Member functions like startup() and shutdown() are not the only items that can be static. You can also declare static data members. For example, look at line 32 in window.h. There you see the declaration

```
static int dispInitialized;
```

A *static data member* is similar in some ways to a global variable. In contrast to other data members such as int wbr or unsigned wca at lines 36–37, only one copy of a static data member exists in memory, no matter how many objects of the class a program creates. As with all global variables, a static data member takes up permanent storage, and it exists for the life of the program.

The static dispInitialized data member in the Window class indicates whether the program called the static startup() function to initialize the class. This object gives the class the means to know whether it has been initialized. When you define an object of type Window, the class constructor checks dispInitialized. If that object is false, the program displays the error message *Window class not initialized* and halts. Together, the static member functions and data member in Window give the class the capability of being initialized, and allow the class to detect whether that initialization has been carried out. This is a powerful device that goes a long way toward making bug-prone global variables unnecessary.

> **Note:** The data type of a static data member can be any common C++ type (`int` or `float`, for example), or it can be an object of another class. That class may have a constructor with or without parameters—a feature not available in some early C++ compilers. If a static data member is declared publicly, then statements outside the class may refer to that object with a statement such as `class::member = x`, where x is a value to assign to the public data. However, as with most data members, and for the same reasons discussed earlier, it's usually best to declare static data in private or protected sections, and to allow only member functions of the class or its derivatives to access the static members.

# Overloaded Constructors

The `Window` class declares two constructors at lines 65–66. As with all constructors, these have the same name as the class. The first constructor declares no parameters. The second declares a reference parameter `&ws` of type `winStruct` and a constant string pointer named `title`.

As I explained earlier for `strItem`, declaring two or more constructors (or other functions) of the same name is called overloading. This C++ feature is merely a convenience that lets you write functions that have the same names but perform different actions. Except for their names, the overloaded functions are not connected in any way. In all cases, overloaded constructors and functions must differ in at least one parameter.

The purpose of overloading constructors and functions is to make it unnecessary to invent a slew of function names that have similar purposes. There's no need in C++ to have functions named `init1()`, `init2()`, `init3()`, and `init4()`. As long as these functions have different parameters, you can name them all `init()` and let the compiler figure out which one to call based on arguments used during the construction of objects. For example, in a program that uses the `Window` class, it's obvious to the compiler which constructor to call in each of the two statements

```
window *default = new window;
window *custom = new window(ws, " Custom Window ");
```

> **Note:** Chapter 9, "Advance Your C++ Knowledge," covers overloading. As you'll discover then, it's also possible to overload many C++ operators such as = and +.

# Reference Functions

One other new element in the Window class is the member function, getInfo(), at lines 71–72. The function returns a reference to a winStruct data type. The reference symbol (&) when applied to a function's return type allows statements to assign the result of the function to an object.

The alternative approach is to return a pointer as the function type. For example, I could have written lines 71–72 like this:

```
winStruct *getInfo()
  { return &ws; }
```

Then, to use the function, I'd need to declare a winStruct pointer and assign to it the function result:

```
window *w = new window();    // Create a window
winStruct *wp;               // Define a winStruct pointer
wp = w->getInfo;             // Address private data with wp ???
```

Although that will work, the effect is to set a pointer to the instance's protected data! This trick goes against the OOP grain by giving statements access to data members that are supposed to be protected or private.

To guard against this condition, it's usually best to return a reference instead of a pointer to private and protected data. Statements can then assign the result of a reference function to an object of the same data type. In the Window class, the getInfo() reference function illustrates the method. Using the function does not pose the same dangers as in the preceding sample code:

```
window *w = new window();    // Create a window
winStruct ws;                // Define a winStruct object
ws = w->getInfo;             // Get copy of data from instance
```

Now, instead of using a winStruct pointer, the program defines a winStruct object ws. Calling the reference function getInfo() *copies* the internal winStruct data from the class instance to ws. This is generally safer because it eliminates the potentially dangerous pointer that peeks into the inner sanctum of the class object's private parts.

The rest of the member functions in Window contain nothing new. You should be able to read and understand the other declarations in the listing.

# Designing Displays with Windows

A short sample program will show how to use most of the Window class's functions.

### Listing 7.12. TWINDOW.CPP.

```
 1:  // twindow.cpp -- Test Window class
 2:
 3:  #include <tscdefs.h>
 4:  #include <stdlib.h>
 5:  #include <window.h>
 6:  #include <conio.h>
 7:
 8:  // Attribute constants
 9:
10:  #define WA_REVERSEVIDEO   0x70
11:  #define WA_NORMAL         0x07
12:
13:  // Test-function prototypes
14:
15:  void pause(void);
16:  void runtest(void);
17:  void overlayTest(void);
18:  void scrollTest(void);
19:
20:  main()
21:  {
22:    Window::startup();
23:    runtest();
24:    Window::shutDown();
25:    return 0;
26:  }
27:
```

All programs that use the Window class must include the window.h header as done here at line 5. Lines 10–11 define two constants for displaying text in reversed and normal video, the default values for all windows. The listed values will work for all display types, but you might want to change them to 0x1e and 0xb4 if you have a color screen.

Function main() shows the bare necessities required to use the Window class. As in WINTOOL, line 22 initializes the class by calling the static startup() function. For a useful experiment, temporarily delete this line and recompile. When you run the modified program, it displays

```
ERROR: 2: Window class not initialized
```

The ERROR module (see Chapter 6, "Building a Class Library—Part 1") displays this message and halts the program. You can trap the error by setting errorignore to true as explained in Chapter 6, but you still must not define or use any Window objects until after calling startup(). Similarly, you must call shutDown() before the program ends. This deinitializes the class and returns the display to normal operation.

After calling startup(), you may not use input- and output-stream statements. After calling shutDown(), you can use those statements again. When the Window class is initialized, *all* program output must go to a Window object. You may call startup() and shutDown() as many times as necessary in a program.

TWINDOW continues after main() with a small function (to pause for a keypress) and the main test function, runtest().

## Listing 7.12. TWINDOW.CPP. (continued)

```
28:  // Wait for and discard keypress
29:  void pause(void)
30:  {
31:    while (getch() != ' ') ;
32:  }
33:
34:  // Execute main test procedures
35:  void runtest(void)
36:  {
37:    int i;
38:    Window *win = new Window;
```

*continues*

**483**

## Listing 7.12. continued

```
39:    winStruct ws;
40:    int row;
41:
42:    win->setTitle(" Press <Spacebar> to Advance Test ");
43:    win->showWindow();
44:    ws = win->getInfo();
45:    for (row = 0; row < ws.height - 2; row++) {
46:      win->gotorc(row, row);
47:      win->puts("This line should end here: abcdefghijklmnop");
48:      win->gotorc(row, 75);
49:      win->puts("Endoftheline");
50:      if (row & 1)
51:        win->normalVideo();
52:      else
53:        win->reverseVideo();
54:      pause();
55:    }
56:    win->setTitle(" Pop-Up Overlay Test ");
57:    overlayTest();
58:    win->normalVideo();
59:    win->setTitle(" Erase to End of Line Test ");
60:    pause();
61:    for (row = 0; row < ws.height - 2; row++) {
62:      win->gotorc(row, row + 26 );
63:      win->eeol();
64:      pause();
65:    }
66:
67:    win->normalVideo();
68:    win->gotorc(0, 0);
69:    win->puts("Scroll down 4x test");
70:    win->eeol();
71:    win->setTitle(" Scroll DOWN 4x test ");
72:    pause();
73:    for (i = 1; i <= 4; i++) {
74:      win->scrollDown(1);
75:      pause();
76:    }
77:
```

```
78:    win->gotorc(4, 0);
79:    win->puts(" Scroll up 4x test ");
80:    win->eeol();
81:    win->setTitle(" Scroll UP 4x test ");
82:    for (i = 1; i <= 4; i++) {
83:      pause();
84:      win->scrollUp(1);
85:    }
86:
87:    win->setTitle(" Erase Window Test " );
88:    pause();
89:    win->gotorc(0, 0);
90:    win->eeow();
91:    win->setTitle(" Null Title Test ");
92:    pause();
93:    win->setTitle("");
94:    pause();
95:    win->setTitle(" Hide Window Test " );
96:    pause();
97:    win->hideWindow();
98:    delete win;
99:  }
100:
```

Run TWINDOW and press Space repeatedly while examining the runtest() function's implementation. This will give you a good feel for how to use the Window class's member functions. Near the beginning of runtest(), the function creates a default window by executing

```
Window *win = new Window;
```

Variable win is a pointer to a object of type Window. The statement allocates memory for a Window object and assigns the address of that object to win. To construct the object, C++ calls the Window's default constructor—the one with no parameters. This creates a window that fills the entire display and does not save any covered text. The program can then use win to execute various functions for this window.

Among those functions are those listed in Table 7.1. Run the program, examine each statement, and use this table as a guide to learn what the various functions do. You'll learn more about how these functions operate internally when you examine the Window class module later.

## Table 7.1. Window functions used in TWINDOW.

| Window Function | Description |
|---|---|
| eeol | Erase from cursor to end of line |
| eeow | Erase from cursor to end of window |
| getInfo | Get winStruct details from window |
| gotorc | Position cursor to a row and column |
| hideWindow | Remove window from display |
| normalVideo | Select normal text attributes |
| puts | Display (put) a string in a window |
| reverseVideo | Select reversed text attributes |
| scrollDown | Scroll window down one or more lines |
| scrollUp | Scroll window up one or more lines |
| setTitle | Change the window's title |
| showWindow | Display the window |

## Listing 7.12. TWINDOW.CPP. (continued)

```
101:    // Display pop-up window over main window
102:    void overlayTest(void)
103:    {
104:      winStruct ws = {
105:        6, 20, 32, 12,
106:        WA_REVERSEVIDEO, WA_NORMAL, WA_NORMAL, 1
107:      };
108:      Window *win = new Window(ws, " Pop-Up ");
109:
110:      win->showWindow();
111:      win->gotorc(4, 2);
112:      win->puts("Pop-Up window!");
113:      win->gotorc(6, 2);
114:      win->puts("Press Space twice to erase");
115:      pause();
```

```
116:    win->gotorc(0, 0);
117:    win->eeow();
118:    pause();
119:    delete win;
120:  }
```

TWINDOW ends with a subfunction `overlayTest()` that displays a small pop-up window over the main one that fills the display. Lines 104–108 illustrate an alternate way to create a window. Instead of the default method used in `runtest()`, a `winStruct` named `ws` is created and assigned the position, size, attributes, and type values to use for this window. Line 108 declares a `win` pointer, using `new` to allocate memory for a `Window` object. The two arguments in this statement, `ws` and `" Pop-Up "`, are passed to the `Window` class's second constructor—the one that declares parameters to match these arguments.

Line 119 uses `delete` to deallocate the memory assigned to the `win` pointer. At this time, the `Window` destructor cleans up any structures inserted on the heap by the constructor or other `Window` member functions. It's especially important to delete objects addressed by pointers that are local to a function such as `overlayTest()`. When the function ends, its local variables such as the `win` pointer no longer exist. If you forget to `delete` space assigned to a local pointer, that pointer will be lost when the function ends. This mistake would destroy the only means the program has to refer to the `Window` object in memory and would leave that space unrecoverable. If you run out of memory while using a program, check whether you've deleted all memory allocated to pointers defined locally in functions.

# The WINDOW.CPP Module

At about 300 lines, the implementation of the `Window` class in WINDOW.CPP, Listing 7.13, is one of the longest modules in this book. Even so, the functions contain mostly conventional C++ programming, most of which you've seen in other samples. Because `Window` is the most complex class in the class library, I laced the source with many comments, which you can read for a better understanding of how the program works. I'll point out only a few highlights and new items here.

## Listing 7.13. WINDOW.CPP.

```
1:    // window.cpp -- Window class
2:
3:    #include <tscdefs.h>
4:    #include <string.h>
5:    #include "error.h"
6:    #include "window.h"
7:
8:
9:    // Disable Microsoft warning about unreferenced member functions
10:   // that have been removed. The functions are inline and are used
11:   // by other modules.
12:
13:   #if (defined __TSC_MSC__)
14:   #pragma warning( disable : 4505 )
15:   #endif
16:
17:   extern disp_numrows;  // Gain access to normally hidden
18:   extern disp_numcols;  //  display package variables.
19:
```

Like most modules, this one begins with several miscellaneous items. Lines 17–18 declare two variables, disp_numrows and disp_numcols as extern. These variables are part of the display package described in Chapter 10, "Cross-Compilation Tools," and they are usually hidden. The variables represent the number of rows and columns available on the display. The display package must be initialized before using them.

Notice there are no data types listed with disp_numrows and disp_numcols, and therefore, C++ assumes the unstated data types to be int. I wrote these lines without types to demonstrate that it is possible to do so and because this is the format that the Zortech display package uses. (As explained in Chapter 10, the display package is emulated for other compilers.) I do not recommend this practice. A short test shows why the technique, although legal (and unfortunately required in this case), is flawed:

```
#include <tscdefs.h>
#include IOSTREAM_H
main()
{
  extern x;
  cout << "size of x = " << sizeof(x);
}
int x;
```

When you compile and run this small program, it reports that x's size is 2 bytes, the size of an int (correct, at least, for most MS-DOS C++ compilers). The extern directive tells the compiler that x is defined elsewhere. In this case, the definition (int x) comes after main(), but the definition could be in another module. Because the extern x; declaration does not specify x's data type, C++ assumes that x is type int.

Change int x to long x and you'll see the problem with the technique. When you attempt to compile the modified listing, the compiler reports an error when it discovers that it has made the wrong assumption about x. However, if the long x; declaration were in another module, the compiler would not report this same error. Worse, the linker would not notice that the program has used a variable that's defined as a different type in another module!

If you use typeless declarations like those at lines 17–18, make sure that the variables are actually type int (a fact that I am sure of here). Better still, don't use the technique. Give all variables explicit data types. If you don't, you're just asking for trouble.

## Listing 7.13. WINDOW.CPP. (continued)

```
20:  // Define and initialize the static class member member, which indicates
21:  // whether the display package has been initialized.  This variable is
22:  // global--it is shared by all objects of the window class. But,
23:  // because it's declared private to the class, only class member
24:  // functions have access to it.
25:
26:  int Window::dispInitialized = FALSE;
27:
```

Line 26 defines space for the static data member dispInitialized. The definition also assigns an initial value to the member, setting the flag to FALSE (0). Because the variable is global (though not globally visible outside the WINDOW module), the assignment isn't necessary. All global objects are initialized to 0 by default. However, I wrote the line in full to demonstrate how to initialize static data members.

Static data members like dispInitialized differ from common definitions in one key way. As you recall, if a module defines a variable, another module can access that variable by declaring it to be extern. But the same trick does not work for private static data members like dispInitialized. Because dispInitialized is private to the

Window class, no statements outside the class can use the variable; therefore, a future change to the module could safely eliminate dispInitialized without requiring changes to any other statements outside of the WINDOW module.

## Listing 7.13. WINDOW.CPP. (continued)

```
28:  // Private routine (not a member of the Window class). Display a string
29:  // at an absolute row and column position using the specified
30:  // attribute. Limit length of string to len characters. Ideally, this
31:  // routine should display all possible ASCII symbols--it should not
32:  // respond to control codes such as carriage returns and line feeds.
33:
34:  void putsat(int row, int col, int len, unsigned attr, char *s)
35:  {
36:    unsigned char buffer[264];
37:    int i, j;
38:
39:    if (len == 0) return;
40:    for (i = 0, j = 0; i < len; i++, j += 2) {
41:      buffer[j] = s[i];
42:      buffer[j + 1] = (unsigned char)attr;
43:    }
44:    disp_pokebox((unsigned short *)buffer, row, col, row, col + len - 1);
45:  }
46:
```

Function putsat() displays strings at an absolute row and column on-screen. The function calls the disp_pokebox() function (described in Chapter 10) to push characters and attributes directly into the PC's video-display buffer.

The function demonstrates that a module may include conventional functions. Not everything in a C++ program has to be in a class. Support functions like putsat() are convenient and common.

They are also a little risky. To understand why, add this line to TWINDOW.CPP (Listing 7.12) just above line 19:

```
extern void putsat(int row, int col, int len, unsigned attr, char *s);
```

Next, insert this line just above line 23 (before Window::shutDown();):

```
putsat(3, 4, 23, WA_NORMAL, "Hello from outer space!");
```

When you run the modified program, all is well. But just before the code ends, the message Hello from outer space! appears on-screen. This alien visitor shows how easy it is for a program to gain access to supposedly private support functions like putsat(). All the program has to do is declare the function extern. A statement is then free to call the function.

At times, you might want to use this technique to gain access to functions that are normally hidden from view. But be aware that if you use this method, you will not be able to take out functions like putsat() from the WINDOW module without also modifying all programs that call the function. A better plan might be to declare functions like putsat() private to the class. That way, no statements outside the class will be able to peek into the module with an extern declaration.

> **Note:** Another way to prevent access to private functions like putsat() is to declare the function static. To do this in the WINDOW.CPP module, add the static keyword to the front of the putsat() declaration at line 29. It is then impossible for another module to use extern to gain access to the function.

### Listing 7.13. WINDOW.CPP. (continued)

```
47:  // Program must call the class static startup function to initialize
48:  // the display package (or another display library if porting the
49:  // code). Because startup is a static member function, it can access
50:  // only static data members of the class. It has no access whatsoever
51:  // to other data members in Window class objects.
52:
53:  void Window::startup(void)
54:  {
55:    if (!dispInitialized) {     // If not initialized yet
56:      disp_open();              //  then initialize display
57:      disp_hidecursor();        // Turn off system cursor
58:      dispInitialized = TRUE;   // Set the static flag
59:    }
60:  }
```

*continues*

## Listing 7.13. continued

```
61:
62:    // Program must call the class static shutDown function to deinitialize
63:    // the display package. Failure to call this routine could lead to
64:    // display problems after the program ends. (This may or may not be the
65:    // case after porting the code to a system that doesn't use the Zortech
66:    // display package.)
67:
68:    void Window::shutDown(void)
69:    {
70:      if (dispInitialized) {              // If previously initialized
71:        disp_move(disp_numrows - 1, 0 );  // Set cursor to bottom row
72:        disp_showcursor();                // Display cursor
73:        disp_close();                     // Shut down display package
74:        dispInitialized = FALSE;          // Reset the static flag
75:      }
76:    }
77:
```

The static member functions startup() and shutDown() are implemented next. Note that the static keyword does not reappear in the implementations, only in the declarations.

The two functions perform simple jobs. Function startup() initializes the display package. Function shutDown() shuts the package down. Most important, when porting the code to another compiler, the two functions can be gutted. All the low-level details concerning a specific compiler's display functions are neatly hidden in the class.

## Listing 7.13. WINDOW.CPP. (continued)

```
78:    // Create and return pointer to a buffer for saving text behind Window.
79:    // Returns null if enough memory is not available.
80:
81:    unsigned short *Window::saveBuf(void)
82:    {
83:      return new unsigned short[(ws.height * ws.width) * sizeof(unsigned)];
84:    }
```

```
85:
86:    // Perform various common initialization steps for all new windows.
87:    // Called by all class constructors. Aborts program if Window class
88:    // startup function was not called, or if the class was shut down.  If
89:    // you add new constructors to the Window class, be sure to call this
90:    // routine, or failing that, at least test the dispInitialized flag and
91:    // take appropriate actions if the flag is false.
92:
93:    void Window::commonInits(void)
94:    {
95:      if (!dispInitialized)                 // Test if display initialized
96:        error(ERRWININIT);                  // Halt or report error if not
97:      cr = cc = 0;                          // Home logical cursor
98:      save = NULL;                          // Text behind not saved
99:      isOpen = FALSE;                       // Window is not open
100:     if (ws.row > disp_numrows - 3)        // Limit smallest window
101:       ws.row = disp_numrows - 3;          //   to one row, one column
102:     if (ws.col > disp_numcols - 3)
103:       ws.col = disp_numcols - 3;
104:     if (ws.width < 1) ws.width = 1;       // Window width must be >= 1
105:     if (ws.height < 1) ws.height = 1;     // Window height must be >= 1
106:     wbr = ws.row + ws.height - 1;         // Window's bottom row number
107:     wrc = ws.col + ws.width - 1;          // Window's right column number
108:     wca = ws.wtattr;                      // Current attr = normal text
109:     wtitle = NULL;                        // No window title (yet)
110:   }
111:
112:   // Default constructor. Creates full-screen window. The save pointer is
113:   // set to NULL, which causes the window not to save the text behind it.
114:   // Because the default window is full screen, this saves at least 4K of
115:   // memory.
116:
117:   Window::Window()
118:   {
119:     ws.row = ws.col = 0;                   // Upper left corner
120:     ws.width = disp_numcols;               // Full width of display
121:     ws.height = disp_numrows;              // Full height of display
```

*continues*

493

## Listing 7.13. continued

```
122:    ws.wtattr = DISP_NORMAL;         // Normal text attribute
123:    ws.wbattr = DISP_NORMAL;         // Normal border attribute
124:    ws.whattr = DISP_REVERSEVIDEO;   // Highlight in reverse video
125:    ws.wtype = 0;                    // Select double-line border
126:    commonInits();                   // Do other init steps
127:  }
128:
129:  // Alternate constructor. Allows sizing window and selecting various
130:  // attributes. Saves text behind window.
131:
132:  Window::Window(winStruct &ws, const char *title)
133:  {
134:    Window::ws = ws;
135:    commonInits();
136:    setTitle(title);
137:    save = saveBuf();
138:  }
139:
140:  // Destructor. Deallocates save-text buffer (if allocated). Note that
141:  // it is legal to pass a null pointer to free, but it is not okay to do
142:  // the same with delete--a minor inconsistency in this version of C++
143:  // that can lead to trouble. Deleting a null pointer may cause the
144:  // program to crash.
145:
146:  Window::~Window()
147:  {
148:    if (isOpen) hideWindow();    // Close window if open
149:    delete save;                 // Dispose save buffer (if any)
150:    delete wtitle;               // Dispose old title (if any)
151:  }
152:
```

The Window destructor at lines 146–151 cleans up a deleted Window object. Line 145 deletes wtitle, a variable of type strItem *. In window.h, wtitle is declared as

strItem *wtitle;

You examined the strItem class earlier. The wtitle member is a pointer to an object of that class. There's nothing unusual about this construction, and classes often have many data members of other class types. Beginners to OOP sometimes neglect this technique, and assume that class data members must be only simple types like int and float. Not so. You can use any data types for members in classes, including other classes.

Be sure to initialize any members of class data types. Usually, the class that declares the members will perform initializations in the constructor. For example, line 109 sets wtitle to NULL, indicating that the pointer does not address a valid strItem object.

The rest of the Window class follows. There are no new elements here, and you should be able to read and understand the code by scanning the comments in the listing.

### Listing 7.13. WINDOW.CPP. (continued)

```
153:  // Display window outline and title if one was assigned. Called
154:  // by showWindow and if the title is changed after window is opened.
155:
156:  void Window::showOutline(void)
157:  {
158:    int len;    // String length
159:
160:    disp_box(ws.wtype, ws.wbattr, ws.row, ws.col, wbr, wrc);
161:    if (wtitle != NULL) {
162:      len = strlen(wtitle->getString());
163:      if (len > 0) {
164:        putsat(ws.row, ws.col + ((ws.width - len) / 2), len,
165:          ws.wbattr, wtitle->getString());
166:        gotorc(cr, cc);
167:      }
168:    }
169:  }
170:
171:  // Save text behind window (optional), draw window's border, erase the
172:  // contents. Cursor is positioned inside window at top left corner.
173:  // The host program is expected to display the window's contents.
```

*continues*

## Listing 7.13. continued

```
174:  // Prevents accidentally opening an already open window, which would
175:  // destroy the save buffer.
176:
177:  void Window::showWindow()
178:  {
179:    if (isOpen) return;  // Prevent multiple openings
180:    if (save) disp_peekbox(save, ws.row, ws.col, wbr, wrc);
181:    showOutline();
182:    isOpen = TRUE;
183:    gotorc(0, 0);
184:    normalVideo();
185:    eeow();
186:  }
187:
188:  // Restore any saved text behind window and mark window closed. If
189:  // there is no save buffer, the display will not change, although the
190:  // window will still be closed.
191:
192:  void Window::hideWindow()
193:  {
194:    if (!isOpen) return; // Exit if window is closed
195:    if (save) disp_pokebox(save, ws.row, ws.col, wbr, wrc);
196:    isOpen = FALSE;
197:  }
198:
199:  // Change window title. You may call this routine whether or not you
200:  // specified a title when creating the Window object. Window may be
201:  // open or closed.
202:
203:  void Window::setTitle(const char *s)
204:  {
205:    delete wtitle;
206:    wtitle = new strItem(s, ws.width - 2);
207:    if (isOpen) showOutline();
208:  }
209:
210:  // Assign new attributes to window. Use this function to move and
211:  // resize windows, or just to change their colors, border types, etc.
212:  // Selects normalVideo output.
```

```
213:
214:   void Window::setInfo(winStruct &ws)
215:   {
216:     int wasOpen = isOpen;
217:
218:     if (isOpen) hideWindow();
219:     delete save;
220:     Window::ws = ws;
221:     save = saveBuf();
222:     if (wasOpen) {
223:       normalVideo();
224:       showWindow();
225:     }
226:   }
227:
228:   // Move cursor to position inside window border. Top left position is
229:   // 0, 0 (home). Row and column values are relative to window
230:   // boundaries. Note: Does not make system cursor visible--instead, this
231:   // function prepares the location where text will appear for the next
232:   // call to puts(). Cursor is allowed to rest on the right border, but
233:   // otherwise must remain within the window's boundaries.
234:
235:   void Window::gotorc(int row, int col)
236:   {
237:     if (!isOpen) return;       // Exit if window is closed
238:     cr = row; cc = col;        // Save relative values
239:     if (cc < 0) cc = 0;        // Prevent negative
240:     if (cr < 0) cr = 0;        //   cursor positions
241:     if (cc > ws.width - 2)
242:       cc = ws.width - 2;       // Limit col to window width
243:     if (cr > ws.height - 3)
244:       cr = ws.height - 3;      // Limit row to window height
245:     disp_move(ws.row + cr + 1, ws.col + cc + 1);
246:   }
247:
248:   // Display string at current cursor position. String is truncated to
249:   // fit within the window boundaries. Cursor is positioned at the end of
250:   // the string. (It is possible for the cursor to be on the right
251:   // border, but it is not possible to display text there.)
252:
```

*continues*

## Listing 7.13. continued

```
253:  void Window::puts(char *s)
254:  {
255:    int len = strlen(s);          // String length
256:    int nc = ws.width - cc - 2;   // Number chars right of cursor
257:
258:    if (!isOpen) return;      // Exit if window is closed
259:    if (nc <= 0) return;      // Exit if no space to cursor's right
260:    if (len == 0) return;     // Exit if length of string is 0
261:    if (len > nc) len = nc;   // Truncate too-long strings
262:    putsat(ws.row + cr + 1, ws.col + cc + 1, len, wca, s);
263:    gotorc(cr, cc + len);      // Position cursor to end of string
264:  }
265:
266:  // Scroll contents of current window up by the number of lines
267:  // specified in nrows. Blanks that many lines at bottom using the
268:  // current display attribute.
269:
270:  void Window::scrollUp(int nrows)
271:  {
272:    if (!isOpen) return; // Exit if window is closed
273:    disp_scroll(nrows, ws.row + 1, ws.col + 1, wbr - 1, wrc - 1, wca);
274:  }
275:
276:  // Scroll contents of current window down by the number of lines
277:  // specified in nrows. Blanks that many lines at top using the current
278:  // display attribute.
279:
280:  void Window::scrollDown(int nrows)
281:  {
282:    if (!isOpen) return;  // Exit if window is closed
283:    disp_scroll(-nrows, ws.row + 1, ws.col + 1, wbr - 1, wrc - 1, wca);
284:  }
285:
286:  // Erase from current cursor position to end of line, that is, to just
287:  // before the window's right border. Uses the current attribute for the
288:  // blanked area.
289:
```

```
290:  void Window::eeol(void)
291:  {
292:    unsigned attr = wca * 256 + ' ';   // Attribute for blank line
293:    int nc = ws.width - cc - 3;        // Number of chars to erase
294:    int acr = ws.row + cr + 1;         // Absolute cursor row
295:    int acc = ws.col + cc + 1;         // Absolute cursor column
296:    if (!isOpen) return;     // Exit if window is closed
297:    if (nc < 0) return;      // Exit if no space to cursor's right
298:    disp_fillbox(attr, acr, acc, acr, acc + nc);
299:  }
300:
301:  // Erase from current cursor position to end of window, that is, to
302:  // just before the window's bottom border. Uses the current attribute
303:  // for the blanked area.
304:
305:  void Window::eeow(void)
306:  {
307:    int ocr = cr;          // Save old cr (cursor row)
308:    int occ = cc;          // Save old cc (cursor col)
309:
310:    if (!isOpen) return;             // Exit if window is closed
311:    eeol();                          // Erase to end of current line
312:    while (++cr < ws.height - 2) {   // Erase other full lines if any
313:      gotorc(cr, 0);
314:      eeol();
315:    }
316:    cr = ocr;              // Restore saved cursor position
317:    cc = occ;
318:  }
```

# A Class for Selections

**P**rograms commonly prompt operators to choose from lists of items. A database might ask for a data field's storage type, or present options for reports. A compiler might solicit options such as whether to include debugging information in the output, or whether to generate a map file of a program's symbols. Lists are tailor-made for organizing these and other data sets from which people will need to make selections.

Because selection lists are so common, a general-purpose tool for creating and displaying them is invaluable, as several examples in this chapter and the next demonstrate. Naturally, you'll want your selectors to look good and be capable of handling any number of items.

Those requirements are easily met by marrying some of the classes you already know about. A selector will need to list strings and let people select one of those strings from a window. With that thought in mind, you can begin to create a selector based on the Window class. Or, should you use the list class for the base? Apparently, the selector will need to borrow elements from list *and* Window. Unlike in previous examples, where derived classes inherited from only a single class, a process known as *single inheritance,* the selector will need to inherit from more than one base class, a feature known as *multiple inheritance.* With single inheritance, derived classes may have only one immediate ancestor. With multiple inheritance, a derived class may inherit the properties of two or more parents.

## The selector.h Header

The selector class declaration in selector.h, Listing 7.14, shows how multiple inheritance allows derived classes to inherit the properties from more than one base class.

### Listing 7.14. selector.h.

```
 1:   // selector.h -- Header for selector.cpp
 2:
 3:   #ifndef __SELECTOR_H
 4:   #define __SELECTOR_H    1      // Prevent multiple #includes
 5:
 6:   #include <stritem.h>
 7:   #include <list.h>
 8:   #include <window.h>
 9:
10:   class selector: public Window, public list {
11:   private:
12:     int showHide;              // True==pop-up, false==stationary
13:     int row;                   // Current row, -1==not initialized
```

```
14:     void highlight(int row);
15:     void showItem(int row);
16:     void moveUp(int &row);
17:     void moveDown(int &row);
18:   public:
19:     selector(winStruct &ws, const char *title, int popup = 1);
20:     strItem *getSelection(void);
21:   };
22:
23:   #endif    // __SELECTOR_H
```

# Multiple Inheritance

Line 10 in selector.h specifies two base classes, Window and list, separated by a comma. The classes are declared to be public, and therefore inherited members retain their private, protected, or public status. Because the two base classes are in turn derived from item, a selector is also an item. Among other benefits, this means that selector objects inherit the properties of list *and* the objects can be stored on another list. Putting that another way, a list of selectors is a multiway structure—in essence, a list of lists. Using conventional techniques to code similar complex structures is possible, but the results are rarely as concise as in the selector class shown here.

A derived class might inherit the properties of any number of base classes, though you'll rarely need to design classes that inherit from more than two or three bases. The result of a multiply-derived class is a new class that combines the properties of two or more ancestors.

Despite what you may have heard or read about multiple inheritance, the technique isn't difficult to use and understand. Detractors will tell you, however, that there are no compelling reasons to use multiple inheritance in derived classes. According to the popular argument against the technique, I could have created selector with two private or protected members, one a list and the other a Window. This would give the selector the same capabilities that multiple inheritance provides.

That argument is difficult to refute. Still, multiple inheritance can be useful for creating classes that combine the properties of two or more other classes, and those new classes may call inherited functions without having to refer to a named instance of the base classes. If I had created a member named theSelectorList of type list, then I would have to execute commands such as theSelectorList->currentItem(). By inheriting from list, I can simply write currentItem(). When inheriting from several base classes, not having to refer to member names is tremendously more convenient.

The other members in selector are best explained by examining and running the test program in the next section.

## Using the *selector* Class

TSELECT.CPP, Listing 7.15, shows how to use the selector class. Run TSELECT and use the cursor keys to scroll up and down in the sample list. Press Enter to choose an item. Press Esc to close the test window and quit without making a selection.

### Listing 7.15. TSELECT.CPP.

```
 1:  // tselect.cpp -- Test selector class
 2:
 3:  #include <tscdefs.h>
 4:  #include IOSTREAM_H
 5:  #include <stdlib.h>
 6:  #include <string.h>
 7:  #include <conio.h>
 8:  #include <selector.h>
 9:
10:  // Test function prototypes
11:  void pause(void);
12:  void runtest(void);
13:
14:  // Pointer to a selected string
15:  char *selection;
16:
17:  main()
18:  {
19:    Window::startup();
20:    runtest();
21:    Window::shutDown();
22:    if (selection == NULL)
23:      cout << "\nNo item selected";
```

```
24:     else
25:       cout << "\nItem selected: " << selection;
26:     return 0;
27:   }
28:
29:   // Wait for a keypress
30:   void pause(void)
31:   {
32:     while (getch() != ' ') ;
33:   }
34:
35:   // Perform the test
36:   void runtest(void)
37:   {
38:     winStruct ws = {
39:       4, 20, 18, 7,   // row, column, width, height
40:       0x07,           // text attribute
41:       0x1e,           // border attribute
42:       0x70,           // highlight attribute
43:       1               // type
44:     };
45:     selector *sel = new selector(ws, " Items ");
46:     strItem *p;
47:
48:     sel->insertItem(new strItem("Elephants"));
49:     sel->insertItem(new strItem("Tigers"));
50:     sel->insertItem(new strItem("Lions"));
51:     sel->insertItem(new strItem("Polar Bears"));
52:     sel->insertItem(new strItem("Deer"));
53:     sel->insertItem(new strItem("Rabbits"));
54:     sel->insertItem(new strItem("Loons"));
55:     sel->insertItem(new strItem("Eagles"));
56:     sel->insertItem(new strItem("Beavers"));
57:     sel->insertItem(new strItem("Peacocks"));
58:     sel->insertItem(new strItem("Quit <Esc>"));
59:
60:     p = sel->getSelection();
61:     if (p) selection = strdup(p->getString());
62:     delete sel;
63:   }
```

Function `runtest()` at lines 36–63 demonstrates how to create and use a `selector` class object. The statements resemble those you used earlier to create `Window` objects. But that shouldn't come as a surprise. A `selector` *is* a `Window`, and you therefore use nearly identical `winStruct` structures and techniques to create `selector` objects as you do `Window` objects.

Line 45 creates a pointer `sel` to a `selector` object, and uses `new` to allocate memory for that object. The `selector` constructor adds a default parameter to those declared in `Window`'s alternate constructor. Passing 0 to the new parameter causes the window to stay visible after you select a command from it. This way, a `selector` allows you to make a selection, perform some action, and then select another item without having to scroll back to the one you selected previously. To use this feature, you can change line 45 to

```
selector *sel = new selector(ws, " Items ", 0);
```

However, you won't notice any difference when you run the test program, because it lets you make only one selection at a time. For a better example of this technique, see WINTOOL in Chapter 6. WINTOOL's main menu uses this method to stay visible so you can select commands without the menu's window disappearing after each new selection.

Lines 48–58 show how to insert new items into a `selector` object. Each item in a selection list must be a `strItem` object or an object of a derived class. In the test program, the statements insert plain `strItem` objects, initializing each with the literal string shown in quotes. Notice that member function `insertItem()` handles the duty of inserting the items into the list. The `selector` class inherited `insertItem` from `list`.

Line 60 calls the `getSelection()` function for the `selector` instance addressed by `sel`. The result of this function is a pointer to one of the inserted `strItem` objects. If `getSelection()` returns null, then the program's user pressed Esc and did not choose an item. Line 61 tests for that condition by checking whether `p` is null. If not, a global `char *` object `selection` (see line 15) is set to address a copy of the string inserted into the list, using the `getString()` member function in the class to obtain the string's characters.

It's important to use `strdup()` at line 61 to copy the selected string, because the next line deletes the `selector` from memory. When you use the `selector` class, be careful not to set a pointer to an item you will delete before using!

# The SELECTOR.CPP Module

There are few new features in the selector implementation module, SELECTOR.CPP, Listing 7.16. Most of the programming is conventional C++ and should be easy to understand from the comments. I'll point out the more interesting sights as you tour the listing.

### Listing 7.16. SELECTOR.CPP.

```
 1:  // selector.cpp -- Selector class
 2:
 3:  #include "key.h"
 4:  #include "selector.h"
 5:
 6:  #define KEY_ENTER    13  // Enter key value
 7:  #define KEY_ESC      27  // Esc key value
 8:  #define KEY_UP     -184  // Cursor Up key value
 9:  #define KEY_DOWN   -176  // Cursor Down key value
10:  #define KEY_PGUP   -183  // Page Up key value
11:  #define KEY_PGDN   -175  // Page Down key value
12:
13:  // Disable Microsoft warning about unreferenced member functions
14:  // that have been removed. The functions are inline and are used
15:  // by other modules.
16:
17:  #if (defined __TSC_MSC__)
18:  #pragma warning( disable : 4505 )
19:  #endif
20:
21:  // Constructor. Passes arguments to the window class's alternate
22:  // constructor, and initializes its own data members.
23:
24:  selector::selector(winStruct &ws, const char *title, int popup)
25:    : Window(ws, title)
26:  {
27:    showHide = popup;     // Select pop-up or stationary style
28:    selector::row = -1;   // i.e. not initialized
29:  }
30:
```

The constructor (lines 24–29) passes the first two of its parameters, ws and title, to the Window class constructor. This is a typical design, and you've seen the technique in other examples. A constructor in a derived class will usually pass the necessary arguments to the base-class constructor in order to initialize members inherited from the base.

But selector is not a typical class. The selector class inherits from *two* base classes. As you can see at lines 24–25, however, the derived constructor calls only one of the constructors in the inherited Window base, not the constructor in list. The reason for this apparent discrepancy is that list's constructor declares no parameters; therefore, C++ calls the constructor by default. Even though you don't name parameterless constructors, they still run before the derived constructor executes.

If a class inherits from two or more base classes that have constructors requiring parameters, then you can call those constructors in the derived class by separating the base constructor calls with commas. For example, suppose selector derives from a third class named dummy with a constructor dummy(int popup). There is no such class in the book's class library, but if there were, the derived constructor declaration would be

```
selector::selector(winStruct &ws, const char *title, int popup)
  : window(ws, title), dummy(popup)
```

In general, in a class derived that inherits from multiple base classes base1, base2, and base3, design the constructor's implementation like this:

```
derived::derived(int x, int y, int z, int a)
  : base1(x), base2(y), base3(z)
{
  // ... statements in derived constructor
}
```

Parameters x, y, and z represent the arguments to be passed to the base-class constructors. Parameter a represents any data required by the derived constructor. C++ calls class constructors in declaration order.

## Listing 7.16. SELECTOR.CPP. (continued)

```
31:  // Display current item at window row, col == 0, using the current
32:  // attribute.
33:
34:  void selector::showItem(int row)
35:  {
```

```
36:      gotorc(row, 0);
37:      Window::puts(((strItem *)currentItem())->getString());
38:      eeol();
39:  }
40:
```

The `showItem()` member function displays the current item in the `selector` object at the specified row. I purposely wrote line 37 differently from lines 36 and 38 to illustrate two ways to call base class member functions. Because `selector` inherits from `Window`, it can call that class's `gotorc()`, `puts()`, and `eeol()` functions as though they were declared directly in `selector`. There is no need to preface such function calls with the class name, as I did at line 37. Specifying `Window::` in front of the statement is allowed but is usually unnecessary. This would be necessary if two or more base classes from which `selector` is derived declared `puts()` member functions. In that case, you would have to preface the function calls with `Window::` or another class name and scope resolution operator (`::`) to indicate which of the identically named functions you want to use.

In the following functions, you'll see other unadorned examples of calls to member functions from the two inherited base classes, `Window` and `list`.

## Listing 7.16. SELECTOR.CPP. (continued)

```
41:  // Display current item at window row, col == 0 using the highlight
42:  // attribute. This procedure displays the "selector bar."
43:
44:  void selector::highlight(int row)
45:  {
46:    reverseVideo();
47:    showItem(row);
48:  }
49:
50:  // Move selector bar up to previous item. Scrolls window contents down
51:  // if necessary.
52:
53:  void selector::moveUp(int &row)
54:  {
55:    if (!listEmpty() && !atHeadOfList()) {
56:      normalVideo();
```

*continues*

## Listing 7.16. continued

```
57:       showItem(row);
58:       if (row > 0) row--; else scrollDown(1);
59:       prevItem();
60:       highlight(row);
61:    }
62: }
63:
64: // Move selector bar down to next item. Scrolls window contents up if
65: // necessary.
66:
67: void selector::moveDown(int &row)
68: {
69:   if (!listEmpty() && !atEndOfList()) {
70:     normalVideo();
71:     showItem(row);
72:     if (row < ws.height - 3) row++; else scrollUp(1);
73:     nextItem();
74:     highlight(row);
75:    }
76: }
77:
78: // Display selector window, list items, and let operator move
79: // selector bar to any item, scrolling up and down as necessary if there
80: // are more items than can fit in the window. Returns a pointer to the
81: // selected item if operator presses Enter. Returns NULL if operator
82: // presses Esc.
83:
84: strItem *selector::getSelection(void)
85: {
86:   int key;     // Keypress value
87:   int i;       // for-loop control variable
88:
89:   if (listEmpty()) return NULL;
90:   if (!isOpen) row = -1;   // Reset newly opened windows
91:   showWindow();            // Make sure window is visible
92:   normalVideo();           // Select normal text attribute
93:   if (row < 0) {           // Initialize first time
94:     row = 0;
95:     resetList();
```

```
 96:     do {
 97:       showItem(row);
 98:       nextItem();
 99:     } while (!atHeadOfList() && (++row <= ws.height - 3));
100:     row = 0;
101:     resetList();
102:   }
103:   highlight(row);
104:
105: // Get keypress and move up or down. Return null for Esc, or
106: // pointer to selected item for Enter.
107:
108:   for (;;) {
109:     switch (key = getKey()) {
110:       case KEY_ESC:
111:       case KEY_ENTER:
112:         if (showHide) {
113:           hideWindow();
114:           row = -1;
115:         }
116:         if (key == KEY_ESC)
117:           return NULL;
118:         else
119:           return (strItem *)currentItem();
120:       case KEY_UP:
121:         moveUp(row);
122:         break;
123:       case KEY_DOWN:
124:         moveDown(row);
125:         break;
126:       case KEY_PGUP:
127:         for (i = 0; i < (ws.height - 2) / 2; i++)
128:           moveUp(row);
129:         break;
130:       case KEY_PGDN:
131:         for (i = 0; i < (ws.height - 2) / 2; i++)
132:           moveDown(row);
133:         break;
134:     }
135:   }
136: }
```

# A Class for Commands

**M**ost programs prompt for and respond to commands from users. To have programs react to commands, programmers typically write code that reads keystrokes and then calls one of several functions. Usually, a `switch` statement controls the process, running a function after someone types a command's letter, or selects a menu item, which the program translates to a number.

The problem with this approach comes when it's time to upgrade the software. To add a new command requires tedious work: modifying `switch` statements, changing prompts in menu functions, and so on. Also, the conventional way makes it difficult to create dynamic menus, which insert and delete commands based on other input. For example, in a *File* menu there might be a command to *Open* a disk file. After you select *Open,* new commands to *Save* and *Close* the file appear in the menu. This design makes programs easier to use by listing only the commands that are possible to select rather than listing every command including disabled ones.

A solution to this problem jumps out of the answer to a simple question: What is a command? There may be many correct answers, but in most programs, a *command* usually has three parts:

- A name

- An action

- A selector

The *name* of a command is what you see in the menu. The *action* represents what the command does. The *selector* might be the letter of the key you press to select the command. Or the selector could be a unique value assigned by the program.

When faced with other problems to solve, it might help to make a similar list of observations. List the properties of the task you need to perform or the structure you need to build. Then, look for a class that comes as close to meeting your requirements as possible.

Applying that thought to this book's class library, the class that comes closest to meeting a command's requirements is `strItem`. A `strItem` object can store a string, which might represent the command's name. The command's action can be a new member function in the derived class. The selector might as well be the `selector` class described in the preceding section. Because `selector` derives from `list`, this design makes it easy to create lists of commands in a window—in other words, a pop-up menu.

# The command.h Header

Chapter 6 introduced the concept of an abstract class. Programs can never create objects of an abstract class, which serves only as the design for other derived classes. The command class, declared in command.h, Listing 7.17, is an abstract class. Instead of defining objects of command, you must derive new classes from command. Those derivatives become the commands in your program.

**Listing 7.17. command.h.**

```
 1:  // command.h -- Header for command.cpp
 2:
 3:  #ifndef __COMMAND_H
 4:  #define __COMMAND_H  1     // Prevent multiple #includes
 5:
 6:  #include <stritem.h>
 7:
 8:  // The abstract command class is an strItem with an associated action
 9:  // in the form of a "pure" virtual function. Selecting a command object
10:  // derived from the command class calls the derived virtual function.
11:  // With this design, all commands are objects, eliminating the need for
12:  // the large switch statements typically found in menu-driven programs.
13:
14:  class command : public strItem {
15:  protected:
16:    int cmdNum;     // Unique number to identify command
17:  public:
18:    command(const char *s, int cn = 0) : strItem(s) { cmdNum = cn; }
19:    virtual void performCommand(void) = 0;
20:  };
21:
22:  #endif   // __COMMAND_H
```

The command class has only three members. The int member cmdNum (line 16) uniquely identifies multiple instances of a class derived from command. For commands that have only one object for their class, this member isn't used. Unlike some menu systems, this one does not assign a unique value to every command in a program. The cmdNum member might be used that way, but its purpose is to distinguish between objects of the same derived class. This means that, in one program, many commands might have the same cmdNum value. (A sample program, TCOMMAND.CPP, near the end of this chapter demonstrates how to use cmdNum.)

The command constructor at line 18 is implemented as an inline function. I could have implemented the constructor in the usual way. However, I wrote command inline to demonstrate that in some cases a class may be declared in a header but have no corresponding implementation module. Many of the classes in this book are stored in corresponding .h and .CPP files. But command is different. The entire class declaration and implementation for command are stored in the command.h header file.

The pure virtual-member function performCommand() at line 19 fulfills the requirement that a command perform an action. Being virtual, a derived class can replace performCommand() and be confident that a pointer to a command object will call the correct replacement function in an object of any class derived from command. Being *purely* virtual (the function ends with the assignment = 0), it's not necessary to implement the function at this time. In fact, the presence of the pure virtual function is what makes the class abstract (unable to be defined as a object). If the function were not declared to be purely virtual, you would have to provide a do-nothing function implementation such as the following:

```
void performCommand(void)
{
}
```

Declaring pure virtual functions eliminates the need for these sorts of empty shells. However, in nonabstract classes, it may be necessary to declare do-nothing virtual functions that a derived class is expected to replace. In such cases, you'll need to supply a shell for the normal virtual function in the base class in order to allow objects of the base class to be defined. When doing this, you might want to create a global function named abstract that goes something like this:

```
void abstract(void)
{
  cout << "\n\nAbstract function called";
  exit(1);
}
```

Then, instead of the do-nothing function shell listed previously, write

```
void performCommand(void)
{
  abstract();    // Signal error in derived class
}
```

With this arrangement, if any statement accidentally calls the impure virtual `performCommand()` function, the program will display an error message and halt. This debugging device can help locate derived classes that fail to provide required replacement functions inherited from a base class.

# Using the *command* Class

TCOMMAND.CPP, Listing 7.18, shows how to use the `command` and `selector` classes to create pop-up menus in programs. Remember, there is no corresponding COMMAND.CPP file to accompany a command.h header file. To use the `command` class, programs need only to `#include` the command.h header file, as done here at line 9.

## Listing 7.18. TCOMMAND.CPP.

```
 1:  // tcommand.cpp -- Test command class
 2:
 3:  #include <tscdefs.h>
 4:  #include IOSTREAM_H
 5:  #include IOMANIP_H
 6:  #include DISP_H
 7:  #include <key.h>
 8:  #include <selector.h>
 9:  #include <command.h>
10:  #include <conio.h>
11:
12:  // Test-function prototypes
13:  void pause(void);
14:  void runtest(void);
15:
16:  // Derived command classes
17:  class openCommand : public command {
18:  public:
19:    openCommand() : command("Open") { }
20:    virtual void performCommand(void);
21:  };
22:
23:  class closeCommand : public command {
24:  public:
```

*continues*

**Listing 7.18. continued**

```
25:    closeCommand() : command("Close") { }
26:    virtual void performCommand(void);
27:  };
28:
29:  class saveCommands : public command {
30:  public:
31:    saveCommands(const char *s, int cn) : command(s)
32:      { cmdNum = cn; }
33:    virtual void performCommand(void);
34:  };
35:
36:  class quitCommand : public command {
37:  public:
38:    quitCommand() : command("Quit Esc") { }
39:    virtual void performCommand(void);
40:  };
41:
```

Lines 17–40 show how to create derived command classes. Typically, a class derived from command will contain only two items: a constructor and a replacement for the performCommand() virtual function inherited from the base class. Of course, the derived class may declare other member functions and data members.

The most common type of derived command will appear similar to openCommand() at lines 17–21. Line 19 declares the derived class's constructor, a do-nothing shell with the sole purpose of passing the command's name to the base-class constructor. Lines 25 and 38 show two other examples of similar constructors.

Class saveCommands (lines 29–34) shows an alternate method for creating commands. As in the other three classes, the new class is derived from the abstract base class command. The derived class declares a replacement performCommand() function. The constructor at lines 31–32, however, is not like other command constructors. Instead of specifying the command's name directly, the derived constructor in saveCommands lists two parameters: a constant string pointer s and an integer cn. The constructor passes the first parameter (representing the command's name) to the base class constructor and assigns the second parameter to cmdNum. The constructor can make this assignment because cmdNum is declared in a protected section in the base class; therefore, the inherited member is visible in the derived class. However, cmdNum is not visible to statements outside the class.

The purpose of this alternate construction is to give programs a way to invent classes that can handle more than one command in a menu. In the implementation of the command's replacement performCommand function, you can use the protected cmdNum as a selector to distinguish among the multiple commands.

The main() function comes next. Always remember to initialize the Window class, as shown here. You must do so because selector inherits from Window, even though the program doesn't include the window.h header and doesn't create any Window objects.

### Listing 7.18. TCOMMAND.CPP. (continued)

```
42:  main()
43:  {
44:    Window::startup();
45:    runtest();
46:    Window::shutDown();
47:    return 0;
48:  }
49:
50:  // Wait for Spacebar
51:  void pause(void)
52:  {
53:    cout << " Press <Spacebar>..." << flush;
54:    while (getch() != ' ') ;
55:  }
56:
57:  // Perform tests
58:  void runtest(void)
59:  {
60:    winStruct ws = {
61:      4, 20, 18, 7,  // row, column, width, height
62:      0x07,          // text attribute
63:      0x1e,          // border attribute
64:      0x70,          // highlight attribute
65:      1              // type, save text (yes)
66:    };
67:    selector *sel = new selector(ws, " Items ");
68:    command *cp;
69:    sel->insertItem(new openCommand());
```

*continues*

**Listing 7.18. continued**

```
70:    sel->insertItem(new closeCommand());
71:    sel->insertItem(new saveCommands("Save", 1));
72:    sel->insertItem(new saveCommands("Save-as", 2));
73:    sel->insertItem(new quitCommand());
74:    while ((cp = (command *)(sel->getSelection())) != NULL) {
75:      cp->performCommand();
76:    }
77:    delete sel;
78: }
79:
```

Function `runtest()` shows how to create a pop-up menu and to perform commands as you select them. The `winStruct` declaration at lines 60–66 should be familiar by now. The assignments specify the size, location, colors, and type of the window used to display the menu. Use WINTOOL from Chapter 6 to choose values for the text, border, and highlight attributes in your own menus.

Line 67 creates a `selector` object for the pop-up menu. The title can be anything you like, or it can be null if you don't want to give the menu a title. (For example, you might use untitled menus to create a series of "pull-down" menus at the top of the display.) Line 68 defines a pointer `cp` to a `command` class object. The program will use `cp` to execute commands in the menu.

After preparing the menu's `selector`, using the menu requires three basic steps:

1. Insert derived command instances into the `selector`.

2. Call the `selector`'s `getSelection()` function to prompt for a command.

3. If `getSelection()` does not return null, use the pointer to call the command's replacement `performCommand()` virtual function. This will run the selected command.

Lines 69–73 take care of the first step. The statements insert derived `command` class objects into the `selector` object addressed by the `sel` pointer. Notice the difference between lines 69–70 (also 73) and 71–72. The `openCommand()`, `closeCommand()`, and `quitCommand()` classes require no arguments for their constructors. But there are two objects of the `saveCommands` class—one for a command named "Save" and another for a command "Save-as." Multiple objects of the same class are inserted into the menu, using different command numbers (the arguments 1 and 2) to distinguish one command from another.

Next come the derived class implementations. These are the functions that perform the command actions.

**Listing 7.18. TCOMMAND.CPP (continued)**

```
80:  // The derived command-class implementations
81:  void openCommand::performCommand(void)
82:  {
83:    disp_move(24, 0);
84:    cout << "\nOpen command." << endl;
85:    pause();
86:  }
87:
88:  void closeCommand::performCommand(void)
89:  {
90:    disp_move(24, 0);
91:    cout << "\nClose command." << endl;
92:    pause();
93:  }
94:
95:  void saveCommands::performCommand(void)
96:  {
97:    disp_move(24, 0);
98:    if (cmdNum == 1)
99:      cout << "\nSave command." << endl;
100:   else if (cmdNum == 2)
101:     cout << "\nSave-as command." << endl;
102:   pause();
103: }
104:
105: void quitCommand::performCommand(void)
106: {
107:   ungetKey(27);     // "Press" the Esc key
108: }
```

The derived command functions simply display a message indicating which function is running. In your own code, you'll need to write similar functions to perform your program's commands. Simple cases like openCommand's performCommand()

function (lines 81–86) carry out a single action. More complex cases like `saveCommands'` `performCommand()` function (lines 95–103) use the value of `cmdNum` to detect which of the several command objects was used to call the function.

# Recap

Y ou've now examined every scrap of code in this book's class library. You can use the classes in the library as foundations for your own projects, or you can use the experience you've gained in this chapter and in Chapter 6 to help you explore a more complex commercial library. You may also want to start your own library, using the classes here as blueprints for your own designs.

You've also encountered nearly all of C++'s features, although a few details remain to be covered in the next two chapters. With what you know so far, you can write sophisticated C++ programs that put OOP techniques to good use. There is, however, one essential programming topic that I still haven't covered: file handling. It's the rare program that doesn't have to read or write at least one disk file. As you'll learn in the next chapter, C++ has an extensive array of functions designed for just that purpose.

# Questions and Exercises

7.1. From Figure 7.1, what class (or classes) does `strItem` derive from? What class (or classes) does `selector` derive from?

7.2. How does multiple inheritance differ from single inheritance?

7.3. Design a new class derived from `item` that can hold four floating point values. What member functions are needed to allow access to the class's data?

7.4. Write a program to create and display a list of your class instances from Exercise 7.3.

7.5. In the following class, which members are accessible by statements in a derived class? Which members are accessible to other members in the same class? Which members are accessible to statements outside of the class?

```
class room {
private:
  int numChairs;
  int numTables;
protected:
  int numBooks;
public:
  void putInfo(int chairs, int tables, int books);
  void getInfo(int &chairs, int &tables, int &books);
};
```

7.6. Redesign the room class in Exercise 7.5 to eliminate the multiple parameters in member functions putInfo() and getInfo(). (Hint: use a struct.) Why make this change?

7.7. Describe the main difference between a constructor and a destructor. In general terms, what should constructors and destructors do?

7.8. Suppose class B derives from class A and that each class declares a constructor and a destructor. In what order do the constructors and destructors run when instances of class B are defined?

7.9. What does the this pointer address? From where can you use this? Inside the implementation to getInfo() in the class from Exercise 7.5, what is the this pointer's data type?

7.10. Create a derivation of the list class that can report how many items are currently listed.

7.11. Create a derivation of the strItem class that converts its strings to uppercase.

7.12. In Chapter 6, you filled in WINTOOL's Help command to display text inside a window. To accomplish this, you had to use wasteful pairs of gotorc() and puts() functions. Improve the Window class by adding a new function that eliminates the need to use gotorc() before every puts operation. (Hint: You may want to design your function to simulate carriage return and line feed operations.)

7.13. How does a static data member differ from a global variable?

7.14. Why is it dangerous to return pointers as member function data types? Instead of a pointer, what should these kinds of functions return?

7.15. Write a program that lets you choose a window border type (0 to 4) and shows the result. Use the Window class in your answer.

# Files and Directories

T he C++ language has no facilities for file and directory handling, but don't let that fact surprise you. You can write C++ programs to read and write files, and to list and change file-name entries in disk directories. The routines for these and other disk operations, however, are stored in the standard library—file and directory handling capabilities are not native to C++.

There's a good reason for omitting file and directory commands from C++ (and from other languages). Because C++ doesn't have any native disk commands, programs written in "pure" C++ can be ported to other systems, which may store information in files and directories in widely different formats. If C++ did have a set of file commands, then those commands would either have to be translated for a different system, or you would have to modify your programs extensively to run on multiple platforms.

C++ minimizes these unappealing chores by using the same file and directory routines available to most modern C compilers. For that reason, except for the discussion of directory classes near the end of this chapter, most of the information that follows applies equally to C and C++. Because the compilers supported by this book run under MS-DOS, I'll focus on MS-DOS file and directory techniques.

The preceding three chapters described object-oriented programming methods in C++. In the first part of this chapter, you'll learn conventional approaches for file and directory handling. Then, you'll return to OOP, using the book's class library from Chapters 6 and 7, "Building a Class Library" (Parts 1 and 2), to create classes for listing file information in disk directories. You'll also use those classes to write two useful utilities, a directory navigator, NAV, and a text-file lister, READ.

> **Note:** You probably ran the READ program to view the README file on disk. This chapter lists READ's source code and explains how the program works.

# File and DOS Functions

The C++ library contains over 60 functions you can use to write a variety of file and directory programs. Some of these functions call low-level DOS and BIOS subroutines to perform system-dependent operations. For example, the dos_abs_disk_read() and dos_abs_disk_write() functions in Zortech C++ read and write disk sectors without regard to whether those sectors belong to files. With another function, _bios_disk(), you can call even lower-level ROM BIOS disk routines.

Although these and other low-level routines are available, you will rarely need them. For most file and directory handling, higher-level library functions are safer and easier to use. These functions exist in pretty much the same forms on a wide variety of C and C++ compilers (even those that run under different operating systems). So, if you stick to the higher ground explained in this chapter, you'll be able to port your programs more easily to other systems later.

# Text Files

A text file is the most common file-storage format on most computer systems. By *text file,* I mean any file that contains bytes representing ASCII characters. Usually, a text file on MS-DOS systems will organize its data into lines separated by carriage-return (0x0d) and line-feed (0x0a) control codes. However, some text files may contain a stream of ASCII data that's not divided into lines.

Other computer operating systems and programs may store ASCII text in files but represent new lines differently. Still other programs modify the ASCII standard. For example, word processors usually add formatting codes to represent boldface, italics, and other special symbols. These facts complicate ASCII file processing, but in general, the techniques in this section apply to most kinds of text files.

# Basic Text-File Techniques

A simple program that creates a new text file will demonstrate some of the basics of text-file handling techniques. You've already seen many examples of programs that display text on-screen. To store text in files, you can use similar methods. But instead of sending text to the console, you'll call routines that direct the text to a disk file. In most text-writing programs, there are three steps to follow:

- Open a text file by preparing a variable that other functions can use to access that file.

- Write information to the file by specifying the file variable opened previously.

- Close the file to update the file's directory information including the file's name, size, and other facts.

This final step is critical. Always close files when you're finished using them. In addition to updating the file entry in the disk directory, closing a file flushes any data held in memory. This step is necessary because DOS, various file routines, and other operating systems usually read and write data in chunks. When you write information to a file, the operating system may store that data temporarily in memory until a full chunk is available for sending to the actual file. This buffering action helps keep file I/O running fast, but it also means you must close files properly. If you end a program prematurely, you might lose any data that wasn't transferred to disk.

> **Note:** When a program ends, internal shutdown subroutines close any open files. Even so, a serious bug could cause these subroutines to be skipped, and many programmers prefer to close open files explicitly.

# Creating Text Files

Listing 8.1, MAKETXT.CPP, shows how to open, write, and close text files. Run MAKETXT by entering a command such as **maketxt test.txt**. That will create a new file, TEST.TXT, in the current directory. Next, enter several lines to store in the new file. Type a blank line to quit. After the DOS prompt returns, enter **type test.txt** to display TEST.TXT's contents and verify that MAKETXT holds the text you entered.

### Listing 8.1. MAKETXT.CPP.

```
 1:  // maketxt.cpp -- Create a new text file
 2:
 3:  #include <tscdefs.h>
 4:  #include IOSTREAM_H
 5:  #include <stdio.h>
 6:  #include <stdlib.h>
 7:  #include <string.h>
 8:  #include <form.h>
 9:
10:  // Function prototypes
11:  void error(const char *message);
12:  void instruct(void);
13:
14:  main(int argc, char *argv[])
15:  {
16:    FILE *fp;
17:    char s[129];
18:
19:    if (argc == 1) instruct();
20:    cout << "\nCreating file " << argv[1] << flush;
21:    cout << "\nEnter a blank line to end\n" << endl;
22:    fp = fopen(argv[1], "w");
23:    if (!fp) error("Creating file");
24:    while (strlen(gets(s)) > 0) {
25:      fputs(s, fp);
26:      fputc('\n', fp);
27:    }
28:    fclose(fp);
29:    return 0;
30:  }
31:
```

```
32:   // Display error message and exit
33:   void error(const char *message)
34:   {
35:     char buf[80];
36:     cout << form(buf, "\n\nERROR: %s\n\n", message);
37:     exit(1);
38:   }
39:
40:   // Display instructions and exit
41:   void instruct(void)
42:   {
43:     cout << "\nMAKETXT <filename>";
44:     cout << "\nInstructions: Enter a filename, then type";
45:     cout << "\nlines of text. End with a blank line. Note:";
46:     cout << "\nan existing <filename> will be erased!\n";
47:     exit(1);
48:   }
```

Most of C++'s file-handling functions are declared in the stdio.h header file, which isincluded into MAKETXT at line 5. You'll almost always include this header file in any program that needs to read and write disk files. MAKETXT's main() function uses a struct declaration from stdio.h to create a file-variable pointer fp. Here's the definition:

```
FILE *fp;
```

The uppercase FILE is a struct that stores various details required by DOS and C++ library functions to read and write data in files. Variable fp is declared as a pointer to an object of the FILE data type. You can safely ignore FILE's contents, although you can read the structure's declaration in stdio.h if you want. Most file routines in the C++ library require a pointer to a FILE object created by a library function; therefore, you'll rarely allocate space directly for a FILE variable. (A FILE structure's contents differ greatly among Borland, Microsoft, and Zortech C++ compilers.)

Line 19 checks whether you entered a filename on the DOS command line. If not, function instruct() displays instructions and halts the program. This is a typical design for simple programs that operate on single files.

Line 22 shows how to open a file. The statement calls function fopen(), declared in stdio.h. That function returns a pointer to a new FILE object, and you should always save that pointer, as done here by assigning the result of fopen() to fp. The file pointer gives other routines the means to process the newly opened file.

Function fopen() requires two char * arguments. The first argument represents the file's name. The second is a short command that selects one of several options listed in Table 8.1. The options affect whether and how other routines may read and write information in files. If you specify *reading only* with "r", for example, you can't write data to the file; you can only read information already stored there. If you create a new file with "w", any existing file of the same name will be erased. If you open a file with the append option, "a", new data written to the file will be attached to the end of any information currently stored in the file. Adding a plus sign to these three basic options opens the file for reading *and* writing.

**Table 8.1. Text-file options for fopen.**

| Option | Description |
| --- | --- |
| "r" | Open file for reading only |
| "w" | Create new file for writing only |
| "a" | Append file for writing only |
| "r+" | Open file for reading and writing |
| "w+" | Create new file for reading and writing |
| "a+" | Append file for reading and writing |

When you run MAKETXT two or more times, each session creates a new file on disk, erasing the old file. To have MAKETXT preserve existing text in a file, change the "w" option at line 22 to "a", which instructs fopen() to append new data to information currently in the file. Compile and run the modified MAKETXT, and enter a few new lines. When you examine the appended text file, you'll see that the new text is added to the old. Simply changing the way you open the file affects how other file-handling functions operate.

After opening a file with an append or write option, you can store text in that file by calling two functions: fputs() (file put string) and fputc() (file put character). (See lines 25–26.) Function fputs() writes a string of characters. The first argument to fputs() must be a pointer that addresses the string to be written. The second argument must be a pointer to a FILE struct. Function fputc() is similar to fputs(), but writes a single character to an open file. For both functions, the file must have been opened by fopen() for writing or appending. (By the way, most file-handling functions in stdio.h begin with the letter f to remind you that these routines require a FILE * argument.)

When you press Enter without entering text on a new line, the while loop in MAKETXT at lines 24–27 ends. Immediately thereafter, line 28 calls fclose() to close the file addressed by the fp pointer. Closing the file updates the disk directory and flushes any buffered information to disk.

> **Note:** As I mentioned earlier, when a program ends, any open files are automatically closed. For this reason, line 28 in MAKETXT is not strictly required.

# Formatted Output

Another useful function for writing text to files is fprintf(). The function operates similarly to printf(), supplied with most C and C++ compilers. The fprintf() function is also similar to the form() function that you can use to display formatted text in output-stream statements (see Chapter 10, "Cross-Compilation Tools.")

To use fprintf(), supply a pointer to an open FILE. Next, specify a formatting string containing various escape codes prefaced with a percent sign (%). Each such code represents a value to appear at this position in the output. Finally, supply one variable or constant for each escape code in the formatting string. For example, to write a string to a file, you can use the statement:

```
fprintf(fp, "%s\n", s);
```

That line is functionally equivalent to the two statements at lines 24–25 in MAKETXT. However, the file pointer fp comes first; in fputs() and fputc(), the pointer is last. This inconsistency exists because fprintf() accepts a variable number of arguments—one for each escape code in the formatting string; therefore, fixed parameters like fp must come ahead of those that will vary in number.

# Errors from File Functions

With one exception, MAKETXT ignores the possibility that an error will occur during a file operation. Generally, this omission is a very bad practice, and you should *always* consider what will happen if a problem develops when a program writes data to disk. Reading data from disk files is not as critical, but programs should still include statements to recover gracefully from mishaps that occur during file reads. When it comes to working with disk drives, just about anything that can go wrong probably will sooner or later.

A typical error occurs when you tell `fopen()` to read a file that doesn't exist. Or you might accidentally ask the function to create a file on a nonexistent disk drive. To simulate this kind of error, run MAKETXT and supply the name of a file on a floppy disk that has its drive door open. For example, type **maketxt a:\dummy.dat**. In a few seconds, you'll see the *critical error message*

```
Not ready error reading drive A
Abort, Retry, Fail?
```

Enter **A** to abort the critical error. This will end MAKETXT and return you directly to the DOS prompt. If you press **R**, DOS will retry the failed operation, though this won't always recover from the error, depending on what caused the problem originally. If you enter **F**, DOS returns an error code to the program that started the ball rolling. Recognizing this error, function `fopen()` returns null, causing line 23 to call MAKETXT's `error()` function.

> **Note:** Of all the error messages from DOS, the "Not ready error..." is one of the most confusing. To "Abort" this critical DOS error means to return control immediately to DOS (that is, to COMMAND.COM). To "Retry" means just that—to retry the same *DOS* operation that failed. Retrying does *not* cause your program to repeat the statement that led to the failure. That's what "Fail" does. Unfortunately, some programs silently repeat a failed file statement, causing Retry and Fail to give identical results. Such unfriendly error-handling in programs has led to much confusion about how to respond to critical DOS errors. You can minimize similar confusion with your programs by using good error-handling methods.

Although MAKETXT detects errors from `fopen()`, the program does not test for similar errors from `fputs()` and `fputc()`. In this simple example, that omission probably will do no harm. Since `fopen()` has to succeed before the other two functions are even called, it's unlikely that any errors will occur. Besides, the worst that can happen is a critical DOS error, forcing you to abort back to the DOS prompt.

Of course, finished commercial applications must deal sensibly with file errors. Like `fopen()`, functions such as `fputs()` and `fputc()` also return a value that indicates whether the operation succeeded. Unlike `fopen()`, which returns a `FILE` pointer or null, `fputs()` and `fputc()` return nonnegative `int` values if successful. If an error occurs, these and other `int` file functions in stdio.h return a symbol called `EOF` (for "End of File.") `EOF` is also used to detect when a program has reached the last byte stored in a file.

In place of lines 25–26 in MAKETXT, you can use the following statements to check for any errors that occur while writing data to disk:

```
if (fputs(s, fp) == EOF) error("Writing to file");
if (fputc('\n', fp) == EOF) error("Writing to file");
```

Now, if any errors occur during either of these two function calls, the program will call the `error()` function (see lines 33–38), display a suitable message, and end.

Unfortunately, however, the modified statements probably *won't* have the chance to detect most errors! Why? Because data is buffered somewhere in memory, and a problem such as a disk-full error may go unnoticed until the program closes the file. Therefore, line 28 also needs rewriting. This is better:

```
if (fclose(fp) == EOF) error("Closing file");
```

# Reading Text Files

Writing text to files is, of course, only half the story. The other half is reading text from files stored on disk. There are two ways to proceed: read text files one *character* at a time, or read text files one *line* at a time. As you'll see, there are pluses and minuses to both approaches.

# Reading Text One Character at a Time

Listing 8.2, READTXT.CPP, shows how to read text files one character at a time. Compile the program and enter a command such as **readtxt readtxt.cpp** to read and display the program's own text. Or, enter **readtxt test.txt** to read and display the file you created earlier with MAKETXT.

## Listing 8.2. READTXT.CPP.

```
 1:  // readtxt.cpp -- Read and display a text file a character at a time
 2:
 3:  #include <tscdefs.h>
 4:  #include IOSTREAM_H
 5:  #include <stdio.h>
 6:  #include <stdlib.h>
 7:  #include <form.h>
 8:
 9:  // Function prototypes
10:  void error(const char *message);
11:  void instruct(void);
12:
13:  main(int argc, char *argv[])
14:  {
15:    FILE *fp;
16:    char c;
17:
18:    if (argc == 1) instruct();
19:    fp = fopen(argv[1], "r");
20:    if (!fp) error("Opening file");
21:    while ((c = fgetc(fp)) != EOF)
22:      cout << c;
23:    fclose(fp);
24:    return 0;
25:  }
26:
27:  // Display error message and exit
28:  void error(const char *message)
29:  {
30:    char buf[80];
31:
32:    cout << form(buf, "\n\nERROR: %s\n\n", message);
33:    exit(1);
34:  }
35:
36:  // Display instructions and exit
37:  void instruct(void)
38:  {
39:    cout << "\nREADTXT <filename>";
```

```
40:     cout << "\nInstructions: Enter the name of a text file.";
41:     cout << "\nEnter `READTXT <filename> ¦ more' to display";
42:     cout << "\nlengthy files (requires DOS's MORE.COM to be";
43:     cout << "\nin the current PATH).\n";
44:     exit(1);
45:  }
```

As in MAKETXT, READTXT includes the header file stdio.h. The program also defines a pointer fp to a FILE struct. Whether you are reading or writing files, you include the same stdio.h header and you define FILE pointers in the same way.

Line 19 is also nearly the same as the similar fopen() statement in MAKETXT. This time, however, the "r" option tells the function to open the file for reading. Because the program uses this option, any attempts to write data to the file will be rejected.

The while loop at lines 21–22 shows the correct way to read every character from a file. The expression (c = fgetc(fp)) calls function fgetc(), which reads the next character from the file addressed by FILE pointer fp. The result of fgetc() is assigned to c for displaying characters individually with an output-stream statement at line 22.

If fgetc() attempts to read past the last byte in a file, or if an error occurs during reading, the function returns EOF. When this happens in READTXT, the while loop ends. Immediately thereafter, line 23 calls fclose() to close the file before the program ends. Since the file was opened for reading only, there's no good reason to test whether fclose() succeeded in closing the file as I suggested earlier.

When you run READTXT, you'll notice that the program's output is divided into lines on-screen. This happens because fgetc() reads not only visible ASCII characters, but also any control codes embedded in the text file. As a result, carriage-return and line-feed control characters are passed to cout at line 21 along with visible characters. Because output-stream statements recognize those controls as commands to start new lines, the text displays normally.

# Reading Text One Line at a Time

There are two main disadvantages associated with reading text files one character at a time. For one, many programs will need to process words and symbols in text files, and you'll have to write statements to build strings of single characters in memory. For another, reading files one character at a time causes the program to execute an entire loop for *every* character in a file. Processing a large file one character at a time may cause the program to run slowly.

Reading text a line at a time solves these problems. Because the program reads entire strings, you do not have to write code to construct those strings in memory. Also, the number of loops and functions needed to process an entire file is likely to be drastically reduced, improving performance.

The primary disadvantage of the line-at-a-time approach to text-file handling is the definition of a "line." Most text files have lines no longer than 80 or 132 characters, two popular column widths for many computer terminals and PCs. But there's no guarantee that a file won't have longer lines. Also, some programs mark the ends of *paragraphs* with carriage returns. Processing such files with a program designed to read lines of a fixed maximum length will either fail or chop off words in mid-sentence.

Many times, however, the line-at-a-time approach to text-file reading gives enough of a performance boost to make the disadvantages worth enduring. Listing 8.3, READLN.CPP, shows the result. Compile the program, then run it with a command such as **readln readln.cpp**.

### Listing 8.3. READLN.CPP.

```
 1:  // readln.cpp -- Read and display a text file a line at a time
 2:
 3:  #include <tscdefs.h>
 4:  #include IOSTREAM_H
 5:  #include <stdio.h>
 6:  #include <stdlib.h>
 7:  #include <form.h>
 8:
 9:  // Function prototypes
10:  void error(const char *message);
11:  void instruct(void);
12:
13:  main(int argc, char *argv[])
14:  {
15:    FILE *fp;
16:    char buffer[256];
17:
18:    if (argc == 1) instruct();
```

```
19:    fp = fopen(argv[1], "r");
20:    if (!fp) error("Opening file");
21:    while (fgets(buffer, 255, fp) != NULL)
22:      cout << buffer;
23:    fclose(fp);
24:    return 0;
25:  }
26:
27:  // Display error message and exit
28:  void error(const char *message)
29:  {
30:    char buf[80];
31:
32:    cout << form(buf, "\n\nERROR: %s\n\n", message);
33:    exit(1);
34:  }
35:
36:  // Display instructions and exit
37:  void instruct(void)
38:  {
39:    cout << "\nREADLN <filename>";
40:    cout << "\nInstructions: Enter the name of a text file.";
41:    cout << "\nEnter `READLN <filename> ¦ more' to display";
42:    cout << "\nlengthy files (requires DOS's MORE.COM to be";
43:    cout << "\nin the current PATH).\n";
44:    exit(1);
45:  }
```

There are only a few differences between READTXT and the new READLN. Line 16 in the new listing defines a `buffer` of 256 characters. That should be enough space to handle the lines in most text files.

Lines 19–20 open the file as READTXT does. You don't have to open a text file any differently in order to read its contents a line or a character at a time.

The `while` loop at lines 21–22 calls `fgets()` to read a string of characters from the open file. (The character-by-character READTXT program called `fgetc()` at this place to read a single character.) Function `fgets()` reads text from a file into a location specified by the first argument; in this example, `buffer`. The parameter's type is `char *`, so you can use either a string buffer as defined at line 16, or you can allocate memory and pass a `char` pointer as the argument. The second argument represents the maximum number of bytes you want `fgets()` to read.

READLN's `while` loop ends when `fgets()` returns null, indicating that all text has been read from the file. After that, `fclose()` closes the file.

> **Note:** Always remember that `fgetc()` returns `EOF` to indicate that the last character from a file has been read. Function `fgets()` returns null to indicate the same condition. The compiler will accept expressions that compare `fgetc()` to the `NULL` macro, even though that will not correctly locate a file's end.

# Sorting Text Files

Many text-processing programs combine the methods described in the preceding sections. A typical text-processing program reads text from a file, performs an operation on that text, and writes the result to another file.

Listing 8.4, SORTTXT.CPP, demonstrates these techniques by alphabetically sorting lines in any text file containing up to about 500 lines. SORTTXT illustrates a useful method for storing strings efficiently in memory. The program also fulfills a promise I made back in Chapter 4—to show how a function pointer makes it possible to call custom functions from within precompiled library routines; in this case, a routine named `qsort()`.

**Listing 8.4. SORTTXT.CPP.**

```
 1:  // sorttxt.cpp -- Sort lines in a text file
 2:
 3:  #include <tscdefs.h>
 4:  #include IOSTREAM_H
 5:  #include <stdio.h>
 6:  #include <stdlib.h>
 7:  #include <string.h>
 8:  #include <form.h>
 9:
10:  #define MAXLINES 500
11:
12:  // Function prototypes
```

```
13:   void error(const char *message);
14:   void instruct(void);
15:   void readText(const char *fname);
16:   void sortText(void);
17:   void writeText(const char *fname);
18:
19:   // Global variables
20:   char *strings[MAXLINES];    // Array of pointers to strings
21:   int index;                  // strings[] array index
22:
23:   // Comparison function, called by qsort(). C++ requires
24:   // the linkage directive extern "C" to allow the function to be linked
25:   // and called correctly.
26:   extern "C" int compare(const void *a, const void *b)
27:   {
28:     return strcmp(*(char **)a, *(char **)b);
29:   }
30:
31:   main(int argc, char *argv[])
32:   {
33:     if (argc <= 2)
34:       instruct();
35:     readText(argv[1]);
36:     sortText();
37:     writeText(argv[2]);
38:     return 0;
39:   }
40:
41:   // Display error message and exit
42:   void error(const char *message)
43:   {
44:     char buf[80];
45:
46:     cout << form(buf, "\n\nERROR: %s\n\n", message);
47:     exit(1);
48:   }
49:
```

*continues*

## Listing 8.4. continued

```
50:   // Display instructions and exit
51:   void instruct(void)
52:   {
53:     cout << "\nSORTTXT <infile> <outfile>";
54:     cout << "\nInstructions: Enter the name of a text file";
55:     cout << "\nto sort plus the name of a new file to create.";
56:     cout << "\nThe SORTTXT program will read <infile>, sort its";
57:     cout << "\nlines alphabetically, and write the results to";
58:     cout << "\n<outfile>. File size is limited by available";
59:     cout << "\nfree memory, or to " << MAXLINES << " lines.\n";
60:     cout << "\nThe original file is not changed provided you enter";
61:     cout << "\ndifferent filenames for <infile> and <outfile>.\n";
62:     exit(1);
63:   }
64:
65:   // Read lines from a text file, store the text on the heap, and
66:   // insert the address of each line into the global strings array of char
67:   // pointers.
68:   void readText(const char *fname)
69:   {
70:     FILE *fp;
71:     char buffer[256];
72:
73:     fp = fopen(fname, "r");
74:     if (!fp) error("Opening file");
75:     while ((index < MAXLINES) && (fgets(buffer, 255, fp) != NULL))
76:       if ((strings[index++] = strdup(buffer)) == NULL)
77:         error("Out of memory");
78:     fclose(fp);
79:   }
80:
81:   // Using the global strings array of char pointers, sort the
82:   // strings in memory. Rearranging the char pointers and not the actual
83:   // strings saves time--a LOT of time.
84:
85:   void sortText(void)
86:   {
```

```
87:     cout << "Sorting " << index << " lines\n";
88:     qsort((void *)strings, index, sizeof(strings[0]), compare);
89:   }
90:
91:  // Create a new file and write the sorted text lines to it.
92:  void writeText(const char *fname)
93:  {
94:     int i;
95:     FILE *fp;
96:
97:     fp = fopen(fname, "w");
98:     if (!fp) error("Creating file");
99:     for (i = 0; i < index; i++)
100:       fputs(strings[i], fp);
101:     fclose(fp);
102:  }
```

Line 20 in SORTTXT defines an array of 500 char pointers. Each of these pointers will address one string in memory. This is a convenient data structure for any program that needs to sort a series of strings (see Figure 8.1). By rearranging only the pointers, the strings can be alphabetized without having to move a single character. The pointers are probably shorter than the associated strings; therefore, the program will operate more quickly, because it takes less time to shuffle small pointers than to move long character strings from location to location.

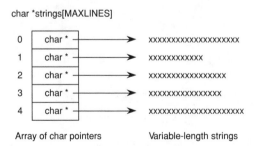

**Figure 8.1.** An array of char pointers (left) addresses a series of variable-length strings (right).

Any program that uses the qsort() library function must implement a function named compare() declared as

```
extern "C" int compare(const void *a, const void *b)
{
  // return result of comparison
}
```

The compare() function must return one of three integer values: −1 if the item addressed by parameter a is less than the item addressed by b; 0 if the two items are identical; or +1 if the first item is greater than the second. The nature of the items being compared, and the method you use to compare them, are entirely up to you. In C++ programs, the function must be prefaced by extern "C", because the qsort() library function is compiled for use in C and C++ modules.

> **Note:** The extern "C" directive in this case disables *name mangling*, the process by which C++ combines function names and their data types. The resulting "mangled" names uniquely identify C++ functions (including class member functions). Name mangling permits common linkers, which have no special C++ capabilities, to join C++ object-code files. Because the qsort() library function is compiled for use with straight C programs (as well as C++), the compare() function's name must not be mangled.

Because the program will rearrange the array of char pointers, but will need to do that by comparing the strings those pointers address, it's necessary to use a type cast inside compare() (see lines 26–29). The program calls the standard library function strcmp() to compare two strings addressed by parameters a and b, each declared as the type const void * (constant typeless pointer). To tell the compiler what type of data those pointers address, the compare() function uses typecast expressions:

```
return strcmp(*(char **)a, *(char **)b);
```

The typecast expression (char **) literally means (pointer to a char pointer). The typecast result is dereferenced by a leading asterisk to address the each char pointer, and thus pass the string addresses to strcmp(). Remember, SORTTXT stores an array of char pointers, and it is those pointers, not the data they address, that are actually sorted. The strings don't move, but are used in the sorting function's comparison. Only the pointers in the array are shuffled, and because pointers take less memory than strings (probably), the results should be faster than sorting the actual character data.

The `main()` function (lines 31–39) calls three other functions: `readText()` to read lines from a text file, `sortText()` to sort those lines alphabetically, and `writeText()` to write the sorted lines to a new file. Run the program by entering a command such as **`sorttxt file.txt new.txt`**. SORTTXT will read and sort lines from FILE.TXT, and then write the sorted text to NEW.TXT.

> **Warning:** SORTTXT does not warn you about overwriting an existing target file, so type your filenames carefully and keep backup copies of your original data.

Function `readText()` (lines 68–79) shows one way to read lines from a text file and store those lines as strings on the heap. The `while` loop at lines 75–77 calls `fgets()` to read one line into a local `buffer` defined as a local variable at line 71. (This is similar to how READLN.CPP read lines from text files.) The `while`-loop's conditional expression also prevents reading more than the number of lines specified by the `MAXLINES` constant.

Line 76 uses the `strdup()` library function to duplicate the characters of each string loaded into `buffer`. If the result of `strdup()` is null, then there wasn't enough memory to hold the new string, and line 77 aborts the program by calling `error()`. If enough memory was available, `strdup()` copies the characters from `buffer` to that space and returns a pointer to the first byte. The assignment saves this pointer in the `strings` array, advancing `index` by one for the next loop.

All of this preparatory work makes `sortText()`'s job easy. Line 87 displays a message telling you how many lines are about to be sorted. Then, the next line calls `qsort()`. Four arguments are passed to `qsort()`:

- `(void *)strings`—the address of the data to be sorted, here the array of `char` pointers, cast to a `void` pointer. (Remember, the pointers will be rearranged, not the strings those pointers address; thus we need to pass the address of the array.)

- `index`—representing the number of items to be sorted.

- `sizeof(strings[0])`—equal to the size of one item. All items to be sorted *must* be of the same size.

- `compare`—the address of the compare function explained earlier.

Note that `compare()` is passed to `qsort()` simply by stating the function's name. Functions have addresses, and therefore you can pass them to other functions that declare function pointers.

After sorting, function `writeText()` at lines 92–102 writes the rearranged strings to disk. The `for` loop at lines 99–100 calls `fputs()` to write each line via the `char` pointers in `strings`.

# Data Files

**T**ext files are only one of the many kinds of files C++ programs can process. Other *data files* are more general in nature. A data file is just a collection of bytes stored on disk. It's completely up to you to decide what those bytes represent.

The following sections describe techniques for reading and writing information in data files. One of the most common uses for these techniques is to process records in a database. You can also use data-file methods for reading and writing binary values. Just about anything you can represent in memory can be stored in a data file.

## Basic Data-File Techniques

Open and close data files similar to the way you perform those operations on text files. First, you'll need a `FILE` pointer defined like the following:

```
FILE *fp;
```

Next, call `fopen()` to open or create a data file. Use the same text-file options listed in Table 8.1, but add the lowercase letter `b` to indicate that the file consists of binary bytes. For example, to open a data file named STUFF.DAT for reading, use these statements:

```
fp = fopen("stuff.dat", "rb");
if (fp == NULL) error("Can't open file");
```

To create a fresh data file and prepare for writing new information to that file, use the option `"wb"`. To append new data onto the end of an existing file, use `"ab"`. To open a data file for reading and writing, use `"rb+"`. Table 8.2 lists the complete set of data-file options available for `fopen`. These are the same options as listed for text files in Table 8.1, but include the letter `b` in the option argument.

**Table 8.2. Data-file options for** `fopen`.

| Option | Description |
|--------|-------------|
| `"rb"` | Open file for reading only |
| `"wb"` | Create new file for writing only |
| `"ab"` | Append file for writing only |
| `"rb+"` | Open file for reading and writing |
| `"wb+"` | Create new file for reading and writing |
| `"ab+"` | Append file for reading and writing |

When done using a data file, always remember to call `fclose(fp)` where `fp` is your `FILE` pointer. As with text files, calling `fclose` updates the file's directory entry and transfers to disk any buffered data temporarily held in memory.

# Reading and Writing Data Files

After opening a data file using one of the options from Table 8.2, you can read and write data using one of three functions. To read bytes from a data file opened for reading, use `fread()`. To write bytes to a disk file opened for writing or appending, use `fwrite()`. To reposition the file to a specific record by number, use `fseek()`. Sample listings in the next several sections show these three functions in action.

# Writing Binary Values to Disk

Data files are useful for storing disk information in binary form. Binary representations often take less space than equivalent ASCII character forms of the same values. For example, the `int` value 12345 occupies two bytes, but the *string* `"12345"` requires six bytes including the null terminator character at the end. Also, because binary data usually takes less disk space than text, binary file I/O tends to be faster than text I/O, although extra time may be required to translate binary information to and from ASCII for display and other purposes.

Listing 8.5, WDATA.CPP, demonstrates how to create a data file and write an array of floating-point values to disk. You can use similar techniques to write other kinds of variables.

## Listing 8.5. WDATA.CPP.

```
1:  // wdata.cpp -- Write data file
2:
3:  #include <tscdefs.h>
4:  #include IOSTREAM_H
5:  #include <stdio.h>
6:  #include <stdlib.h>
7:  #include <time.h>
8:  #include <form.h>
9:
10: #define MAX 100    // Number of values to write
11:
12: void error(const char *s);
13:
14: main()
15: {
16:   double fpArray[MAX];
17:   int i, n;
18:   FILE *fp;
19:   char buf[80];
20:
21:   srand((unsigned)time(NULL));   // Scramble random number generator
22:   cout << "Filling array with values\n";
23:   for (i = 0; i < MAX; i++) {
24:     fpArray[i] = 1.0 / rand();
25:     cout << form(buf, "%16.8f", fpArray[i]);
26:   }
27:   cout << "\nWriting array to TEST.DAT...\n";
28:   fp = fopen("TEST.DAT", "wb");
29:   if (fp == NULL) error("Can't create TEST.DAT");
30:   for (i = 0; i < MAX; i++) {
31:     n = fwrite(&fpArray[i], sizeof(double), 1, fp);
32:     if (n != 1) error("Writing data");
33:   }
34:   fclose(fp);
35:   return 0;
36: }
37:
38: void error(const char *s)
```

```
39:  {
40:    cout << "\nERROR: " << s;
41:    exit(1);
42:  }
```

After the program fills an array fpArray of double elements with random values (see lines 23–26), fopen() at line 28 creates a new file named TEST.DAT. The "wb" option in this statement creates a fresh data file, erasing any existing file named TEST.DAT. Be aware of this side effect. You may want to warn people before they erase existing files.

With the newly created file open, a for loop at lines 30–33 writes individual values from fpArray to disk. Line 31 calls fwrite() to transfer one value from memory to the file. Function fwrite() requires four arguments:

- &fpArray[i]—A pointer to the value stored in memory. Either pass a pointer variable as this argument, or use the & operator to find the address of a variable.

- sizeof(double)—The size in bytes of one element. Using sizeof is optional, but ensures that the program will work correctly if compiled with a different C++ compiler that uses a different number of bytes to represent a data type.

- 1—The number of elements to write to disk.

- fp—A pointer to a FILE struct opened by fopen() for writing or appending.

Function fwrite() returns an int value equal to the number of items transferred successfully to disk. Usually you should use this number to verify that the correct number of elements was written, as the sample listing does at line 28.

I purposely constructed the for loop at lines 30–33 the "long way" to show how to write individual values to disk. Other variations, however, are possible. For example, you can replace the entire loop with a single statement:

```
if (fwrite(fpArray, sizeof(double), MAX, fp) != MAX)
  error("Writing data");
```

Simply altering the arguments passed to fwrite() makes it possible to write all of fpArray to disk with one statement. The first fwrite() argument fpArray addresses the first byte of the data to write. The second argument equals the size in bytes of one element. The third argument specifies the number of elements. And the fourth argument is the ever-present FILE pointer.

Usually the single-statement form is faster than writing individual elements, though the actual speed advantage may be minor for small files. Also, be aware that, due to any errors that might occur, `fwrite()` might write only *some* of the requested number of elements to disk. As written here, the single-statement solution would report a fatal error unless all data was written successfully. This approach might not be the best in all situations, and you may want to recode the single statement to this slightly longer form:

```
n = fwrite(fpArray, sizeof(double), MAX, fp);
if (n == 0) error("Writing data");
cout << "\n" << n << " elements written to disk";
```

**Note:** When writing single multibyte elements to disk with `fwrite()`, the second and third arguments can be reversed. For example, to write a 4-byte `long` value v, you might use the statement `fwrite(&v, sizeof(long), 1, fp)`. Technically, that's the correct form—the second argument specifies the size in bytes of one element, and the third argument states how many of those elements to write. But the following alternate statement has the identical effect: `fwrite(&v, 1, sizeof(long), fp)`. If a `long` value takes four bytes, that statement writes to disk four single-byte elements starting at the address of v. Writing the statement in this alternate way reduces the *granularity* of the output to single-byte transfers; therefore, if an error occurs, the program can report exactly at which byte the problem developed. However, the first form (stating the size of the elements) ensures that only whole elements will be written. Be aware of this subtle difference in `fwrite()` arguments—you'll see the alternate trick often in C and C++ listings.

# Reading Binary Values from Disk

WDATA's counterpart is RDATA.CPP in Listing 8.6. Run the program to read the TEST.DAT file that you created when you ran WDATA.

### Listing 8.6. RDATA.CPP.

```
1:  // rdata.cpp -- Read data file
2:
3:  #include <tscdefs.h>
```

```
 4:  #include IOSTREAM_H
 5:  #include <stdio.h>
 6:  #include <stdlib.h>
 7:  #include <form.h>
 8:
 9:  #define MAX 100    // Number of values to write
10:
11:  void error(const char *s);
12:
13:  main()
14:  {
15:    double fpArray[MAX];
16:    int i, n;
17:    FILE *fp;
18:    char buf[80];
19:
20:    fp = fopen("TEST.DAT", "rb");
21:    if (fp == NULL)
22:      error("Can't open TEST.DAT");
23:    cout << "Reading array from TEST.DAT...\n";
24:    for (i = 0; i < MAX; i++) {
25:      if feof(fp)
26:        error("Unexpected end of file");
27:      n = fread(&fpArray[i], sizeof(double), 1, fp);
28:      if (n != 1)
29:        error("Reading data");
30:    }
31:    fclose(fp);
32:    cout << "\nValues read from disk:\n";
33:    for (i = 0; i < MAX; i++)
34:      cout << form(buf, "%16.8f", fpArray[i]);
35:    return 0;
36:  }
37:
38:  void error(const char *s)
39:  {
40:    cout << "\nERROR: " << s;
41:    exit(1);
42:  }
```

Here again, `fopen()` opens TEST.DAT (see line 20), but this time using the option `"rb"` to specify read-only status. The `for` loop at lines 24–30 reads values stored in the file. Because the file might not have as many values as expected, line 25 calls `feof()` (*eof* stands for end of file). If this function returns true, then the program has reached the end of the file, and no statement should call `fread()` to read any more elements. In this sample, reaching the end of the file too soon is considered to be an error. In another situation, you might simply continue the program with a message that reports how many items were read.

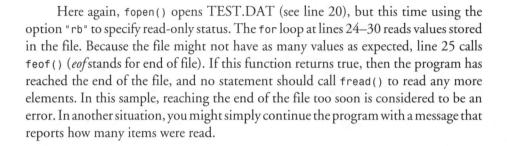

**Note:** To simulate the unexpected-end-of-file error, change MAX in a copy of WDATA (Listing 8.5) to 50. Recompile and run. Then, rerun RDATA. This time, the `feof()` function will return true before 100 values are read, and the program will display an error message and halt.

Line 27 shows how to read a single element from a data file. As with `fwrite()`, the statement requires four arguments. In fact, they are the *same* arguments (see line 31 in WDATA.CPP). Of course, the effect is different. The function stores data in memory at the address represented by the first argument, here `&fpArray[i]`. The second argument specifies the size in bytes of one element. The third argument is the number of those elements to read. The final element is the `FILE` pointer.

Function `fread()` returns an `int` value equal to the number of elements read from disk. Usually, you should compare this value with the number of requested values, as done here at line 28. If the two values do not agree, then something went wrong during the transfer from disk to memory.

As with WDATA, the `for` loop at lines 24–30 is written the long way, showing how to read values from disk one-by-one. You can do away with the loop altogether by telling `fread()` to load all values with a single statement:

```
if (fread(fpArray, sizeof(double), MAX, fp) != MAX)
  error("Reading data");
```

Specifying the address of `fpArray` as the destination for `fread()`, and requesting MAX values, reads the entire array from disk. (If you try this and receive an error message, run WDATA to make sure that there are 100 values stored in TEST.DAT.)

# Creating Database Files

The data-file techniques described in the preceding sections can be used to save and retrieve records in database files. In general, the method is simple. First, design a struct data type containing the fields for your records. Then, read and write struct variables in binary form.

You'll usually want to store your struct declaration in a header file so that other programs can use the same data type. Listing 8.7, sample.h, shows an example of a struct that other programs in this section will use.

### Listing 8.7. sample.h.

```
 1:  // sample.h -- Sample data base header file
 2:
 3:  #include <tscdefs.h>
 4:  #include <stdio.h>
 5:  #include <stdlib.h>
 6:  #include <string.h>
 7:
 8:  #define NAMELEN 30
 9:  #define STATELEN 2
10:
11:  struct rec {
12:     long custnum;              // Customer number
13:     char name[NAMELEN + 1];    // Name in string form
14:     char state[STATELEN + 1];  // State in string form
15:     double balance;            // Account balance
16:  };
```

The members of the struct, and its name, are up to you. In sample.h, the rec struct has four members, custnum, name, state, and balance. Note that the two string members, name and state, are declared as char arrays, not as char * (pointers). There's nothing wrong with pointer members in structs, of course, but when designing records for disk storage, pointers complicate the works. Simple structs like rec exactly match the bytes that will be stored on disk. If the struct had pointer members, however, it would make no sense to store those pointers on disk. Instead, you would have to write statements to read and write the data addressed by those pointers. The extra work involved to allocate space on the heap, assign addresses to pointer members, and read and write data in files may be more trouble than it's worth.

After designing a record as a struct, the next step is to run a program that writes a few records to disk. Listing 8.8, MAKEDB.CPP, outlines the necessary steps.

**Listing 8.8. MAKEDB.CPP.**

```
1:  // makedb.cpp -- Make sample data base
2:
3:  #include <tscdefs.h>
4:  #include IOSTREAM_H
5:  #include IOMANIP_H
6:  #include "sample.h"
7:
8:  // Function prototypes
9:  int getNewRec(rec &oneRec);
10: void error(const char *s);
11:
12: main()
13: {
14:   FILE *fp;
15:   rec oneRec;
16:
17:   cout << "\nCreating or updating sample data base" << flush;
18:   fp = fopen("sample.dat", "ab");
19:   if (!fp)
20:     error("Opening file");
21:   for (;;) {
22:     cout << "\n\nEnter new record. (<Enter> quits)." << endl;
23:     if (!getNewRec(oneRec))
24:       break;
25:     if (fwrite(&oneRec, sizeof(rec), 1, fp) < 1)
26:       error("Writing to file");
27:   }
28:   if (fclose(fp) != 0)
29:     error("Closing file");
30:   cout << "\nFile created or updated" << flush;
31:   return 0;
32: }
33:
34: // Prompt for and let user enter one record. Return false if user
35: // presses Enter for first field. Return true otherwise.
36:
```

```
37:  int getNewRec(rec &oneRec)
38:  {
39:    char buf[129];
40:
41:    memset(&oneRec, 0, sizeof(rec));    // Zero fill record
42:
43:    cout << "\nCustomer #  : " << flush;
44:    gets(buf);
45:    if (strlen(buf) == 0) return FALSE;
46:    oneRec.custnum = atol(buf);
47:
48:    cout << "Name ...... : " << flush;
49:    gets(buf);
50:    strncpy(oneRec.name, buf, NAMELEN);
51:
52:    cout << "State ..... : " << flush;
53:    gets(buf);
54:    strncpy(oneRec.state, buf, STATELEN);
55:
56:    cout << "Balance ... : " << flush;
57:    gets(buf);
58:    oneRec.balance = atof(buf);
59:
60:    return TRUE;
61:  }
62:
63:  void error(const char *s)
64:  {
65:    cout << "\nERROR: " << s << flush;
66:    exit(1);
67:  }
```

To keep the program short, MAKEDB doesn't include all the programming required to make record-entry easy. A more sophisticated database system would allow stepping from field to field, making corrections to fields entered earlier, and other operations. Run MAKEDB and enter a few test records. You can enter any characters for the customer "number"; for example, A10 or 99X. After typing a few sample records, press Enter at the "Customer #" prompt to end.

Line 18 shows a typical way to open a database file, using the "ab" option and fopen() to prepare for appending new records. Line 25 writes a single record to disk with `fwrite()`, similar to the way WDATA wrote floating-point values. In this case, however, the first argument to `fwrite()` is the address of a `rec` variable, `oneRec`. The second argument, `sizeof(rec)`, specifies the size, in bytes, of one record. The third argument tells `fwrite()` to write one of those records to disk. The final argument is, of course, the file pointer `fp`.

## Reading Database Files

For a simple way to process records created by MAKEDB, open the sample database file with `fopen()` and then use `fread()`. Listing 8.9, ALLRECDB, plots the game plan.

### Listing 8.9. ALLRECDB.CPP.

```
 1:  // allrecdb.cpp -- Read all records in sample database
 2:
 3:  #include <tscdefs.h>
 4:  #include IOSTREAM_H
 5:  #include <form.h>
 6:  #include "sample.h"
 7:  #include "stdlib.h"
 8:
 9:  void showRec(rec &oneRec, long recnum);
10:  void error(const char *s);
11:
12:  main()
13:  {
14:    FILE *fp;
15:    rec oneRec;
16:    long recnum = 0L;
17:
18:    fp = fopen("sample.dat", "rb");
19:    if (!fp)
20:      error("Opening file");
21:    while (fread(&oneRec, sizeof(rec), 1, fp) == 1)
22:      showRec(oneRec, recnum++);
23:    fclose(fp);
24:    return 0;
25:  }
26:
27:  void showRec(rec &oneRec, long recnum)
```

```
28:  {
29:    char buf[80];
30:
31:    cout << form(buf, "\n%04ld: %-30s %-2s %+8.2f",
32:      recnum, oneRec.name, oneRec.state, oneRec.balance);
33:  }
34:
35:  void error(const char *s)
36:  {
37:    cout << "\nERROR: " << s;
38:    exit(1);
39:  }
```

After `fopen()` successfully opens SAMPLE.DAT, a `while` loop calls `fread()` to load successive records from disk. Each record is stored into `oneRec`. Function `showRec()` displays the record's contents and record number on a single line.

The number of the first record in a file is always 0. By using that number as an index, another function, `fseek()`, prepares a file for reading or writing a specific record. The `fseek()` function makes it possible to write *random-access database programs*, as Listing 8.10, READDB.CPP, demonstrates.

### Listing 8.10. READDB.CPP.

```
1:  // readdb.cpp -- Read records from sample data base
2:
3:  #include <tscdefs.h>
4:  #include IOSTREAM_H
5:  #include <form.h>
6:  #include "sample.h"
7:
8:  #define FATAL 1        // Pass to error to halt
9:  #define NONFATAL 0     // Pass to error to continue
10:
11: int getRec(FILE *fp, rec &oneRec, long recnum);
12: void showRec(rec &oneRec, long recnum);
13: void error(const char *s, int halt);
14:
```

*continues*

## Listing 8.10. continued

```
15:   main()
16:   {
17:     FILE *fp;
18:     rec oneRec;
19:     long recnum = 0;
20:     char s[80];
21:
22:     fp = fopen("sample.dat", "rb");
23:     if (!fp)
24:       error("Opening file", FATAL);
25:     for (;;) {
26:       cout << "\nEnter record number (-1 to quit): ";
27:       cin >> s;
28:       recnum = atol(s);
29:       if (recnum < 0)
30:         break;
31:       if (getRec(fp, oneRec, recnum))
32:         showRec(oneRec, recnum);
33:       else
34:         error("Reading record", NONFATAL);
35:     }
36:     fclose(fp);
37:     return 0;
38:   }
39:
40:   // Read one record from file fp at specified recnum. Return FALSE if any
41:   // errors are detected; otherwise, return TRUE. If FALSE, then contents
42:   // of oneRec are not defined.
43:
44:   int getRec(FILE *fp, rec &oneRec, long recnum)
45:   {
46:     if (fseek(fp, recnum * sizeof(rec), SEEK_SET) != 0)
47:       return FALSE;
48:     if (fread(&oneRec, sizeof(rec), 1, fp) != 1)
49:       return FALSE;
50:     return TRUE;
51:   }
52:
53:   // Display record number and contents of one record
54:
55:   void showRec(rec &oneRec, long recnum)
```

```
56:  {
57:    char buf[80];
58:    cout << form(buf, "%04ld:%-30s %-2s %+8.2f",
59:      recnum, oneRec.name, oneRec.state, oneRec.balance);
60:  }
61:
62: void error(const char *s, int halt)
63:  {
64:    cout << "\nERROR: " << s;
65:    if (halt)
66:      exit(1);
67:  }
```

The `main()` function in READDB opens the database file, and prompts for record numbers (lines 22–30). Enter the number of a record to view, or enter –1 to quit.

Function `getRec()` shows how to use `fseek()` to find a specific record by its number. Lines 46–47 call `fseek()` in an `if` statement, returning `FALSE` if the specified record number is out of range. (`TRUE` and `FALSE` are defined in tscdefs.h.) Function `fseek()` requires three arguments:

- `fp`—A `FILE` struct pointer returned by `fopen()`.

- `recnum * sizeof(rec)`—A `long` integer offset representing the number of bytes relative to a fixed location where the record is located. Typically, you'll multiply the record number by the size of one record to determine the offset from the beginning of the file to that record.

- `SEEK_SET`—A predeclared constant that tells `fseek()` to treat the offset value in the second argument relative to the beginning of the file. Use `SEEK_CUR` to position the file pointer relative to the *current* position. Use `SEEK_END` to position the file backwards relative to its end.

The `fseek()` function returns 0 if the sought position is available in the file. The function returns an unspecified nonzero value if an error was detected, usually because an argument requested a record not stored in the file.

If you open a file for reading and writing, you can use `fseek()`, `fread()`, and `fwrite()` to find records, display their values, and then write modified values back to disk. Before writing a numbered record this way, always call `fseek()` before `fwrite()`. Doing that positions the file to the correct record to be changed.

# Working with Directories

**W**ell-designed file programs should give people ways to view filenames in disk directories. Amazingly, some commercial programs don't provide even the basic capability to list filenames in the current directory—not to mention changing directories and listing files in other locations. Be kind to your users. Add directory commands to your programs as suggested in the following sections.

> **Note:** Programs that list filenames in directories and perform other related operations are firmly tied to the operating system for which those programs were designed. The directory listings in the following sections require MS-DOS; they are unlikely to run correctly under other operating systems.

## Determining Free Space on Disk

Before storing large amounts of data on disk, it may be a good idea to test how much free space is available. It's frustrating to start a lengthy operation—sorting a large database, for example—only to discover 20 minutes later that the operation has failed due to insufficient disk space.

Finding the amount of free space on a disk is easy. Just call function `dos_getdiskfreespace()`, prototyped in the dos.h header file for Zortech C++, and in dosgfree.h for Borland and Microsoft compilers. Pass an `int` argument representing the drive number to check. 0 represents the current drive. 1 represents drive A:, 2 stands for B:, 3 for C:, 4 for D:, and so on. Listing 8.11, FREE.CPP, shows how to use `dos_getdiskfreespace()`. The program also makes a handy utility to keep around. (I use it to check the amount of free room available on floppy disks before I copy a large number of files from my hard drive to a backup diskette.)

### Listing 8.11. FREE.CPP.

```
1:   // free.cpp -- Report free space on drive
2:
3:   #include <tscdefs.h>
```

```
 4:  #include IOSTREAM_H
 5:  #include <dos.h>
 6:  #include <ctype.h>
 7:  #include <form.h>
 8:
 9:  #if (defined __TSC_BTC__) ¦¦ (defined __TSC_MSC__)
10:  #include <dosgfree.h>
11:  #endif
12:
13:  main(int argc, char *argv[])
14:  {
15:    int drive = 0;
16:    unsigned long freeSpace;
17:    char buf[80];
18:
19:    if (argc > 1)
20:      drive = toupper(*argv[1]) - ('A' - 1);
21:    freeSpace = dos_getdiskfreespace(drive);
22:    if (freeSpace == -1)
23:      cout << "Error reading drive";
24:    else
25:      cout << form(buf, "Free space on drive = %lu", freeSpace);
26:    return 0;
27:  }
```

To run FREE, enter **free** at the DOS prompt plus an optional drive letter. For example, to display the amount of free space on drive A:, enter **free a:**. (The colon is optional—**free a** is just as good.) Lines 19–20 detect the optional drive-letter argument and convert the letter into a value, 1 for A:, 2 for B:, 3 for C:, and so on. That value is assigned to drive, which is initialized to 0, the value that refers to the current drive.

Line 21 passes drive to dos_getdiskfreespace(), which returns the number of bytes available. FREE saves that result in a variable called freeSpace, displayed at line 25. If freeSpace equals –1, then an error occurred (perhaps due to an open drive door).

# Changing the Current Directory

Another simple function, cdir() (change directory) changes the current directory, also called the *working directory*. Adding a change-directory command to your programs makes them much easier to use, especially if the code reads and writes files that users might store in many different subdirectories.

Naturally, from DOS, you may as well use the CD command to change directories. But it's a useful exercise to duplicate that command as a demonstration of how to perform the same operation in a C++ program. Listing 8.12 demonstrates the basic idea. Compile the program, then run it by entering **cdir** and a pathname to change the current directory.

## Listing 8.12. CDIR.CPP.

```
 1:  // cdir.cpp -- Change directories
 2:
 3:  #include <tscdefs.h>
 4:  #include IOSTREAM_H
 5:  #include <stddef.h>
 6:  #include <direct.h>
 7:
 8:  #if (defined __TSC_BTC__) ¦¦ (defined __TSC_MSC__)
 9:  #include <malloc.h>
10:  #elif (defined __TSC_ZTC__)
11:  #include <stdlib.h>  // defines malloc() and free()
12:  #endif
13:
14:  #define MAXLEN 128
15:
16:  main(int argc, char *argv[])
17:  {
18:    char *buf;
19:
20:    if (argc <= 1) {
21:      if ((buf = getcwd(NULL, MAXLEN)) != NULL) {
22:        cout << buf;
23:        free(buf);
24:      }
25:    } else {
26:      if (chdir(argv[1]) != 0)
27:        cout << "Can't change to " << argv[1];
28:    }
29:    return 0;
30:  }
```

For Borland, Microsoft, and Zortech compilers, `cdir()` is prototyped in direct.h (line 6). The program also calls memory allocation routines (`free()` directly; `malloc()` indirectly), and must include prototypes for those functions as well. Unfortunately, Borland and Microsoft declare these functions in malloc.h, while Zortech declares them in stdlib.h. Lines 8–12 included the correct header for each compiler.

CDIR relies on two functions to duplicate DOS's CD command. The first is `getcwd()`, which returns a string equal to the current working directory (hence the *cwd* in the function's name). This is the string that CDIR displays if you run the program with no arguments. Line 21 assigns the address of the current directory string to `buf`, a char pointer defined earlier at line 8. Passing NULL to `getcwd()` instructs the function to allocate memory for a buffer of size MAXLEN. The function does this by calling `malloc()`. Line 23 deletes the buffer by calling `free()`.

Line 26 calls `chdir()`, the function that switches to a new directory specified as an argument. If `chdir()` returns 0, then the function successfully changed directories; otherwise, an error occurred (probably due to a nonexistent pathname), and line 27 displays an error message.

# Displaying a Directory

DOS includes internal subroutines that programs can use to retrieve filenames in directories. Borland, Microsoft, and Zortech C++ compilers provide functions that call these subroutines, but unfortunately, each company handles the process differently.

In this and the next few sections, you'll examine the standard methods for accessing directory information. To accommodate each compiler, sample programs use conditional compilation directives to select the proper syntax. Unfortunately, this approach to writing compatible programs leads to messy results, so after learning the basic techniques, you'll extend the book's class library with classes that any C++ program can use to access filenames and related information in disk directories.

**Note:** I could have added directory functions to the book's cross-compilation tools, but I chose to take a different course here in order to demonstrate how, with classes, you can write portable programs.

In general, to read a directory, programs follow two basic steps. To start the ball rolling, they call call a function named findfirst(), which begins a directory search and recognizes the same wild-card characters * and ? as does the DOS DIR command. After that step, a loop repeatedly calls findnext() to continue searching the directory until no more matching entries are found. (Microsoft programs use functions dos_findfirst() and dos_findnext(), but the idea is the same.)

Listing 8.13, SDIR.CPP, demonstrates how to use these functions to display a simple directory.

## Listing 8.13. SDIR.CPP.

```
 1:  // sdir.cpp -- Show directory
 2:
 3:  #include <tscdefs.h>
 4:  #include IOSTREAM_H
 5:  #include IOMANIP_H
 6:  #include <string.h>
 7:  #include <dos.h>
 8:
 9:  #if (defined __TSC_BTC__)
10:  #include <dir.h>
11:  #endif
12:
13:  main(int argc, char *argv[])
14:  {
15:    char wildCard[13] = "*.*";
16:    if (argc > 1)
17:      strncpy(wildCard, argv[1], 12);
18:
19:  // Zortech C++
20:  #if (defined __TSC_ZTC__)
21:    TSC_FIND *fp;      // Pointer to DOS search-directory info
22:    fp = findfirst(wildCard, FA_DIREC);
23:    while (fp) {
24:      cout << fp->NAME << endl;
25:      fp = findnext();
26:    }
27:
28:  // Borland C++, Turbo C++
29:  #elif (defined __TSC_BTC__)
```

```
30:     TSC_FIND fb;      // DOS search-directory info
31:     int done = findfirst(wildCard, &fb, FA_DIREC);
32:     while (!done) {
33:       cout << fb.NAME << endl;
34:       done = findnext(&fb);
35:     }
36:
37:  // Microsoft C/C++
38:  #elif (defined __TSC_MSC__)
39:     TSC_FIND fb;       // DOS search-directory info
40:     int done = _dos_findfirst(wildCard, FA_DIREC, &fb);
41:     while (!done) {
42:       cout << fb.NAME << endl;
43:       done = _dos_findnext(&fb);
44:     }
45:
46:  #endif
47:
48:     return 0;
49:  }
```

To simplify the code, tscdefs.h defines TSC_FIND as the structure required by directory searches. DOS fills in the members of this structure with filenames, dates, times, sizes, and so on. Header file tscdefs.h also defines symbols such as NAME for accessing these members (all have different names among the Borland, Microsoft, and Zortech compilers).

Even with the help of these symbols, each compiler requires its own method of performing the directory search. Lines 19–26 show the solution for Zortech C++. A pointer fp is defined of type TSC_FIND, after which findfirst() begins the search. The result of the function is a pointer to a TSC_FIND structure (stored internally), or null if no files match the wildCard string argument and the selected attributes (FA_DIREC, meaning directory and filenames).

Line 24 displays matching filenames, accessing the NAME member in the structure addressed by fp. Line 25 continues the search by calling findnext().

Borland C++ and Turbo C++ handle these steps differently. For this compiler, findfirst() returns an int value that indicates whether the search was successful. The TSC_FIND structure, which the program must define, is passed by address to findfirst()'s second parameter. Line 34 continues the search by calling findnext(), which in

Borland's compilers requires a `TSC_FIND` structure and returns an int success-or-fail value.

Finally, there's Microsoft C++. The directory search closely resembles Borland's, but `_dos_findfirst()` and `_dos_findnext()` are the function names. The parameters are the same as in the Borland code, but they are in different positions.

# Decoding Directory Information

A great way to become more familiar with DOS directories is to write a program that duplicates the DIR command's output. Listing 8.14, FSIZE.CPP, does that, with an added twist. The program also totals all listed file sizes, showing you how many bytes the files occupy on disk.

> **Note:** Because DOS stores files in clusters of fixed-size sectors, most files actually occupy more space than their file sizes indicate. Therefore, a set of files may not fit on a disk even though DIR reports that enough space is available.

### Listing 8.14. FSIZE.CPP.

```
 1:  // fsize.cpp -- Show file sizes, dates, times, and total size
 2:
 3:  #include <tscdefs.h>
 4:  #include IOSTREAM_H
 5:  #include IOMANIP_H
 6:  #include <string.h>
 7:  #include <dos.h>
 8:  #include <form.h>
 9:
10:  #if (defined __TSC_BTC__)
11:  #include <dir.h>
12:  #endif
13:
14:  // Function prototypes
15:  void showFileInfo(TSC_FIND *fp);
```

```
16:    void adjustTime(TSC_FIND *fp, char &ampm);
17:
18:    // Date and time bitfield structures
19:    struct dateStruct {
20:      unsigned day : 5;
21:      unsigned month : 4;
22:      unsigned year : 7;
23:    };
24:    typedef dateStruct *dsp;
25:
26:    struct timeStruct {
27:      unsigned seconds : 5;
28:      unsigned minutes : 6;
29:      unsigned hours : 5;
30:    };
31:    typedef timeStruct *tsp;
32:
33:    main(int argc, char *argv[])
34:    {
35:      char wildCard[129] = "*.*";
36:      unsigned long total = 0L;
37:      int count = 0;
38:
39:      if (argc > 1)
40:        strcpy(wildCard, argv[1]);
41:
42:    // Zortech C++
43:    #if (defined __TSC_ZTC__)
44:      TSC_FIND *fp;      // Pointer to DOS search-directory info
45:      fp = findfirst(wildCard, 0);
46:      while (fp) {
47:        showFileInfo(fp);
48:        total += fp->SIZE;
49:        count++;
50:        fp = findnext();
51:      }
52:
53:    // Borland C++, Turbo C++
54:    #elif (defined __TSC_BTC__)
55:      TSC_FIND fb;      // DOS search-directory info
56:      int done = findfirst(wildCard, &fb, 0);
```

*continues*

## Listing 8.14. continued

```
57:     while (!done) {
58:       showFileInfo(&fb);
59:       total += fb.SIZE;
60:       count++;
61:       done = findnext(&fb);
62:     }
63:
64:  // Microsoft C/C++
65:  #elif (defined __TSC_MSC__)
66:     TSC_FIND fb;        // DOS search-directory info
67:     int done = _dos_findfirst(wildCard, 0, &fb);
68:     while (!done) {
69:       showFileInfo(&fb);
70:       total += fb.SIZE;
71:       count++;
72:       done = _dos_findnext(&fb);
73:     }
74:
75:  #endif
76:
77:     if (count == 0)
78:       cout << "no matching files";
79:     else {
80:       cout << setw(21) << dec << total << "  byte(s) in ";
81:       cout << count << " file(s)";
82:     }
83:     return 0;
84:  }
85:
86:  // Display formatted file entry using information addressed by the
87:  // TSC_FIND structure pointer fp.
88:  void showFileInfo(TSC_FIND *fp)
89:  {
90:     static char buf[65];
91:     static char dirStr[] = "<DIR>    ";
92:     char ampm;
93:
94:     adjustTime(fp, ampm);
95:     form(buf, "%-14s%7lu  %2d-%02d-%02d   %2d:%02d%c",
96:       fp->NAME,
```

```
 97:       fp->SIZE,
 98:       dsp(&fp->DATE)->month,
 99:       dsp(&fp->DATE)->day,
100:       dsp(&fp->DATE)->year + 80,
101:       tsp(&fp->TIME)->hours,
102:       tsp(&fp->TIME)->minutes,
103:       ampm);
104:    if ((fp->ATTRIBUTE & FA_DIREC) != 0)
105:      memcpy(buf+13, dirStr, 8);
106:    cout << buf << '\n';
107:  }
108:
109:  // Adjust 24-hour time field in FIND structure addressed by fp
110:  // to 12-hour format. Return AM or PM character in ampm.
111:  void adjustTime(TSC_FIND *fp, char &ampm)
112:  {
113:    unsigned theHour;
114:
115:    theHour = tsp(&fp->TIME)->hours;
116:    if (theHour < 12) {
117:      if (theHour == 0)
118:        theHour = 12;  // Midnight
119:      ampm = 'a';
120:    } else {
121:      if (theHour > 12)
122:        theHour -= 12;
123:      ampm = 'p';
124:    }
125:    ((tsp)&fp->TIME)->hours = theHour;
126:  }
```

Here again, conditional directives are needed to select directory-search statements for each compiler. There are a couple of new elements—line 48, for example, adds fp->SIZE to the accumulated total of file sizes. In general, however, the while loops are similar to those you examined before.

Two bit-mapped structs at lines 19–31 make it easy to decode date and time information in a TSC_FIND structure. Figure 8.2 shows how this structure's date and time information is packed into two 16-bit words. The dateStruct and timeStruct structures in FSIZE help programs easily extract this data.

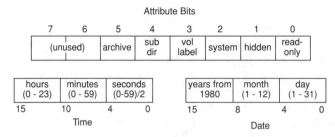

**Figure 8.2.** Various bit fields are packed inside a TSC_FIND structure.

Notice how at lines 24 and 31 typedef is used to declare dsp and tsp as pointer types to their respective structs. This simplifies the type casting that's necessary to access the packed date and time information. For example, see lines 98–102. The statements there dereference the DATE and TIME members in the TSC_FIND structure addressed by fp, and use the & symbol to locate the address of each member.

An example of a similar cast appears at line 115 inside function adjustTime(). The function returns a char equal to 'a' or 'p', representing am or pm. In addition, the function adjusts the hours value in the TSC_FIND TIME member to keep that value within the range 1 to 12. The adjusted value is stored back into the TIME member, again using a cast and pointer dereferences to refer to the hours bit field packed in the TIME value.

Other members such as SIZE, NAME, and ATTRIBUTE are used directly (see lines 48, 96–97, and 104). Line 104 checks whether the directory bit (represented by the constant FA_DIREC) is set in the file's ATTRIBUTE. If so, memcpy() copies the string "<DIR>" plus a few extra blanks to the output buffer, buf. Function showFileInfo() constructs and displays buf with an output statement at line 106.

# Modifying Directory Entries

In addition to being able to read a directory, on occasion, you'll also want to modify some of a directory's information. For instance, after backing up, it's helpful to update all file dates and times. That way, any new or modified files will be easy to spot in a directory listing. Listing 8.15, TOUCH.CPP, shows how to change a directory entry's date and time.

## Listing 8.15. TOUCH.CPP.

```
1:   // touch.cpp -- Update file dates and times
2:
3:   #include <tscdefs.h>
4:   #include IOSTREAM_H
5:   #include <stdlib.h>
6:   #include <time.h>
7:   #include <string.h>
8:   #include <errno.h>
9:   #include <dos.h>
10:
11:  #if (defined __TSC_BTC__)
12:  #include <dir.h>
13:  #include <utime.h>
14:  #elif (defined __TSC_MSC__)
15:  #include <sys\utime.h>
16:  #endif
17:
18:  main(int argc, char *argv[])
19:  {
20:    char wildCard[129] = "*.*";
21:    if (argc > 1)
22:      strcpy(wildCard, argv[1]);
23:
24:  // Zortech C++
25:  #if (defined __TSC_ZTC__)
26:    TSC_FIND *fp;
27:    cout << "\nUpdating " << wildCard;
28:    fp = findfirst(wildCard, 0);
29:    while (fp) {
30:      cout << endl << fp->NAME;
31:      if (utime(fp->NAME, NULL) == -1) {
32:        cout << "\nError setting time for file " << fp->NAME;
33:        cout << "\nERROR #" << errno << ": " << strerror(errno);
34:        exit(errno);
35:      }
36:      cout << " updated";
37:      fp = findnext();
38:    }
```

*continues*

## Listing 8.15. continued

```
39:
40:  // Borland C++, Turbo C++
41:  #elif (defined __TSC_BTC__)
42:    TSC_FIND fb;
43:    cout << "\nUpdating " << wildCard;
44:    int done = findfirst(wildCard, &fb, 0);
45:    while (!done) {
46:      cout << endl << fb.NAME;
47:      if (utime(fb.NAME, NULL) == -1) {
48:        cout << "\nError setting time for file " << fb.NAME;
49:        cout << "\nERROR #" << errno << ": " << strerror(errno);
50:        exit(errno);
51:      }
52:      cout << " updated";
53:      done = findnext(&fb);
54:    }
55:
56:  // Microsoft C/C++
57:  #elif (defined __TSC_MSC__)
58:    TSC_FIND fb;
59:    cout << "\nUpdating " << wildCard;
60:    int done = _dos_findfirst(wildCard, 0, &fb);
61:    while (!done) {
62:      cout << endl << fb.NAME;
63:      if (_utime(fb.NAME, NULL) == -1) {
64:        cout << "\nError setting time for file " << fb.NAME;
65:        cout << "\nERROR #" << errno << ": " << strerror(errno);
66:        exit(errno);
67:      }
68:      cout << " updated";
69:      done = _dos_findnext(&fb);
70:    }
71:
72:  #endif
73:
74:    return 0;
75:  }
```

TOUCH is similar to the previous two programs, SDIR and FSIZE. As before, each compiler has its own section of code for perusing directory information. Lines 31, 47, and 63 call utime() (Microsoft calls it _utime()) to update a file's date and time. If the function returns −1, an error occurred. Otherwise, you can assume that the change took hold.

The utime function requires two arguments. The first is the file's pathname. The second is always NULL. That second argument is for compatibility with operating systems that can associate last-access and last-modified date and time values with files. DOS has no such capability, and for that reason, the second utime() argument must be NULL.

# A Class for Directories

T he preceding examples outline the basic steps for reading and writing directory information from disk. But they also demonstrate serious flaws in the conventional methods. For one, each compiler requires its own programming techniques to access directory information. For another, the programs are likely to work correctly only on PCs running MS-DOS. The same programs may not even compile with other C++ compilers, and they probably won't give meaningful results under other operating systems even if the listings compile. When it comes to disk directories, there are no standards—except, perhaps, to use readable characters for filenames.

For better portability, it makes good sense to relegate system-dependent details in classes. By hiding the specific file-entry details, a class can provide common directory services to programs. Of course, the class's programming will need revisions to work under other operating conditions. But programs that *use* the class will not require similar changes.

In the following sections, you'll develop a class module TSCDIR, which you can use to access directory information. Then, after investigating how TSCDIR's classes work, you'll build a disk-navigator program that uses those classes along with others from the book's class library described in Chapters 6 and 7.

## The tscdir.h Header

Like other classes in this book, the fileItem and directory classes are declared in a separate header file, Listing 8.16, tscdir.h. Make sure to include that file in all programs that use the TSCDIR module's classes. (The file is located in C:\TSC\LIB\SOURCE.)

## Listing 8.16. tscdir.h.

```
 1:   // tscdir.h -- Header for tscdir.cpp
 2:
 3:   #ifndef __TSCDIR_H
 4:   #define __TSCDIR_H         1      // Prevent multiple #includes
 5:
 6:   #include <tscdefs.h>
 7:   #include <dos.h>
 8:   #include <stritem.h>
 9:   #include <selector.h>
10:
11:   #if (defined __TSC_BTC__)
12:   #include <dir.h>
13:   #endif
14:
15:   class fileItem: public strItem {
16:   private:
17:     char ampm;                // AM or PM indicator ('a' or 'p')
18:     char attribute;           // File entry's attribute
19:     unsigned time, date;      // Time and date of last update
20:     unsigned long size;       // Size of file in bytes
21:   public:
22:     fileItem(TSC_FIND *fp);
23:     virtual char *getString(void);
24:   };
25:
26:   class directory: public selector {
27:   public:
28:     directory(winStruct &ws, char *wildCard, int popup = 1);
29:     void resetDirectory(char *wildCard);
30:   };
31:
32:   #endif    // __TSCDIR_H
```

The TSCDIR module uses declarations from the STRITEM and SELECTOR modules listed in Chapter 7, "Building a Class Library—Part 2." Any program that includes tscdir.h gets a copy of stritem.h and selector.h free of charge.

Two classes are declared in tscdir.h. The first is fileItem, which derives from strItem. A directory's file entry is, after all, mostly a string of characters plus other data; therefore, it makes sense to build fileItem using strItem as a base. Lines 17–20 add other data members to the fileItem class for storing details about each directory entry.

Class fileItem has only two member functions. The first is a constructor at line 22, which initializes an object of the fileItem class. To this constructor you must pass a TSC_FIND pointer returned by findfirst() or findnext(). (Or by Microsoft's _dos_findfirst() or _dos_findnext().)

The second member function replaces strItem's getString(). The replacement returns a pointer to a string with all the details for this file entry spelled out. Because getString() is virtual, existing code that calls getString() can display and process directory entries.

The second class in TSCDIR, directory (lines 26–30), uses the virtual getString() to good advantage. The directory class derives from selector, which, as you'll see, is able to call the replacement getString() function without requiring recompilation of the SELECTOR module. The directory class's constructor at line 28 initializes a directory-selection list, reading matching filenames into memory. The second member function, resetDirectory(), changes the current wild-card string and reloads matching filenames. Remember, selector derives from list, and therefore, the mechanisms for storing and retrieving listed files are inherited. There is no need to duplicate those mechanisms in the new class. After all, what is a directory but a list of strings?

## Using the Directory Classes

The next three listings demonstrate how to write, compile and run programs that use the two classes in the TSCDIR module. You'll find these programs in directory C:\TSC\C08 along with other sample programs in this chapter.

The test program, TDIR.CPP, Listing 8.17, demonstrates how to use the fileItem and directory classes in the TSCDIR module. After compiling, run TDIR. You should see a pop-up window listing the current directory's filenames. Select a file by pressing Enter, or press Esc to quit to DOS and not make a selection. The program merely displays the selection you make—it doesn't write any data to disk, so feel free to experiment.

## Listing 8.17. TDIR.CPP.

```
1:  // tdir.cpp -- Test TSCDIR module classes
2:
3:  #include <tscdefs.h>
4:  #include IOSTREAM_H
5:  #include <tscdir.h>
6:  #include <string.h>
7:  #include <conio.h>
8:
9:  void pause(void);
10: void runtest(void);
11:
12: char *selection;
13:
14: main()
15: {
16:   Window::startup();
17:   runtest();
18:   Window::shutDown();
19:   if (selection == NULL)
20:     cout << "\nNo file selected";
21:   else
22:     cout << "\nFile selected: " << selection;
23:   return 0;
24: }
25:
26: // Pause until user presses <Spacebar>
27: void pause(void)
28: {
29:   while (getch() != ' ') ;
30: }
31:
32: // Execute the test. Assign a selected filename string to the
33: // global selection pointer, or if no file is selected, assign NULL.
34:
35: void runtest(void)
36: {
37:   winStruct ws = {
38:     4, 4, 41, 18,  // Row, column, width, height
39:     0x1f,          // Text attribute
```

```
40:        0x70,          // Border attribute
41:        0x70,          // Highlight attribute
42:        1              // Type
43:      };
44:      directory *dir = new directory(ws, "*.*");
45:      strItem *p;
46:      p = dir->getSelection();
47:      if (p) selection = strdup(p->getString());
48:      delete dir;
49:    }
```

If you studied the listings in Chapters 6 and 7, most of TDIR should be familiar. The main() function initializes the Window class and calls a local function runtest(). That function (see lines 35–49) displays the directory window and lets you select a filename.

Notice that nowhere in this program are there any conditional directives for selecting among each compiler's peculiar requirements. These items are tucked away inside the class (which you'll examine later). By using classes, the program hides the messy details, and the same code works identically for all supported compilers.

As with all windows, a winStruct variable at lines 37–43 specifies the position, size, and attributes for the directory window. Line 44 uses new to construct an object of the directory class, and assigns the object's address to dir. To the directory object's constructor, the statement passes a winStruct structure and a wild-card string. The next line defines a pointer to an object of the strItem class for saving the address of a selected item.

Most of the directory action is triggered at line 46. There, function getSelection() is called for the directory class object addressed by dir. This is a good example of polymorphism at work. The getSelection() function was written and compiled in the SELECTOR module. Still, because getString() in fileItem is virtual, the precompiled code in the selector class is able to list directory information and let you choose filenames.

After you press Enter or Esc, the pop-up window closes and getSelection() returns null or, if you selected a directory item, the address of that item. Line 47 tests the value of p, and if it's not null, calls strdup() to create and assign the selected item's string to the global selection pointer.

There's an important lesson to learn from line 47. Because the next line deletes the directory from the heap, the program *must* copy any information that it needs to use later on. It would be a serious mistake to assign getString() directly to the global selection pointer. After deleting dir, the addressed information would no longer be valid, leading to a serious bug.

## The TSCDIR.CPP Module

Now that you've seen how to use the fileItem and directory classes, you'll be able to understand how the class functions work. Listing 8.18, TSCDIR.CPP, implements the classes. (As I have for other large listings, I'll explain the entire listing in segments.)

### Listing 8.18. TSCDIR.CPP.

```
 1:  // tscdir.cpp -- directory class
 2:
 3:  #include "tscdir.h"
 4:  #include IOSTREAM_H
 5:  #include <direct.h>
 6:  #include <dos.h>
 7:  #include <string.h>
 8:  #include <form.h>
 9:
10:  #define BUFLEN 128
11:
12:  // Date and time structures, plus pointer types to those structures.
13:  // The module uses these structures to extract the packed fields in the
14:  // unsigned date and time integer fields passed to a fileItem object
15:  // during its construction.
16:
17:  struct dateStruct {
18:    unsigned day : 5;
19:    unsigned month : 4;
20:    unsigned year : 7;
21:  };
22:  typedef dateStruct *dsp;
23:
24:  struct timeStruct {
25:    unsigned seconds : 5;
```

```
26:    unsigned minutes : 6;
27:    unsigned hours : 5;
28:  };
29:  typedef timeStruct *tsp;
30:
```

The TSCDIR module declares the same dateStruct and timeStruct structures, plus the dsp and tsp pointer types, from FSIZE.CPP in Listing 8.14. The structures could go in the tscdir.h header, but since you don't have to use them with the module's classes, they are probably best hidden inside the module's implementation file. If you need the structs, copy their declarations to another file.

### Listing 8.18. TSCDIR.CPP. (continued)

```
31:  // Constructor for fileItem. Passes the directory filename to the base
32:  // strItem constructor, and initializes its own members. Also adjusts
33:  // the time from 24- to 12-hour format.
34:
35:  fileItem::fileItem(TSC_FIND *fp) : strItem(fp->NAME)
36:  {
37:    unsigned theHour;
38:
39:    attribute = fp->ATTRIBUTE;
40:    time = fp->TIME;
41:    date = fp->DATE;
42:    size = fp->SIZE;
43:    theHour = tsp(&time)->hours;
44:    if (theHour < 12) {
45:      if (theHour == 0)
46:        theHour = 12;  // Midnight
47:      ampm = 'a';
48:    } else {
49:      if (theHour-> 12)
50:        theHour -= 12;
51:      ampm = 'p';
52:    }
53:    ((tsp)&time)->hours = theHour;
54:  }
55:
```

The fileItem class constructor assigns values to private data members. Line 35 passes a directory entry's filename to the base class strItem constructor. This name can be retrieved later with a call to getString(). The other members are simply copied from the TSC_FIND structure addressed by fp. The constructor also adjusts the time's hour value to 12-hour format. Using symbols such as ATTRIBUTE and NAME defined in tscdef.h avoids having to use conditional compilation directives to select different identifiers for various compilers.

As in TDIR, casts and pointer dereferences are used to extract and change directory information packed into bit-field members. See Figure 8.2 for the locations of values packed in date and time.

### Listing 8.18. TSCDIR.CPP. (continued)

```
56:   // Return string stored by object plus the file size, date, and time of
57:   // the most recent update to the file. This function is called by the
58:   // selector class even though the fileItem class is declared after the
59:   // selector module was compiled--a feature made possible by declaring
60:   // the getString function virtual.
61:
62:   char *fileItem::getString(void)
63:   {
64:     static char buf[65];
65:     static char dirStr[] = "<DIR>    ";
66:
67:   // Insert filename, size, date, and time into the static buffer using
68:   // the form function to convert coded information into text. Note the
69:   // call to the base class (strItem) getString function. This
70:   // demonstrates how a derived class can access the base class's public
71:   // members.
72:
73:     form(buf, "%-14s%7lu  %2d-%02d-%02d  %2d:%02d%c",
74:       strItem::getString(),
75:       size,
76:       dsp(&date)->month,
77:       dsp(&date)->day,
78:       dsp(&date)->year + 80,
79:       tsp(&time)->hours,
80:       tsp(&time)->minutes,
81:       ampm);
82:
```

```
83:  // Check if a file is a directory. If so, replace the size of the file
84:  // in the newly created string with "<DIR>".
85:
86:    if ((attribute & FA_DIREC) != 0)
87:      memcpy(buf+13, dirStr, 8);
88:    return buf;
89:  }
90:
```

Function getString() demonstrates a classic use for virtual functions—augmenting existing code with new capabilities. In this case, the basic getString() member function inherited from the strItem class is enhanced to include string representations of the directory information stored in the fileItem class object.

Lines 64–65 define two static variables, buf and dirStr. The getString() function will assemble the directory string in buf, adding the characters from dirStr for subdirectory names. The two variables are declared static because getString() returns a pointer to buf. If buf were local to getString(), returning buf's address would be a serious mistake. Remember, local variables exist only as long as their defining functions are active. After getString() ends, a pointer to a local variable addresses stack space that is available for other functions to use.

The basic buf string is assembled by a call to form() at lines 73–81. Line 74 calls the strItem base class getString() function to obtain a filename. The other members are decoded as in FSIZE.CPP (see Listing 8.14).

## Listing 8.18. TSCDIR.CPP. (continued)

```
 91:  // Constructor for directory. Passes the window struct variable, NULL
 92:  // for the window title (changed later by resetDirectory), and 1 (true)
 93:  // for a pop-up style window to the base class selector constructor.
 94:
 95:  directory::directory(winStruct &ws, char *wildCard, int popup)
 96:    : selector(ws, NULL, popup)
 97:  {
 98:    resetDirectory(wildCard);
 99:  }
100:
101:  // Dispose any current list of directory items, then read the current
```

*continues*

## Listing 8.18. continued

```
102:  // directory into the list. Set the window's title to the current
103:  // working directory (cwd).
104:
105:  void directory::resetDirectory(char *wildCard)
106:  {
107:    char *buf;    // Current working directory string
108:
109:  // Read directory into a list of fileItems
110:
111:    hideWindow();
112:    disposeList();
113:
114: #if (defined __TSC_ZTC__)
115:    TSC_FIND *fp;    // Pointer to DOS search-directory info
116:    fp = findfirst(wildCard, FA_NORMAL | FA_DIREC);
117:    while (fp) {
118:      insertItem(new fileItem(fp));
119:      fp = findnext();
120:    }
121: #elif (defined __TSC_BTC__)
122:    TSC_FIND fb;    // DOS search-directory info
123:    int done = findfirst(wildCard, &fb, FA_NORMAL | FA_DIREC);
124:    while (!done) {
125:      insertItem(new fileItem(&fb));
126:      done = findnext(&fb);
127:    }
128: #elif (defined __TSC_MSC__)
129:    TSC_FIND fb;    // DOS search-directory info
130:    int done = _dos_findfirst(wildCard, FA_NORMAL | FA_DIREC, &fb);
131:    while (!done) {
132:      insertItem(new fileItem(&fb));
133:      done = _dos_findnext(&fb);
134:    }
135: #endif
136:
137:  // Set window title to current directory
138:
139:    if ((buf = getcwd(NULL, BUFLEN)) != NULL) {
```

```
140:      setTitle(buf);
141:      free(buf);
142:    }
143:  }
```

The rest of the TSCDIR module implements the constructor and resetDirectory() member function in the directory class. The constructor at lines 95–99 simply passes the ws and popup members to the selector base class constructor. The NULL value for the second argument tells the selector not to assign a title string to the window. After constructing this much of the base-class portion of the directory object, the constructor calls resetDirectory() with the current wildCard argument. This statement (line 98) performs all of the work of loading directory information into memory.

Here is where the code gets messy again. As in earlier examples such as SDIR.CPP, conditional compilation directives select sections for Borland, Microsoft, and Zortech compilers (lines 114–135). Fortunately, these unattractive sections are now buried deeply inside the directory class. With any luck, we never have to look at them again!

Notice how the inherited insertItem() member function (lines 118, 125, and 132) is used to insert new fileItem class objects into the selection list. The program trusts the list class to collect the directory entries, so there's no need to spend mental energy figuring out how to store those entries in memory. Programming with classes tends to lead to similar situations. You've already invested time and effort in constructing or learning about various classes. Don't rewrite those classes. *Reuse them.*

# Directory Navigator

The directory class makes a useful addition to any program that needs basic directory services. The next three listings demonstrate how to incorporate directory into a finished product; in this case, a directory navigator nicknamed NAV.

After compiling, run NAV and select a directory name. The program will switch to that directory. Select the double-dot entry, if listed, to move up one level in the directory hierarchy. Selecting filenames has no effect.

## Listing 8.19. NAV.CPP.

```
1:  // nav.cpp -- Directory navigator
2:
3:  #include <tscdefs.h>
4:  #include IOSTREAM_H
5:  #include <tscdir.h>
6:  #include <string.h>
7:
8:  #if (defined __TSC_MSC__) || (defined __TSC_ZTC__)
9:  #include <direct.h>  // defines chdir()
10: #endif
11:
12: void navigate(void);
13:
14: main()
15: {
16:   Window::startup();
17:   navigate();
18:   Window::shutDown();
19:   return 0;
20: }
21:
22: void navigate(void)
23: {
24:   winStruct ws = {
25:     4, 4, 41, 18,   // row, column, width, height
26:     0x0f,           // text attribute
27:     0x70,           // border attribute
28:     0x70,           // highlight attribute
29:     1               // type
30:   };
31:   directory *dir;  // Directory object
32:   strItem *p;      // Pointer to strItem returned by getSelection
33:   char buf[13];    // Filename returned by getString
34:   char *t;         // Temporary pointer to char
35:
36: // Read directory. Then, while user makes a selection, change to that
37: // new directory. Ignore any errors (user may select a file instead of a
38: // directory). The 'if' statement truncates the directory name returned
39: // by getString at the first blank (if any).
40:
```

```
41:    dir = new directory(ws, "*.*");
42:    while ((p = dir->getSelection()) != NULL) {
43:      strncpy(buf, p->getString(), 12);
44:      if ((t = strchr(buf, ' ')) != NULL) *t = 0;
45:      chdir(buf);
46:      dir->resetDirectory("*.*");
47:    }
48:    delete dir;
49: }
```

For such a complex program, NAV's source code is relatively simple—a good sign that the classes used by NAV are doing their jobs. Most of the listing should be familiar. The only new business appears at lines 41–47. After the program creates a new directory object (addressed by dir), a while loop calls getSelection() to display the pop-up directory window and let you select a directory name. The call to strncpy() at line 43 copies the selected string to a local buf character array. Line 44 inserts 0 at the location of the first blank space after the filename. That's necessary because chdir(), called at line 45 to switch to a new directory, chokes when fed blanks. After the change, line 46 calls resetDirectory() to load the file entries from the new location.

# READ: An OOP Text-File Reader

The final listing in this chapter combines features from the book's class library described in Chapters 6 and 7 with the TSCDIR module. The result is the READ.EXE program that you probably used to browse the README file on the accompanying diskette. You can also use READ to browse any text file up to 500 lines long. (As a project, you might want to consider removing this limitation.) The listings in the following sections describe how to compile and use READ.

## Compiling and Using READ

After compiling, run READ by typing the program's name at the DOS prompt. You should see a directory window in the middle of the display. Select a file to read and press Enter, or press Esc to quit. You can also select a directory name, and READ will switch to that directory so you can read text files there.

While reading a file, use the cursor, Page Up, and Page Down keys to browse. Press Esc or Enter to return to the directory window.

Another way to start READ is to specify a wild-card argument. For example, enter **read \*.cpp** to list all the .CPP files in the current directory. You can then select and read one or more of the listed files. When using READ this way, you can't change directories (unless, that is, a directory name matches the wild-card argument).

Lastly, you can read an individual file by entering its name. For example, type **read readme** to read a README text file in the current directory. When you specify an individual filename, READ bypasses its directory display and shows you the file's contents. Press Esc or Enter to return to DOS.

# The READ.CPP Program

You may be surprised by the small size of READ.CPP's source code in Listing 8.20. Even counting blanks, it's only 100 lines long. You should *not* be surprised to discover that READ's streamlined appearance is due to the use of classes for just about every significant operation. Naturally, to display a directory of filenames, READ uses the directory class from the TSCDIR module you examined earlier in this chapter. But the program also uses the selector object from Chapter 7 to list the text file's contents! After all, the selector class already knows how to scroll lines of text. Since those operations are just what READ needs to display text files, using the selector class in this new way eliminates the need to duplicate code that's already written and tested.

**Listing 8.20. READ.CPP.**

```
 1:   // read.cpp -- Text file lister
 2:
 3:   #include <tscdefs.h>
 4:   #include IOSTREAM_H
 5:   #include <tscdir.h>
 6:   #include <stdio.h>
 7:   #include <direct.h>
 8:   #include <string.h>
 9:
10:   // Function prototypes
11:
12:   void listFiles(char *wildCard);
```

```
13:   int listOneFile(char *fname);
14:
15:   // The main program calls listFiles with a wild-card argument such as
16:   // *.cpp or ??.bak. Or, if only a single file is listed, it calls
17:   // listOneFile, bypassing the directory display. If no arguments are
18:   // entered on the command line, the program calls listFiles with the
19:   // default *.* wild-card string.
20:
21:   main(int argc, char *argv[])
22:   {
23:     Window::startup();
24:     if (argc == 2)
25:       if ( (strchr(argv[1], '*') != NULL) ||
26:            (strchr(argv[1], '?') != NULL) )
27:         listFiles(argv[1]);
28:       else
29:         listOneFile(argv[1]);
30:     else
31:       listFiles("*.*");
32:     Window::shutDown();
33:     return 0;
34:   }
35:
```

READ's main() function initializes the Window class in the usual way, and then calls listFiles() or listOneFile() depending on whether you enter a wild-card character. The program calls strchr() to search the argument string for one of those symbols. If you enter no arguments, line 31 passes the default wild-card string "*.*" to listFiles()..

## Listing 8.20. READ.CPP. (continued)

```
36:   void listFiles(char *wildCard)
37:   {
38:     winStruct dwin = {  // Directory window
39:       3, 19, 41, 18,    // row, column, width, height
40:       0x1f,             // text attribute
41:       0x70,             // border attribute
```

*continues*

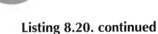

**Listing 8.20. continued**

```
42:       0x70,              // highlight attribute
43:       0                  // type
44:     };
45:     winStruct mwin = {   // Main window
46:       0, 0, 80, 24,      // row, column, width, height
47:       0x4f,              // text attribute
48:       0x0f,              // border attribute
49:       0x70,              // highlight attribute
50:       3                  // type
51:     };
52:     directory *dir;      // Directory window object
53:     Window *mainWin;     // Main display window
54:     strItem *p;          // Ptr to strItem returned by getSelection
55:     char buf[13];        // Filename returned by getString
56:     char *t;             // Temporary pointer to char
57:
58:     buf[12] = 0;         // Make sure strings are terminated
59:     mainWin = new Window(mwin,
60:       " File Lister from \"Tom Swan's C++ Primer\" ");
61:     mainWin->showWindow();
62:     dir = new directory(dwin, wildCard, 0);  // 0 == no popup
63:     while ((p = dir->getSelection()) != NULL) {
64:       strncpy(buf, p->getString(), 12);
65:       if ((t = strchr(buf, ' ')) != NULL) *t = 0;
66:       if (!listOneFile(buf)) {
67:         chdir(buf);
68:         dir->resetDirectory(wildCard);
69:       }
70:     }
71:     delete dir;
72:     delete mainWin;
73:   }
74:
```

Function `listFiles()` operates much like NAV (see Listing 8.19). Two windows are used to cover the entire screen and display a title at the top. A `while` loop at lines 63–70 calls `getSelection()` to display the current directory, from which you can select a file to list. If you do that, the next lines copy the filename to `buf`, fix up the end of the string (see line 65), and call `listOneFile()`. If that function returns false, lines 67–68 assume that you selected a directory name. In that event, chdir() switches to that directory, and resetDirectory() loads and displays the filenames from the new location.

## Listing 8.20. READ.CPP. (continued)

```
 75:  int listOneFile(char *fname)
 76:  {
 77:    winStruct ws = {
 78:      0, 0, 80, 24,   // row, column, width, height
 79:      0x1f,           // text attribute
 80:      0x70,           // border attribute
 81:      0x70,           // highlight attribute
 82:      3               // type
 83:    };
 84:    FILE *fp;
 85:    char buffer[256];
 86:    selector *listWindow = new selector(ws, fname, 1);
 87:    int n;
 88:
 89:    fp = fopen(fname, "r");
 90:    if (!fp) return FALSE;
 91:    while (fgets(buffer, 255, fp) != NULL) {
 92:      n = strlen(buffer);
 93:      if (n > 0) buffer[n - 1] = 0;   // Kill newline at end
 94:      listWindow->insertItem(new strItem(buffer));
 95:    }
 96:    fclose(fp);
 97:    listWindow->getSelection();
 98:    delete listWindow;
 99:    return TRUE;
100:  }
```

Function listOneFile() handles the display of a text file's contents. Line 86 prepares a selector object in which the file's lines will appear. Then, lines 89–96 execute standard text-file commands to read the strings in the file. Lines 92–93 delete the new-line character appended to the end of each string. After that, for each string, insertItem() inserts new strItem objects (one per string) into the selector list addressed by listWindow.

The `selector` class completely handles the display of lines in the text file. Line 97 simply calls `getSelection()` to let you browse through the list of strings. When you are done, a single call to `delete` at line 98 erases the text from memory, along with the `selector` object. All data is properly disposed of because the classes have any necessary destructors to clean up after themselves. The program ignores `getSelection()`'s result; therefore, pressing Enter or Esc ends the function.

Finding new uses for old classes like `selector` is one of the hallmarks of OOP. In this and preceding chapters, you have used the `selector` class to build simple selection lists, to write menu-driven programs, to display filenames in a directory, and now, to list the contents of text files. What a remarkable array of jobs for a single class! But that's exactly what OOP is supposed to do—make reusing existing code as easy as bending a few classes to suit the job at hand.

Of course, every programmer eventually runs into at least one job that needs special handling. Not every programming problem can be solved neatly with the conventional and class techniques described in this and the preceding chapters. In the next chapter, you'll learn several advanced C++ tools that fall into the special-use category—tools that come in handy for those rare moments when standard approaches fail. You may not need these tools often, but when you do, you'll be glad you took the time at least to learn of their existence. Before continuing, however, make sure that you understand the concepts discussed in previous chapters, especially Chapters 6, 7, and 8.

# Questions and Exercises

8.1. Write a program that converts text in files to all uppercase letters.

8.2. On PCs, new lines are represented by carriage return and line feed control codes. On UNIX systems, new lines are represented by line feeds alone. Write two programs that convert text files in each format to the other.

8.3. What are the main advantages and disadvantages of reading text files a character or a line at a time?

8.4. Write a program that can display text files containing embedded tab characters.

8.5. Store help text in a file and read that text into WINTOOL's `helpCommand::performCommand()` function from Chapter 6 (Listing 6.3, lines 114–132).

8.6. Give the commands needed to read and write an array named `fparray` that contains 100 `double` values.

8.7. Listing 8.10, READDB.CPP, lets you enter a record number to view that record's information. Using that program as a guide, write a new program that lets you modify records by number.

8.8. Write a program that prompts for a customer number and searches SAMPLE.DAT (created by MAKEDB.CPP, Listing 8.8) for a record with a matching customer number member.

8.9. Write a program that displays only the subdirectory names in the current directory.

# Advancing Your C++ Knowledge

I n a famous study of chess masters, researchers were handed a surprise. During play, masters and lesser players were asked to explain how they selected their next moves. To everyone's amazement, the results of the study showed that players of all levels examined about the same number of possibilities. From that evidence, researchers distilled what can only be classed as a pristine example of restating the obvious: master chess players, they said, become masters because they invariably select better moves.

There's more wisdom in that conclusion than you might suppose. The message is simple. You can memorize openings, closings, and situations until you turn blue. You can study past games, positions, and responses until the cows come home. But you'll become a better chess player only when you learn to apply your knowledge skillfully.

The same observation holds true for master programmers. The whiz kids in the programming shops don't necessarily know more about programming languages than their less capable colleagues; expert programmers are somehow able to *apply* in more creative ways the same commands that anyone can easily learn. How do expert programmers become experts? Perhaps those same researchers would say *"They select better programming commands."*

Developing that level of skill will take time, patience, and lots of practice. The previous eight chapters provide the raw material. The next step is yours. Write programs. Then write more programs. Use C++ to solve problems. Choose a game plan and implement your strategies. You'll fail plenty of times, but you'll also gain valuable experience from spending long hours at the computer terminal.

Along with that experience, you'll pick up numerous tidbits such as those in this chapter, which brings the C++ story to a close. (The next chapter describes my cross-compilation tools for Borland, Microsoft, and Zortech C++ compilers.) In the following sections, you'll learn how to use friends, how to customize C++'s memory management routines new and delete, how to overload functions and operators, and how to use other advanced C++ techniques. You won't use these special tools often, but when the need arises—when the King is in check—look here for hints. You may find just the method that will turn a losing situation to your advantage.

# Good Friends and Neighbors

One of the main reasons for using OOP techniques is to isolate data inside classes. By doing that, only member functions can access critical values. Most of the time, hiding data in classes gives programs a good measure of control by preventing processes from modifying critical values indiscriminately.

You've seen many examples of the *data-hiding* concept in previous listings. For example, the Window class described in Chapter 7, "Building a Class Library—Part 2," hides many of the values that store a window's position, title, and text saved from "behind" a covered area. Other Window data members are protected, providing access to those fields from derived classes, but not from the main program. Because Window isolates its design details inside the class declaration, if you need to modify any of the class's private members, you can do so without concern that you'll affect any statements outside the class.

Like many rules in life and programming, however, those of data hiding are made to be broken. In C++, you can break the rules for hiding data by using *friends*. Declaring a friend of a class is like giving a pal a copy of your house key. If you go away for the weekend, you shouldn't be surprised on returning to discover your buddy asleep on the couch and the 'fridge seriously depleted.

C++ classes can declare two kinds of friends. An entire class may be a friend of another class. Or, a single function may be declared a friend. The following sections describe both kinds.

**Note:** If friends have a counterpart in C++, it's the goto statement. Like goto, a friend lets you break the very rules of C++ that help you to write reliable programs. You should learn about friends, if for no other reason because the technique is available, and you'll undoubtedly see friends used in published listings. But don't take the following sections as an endorsement of friends. Top C++ programmers *avoid* using friends unless absolutely necessary.

# Friend Classes

A class may declare another class as a friend. By doing that, the first class (the one doing the declaring) gives another class (the friend) permission to access all of the first class's private and protected members. Public members are, of course, always accessible, so they don't enter into the discussion. Any statement, including those in friend classes, may always access the public members in class objects.

Typically, friend classes are used when two unrelated classes require access to one of the class's private or protected members. A simple example explains the process. Suppose you declare a class like this:

```
class AClass {
private:
  float value;
public:
  AClass() { value = 3.14159; }
};
```

Class AClass contains a single private member, value, of type float. To that member, the class constructor assigns the value 3.14159. Except for that action, the class provides no means to change or even to inspect value.

Next, suppose you declare another class that stores an object of AClass in a member member:

```
class BClass {
private:
  AClass A;
public:
  void showValue(void)
```

```
  { cout << A.value; }    // ???
};
```

Member A of type AClass is private to BClass. In addition to that member, function showValue displays A's value. However, the declaration won't compile because value is private to AClass; therefore, *only* member functions in AClass may access value. Functions in BClass are prevented from using value directly as the inline statement here attempts to do.

Changing the status of value to protected would not solve the problem. A protected member is available to its declaring class and to any derived class. AClass and BClass are unrelated, and for that reason, the two classes have no special access to each other's private and protected members. You could change the status of value to public, but doing so would then make value available to *any* statement, an unhealthful remedy.

A better solution is to declare BClass to be a friend of AClass. Objects of BClass then can access value, but other statements outside the two classes are still prevented entry to AClass's private section. To make this change, use the friend keyword inside the class to which the *other* class needs access. In this example, BClass needs to access the private value member inside AClass. So to give BClass permission to use that private data, AClass can declare BClass to be a friend. Here's the new AClass declaration:

```
class AClass {
  friend class BClass;
private:
  float value;
public:
  AClass() { value = 3.14159; }
};
```

The only difference from before is the line friend class BClass. This tells the compiler that BClass should be granted access to AClass's private and protected members. Other statements in other classes and in the main program still can't use AClass's private and protected items; only BClass is given a backstage pass to AClass's private rooms. You may declare any number of classes to be friends this way. The only restriction is that the friend keyword must appear inside a class declaration. A few other facts are worth remembering:

- A class must name all of its friends in advance.

- The class that contains the private and protected data is the one that declares another class to be a friend, thus giving that friend special access to the declaring class's normally hidden members. A class can never declare *itself* to be a friend of another class.

- The friend class may be declared before or after the class that declares the friend. The order of the declarations is unimportant.

- Derived classes of the friend do *not* inherit special access to the original class's private and protected members. Only the specifically named friend has those permissions.

- A derived class may be a friend of its base class, although in such cases, using protected members in the base will accomplish the same goal of giving the friend access to hidden members in the base.

A second example, Listing 9.1, FRIEND.CPP, demonstrates how friends can be used to access private data in class objects that are stored in another class or created as variables.

### Listing 9.1. FRIEND.CPP.

```
 1: // friend.cpp -- Demonstrate friends
 2:
 3: #include <tscdefs.h>
 4: #include IOSTREAM_H
 5:
 6: class pal {
 7: private:
 8:    friend class buddy;      // buddy is a friend of pal
 9:    int x;
10: protected:
11:    void doublex(void) { x *= x; }
12: public:
13:    pal() { x = 100; }
14:    pal(int n) { x = n; }
15: };
16:
17: class buddy {
18: private:
19:    pal palInstance;
20: public:
```

*continues*

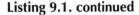
**Listing 9.1. continued**

```
21:     void showValues(void);
22:  };
23:
24:  main()
25:  {
26:    buddy abuddy;
27:
28:    abuddy.showValues();
29:    return 0;
30:  }
31:
32:  void buddy::showValues(void)
33:  {
34:    pal apal(1234);
35:
36:    cout << "\nBefore, palInstance.x == " << palInstance.x;
37:    palInstance.doublex();
38:    cout << "\nAfter, palInstance.x  == " << palInstance.x;
39:    cout << "\napal.x == " << apal.x << endl;
40:  }
```

FRIEND begins by declaring a class named pal. Line 8 states that a second class buddy is a friend of pal. Because of this line, statements in buddy's member functions may access the private and protected members in pal. However, pal may *not* access any private or protected items in buddy.

At line 19, the buddy class declares an object of type pal. As you can see when you run the code, even though buddy is unrelated to pal, the function showValues can directly access pal's private member x. The function also can call the protected member function doublex.

Those actions are demonstrated in the showValues() member function at lines 32–40. Because buddy is a friend of pal, statements may directly refer to private and protected members and functions in palInstance. Similarly, line 39 shows that inside a buddy function, a statement may refer to a local variable's private data. Normally, the compiler would reject the expression apal.x because x is private to the pal class. No error occurs because buddy is a friend of pal and therefore, statements inside any of buddy's function may use the normally hidden members.

Keep in mind that outside of buddy, nothing has changed about the status of pal's private and protected members. To demonstrate that fact, declare a variable of type pal in main and try to access the private x member. For example, you might revise main to this:

```
main()
{
  buddy abuddy;
  pal mypal(4321);
  abuddy.showValues();
  cout << mypal.x;     // ???
}
```

Compiling now gives a syntax-error message similar to *Member 'x' of class 'pal' is private*. Class pal declares buddy as a friend; therefore, buddy may access pal's private and protected members. However, statements outside of pal and buddy, either in the main program or in another class, still may not access pal's hidden members.

# Mutual Friend Classes

Two classes may declare each other as friends. Doing that gives each class access to the other's private and protected members. Of course, this also destroys the barriers that prohibit unrestricted access to hidden members. If you discover that you often need to make classes friends of each other, you probably need to redesign your program. Most classes are better off as strangers to one another.

Use a similar format as in the preceding examples to declare two classes to be friends of each other. Each class lists the other as a friend, giving both classes access to each other's private and protected members. For AClass and BClass to be friends of each other, their declarations could be written this way:

```
class AClass {
  friend class BClass;
  // ... other members
};

class BClass {
  friend class AClass;
  // ... other members;
};
```

Any member functions in either class may now access private and protected data in an object of the other class. Typical uses for this design include array classes to which a member function in another class needs direct access. Another example is a list class that gives other classes direct access to its pointer members.

If the first class refers to the second class by name—in a member function parameter, for example—you may declare the second class in a *forward class declaration*. The declaration tells the compiler the name of a class that you'll fill in later. To declare BClass forward, insert this line ahead of AClass.

```
class BClass;
```

The compiler then allows you to create member members and function parameters of type BClass although that class has not yet been formally declared.

# Friend Functions Part 1

A friend function is similar to but less onerous than a friend class. A friend function is given access to a class's private and protected members. If that function is a member of another class, as it usually will be, only that function and not any other members of the class have permission to access the declaring class's private members.

By declaring a specific function as a friend to two classes, you give that function access to private and protected members in objects of *both* class data types. The friend function may be a global C++ function or a member of another class. In a typical design, the friend function declares parameters of the two classes to which the function owes its friendship. Inside the friend function, statements can then access normally hidden members in the parameters passed as arguments to the function.

Listing 9.2, FRIENDFN.CPP, demonstrates how to declare and use this kind of typical friend function.

### Listing 9.2. FRIENDFN.CPP.

```
1:  // friendfn.cpp -- Demonstrate global friend functions
2:
3:  #include <tscdefs.h>
4:  #include IOSTREAM_H
5:
6:  class two;
7:
8:  class one {
```

```
 9:  private:
10:    friend void show(one &c1, two &c2);
11:    char *s1;
12:  public:
13:    one() { s1 = "Testing "; }
14:  };
15:
16:  class two {
17:  private:
18:    friend void show(one &c1, two &c2);
19:    char *s2;
20:  public:
21:    two() { s2 = "one, two, three"; }
22:  };
23:
24:  main()
25:  {
26:    one c1;
27:    two c2;
28:
29:    show(c1, c2);
30:    return 0;
31:  }
32:
33:  void show(one &c1, two &c2)
34:  {
35:    cout << c1.s1 << c2.s2 << '\n';
36:  }
```

FRIENDFN declares two classes one and two. Because both of those classes refer to the other, and because C++ requires you to declare identifiers before using them, line 6 declares class two forward of one. Declaring a class forward tells the compiler to allow references to the class name before the class is formally declared.

Lines 10 and 18 list the prototype for a friend function named show(). Because each class declares show() to be a friend, statements in show() are granted access to the private and protected members in classes one and two. (The classes have no protected sections, but if they did, the friend declaration would allow access to those members.)

Function show()'s declarations list reference parameters c1 and c2 of the two class types. Because show() is a friend of those two classes, statements inside show() can access private and protected members in arguments passed to show(). The reason for the forward declaration at line 6 should now be clear. Line 10 needs to declare a parameter of class two, which is declared later in the file. The forward reference allows the reference to the as yet undeclared two class.

The implementation for function show() appears at lines 33–36. In this simple example, the code merely displays the value of the string pointers s1 and s2. Because show() is a friend of the two classes, it may directly refer to the s1 and s2 members, which are hidden in their respective classes. Other less friendly functions would not be allowed similar access to those members.

It's important to realize that show() is a common C++ function. The program can therefore call show() in the usual way, as shown here at line 28. Because show() is a common function and not a member of a class, it does not have a this pointer, and it is not called in conjunction with a variable of the class type. The next section explains how to create similar friend functions as class members.

## Friend Functions Part 2

A friend function does not have to be a common C++ function as demonstrated in the preceding section. Friend functions can also be members of a class. In a typical case, one class will declare a function in another class as a friend. The friend function will then have access to the original class's private and protected members.

Listing 9.3, FRIENDMF.CPP (the MF stands for Member Function), outlines the basic strategy of friend member functions. The program is similar to FRIENDFN in the previous section. Comparing the two programs reveals several key differences between global friend functions and those that are members of a class.

### Listing 9.3. FRIENDMF.CPP.

```
1:  // friendmf.cpp -- Demonstrate friend member functions
2:
3:  #include <tscdefs.h>
4:  #include IOSTREAM_H
5:
6:  class one;
7:
8:  class two {
9:  private:
10:    char *s2;
11:  public:
12:    two() { s2 = "one, two, three"; }
```

```
13:    void show(one &c1);
14:  };
15:
16:  class one {
17:  private:
18:    friend void two::show(one &c1);
19:    char *s1;
20:  public:
21:    one() { s1 = "Testing "; }
22:  };
23:
24:  main()
25:  {
26:    one c1;
27:    two c2;
28:
29:    c2.show(c1);
30:    return 0;
31:  }
32:
33:  void two::show(one &c1)
34:  {
35:    cout << c1.s1 << s2 << '\n';
36:  }
```

The first rule to remember about friend member functions concerns the order of the class declarations. The class that prototypes the member function must come *before* the class that declares that function as a friend. Using a forward declaration as at line 6 in Listing 9.2 is not enough. For example, this does not work:

```
class forward;
class aClass {
  friend int forward::fn(aClass &a);   // ???
  // ...
}
```

The goal here is to declare fn(), a member function of class forward, as a friend of aClass. The purpose of the declaration is to give fn() access to private and protected members in an argument of type aClass passed to fn's a reference parameter. But even though fn() is declared to be a friend of aClass, inside fn()'s implementation (not shown here), the compiler rejects access to aClass's hidden items. Declaring the forward class ahead of aClass does not remove the conflict, even though it does allow the declaration to be compiled.

One solution to this sticky problem is to declare the entire class `forward` as a friend. This works:

```
class forward;
class aClass {
  friend class forward;
  // ...
}
```

Now function `fn()` in `forward` may access `aClass`'s private and protected members. However, declaring the entire class a friend of `aClass` also means that *every* member function in `aClass` can access the same private and protected items in the class. Such unrestricted access may be dangerous to your program's health, and an alternate solution may be less toxic. At such times, you should be able to rearrange the class declarations as in FRIENDMF to allow the program to compile.

To solve this problem for Listing 9.3, FRIENDMF.CPP, I reversed the two class declarations from Listing 9.2 so that `two` comes before `one`. That satisfies the rule that a friend member function must be declared before being listed as a friend. For example, see line 18. There, `two::show()` is declared as a friend of class `one`. The compiler allows this because class `two` was declared previously. If `two` came *after* `one`, as it did in Listing 9.2, even declaring `two` forward would not permit the program to compile. (Try this. Reverse the class declarations and change line 6 to `class two;`. You'll receive an error message when the compiler rejects the illegal friend declaration.)

Another difference in Listing 9.3 is the way the `show()` function refers to private data in the two classes. The function now has only one parameter, `one &c1`. Because the function is a member of class `two`, it doesn't need to list an argument of type `two`. In fact, doing so would be a mistake. The function is encapsulated in `two`; therefore, the statement at line 35 can refer to `two`'s private `s2` member directly. The reference to `c1.s1` is allowed as in Listing 9.2 because `show()` is a friend of class `one`.

Because function `show()` is a member of `two`, it now has a `this` pointer that addresses the object for which the function was called. Consequently, the program can no longer call the friend function directly. The program now has to define a variable of type `two` and call `show()` for that variable (see line 29).

One final note: Friends are attractive for giving objects access to private data in other objects. Used carefully, friends can improve performance by eliminating the overhead associated with calling member functions. (Inline functions may give similar advantages, however.) But friends also break down the barriers that protect data in classes. Using friends reduces OOP's advantages of data hiding, encapsulation of function and data, and isolation of statements that access critical values. By all means, use friends. But use them carefully. Don't let your best friends become your worst enemies!

# Function Overloading

**I**n most computer programming languages, when you declare identifiers like myValue or showResults, those symbols have one and only one meaning. But in C++, two or more functions may have the same name without causing a conflict. This unique feature, known as *function overloading,* is possible because C++ considers a function and its parameters to be inseparable. As long as multiple functions differ in at least one parameter, they may have the same name. For example, C++ allows you to write programs with functions declared like these:

```
void showResults();
void showResults(int count);
void showResults(int count, int max);
```

Each of these four functions has the same name but differs in at least one parameter. A single difference in a parameter's data type or the number of parameters are all that C++ needs to distinguish between functions named the same. For the three sample functions here, if you write the statement showResults();, C++ correctly determines that it should call the first function. If you write showResults(k) where k is a variable of type int, C++ calls the function that lists a single int parameter.

Even though functions like showResults() have the same name, they are still distinct functions and are not related in any way. Function overloading is merely a convenience that eliminates some of the need to invent new symbols for similar operations. In many languages, you would have to create functions named showResults1(), showResults2(), showResults3(), and showResults4() so that the compiler can distinguish between them. In C++, if similar functions require a different number or type of parameters, they may have the same name. Usually, you'll want to make those functions perform similar jobs. But that's only a suggestion, not a requirement.

## Name Mangling Revisited

Chapter 8, "Files and Directories," introduced the term *name mangling,* otherwise known as *type-safe linkage.* When C++ compiles a listing, it combines (mangles)

**599**

function names and parameters using a complex scheme that pretty much guarantees every overloaded function will have a unique symbol for use internally during compilation and linking.

The mangled symbols make it possible for common linkers to join modules containing overloaded function names. Name mangling also allows common linkers to reject many sorts of illegal function calls, for example, a statement that passes a float argument to a char * parameter. This high degree of type checking across compiled modules (hence the term type-safe linkage) helps you avoid common mistakes caused by passing the wrong types of data to functions in precompiled modules.

Listings 9.4 (SUBBUG.CPP) and 9.5 (MAINBUG.CPP) demonstrate how type-safe linkage and name mangling can keep you out of trouble. The two modules illustrate a typical C and C++ trick: declaring in a source listing a prototype to a precompiled function in a library module. You can compile the listings separately, but during linking, you'll receive an error message because the linker is unable to resolve references to function fn(). Make C:\TSC\C09 the current directory, and follow these instructions to attempt compiling, and to see the error. Enter the commands exactly as shown, using upper- and lowercase letters:

Borland C++ and Turbo C++: **bcc -D__TSC_BTC__ mainbug subbug**

Microsoft C++: **cl -D__TSC_MSC__ mainbug.cpp subbug.cpp**

Zortech C++: **ztc -D__TSC_ZTC__ mainbug.cpp subbug.cpp**

## Listing 9.4. SUBBUG.CPP.

```
1:   // subbug.cpp -- Sub module for mainbug.cpp
2:
3:   #include <tscdefs.h>
4:   #include IOSTREAM_H
5:
6:   void fn(char *string)
7:   {
8:     cout << "\nstring = " << string;
9:   }
```

### Listing 9.5. MAINBUG.CPP.

```
 1:   // mainbug.cpp -- Demonstrate type-safe linkage
 2:
 3:   #include <tscdefs.h>
 4:   #include IOSTREAM_H
 5:
 6:   void fn(float f);      // ???
 7:
 8:   main()
 9:   {
10:     fn(3.14159);
11:     return 0;
12:   }
```

Examine the two listings carefully and you'll see why the linker refuses to join them. SUBBUG.CPP implements function fn() with a char * parameter string. MAINBUG.CPP calls fn(), but passes to the function the wrong type of data—a floating point value, not the expected pointer. Usually, this kind of mistake is easily avoided by including in MAINBUG a header file (not shown) that prototypes fn().

Whether or not such a header file exists, however, MAINBUG.CPP ignores it, choosing instead to prototype fn() directly in the main program's source listing at line 6 in Listing 9.5. Avoiding an #include of a lengthy header file this way is a common trick for reducing compilation times. Rather than include many long header files, a program can prototype only the functions and other declarations that it needs. However, the prototype at line 6 differs from the function declaration in SUBBUG.CPP, a serious mistake that the compiler misses. To allow separate compilation of related modules, the compiler assumes that all function prototypes are correct. That's why you can compile the modules with no errors.

If you compile similar programs with many C compilers, you'll be able to link the object-code files, though running the code may produce disastrous results when the program passes a floating point value to the expected character pointer. If you compile with C++, however, the linker will receive different mangled symbols for function fn() in the two modules. The linker will therefore reject the function call in MAINBUG, not because of the mismatched parameter and argument, but because the linker will fail to find a mangled symbol for a void function named fn() that requires a single floating point argument. You can't run the buggy program because the linker will refuse to create the final executable code file.

# The *overload* Keyword

Early versions of C++ required the `overload` keyword to specify multiple functions with the same names. To declare the `showResults` functions from the preceding section, you had to write

```
overload void showResults();
overload void showResults(int count);
overload void showResults(int count, int max);
```

In newer C++ versions (including the compilers supported by this book), the `overload` keyword is not needed. If you find this word in older C++ listings, remove it.

# Overloading Conventional Functions

Overloading conventional functions—those that are not members of a class—is often convenient for simulating inheritance without using OOP techniques. For instance, suppose that you are using a library function named `glitch()` prototyped like this:

```
void glitch(float value);
```

You want to add a new statement to `glitch()`, but you don't have the original source code. The solution is simple—just overload `glitch()` with a new prototype that lists the same parameters as the original, but adds a new one:

```
void glitch(float value, int DEBUG);
```

Adding the `int DEBUG` parameter (the name and type are not important) overloads the `glitch()` function. You can then implement the function, add the new statement, and call the original code this way:

```
void glitch(float value, int DEBUG)
{
  cout << "\nNew statement added to glitch";
  glitch(value);  // call original glitch function
}
```

In the main program, use a statement such as `glitch(10, 1);` to call the new overloaded function. Use a statement such as `glitch(10)` to call the original. Of course, you could achieve the same result simply by creating a function with a different name. But using the same name helps you remember that the two `glitch()`es are related.

# Overloading Class Member Functions

Starting with Chapter 7, you've seen several class declarations that have more than one constructor. For example, Listing 7.7 (stritem.h) and Listing 7.11 (window.h) declare the strItem and Window classes. In each of these classes, two constructors initialize class objects in different ways. Because constructors must have the same names as their classes, multiple constructors in a class are overloaded by default. It's not possible to name multiple constructors differently in the same class. Multiple constructors in the same class *must* have the same name.

In addition to constructors, classes may also overload member functions. As with common functions, overloaded members have the same names but must differ in at least one parameter.

Overloading member functions can improve a program's readability by using the same function name for similar operations. In a graphics program, for example, you might have separate classes for lines, circles, squares, and other shapes. In another class, you may want to create an object that knows how to draw objects of those shapes. Rather than invent separate function names for each shape class (drawLine(), drawCircle(), and so on), you can overload a draw() function like this:

```
class overdrawn {
public:
  void draw(line &q);
  void draw(circle &q);
  void draw(square &q);
}
```

Class overdrawn declares three member functions all named draw(). Each function is separate and distinct, and the only reason for overloading the names is to improve the program's clarity. Because of the overloaded functions, you can write these kinds of statements for an overdrawn object od:

```
od.draw(aLine);
od.draw(aCircle);
od.draw(aSquare);
```

where aLine, aCircle, and aSquare are objects of the line, circle, and square classes (not shown here). Derived classes can then add new draw() functions for others kinds of shapes. In a program with dozens or more such functions, it's much easier to remember one function name like draw() than it is to look up which kind of draw() function goes with this or that shape.

> **Note:** The only member function that may not be overloaded is a destructor. This restriction is a consequence of the rule that a class may have one and only one destructor, which may not declare a return type or any parameters. If you need multiple ways to destroy class objects, divide the code among other member functions, which the destructor can then call.

# Operator Overloading

The topic of *operator overloading* in C++ has been needlessly smothered in mysterious explanations that require a graduate degree in mathematics to understand. Like most programming subjects, however, once you cut through the mustard, operator overloading is as simple as a ham sandwich.

Before devouring operator overloading, it will help for you to review what you know about operators in general. Of course, you know what an operator is. For example, the plus sign (+) is an operator that sums two values. The minus sign (-) is an operator that subtracts two values. These and other similar operators are called *binary operators* because they operate on two arguments. Some others, such as the *not* operator, (!) are *unary*—they require only one argument. The unary minus (-) is another good example of a unary operator. In the expression -count, the unary minus negates count's value.

> **Note:** A question mark (?) represents the only ternary (that is, "three-argument") operator in C and C++. The ternary operator doesn't enter into the discussion about operator overloading. See "Conditional Expressions" later in this chapter.

Most people have no trouble using common binary and unary operators. But consider an interesting fact about common operators like +, -, *, /, and others. In the expression 1234 + fp + count, if count is type long and fp is type float, the expression actually sums values of three *different* data types. Somehow, the plus operator can operate with arguments of different types. That observation may seem natural and intuitive, but mixing different types of data and operators is what operator overloading is all about.

Operator overloading is a mechanism that lets you add new data types to those that C++ operators are designed to handle. With operator overloading, you can create a class and write functions that implement a plus operation for two objects of the class type. After overloading the plus operator, you can write expressions using the familiar plus sign, and C++ calls your custom operator functions to sum the class objects.

Overloaded operators are C++ functions, which may or may not be members of a class. You write an overloaded operator function as you do other functions, although there are a few unique rules to memorize and follow. A hypothetical example will introduce those rules. Here's a partial declaration for a class named ZZ:

```
class ZZ {
public:
  friend ZZ operator+(ZZ a, ZZ b);
  friend ZZ operator-(ZZ a, ZZ b);
  friend ZZ operator*(ZZ a, ZZ b);
  friend ZZ operator/(ZZ a, ZZ b);
  // ... other members
};
```

ZZ declares four overloaded operator functions. (Like all classes, in practice, ZZ would probably declare other public, private, and protected members.) The overloaded function names are: operator+, operator-, operator*, and operator/. Normally, you can't use symbols like +, -, *, and / in identifiers, but for the special case of overloading an operator, C++ allows the function name to consist of the word operator and one of the following symbols:

| | | | | | | | |
|---|---|---|---|---|---|---|---|
| + | – | * | / | % | ^ | & | ¦ |
| ~ | ! | , | = | < | > | <= | >= |
| ++ | -- | << | >> | == | != | && | ¦¦ |
| += | -= | /= | *= | %= | ^= | &= | ¦= |
| <<= | >>= | [] | () | -> | ->* | new | delete |

The hypothetical class ZZ defines operator functions for the first four operators in the table. Each function has the general form

```
friend ZZ operator+(ZZ a, ZZ b);
```

The function is declared as a friend of the class, giving the function access to the class's private and protected members. The function returns type ZZ (it could return another type). Most important, the function's name is operator+, which identifies the function as the method by which expressions using + can process objects of the class. To the function, a statement must pass two parameters, a and b, each of type ZZ.

The `operator+` function name confuses some people. Remember, `operator+` is simply the function's name. If you named the function `feeblewitz` rather than `operator+`, you could write a statement such as

```
feeblewitz(a, b);
```

where a and b are objects of type ZZ. If you change `feeblewitz` back to `operator+`, you can call the function with the statement

```
operator+(a, b);
```

There is no difference between those two function calls—only the function names were changed. The symbol `operator+` is the function's name, and you can call the function in the same way you could if it were named `feeblewitz`. However, as an overloaded operator, the function can also be called from an expression. For example, this statement is *exactly* equivalent to the preceding function call:

```
a + b;
```

The expression a + b and the statement `operator+(a, b)` do exactly the same jobs, and they generate exactly the same object code. The only reason for using one form over the other is clarity. Operator overloading adds nothing to C++ that you don't already know. It simply lets you write expressions rather than the equivalent function calls.

But don't discount operator overloading too quickly just because it's only new clothing on the same old wolf. It took centuries for mathematicians to develop an efficient symbology for representing complex formulas like `((a + b) * c) / q`. That's a very concise way to state a potentially confusing combination of symbols. The equivalent function calls—let's name them add, multiply, and divide—are much less clear:

```
divide(multiply(add(a, b), c), q)
```

Even separating the expressions and assigning the function calls to a temporary variable isn't much better:

```
x = add(a, b);
x = multiply(x, c);
x = divide(x, q);
```

That's a bit easier to read, but now the relationship between the elements is lost. But that's exactly the sort of code that programmers have been writing since the first high-level languages appeared on the programming scene. Operator overloading lets you write familiar expressions that can operate with custom data types implemented as C++ classes.

A working example of a class that uses overloaded operators will help make these concepts clearer. Listing 9.6, STROPS.CPP, illustrates the beginnings of a class that can store integer values in string form. By using overloaded operators, the program can evaluate expressions that add strings without having to convert those strings to numeric values.

### Listing 9.6. STROPS.CPP.

```
 1:  // strops.cpp -- Demonstrate operator overloading
 2:
 3:  #include <tscdefs.h>
 4:  #include IOSTREAM_H
 5:  #include IOMANIP_H
 6:  #include <stdlib.h>
 7:  #include <string.h>
 8:
 9:  class strop {
10:  private:
11:    char value[12];
12:  public:
13:    strop() { value[0] = 0; }
14:    strop(const char *s);
15:    friend long operator+(strop a, strop b);
16:    friend long operator-(strop a, strop b);
17:  };
18:
19:  main()
20:  {
21:    strop a = "1234";
22:    strop b = "4321";
23:
24:    cout << "a + b +  6 == " << (a + b + 6) << endl;
25:    cout << "a - b + 10 == " << (a - b + 10) << endl;
26:    return 0;
27:  }
28:
```

*continues*

**Listing 9.6. continued**

```
29:  strop::strop(const char *s)
30:  {
31:    strncpy(value, s, 11);
32:    value[11] = 0;
33:  }
34:
35:  long operator+(strop a, strop b)
36:  {
37:    return (atol(a.value) + atol(b.value));
38:  }
39:
40:  long operator-(strop a, strop b)
41:  {
42:    return (atol(a.value) - atol(b.value));
43:  }
```

STROPS is only a simple example of operator overloading, and the program would require extensive work to be practical. Even so, the strop class at lines 9–17 demonstrates several important rules for overloaded operators.

The class stores characters in a small char array, which is large enough to hold eleven digits and a null terminator—room for the smallest possible long value, –2147483648L, in string form. The largest possible long value is 2147483647L, which takes ten digits. So with its twelve-character array, strop can store any long value as a string.

Two constructors at lines 13–14 provide the means to initialize new objects of type strop. The first constructor takes care of a default variable definition. The second allows variables to be created with lines such as these:

```
strop v1 = "64";
strop v2 = "-1000";
```

The strop class does not specify member functions to retrieve and change the private value member. I left these out to keep the example short; in practice, you would need many more functions than those shown here.

The two friend functions at lines 15–16 overload the plus and minus operators for objects of the class. The declarations are similar to those in the hypothetical zz class mentioned earlier. However, in this case, the functions return long values. Typically, overloaded operator functions return the same type of value as their class (or a reference to an object of the class). But that's not a requirement. Overloaded operator functions, just like other functions, can return any data types.

Lines 21–25 in the main() function show how useful overloaded operators can be. First, the program defines two objects a and b of the class type, assigning to those objects the strings "1234" and "4321", respectively. Two output stream statements then use those objects in the expressions a + b + 6 and a - b + 10.

Think about what those expressions are doing: They are adding and subtracting strings and integer values. Normally, the plus and minus operators can't do that; those operators were designed to operate only on numeric values. By overloading the two operators, the program teaches C++ how to evaluate expressions involving objects of the strop class type. C++ now can add and subtract string representations of long values—a capability not built into the language.

Examine the implementations at lines 29–38 for the overloaded operator functions. Because the functions were declared as friends and not as member functions, their implementations are identical to other common C++ functions. The only differences are the special function names operator+ and operator-, which permit the compiler to evaluate expressions with the plus and minus operators and objects of the strop class.

Because the operator functions are friends, they can access the private and protected parts of strop objects. That fact allows the functions to convert to a long the value string member in the two parameters a and b. Those conversions are handled by calling the standard atol() (ASCII to long) function in the C++ library. The functions then return the addition or subtraction of the converted values.

# Overloading Operator Member Functions

In Listing 9.6, the two overloaded operator functions operator+ and operator- are declared as common friends. Another way to accomplish the same goal of overloading the plus and minus operators (and others) is to list the functions as members of the class.

Listing 9.7, STROPS2.CPP, is similar to the original STROPS, but shows how to overload operators as member functions. Comparing the two programs will help you decide which of the two methods is appropriate for your own code.

## Listing 9.7. STROPS2.CPP.

```
 1:  // strops2.cpp -- Demonstrate member operator overloading
 2:
 3:  #include <tscdefs.h>
 4:  #include IOSTREAM_H
 5:  #include IOMANIP_H
 6:  #include <stdlib.h>
 7:  #include <string.h>
 8:
 9:  class strop {
10:  private:
11:    char value[12];
12:  public:
13:    strop() { value[0] = 0; }
14:    strop(const char *s);
15:    long operator+(strop b);
16:    long operator-(strop b);
17:  };
18:
19:  main()
20:  {
21:    strop a = "1234";
22:    strop b = "4321";
23:
24:    cout << "a + b + 6  == " << (a + b + 6) << endl;
25:    cout << "a - b + 10 == " << (a - b + 10) << endl;
26:    return 0;
27:  }
28:
29:  strop::strop(const char *s)
30:  {
31:    strncpy(value, s, 11);
32:    value[11] = 0;
33:  }
34:
35:  long strop::operator+(strop b)
36:  {
37:    return (atol(value) + atol(b.value));
38:  }
39:
40:  long strop::operator-(strop b)
```

```
41:  {
42:    return (atol(value) - atol(b.value));
43:  }
```

Compare the overloaded operator function prototypes at lines 15–16 with the equivalent friend functions in Listing 9.6. Because the functions in STROPS2 are members, they already have access to the class's private and protected members, so there's no need to specify them as friends of the class. In addition, because they are members of the class, they receive a `this` pointer to the object for which a statement calls the functions. They therefore need only single parameters. To add two string values, the functions combine `this->value` with `b.value`. There's no need to pass two parameters to the functions as there was in STROPS. In fact, doing so is an error because binary operators such as + and - *require* two, and only two, parameters. You could not write line 15 like this:

```
long operator+(strop a, strop b);  // ???
```

If that were possible (it's not), the prototype would define a ternary operation for the plus operator, involving three values of type `strop`: `*this`, `a`, and `b`. No such operation is possible. In the original STROPS.CPP, the two parameters are required because the friend functions are not members; therefore, they do not receive `this` pointers to objects of the class.

Getting back to Listing 9.7, notice that the `main()` function is exactly the same as the `main()` function in Listing 9.6. Whether the overloaded operator functions are declared as friends or as members of the class does not affect how those operators are used in expressions.

The function implementations at lines 35–43 differ only slightly from those in the original STROPS. Because the new functions are members, they are tagged with the class name `strop::`. In addition to that change, the statements at lines 37 and 42 now refer directly to the `value` member in the objects for which the functions were called. The reference to the second argument, `b.value`, is the same as before.

# Overloading Unary Operators

Unary operators, such as unary minus and ! operate on one argument. You can overload these and other unary operators with techniques similar to those illustrated in the preceding sections.

As with binary operators, you can declare an overloaded unary operator function as a friend or a member of the class. To overload a unary operator as a friend function, you must list only one parameter of the class type. For example, add this declaration to STROPS.CPP, Listing 9.6, (above line 16 is a good location):

```
friend long operator-(strop a);
```

Even though the original line 16 already overloads the minus operator, because the new declaration specifies only one parameter, there is no conflict. This is not a special rule. It's just a consequence of function overloading, which allows multiple functions to share the same name as long as the function declarations differ in at least one parameter.

The overloaded function implementation returns the negation of the value member in parameter a. Add the function's implementation anywhere after main():

```
long operator-(strop a)
{
  return -atol(a.value);
}
```

Because the unary operator- is a friend of the class, the return statement may directly access the private value member in parameter a. The function is now complete, and the compiler can evaluate unary expressions involving objects of the class type. For an example of how that works, add the following statement to main() just above return:

```
cout << "     - a == " << -a << endl;
```

Compile the modified program and run. As you can see, the expression -a is replaced by the long negation of a's string member value, "1234". You have taught C++ how to negate a long value that's represented in string form.

As with overloaded binary operators, you can also declare overloaded unary operators as member functions. In STROPS2.CPP add the following declaration above line 16:

```
long operator-();
```

This is equivalent to the friend unary function you added to STROPS earlier. In this case, however, the function is declared as a member of the strop class. Because all member functions receive a this pointer that addresses the object for which the functions are called, the operator- function can operate directly on the value member in a strop object. For that reason, the function does not need any parameters. In fact, it must have *no* parameters, or C++ won't recognize the function as an overloaded unary operator.

To implement the function, add the following lines to STROPS2.CPP after `main()`:

```
long strop::operator-(void)
{
  return -atol(value);
}
```

The overloaded unary minus operator for `strop` is a member function, and therefore, it is tagged with the class name `strop::`, as are all member function implementations. The function simply returns the `long` negation of `value` after passing that string to the standard `atol` function in the C++ library.

To use the new unary member function, add the same statement you added to STROPS earlier. Insert this line above the `main()` function's `return` statement in STROPS2.CPP:

```
cout << "       - a == " << -a << endl;
```

Whether you declare an overloaded unary operator function as a friend or as a class member, you can use that function in the same way. Because the class defines an operation for unary minus, C++ can evaluate the expression -a to give the negation of a `long` value represented as a character string.

## Tips for Successful Operator Overloading

STROPS and STROPS2 demonstrate some of the fundamentals of operator overloading. The following sections in this chapter explain a few twists for special operators such as array index brackets, type conversion parentheses, the assignment operator, and memory management operators `new` and `delete`.

The following tips will help you design classes with overloaded operators. (Assume that a and b are objects of appropriate class types.)

- C++ does not "understand" the meaning of an overloaded operator. It's your responsibility to provide meaningful overloaded functions. For example, if you change + to * at line 37 in STROPS2.CPP, the expression a + b will *multiply* the two objects. C++ makes no guarantee that an overloaded plus operator will actually add values. This means that operator overloading can be used to obscure meaning (a common criticism), but it also means that you are free to redefine the traditional meaning of an operator, which may be handy.

- C++ is not able to derive complex operators from simple ones. If you define overloaded operator functions operator* and operator=, you can't expect C++ to evaluate the expression a *= b correctly. For that and similar expressions to work, you must declare an overloaded operator function for the symbol *= as well *&=.

- You may never change the syntax of an overloaded operator. Operators that are binary must remain binary. Unary operators must remain unary. Because of this rule, it is not possible, for example, to create a unary division operator. The division operator / must be defined to operate on two arguments. The unary operator ! must be defined to operate on only one value.

- You can't invent new operators for use in expressions. You may overload *only* the operators listed earlier. You can, however, always write functions for special cases. For example, it might be nice if you could redefine ! (or, perhaps, !!, to avoid a conflict with the standard ! symbol) to mean "factorial of." Although that's not possible, you can just as easily write a function named factorial.

## Increment and Decrement Operators

In earlier versions of C++, it was not possible to define separate overloaded operations for postfix and prefix ++ and -- operators. Now it is, as TAnyClass shows:

```
class TAnyClass {
  int x;
public:
  TAnyClass(int xx) { x = xx; }
  int operator++() { return ++x; }      // Prefix ++object
  int operator++(int) { return x++; }   // Postfix object++
  int operator--() { return --x; }      // Prefix --object
  int operator--(int) { return x--; }   // Postfix object--
  int GetX() { return x; }
};
```

Member function operator++() defines a prefix increment operator for an object of type TAnyClass. This member function has no parameters. Member function `operator++(int)` defines a postfix increment operator for a `TAnyClass` object. The single `int` parameter is assigned zero by C++.

The demonstration functions are implemented inline, but they could be implemented separately. For an object v of type `TAnyClass`, the expression ++v calls the overloaded prefix ++ operator, in effect executing the statement `x.operator++();`. The expression v++ calls the overloaded postfix ++ operator, and executes as though written `x.operator++(0);`. The decrement operators work similarly.

To experiment with the above class, add it to a C++ program with the following `main()` function:

```
main()
{
  TAnyClass t(100);
  cout << "t == " << t.GetX() << "; ++t == " << ++t << '\n';
  cout << "t == " << t.GetX() << "; t++ == " << t++ << '\n';
  cout << "t == " << t.GetX() << "; --t == " << --t << '\n';
  cout << "t == " << t.GetX() << "; t-- == " << t-- << '\n';
  return 0;
}
```

# Overloading Array Indexing

When overloading the array-indexing operator [] (also known as the *subscript* operator), you are expected to provide a function that returns a reference to one of several values stored by a class. The index value may be any data type that can be passed to the `operator[]` function as a parameter. For example, this declaration overloads [] as a friend function that returns a reference to class ZZ:

```
friend ZZ &operator[](int i);
```

The index value for an array element is the parameter `int i`. If the declaration appears in a class ZZ, you could then use expressions such as a[10] and a[i] for an object a of type ZZ.

Overloaded array indexing makes it possible to write expressions that appear to access arrays but that actually call a class function to perform the indexing. Because the array-indexing mechanism is neatly stowed inside the class, if you later change the way the class stores its data, you can simply update the overloaded `operator[]` function without having to modify programs that use the class.

A list class is a good example of where overloaded array indexing is useful. Programmers with limited experience find list functions confusing to use. In such cases, an array index function lets programmers write expressions like `array[i]` and `array[10]` rather than the equivalent function calls to step through a list and locate a specific element. The simpler array expressions may also help you convert array-based algorithms such as sorting routines to work with linked lists.

Listing 9.8, ARRAYLST.CPP, demonstrates how to add array-indexing to a derivative of the `list` class from Chapter 7. The program also shows how to create reference aliases to variables in C++—a topic I'll explain after the listing.

## Listing 9.8. ARRAYLST.CPP.

```
 1:  // arraylst.cpp -- List class with array-indexing operator
 2:
 3:  #include <tscdefs.h>
 4:  #include IOSTREAM_H
 5:  #include IOMANIP_H
 6:  #include <error.h>
 7:  #include <stritem.h>
 8:  #include <list.h>
 9:
10:  class stringArray : public list {
11:  public:
12:    const char *operator[](int i);
13:  };
14:
15:  void error(void);
16:
17:  main()
18:  {
19:    stringArray *a = new stringArray;
20:    stringArray &sa = *a;
21:
22:    a->insertItem(new strItem("First string"));
23:    a->insertItem(new strItem("Second string"));
24:    a->insertItem(new strItem("Third string"));
25:    a->insertItem(new strItem("Fourth string"));
26:    for (int i = 1; i <= 4; i++)
27:      cout << endl << sa[i];
28:    cout << "\n\nString #2 == " << sa[2];
```

```
29:    delete a;
30:    return 0;
31:  }
32:
33:  const char *stringArray::operator[](int i)
34:  {
35:    if (listEmpty() || (i <= 0)) error();
36:    resetList();
37:    for (int count = 1; count < i; count++) {
38:      nextItem();
39:      if (atHeadOfList()) error();
40:    }
41:    return ((strItem *)currentItem())->getString();
42:  }
43:
44:  void error(void)
45:  {
46:    error(99, "Index out of range");
47:  }
```

To the items inherited from list, the derived stringArray class adds an overloaded operator function for the [ ] subscript operator. The index value is type int, and the function returns a char pointer. To prevent the function from being used to alter private data in a class object, the function is prefaced with the keyword const.

Lines 19–20 use the new operator to construct a stringArray object, assigning to pointer a the object's address. The statement stringArray &sa = *a creates a reference variable named sa that refers to the object addressed by a. The reference sa variable is an alias for *a, and it is possible to index the list using array-like expressions sa[i] and sa[2]. I'll explain the reason for creating the alias in a moment.

After inserting a few string items into the list addressed by a, two statements demonstrate how to use the overloaded subscript operator. Lines 26–27 execute a for loop that displays the four strings in the array. Line 28 displays the second string. Notice that in this example, the "arrays" are indexed starting with 1, not with 0 as is common in C and C++. I purposely wrote the program this way to demonstrate that C++ does not enforce its usual array-indexing rules for the overloaded subscript operator. If you want to begin array indexing at 0, 1, or 100, that's up to you.

Notice how much simpler the expressions sa[i] and sa[2] are when compared to the equivalent steps required to peruse the stringArray list. For example, to display the third string (pretending again that the first array index is 1), you would normally have to write all of this:

```
a->resetList();
for (int i = 1; i < 3; i++) {
  a->nextItem();
  if (a->atHeadOfList())
    exit(1);  // Range error
}
cout << ((strItem *)a->currentItem())->getString();
```

With the overloaded subscript operator—and with the help of the sa alias—the equivalent statement is far simpler:

```
cout << sa[3];
```

The overloaded operator takes care of the messy list-processing details, thus clarifying the program's text. Of course, you could also hide the details inside a function. But the overloaded array operator is highly descriptive. There's no mistaking the purpose of the expression—to output the third element of the sa array. (With zero-based indexing, the expression would output the fourth element.)

The reason for using the sa alias is because of the list class's requirement that objects of the list class or of any derived classes such as stringArray *must* be stored on the heap and addressed by pointers. Line 19 fulfills that requirement, creating a pointer a to a stringArray list allocated memory on the heap by new. However, it is *not* possible to use overloaded array subscripting directly with pointers. For example, this does not compile:

```
cout << a->[3];    // ???
```

That seems reasonable enough, but is not permitted. To use the pointer with the overloaded subscript operator function, you must instead write the equivalent function call in longhand:

```
cout << a->operator[](3);
```

Study that line carefully and you'll see how C++ implements an overloaded subscript. If you find the statement confusing, replace the function name with something else. For instance, just for illustration, suppose that the function were named lookup(). The statement would then become

```
cout << a->lookup(3);
```

Looks more familiar, doesn't it? Remember, like `operator+` from earlier, `operator[]` is simply a function name—the brackets have no special meaning except to identify the function as an overloaded operator. You can always call an overloaded operator function just as you can call any other function.

But the goal of creating an overloaded operator is to *avoid* writing statements that look like function calls. Because a is a pointer, however, it's not possible to use the expression a->[3]. To take advantage of the overloaded subscript operator, you can define a reference alias like sa that means the same as *a, but meshes with C++'s syntax requirements. As line 20 in ARRAYLST.CPP demonstrates, you create a reference variable with the & symbol. This states that sa is a `stringArray` alias for *a:

```
stringArray &sa = *a;
```

You can now use sa as an alias for *a. C++ will accept the alias where it would reject a pointer. With the alias, you can write array-like expressions such as sa[3], which is *exactly* equivalent to a->operator[](3). Both expressions call the `operator[]` function for the object addressed by a.

The final step in overloading the subscript operator is to implement the overloaded function. Lines 33–42 in ARRAYLST take care of that remaining detail, using code that's similar to the lengthy list-processing steps outlined previously. Lines 35 and 39 call `error()` for out-of-range indexes. The other statements reset the list and step through items one-by-one to find the element at the requested index. Line 41 returns a pointer to the string item's characters.

As `stringArray` illustrates, it takes some work to implement overloaded subscripts. But hiding messy list-processing statements inside a class member and being able to use simple array-like expressions such as sa[3] may make the extra programming more than worthwhile.

# User-Defined Type Conversions

The phrase *automatic type conversion* describes the internal steps that C++ takes when converting data types from one form to another. C++ compiler manuals (and the documentation for other languages) usually list a dozen or more rules that describe what happens, for example, when you pass a char to an int parameter, or when you mix data types in expressions such as a + b + c where the three variables a, b, and c are of different, but compatible, numeric types.

To handle such cases, C++ generally *promotes* values to a common form. C++ can't actually add integer and floating point values directly, though it may appear to do so. To evaluate this and similar multitype expressions, C++ converts the integer to an equivalent floating point value, then calls an internal routine that can add variables of type double (probably). All these actions happen behind the scenes—you rarely even need to think about them.

At times, however, it's necessary to add your own type-conversion rules to those built into the C++ language. For example, return to the strop class in Listing 9.6 (STROPS.CPP). The main() function in that test program initialized strop objects with the definitions:

```
strop a = "1234";
strop b = "4321";
```

Those commands work well enough, but what if you wanted to initialize a strop object with a binary value, not a string? For example, suppose that you want to write

```
strop c = 9876;    // ???
```

That will not compile because the strop class does not provide a mechanism for converting an integer data type to a string. One way to solve that problem is to add a new constructor that takes a long parameter. For example, you could use this inline constructor:

```
strop(long i) { strcpy(value, form("%d", i)); }
```

The new constructor takes a single long parameter. The constructor's inline statement converts that parameter's value to a string, which is copied to the private value char array. As a result, you can now use the statement

```
strop c = 9876;
```

The new constructor tells the compiler how to convert a long value to a strop data type—in other words, to a string. You have just added a new type-conversion rule to C++ for the strop class.

But there's a flaw in the solution because the reverse conversion is not possible. After initializing the strop object, some way is needed to use the value stored in string form. As written, strop does not provide a function that returns the value of its private value member. For that reason, statements like these fail:

```
strop c = 9876;
cout << c;         // ???
```

The first line compiles and runs just fine. Using the new constructor, C++ is able to convert 9876 to string form and store that string inside the strop object c. But the output statement fails. Output stream statements don't know how to handle values of type strop, and attempting to display such values doesn't compute.

There are several possible solutions to problems such as these. The standard approach is to provide a member function that returns the value character string converted to a long data type. For example, you could insert this inline function into strop:

```
long getValue(void) { return atol(value); }
```

You can then assign a value to c and display that value with statements such as

```
strop c = 9876;
cout << "\nc     == " << c.getValue();
```

There's nothing wrong with this method—it's a classic solution for accessing private data via member functions. However, there's another less obvious solution that uses an overloaded *conversion operator* to translate a class object to another data type.

Conversion operators take the form *operator TYPE()* where *TYPE* is the data type to which you want to convert objects of the class. For example, to provide a type conversion operation for translating strop objects to type long, insert this inline function inside the class's public section:

```
operator long() { return atol(value); }
```

This is a special use for the operator keyword that C++ provides specifically for creating new type-conversion rules. In this example, the new rule lists the steps required to convert strop's private value member from character format to long. (There's only one such step in this sample. In another setting, the type-conversion function might have many statements, and it doesn't have to be implemented inline.) Here, the actual conversion is handled by the standard atol() library function. With the new type-conversion rule in place, it's now possible to write statements like these:

```
strop c = 9876;
cout << "\nc     == " << (long)c;
```

The type-cast expression (long)c converts the strop object c to a long value. The expression calls the new type-conversion operator function in the strop class. You may also notice that by stating a type-conversion rule, it's now possible to access strop's value *without* explicitly calling a member function! In fact, other than the new type-conversion function, strop provides no means to get to its value member.

**621**

Another interesting benefit of the new type-conversion rule is the capability to pass variables of type strop to function parameters of type long. After all, the type-conversion rule tells C++ how to convert an object of strop to a long value; therefore, it should be possible to use a strop object wherever a long value is expected.

And that's exactly true. To see how the trick works, examine Listing 9.9, NEWOPS.CPP. The listing is similar to STROPS.CPP, but adds most of the modifications suggested previously in this section. To keep the listing short, I removed the friend overloaded operator functions from STROPS, but those functions could be reinserted without changing the way the new type-conversion function operates.

### Listing 9.9. NEWOPS.CPP.

```
 1:  // newops.cpp -- Demonstrate type-conversion rules
 2:
 3:  #include <tscdefs.h>
 4:  #include IOSTREAM_H
 5:  #include <stdlib.h>
 6:  #include <string.h>
 7:  #include <form.h>
 8:
 9:  class strop {
10:  private:
11:    char value[12];
12:  public:
13:    strop() { value[0] = 0; }
14:    strop(const char *s);
15:    strop(long i) { form(value, "%d", i); }
16:    operator long() { return atol(value); }
17:  };
18:
19:  void showValue(long v);
20:
21:  main()
22:  {
23:    strop c = 9876;
24:
25:    cout << "\nc == " << (long)c;
26:    showValue(c);
27:    return 0;
28:  }
```

```
29:
30:   void showValue(long v)
31:   {
32:     cout << "\nValue of v == " << v;
33:   }
```

Because of the type-conversion function at line 16, it's now possible to use type-cast expressions such as (long)c at line 25. It's also possible to pass strop objects directly to functions that declare long arguments. For example, the program calls function showValue() to display c's value. When line 26 executes, C++ consults the rules it knows for converting data types to long. In this example, the compiler uses the inline statement for the operatorlong() function at line 16 to perform the conversion.

That line shows how to write an inline type-conversion function. As with other member functions, it's also possible to code type-conversions as callable functions. To do this for strop, change line 16 to

```
operator long();
```

Then insert the function implementation somewhere after function main():

```
strop::operator long()
{
  return atol(value);
}
```

The result is the same, but now conversions of strop objects to long values are handled by calling the type-conversion function. The inline code is probably best to reduce the number of such function calls, except when the conversion code is lengthy.

# Overloading the Assignment Operator

Assigning one variable to another of a compatible type is an operation that most programmers perform without much thought. However, when the copied variables are class objects, you need to consider a few obscure consequences of assigning one object to another. Although the compiler will allow you to write a = b; where a and b are class objects, the effects of that assignment might not be what you expect.

Before explaining why assignments of class objects can cause trouble—and describing how to deal sensibly with those situations—it will help to review how assignments work for variables of common C++ data types. For example, examine these lines:

```
float a, b;
a = 3.14159;
b = 100.0;
a = b;
```

After defining two `float` variables a and b, the program assigns 3.14159 to a and 100.0 to b. Upon assigning b to a, the two variables hold copies of the same value (see Figure 9.1). The variables, however, remain distinct. If one should go out of scope—perhaps because the function that defined the variable ends—the other variable will remain valid. Even though both variables hold the same value, they are stored separately in memory.

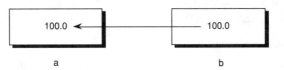

**Figure 9.1.** For simple data types, after the assignment a = b;, the variables a and b hold copies of the same value.

Next, consider a similar assignment that involves pointers. If p1 and p2 are *pointers* to variables of type `float`, the following assignments have a subtle and potentially dangerous effect that's not immediately obvious from reading the program's text:

```
float *p1 = new float;
float *p2 = new float;
*p1 = 3.14159;
*p2 = 100.0;
p1 = p2;        // ???
```

In this case, the variables p1 and p2 are pointers to the actual `float` variables allocated space on the heap. The two literal values are assigned to those variables by dereferencing the pointers. Copying the *pointer* p2 to the *pointer* p1 causes the two variables to address the same value in memory (see Figure 9.2). Usually it's best to avoid this situation. The space formerly addressed by p1 is disconnected from the pointer, and there is no way to recover that space. Worse, if the program `deletes` the space addressed by p2, the pointer p1 will address an invalid memory location.

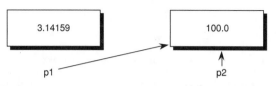

**Figure 9.2.** Assigning one pointer to another causes the two pointers to address the same location in memory.

The correct way to copy values addressed by pointers is to dereference the point-er variables. The correct assignment of p2's addressed value to the space addressed by p1 is

```
*p1 = *p2;
```

As Figure 9.3 shows, by dereferencing each pointer, C++ copies the value addressed by p2 to the space addressed by p1. Now, the two pointers continue to address unique locations in memory, and, therefore, deleting one will not cause the other to point to an invalid location.

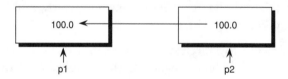

**Figure 9.3.** Dereferencing the pointers assigns the value addressed by one to the space addressed by the other.

# Copying Class Objects

When copying one class object to another object of a compatible class, the results can be unexpected. C++ makes copies of objects not only in assignment expressions but at other times. So you must be aware of the consequences of copying class objects, even if you don't explicitly assign them with the = operator. There are four times when a copy of a class object will be made:

- When one object is used to initialize a newly defined object of the same class.

- When an object is passed to a function's value parameter of the class type.

- When a function returns a class object directly (not a reference or pointer to the class).

- When a statement assigns one object to another.

The first three of these cases initialize *new* copies of class objects using the value of an existing object. The fourth case assigns the value of an existing object to another object that was previously defined. In all cases, the result is an object that contains copies of the data members of another object.

After making such copies, all may seem well, but trouble brews when the classes declare pointer members. Problems can also arise when creating copies of objects that contain members of other class types, which may contain their own pointer members. As I explained in the previous section (see Figure 9.2), if two or more pointers happen to address the same location in memory, deleting one of those pointers will cause the others to address invalid data. Worse, deleting the same space more than once can corrupt the heap and cause a major bug. Because classes often inherit properties of many other classes, a simple assignment or function call might create dozens of duplicate pointers. And if those pointers address objects allocated by new, class destructors might deallocate the same memory spaces multiple times, which will almost always corrupt the heap.

C++ provides two mechanisms for ensuring that classes with pointer members may be copied safely. Those two mechanisms are called *memberwise initialization* and *memberwise assignment*.

## Memberwise Initialization

When a class object is used to initialize another object, C++ copies each data member from the existing object to the new one. For example, here's a simple class with no pointer members:

```
class simple {
private:
  int i;
  float r;
public:
  simple()
    { i = 0; r = 0; }
  simple(int ii, float rr)
    { i = ii; r = rr; }
};
```

In practice, simple would need other member functions to access its private data members i and r, but the example illustrates how object copying works. The class declares two inline constructors. The default constructor (simple()) initializes members i and r to 0. An alternate constructor allows a program to initialize a class object with explicit values. The two constructors make these definitions possible:

```
simple v1;
simple v2(100, 3.14159);
```

The first line creates an object v1 of type simple with members i and r initialized to 0. The second line creates a second object v2 with its members initialized to 100 and 3.14159 respectively.

Suppose that you need to create another object v3 somewhere else in the program. You want the new object to have the same value as v2. To accomplish that, C++ allows you to use the existing object (v2) to initialize the new object v3 in its definition line like this:

```
simple v3 = v2;
```

That creates v3 as a copy of v2. For such definitions, C++ performs a memberwise initialization of v3's data members by copying the member values one-by-one from v2 to v3. C++ does *not* call the class constructor for v3! Always be aware of these facts when using an object to initialize another. Although the definition appears to copy the bytes from v2 to the bytes of v3, C++ actually performs the equivalent of the two statements:

```
v3.i = v2.i;
v3.r = v2.r;
```

In other words, when one object is used to initialize a new object of the same class, C++ copies the existing object's member members to the new objects's members. (The statements are for illustration only. The class members are private, and the statements would not compile.)

The identical memberwise initialization occurs also when you pass an object to a function's value parameter. For example, suppose that the program contains this function prototype:

```
void doSomething(simple x);
```

Value parameters, as you learned in Chapter 3, "Functions: Programming in Pieces," are passed as *copies* of arguments. When the arguments are class objects, C++ copies them to the function parameters using the identical memberwise initialization steps executed when initializing a new object with another. For example, if the program calls a function

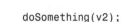
```
doSomething(v2);
```

inside doSomething()'s implementation (not shown), parameter x will contain a copy of the data members from v2. In addition, the class constructor for x will not be called—an important fact to consider when passing objects to functions.

> **Note:** Class objects are *not* copied when passing them to reference parameters or when passing them by address to pointers. To prevent copies of objects from being made, declare the function parameter as simple &x (a reference) or simple *x (a pointer). However, in those cases, the function directly addresses the original object passed as an argument. If the function changes the object, the original will also change.

The third and final situation where C++ makes a memberwise initialization of a copied object is when a function returns a class value. To see how this works, consider a function that's prototyped like this:

```
simple returnSomething();
```

The function returnSomething() returns an object of type simple. That object will be a *copy* of the object listed in the function's return statement. Suppose that the function is implemented as

```
simple returnSomething()
{
  simple q(1234, 43.21);
  return q;
}
```

Inside the function, a local simple variable is initialized with the values 1234 and 43.21. That variable is returned as the function result. However, and this is important, what's actually returned is a *copy* of q, not q itself. Returning q directly would be a serious error—that variable is local to the function, and after the function ends, q no longer exists. For that reason, C++ must copy the object to a new location (probably on the stack) and return that copy. To create the copy, C++ performs a memberwise initialization of the new object, using the members in q to make that copy. As in the previous two situations—initializing an object with another and passing objects to value parameters—C++ does *not* call the class constructor for the copied object.

Memberwise initialization is automatic, and for uncomplicated classes like `simple`, you do not need to consider the effects on the object copies that C++ makes. When classes declare pointer members, however, memberwise initialization can cause serious problems. The next section demonstrates how this can lead to major bugs.

# Copying Pointer Members

When a class contains or inherits one or more pointer members, you must carefully consider the consequences of memberwise initialization for the three situations outlined in the preceding sections. This is doubly important when the class also declares a destructor, as it probably will do in order to delete memory assigned to the pointers.

As an example of the problems that can arise, Listing 9.10 declares the same `simple` class you examined earlier. To that class, the program adds a destructor. Although the purpose of the demonstration is to illustrate why copying pointer members is dangerous, the class does *not* declare such members. (Doing so might corrupt the heap, and though unlikely, could cause your computer to hang.) After the listing, I'll show you why the program is a potential troublemaker.

**Listing 9.10. TROUBLE.CPP.**

```
 1:  // trouble.cpp -- Trouble with memberwise initialization
 2:
 3:  #include <tscdefs.h>
 4:  #include IOSTREAM_H
 5:
 6:  class simple {
 7:  private:
 8:    int i;
 9:    float r;
10:  public:
11:    simple()
12:      { i = 0; r = 0; }
13:    simple(int ii, float rr)
14:      { i = ii; r = rr; }
15:    ~simple();
16:  };
17:
```

*continues*

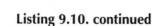

## Listing 9.10. continued

```
18:  main()
19:  {
20:    cout << "\nsimple v1;";
21:    simple v1;
22:
23:    cout << "\nsimple v2(100, 3.14159);";
24:    simple v2(100, 3.14159);
25:
26:    cout << "\nsimple v3 = v2;";
27:    simple v3 = v2;
28:    return 0;
29:  }
30:
31:  simple::~simple()
32:  {
33:    cout << "\nInside simple's destructor";
34:  }
```

When you run TROUBLE, you'll see that `simple`'s destructor is called three times, once for each constructed object of the class—v1, v2, and v3. The first two objects are defined normally at lines 21 and 24. The third object v3 is initialized by making a copy of v2 (line 27).

So far, TROUBLE is trouble free. But suppose you declared the class to contain a pointer member:

```
class simple {
private:
  char *s;
  // ... other members
}
```

In the constructors, you might then allocate space to the char pointer s using new. For example, the constructor could execute the statement

```
s = new char[129];
```

After that, s addresses a 129-byte space on the heap. So far so good. Of course, you'll also want to delete that space in the class destructor. Doing that will reclaim the allocated space for other uses—generally a wise move. The destructor will need a statement such as

```
delete[] s;
```

That seems harmless enough, but you have just introduced a nasty bug into the code! When the program initializes v3 at line 27, C++ copies each data member from v2 to v3, *including* the pointer member s. The s members in v2 and v3 now address the same location in memory. When the destructor for v2 runs, that space is deleted. But the destructor will also run for v3, causing the program to delete that *same* space twice. The memberwise initialization of v3 caused the s pointer member to address the same location in the heap, a dangerous condition to be avoided at all costs.

# The Copy Constructor

The solution to the duplicate pointer member problem is to prevent the condition from ever occurring. Doing that is possible by overriding C++'s default memberwise initialization of copied objects. As I mentioned earlier, when such copies are made, C++ does not call the class constructor. Rather, C++ copies each member from one object to the other. By providing a special *copy constructor* in a class, you can override that default action, thus preventing C++ from copying pointer members.

To create a copy constructor, use the prototype form *CLASS(const CLASS&)* where *CLASS* is the class in which the prototype appears. The prototyped function may be inline or declared as a callable function. It may not be virtual, and it is not inherited by derived classes, though a copy constructor in a derivation may call its base copy constructor (see "Copying Derived Class Objects" later in this chapter).

To add a copy constructor to the simple class from Listing 9.10, modify the class declaration to the following:

```
class simple {
private:
  int i;
  float r;
  char *s;
public:
  simple()
    { i = 0; r = 0; s = new char[129]; }
  simple(int ii, float rr)
    { i = ii; r = rr; s = new char[129]; }
  ~simple();
  simple(simple &copy);
};
```

The next-to-last line declares the copy constructor. Like all constructors, a copy constructor has the same name as its class (`simple`). Because the constructor receives a reference to another class object—the one that's being copied to this one—the constructor must declare a single reference parameter of the class type. The parameter name copy can be anything you like. Later in the program, implement the copy constructor with code such as

```
simple::simple(simple &copy)
{
  cout << "\nInside simple's copy constructor";
  i = copy.i;
  r = copy.r;
  s = strdup(copy.s);
}
```

The output stream statement isn't necessary, but if you try these changes, the statement will show you when the copy constructor runs. The three assignments illustrate the correct way to override C++'s default memberwise initialization of copied class objects. The statements copy each member from the reference parameter copy to the new object's data members of the same names. To handle the pointer member s, the final assignment allocates new space on the heap and copies the *value* addressed by the reference object. (In a real program, you'd also want to include error-handling checks to deal with out-of-memory conditions.) The pointer members now address distinct locations that hold copies of the appropriate values. Bugs will no longer fly in when the class destructor deletes the space allocated to the pointer members.

The copy constructor runs automatically for the three cases listed earlier: when an object is used to initialize a newly defined object of the same class, when a statement passes an object to a function's value parameter of that class, and when a function returns an object of the class data type. The other constructors still operate as before.

Unfortunately, the solution is not yet perfect. Although the copy constructor deals sensibly with the three situations when C++ makes a copy of a class object, a possible hot spot remains. When a statement directly assigns one object to another, you must again consider what will happen if those objects contain pointer members. The next section explains how to handle these situations.

# Memberwise Assignment

C++ always permits direct assignment of one variable to another of the same or a compatible type. Because one of the goals of OOP features and classes in C++ is to give programmers the means to invent new data types, it should be no surprise that C++ allows you to assign objects of the same classes to each other. As explained in the previous sections, however, such assignments might cause pointers to address the same locations in memory, a dangerous situation to avoid at all costs.

Consider the simple case of defining a couple of objects of type `simple` (from Listing 9.10) and then copying one of those objects to the other. For example, you could write these lines:

```
simple v1;
simple v2(9876, 1.2345);
v1 = v2;
```

After defining v1 with default values and defining v2 with explicit values, 9876 and 1.2345, an assignment statement copies v2 to v1. As before, when making such copies, C++ transfers the individual members from v2 to v1. It does *not* call any class constructor for v1. If the class contains or inherits a pointer member, the copied pointers will now address the same location in memory, which almost certainly will lead to problems.

A copy constructor can't solve this problem because the objects involved have already been constructed. In the case of the assignment of v2 to v1, no new object is created. Rather, the one object is merely copied to the other.

The cure is to overload the assignment operator. By doing that, any assignments of one object to an object of the same class will cause the overloaded function to run, replacing C++'s default memberwise assignment and giving you the opportunity to prevent pointer members from addressing identical locations in memory.

Overloading the assignment operator is similar to overloading other operators. The overloaded function's prototype must be in the general form *void operator=(const CLASS&)*, where *CLASS* is the name of the class that declares the overloaded function.

To add an overloaded assignment operator function to the `simple` class, insert this line in the class's public section:

```
void operator=(const simple &copy);
```

That overloads the = operator and specifies a reference parameter named copy of type `simple`. The parameter is the one being copied to the object for which a statement calls the operator= function. In the assignment a = b, copy would refer to b. The const keyword tells the compiler to disallow any changes to the object passed by reference to the overloaded function. You may change copy to a different name if you want.

Implement the overloaded assignment function using code that's similar to the statements you inserted earlier into the copy constructor:

```
void simple::operator=(const simple &copy)
{
  cout << "\nInside simple's operator= function";
  if (this == &copy) return;
  if (s != NULL) delete s;
  i = copy.i;
  r = copy.r;
  s = strdup(copy.s);
}
```

As before, the output statement is just for illustration. If you are making these changes, when you run the program, the statement will show you exactly when the overloaded function runs. The first if statement compares the this pointer to the address of the copy reference parameter. This catches the assignment of the *same* object to itself. For example, suppose that you execute the statements

```
simple v1, v2;
v1 = v1;
```

That may be a mistake, but you certainly wouldn't want to have the code duplicate the same object on top of itself. Comparing this to the assignment operator function's reference parameter prevents executing wasteful code. (In a program that uses aliases to address objects, copying an object to itself might occur either by accident or by design, so this rule is an important one to remember for overloaded assignment functions.)

The second if statement in the assignment function deletes the space (if any) currently allocated to pointer s. Remember that the two objects have already been constructed; therefore, any pointer members might have been allocated space on the heap. You'll probably want to delete that space in the object receiving the copy (the object to the left of =).

The other assignments in the overloaded function are the same as in the copy constructor. Each statement simply copies the member from the reference parameter to the object for which the function was called. The result is a copy of the values, but not the pointers. Both object's destructors can now safely delete any space allocated to pointer members in the class objects without worry that the same space will be deleted more than once.

With the overloaded `operator=` function in place, assignments of `simple` objects now call the function to perform the copy. When you write

```
a = b;
```

C++ actually executes the statement

```
a.operator=(b);
```

In other words, a reference to b is passed to object a's `operator=` function, which is expected to copy the members from b into a.

> **Note:** The preceding discussions about copying objects imply that only pointer members can lead to trouble. That's the typical case; however, you should also consider *every* possible consequence that might arise when a copy of an object is made. For example, a constructor might perform some other critical action that will be skipped for a copied object. In that case, you might need to include a copy constructor and an overloaded assignment operator function to execute that same critical action for copies of the class objects.

# Calling *operator=* from a Copy Constructor

Because a copy constructor and an overloaded assignment operator function `operator=` perform similar jobs, supplying both functions for a class is wasteful. Each of the functions copies the members of one object to another; the only significant difference is that the copy constructor creates a new object. The assignment function copies values to an *existing* object of the class.

Here's one way to combine the two functions to reduce duplication. First, declare the class as usual:

```
class simple {
private:
  int i;
  float r;
  char *s;
public:
  simple();
  ~simple();
```

```
  simple(simple &copy);
  void operator=(const simple &copy);
};
```

To keep `simple` even more simple, I've left out some of the details from earlier examples. The last two prototypes declare the copy constructor and overloaded `operator=` function. The copy constructor will run when

- A definition initializes a new object with a copy of another object.

- A statement passes a class object to a function's value parameter.

- A function returns an object of type `simple`.

Those are the same three cases listed earlier. The overloaded `operator=` function runs when a statement assigns an existing object of type `simple` to another objects of the same class.

To avoid duplicating the efforts of copying members in both functions, you can have the copy constructor call the overloaded `operator=` function. The implementations for both functions show one way to accomplish this:

```
simple::simple(simple &copy)
{
  s = NULL;
  *this = copy;
}

void simple::operator=(const simple &copy)
{
  if (this == &copy) return;
  delete[] s;
  i = copy.i;
  r = copy.r;
  s = strdup(copy.s);
}
```

The copy constructor (the first of the two functions) sets pointer member s to NULL and then assigns the reference parameter copy to *this. Because this addresses the object under construction, the assignment would normally kick C++'s default memberwise initialization code into action. But since the = operator has been overloaded by the `operator=` function, that function takes over C++'s default assignments to copy each member from the object being copied to the new one's members.

When pulling this trick, be sure to set all pointer members to NULL in the copy constructor, as done here to member s. This way, when the operator= function carries out the assignment of *this = copy, any deleted null pointers will have a harmless effect. Obviously, deleting unallocated space would be a serious error and would probably lead to a colossal crash.

## Copying Derived Class Objects

A significant concern is the effect in a derived class of a copy constructor and overloaded operator= function in a base class declaration. The derived class inherits the copy constructor just as it inherits all other member functions from the base. And that constructor will be called automatically at the appropriate times. However, derived classes do *not* inherit overloaded operator functions, thus complicating assignments of derived class objects.

To handle those situations, when the derived class adds pointer members, it too should have a copy constructor and an overloaded operator= function. The designs of those functions may be similar to those for simple. However, in the new operator= function, it's possible to call the base class function for copying values of inherited data members. Assuming the derived class's function prototype is

```
void operator=(const complex &copy);
```

to call the base class's similar function, use a statement such as

```
simple::operator=(copy);
```

# Overloading and Memory Management

The C++ memory manager is capable enough to handle memory allocations for most programs. However, there are times when you'll want to exercise greater control over memory resources. For instance, you may want to provide for virtual memory, storing some objects in memory and others on disk until needed. Or you may want to allocate space from a fixed pool that the program reserves for specific class objects, a method that may reduce the potential for heap fragmentation.

To satisfy these and other special requirements, you can overload the new and delete operators. Doing this gives you the means to trap memory allocation requests for objects of a specific class. Other allocations continue to use the standard C++ heap management facilities. Overloading new and delete in a class declaration does not affect how those operators work for other data types.

## Assignments to *this*

In past versions of C++, a constructor could assign the address of a memory buffer to the this pointer. That space would then be used to store the constructed object's data members. In that way, the constructor took over operator new's allocation of memory to provide custom allocations for class objects.

File THISIS.CPP on disk demonstrates how the technique was used. The compilers supported by this book no longer permit assigning values to this, and this file is provided for your information only. If you run into the method in an older C++ program, you'll have to convert the code to use the more modern custom memory management tool described in the next section.

## Overloading *new*

You may overload the new operator just as you can any other operator such as + or =. Overloading new in a class declaration tells the compiler that from now on you will take care of memory allocation requests for objects of the class.

To overload new, insert a function prototype of the form *void * operator new(size_t size);*. Future uses of new to allocate space for class objects will then be directed to the overloaded function. The function should return the address of space allocated for the object. If no space is available, the function should return 0.

Listing 9.11, OVERNEW.CPP, is a simple though complete example showing how to customize new to allocate space for objects of a class. Instead of storing the objects on the heap in the usual way, for the demonstration, the program stuffs the objects into a global buffer.

### Listing 9.11. OVERNEW.CPP.

```
1:  // overnew.cpp -- Overload the new operator
2:
```

```
 3:   #include <tscdefs.h>
 4:   #include IOSTREAM_H
 5:   #include <stddef.h>
 6:
 7:   class brandNew {
 8:   private:
 9:     int x;
10:   public:
11:     brandNew();
12:     void * operator new(size_t size);
13:     void operator delete(void *) { }
14:   };
15:
16:   char buf[512];
17:   int index;
18:
19:   main()
20:   {
21:     cout << "\nCreating local object";
22:     brandNew b1;
23:
24:     cout << "\nAllocating space via new";
25:     brandNew *b2 = new brandNew;
26:     brandNew *b3 = new brandNew;
27:     brandNew *b4 = new brandNew;
28:     brandNew *b5 = new brandNew;
29:     delete b2;
30:     delete b3;
31:     delete b4;
32:     delete b5;
33:     return 0;
34:   }
35:
36:   brandNew::brandNew()
37:   {
38:     cout << "\nInside constructor";
39:     x = index;
40:   }
41:
42:   void *brandNew::operator new(size_t size)
43:   {
44:     cout << "\nInside overloaded new. Size == " << size;
```

```
45:    if (index >= 512 - sizeof(brandNew))
46:      return 0;
47:    else {
48:      int k = index;
49:      index += sizeof(brandNew);
50:      return &buf[k];
51:    }
52:  }
```

The overloaded new operator function at lines 42–52 checks whether space is available in the global buffer. If not, the function returns 0, causing new to return null. (The program doesn't check for this condition, but you should do that in a real setting.) If space is available, the global index is incremented by the size of the memory request, passed to the new function in the size parameter. In that event, the function returns the address of the newly allocated space.

OVERNEW is a complete demonstration of an overloaded new operator, but the program lacks the sophistication of a finished product. In your own programs, you'll undoubtedly have to provide more extensive programming for keeping track of allocated space. Also, it probably makes little sense to store objects in a global buffer, used here only for illustration. Instead, you might allocate space for the buffer in another location, perhaps on the heap or on disk.

## Overloading *delete*

Of course, the other side of the memory allocation coin is the delete operator. As with new, you can overload delete to trap deletions of objects addressed by pointers.

An overloaded delete function's prototype must be in the form *void operator delete(void *p)*, where p is the address of the object being deleted. Alternatively, you may declare the function using the form *void operator delete(void *p, size_t size)*. When using this second format, the compiler will pass in *size* the number of bytes to dispose.

To add an overloaded delete function to the brandNew class in Listing 9.11, add this prototype to the class's public section:

```
void operator delete(void *p);
```

Next, append the function's implementation to the end of the listing:

```
void brandNew::operator delete(void *p)
{
  cout << "\nInside overloaded delete.";
}
```

The overloaded function doesn't do anything except display a message. When you run the program, the message tells you exactly when the overloaded `delete` operator is called to action.

As this experiment shows, it's fairly simple to override `delete`. It's another matter to manage the deletion of memory or other space allocated to class objects. Don't attempt this technique unless absolutely necessary. In most cases, the default `new` and `delete` operators are more than adequate.

> **Note:** To use the C++ memory manager to allocate heap space for objects that override `new`, preface the operator with a double colon. For example, the statement `brandNew *x = ::new brandNew;` bypasses the overloaded `new` operator function. Similarly, the statement `::delete x;` calls the C++ deletion routine, not the overloaded `delete` operator function.

# Overloading Streams

S ample listings throughout this book use input and output stream statements for reading and displaying values. You may be surprised to discover that streams are not part of the C++ language, but are implemented as classes in the C++ library. The declarations for those classes are stored in the header file iostream.h (iostream.hpp in Zortech C++), which nearly every program in this book includes by using the macro IOSTREAM_H.

The following sections explain how to tap into input and output stream statements for your own classes. As you'll see, by overloading the input and output stream operators, it's possible to teach C++ how to handle stream statements that include any type of class object.

# Overloading Output Streams

Normally, output streams can handle only simple data types, `int`, `long`, `float`, `char *`, and so on. However, by overloading the output stream operator `<<`, you can easily add your own classes to the data types that output stream statements are designed to use.

Listing 9.12 shows a typical example. The program declares a class named `point` that stores two `int` values `x` and `y`, representing the coordinate value of a location, perhaps on a graphics display. Usually, to display the values of private data members like `x` and `y`, you would have to call member functions such as `getx` and `gety`. But by adding the `point` class to those that output streams can handle, it's possible to display `point` variables without going to all that trouble.

### Listing 9.12. POINTOUT.CPP.

```
1:  // pointout.cpp -- Demonstrate overloading output streams
2:
3:  #include <tscdefs.h>
4:  #include IOSTREAM_H
5:
6:  class point {
7:  private:
8:    int x, y;
9:  public:
10:   point() { x = y = 0; }
11:   point(int xx, int yy) { x = xx; y = yy; }
12:   void putx(int xx) { x = xx; }
13:   void puty(int yy) { y = yy; }
14:   int getx(void) { return x; }
15:   int gety(void) { return y; }
16:   friend ostream& operator<<(ostream& os, point &p);
17:  };
18:
19:  main()
20:  {
21:    point p;
22:
23:    cout << p << '\n';
24:    p.putx(100);
25:    p.puty(200);
```

```
26:    cout << p << '\n';
27:    return 0;
28: }
29:
30: ostream& operator<<(ostream& os, point &p)
31: {
32:   os << "x == " << p.x << ", y == " << p.y;
33:    return os;
34: }
```

Line 16 overloads the output stream operator with a friend function named operator<<. The function returns a reference to ostream—one of the classes declared in the I/O stream library. Two parameters are also listed for the overloaded function: os, a reference to ostream, and p, a reference to a point object. In other classes, use this same format, but replace point with your own class name. The other elements remain the same.

The implementation of the friend function appears at lines 30–34. Because the function is a friend of class point, the statement at line 32 may directly access the x and y data members in the parameter p. Notice that this line is itself an output stream statement, which writes the values of the two data members plus two literal strings to the ostream reference os. Finally, the function returns os.

As a result of these steps, the statements at lines 23 and 26 may now pass objects of class point to the output stream cout. When those statements run, they display

```
x == 0, y == 0
x == 100, y == 200
```

Because the operator<< friend function returns an ostream reference, it's also possible to nest multiple uses of the output stream operator. For example, if p1, p2, and p3 are objects of type point, you can display their values with the single statement

```
cout << p1 << "; " << p2 << "; " << p3;
```

Technically, such statements are executed as multiple function calls to various overloaded output-stream operators. For example, the above line is executed as though it were written

```
((((cout << p1) << "; ") << p2) << "; ") << p3;
```

Luckily, there's no need to use all those confusing parentheses, although the statement will compile and run.

> **Note:** Overloading output stream statements is a handy technique to remember for debugging. To display a series of member members in a complex class, it may be easier to provide an output stream function rather than call member functions for every value you want to examine.

# Overloading Input Streams

Overloading the input stream operator >> is similar to overloading output streams. Providing an overloaded input stream function effectively teaches C++ how to read objects of a specific class type.

Listing 9.13 adds input stream capability to the POINTOUT.CPP sample program.

### Listing 9.13. POINTIN.CPP.

```
1:  // pointin.cpp -- Demonstrate overloading input streams
2:
3:  #include <tscdefs.h>
4:  #include IOSTREAM_H
5:
6:  class point {
7:  private:
8:    int x, y;
9:  public:
10:   point() { x = y = 0; }
11:   point(int xx, int yy) { x = xx; y = yy; }
12:   void putx(int xx) { x = xx; }
13:   void puty(int yy) { y = yy; }
14:   int getx(void) { return x; }
15:   int gety(void) { return y; }
16:   friend ostream& operator<<(ostream& os, point &p);
17:   friend istream& operator>>(istream& is, point &p);
18: };
19:
20: main()
21: {
22:   point p;
```

```
23:
24:    cout << p << '\n';
25:    p.putx(100);
26:    p.puty(200);
27:    cout << p << '\n';
28:    cout << "\nEnter x and y values: ";
29:    cin >> p;
30:    cout << "\nYou entered: " << p;
31:    return 0;
32:  }
33:
34:  ostream& operator<<(ostream& os, point &p)
35:  {
36:    os << "x == " << p.x << ", y == " << p.y;
37:    return os;
38:  }
39:
40:  istream& operator>>(istream& is, point &p)
41:  {
42:    is >> p.x >> p.y;
43:    return is;
44:  }
```

Line 17 declares the input-stream friend function, overloading operator>> for the point class. Except for the reference to istream and the function result type, the input stream function is similar to the output function above.

The new function's implementation reads values for x and y via the istream reference parameter is. After that, a return statement returns the istream so that input statements may be nested.

When you run the program, you'll be prompted to enter x and y values. Type two integers separated by a space. As you'll see, the input stream statement at line 29 stores both values you enter in the class object. Line 30 displays those values.

# Miscellany

In any toolchest, there are always a few odds and ends that you'll rarely use, but that when the need arises, you'll be glad to have. The following C++ tips fall into this category.

# Other I/O Streams

The I/O stream library declares one input stream object, cin, of type istream. As you've seen in earlier chapters, you can input values with input-stream statements such as

```
cin >> v;
```

The same header file also declares four output streams of type ostream: cout, cerr, cprn, and caux. You'll recognize the first; it's attached to the system's standard output device, usually the console. The statement

```
cout << v;
```

sends v's value in character form to cout. You can use the other three output streams in similar statements. To write an error message, use a statement like this:

```
cerr << "ERROR: Trouble in paradise!";
```

You can, of course, write error messages via cout. However, if the program's user redirects standard output to a file, the messages will also be redirected and they might be missed. When you don't want that to happen, write the messages to cerr, which can't be redirected away from the console (at least not as easily as the system's standard output can).

To send output streams to the printer, use cprn in place of cout. For example, this prints a line of text:

```
cprn << "This appears on the printer\n";
```

To send output streams to the system's auxiliary output, often attached to a serial output port, use caux:

```
caux << "This line is directed to the auxiliary output\n";
```

> **Note:** Writing text to caux may not be a reliable method for communicating between two computers linked via a serial cable. It may be possible to use caux informally to display text on a terminal, but it probably is not possible to use output stream statements to communicate with remote systems via modems.

# Conditional Expressions

C++ and C share a shorthand form of the common if statement. Both forms perform identical jobs, but the shorthand version can be useful at times, and it may even generate slightly smaller, though not necessarily more efficient, compiled code.

Suppose that you have defined a symbol DEBUGGING. If the symbol is true, you want a char * variable named version to address the string "0.10b"; otherwise, you want version to address the string "1.00". You could initialize version with an if statement like this:

```
if (DEBUGGING)
  version = "0.10b";
else
  version = "1.00";
```

That requires the compiler to create instructions that reference version twice. The equivalent shorthand conditional expression eliminates the duplicate reference:

```
version = DEBUGGING ? "0.10b" : "1.00";
```

The shorthand statement has the same effect as the longer if version. Actually, there are two statements: the conditional expression DEBUGGING ? "0.10b" : "1.00" and the assignment to version. Conditional expressions have values and therefore are typically assigned to variables. In general, the conditional expression has the form

```
condition ? default : alternate
```

The *condition* may be any expression that evaluates to a true (nonzero) or false (0) result. The question mark is required. The *default* value will be the final value of the entire expression if *condition* is true. Otherwise, the *alternate* value will be the value of the expression. The two selection values, *default* and *alternate*, must be separated with a colon. A typical use for a conditional expression is to select the lesser of two values:

```
result = (v1 < v2) ? v1 : v2;
```

That sets result to v1 only if v1 is less than v2. If v1 is greater or equal to v2, v2 will be assigned to result. The conditional expression has the identical effect as this if statement:

```
if (v1 < v2)
  result = v1;
else
  result = v2;
```

Shorthand conditional expressions are useful for assigning choices of values to arrays. For example, this expression sets the first character of a string to a British pound sign if an `int` variable `dollars` is false, otherwise the first character will be a dollar sign:

```
string[0] = (dollars == 0) ? '£' : '$';
```

The compiler may be able to generate smaller code because it has to create instructions to reference `string[0]` only once. The equivalent `if` statement requires two references to `string`:

```
if (dollars == 0)
  string[0] = '£';
else
  string[0] = '$';
```

Because only one of the references executes based on the value of `dollars`, both expressions take about the same amount of time to run. However, the conditional expression may occupy slightly less space in the finished program's code file.

It's also possible to nest conditional expressions, creating statements like this:

```
char c = (index > 100) ? 'c' : (index <= 50) ? 'a' : 'b';
```

When that statement executes, it will set `char c` to `'a'` if `index` is 50 or less, to `'b'` if `index` equals from 51 to 100, or to `'c'` if `index` is greater than 100. The equivalent `if` statement is

```
char c;
if (index > 100)
  c = 'c';
else if (index <= 50)
  c = 'a';
else
  c = 'b';
```

Complex nested conditional expressions can be extremely difficult to read. For that reason, I usually prefer the longer `if` statements even though they may increase the size of the compiled code file.

# Resolving Global Function Conflicts

Because classes encapsulate code and data, you are free to use any names you like for member functions and data members. Those names are permanently associated with a class name, and therefore, the names can't conflict with others in the program.

However, if you use an existing identifier for a class member function or member, you may have to explain to the compiler which of the similar names you intend to use. For example, suppose you create this class:

```
class conflict {
private:
  int x, y;
public:
  conflict();
  int getx(void) { return x; }
  int gety(void) { return y; }
};
```

The class stores two private variables, x and y. Because those identifiers are stowed away inside the class, there's no possibility of a conflict with any other variables of the same name. But suppose that the program defines these two global values:

```
int x = 100;
int y = 200;
```

In the class constructor, you want to set a new conflict object's x and y members to the global default values. But you can't write the constructor this way:

```
conflict::conflict()
{
  x = x;   // ???
  y = y;   // ???
}
```

There's no way the compiler can know what those two statements are supposed to do. To tell the compiler to use the global x and y values, preface their names with the scope resolution operator :: as shown here:

```
conflict::conflict()
{
  x = ::x;
  y = ::y;
}
```

When an identifier is prefaced with ::, the compiler looks outside of the current scope for that symbol. In this example, the scope resolution operator tells the compiler to use the global symbols. Without the operator, the references to x and y are directed to those members in the class object.

You can use a double colon also to call functions. For example, if `int getx(void)` is a member function and if there is a global function of that same name, `::getx()` calls the global function; `getx()` inside another member of the class refers to the member function.

## Default Status of Inherited Classes

It's best always to use the `private`, `public`, and `protected` keywords to mark the status of class members. In general, design your classes with this format:

```
class name {
private:
  // private members
protected:
  // protected members
public:
  // public members
};
```

The order and number of sections in the class are not important. (Some C++ programmers prefer to list public members first, private ones last.) In the absence of an explicit status keyword, members default to private status. In this class, the two data members count and value are private:

```
class reference {
  int count;    // private member
  float value;  // private member
public:
  reference();
  // other public members
};
```

It's also a good idea always to specify whether an inherited base class's members are to be `public` or `private`. Suppose, for example, that `newClass` inherits the reference class. You can write the new class declaration this way:

```
class newClass : public reference {
  // members for newClass
};
```

By stating that reference is public, all members inherited from reference retain their original public, private, or protected status. Changing the public keyword to `private` in the derivation list causes the inherited members to become private to the new class:

```
class newClass : private reference {
  // members for newClass
};
```

The significance of this change becomes important only if *another* class inherits from `newClass`. Because the `reference` base class was converted to `private` status, a further derivation of `newClass` cannot access any of `reference`'s members. The `private` keyword says "inherit the members from the base, but prevent any future derivations from using any of those same members."

You can also declare a `protected` class. For example, in the declaration

```
class newClass : protected reference {
  // members for newClass
};
```

`reference`'s public members become protected members in `newClass`. Any private and protected members in `reference` retain their original status.

If you do not state `public`, `protected`, or `private` in a derivation list, the default status is private. If you write the derived `newClass` like this:

```
class newClass : reference {
  // members for newClass
};
```

future derivations of `newClass` will not be able to refer to any members inherited from `reference`.

# Pointers to Member Functions

As you learned in Chapter 4, "Pointers About Pointers," it's possible to address conventional functions with pointers. To create a pointer to a function, use a definition such as this:

```
float (* myfnptr)(int k);
```

That defines a pointer named `myfnptr` to address any function that accepts one `int` parameter and returns a `float` value. If the program defines a function `theFunction()` with that same type of parameter and return type, this statement assigns the address of that function to the pointer and then calls the function through the pointer:

```
myfnptr = &theFunction;
float fp = (* myfnptr)(100);
```

Calling functions via pointers provides a convenient method for programs to attach custom functions for critical operations. For instance, a graphics program might define a pointer to a `putPixel()` function. By writing your own `putPixel()` function and assigning that function's address to the function pointer, the compiled program can call your custom code.

The same techniques do not work for functions that are members of a class. The reason you can't create common function pointers to class members is that those members *must* be called in reference to an object of the class. A pointer to a function may be called outside of the context of a class object; therefore, common function pointers can't call member functions.

However, it is possible to create a member function pointer by binding the pointer to the class name. For example, for a class named `firstClass`, to design a pointer to a member function that requires no input and returns `float`, use the definition

```
float (firstClass::*myfnptr)(void);
```

To design `myfnptr` to address a member function that accepts two `int` parameters and returns `void`, use this instead:

```
void (firstClass::*myfnptr)(int, int);
```

Those two definitions do not specify *which* member function `myfnptr` addresses, only the *form* of the function that may be assigned to the pointer variable. It's still necessary to create an object of the class and to assign to the pointer the address of a class member of the appropriate form.

Listing 9.14, MFNPTR.CPP, shows the basic steps that are required to define and use pointers to member functions.

### Listing 9.14. MFNPTR.CPP.

```
1:   // mfnptr.cpp -- Member function pointers
2:
3:   #include <tscdefs.h>
4:   #include IOSTREAM_H
5:   #include IOMANIP_H
6:
```

```
 7:  class firstClass {
 8:  private:
 9:    int count;
10:  public:
11:    firstClass() { count = 0; }
12:    int access(void);
13:  };
14:
15:  int (firstClass::*myfnptr)(void);
16:
17:  main()
18:  {
19:    int i;
20:    firstClass fc;
21:
22:    cout << "\nCall access the normal way:\n";
23:    for (i = 0; i < 9; i++)
24:      cout << setw(8) << dec << fc.access();
25:
26:    cout << "\n\nCall access via the member function pointer\n";
27:    myfnptr = &firstClass::access;
28:    for (i = 0; i < 9; i++)
29:      cout << setw(8) << dec << (fc.*myfnptr)();
30:
31:    cout << "\n\nMember function pointer and a dynamic object\n";
32:    firstClass *fp = new firstClass;
33:    for (i = 0; i < 9; i++)
34:      cout << setw(8) << dec << (fp->*myfnptr)();
35:    return 0;
36:  }
37:
38:  int firstClass::access(void)
39:  {
40:    return count++;
41:  }
```

Line 15 defines a pointer named myfnptr bound to a function that has no parameters and returns an int value. The pointer may address any function with that design in class firstClass. However, the pointer may *not* address a function even of an appropriate design that's not also a member of firstClass.

After defining a variable `fc` of type `firstClass` (line 20), the test program calls the class's `access()` function in the usual way (see lines 22–24). The expression `fc.access()` calls the `access()` function for the class object `fc`. (The test function increments and returns a private variable, just to give the program something to do.)

Lines 26–29 perform the identical operation as the preceding `for` loop, but use the member function pointer `myfnptr` to call `access()`. Line 27 assigns to `myfnptr` the address of the `access()` member function in `firstClass`. The compiler accepts this statement because `myfnptr` is bound to `firstClass` and is designed to address any function with an appropriate prototype. You could also replace the pointer definition (line 15) and the address assignment (line 27) with the single line

```
int (firstClass::*myfnptr)(void) = firstClass::access;
```

That both defines `myfnptr` and assign's to the pointer the address of the `access` member function. When calling the member function, you must follow two rules: Refer to an object of the class and surround the function call with parentheses. For example, if `n` is an `int` variable and `fc` is an object of `firstClass`, this copies to `n` the result of function `access()` called via the member function pointer:

```
n = (fc.*myfnptr)();
```

That's exactly equivalent to the more common statement

```
n = fc.access();
```

You can also call member functions via pointers when objects are addressed by other pointer variables. Lines 31–34 in MFNPTR show how to do that for a pointer `fp`, to which new allocates a dynamic object of `firstClass` (line 32). The expression at line 34

```
(fp->*myfnptr)();
```

calls the `access()` function for the object addressed by `fp`. The statement is equivalent to

```
fp->access();
```

In addition to addressing member functions with pointers, it's also possible to address other public data members. For example, if `firstClass` had a public `float` member named `balance`, you could define a pointer to that member by writing

```
float firstClass::*dataPtr;
```

That defines a pointer variable named `dataPtr` that can address any public `float` data member in class `firstClass`. The pointer may *not* address a `float` variable outside of the class. To assign the address of the hypothetical `balance` data member to `dataPtr`, execute this statement:

```
dataPtr = &firstClass::balance;
```

Or you could define the pointer and assign the address of the `balance` member with a single line. This replaces the previous two lines:

```
float firstClass::*dataPtr = &firstClass::balance;
```

Either way, `dataPtr` now addresses the `balance` member in `firstClass`. Actually, however, `dataPtr` does not hold the address of a memory location, but rather the offset to where the `balance` member will be stored in an object of the class. As with member function pointers, it is still necessary to refer to the addressed data member through a class object. These two statements assign a floating point value to the `balance` member and then use `dataPtr` to display that value:

```
fc.balance = 3.14159;
cout << "\nBalance=" << fc.*dataPtr;
```

The notation `fc.*dataPtr` is similar to the notation used to call a member function. However, the extra parentheses are not required when referring to data member members.

# Virtual Base Classes

When a derived class inherits from more than one base class—a situation commonly known as *multiple inheritance*—it's possible that somewhere along the line, more than one copy of a distant ancestor class's members will be brought along for the ride. For example, if classes X and Y each inherit the members of A, if a fourth class Z inherits both X and Y, the new class Z will have two copies of every member in A. What's more, to refer to the correct copies of those members, the program will have to use a scope resolution operator for X::member and Y::member; otherwise, the compiler won't be able to resolve plain references to the multiple `member` members.

This situation is not always undesirable, and there is nothing wrong with inheriting multiple copies of a distant class relative. However, when the multiple copies aren't needed, you can use *virtual base classes* to eliminate the duplications. A class that inherits a virtual base class will have only one copy of that base's members, regardless of how many derivations inherit that same base.

A few sample classes illustrate the problem and show how to prevent inheriting multiple base class members. First, here's the granddaddy base class—the one that's about to cause all the trouble:

```
class base {
protected:
  int basex;
public:
  base();
};
```

The class stores a single protected member named base. Next, you declare two derived classes that inherit base:

```
class derived1 : public base {
public:
  void doNothing(void) { }
};

class derived2 : public base {
public:
  void doNothing(void) { }
};
```

Each class inherits a copy of base's basex member. So far so good. But now you create one more class that inherits both of the two derived classes above:

```
class derived3 : public derived1, public derived2 {
public:
  void showValues(void);
};
```

Now there's a thorn in derived3's paw—the new class has just inherited two copies of the base class members. Because of that inheritance, the derived3 class has two basex members, one that came from derived1 and one that came from derived2.

By using expressions such as derived1::basex and derived2::basex, you can easily resolve any ambiguous references to the multiple basex members. However, suppose you need only one copy of basex in derived3. To do away with the unused extra basex copy, you can declare the derived bases to be virtual. To do that, change the declarations for derived1 and derived2 to

```
class derived1 : virtual public base {
public:
  void doNothing(void) { }
};

class derived2 : virtual public base {
public:
  void doNothing(void) { }
};
```

Now when derived3 inherits the derived classes, each of which inherits a virtual copy of base, there will be only one object of base's member members in the final derivation. Additionally, there's no longer any need to use a scope resolution operator and a class name to access the inherited basex member.

# Now That You've Learned C++...

You've come a long way from Chapter 1, "Discovering C++," but your journey into learning C++ is just beginning. Learning a new language is not a goal you will ever finish. There will always be new facts to learn, new tips to pick up, and new tools to acquire. As you write your own programs and learn more about C++, the following brief notes will answer a few questions that may arise.

## Differences Between C and C++

C++ and C are cut from similar molds, so it's not surprising that C++ can compile most C programs. However, the reverse is not true. A C compiler probably will choke on a C++ listing. C++'s unique features, such as classes, stream operators, and function overloading (to name only a few), aren't part of the C language.

You can compile many C-style programs with the C++ compilers supported by this book, and with other brands of C++. However, you will have to follow a few rules that C programmers sometimes break. When writing C-style programs, or when converting a C listing to C++, keep the following key differences between C and C++ in mind.

All functions *must* have prototypes before being called. In C, prototyping is not enforced as strictly as in C++, although ANSI C compilers do encourage prototyping.

C++ is much more strict about mixing data types in expressions. In assignment statements and when passing arguments to function parameters, try to use the same data types for variables.

C++ also insists that calls to functions in other modules have the correct numbers and types of parameters. If all your modules compile with no errors, but the linker refuses to create the finished executable code file, you may have passed the wrong type of argument to a function.

Don't use old-style function declarations where the parameters are listed by type, and then given names on separate lines below. This format is from C's ancient history and should be avoided.

Use `const void *` rather than `void *` as the type of a pointer that addresses a constant value.

Define variables only once. Use `extern` to refer to variables defined elsewhere, perhaps in another module.

Use `new` and `delete` rather than `malloc` and `free` whenever possible. Remember, it's possible to overload the `new` and `delete` operators. The same trick is not possible with `malloc` and `free`, which are functions, not operators.

All strings must end with a null terminating byte. This means that definitions like `char network[3] = "ABC";` will be rejected by C++ because there isn't room in the variable for the null terminator.

# Using Other C++ Compilers

In this book's ancestor, *Learning C++*, this section described hints for converting the programs in this book for use with other C++ compilers. This new and improved book, and accompanying disk, now supports five compilers from Borland, Microsoft, and Zortech. See Chapter 10, "Cross-Compilation Tools," for more information on using my definitions and modules, and for converting these items for other C++ compilers. After modifying these elements, you should be able to compile all of the programs in this book with only minor changes here and there.

# Questions and Exercises

9.1. Suppose that you have two unrelated classes named Engine and Fuel. Using friends, how can you allow Fuel members to access the private and protected members in Engine?

9.2. List one or more disadvantages of friend classes and functions.

9.3. What does function overloading allow you to do?

9.4. What is the one kind of function that may not be overloaded?

9.5. Add times (*) and divide (/) overloaded operator functions to the strop class in STROPS.CPP, Listing 9.6.

9.6. Add ++ and -- overloaded operators to the strop class in STROPS2.CPP, Listing 9.7. Implement the operators as member functions.

9.7. Given the declaration strop *sp, show how to create a reference alias named spAlias for an object addressed by sp.

9.8. Declare and implement a double type-conversion operator for class strop in NEWOPS.CPP, Listing 9.9.

9.9. What are the four times that C++ makes a copy of a class object. What is the primary danger of making such copies?

9.10. Given a class named Fruit and an object of Fruit named Orange, write a definition that uses Orange to initialize a new object named Grapefruit.

9.11. List the prototype for a copy constructor in the hypothetical Fruit class from Exercise 9.10.

9.12. List an overloaded assignment operator for the Fruit class from Exercise 9.10.

9.13. What is the default status of a class member that does not use the private:, protected:, or public: keywords?

9.14. What are the effects of the public and private keywords when applied to a base class in a derived class's derivation list? What is the default status of the inherited class members if neither keyword is used?

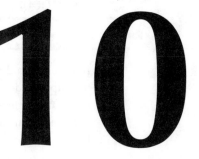

# Cross-Compilation Tools

In writing this book for five C++ compilers from three companies—Borland, Microsoft, and Zortech—I soon realized that "compatibility" is a relative term. Although all of the compilers implement most C++ language features similarly, they differ greatly in their add-on library files, headers, structure declarations, and other items.

When I reached an impasse—a program, for example, that would compile with one C++ compiler but not another—I attempted to solve the problem in a way that would permit me to continue revising the book. Eventually, I realized I had collected a set of cross-compilation tools that might be useful for developing other libraries and software to be used with more than one compiler. In each case, when troubles arose, I followed one of three courses of action:

- I created a macro symbol (typically but not always in all uppercase) to replace a symbol or a header filename. The symbol IOSTREAM_H, for example, is translated during compilation to iostream.h for Borland C++ and Microsoft C/C++, but to iostream.hpp for Zortech C++. This solution is better, I think, than asking you to rename your Zortech header files, or to copy them from .hpp files to new ones ending in .h—the approach favored by at least one C++ software vendor whose software tools I examined while researching this book.

- In other cases, I wrote a new function to emulate a feature in one compiler not supported in another. I also restored features no longer supplied with newer C++ releases. A good example is the `form()` function, which was removed from the newest AT&T C++ specification. (I should learn. The *one* function you rely on most heavily is the one that others decide has no purpose!) Another example is Zortech's `msleep()` function, which I duplicated for Borland and Microsoft. In order to honor each company's copyright, I did not examine the original source code for any such duplicated routines; instead, I wrote my own functions based on my experience with the originals and their descriptions in various references.

- In some programs (directory examples, for instance), I used conditional compilation directives such as `#ifdef` to select sections for each compiler. This is the least desirable solution, as it results in multiple statements that need to be modified should the program require updating. Because I intended to encapsulate directory routines in a class, however, (see Chapter 8, "Files and Directories"), I didn't want to waste time devising a set of compatible directory functions and structures. I did define some compatible directory symbols, though, to ease the pain of writing cross-compatible directory operations.

This chapter lists all of the cross-compilation tools that I developed for the programs in Chapters 1 to 9. I made no attempt to include tools for every language element, and many other incompatibilities undoubtedly remain among the supported compilers. I solved only those problems that needed solving.

You should consider my cross-compilation tools as a starting place, not the final destination. If you develop software for multiple compilers, you probably will add many of your own functions and symbols to mine. Read this chapter for information about how the library is organized, how to use the features in it, how to add your own modules, and how to convert the entire library for use with another C++ compiler.

# Building the Library

When programmers use the word "build," they generally mean "recompile all modules from scratch." You might need to build this book's library for another compiler or an upgraded version. Here's how.

Set up your compiler as explained in this book's introduction. Change to the C:\TSC\LIB directory (or its equivalent if you installed to a directory other than C:\TSC). Then run one of the build batch files:

- *BUILDBCC.BAT* Run this batch file to build the Borland C++ library (compatible with Borland C++ 3.0 and 3.1).

- *BUILDMSC.BAT* Run this batch file to build the Microsoft C/C++ library.

- *BUILDTCC.BAT* Run this batch file to build the Turbo C++ library.

- *BUILDZTC.BAT* Run this batch file to build the Zortech C++ library.

> **Note:** If you are rebuilding the library for more than one compiler, delete all .OBJ files in the directory C:\TSC\LIB\SOURCE before running each batch file.

Every batch file executes similar commands. In general terms, the batch files perform these steps:

1. Change to the SOURCE directory where the library source code files (such as FORM.CPP) are stored.

2. Copy all header files (those with filenames ending in .h) to ..\..\INCLUDE (equivalent to C:\TSC\INCLUDE if you installed to the recommended directory).

3. Run the MAKE utility to compile all library modules.

4. Change back to C:\TSC\LIB.

5. Run the compiler's library utility to install the compiled .OBJ code files into a library file, ending in .LIB.

> **Hint:** No file anywhere in the cross-compilation library refers to the C:\TSC directory by name. Instead, *relative directory references* as in step 2's ..\..\INCLUDE pathname permit batch and MAKE files to work correctly in any drive or directory. Try always to use similar relative paths in your own programs so you can move the files to other locations at will.

The result of running a build batch file is a .LIB file containing all of the library's compiled .OBJ modules. All headers that declare functions and other symbols for these modules are stored in the INCLUDE directory where programs can find them. I copy the headers to a new directory so I can use the library without requiring the original source files to be on line. A similar setup is especially useful for programming teams whose members share common modules that are "frozen"—that is, their sources are no longer in development and must not be changed. You can also delete the library sources to save room, so you can install the library on a small portable computer.

## The Compiler Identifier Symbol

A single header file, tscdefs.h, declares all cross-compilation library function prototypes and other symbols. To select the proper symbols for each compiler, tscdefs.h recognizes a compiler identifier symbol, which you must define to compile programs. These symbols are

- **__TSC_BTC__** Borland C++ or Turbo C++.

- **__TSC_MSC__** Microsoft C/C++.

- **__TSC_ZTC__** Zortech C++.

Use the Borland C++, Turbo C++, or Zortech C++ -D option to define the proper symbol for each compiler. Use the /D option with Microsoft C/C++. If you don't define a symbol, the library defaults to Borland C++ by executing the following conditional expressions:

```
#ifndef __TSC_BTC__
  #ifndef __TSC_MSC__
    #ifndef __TSC_ZTC__
      #define __TSC_BTC__
    #endif
  #endif
#endif
```

If you don't use Borland C++ as your main compiler, you can redefine the innermost symbol to change the default to one of the others. (See Listing 10.1 later in this chapter.)

# The Automated MAKE Files

Automated MAKE files are provided for the library and for the programs in each chapter. The automated MAKE files for each compiler are named MAKEFILE.xxx, where xxx is BTC, MSC, or ZTC. For example, in C:\TSC\LIB\SOURCE, the file MAKEFILE.BTC contains commands for compiling library modules for Borland C++ and Turbo C++.

To compile the library modules and other programs, rather than type a MAKE filename in a command such as

```
make -fmakefile.btc
```

you can rename the appropriate file for your compiler to MAKEFILE and then simply enter **make** (or **nmake** for Microsoft C/C++). Most MAKE utilities automatically search for a file named MAKEFILE in the current directory.

Generally, you should not modify the MAKEFILE.xxx files except to add new modules to the library, or new programs to the sample chapters. The next section explains how to select global options for rebuilding the library.

# MAKE File Options

In the C:\TSC directory are two files that prepare global symbols for use by individual MAKEFILE.xxx files. Each such file begins by reading two other files located in your installation directory (as before, xxx stands for BTC, MSC, or ZTC):

- ROOTxxx.INC Specifies the compiler's root pathname.

- MAKExxx.INC Declares compiler options and common symbols used by individual MAKE files.

These two files select all global compiler options. Changing any settings in these files affects all library modules and programs.

You can probably insert your compiler's pathname into ROOTxxx.INC and then forget about this file. Unless you install your compiler to a different directory, you probably won't ever change ROOTxxx.INC again. The file contains two commands:

```
CPPROOT = C:\borlandc
TSCROOT = C:\tsc
```

Symbol CPPROOT is used by other MAKE files to locate the compiler's executable programs and other files. You may set CPPROOT to any drive or directory, but if you change any of the compiler's default subdirectories, you will have to make additional changes to this book's MAKE files. (I suggest you use the default subdirectories as recommended by your compiler's manufacturer. Change only the drive and installation root directory. Some programmers, for example, install Borland C++ to C:\BC rather than C:\BORLANDC. That's fine, but it is not a good idea to change the name of the C:\BC\INCLUDE subdirectory.)

Symbol TSCROOT specifies the root directory where you installed this book's files. You may install to any drive or directory, or even a multidirectory path. (While writing this book, my working TSCROOT directory was D:\TSWAN\TSC\SOURCE.)

File MAKExxx.INC contains global compiler options listed in the Introduction. The following notes suggest changes you might want to make to these symbols for each compiler.

> **Note:** Global Turbo C++ options are stored in file TURBOC.INC, which you should rename MAKEBTC.INC before compiling. You can rename the file manually, or you can run the supplied SETTCC.BAT batch file to set up for Turbo C++. To change back to Borland C++, run SETBCC.BAT.

Never delete symbols from the MAKExxx.INC files (or from TURBOC.INC). To disable a particular option, set it to a null string. For example, to disable debugging information for Borland C++, in MAKEBTC.INC, change the command

```
CDEBUG = -v
```

to the following null command

```
CDEBUG =
```

> **Note:** The preceding change might also improve runtime performance because, with debugging enabled, inline class member functions are converted to callable functions so they can be traced by debugger commands. Turning off debugging information and compiling reinstates all inline functions.

## Borland C++ Options

In MAKEBTC.INC, the warning level symbol, WARN, is set to enable all compiler warnings. Set this symbol to null to use the compiler's default warnings or those specified in a TURBOC.CFG configuration file.

To change memory models, set MODEL to s (small), m (medium), c (compact), l (large), or h (huge). If you make this change, you *must* rebuild all library files. The library is designed to support only one memory model at a time.

> **Note:** You can easily modify the library to support multiple memory models. First, modify the appropriate BUILDxxx.BAT file to create TSCxxxM.LIB files for each memory model that you use. For Borland C++, you might create library files named TSCBCCS.LIB (small), TSCBCCM.LIB (medium), TSCBCCH.LIB (huge), and so on. In the MAKEBTC.INC file, set TSCLIB to tscbcc$(MODEL).lib. The expression $(MODEL) is translated to the MODEL symbol (m, s, and so forth), creating the appropriate filename for the model in effect. You also need to modify the MODEL setting, perhaps by removing it from MAKEBTC.INC and defining it on the command line using the -D MAKE file option.

To select global options, modify these two MAKEBTC.INC settings:

```
CFLAGS = -c -Od -g1 $(CDEBUG) $(WARN)
CLFLAGS = -Od -g1 $(CDEBUG) $(WARN)
```

Don't delete -c from CFLAGS (compile-only flags)—it's needed to compile separate modules to .OBJ files. Conversely, don't add -c to CLFLAGS (compile and link), or .EXE files won't be created. Except for these restrictions, you can add or subtract whatever options you like. Option -Od specifies no optimizations. Change this to any other optimizations you want—to -O2, for example, to select optimizations designed for faster performance, or to -O1 to generate potentially smaller code files.

Option -g1 halts compilation upon the first error or warning received. Except when learning how to program, this option is a nuisance and you probably should delete it. (When using lengthy MAKE files, however, errors and warnings might scroll out of view. To read these messages, enter a command such as **make >err.txt** and then scan the resulting ERR.TXT file for any problems.)

## Microsoft C/C++ Options

Microsoft C/C++ uses options similar to Borland C++, although of course, the actual settings differ in form. In MAKEMSC.INC, you find the commands

```
CFLAGS = /f /c $(WARN) /A$(MODEL) $(CDEBUG) /D__TSC_MSC__
CLFLAGS = /f $(WARN) /A$(MODEL) $(CDEBUG) $(TSCLIB) /D__TSC_MSC__
```

The /f option selects "fast compilation." This is probably the best setting for testing the library, but you should remove it for production-quality code. You might also want to specify selection optimizations as explained in Microsoft's references.

Notice how the symbol __TSC_MSC__ is defined at this stage. Don't change the /D options unless you modify tscdefs.h to define this symbol by default.

## Turbo C++ Options

Turbo C++ is essentially a stripped version of Borland C++, and it doesn't offer extensive optimizations. The TURBOC.INC file selects between generating .OBJ files and .EXE files and also specifies debugging and warning options:

```
CFLAGS = -c $(CDEBUG) $(WARN)
CLFLAGS = $(CDEBUG) $(WARN)
```

You can add any other Turbo C++ options to these symbols. The only restriction is that CFLAGS must include -c, and CLFLAGS must *not* include that option. For a list of Turbo C++ options, consult the compiler's references or type **tcc** at a DOS prompt.

## Zortech C++ Options

Zortech C++ options are similar to those used for Microsoft C/C++. The MAKEZTC.INC file defines these symbols:

```
CFLAGS = -c $(WARN) -m$(MODEL) $(CDEBUG) -I$(INC) -D__TSC_ZTC__
CLFLAGS = $(WARN) -m$(MODEL) $(CDEBUG) $(TSCLIB) -D__TSC_ZTC__
```

The symbol __TSC_ZTC__ must be defined for tscdefs.h unless you modify that header file to select Zortech C++ by default. You can add any other options to CFLAGS and CLFLAGS, but be sure to define -c as shown here (CFLAGS *must* define the compiler-only option, -c; CLFLAGS must *not* define that option).

# Using the Cross-Compilation Library

ou should now have a good grasp of how the library is organized. This section lists and describes the library's individual modules.

> **Note:** Several class modules in this book's chapters are also stored in the library. See Chapters 6, 7, and 8 for descriptions of modules such as WINDOW.CPP and STRITEM.CPP. Other files not described in those chapters are listed here.

## The tscdefs Header

This file is the main header for the cross-compilation library (see Listing 10.1, tscdefs.h). The file is located in C:\TSC\INCLUDE. All programs in this book include this header file by using the directive

```
#include <tscdefs.h>
```

### Listing 10.1. tscdefs.h.

```
 1:  /* ------------------------------------------------------------ *\
 2:  **   tscdefs.cpp -- Tom Swan's C++ Primer Misc Definitions       **
 3:  **   ------------------------------------------------------------ **
 4:  **                                                                **
 5:  **   This file defines various macros that simplify compiling     **
 6:  **   C++ programs with Borland C++ 3, Microsoft C/C++ 7, and      **
 7:  **   Zortech C++ 3. Programs in the Primer include this file      **
 8:  **   and use defined uppercase symbols such as DOS_GETDATE.       **
 9:  **   These symbols are translated at compile time to the          **
10:  **   appropriate name (e.g. _dos_getdate or dos_getdate).         **
11:  **                                                                **
12:  **   NOTE: Some sections below are position dependent.            **
```

*continues*

## Listing 10.1. continued

```
13:   **                                                          **
14:   ** ---------------------------------------------------------- **
15:   **      Copyright (c) 1992 by Tom Swan. All rights reserved    **
16:   \* ---------------------------------------------------------- */
17:
18:   #ifndef __TSCDEFS_H
19:   #define __TSCDEFS_H        // Prevent multiple includes
20:
21:   // ---------------------------------------------------------- //
22:
23:   //  Directory of conditional symbols
24:   //  At least one of the following symbols MUST be defined
25:   //  or some of the programs might not compile. You may add
26:   //  additional symbols to support other C++ compilers. If you
27:   //  define a new symbol, please let me know!
28:
29:   //  __TSC_xxx__  == Tom Swan's C++ Primer for compiler xxx
30:   //  __TSC_BTC__  == Borland C++ or Turbo C++
31:   //  __TSC_MSC__  == Microsoft C++
32:   //  __TSC_ZTC__  == Zortech C++
33:
34:   // ---------------------------------------------------------- //
35:
36:   //  Test whether at least one conditional symbol is defined.
37:   //  Default to Borland C++ or Turbo C++ (__TSC_BTC__)
38:
39:   #ifndef __TSC_BTC__
40:     #ifndef __TSC_MSC__
41:       #ifndef __TSC_ZTC__
42:         #define __TSC_BTC__
43:       #endif
44:     #endif
45:   #endif
46:
47:   // ---------------------------------------------------------- //
48:
49:   //  General purpose symbols (defined only if not presently defined)
50:   //  FALSE  == zero (0)
51:   //  TRUE   == one (1)
52:
```

```
53:  #ifndef FALSE
54:    #define FALSE 0
55:  #endif
56:  #ifndef TRUE
57:    #define TRUE 1
58:  #endif
59:
60:  // ------------------------------------------------------------ //
61:
62:  //   I/O Stream header
63:  //   IOSTREAM_H  == iostream.h or iostream.hpp
64:
65:  #if (defined __TSC_BTC__) ¦¦ (defined __TSC_MSC__)
66:    #define IOSTREAM_H <iostream.h>
67:    #define IOMANIP_H <iomanip.h>
68:  #elif defined __TSC_ZTC__
69:    #define IOSTREAM_H <iostream.hpp>
70:    #define IOMANIP_H <iomanip.hpp>
71:  #endif
72:
73:  // ------------------------------------------------------------ //
74:
75:  //   Display module header
76:  //   DISP_H == tscdisp.h (BTC, MSC) or disp.h (ZTC)
77:
78:  #if (defined __TSC_BTC__) ¦¦ (defined __TSC_MSC__)
79:    #define DISP_H <tscdisp.h>
80:  #elif defined __TSC_ZTC__
81:    #define DISP_H <disp.h>
82:  #endif
83:
84:  // ------------------------------------------------------------ //
85:
86:  //   Date and time symbols
87:  //   DOS_DATE_T    == DOS date struct
88:  //   DOS_TIME_T    == DOS time struct
89:  //   DOS_GETDATE   == DOS get date function
90:  //   DOS_GETTIME   == DOS get time function
91:
92:  #if defined __TSC_BTC__
93:    #define DOS_DATE_T struct dosdate_t
```

*continues*

671

## Listing 10.1. continued

```
 94:    #define DOS_TIME_T struct dostime_t
 95:    #define DOS_GETDATE _dos_getdate
 96:    #define DOS_GETTIME _dos_gettime
 97: #elif defined __TSC_MSC__
 98:    #define DOS_DATE_T struct _dosdate_t
 99:    #define DOS_TIME_T struct _dostime_t
100:    #define DOS_GETDATE _dos_getdate
101:    #define DOS_GETTIME _dos_gettime
102: #elif defined __TSC_ZTC__
103:    #define DOS_DATE_T struct dos_date_t
104:    #define DOS_TIME_T struct dos_time_t
105:    #define DOS_GETDATE dos_getdate
106:    #define DOS_GETTIME dos_gettime
107: #else error Conditional symbol not defined
108: #endif  // Date and time symbols
109:
110: // ------------------------------------------------------------ //
111:
112: //   DOS findfirst() and findnext() symbols
113: //   NOTE: All compilers MUST include <dos.h> to use these symbols!!!
114: //   NOTE: Borland C++ MUST include <dir.h> to use these symbols!!!
115: //   TSC_FIND     find structure name
116: //   NAME         find-structure filename member
117: //   ATTRIBUTE    find-structure attribute member
118: //   TIME         find-structure time member
119: //   DATE         find-structure date member
120: //   SIZE         find-structure size member
121: //   FA_ARCH      Archive attribute flag
122: //   FA_DIREC     Directory attribute flag
123: //   FA_LABEL     Volume label attribute flag
124: //   FA_NORMAL    Normal (files only) attribute flag
125: //   FA_SYSTEM    System file attribute flag
126: //   FA_HIDDEN    Hidden file attribute flag
127: //   FA_RDONLY    Read-only file attribute flag
128: #if (defined __TSC_ZTC__)
129:    #define TSC_FIND FIND
130:    #define NAME name
131:    #define ATTRIBUTE attribute
132:    #define TIME time
```

```
133:    #define DATE date
134:    #define SIZE size
135: #elif (defined __TSC_BTC__)
136:    #define TSC_FIND ffblk
137:    #define NAME ff_name
138:    #define ATTRIBUTE ff_attrib
139:    #define TIME ff_ftime
140:    #define DATE ff_fdate
141:    #define SIZE ff_fsize
142: #elif (defined __TSC_MSC__)
143:    #define TSC_FIND _find_t
144:    #define NAME name
145:    #define ATTRIBUTE attrib
146:    #define TIME wr_time
147:    #define DATE wr_date
148:    #define SIZE size
149:    #define FA_ARCH _A_ARCH
150:    #define FA_DIREC _A_SUBDIR
151:    #define FA_LABEL _A_VOLID
152:    #define FA_NORMAL _A_NORMAL
153:    #define FA_SYSTEM _A_SYSTEM
154:    #define FA_HIDDEN _A_HIDDEN
155:    #define FA_RDONLY _A_RDONLY
156: #endif
157:
158: // ------------------------------------------------------------ //
159:
160: //   Microsoft doesn't define the value of pi. Zortech C++
161: //   and Borland C++ define the following symbol in math.h.
162: //   Just in case MS decides to define M_PI later on, I
163: //   redefine it only if it is not already defined.
164: //   M_PI   Value of pi
165:
166: #if (defined __TSC_MSC__)
167:   #ifndef M_PI
168:     #define M_PI 3.14159265358979323846
169:   #endif
170: #endif
171:
172: // ------------------------------------------------------------ //
173:
174: #endif   // __TSCDEFS_H
```

Lines 18–19 prevent the header from being included more than once—in case, for example, you compile a multimodule program where more than one individual module includes tscdefs.h. The first time the file is included, the symbol __TSCDEFS_H is not defined, and the file is processed normally. The *next* time tscdefs.h is included, the symbol is defined and the compiler ignores the file's commands.

Comments at lines 29–32 describe the naming convention used to prepare compiler identification symbols. Be sure to define the appropriate symbol for your compiler (usually in a MAKE file such as MAKEBTC.INC). As mentioned earlier, lines 39–45 select __TSC_BTC__ by default for Borland C++. To use a different default compiler, change the compiler identification symbol in line 42.

General-purpose TRUE and FALSE symbols are defined at lines 53–58. Notice how this command tests whether these symbols are already defined. When preparing shared libraries, it's often wise to test whether general-purpose symbols are defined before redefining them, though that isn't always practical.

Lines 65–71 define two symbols IOSTREAM_H and IOMANIP_H for I/O stream header filenames. C++ does not require compiler's to use any specific filename extensions—some even use .CXX and .HXX rather than .CPP and .h or .HPP. After including tscdefs.h, use the symbols like this:

```
#include <tscdefs.h>
#include IOSTREAM_H
#include IOMANIP_H
```

Borland C++, Microsoft C/C++, and Turbo C++ translate these directives to

```
#include <tscdefs.h>
#include <iostream.h>
#include <iomanip.h>
```

Zortech C++ translates the final two filenames to iostream.hpp and iomanip.hpp. Another compiler could translate the symbols to different names. You can specify literal filenames directly, of course, but if you do, your programs might no longer be cross-compatible with other C++ compilers.

Lines 78–82 solve another cross-compilation problem—what to do when a compiler provides a set of tools that aren't available in another compiler. In this case, Zortech C++ provides a display package of text-based functions for writing directly to a PC's video memory buffers. The standard "solution" is not to use such system-dependent code, but rather, to employ only standard I/O techniques.

As most programmers know, however, "standard" usually means "slow," and most if not all commercial-quality programs use direct-video and other system-dependent features to boost performance. To have the best of both worlds—performance and compatibility—I wrote my own display package of functions that mirror most of those in Zortech C++. (I converted only the functions that this book uses.) The functions are named the same for all compilers, and they use the same parameters, but their statements are written using each compiler's *own* high-speed I/O functions.

If you are using Borland C++, Microsoft C/C++, or Turbo C++, line 79 includes my replacement display package header, tscdisp.h. If you are using Zortech C++, line 81 includes the header supplied with that compiler, disp.h. Notice that the filenames can be different—by defining the symbol DISP_H, I did not have to name my package's header disp.h.

To use the display package, a program or module can use the directives:

```
#include <tscdefs.h>
#include DISP_H
```

Later in this chapter, you will examine the display package in detail.

A variety of symbols at lines 92–156 shows one way to solve the nasty problem of a compiler defining similar symbols that differ, sometimes by only one character or two. These sorts of incompatibilities between compilers are among the most aggravating when trying to write cross-compatible code. Borland C++, to name one instance, defines dosdate_t with no leading underscore for its DOS date structure; Microsoft calls the same structure _dosdate_t with a leading underscore; Zortech names it dos_date_t with two embedded underscores.

I imagine these sorts of seemingly minor, but significant, differences are intentionally made in order to avoid copyright infringement claims. Or, perhaps the manufacturers intend to force programmers to write code that works only with their products. Whatever the reason, the result is more work for programmers who have to write cross-compatible code.

Fortunately, there's nothing to prevent *you* from defining another symbol that is translated at compile time into the compiler's unique identifier. In tscdefs.h, for instance, lines 93, 98, and 103 define the symbol DOS_DATE_T. By using that symbol to define a DOS date structure, the same line compiles correctly for all supported compilers:

```
#include <tscdefs.h>
DOS_DATE_T myDate;   // Define myDate DOS date structure
```

Finally in tscdefs.h, I define the symbol M_PI for the literal value of pi to 20 decimal places. Borland and Zortech define this value in the math.h header, but Microsoft doesn't. Just in case Microsoft decides to change their mind about defining M_PI, I define the symbol only if it is not already defined.

## The dosgfree Module

The tscdefs.h header is only one gear of the full cross-compilation engine. Other modules supply various functions for one or another compiler. This and several following sections list the modules in the library and explain how to use them.

> **Note:** With only one exception (ZTCFLUSH.CPP in Listing 10.12), each module has two listings, a header file (name in lowercase) and implementation (name in uppercase). To use a module, include it in your program after including tscdefs.h.

**Listing 10.2. dosgfree.h.**

```
1:  // dosgfree.h -- Header for dosgfree.cpp module
2:
3:  long dos_getdiskfreespace(int d);
```

There's not much to the dosgfree.h header file. It declares a single function, dos_getdiskfreespace(), which returns a long integer equal to the number of free bytes on the drive specified by int d. Set d to 0 for the current drive, 1 for A:, 2 for B:, 3 for C:, and so on.

Listing 10.3, DOSGFREE.CPP, implements the function.

**Listing 10.3. DOSGFREE.CPP.**

```
1:  /* ------------------------------------------------------------ *\
2:  **  dosgfree.cpp -- Dos get free disk space                      **
3:  **  ------------------------------------------------------------ **
4:  **                                                                **
```

```
 5:  **   This function comes with Zortech C++, but not Borland C++,  **
 6:  **   Turbo C++, or Microsoft C++. Here's a replacement           **
 7:  **   function that returns amount of free space available on a    **
 8:  **   disk drive D where D==0==the current drive, 1==A:, 2==B:,    **
 9:  **   and so on.                                                   **
10:  **                                                                **
11:  ** -------------------------------------------------------------  **
12:  **       Copyright (c) 1992 by Tom Swan. All rights reserved      **
13:  \* -------------------------------------------------------------  */
14:
15:  #include <dos.h>
16:
17:  long dos_getdiskfreespace(int d)
18:  {
19:    struct diskfree_t t;
20:
21:    if (_dos_getdiskfree(d, &t) != 0)
22:      return 0;
23:    else
24:      return (long)t.avail_clusters
25:        * (long)t.sectors_per_cluster * (long)t.bytes_per_sector;
26:  }
```

Borland C++ and Microsoft C/C++ programs can include the dosgfree.h header so they can call this function. Zortech C++ already has this function. FREE.CPP in Chapter 8, "Files and Directories," for example, uses the directive

```
#if (defined __TSC_BTC__) || (defined __TSC_MSC__)
#include <dosgfree.h>
#endif
```

The dosgfree.h header is included only if the symbols __TSC_BTC__ or __TSC_MSC__ are defined.

# The tscdisp Module

The direct-video display package is one of the most extensive in the library. The header file, tscdisp.h in Listing 10.4, includes other required headers, defines various symbols and macros, and prototypes the package's functions. The module is patterned after a portion of the Zortech C++ DISP module.

## Listing 10.4. tscdisp.h.

```
 1:  // tscdisp.h -- Header for tscdisp.cpp display module
 2:
 3:  #ifndef __TSCDISP_H
 4:  #define __TSCDISP_H  1       // Prevent multiple #includes
 5:
 6:  #ifndef __TSCDEFS_H          // Include tscdefs.h if it
 7:  #include <tscdefs.h>         //  hasn't already been included
 8:  #endif
 9:
10:  #ifndef __TSC_ZTC__          // Ignore this header for ZTC!
11:
12:
13:  // Include any system dependent headers so that any functions
14:  //  implemented as direct replacement macros compile correctly.
15:
16:  #if (defined __TSC_BTC__) ¦¦ (defined __TSC_MSC__)
17:  #include <conio.h>
18:  #endif
19:
20:  #if (defined __TSC_MSC__)
21:  #include <graph.h>
22:  #endif
23:
24:  #define DISP_REVERSEVIDEO 0x70
25:  #define DISP_NORMAL 0x07
26:
27:
28:  // Define a few direct macro replacements
29:  // In Microsoft C/C++, disp_printf() does not recognize
30:  //  foreground and background colors.
31:
32:  #if (defined __TSC_BTC__)
33:    #define disp_printf cprintf
34:    #define disp_setattr textattr
35:    #define disp_puts cputs
36:    #define disp_startstand() textattr(DISP_REVERSEVIDEO)
37:    #define disp_endstand() textattr(DISP_NORMAL)
38:  #elif (defined __TSC_MSC__)
39:    #define disp_printf _cprintf
40:    #define disp_puts _outtext
```

```
41:     #define disp_startstand() disp_setattr(DISP_REVERSEVIDEO)
42:     #define disp_endstand() disp_setattr(DISP_NORMAL)
43:     void disp_setattr(int);
44: #endif
45:
46: void disp_open(void);
47: void disp_close(void);
48: void disp_move(int,int);
49: void disp_eeol(void);
50: void disp_eeop(void);
51: void disp_box(int,int,unsigned,unsigned,unsigned,unsigned);
52: void disp_pokew(int,int,int);
53: void disp_peekbox(unsigned short*,unsigned,unsigned,unsigned,unsigned);
54: void disp_pokebox(unsigned short*,unsigned,unsigned,unsigned,unsigned);
55: void disp_fillbox(unsigned,unsigned,unsigned,unsigned,unsigned);
56: void disp_hidecursor(void);
57: void disp_showcursor(void);
58: void disp_scroll(int,unsigned,unsigned,unsigned,unsigned,unsigned);
59:
60: int disp_putc(int);
61: int disp_getmode(void);
62:
63:
64: #endif    // __TSC_ZTC__
65:
66: #endif    // __DISP_H
```

Lines 6–8 include tscdefs.h if it is not already included. As I explained earlier, the tscdefs.h header file prevents itself from being included more than once, so the ifndef directive at line 6 and associated #endif at line 8 are technically not needed. Checking whether an include file has been included, however, saves a small amount of time because the compiler doesn't have to load the file from disk only to discover that the file has already been included previously. In programs that include many header files, the technique shown here might save a significant amount of compilation time.

Line 10 prevents the file from being included for Zortech C++, which has its own display package. You can't use the TSCDISP module with Zortech C++, nor would you want to. Programs can never accidentally include the wrong files if you always include the display package with the commands

```
#include <tscdefs.h>
#include DISP_H
```

Lines 17 and 21 include Borland and Microsoft headers required for some of the routines. Some critical functions are coded as macros at lines 32–44. Uppercase isn't used because the goal is to duplicate the Zortech functions. The symbol `disp_printf`, for example, is translated to `cprintf` for Borland C++. In Zortech C++, the statement

```
disp_printf("Value = %d", v);
```

is translated *at compile time* for Borland C++ to

```
cprintf("Value = %d", v);
```

The other macros provide similar one-for-one translations for Borland and Microsoft compilers. There are no runtime performance penalties to pay here because the native direct-video functions (such as `cprintf()`) are used directly.

Other replacement functions that have no direct counterparts are prototyped at lines 43 and 46–61. These functions are implemented in Listing 10.5, TSCDISP.CPP.

## Listing 10.5. TSCDISP.CPP.

```
 1:  /* ------------------------------------------------------------ *\
 2:  **   tscdisp.cpp — Compatibility module for display package    **
 3:  **   ------------------------------------------------------------ **
 4:  **                                                              **
 5:  **   Zortech C++ includes a set of text-display routines        **
 6:  **   prototyped in header disp.h. Borland C++ and Microsoft      **
 7:  **   C/C++ provide similar routines with similar capabilities,   **
 8:  **   but in very different forms. Because Learning C++ used       **
 9:  **   the Zortech C++ compiler, many of the programs in the       **
10:  **   book rely on Zortech's display module. Rather than re-      **
11:  **   write every such program, I developed this module to        **
12:  **   duplicate some (but not all) of the Zortech functions       **
13:  **   for Borland C++ and Microsoft C/C++.                        **
14:  **                                                              **
15:  **   See tscdefs.h in the include directory for macros that      **
16:  **   that include tscdisp.h or disp.h depending on which         **
17:  **   compiler you are using. If you have Zortech C++, of         **
18:  **   course you don't need these replacement functions.          **
19:  **                                                              **
```

```
20:  **  ------------------------------------------------------------  **
21:  **       Copyright (c) 1992 by Tom Swan. All rights reserved      **
22:  \* ------------------------------------------------------------  */
23:
24:  #include <tscdefs.h>
25:  #include <dos.h>
26:  #include "tscdisp.h"
27:
28:  #if (defined __TSC_MSC__)
29:  __segment vidbase;
30:  #endif
31:
32:  #define VIDEO 0x010
33:
34:  // Hidden global variables available in Zortech C++. You can
35:  //   access these by declaring them extern.
36:
37:  int disp_numrows;
38:  int disp_numcols;
39:
40:  // Character sets for disp_box function
41:
42:  char *scul = "╔╦█╔╦";
43:  char *scur = "╗╦█╗╦";
44:  char *scbl = "╚╩█╚╩";
45:  char *scbr = "╝╩█╝╩";
46:  char *schz = "═─█═─";
47:  char *scvt = "║│█║│";
48:
49:  // Limit row and column values (private routine)
50:
51:  void limitrc(int &row, int &col)
52:  {
53:    if ((unsigned)row >= (unsigned)disp_numrows)
54:      row = disp_numrows - 1;
55:    if ((unsigned)col >= (unsigned)disp_numcols)
56:      col = disp_numcols - 1;
57:  }
58:
59:  // Clean up after using display package
60:  void disp_close(void)
```

*continues*

**681**

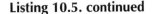
## Listing 10.5. continued

```
61:  {
62:  }
63:
64:  // Initialize display package
65:  void disp_open(void)
66:  {
67:  #if (defined __TSC_BTC__)
68:    text_info info;
69:    gettextinfo(&info);
70:    disp_numrows = info.screenheight;
71:    disp_numcols = info.screenwidth;
72:  #elif (defined __TSC_MSC__)
73:    _videoconfig info;
74:    _getvideoconfig(&info);
75:    disp_numrows = info.numtextrows;
76:    disp_numcols = info.numtextcols;
77:    _wrapon(_GWRAPOFF);  // Do not wrap text lines
78:    if (info.monitor == _MONO)
79:      vidbase = (__segment)0xB000;  // Direct-video mono buffer segment
80:    else
81:      vidbase = (__segment)0xB800;  // Direct-video color buffer segment
82:  #endif
83:  }
84:
85:  // Position cursor at row, col where (0, 0) == upperleft corner
86:  void disp_move(int row, int col)
87:  {
88:    limitrc(row, col);
89:  #if (defined __TSC_BTC__)
90:    gotoxy(col + 1, row + 1);
91:  #elif (defined __TSC_MSC__)
92:    _settextposition((short)row + 1, (short)col + 1);
93:  #endif
94:  }
95:
96:  // Erase from cursor to end of line
97:  void disp_eeol(void)
98:  {
99:  #if (defined __TSC_BTC__)
100:   clreol();
```

```
101:   #elif (defined __TSC_MSC__)
102:     _rccoord xy = _gettextposition();
103:     unsigned attr = (unsigned)_getbkcolor() << 4;
104:     attr += (unsigned)_gettextcolor();
105:     unsigned uattr = attr << 8;
106:     unsigned c = uattr ¦ ' ';
107:     for (int x = xy.col - 1; x < disp_numcols; x++)
108:       disp_pokew(xy.row - 1, x, (int)c);
109:   #endif
110:   }
111:
112:   // Erase from cursor to end of page
113:   void disp_eeop(void)
114:   {
115:     int y;
116:
117:   #if (defined __TSC_BTC__)
118:     int xx, yy;
119:     text_info info;
120:     gettextinfo(&info);
121:     clreol();
122:     yy = wherey();
123:     xx = wherex();
124:     for (y = yy + 1; y <= info.screenheight; y++) {
125:       gotoxy(1, y);
126:       clreol();
127:     }
128:     gotoxy(xx, yy);
129:   #elif (defined __TSC_MSC__)
130:     _rccoord xy = _gettextposition();
131:     disp_eeol();
132:     for (y = xy.row + 1; y <= disp_numrows; y++) {
133:       _settextposition((short)y, 1);
134:       disp_eeol();
135:     }
136:     _settextposition(xy.row, xy.col);
137:   #endif
138:   }
139:
```

*continues*

## Listing 10.5. continued

```
140:  // Draw a box outline
141:  void disp_box(int type, int attr, unsigned trow, unsigned lcol,
142:    unsigned brow, unsigned rcol)
143:  {
144:    int cul, cur, cbl, cbr, chz, cvt;    // Drawing characters
145:    unsigned uattr = attr * 256;         // Attr in high byte
146:
147:  // Create drawing characters based on type and attribute
148:
149:    if (type < 0 || type > 4) type = 0;
150:    cul = uattr + (unsigned char)scul[type];
151:    cur = uattr + (unsigned char)scur[type];
152:    cbl = uattr + (unsigned char)scbl[type];
153:    cbr = uattr + (unsigned char)scbr[type];
154:    chz = uattr + (unsigned char)schz[type];
155:    cvt = uattr + (unsigned char)scvt[type];
156:
157:  // Display four corners of box
158:
159:    disp_pokew(trow, lcol, cul);
160:    disp_pokew(trow, rcol, cur);
161:    disp_pokew(brow, lcol, cbl);
162:    disp_pokew(brow, rcol, cbr);
163:
164:  // Display box outline
165:
166:    for (unsigned x = lcol + 1; x < rcol; x++) {
167:      disp_pokew(trow, (int)x, chz);
168:      disp_pokew(brow, (int)x, chz);
169:    }
170:    for (unsigned y = trow + 1; y < brow; y++) {
171:      disp_pokew((int)y, lcol, cvt);
172:      disp_pokew((int)y, rcol, cvt);
173:    }
174:
175:  }
176:
177:  // Poke unsigned character and attribute into display
178:  void disp_pokew(int row, int col, int attrchar)
179:  {
180:    limitrc(row, col);
```

```
181:  #if (defined __TSC_BTC__)
182:    col = col + 1;
183:    row = row + 1;
184:    puttext(col, row, col, row, &attrchar);
185:  #elif (defined __TSC_MSC__)
186:    int __based(vidbase) *p;
187:    p = (int __based(vidbase) *)( ((row * disp_numcols) * 2) + (col * 2) );
188:    *p = attrchar;
189:  #endif
190:  }
191:
192:  // Read unsigned characters and attributes (Microsoft C++ only)
193:  #if (defined __TSC_MSC__)
194:  int disp_peekw(int row, int col)
195:  {
196:    limitrc(row, col);
197:    int __based(vidbase) *p;
198:    p = (int __based(vidbase) *)( ((row * disp_numcols) * 2) + (col * 2) );
199:    return *p;
200:  }
201:  #endif
202:
203:  // Copy display buffer bytes to buffer at save pointer
204:  void disp_peekbox(unsigned short *save, unsigned trow, unsigned lcol,
205:    unsigned brow, unsigned rcol)
206:  {
207:  #if (defined __TSC_BTC__)
208:    gettext(lcol + 1, trow + 1, rcol + 1, brow + 1, save);
209:  #elif (defined __TSC_MSC__)
210:    for (unsigned row = trow; row <= brow; row++)
211:      for (unsigned col = lcol; col <= rcol; col++)
212:        *save++ = disp_peekw(row, col);
213:  #endif
214:  }
215:
216:  // Copy data saved by disp_peekbox back to display
217:  void disp_pokebox(unsigned short *save, unsigned trow, unsigned lcol,
218:    unsigned brow, unsigned rcol)
219:  {
220:  #if (defined __TSC_BTC__)
221:    puttext(lcol + 1, trow + 1, rcol + 1, brow + 1, save);
```

*continues*

## Listing 10.5. continued

```
222:  #elif (defined __TSC_MSC__)
223:    for (unsigned row = trow; row <= brow; row++)
224:      for (unsigned col = lcol; col <= rcol; col++)
225:        disp_pokew(row, col, *(int *)save++);
226:  #endif
227:  }
228:
229:  // Paint a box on-screen with an attribute and character
230:  void disp_fillbox(unsigned attrchar, unsigned trow, unsigned lcol,
231:    unsigned brow, unsigned rcol)
232:  {
233:    while (trow <= brow) {
234:      for (unsigned i = lcol; i <= rcol; i++)
235:        disp_pokew(trow, i, attrchar);
236:      trow++;
237:    }
238:  }
239:
240:  // Remove cursor from display
241:  void disp_hidecursor(void)
242:  {
243:  #if (defined __TSC_BTC__)
244:    _setcursortype(_NOCURSOR);
245:  #elif (defined __TSC_MSC__)
246:    _settextcursor(0x2000);
247:  #endif
248:  }
249:
250:  // Redisplay hidden cursor
251:  void disp_showcursor(void)
252:  {
253:  #if (defined __TSC_BTC__)
254:    _setcursortype(_NORMALCURSOR);
255:  #elif (defined __TSC_MSC__)
256:    _settextcursor(0x0707);
257:  #endif
258:  }
259:
260:  // Scroll the defined area up or down
261:  void disp_scroll(int lines, unsigned ulrow, unsigned ulcol,
```

```
262:    unsigned lrrow, unsigned lrcol, unsigned attr)
263: {
264: #if (defined __TSC_BTC__)
265:    union REGS regs;
266: #elif (defined __TSC_MSC__)
267:    union _REGS regs;
268: #endif
269:
270:    if (lines < 0){
271:      regs.h.ah = 7;      // Scroll down
272:      lines = -lines;
273:    }
274:    else
275:      regs.h.ah = 6;      // Scroll up
276:    regs.h.ch = (unsigned char) ulrow;
277:    regs.h.cl = (unsigned char) ulcol;
278:    regs.h.dh = (unsigned char) lrrow;
279:    regs.h.dl = (unsigned char) lrcol;
280:    regs.h.bh = (unsigned char) attr;
281:    if (ulrow >= lrrow)
282:      regs.h.al = 0;      // Clear window if top >= bottom row
283:    else
284:      regs.h.al = (unsigned char)lines;  // Else scroll this many lines
285: #if (defined __TSC_BTC__)
286:    int86(VIDEO, &regs, &regs);
287: #elif (defined __TSC_MSC__)
288:    _int86(VIDEO, &regs, &regs);
289: #endif
290: }
291:
292: // Display character c at cursor location
293: int disp_putc(int c)
294: {
295:    return putch(c);
296: }
297:
298: // Return current display mode
299: int disp_getmode(void)
300: {
301: #if (defined __TSC_BTC__)
302:    text_info info;
```

*continues*

**Listing 10.5. continued**

```
303:    gettextinfo(&info);
304:    return info.currmode;
305: #elif (defined __TSC_MSC__)
306:    _videoconfig info;
307:    _getvideoconfig(&info);
308:    return (int)info.mode;
309: #endif
310: }
311:
312: // Set display colors for Microsoft C/C++
313: #if (defined __TSC_MSC__)
314: void disp_setattr(int attr)
315: {
316:    _settextcolor((short)(attr & 0x0f));
317:    _setbkcolor((long)((attr & 0x00f0) >> 4));
318: }
319: #endif
```

Borland provides two useful functions for reading and writing blocks of video memory, gettext() and puttext() (see lines 208 and 221). For Microsoft C/C++, I coded the same operations as nested for loops. Eventually, these sections should be recoded in assembly language for speed.

The functions are commented and there are many examples of their use throughout the book, so you should have little trouble inserting them in your own programs. After you are familiar with the module, you might want to improve it by using your compiler's optimizations, or by rewriting some routines in assembly language. A small improvement to these functions should give a large boost in display performance.

# The form Module

In this book's predecessor, *Learning C++,* I made extensive use of the form() function that used to be supplied with older versions of the C++ I/O stream library. Newer C++ releases no longer have form(), so I wrote my own replacement. All of the compilers supported by this book can use the FORM module. First comes the header file, form.h, in Listing 10.6.

### Listing 10.6. form.h.

```
1:   // form.h -- Header file for form() function
2:
3:   char *form(char *buf, const char *format, ...);
```

My form() function declares an initial char *buf parameter. The original form() did not have a similar buffer, which you must declare. To use form(), include the header file and use statements such as

```
#include <tscdefs.h>
#include IOSTREAM_H
#include <form.h>
...
char buf[80];
cout << form(buf, "%2d", value);
```

You don't have to use form() in an output stream statement as shown here, but that's the most common use. Listing 10.7, FORM.CPP, implements form().

### Listing 10.7. FORM.CPP.

```
 1:   /* ------------------------------------------------------------ *\
 2:   **   form.cpp -- Implement form() function                     **
 3:   ** ------------------------------------------------------------ **
 4:   **                                                              **
 5:   **   The form() function from the older stream.hpp header in    **
 6:   **   Zortech C++ is no longer available, so I wrote my own      **
 7:   **   replacement. Unlike the original function, however,        **
 8:   **   mine requires you to pass it a string buffer, similar      **
 9:   **   to the way sprintf() works. Actually, my form() function   **
10:   **   is identical to sprintf()--it just returns the address    **
11:   **   of the buffer rather than the number of characters         **
12:   **   copied to the buffer.                                      **
13:   **                                                              **
14:   ** ------------------------------------------------------------ **
15:   **      Copyright (c) 1992 by Tom Swan. All rights reserved     **
16:   \* ------------------------------------------------------------ */
17:
18:   #include <stdio.h>
19:   #include <stdarg.h>
```

*continues*

**Listing 10.7. continued**

```
20:
21:   char *form(char *buf, const char *format, ...)
22:   {
23:     if (buf) {
24:       va_list vap;
25:       va_start(vap, format);
26:       vsprintf(buf, format, vap);
27:       va_end(vap);
28:     }
29:     return buf;
30:   }
```

The form() function resembles printf(), and it understands all of the same formatting commands such as %d and %f. (Look up printf() in your compiler's reference if these commands aren't familiar to you.)

Lines 24–27 call variable-argument functions in the standard C library to pass arguments one by one to vsprintf(), which does the actual work of formatting values and storing the resulting string in buf. The form() function then returns the address of buf. If buf is null on entry to form(), the function returns null.

## The msleep Module

Every C and C++ compiler (and probably every computer language) has a command that pauses a program's execution for a length of time. Even though we all want our programs to run as fast as possible, there are times when we have to slow a program down. You might, for example, waste a fraction of a second in a critical function so that programs operating on slower machines run at more or less the same relative speed on faster computers. This trick is common in computer games, where the extra speed of a fast system might make the graphics race by too quickly to be seen.

Zortech C++ defines a useful function, msleep(), that pauses for a number of milliseconds. Borland provides a similar delay() function that requires an unsigned int parameter rather than a long value as in the Zortech C++ version.

Listing 10.8, msleep.h, prototypes a replacement msleep() function for Borland and Microsoft compilers.

## Listing 10.8. msleep.h.

```
1: // msleep.h -- Header file for msleep.cpp
2:
3: void msleep(long msec);
```

Listing 10.9, MSLEEP.CPP, implements the msleep() function. Zortech C++ doesn't need this module.

## Listing 10.9. MSLEEP.CPP.

```
 1: /* ------------------------------------------------------------- *\
 2: **  msleep.cpp -- Millisecond "sleep" (delay) function        **
 3: ** -------------------------------------------------------------- **
 4: **                                                                **
 5: **  A similar function is provided by Zortech C++ in time.h      **
 6: **                                                                **
 7: ** -------------------------------------------------------------- **
 8: **      Copyright (c) 1992 by Tom Swan. All rights reserved      **
 9: \* ------------------------------------------------------------- */
10:
11: #include <tscdefs.h>
12:
13: #if (defined __TSC_BTC__)
14: #include <dos.h>
15: #elif (defined __TSC_MSC__)
16: #include <time.h>
17: #endif
18:
19: // Pause for a specified number of milliseconds
20: void msleep(long msec)
21: {
22: #if (defined __TSC_BTC__)
23:   delay((unsigned)msec);  // Possible loss of significant digits
24: #elif (defined __TSC_MSC__)
25:   clock_t end;
26:   end = clock() + msec / (1000 / CLOCKS_PER_SEC);
27:   while (end > clock()) ;
28: #endif
29: }
```

Lines 13–17 include the dos.h or time.h headers depending on the compiler that you are using. For Borland C++ and Turbo C++, line 23 calls the delay() function, which might result in a loss of significant digits for the long msec parameter. In Borland's compilers, therefore, msleep() is limited to 65,535 milliseconds (about 65 seconds).

For Microsoft C/C++, lines 25–27 use the clock_t structure and clock() function to pause the program at line 27 for the specified number of milliseconds. This code works only on PCs, all of which have a timer interrupt that cycles at the fixed rate of approximately 18.2 times per second.

The msleep() function is woefully inaccurate, but is useful nevertheless for pausing execution for approximate intervals. The elevator simulation in Chapter 5, "Class Objectives," for example, has a few suggested msleep() statements that you can enable to slow execution to more closely resemble real time (see file ELEVSIM.CPP in Chapter 5).

> **Note:** If the limitation of 65,535 milliseconds for Borland's compilers is a problem, you might want to implement msleep() for Borland C++ and Turbo C++ as shown at lines 25–27. The time.h header for those compilers prototypes a clock() function that works similarly to the one in Microsoft C/C++.

## The pbin Module

The Zortech C++ printf() function can format integer values in binary by using the %b option—a useful feature that is sorely missed in Borland and Microsoft compilers. The PBIN module described in this section provides a similar capability, though it's not as handy as the Zortech option. Listing 10.10, pbin.h, prototypes the function.

**Listing 10.10. pbin.h.**

```
1:  // pbin.h -- Header file for pbin() function
2:
3:  void pbin(unsigned int n);
```

Call pbin() to write an unsigned int value as binary digits to the standard output file. (PBIN stands for "print binary.") Even though Zortech C++ already can format binary values with printf() statements, the pbin() function is included in this book's TSCZTC.LIB library file in case you want to use the function with the Zortech compiler.

## Listing 10.11. PBIN.CPP.

```
 1:  /* ------------------------------------------------------------ *\
 2:  **  pbin.cpp -- Print values as binary digits                   **
 3:  ** ------------------------------------------------------------  **
 4:  **                                                               **
 5:  **  Borland C++ and Microsoft C/C++ programs call pbin() to      **
 6:  **  print values as binary digits. In Zortech C++, the           **
 7:  **  printf() function understands a %b option to display         **
 8:  **  values in binary. The pbin() function in this module is      **
 9:  **  included in the Zortech C++ tscztc.lib library, however,     **
10:  **  in case you want to call it.                                 **
11:  **                                                               **
12:  ** ------------------------------------------------------------  **
13:  **     Copyright (c) 1992 by Tom Swan. All rights reserved       **
14:  \* ------------------------------------------------------------ */
15:
16:  #include <tscdefs.h>
17:  #include IOSTREAM_H
18:  #include IOMANIP_H
19:
20:  // Print an 8-bit unsigned char n in binary
21:  void pbinc(unsigned char n)
22:  {
23:    int i;
24:    for (i = 0; i < 8; i++) {
25:      if (n & 0x80)
26:        cout << '1' << flush;
27:      else
28:        cout << '0' << flush;
29:  #ifdef __TSC_MSC__
30:        n = (unsigned char)(n << 1);
31:  #else
32:        n = n << 1;
```

*continues*

**Listing 10.11. continued**

```
33:  #endif
34:    }
35:  }
36:
37:  // Print unsigned integer n in binary
38:  void pbin(unsigned int n)
39:  {
40:  #ifdef __TSC_MSC__
41:    pbinc((unsigned char)(n / 256));
42:    pbinc((unsigned char)(n % 256));
43:  #else
44:    pbinc(n / 256);
45:    pbinc(n % 256);
46:  #endif
47:    cout << endl;
48:  }
```

Some of the programming in the PBIN.CPP file might seem complex, but the process is simple. Function pbin() (lines 38–48) calls a local function, pbinc(), to output each 8-bit half of a full 16-bit value.

The local pbinc() function tests each bit of the target value (line25), and outputs '1' or '0'. Line 30 works around an annoying problem in Microsoft C++. The expression

n = n << 1;

is for some reason rejected when n is type unsigned char, probably because n << 1 is evaluated as an int expression rather than an 8-bit char. Borland C++ and Turbo C++ correctly compile the statement at line 32. Line 30 requires a typecast to compile the statement for Microsoft C/C++.

# The ZTCFLUSH Module

Finally in the library is a module with no header file, ZTCFLUSH.CPP, in Listing 10.12. Only Zortech C++ requires this module, which fills in a serious omission in the Version 3.0 compiler.

## Listing 10.12. ZTCFLUSH.CPP.

```
 1:  /* ----------------------------------------------------------- *\
 2:  **   ztcflush.cpp -- Provide ostream flush routine             **
 3:  **   ----------------------------------------------------------- **
 4:  **                                                              **
 5:  **   Zortech C++ 3.0 declares but fails to implement the        **
 6:  **   overloaded ostream flush function that both returns and    **
 7:  **   accepts a reference to ostream. This file provides the     **
 8:  **   missing function, which is necessary to use the flush      **
 9:  **   manipulator. Without this function, for example, you       **
10:  **   cannot write 'cout << "xxx" << flush;'                     **
11:  **                                                              **
12:  **   ----------------------------------------------------------- **
13:  **      Copyright (c) 1992 by Tom Swan. All rights reserved     **
14:  \* ----------------------------------------------------------- */
15:
16:  #include <tscdefs.h>
17:  #include IOSTREAM_H
18:  ostream &flush(ostream &stream)
19:  {
20:    stream.flush();
21:    return stream;
22:  }
```

As you have learned in earlier chapters, you often need to flush an output stream. This action causes the stream to send any buffered output to its destination file. Not flushing output can cause strange on-screen behavior. Consider this innocent looking fragment:

```
#include <tscdefs.h>
#include IOMANIP_H
char buf[80];
cout << "What is your name? ";
cin >> buf;
```

If the prompt string, "What is your name? ", is buffered, the input statement is executed before the prompt appears! To prevent this mistake, the output statement should be written as:

```
cour << "What is your name? " << flush;
```

**695**

And here a major problem in Zortech C++ 3.0 arises. The compiler prototypes a `flush()` output stream function, used by the `flush` I/O manipulator, but that function's implementation was accidentally left out of the supplied Zortech libraries. The above statement therefore compiles, but the resulting program cannot be linked. Because the proper function is already prototyped in iostream.hpp, this module does not need a ztcflush.h header file.

The repair shown here provides the missing `flush()` function, which returns a reference to `ostream`, and accepts a like reference parameter. The function merely calls the stream's `flush()` member function (which fortunately is provided in the Zortech library), and returns a reference to the stream so `flush()` can be used in multipart output stream statements.

> **Note:** It's entirely possible that Zortech will repair this problem in the future, in which case you can remove the compiled ZTCFLUSH module from the TSCZTC.LIB library file.

# Compiling Your Own Programs

U sing the cross-compilation library is not difficult, and if you have read this book from cover to cover, you probably don't need any help. If, however, you are having trouble getting your own programs to compile, you've come to the right place for advice.

Most programming tutorials begin with a `"Hello world!"` program that displays that very same string—for no good reason except that this is a very nice string to display. I'll follow a different drummer, however, and *end* this book's final chapter with the classic HELLO.CPP program in Listing 10.13. (Maybe I should have titled it GOODBYE.CPP.) The file is located in the C:\TSC installation directory.

> **Note:** The following sections list the commands required to compile HELLO.CPP for each of this book's supported compilers. Use similar commands to compile your own programs. The instructions assume that you have configured your system as explained in the Introduction.

### Listing 10.13. HELLO.CPP.

```
1:   #include <tscdefs.h>
2:   #include IOSTREAM_H
3:   #include IOMANIP_H
4:
5:   int main()
6:   {
7:     cout << "Hello world!" << endl;
8:     return 0;
9:   }
```

# Compiling with Borland C++ 3.0 and 3.1

First, create a text file named TURBOC.CFG in the current directory. Into this file insert the following commands:

```
-D__TSC_BTC__
-ms
-IC:\tsc\include;C:\borlandc\include
-LC:\tsc\lib;C:\borlandc\lib
```

The first line defines the symbol __TSC_BTC__. The second line selects the small memory model, which you must use unless you rebuild this book's library to use a different model. The last two lines specify the locations of various header and library files.

You can now compile HELLO.CPP by entering the command

```
bcc hello
```

To compile and link other programs that use this book's library functions such as form(), specify the library file TSCBCC.LIB in a command such as

```
bcc filename tscbcc.lib
```

## Compiling with Microsoft C/C++ 7.0

To compile HELLO.CPP with Microsoft C/C++, from a DOS prompt, enter the command

```
cl /D__TSC_MSC__ hello.cpp
```

Define the symbol __TSC_MSC__ as shown. Be sure to type the full filename including the .CPP extension. To compile and link other programs that use this book's library functions such as form(), also specify the library file TSCMSC.LIB in a command such as

```
cl /D__TSC_MSC__ filename.cpp tscmsc.lib
```

> **Hint:** If you get tired of typing /D__TSC_MSC__, edit tscdefs.h as explained earlier in this chapter and set the default compiler identifier to __TSC_MSC__ (see Listing 10.1, line 42). You can then omit the /D__TSC_MSC__ option.

## Compiling with Turbo C++ 3.0

First, create a text file named TURBOC.CFG in the current directory. Into this file insert the following commands:

```
-D__TSC_BTC__
-ms
-IC:\tsc\include;C:\tc\include
-LC:\tsc\lib;C:\tc\lib
```

The first line defines the __TSC_BTC__ symbol. The second line selects the small memory model, which you must use unless you rebuild this book's library to use a different model. The last two lines specify the locations of various header and library files.

You can now compile HELLO.CPP by entering the command

```
tcc hello
```

To compile and link other programs that use this book's library functions such as form(), specify the library file TSCTCC.LIB in a command such as

```
tcc filename tsctcc.lib
```

## Compiling with Zortech C++ 3.0

To compile HELLO.CPP with Zortech C++, from a DOS prompt, enter the command

```
ztc -D__TSC_ZTC__ hello
```

Define the symbol __TSC_ZTC__ as shown. To compile and link other programs that use this book's library functions such as form(), specify the library file TSCZTC.LIB in a command such as

```
ztc -D__TSC_ZTC__ filename tscztc.lib
```

> **Hint:** As with Microsoft C/C++, if you get tired of typing **-D__TSC_ZTC__**, edit tscdefs.h as explained earlier in this chapter and set the default compiler identifier to __TSC_ZTC__ (see Listing 10.1, line 42). You can then omit the -D__TSC_ZTC__ option.

# Converting to Other C++ Compilers

To compile this book's programs with another C++ compiler, you should be able to revise tscdefs.h, rewrite some or all modules described in this chapter, and begin compiling. No other changes should be needed.

At least, that's the theory. If you run into barriers, follow the general instructions in this section. If you still run into brick walls, please let me know.

Let's assume you are using a new compiler named *Wonder C++*. The compiler's filename is WONDER.EXE, a control program that compiles .CPP program files and automatically runs the linker to create a finished .EXE code file. The compiler understands one option: -c, which compiles .CPP files to produce .OBJ object-code modules and does *not* call the linker.

Our fictitious *Wonder C++* comes with a MAKE utility named MAKE.EXE, as most MAKE utilities are named. The program understands all the usual MAKE utility commands, and is similar to MAKE.EXE supplied with Borland C++. The compiler also comes with a library utility named WLIB.EXE.

Follow these steps to convert this book's listings for use with *Wonder C++*:

1. Create a file ROOTWON.INC in C:\TSC. Assign the compiler's pathname to a symbol named CPPROOT and this book's installation directory to TSCROOT. Use an existing root file (ROOTBTC.INC, for example) as a guide.

2. Create a file MAKEWON.INC in C:\TSC and insert the following lines, modifying the pathnames as needed:

```
CC = wonder
CCLL = wonder
MODEL = s
INC = $(TSCROOT)\include;$(CPPROOT)\include
LIB = $(TSCROOT)\lib;$(CPPROOT)\lib
TSCLIB = tscwon.lib
CFLAGS = -c
CLFLAGS =
```

3. If your compiler uses environment variables to locate include and library directories, omit the INC and LIB symbols. You might also need to create a SETWON.BAT file to configure your system for compiling programs. Use SETBTC.BAT, SETMSC.BAT, or SETZTC.BAT as guides.

4. Your next step is likely to be the most difficult: building the cross-compilation and class libraries. Edit file tscdefs.h in C:\TSC\LIB. Add an identifying symbol for your compiler, probably __TSC_WON__. Modify each section in tscdefs.h to create appropriate symbols, include headers, and define other items for your compiler. In some cases, you can use the existing definitions. If, for instance, *Wonder C++* uses the I/O stream header file iostream.h, you can simply change line 65 in tscdefs.h (Listing 10.1) to the following (all on one line):

```
#if (defined __TSC_BTC__) ¦¦ (defined __TSC_MSC__)
  ¦¦ (defined __TSC_WON__)
```

5. Create a MAKE file (named MAKEFILE.WON, or just MAKEFILE) for the library modules. Store the file in C:\TSC\ LIB\ SOURCE. Use MAKEFILE.BTC, MAKEFILE.MSC, and MAKEFILE.ZTC in that directory as guides. The first commands in your MAKE file should include the ROOTWON.INC and MAKEWON.INC files that you created in steps 1 and 2. Most MAKE utilities understand similar commands, and your MAKE files might be nearly the same as, if not identical to, the included MAKE files for Borland, Microsoft, or Zortech compilers.

6. Examine each of the library files in this chapter, from Listing 10.2 to Listing 10.12. Also examine the class-library files explained in Chapters 6 and 7, "Building a Class Library" (Parts 1 and 2), and stored in C:\TSC\LIB\SOURCE. (The class modules will be relatively easy to convert if your C++ compiler adheres to the emerging ANSI C++ standard.) You probably will need to modify most .CPP files in the library, but don't modify any .h header files or you might no longer be able to use the library with other C++ compilers.

7. Try to compile the library by changing to C:\TSC\LIB\SOURCE and running your MAKE utility. (Don't attempt to build the .LIB library file at this stage—just try to get the modules to compile.) You can't continue until you successfully compile all modules.

8. Change to C:\TSC\LIB, and create a batch file named BUILDWON.BAT. Using the other batch files in this directory as guides, insert commands to perform the steps outlined earlier under "Building the Library." Use your compiler's library utility (WLIB.EXE for the fictitious *Wonder C++*) to insert all .OBJ object-code files from C:\TSC\LIB\SOURCE into a file named TSCWON.LIB.

9. The rest of the conversion should be easy. Create MAKE files for each chapter, using the existing files as guides (they will be similar to the MAKE file you created in step 5). Compile the programs in each chapter.

10. You might need to modify a few programs that have conditional directives. Program FSIZE.CPP in Chapter 8, for example, will need to be revised to use your compiler's directory-searching functions (if it has them). Other programs that do not use system-dependent functions probably need only minor changes.

**Note:** If you convert the book's files to another C++ compiler, I'd like to hear from you. Write to me in care of the publisher, or send CompuServe mail to my ID number, 73627,3241.

# Reserved Keywords

**D**o not use the following C++ keywords for your own identifiers. Compiler vendors might add additional words to this list. These reserved words are treated specially by the C++ compiler and they may not be redefined:

| | | | | | |
|---|---|---|---|---|---|
| asm | auto | break | case | char | class |
| const | continue | default | delete | do | double |
| else | enum | extern | float | for | friend |
| goto | if | inline | int | long | new |
| operator | overload | private | protected | public | register |
| return | short | signed | sizeof | static | struct |
| switch | template | this | typedef | union | unsigned |
| virtual | void | volatile | while | | |

The overload keyword is a holdover from earlier C++ versions and should no longer be used. In addition to the preceding list, C++ compilers that implement exceptions reserve the keywords catch, throw, and try.

# Operator Precedence

In expressions, operators on lines above other operators in the following table are given priority over operators below. For example, in the expression a + (b + c), because parentheses have a higher precedence (level 1) than + (level 5), the subexpression (b + c) is evaluated before the addition to a.

| Level | Operator | Evaluation order |
|-------|----------|------------------|
| 1.(high) | () . [] -> :: | left-to-right |
| 2. | * & ! ~ ++ -- + - sizeof new delete | right-to-left |
| 3. | .* ->* | left-to-right |
| 4. | * / % | left-to-right |
| 5. | + - | left-to-right |
| 6. | << >> | left-to-right |
| 7. | < <= > >= | left-to-right |
| 8. | == != | left-to-right |

| Level | Operator | Evaluation order |
|---|---|---|
| 9. | & | left-to-right |
| 10. | ^ | left-to-right |
| 11. | ¦ | left-to-right |
| 12. | && | left-to-right |
| 13. | ¦¦ | left-to-right |
| 14. | ?: | right-to-left |
| 15. | = *= /= += -= %= <<= >>= &= ^= ¦= | right-to-left |
| 16.(low) | , | left-to-right |

**Note:** The symbol * at level 2 is the pointer dereference operator. The same symbol * at level 4 is the multiplication operator.

# Bibliography

Eckel, Bruce. *Using C++*. Osborne McGraw-Hill, 1989.

Ellis, Margaret A. and Bjarne Stroustrup. *The Annotated C++ Reference Manual*. AT&T Bell Laboratories, 1990.

Kernighan, Brian W. and Dennis M. Ritchie. *The C Programming Language, 2nd Ed*. Prentice Hall, 1988.

Knuth, Donald E. *The Art of Computer Programming. Vol. 1, Fundamental Algorithms*. Addison-Wesley Publishing Company, 1973.

Lafore, Robert. *Turbo C Programming for the PC. Revised Ed*. Howard W. Sams & Company, 1989.

Paulos, John Allen. *Innumeracy*. Vintage Books, 1988.

Plauger, P.J. and Jim Brodie. *Standard C*. Microsoft Press, 1989.

Stroustrup, Bjarne, *The C++ Programming Language, 2nd Ed*. Addison-Wesley Publishing Company, 1991.

Swan, Tom. *Learning C++*. Sams, 1991.

Swan, Tom. *Mastering Borland C++*. Sams, 1992.

Swan, Tom. *Mastering Turbo Assembler.* Sams, 1988.

Swan, Tom. *Mastering Turbo Pascal 6, 4th Ed.* Hayden Books, 1991.

Wiener, Richard S. and Lewis J. Pinson. *An Introduction to Object-Oriented Programming and C++.* Addison-Wesley Publishing Company, 1988.

# Index

## Symbols

! operator, 73
!= operator, 65
#endif directive, 24
#include directive, 14
%#X formatting instruction, 32
%#x formatting instruction, 32
%+d formatting instruction, 32
%.10f formatting instruction, 33
%10d formatting instruction, 32
%b formatting instruction, 32
%e formatting instruction, 33
%f formatting instruction, 33
%g formatting instruction, 33
%x formatting instruction, 32
& operator, 74
&& operator, 70
&fpArray[i] argument, 543
*/ C-style comment, 8
+ operator, 309
/* C-style comment, 8
// C-style comment, 9
:: button, 302
; string terminator, 6-8
< (take input from) symbol, 90
< operator, 65

<< operator, 74
<= operator, 65
== operator, 65
> (send output to) symbol, 90
> operator, 65
>= operator, 65
>> operator, 74
\ escape code, 42
\\ escape code, 42
^ operator, 74
¦ (pipe), 90
¦ operator, 74
¦¦ operator, 71
~ operator, 74
1 argument, 543

## A

a text file option, 526
a+ text file option, 526
ab data file option, 541
ab+ data file option, 541
abstract classes, 405
accessing system information
  with pointers, 224-226
aClass class, 397
action data type, 299

action( ) function, 312, 317-318, 330-333, 339, 358
ACTION.CPP program, 314-316
action.h header file, 309-310
additem( ) function, 250
addresses
    argument, 259
    pointers, 212
        assigning, 225-226
        segmented, 221
    variables, 182
adjustTime( ) function, 564
algorithms, Quicksort, 195
ALIAS.CPP program, 213-214
aliases, 215
allocation
    core, 253
    memory, 252
ALLRECDB.CPP program, 550-551
alternate values, 647
ancestors, class, 367
anchor member, 454
ANIMAL.CPP program, 367-373
argc parameter, 285
arguments, 157, 178
    &fpArray[i], 543
    1, 543
    addresses, 259
    character, 287-290
    command-line, 284-292
    default, 188-194
    functions, pointers, 259-264
    numeric, 290-292
    recnum * sizeof(rec), 553
    setw, 30
    sizeof, 543
arithmetic pointer, 273

array-indexing operator, overloading, 615-623
ARRAY.CPP program, 127
ARRAYLST.CPP program, 616-617
ARRAYPTR.CPP program, 270-271
arrays, 126-129
    character, initializing, 138
    creating, 127
    deleting, 234
    dynamic, 251-252
    indexes, 126
    initializing, 132-133
    multidimensional, 133-137
    of arrays, 133
    relationship with pointers, 138-140, 270-276
    size, 126
    storing variables, 126
ASC.CPP program, 204-206
ASCII.CPP program, 106-107
asctime( ) function, 277-278
assigning
    addresses to pointers, 225-226
    values to enumerated constants, 52-53
    variables, 17
assignment
    memberwise, 632-635
    operator, overloading, 623-637
    statements, initializing variables, 19-20
atHeadOfList( ) function, 458
atof( ) function, 37
atol( ) function, 37, 609
ATONUMS.CPP program, 36-37
attrCommand class, 394, 419-420
attributes, window, changing, 418
automated MAKE files, 665
automatic type conversion, 619

## B

\b escape code, 42
base classes, 366, 438
   constructors, 448
   destructors, 448
   pointers to, 446-447
batch files
   BUILDBCC.BAT, 663
   BUILDMSC.BAT, 663
   BUILDTCC.BAT, 663
   BUILDZTC.BAT, 663
   TESTYN.BAT, 88
binary operators, 604
binary values
   reading, 544-546
   writing, 541-544
binding
   early, 408
   late, 408
   pointers to variables, 214
_bios_disk( ) function, 522
bit fields, 140-144
bits, setting, 80
bitwise AND operator, 74-80
bitwise exclusive OR operator, 74, 80-81
bitwise inclusive OR operator, 74
bitwise operators, 73-82
blocks, 68
borders
   menu, type values, 392
   window, type values, 392
Borland C++, *see* C++
BOX.CPP program, 186
BP.CPP program, 159-161
break statement, 109
BREAKER.CPP program, 109
buf variable, 575

BUILDBCC.BAT batch file, 663
building class, 374-381
BUILDING.CPP function, 377-380
building.h header file, 375
BUILDMSC.BAT batch file, 663
BUILDTCC.BAT batch file, 663
BUILDZTC.BAT batch file, 663
BUTTON.CPP program, 300-301
BUTTON2.CPP program, 305-306
buttonDown( ) function, 354
buttonUp( ) functions, 354
bytes, keyboard flag, 228

## C

C++
   compared to C, 657-658
   compilers, 658
   compiling
      Borland, 697
      Microsoft, 698
      Turbo, 698
      Zortech, 699
   options
      Borland, 667
      Microsoft, 668
      Turbo, 668
      Zortech, 668
C-style comments, 9
calling
   dashes, 189
   dashes function, 189
   functions, 152
   member functions, 398
calloc( ) function, 252-253
case-sensitivity, 12-13
catch keyword, 703
caux output stream, 646

cdir( ) function, 555-557
CDIR.CPP program, 556
center( ) function, 194
CENTER.CPP program, 192-193
centerText( ) function, 172
cerr output stream, 646
char data type, 16
character arguments, 287-290
character constants, 40-42
characters
    copying, 279
    escape, 11, 31
    newline, 5
chdir( ) function, 557
cin input stream, 646
cip member, 454
class libraries, 387-388
    class hierarchies, 438-439
    command class, *see* command class
    menu-driven programs, creating,
        390-395
    selectors, creating, 413
    Window class, *see* Window class
class member functions, overloading,
    603-604
class objects, *see* objects
class variables, pointers to, 395-399
CLASS( ) function, 631
classes, 297-319
    abstract, 405
    aClass, 397
    as data types, 308-311
    attrCommand, 394, 419-420
    base, 366, 438
        constructors, 448
        destructors, 448
        pointers to, 446-447

building, 374-381
collection, creating, 365
command, 510
    command.h header file, 511-513
    derived class implementations,
        517-518
    derived, creating, 514
    testing, 513-518
constructors, declaring, 399
container, 439
creating, 300-304
derived, 366
    pointers to, 399-400
derivedItem, 446
directory, 569-572
elevator, 353-365
fileItem, 569
floor, 342-352
floorCollection, 344
friends, 588-594
global objects, initializing, 478
helpCommand, 394
hierarchies, 438
inheritance, 365-374
inherited, default status, 650-651
item, 440-448
    this keyword, 448-452
list, 453-462
members, 301
    person data, 328
    private, 301
    public, 301
    timeAtStart, 311
    timeRemaining, 311
myItem, 457
objects, copying, 625-626
persCollection, 328-329

person, 325-342
selector, 439, 499-500
   creating objects, 504
   inserting objects, 504
   multiple inheritance, 500-502
   SELECTOR.CPP program,
     505-509
   selector.h header file, 500-501
   testing, 502-504
stritem, 463-471
   characters, changing, 465-466
   constructors, overloading, 464-466
   string address, obtaining, 465
virtual base, 655-657
Window, 473
   displays, designing, 482-486
   overloaded constructors, 480-481
   private members, 477
   protected members, 477
   public members, 477
   reference functions, 481-482
   static data members, 479-480
   WINDOW.CPP program,
     487-499
   window.h header file, 473-477
clearFunction( ) function, 475
clock( ) function, 692
clock_t structure, 692
closeTopWindow( ) function, 259
CMDLINE.CPP program, 286
cmdNum member, 511-512
cmpkeys( ) function, 229
COCO.CPP program, 175-176
coefficients, combinatorial, 174
colasc( ) function, 207
collection classes, creating, 365
COLUMN.CPP program, 290-291

combinatorial coefficients, 174
combined assignment operator, 84-85
combining values, 208-209
command class, 510
   command.h header file, 511-513
   derived
     class implementations, 517-518
     creating, 514
   testing, 513-518
command-line arguments, 284-292
command.h header file, 511-513
COMMENT.CPP program, 10
comments, 8-12
COMP1.CPP program, 119-120
COMP2.CPP program, 121-122
compare( ) function, 538
comparing strings, 281-282
compdb.h header file, 119
compiler identifier symbol, 664
compilers, 658
   switching, 699-701
compiling
   elevator simulation, 319-321
   programs, 696-699
   WINTOOL program, 389-390
   with C++
     Borland, 697
     Microsoft, 698
     Turbo, 698
     Zortech, 699
compound statements, *see* blocks
concatenate, 281
conditional directives, 24, 310
conditional expressions, 647-648
cone( ) function, 202
CONE.CPP program, 201-202
confusingFunction( ) function, 475

connecting multiple filters, 90
CONST.CPP program, 46-47
constants, 38-53
    declared, 46-48
    defined, 44-46
    enumerated, 48-52
        assigning values, 52-53
    literal, 40-44
        character, 40-42
        floating point, 43-44
        string, 42-43
        whole number, 43
constructors, 311-314, 445-448
    copy, 631-632
        creating, 631
        declaring, 632
    declaring, 399
    overloaded, 480-481
    stritem class, overloading, 464-466
container classes, 439
continue statement, 111
CONTINUE.CPP program, 110-111
continues( ) function, 299, 313, 376-378
control structures, 85
control variables, 107
conversion operators, 621
CONVERT.CPP program, 38-46
copy constructors
    creating, 631
    declaring, 632
copying
    characters, 279
    class objects, 625-626
    derived class objects, 637
    MAKEFILE, 2
    pointer members, 629-631
core allocation, 253
countchars( ) function, 158

cout output stream, 5, 646
cprn output stream, 646
createMainWindow( ) function, 411
createSampWindow( ) function, 412
creating
    arrays, 127
    classes, 300-304
    collection classes, 365
    combined assignment operator, 84
    copy constructors, 631
    data files, 540
    data types, 115
    database files, 547-550
    dynamic lists, 241-251
    function pointers, 265
    inline functions, 200
    member function pointers, 652
    pointers, 212
        to class objects, 396-397
    pop-up menus, 513-518
    selectors, 413
    string lists, 471-473
    text files, 524-527
    union variables, 125
    void pointers, 218
critical error message, 528
cross-compilation tools, 662
CRTSTAT.CPP program, 224
current directories, switching, 555-557

D

dashes, calling, 189
dashes function, 189
data files, 540-553
    creating, 540
    fopen( ) function options, 541
    handling techniques, 540-541

reading, 541
writing, 541
data structures, *see* structures
data types
  action, 299
  char, 16
  classes, 308-311
  creating, 115
  double, 16
  float, 16
  int, 16
  long, 16
  long double, 16
  of static data members, 480
  short, 16
database files
  creating, 547-550
  opening, 549
  random-access, 551
  reading, 550-553
dataPtr variable, 654
declarations, 4
  forward class, 594
  function, 152
declared constants, 46-48
declaring
  action( ) function, 339
  copy constructor, 632
  pointers, 212-213
  variables
    external, 167
    local, 165
    register, 168
decoding directory information, 560-564
decrement operators, 54-57
  overloading, 614-615
default arguments, 188-194

default values, 647
deferencing pointers, 213-216
DEFINE.CPP program, 45-46
defined constants, 44-46
defining
  list instances, 457
  pointers to class objects, 397
  string pointers, 233
definitions, 4, 17
  in main( ) function, 21
  initializing variables, 17-19
delay( ) function, 690-692
delete operator, overloading, 640-641
deleting
  arrays, 234
  lines, temporarily, 9
  memory, 234
  objects, 419, 455, 460
delitem( ) function, 250
derived classes, 366
  copying objects, 637
  pointers to, 399-400
derivedItem class, 446
descendants, class, 367
designing functions, top-down
  method, 153-162
destructors, 312, 444-448
determining disk free space, 554-555
directives
  #endif, 24
  #include, 14
  conditional, 24, 310
directories, 554
  classes, 570-572
  current, switching, 555-557
  displaying, 557-560
  modifying, 564-567
  navigators, 577-579

directory class, 569
directory information, decoding, 560-564
dirStr variable, 575
discharge( ) function, 336
disks
  binary values
    reading, 544-546
    writing, 541-544
  determining free space, 554-555
disp_box( ) function, 188
disp_numcols variable, 488
disp_numrows variable, 488
disp_pointer( ) function, 221
disp_pokew( ) function, 207
disp_printf( ) function, 229
dispInitialized member, 479, 489-490
display( ) function, 299, 313, 376-380
displaying
  directories, 557-560
  text within window, 416
displays, designing with Window class, 482-486
disposeList( ) member function, 455, 460
dnwaiting( ) function, 333, 340
do-forever loop, 108-109
do-nothing loop, 108
do/while loop, 102-105
DOS functions, 522
dos_abs_disk_read( ) function, 522
dos_abs_disk_write( ) function, 522
dos_findfirst( ) function, 558
dos_findnext( ) function, 558
dos_getdiskfreespace( ) function, 554, 676
DOSGFREE.CPP program, 676-677

dosgfree.h header file, 676
double data type, 16
doublex function, 592
draw( ) member function, 405-407
drawbox( ) function, 188
DSTRUCT.CPP program, 236-237
DT.CPP program, 26
dynamic
  arrays, 251-252
  lists, creating, 241-251
  structures, 322
  variables, 232-235
    advantages, 239-241

# E

early binding, 408
eeol( ) member function, 486
eeow( ) member function, 418, 486
elevator class, 353-365
elevator simulation, 381-385
  compiling, 319-321
  files, 320-344
ELEVATOR.CPP program, 355-364
elevator.h header file, 353-354, 354
ELEVSIM.CPP program, 381-385
elevsim.h header file, 322-324
elevStopping( ) function, 358
encapsulation, 297
encryption, 82
endl manipulator, 94
ENUM.CPP program, 50
enumerated constants, 48-52
  assigning values, 52-53
equal operator, 65
EQUIP.CPP program, 142-143

error messages
  critical, 528
  type mismatch, 216
  unexpected-end-of-file, 546
  writing, 646
ERROR module, 428-433
  testing, 433-435
error( ) function, 429-435
ERROR.CPP program, 429-433
error.h header file, 428-429
errorignore variable, 430
errornumber variable, 430
errors, handling, 428-433
escape characters, 11, 31
escape codes, 41-42
evaluation, short-circuit expression, 70
exit( ) function, 72, 86-88
expression1, 105
expression2, 105
expressions, 4, 57-59
  conditional, 647-648
  fully qualified, 118
extern keyword, 167, 325
EXTERN1.CPP program, 166
EXTERN2.CPP program, 166-167
external variables, 165-167

# F

\f escape code, 42
factorial( ) function, 176
factorials, 174
far pointers, 222-223
  and keyboard, 226-232
fclose( ) function, 156, 527, 531
feof( ) function, 546
fgetc( ) function, 156, 531
fgets( ) function, 533
fields, bit, 140-144
file functions, 522
  error, 527-529
fileItem class, 569
files
  batch
    BUILDBCC.BAT, 663
    BUILDMSC.BAT, 663
    BUILDTCC.BAT, 663
    BUILDZTC.BAT, 663
    TESTYN.BAT, 88
  data, 540-553
    creating, 540
    fopen( ) function options, 541
    handling techniques, 540-541
    reading, 541
    writing, 541
  database
    creating, 547-550
    opening, 549
    reading, 550-553
  elevator simulation, 320-344
  handles, 156
  header, 14-15, 322-325
    command.h, 511-513
    compdb.h, 119
    dosgfree.h, 676
    error.h, 428-429
    item.h, 440-441
    key.h, 421
    list.h, 453-455
    msleep.h, 691
    pbin.h, 692
    sample.h, 547
    selector.h, 500-501
    stritem.h, 463-464

tscdefs.h, 559, 664, 669-676
tscdir.h, 567-569
tscdisp.h, 678-679
window.h, 474-477
wintool.h, 390-395
include, 14
MAKEFILE
automated, 665
copying, 2
options, 665-669
object-code, 317
text, 522-540
creating, 524-527
fopen( ) function options, 526
formatted output, 527
handling techniques, 523
reading, 529-534
sorting, 534-540
WINTOOL program, 390
fillArray( ) function, 199
FILTER.CPP program, 92
filters, 90-93
findfirst( ) function, 558
findnext( ) function, 558
firstClass( ) function, 346
flags, 96
float data type, 16
floating point constants, 43-44
floating point variables, formatting, 417
floor class, 342-352
FLOOR.CPP program, 344-352
floor.h header file, 343-344
floorCollection class, 344
floorNumber parameter, 334
flush manipulator, 94
flush( ) function, 696
fn( ) function, 597

FNCOUNT.CPP program, 151
fopen( ) function, 161-162, 525-528
for loop, 105-107
form one's complement operator, 74, 83
form( ) function, 30-35, 417, 689-690
FORM.CPP program, 689-690
form.h header file, 689
FORMAT.CPP program, 30-31
formatted
input, 35-37
output, 28-34, 527
formatting
floating-point variables, 417
instructions, 32-33
integer variables, 417
forward class declarations, 594
fp pointer, 527, 543
fp variable, 161-162
FP_OFF( ) function, 221
FP_SEG( ) function, 221
fprintf( ) function, 527
fputc( ) function, 526-529
fputs( ) function, 526-529
fragmentation, 240
fread( ) function, 541, 546, 551-553
free( ) function, 278
FREE.CPP program, 554-555
FRIEND.CPP program, 591-592
FRIENDFN.CPP program, 594-595
FRIENDMF.CPP program, 596-597
friends, 443, 588
class, 589-594
function, 594-599
fseek( ) function, 541, 551-553
FSIZE.CPP program, 560-563
fully qualified expressions, 118

function keys
    converting to negative values, 423-424
    values returned by getKey( ) function,
    424
function prototypes, 152
functions, 3, 149-150
    _bios_disk( ), 522
    action( ), 312, 317-318, 330-333,
        339, 358
    additem( ), 250
    adjustTime( ), 564
    arguments, pointers, 259-264
    asctime( ), 277-278
    atHeadOfList( ), 458
    atof( ), 37
    atol( ), 37, 609
    buttonDown( ), 354
    buttonUp( ), 354
    calling, 152
    calloc( ), 252-253
    cdir( ), 555-557
    center( ), 194
    centerText( ), 172
    chdir( ), 557
    CLASS( ), 631
    clearFunction( ), 475
    clock( ), 692
    closeTopWindow( ), 259
    cmpkeys( ), 229
    colasc( ), 207
    compare( ), 538
    cone( ), 202
    confusingFunction( ), 475
    constructors, 311-314
    continues( ), 299, 313, 376-378
    countchars( ), 158
    createMainWindow( ), 411

createSampWindow( ), 412
dashes, 189
declarations, 152
delay( ), 690, 692
delitem( ), 250
designing, top-down method,
    153-162
destructors, 312
discharge( ), 336
disp_box( ), 188
disp_pointer( ), 221
disp_pokew( ), 207
disp_printf( ), 229
display( ), 299, 313, 376-380
dnwaiting( ), 333, 340
DOS, 522
dos_abs_disk_read( ), 522
dos_abs_disk_write( ), 522
dos_findfirst( ), 558
dos_findnext( ), 558
dos_getdiskfreespace( ), 554, 676
doublex, 592
drawbox( ), 188
eeol( ), 486
eeow( ), 486
elevStopping( ), 358
error( ), 429-435
exit( ), 72, 86-88
factorial( ), 176
fclose( ), 156, 527, 531
feof( ), 546
fgetc( ), 156, 531
fgets( ), 533
file, 522
    error, 527-529
fillArray( ), 199
findfirst( ), 558

findnext( ), 558
firstClass( ), 346
flush( ), 696
fn( ), 597
fopen( ), 161-162, 525-528
form( ), 30-35, 417, 688-690
FP_OFF( ), 221
FP_SEG( ), 221
fprintf( ), 527
fputc( ), 526-529
fputs( ), 526-529
fread( ), 541, 546, 551-553
free( ), 278
friend, 594-596
friends, 596-599
fseek( ), 541, 551-553
fwrite( ), 541-546, 553
get( ), 92
getch( ), 423
getcoords( ), 188
getcwd( ), 557
geterror( ), 429, 433
getfloat( ), 167
getInfo( ), 486
getKey( ), 419, 423-425
getName( ), 367, 372
getRec( ), 553
gets( ), 161
getSelection( ), 504, 571
getString( ), 571, 575
gettext( ), 688
getTime( ), 313, 376
global, conflict resolution, 648-650
gotorc( ), 486
hideWindow( ), 486
implementation, 152
initDisplay( ), 382-383

inline, 200-203
insertItem( ), 458, 577
instruct( ), 525
isalpha( ), 96
isdigit( ), 96
islower( ), 96
isspace( ), 96
isupper( ), 96
kbhit( ), 378
keyWaiting( ), 419, 425
library, 150
listEmpty( ), 455
listFiles( ), 581-582
listOneFile( ), 581-583
loadAny( ), 341
loadIfGoing( ), 335-336
loadIfWaiting( ), 335
loadOne( ), 341
localtime( ), 277
main( ), 3-4, 150
    definitions in, 21
malloc( ), 252
mammal( ), 372
member, 301-304
    calling, 398
    inline, 305-308
    pointers to, 651-655
    replacement, 376-377
    static, 410-420
    virtual, 402-407
    see also member functions
memcpy( ), 564
msleep( ), 258, 384, 690-692
normalVideo( ), 486
numWaiting( ), 339, 348
openfile( ), 161
openWindow( ), 258

operator TYPE( ), 621
overlayTest( ), 487
overloading, 599-604
    class member, 603-604
    conventional, 602
    operator member, 609-611
pause( ), 164
pbin( ), 76, 693-694
pbinc( ), 694
perform( ), 299-300, 313, 376-379
performCommand( ), 418-420
performCommands( ), 413-414
person( ), 329-330
pointers to, 264-269
pop( ), 247-250
pow( ), 174
printf( ), 27, 34, 692
prompt( ), 181
prototypes, 157
push( ), 247-248, 302-304
put( ), 92
putPixel( ), 652
puts( ), 486
putsat( ), 490-491
puttext( ), 688
qsort( ), 538
quicksort( ), 199-200
rand( ), 199, 324
readstring( ), 275
readText( ), 539
recordtemp( ), 260
recount( ), 196-197
recursion, 194-200
reduceTime( ), 313, 379
resetDirectory( ), 577
results( ), 299, 313

returning
    string pointers, 276-278
    values, 172-178
reverseVideo( ), 486
rowasc( ), 207
running, 179
runtest( ), 483-485, 504, 571
scope, 158
scrollDown( ), 486
scrollUp( ), 486
SEEK_CUR, 553
SEEK_END, 553
SEEK_SET, 553
setDirection( ), 358
setDownButton( ), 348-349
setelevNumber( ), 364
setFloorNumber( ), 346, 350
setTime( ), 313, 376
setTitle( ), 486
setUpButton( ), 348-349
show( ), 595-596
showBird( ), 372
showColors( ), 416
showElevators( ), 364
showFileInfo( ), 564
showFirst( ), 271
showFloor( ), 347-351
showList( ), 457
showlist( ), 250
showMammal( ), 372
showRec( ), 551
showSample( ), 418
showValues, 592
showWindow( ), 486
sin( ), 174
sortText( ), 539
srand( ), 199

state( ), 302-303
strcat( ), 281
strchr( ), 282-283
strcmp( ), 282, 538
strcmpi( ), 282
strcpy( ), 118, 279
strdup( ), 280, 539
string, 278-284
strlen( ), 280
strlwr( ), 283-284
strncat( ), 281
strncpy( ), 280, 373
strrchr( ), 283
strstr( ), 283
strupr( ), 284
swapbytes( ), 263-264
theFunction( ), 651
threesum( ), 173
time( ), 277
tolower( ), 87
toupper( ), 87, 290
ungetKey( ), 425
upwaiting( ), 333, 340
useregister( ), 170
usevolatile( ), 170
utime( ), 567
variables, 162-163
    external, 165-167
    local, 163-165
    register, 168-170
    static, 170-172
writeText( ), 539-540
writing, 150-153
yplot( ), 269
fwrite( ) function, 541-546, 553

# G

garbage collectors, 240
GAS.CPP program, 71-72
get( ) function, 92
getch( ) function, 423
getcoords( ) function, 188
getcwd( ) function, 557
geterror( ) function, 429, 433
getfloat( ) function, 167
getInfo( ) function, 486
getInfo( ) member function, 481-482
getKey( ) function, 419, 423-425
getName( ) function, 367, 372
getRec( ) function, 553
gets( ) function, 161
getSelection( ) function, 504
getString( ) function, 571, 575
getString( ) member function, 465-467
gettext( ) function, 688
getTime( ) function, 313, 376
getValue( ) member function, 397
global functions, conflicts, resolving,
    648-650
global variables, 23-25, 158, 232, 322
    side effects, 433
GLOBAL.CPP program, 23-24
goto statements, 113-114
gotorc( ) member function, 416, 486
GRADE.CPP program, 130-131
granularity, reducing, 544
greater than operator, 65
greater than or equal to operator, 65

# H

handles, file, 156
HEAD.CPP program, 104
header files, 14-15, 322-325
   command.h, 511-513
   compdb.h, 119
   dosgfree.h, 676
   error.h, 428-429
   item.h, 440-441
   key.h, 421
   list.h, 453-455,
   msleep.h, 691
   pbin.h, 692
   sample.h, 547
   selector.h, 500-501
   stritem.h, 463-464
   tscdefs.h, 559, 664, 669-676
   tscdir.h, 567-569
   tscdisp.h, 678-679
   window.h, 474-477
   wintool.h, 390-395
heap, 232
   allocating space for class objects, 396-397
HELLO.CPP program, 696
helpCommand class, 394
hideWindow( ) function, 486
hiding data, 588
holders, place, 141
hybrid languages, 296

# I

I/O (input & output), 25-38
I/O manipulators, 28, 94
identifiers, 12
if/else statement, 67-70

implementation, function, 152
implementing
   building class, 377-381
   elevator class, 355
   floor class, 344-355
INCDEC.CPP program, 57
include files, 14
increment operators, 54-57
   overloading, 614-615
indexes, 126
inheritance, 365-374
   multiple, 501, 655
inherited classes, default status, 650-651
initDisplay( ) function, 382-383
initialization, memberwise, 626-629
initializing
   arrays, 132-133
   character arrays, 138
   classes, global objects, 478
   objects, 398
   pointers, 213
   variables
      global, 23-25
      local, 23-25
      with assignment statements, 19-20
      with definitions, 17-19
   Zortech C++ display package, 187
inline keyword, 308
inline member functions, 200-203, 305-308
   creating, 200
   restrictions & suggestions, 202
inner variable, 22
input/output, *see* I/O
input streams, 34-35
   cin, 646
   overloading, 644-645

insertItem( ) member function, 414-415,
    455-458, 577
instruct( ) function, 525
instructions, 4
int data type, 16
integer variables, formatting, 417
isalpha( ) function, 96
isdigit( ) function, 96
islower( ) function, 96
isspace( ) function, 96
isupper( ) function, 96
item class, 440-441, 445-448
    this keyword, 448-452
    virtual functions, 472-473
ITEM.CPP program, 448-452
item.h header file, 440-441

# J-K

joining strings, 281
JUSTIFY.CPP program, 29

kbhit( ) function, 378
KEY module, 420-425
    defining KEY values, 425
    testing, 426-427
KEY.CPP program, 421-427
KEY.DOC program, 426
key.h header file, 421
keyboard flag byte, 228
keyboards, and far pointers, 226-232
keypresses
    getting, 422-423
    pausing for, 483-485
    ungetting, 425
keys, values, testing, 426-427
KEYSTAT.CPP program, 226-228
keyWaiting( ) function, 419, 425

keywords, 13
    catch, 703
    extern, 167, 325
    inline, 308
    overload, 602, 703
    register, 168-170
    reserved, 703
    switch, 98
    this, 448-452
    throw, 703
    try, 703
    void, 157

# L

languages, hybrid, 296
late binding, 408
left shift operator, 82
less than operator, 65
less than or equal operator to, 65
library functions, 150
LINENUM.CPP program, 93
lines, deleting temporarily, 9
link( ) member function, 440-441, 447,
    451-452
list class, 453-462
    deleting objects, 472
    virtual functions, 472-473
list heads, 247, 457
list parameter, 248
LIST.CPP program, 459-462
list.h header file, 453-455
listEmpty( ) function, 455
listFiles( ) function, 581-582
Listings
    1.1. WELCOME.CPP, 2
    1.2. COMMENT.CPP, 10
    1.3. NOTHING.CPP, 11-12

1.4. VARIABLE.CPP, 18
1.5. SCOPE.CPP, 22
1.6. GLOBAL.CPP, 23-24
1.7. DT.CPP, 26
1.8. JUSTIFY.CPP, 29
1.9. FORMAT.CPP, 30-31
1.10. NUMIN.CPP, 35
1.11. ATONUMS.CPP, 36-37
1.12. CONVERT.CPP, 38
1.13. DEFINE.CPP, 45-46
1.14. CONST.CPP, 46-47
1.15. ENUM.CPP, 50
1.16. INCDEC.CPP, 57
1.17. TAX.CPP, 58
2.1. MILES.CPP, 66-67
2.2. GAS.CPP, 71-72
2.3. TAND.CPP, 75-76
2.4. TOR.CPP, 77-78
2.5. TXOR.CPP, 79
2.6. TCOMP.CPP, 83-84
2.7. YESNO.CPP, 8-87
2.8. TESTYN.BAT, 88
2.9. YESNO2.CPP, 89-90
2.10. FILTER.CPP, 92
2.11. LINENUM.CPP, 93
2.12. WORDS.CPP, 95-96
2.13. MENU.CPP, 101-102
2.14. HEAD.CPP, 104
2.15. ASCII.CPP, 106-107
2.16. BREAKER.CPP, 109
2.17. CONTINUE.CPP, 110-111
2.18. compdb.h, 119
2.19. COMP1.CPP, 119-120
2.20. COMP2.CPP, 121-122
2.21. UNION.CPP, 125
2.22. ARRAY.CPP, 127
2.23. GRADE.CPP, 130-131

2.24. MEETING.CPP, 135-136
2.25. EQUIP.CPP, 142-143
2.26. SIZEOF.CPP, 145
3.1. FNCOUNT.CPP, 151
3.2. BP.CPP, 159-161
3.3. LOCAL.CPP, 164-165
3.4. EXTERN1.CPP, 166
3.5. EXTERN2.CPP, 166-167
3.6. REG.CPP, 169
3.7. STATIC.CPP, 171
3.8. COCO.CPP, 175-176
3.9. REF.CPP, 183
3.10. BOX.CPP, 186
3.11. CENTER.CPP, 192-193
3.12. RECOUNT.CPP, 195-196
3.13. SORTER.CPP, 197-199
3.14. CONE.CPP, 201-202
3.15. ASC.CPP, 204-206
4.1. ALIAS.CPP, 213-214
4.2. VOID.CPP, 219-220
4.3. NEARFAR.CPP, 222-223
4.4. CRTSTAT.CPP, 224
4.5. KEYSTAT.CPP, 226-228
4.6. DSTRUCT.CPP, 236-237
4.7. STACK.CPP, 243-246
4.8. popup.h, 253-254
4.9. POPUP.CPP, 254-257
4.10. SWAP.CPP, 262-263
4.11. PLOT.CPP, 267-269
4.12. ARRAYPTR.CPP, 270-271
4.13. PTRARRAY.CPP, 272
4.14. READSTR.CPP, 274-275
4.15. THEDATE.CPP, 276-277
4.16. CMDLINE.CPP, 286
4.17. OPTIONS.CPP, 288-289
4.18. COLUMN.CPP, 290-291
5.1. SIMULATE.CPP, 298

5.2. BUTTON.CPP, 300-301
5.3. BUTTON2.CPP, 305-306
5.4. action.h, 309-310
5.5. ACTION.CPP, 314-316
5.6. elevsim.h, 322-324
5.7. person.h, 326-327
5.8. PERSON.CPP, 329-342
5.9. floor.h, 343-344
5.10. FLOOR.CPP, 344-352
5.11. elevator.h, 353-354
5.12. ELEVATOR.CPP, 355-364
5.13. ANIMAL.CPP, 367-373
5.14. building.h, 375
5.15. BUILDING.CPP, 377-380
5.16. ELEVSIM.CPP, 381-385
6.1. wintool.h, 391-393
6.2. POLY.CPP, 404-407
6.3. WINTOOL.CPP, 409-420
6.4. key.h, 421
6.5. KEY.CPP, 421-422
6.6. KEY.DOC, 426
6.7. TKEY.CPP, 427
6.8. error.h, 428-429
6.9. ERROR.CPP, 429-433
6.10. TERROR.CPP, 434-435
7.1. item.h, 440-441
7.2. TITEM.CPP, 445-448
7.3. ITEM.CPP, 448-452
7.4. list.h, 453-455
7.5. TLIST.CPP, 455-459
7.6. LIST.CPP, 459-462
7.8. TSTRITEM.CPP, 466-467
7.9. STRITEM.CPP, 467-471
7.10. TSTRLIST.CPP, 471-473
7.11. window.h, 474-477
7.12. TWINDOW.CPP, 482-487
7.13. WINDOW.CPP, 488-499

7.14. selector.h, 500-501
7.15. TSELECT.CPP, 502-504
7.16. SELECTOR.CPP, 505-509
7.17. command.h, 511-513
7.18. TCOMMAND.CPP, 513-517
8.1. MAKETXT.CPP, 524-525
8.2. READTXT.CPP, 530-531
8.3. READLN.CPP, 532-533
8.4. SORTTXT.CPP, 534-537
8.5. WDATA.CPP, 542-543
8.6. RDATA.CPP, 544-545
8.7. sample.h, 547
8.8. MAKEDB.CPP, 548-549
8.9. ALLRECDB.CPP, 550-551
8.10. READDB.CPP, 551-553
8.11. FREE.CPP, 554-555
8.12. CDIR.CPP, 556
8.13. SDIR.CPP, 558-559
8.14. FSIZE.CPP, 560-563
8.15. TOUCH.CPP, 565-566
8.16. tscdir.h, 568
8.17. TDIR.CPP, 570_571
8.18. TSCDIR.CPP, 572-577
8.19. NAV.CPP, 578-579
8.20. READ.CPP, 580-583
9.1. FRIEND.CPP, 591-592
9.2. FRIENDFN.CPP, 594-595
9.3. FRIENDMF.CPP, 596-597
9.4. SUBBUG.CPP, 600
9.5. MAINBUG.CPP, 601
9.6. STROPS.CPP, 607-608
9.7. STROPS2.CPP, 610-611
9.8. ARRAYLST.CPP, 616-617
9.9. NEWOPS.CPP, 622-623
9.10. TROUBLE.CPP, 629-630
9.11. OVERNEW.CPP, 638-640
9.12. POINTOUT.CPP, 642-643

9.13. POINTIN.CPP, 644-653
9.14. MFNPTR.CPP, 652-653
10.1. tscdefs.h, 669-673
10.2. dosgfree.h, 676
10.3. DOSGFREE.CPP, 676-677
10.4. tscdisp.h, 678-679
10.5. TSCDISP.CPP, 680-688
10.6. form.h, 689
10.7. FORM.CPP, 689-690
10.8. msleep.h, 691
10.9. MSLEEP.CPP, 691
10.10. pbin.h, 692
10.11. PBIN.CPP, 693-694
10.12. ZTCFLUSH.CPP, 695
10.13. HELLO.CPP, 696
listOneFile( ) function, 581-583
lists, 439
    defining instances, 457
    deleting objects, 455, 460
    dynamic, creating, 241-251
    inserting objects, 455-458
    resetting, 458
    scanning objects, 455
    string, creating, 471-473
literal constants, 40-44
    character, 40-42
    floating point, 43-44
    string, 42-43
    whole number, 43
loadAny( ) function, 341
loadIfGoing( ) function, 335-336
loadIf Waiting( ) function, 335
loadOne( ) function, 341
local variables, 23-25, 163-165, 232, 322
LOCAL.CPP program, 164-165
localtime( ) function, 277

logical AND operator, 70
logical operators, 70-73
logical OR operator, 71
long data type, 16
long double data type, 16
loops
    do-forever, 108-109
    do/while, 102-105
    for, 105-107
    while, 90-93, 251
lvalues, 53

# M

machines, state, 333
macros, 15, 87
main( ) function, 3-4, 150
    definitions in, 21
MAINBUG.CPP program, 601
MAKE utility, 2
MAKEDB.CPP program, 548-549
MAKEFILE
    automated, 665
    copying, 2
    options, 665-669
MAKETXT.CPP program, 524-525
malloc( ) function, 252
mammal( ) function, 372
mangling names, 538, 599-601
manipulators, I/O, 28, 94
masks, 77
MEETING.CPP program, 135-136
member functions, 301-304
    calling, 398
    disposeList( ), 455, 460
    draw( ), 405-407

eeow( ), 418
getInfo( ), 481-482
getString( ), 465-467
getValue( ), 397
gotorc( ), 416
inline, 305-308
insertItem( ), 414-415, 455
link( ), 440-441, 447, 451-452
nextItem( ), 455
performCommand( ), 394, 512-513
pointers to, 651-655
prevItem( ), 455
puts( ), 417
putString( ), 465-470
removeItem( ), 455
replacement, 376-377
reverseVideo( ), 418
setInfo( ), 418
showItem( ), 507
shutDown( ), 410-411, 478, 492
startup( ), 410-411, 478, 492
static, 410-420, 478-479
unlink( ), 440-441, 447, 452
virtual, 402-407
  early binding, 408
  late binding, 408
members, 301
 anchor, 454
 cip, 454
 cmdNum, 511-512
 dispInitialized, 479, 489-490
 person data, 328
 pointer, copying, 629-631
 private, 301, 443-444, 650-651
  sp, 464
  Window class, 477
 protected, 441-444

Window class, 477
public, 301, 443-444, 650-651
  Window class, 477
static member, 479-480
timeAtStart, 311
timeRemaining, 311
wtitle, 495
memberwise
 assignment, 632-635
 initialization, 626-629
memcpy( ) function, 564
memory
 allocation, 252
 deleting, 234
 managing, 232-235
 overloading, 637-641
 reserving, 252-259
 running out of, 238-239
 storing strings in, 462-470
menu-driven programs, creating,
 390-395
MENU.CPP program, 101-102
menus, border type values, 392
messages
 error
  critical, 528
  type mismatch, 216
  unexpected-end-of-file, 546
  writing, 646
 passing, 300
MFNPTR.CPP program, 652-653
Microsoft C/C++
 compiling with, 698
 options, 668
 pointers, assigning addresses to,
  225-226
MILES.CPP program, 66-67

MK_FP macro, 225
modifying directory entries, 564-567
modules
    ERROR, 428-433
        testing, 433-435
    KEY, 420-425
        defining values, 425
        testing, 426-427
msleep( ) function, 258, 384, 690-692
MSLEEP.CPP program, 691
msleep.h header file, 691
multidimensional arrays, 133-137
multiple inheritance, 439, 500-502, 655
myfnptr pointer, 654
myItem class, 457
myItem object, 395

## N

\n escape code, 42
\n switch, 5
named keys, values returned by getKey( )
    function, 424
names, mangling, 538, 599-601
NAV.CPP program, 578-579
navigators, directory, 577-579
near pointers, 222-223
NEARFAR.CPP program, 222-223
nested structures, 122-123
new operator, overloading, 638-640
newitem parameter, 248
newline characters, 5
NEWOPS.CPP program, 622-623
nextItem( ) member function, 455
no statements, 304
normalVideo( ) function, 486

noseeum variable, 22
not equal operator, 65
not operator, 73
NOTHING.CPP program, 11-12
null pointers, 216-218
numbers, factorials, 174
numeric arguments, 290-292
NUMIN.CPP program, 35
numWaiting( ) function, 339, 348

## O

object-code files, 317
object-oriented programming, see OOP
objects
    deinitializing, 444
    deleting, 419, 455, 460
    heap space, allocating, 396-397
    initializing, 398
    inserting in lists, 455
    list head, 457
    myItem, 395
    pointers, defining, 397
    public members, accessing, 396
    scanning in lists, 455
old-style output, 27
oldkeys variable, 230-231
OOP (object-oriented programming),
    296
openfile( ) function, 161
opening database files, 549
openWindow( ) function, 258
operator member functions, overloading,
    609-611
operator TYPE( ) function, 621
operator<< function, 643

operator= function, 635-637
operators, 53-59
   array-indexing, overloading, 615-623
   assignment, overloading, 623-637
   binary, 604
   bitwise, 73-82
   bitwise AND, 74-80
   bitwise exclusive OR, 74, 80-81
   bitwise inclusive OR, 74
   bitwise OR, 78-80
   combined assignment, 84-85
   conversion, 621
   decrement, 54-57
     overloading, 614-615
   delete, overloading, 640-641
   equal, 65
   form one's complement, 74, 83
   greater than, 65
   greater than or equal to, 65
   increment, 54-57
     overloading, 614-615
   left shift, 82
   less than, 65
   less than or equal to, 65
   logical, 70-73
   logical AND, 70
   logical OR, 71
   new, overloading, 638-640
   not, 73
   not equal, 65
   overloading, 604-615
   precedence, 54, 705-706
   relational, 65-67
   right shift, 82
   shift bits left, 74
   shift bits right, 74
   sizeof, 144-147
   ternary, 604
   unary, 604

   overloading, 611-613
options
   C++
     Borland, 667
     Microsoft, 668
     Turbo, 668
     Zortech, 668
   MAKE files, 665-669
OPTIONS.CPP program, 288-289
outer variable, 22
output, formatted, 527
output streams
   caux, 646
   cerr, 646
   cout, 646
   cprn, 646
   overloading, 642-644
output-stream statements, 5, 25
overlayTest( ) function, 487
overload keyword, 602, 703
overloaded constructors, 480-481
overloading
   and memory management, 637-641
   array-indexing operator, 615-623
   delete operator, 640-641
   functions, 599-604
     class member, 603-604
     conventional, 602
     operator member, 609-611
   input streams, 644-645
   new operator, 638-640
   operators, 604-615
     assignment, 623-637
     decrement, 614-615
     increment, 614-615
     unary, 611-613
   streams, output, 642-644
OVERNEW.CPP program, 638-640

# P

paradigms, 295
parameters, 157
  argc, 285
  default arguments, 188-194
  floorNumber, 334
  list, 248
  newitem, 248
  passing, 178-194
    by reference, 179-188
    by value, 179-188
  reference, 184
  value, 184
parsing strings, 282
passing
  messages, 300
  parameters, 178-194
    by reference, 179-188
    by value, 179-188
pause( ) function, 164
pbin( ) function, 76, 693-694
PBIN.CPP program, 693-694
pbin.h header file, 692
pbinc( ) function, 694
perform( ) function, 299-300, 313,
  376-379
performCommand( ) member function,
  394, 418-420, 512-513
performCommands( ) function, 413-414
persCollection class, 328-329
person class, 325-342
person data members, 328
person( ) function, 329, 330
PERSON.CPP program, 329-342
person.h header file, 326-327
pipes, 90
place holders, 141

PLOT.CPP program, 267-268
pointer arithmetic, 273
pointer members, copying, 629-631
pointer-addressable variables, *see* dynamic
  variables
pointers, 120
  addresses, 212
    assigning, 225-226
    segmented, 221
  as function arguments, 259-264
  binding to variables, 214
  creating, 212
    to class objects, 396-397
  declaring, 212-213
  deferencing, 213-216
  defining to class objects, 397
  far, 222-223
    and keyboard, 226-232
  fp, 527, 543
  initialzing, 213
  myfnptr, 654
  near, 222-223
  null, 216-218
  relationship to arrays, 138-140
  relationship with arrays, 270-276
  root, 247
  string, 233
    returning, 276-278
  this, 448-452, 638
  to base classes, 446-447
  to class variables, 395-399
  to derived classes, 399-400
  to functions, 264-269
  to member functions, 651-655
  to structures, 236-238
  to system locations, 224-226
  type casts, 218-222
  type checking, 216
  void, 216-218

POINTIN.CPP program, 644-653
POINTOUT.CPP program, 642-643
POLY.CPP program, 404-407
polymorphism, 400-407
pop( ) function, 247-250
pop-up menus
    creating, 513-518
    selector objects, creating, 516
popping variables, 242
POPUP.CPP program, 254-257
popup.h header file, 253-254
pow( ) function, 174
precedence, operator, 54, 705-706
prevItem( ) member function, 455
printf( ) function, 27, 34, 692
private members, 301, 443-444, 650-651
    sp, 464
    versus protected members, 441-442
    Window class, 477
program flow statements, 85
programming
    OOP, 296
    top-down, 153-162
programs
    ACTION.CPP, 314-316
    ALIAS.CPP, 213-214
    ALLRECDB.CPP, 550-551
    ANIMAL.CPP, 367-373
    ARRAY.CPP, 127
    ARRAYLST.CPP, 616-617
    ARRAYPTR.CPP, 270-271
    ASC.CPP, 204-206
    ASCII.CPP, 106-107
    ATONUMS.CPP, 36-37
    BOX.CPP, 186
    BP.CPP, 159-161
    BREAKER.CPP, 109

BUTTON.CPP, 300-301
BUTTON2.CPP, 305-306
CDIR.CPP, 556
CENTER.CPP, 192-193
CMDLINE.CPP, 286
COCO.CPP, 175-176
COLUMN.CPP, 290-291
COMMENT.CPP, 10
COMP1.CPP, 119-120
COMP2.CPP, 121-122
compiling, 696-699
CONE.CPP, 201-202
CONST.CPP, 46-47
CONTINUE.CPP, 110-111
CONVERT.CPP, 38-46
CRTSTAT.CPP, 224
database, random-access, 551
DEFINE.CPP, 45-46, 46
DOSGFREE.CPP, 676-677
DSTRUCT.CPP, 236-237
DT.CPP, 26
ELEVATOR.CPP, 355-364
elevator.h, 353-354
ELEVSIM.CPP, 381-385
ENUM.CPP, 50
EQUIP.CPP, 142-143
ERROR.CPP, 429-433
EXTERN1.CPP, 166
EXTERN2.CPP, 166-167
FILTER.CPP, 92
FLOOR.CPP, 344-352
FNCOUNT.CPP, 151
FORM.CPP, 689-690
FORMAT.CPP, 30-31
FREE.CPP, 554-555
FRIEND.CPP, 591-592, 592
FRIENDFN.CPP, 594-595

FRIENDMF.CPP, 596-597
FSIZE.CPP, 560-563
GAS.CPP, 71-72
GLOBAL.CPP, 23-24
GRADE.CPP, 130-131
HEAD.CPP, 104
HELLO.CPP, 696
INCDEC.CPP, 57
ITEM.CPP, 448-452
JUSTIFY.CPP, 29
KEY.CPP, 421-427
KEY.DOC, 426
KEYSTAT.CPP, 226-228
LINENUM.CPP, 93
LIST.CPP, 459-462
LOCAL.CPP, 164-165
MAINBUG.CPP, 601
MAKEDB.CPP, 548-549
MAKETXT.CPP, 524-525
MEETING.CPP, 135-136
menu-driven, creating, 390-395
MENU.CPP, 101-102
MFNPTR.CPP, 652-653
MILES.CPP, 66-67
MSLEEP.CPP, 691
NAV.CPP, 578-579
NEARFAR.CPP, 222-223
NEWOPS.CPP, 622-623
NOTHING.CPP, 11-12
NUMIN.CPP, 35
OPTIONS.CPP, 288-289
OVERNEW.CPP, 638-640
PBIN.CPP, 693-694
PERSON.CPP, 329-342
PLOT.CPP, 267-268
POINTIN.CPP, 644-653
POINTOUT.CPP, 642-643

POLY.CPP, 404-407
POPUP.CPP, 254-257
PTRARRAY.CPP, 272
RDATA.CPP, 544-545
READ.CPP, 579-584
READDB.CPP, 551-553
READLN.CPP, 532-533
READSTR.CPP, 274-275
READTXT.CPP, 530-531
RECOUNT.CPP, 195-196
REF.CPP, 183
REG.CPP, 169
SCOPE.CPP, 22
SDIR.CPP, 558-559
SELECTOR.CPP, 505-509
SIMULATE.CPP, 298
SIZEOF.CPP, 145
SORTER.CPP, 197-199
SORTTXT.CPP, 534-537
STACK.CPP, 243-246
STATIC.CPP, 171
STRITEM.CPP, 467-471
STROPS.CPP, 607-608
STROPS2.CPP, 610-611
SUBBUG.CPP, 600
SWAP.CPP, 262-263
TAND.CPP, 75-76
TAX.CPP, 58
TCOMMAND.CPP, 513-518
TCOMP.CPP, 83-84
TDIR.CPP, 570-571
TERROR.CPP, 434-435
THEDATE.CPP, 276-277
TITEM.CPP, 445-448
TKEY.CPP, 427
TLIST.CPP, 455-459
TOR.CPP, 77-78

TOUCH.CPP, 565-566
TROUBLE.CPP, 629-630
TSCDIR.CPP, 572-577
TSCDISP.CPP, 680-688
TSELECT.CPP, 502-504
TSTRITEM.CPP, 466-467
TSTRLIST.CPP, 471-473
TWINDOW.CPP, 482-487
TXOR.CPP, 79
UNION.CPP, 125
VARIABLE.CPP, 18
VOID.CPP, 219-220
WDATA.CPP, 542-543
WELCOME.CPP, 2
WINDOW.CPP, 487-499
WINTOOL.CPP, 409-420
   compiling, 389-390
   files, 390
WORDS.CPP, 95-96
YESNO.CPP, 86-87
YESNO2.CPP, 89-90
ZTCFLUSH.CPP, 695
prompt( ) function, 181
protected members, 441-444
   versus public members, 441-442
   Window class, 477
prototypes, 658
   function, 152, 157
pseudocode, 155
ptr variable, 212
PTRARRAY.CPP program, 272
public members, 301, 443-444, 650-651
   versus protected members, 441-442
   Window class, 477
punctuators, 13
push( ) function, 247-248, 302-304
pushing variables, 242

put( ) function, 92
putPixel( ) function, 652
puts( ) member function, 417, 486
putsat( ) function, 490-491
putString( ) member function, 465-470
puttext( ) function, 688

## Q

qsort( ) function, 538
Quicksort algorithm, 195
quicksort( ) function, 199-200

## R

\r escape code, 42
r text file option, 526
r+ text file option, 526
rand( ) function, 199, 324
random-access database programs, 551
rb data file option, 541
rb+ data file option, 541
RDATA.CPP program, 544-545
READ.CPP program, 579-584
READDB.CPP program, 551-553
reading
   binary values, 544-546
   data files, 541
   database files, 550-553
   text files, 529
      a character at a time, 529-531
      a line at a time, 531-534
READLN.CPP program, 532-533
READSTR.CPP program, 274-275
readstring( ) function, 275
readText( ) function, 539
READTXT.CPP program, 530-531

recnum * sizeof(rec) argument, 553
recordtemp( ) function, 260
recount( ) function, 196-197
RECOUNT.CPP program, 195-196
recursion, 194-200
recursive data structures, 246
redirection symbols, 90
reduceTime( ) function, 313, 379
reducing granularity, 544
REF.CPP program, 183
reference parameters, 184
REG.CPP program, 169
register keyword, 168-170
register variables, 168-170
relational operators, 65-67
removeItem( ) member function, 455
replacement member functions, 376-377
reserved keywords, 703
reserving memory, 252-259
resetDirectory( ) function, 577
resolving global function conflicts,
   648-650
results( ) function, 299, 313
retrieving command-line options, 287
returning
     string pointers, 276-278
     values with functions, 172-178
reverseVideo( ) member function, 418,
   486
right shift operator, 82
root pointers, 247
rowasc( ) function, 207
running functions, 179
runtest( ) function, 483-485, 504, 571
rvalues, 53

## S

sa variable, 617
sample.h header file, 547
savedChar variable, 423
scanning objects in lists, 455
scope, 20-23
   function, 158
SCOPE.CPP program, 22
scrollDown( ) function, 486
scrollUp( ) function, 486
SDIR.CPP program, 558-559
searching strings, 282-284
SEEK_CUR function, 553
SEEK_END function, 553
SEEK_SET function, 553
selector class, 499-500
   creating objects, 504
   inserting objects, 504
   multiple inheritance, 500-502
   SELECTOR.CPP program, 505-509
   selector.h header file, 500-501
   testing, 502-504
selector classes, 439
SELECTOR.CPP program, 505-509
selector.h header file, 500-501
selectors, creating, 413
separators, 13-14
setDirection( ) function, 358
setDownButton( ) function, 348-349
setelevNumber( ) function, 364
setFloorNumber( ) function, 346, 350
setInfo( ) member function, 418
setTime( ) function, 313, 376
setting bits, 80
setTitle( ) function, 486

setUpButton( ) function, 348-349
setw arguments, 30
shift bits left operator, 74
shift bits right operator, 74
short data type, 16
short-circuit expression evaluation, 70
shorthand conditional expressions, 648
show( ) function, 595-596
showBird( ) function, 372
showColors( ) function, 416
showElevators( ) function, 364
showFileInfo( ) function, 564
showFirst( ) function, 271
showFloor( ) function, 347-348, 351
showItem( ) member function, 507
showList( ) function, 457
showlist( ) function, 250
showMammal( ) function, 372
showRec( ) function, 551
showSample( ) function, 418
showValues function, 592
showWindow( ) function, 486
shutDown( ) member function, 410-411,
  478, 492
side effects, 433
SIMULATE.CPP program, 298
simulations, elevator
    compiling, 319-321
    files, 320-344
sin( ) function, 174
single inheritance, 500
sizeof argument, 543
sizeof operator, 144-147
SIZEOF.CPP program, 145
SORTER.CPP program, 197-199
sorting text files, 534-540
sortText( ) function, 539

SORTTXT.CPP program, 534-537
sp private member, 464
srand( ) function, 199
STACK.CPP program, 243-246
stacks, 23, 242
startup( ) member function, 410-411,
  478, 492
state machines, 333
state( ) function, 302-303
statements, 105
    assignment, initializing variables,
      19-20
    break, 109
    continue, 111
    exit( ), 86-88
    goto, 113-114
    if/else, 67-70
    input-stream, 34-35
    no, 304
    output-stream, 5, 25
    program flow, 85
    switch, 97-102
    see also loops
static data members, 479-480
    dispInitialized, 489-490
static member functions, 410-420,
  478-479
static variables, 170-172
STATIC.CPP program, 171
storing
    strings in memory, 462-470
    variables in structures, 114-122
strcat( ) function, 281
strchr( ) function, 282-283
strcmp( ) function, 282, 538
strcmpi( ) function, 282
strcpy( ) function, 118, 279

strdup( ) function, 280, 539
streams, 5-7
    input
        cin, 646
        overloading, 644-645
    output
        caux, 646
        cerr, 646
        cout, 646
        cprn, 646
        overloading, 642-644
string constants, 42-43
string functions, 278-284
string pointers, 233
    returning, 276-278
strings, 137-138
    comparing, 281-282
    joining, 281
    lists, creating, 471-473
    parsing, 282
    pointers to, 277
    searching, 282-284
    storing in memory, 462-470
STRITEM.CPP program, 467-471
stritem.h header file, 463-464, 464
strlen( ) function, 280
strliem class, 463-464
    constructors, overloading, 464-466
stritem class, 466-471
    characters, changing, 465-466
    string address, obtaining, 465
strlwr( ) function, 283-284
strncat( ) function, 281
strncpy( ) function, 280, 373
STROPS.CPP program, 607-608
STROPS2.CPP program, 610-611
strrchr( ) function, 283

strstr( ) function, 283
structures, 114
    clock_t, 692
    control, 85
    dynamic, 322
    nested, 122-123
    pointers to, 236-238
    recursive data, 246
    storing variables, 114-122
    winStruct, 474-475, 481-482
strupr( ) function, 284
SUBBUG.CPP program, 600
subscript operator, *see* array-indexing
    operator
SWAP.CPP program, 262-263
swapbytes( ) function, 263-264
switch statements, 97-102
switches, 287
switching
    compilers, 699-701
    current directories, 555-557
symbols
    < (take input from), 90
    > (send output to), 90
    compiler identifier, 664

# T

\t escape code, 42
TAND.CPP program, 75-76
TAX.CPP program, 58
TCOMMAND.CPP program, 513-518
TCOMP.CPP program, 83-84
TDIR.CPP program, 570-571
ternary operator, 604
TERROR.CPP program, 434-435

testing
    command class, 513-518
    ERROR module, 433-435
    key values, 426-427
    selector class, 502-504
TESTYN.BAT batch file, 88
text, displaying within window, 416
text files, 522-540
    creating, 524-527
    fopen( ) function options, 526
    formatted output, 527
    handling techniques, 523
    reading, 529
        character at a time, 529-531
        line at a time, 531-534
    sorting, 534-540
THEDATE.CPP program, 276-277
this keyword, 448-452
this pointer, 638
threesum( ) function, 173
throw keyword, 703
time( ) function, 277
timeAtStart member, 311
timeRemaining member, 311
TITEM.CPP program, 445-448
TKEY.CPP program, 427
TLIST.CPP program, 455-459
tolower( ) function, 87
tools, cross-compilation, 662
top-down programming, 153-162
TOR.CPP program, 77-78
TOUCH.CPP program, 565-566
toupper( ) function, 87, 290
TROUBLE.CPP program, 629-630
try keyword, 703
tscdefs.h header file, 559, 664, 669-676
TSCDIR.CPP program, 572-577

tscdir.h header file, 567-569
TSCDISP.CPP program, 680-688
tscdisp.h header file, 678-679
TSELECT.CPP program, 502-504
TSTRITEM.CPP program, 466-467
TSTRLIST.CPP program, 471-473
Turbo C++
    compiling with, 698
    options, 668
TWINDOW.CPP program, 482-487
TXOR.CPP program, 79
type casts, 27
    pointers, 218-222
type checking, 216
type conversions
    automatic, 619
    user-defined, 619-623
type mismatch error message, 216
type-safe linkage, *see* name mangling

# U

unary operators, 604
    overloading, 611-613
unexpected-end-of-file error message,
    546
ungetKey( ) function, 425
union variables, creating, 125
UNION.CPP program, 125
unions, 123-126
unlink( ) member function, 440-441,
    447, 452
upwaiting( ) function, 333, 340
user-defined type conversions, 619-623
useregister( ) function, 170
usevolatile( ) function, 170
utime( ) function, 567

# V

\v escape code, 42
value parameters, 184
values
 alternate, 647
 assigning to enumerated constants,
  52-53
 binary
  reading, 544-546
  writing, 541-544
 combining, 208-209
 default, 647
 returning with functions, 172-178
VARIABLE.CPP program, 18
variables, 15-25
 addresses, 182
 assigning, 17
 buf, 575
 control, 107
 dataPtr, 654
 dirStr, 575
 disp_numcols, 488
 disp_numrows, 488
 dynamic, 232-235
  advantages, 239-241
 errorignore, 430
 errornumber, 430
 floating-point, formatting, 417
 fp, 161-162
 function, 162-163
  external, 165-167
  local, 163-165
  register, 168-170
  static, 170-172
 global, 23-25, 158, 232, 322
  side effects, 433

initializing
 with assignment statements, 19-20
 with definitions, 17-19
inner, 22
integer, formatting, 417
local, 23-25, 232, 322
noseeum, 22
oldkeys, 230-231
outer, 22
pointers bound to, 214
popping, 242
ptr, 212
pushing, 242
sa, 617
savedChar, 423
static, 170-172
storing in structures, 114-122
union, creating, 125
virtual base classes, 655-657
virtual member functions, 400-408
 early binding, 408
 late binding, 408
void keyword, 157
void pointers, 216-218
VOID.CPP program, 219-220

# W

w text file option, 526
w+ text file option, 526
wb data file option, 541
wb+ data file option, 541
WDATA.CPP program, 542-543
WELCOME.CPP program, 2
while loop, 90-93, 251
white space, 13, 96
whole number constants, 43

Window class, 473
  displays, designing, 482-486
  overloaded constructors, 480-481
  private members, 477
  protected members, 477
  public members, 477
  reference functions, 481-482
  static data members, 479-480
  static member functions, 478-479
  WINDOW.CPP program, 487-499
  window.h header file, 473-477
WINDOW.CPP program, 487-499
window.h header file, 474-477
windows
  attributes, changing, 418
  border type values, 392
  displaying text within, 416
winStruct structure, 474-475
  returning reference to, 481-482
WINTOOL.CPP program, 388,
  409-420
  compiling, 389-390
  files, 390
wintool.h header file, 390-395
WORDS.CPP program, 95-96

working directories, *see* current
  directories
writeText( ) function, 539-540
writing
  binary values, 541-544
  data files, 541
  error messages, 646
  functions, 150-153
wtitle member, 495

## X-Y

YESNO.CPP program, 86-87
YESNO2.CPP program, 89-90
yplot( ) function, 269

## Z

Zortech C++
  compiling with, 699
  initializing, 187
  options, 668
ZTCFLUSH.CPP program, 695